R A

Torres Strait

C. York

CORAL

SEA

Cape

York

Peninsula

Cooktown

roote
landt

Gulf of
Carpentaria

Wellesley Is

Cairns

Mt. Bartle Frere
1,622 ▲

Mitchell

Gilbert

Normanton

Townsville

Burdekin

Flinders

Barkly Tableland

Cloncurry

Mount
Isa

Selwyn Range

Repulse
Bay

Mackay

Great Barrier Reef

Georgina

QUEENSLAND

Rockhampton

PACIFIC

mpson

Charleville

Bundaberg

Maryborough

Fraser I.

OCEAN

esert

Lake Eyre Basin

Warrego

Grey Range

Toowoomba

Ipswich   ● Brisbane

Lake
Eyre N

Sturt
Desert

Gold Coast

Lake
Eyre S

Darling

New England Range

Round Mt.
▲1,615

LIA

Lake
Torrens

Flinders Ranges

Lake
Frome

Tamworth

Barrier Range

NEW SOUTH

Mt.
Barrington
▲1,585

anges

Broken Hill

WALES

Port Augusta

Bathurst

Newcastle

Port
Pirie

re
en.

Spencer Gulf

Mt. Lofty Range

MURRAY

Lachlan

Blue Mtns

● Sydney

Mildura

Murrumbidgee

Wollongong

Adelaide

RIVER

Wagga Wagga
RIVERINA

Murray

Canberra
(A.C.T.)

Kangaroo I.

BASIN

Albury

Mt. ▲
Kosciusko
2,228

Bendigo

Australian Alps

VICTORIA

Mount
Gambier

Ballarat   ● Melbourne

C. Howe

Geelong

Portland

Bass Strait

King I.

Flinders I.

Launceston

▲ *Mt. Ossa*
1,617

TASMANIA

● Hobart

The Cambridge Encyclopedia of Australia is the most comprehensive single-volume reference on Australia yet to appear. It not only looks at life in today's Australia, but also provides a host of insights into contemporary culture, the Aboriginal heritage, the natural world, and the continent's colourful past.

The states and territories – New South Wales, Queensland, South Australia, Tasmania, Victoria, Western Australia, the Australian Capital Territory and the Northern Territory – receive individual attention although the emphasis throughout is on Australia-wide trends and the way these interact with developments in the world outside. Illustrated panels highlight renowned landmarks such as Uluru (Ayers Rock) and the Great Barrier Reef, and the work of well-known Australians such as Sidney Nolan and Patrick White. In addition, Susan Bambrick and her team of 91 contributors supplement the overview with a mass of facts, figures and photographs to make this the essential source of reference for everyone with an interest in Australia.

The Cambridge Encyclopedia of Australia

The Cambridge Encyclopedia of

Australia

Contents

Published by the Press Syndicate of the University of Cambridge
The Pitt Building, Trumpington Street, Cambridge CB2 1RP
40 West 20th Street, New York, NY 10011-4211, USA
10 Stamford Road, Oakleigh, Melbourne 3166, Australia

© Cambridge University Press 1994

First published 1994

Printed in Great Britain at the University Press, Cambridge
Colour origination by Kestrel Digital Colour, Chelmsford

A catalogue record for this book is available from the British Library

Library of Congress cataloguing in publication data available

ISBN 0 521 36511 2

A CAMBRIDGE REFERENCE BOOK

Editor Peter Richards
Project development Sarah Bunney, Lyn Collingwood,
  Cameron Hazlehurst, Clare Orchard
Design Dale Tomlinson (Peter Ducker and David Seabourne)
Maps and diagrams European Map Graphics Limited
Picture Research Stephen Adamson, Susan Bambrick,
  Lyn Collingwood, Callie Kendall

Half-title illustration: Kangaroo road sign, the Nullarbor,
South Australia (Debbie Perrin/Planet Earth Pictures).
Title: Sand dunes in the Petermann Ranges, Northern Territory
(Ron Ryan/Coo-ee Picture Library).

CONTRIBUTORS

AB ALAN BURNETT
The Australian National University

AC ASSOCIATE PROFESSOR ATHOL CHASE
Griffith University

AD ASSOCIATE PROFESSOR ANN DANIEL
University of New South Wales

AG DR ALAN GIBSON
CSIRO Division of Plant Industry

AH DR ANDREW HOPKINS
The Australian National University

AHC PROFESSOR ANTHONY H CHISHOLM
La Trobe University

AJB PROFESSOR ARTHUR J BIRCH
The Australian National University

AM ASSOCIATE PROFESSOR ADRIAN MITCHELL
University of Sydney

APK DR A PETER KERSHAW
Monash University

AR DR ANDRÉE ROSENFELD
The Australian National University

AW SIR ALAN WALSH
Formerly CSIRO Division of Chemical Physics

BC BARBARA CHAMBERS
University of Canberra

BG DR BILL GAMMAGE
University of Adelaide

BH BARBARA HILLIARD
Sydney

BHF PROFESSOR BRIAN H FLETCHER
University of Sydney

BM PROFESSOR BILL MANDLE
University of Canberra

BTCE BUREAU OF TRANSPORT AND
COMMUNICATIONS ECONOMICS
Canberra

CA DR CHRISTOPHER ANDERSON
South Australian Museum, Adelaide

CC CATRIONA COOK
The Australian National University

CF DR CHRISTOPHER FINDLAY
University of Adelaide

CJ CHRISTINE JENNETT
Charles Sturt University

CKC CLIVE COOGAN
Formerly CSIRO Science and Industry Liaison Division

CM PROFESSOR CAMPBELL MACKNIGHT
University of Tasmania

CO EMERITUS PROFESSOR CLIFF D. OLLIER
The Australian National University

CR DR CLAIRE RUNCIMAN
Queensland Health

DB DR DEBORAH BRENNAN
University of Sydney

DFB DR DAVID F BRANAGAN
Formerly University of Sydney

DHB DR DOROTHY H BROOM
The Australian National University

DJM EMERITUS PROFESSOR JOHN MULVANEY
Australian Academy of the Humanities

DKR ASSOCIATE PROFESSOR DAVID K ROUND
University of Adelaide

DP PROFESSOR DAVID POPE
The Australian National University

DR DR DON RAWSON
The Australian National University

DTR DR DONALD T ROWLAND
The Australian National University

EY DR ELSPETH A YOUNG
The Australian National University

FF EMERITUS PROFESSOR FRANK FENNER
The Australian National University

FL DR FRANK LEWINS
The Australian National University

GC GRACE COCHRANE
Powerhouse Museum, Sydney

HM HELEN MILLS
Communications Law Centre, University of New South Wales

HMB DR H M BOOT
The Australian National University

HS HELEN SIM
CSIRO Australia Telescope National Facility

IG DR IAN GRAY
Charles Sturt University

II DR IAN INKSTER
University of New South Wales

IK DR IAN KEEN
The Australian National University

JAC DR JOHN A CARNAHAN
Formerly The Australian National University

JB DR JOHN BARRETT
Formerly La Trobe University

JC ASSOCIATE PROFESSOR JOHN CARMODY
University of New South Wales

JDP PROFESSOR JOHN D PITCHFORD
The Australian National University

JI JENNIFER ISAACS
Sydney

JM   DR JOHN MERRITT
      The Australian National University

JMcC JOHN McCALLUM
      University of New South Wales

J-PLF DR J-P L FONTEYNE
      The Australian National University

JPW   DR PAUL WILD
      Formerly CSIRO

JS   JILL SYKES
      Dance Critic, The Sydney Morning Herald

JWK   DR J W KNOTT
      The Australian National University

JWZ   DR J W ZILLMAN
      Bureau of Meteorology

KB   KATHARINE BRISBANE
      The Currency Press, Sydney

KP   DR KEITH POWELL
      *Formerly Director, Alcohol and Drug Service of the
      ACT Health Services, Canberra*

KSWC PROFESSOR K S W CAMPBELL
      The Australian National University

LJS   DR LAWRENCE J SAHA
      The Australian National University

LRZ   EMERITUS PROFESSOR LESLIE ZINES
      The Australian National University

MAH   DR M A HABERMEHL
      Australian Geological Survey Organisation

MC   PROFESSOR MICHAEL CLYNE
      Monash University

MD   DR M F DAY
      Formerly CSIRO Division of Forest Research

MJS   DR MARIAN J SIMMS
      The Australian National University

ML   DR MILES LEWIS
      University of Melbourne

MP   DR MAX PETTINI
      Royal Greenwich Observatory, Cambridge, England

MS   DR MARIAN SAWER
      University of Canberra

MStL MARK ST LEON
      Australia Council

PD   PROFESSOR PETER J DAVIES
      University of Sydney

PGQ   PROFESSOR PATRICK G QUILTY
      Australia Antarctic Division, Tasmania

PMF   P M FLEMING
      CSIRO Division of Water Resources

PR   DR PETER READ
      The Australian National University

PS   DR PETER SUTTON
      Formerly South Australian Museum, Adelaide

PSV   PETER VALENTINE
      James Cook University of North Queensland

RB   ROBIN BURNETT
      The Australian National University

RE   RAY EDMONDSON
      National Film and Sound Archive

RFI   MR R F ISBELL
      CSIRO Division of Soils

RLM   EMERITUS PROFESSOR RUSSELL L MATHEWS
      The Australian National University

RM   DR ROBIN MARKS
      St Vincent's Hospital, Melboune

RNB   DR R N BYRON
      The Australian National University

RS   DR RICHARD SCHODDE
      CSIRO Division of Wildlife and Ecology

RVB   PROFESSOR R V BLANDEN
      The Australian National University

RVJ   DR R V JACKSON
      The Australian National University

SB   PROFESSOR SUSAN BAMBRICK
      La Trobe University

SCBG EMERITUS PROFESSOR S C B GASCOIGNE
      The Australian National University

SEB   SARAH BUNNEY
      Reading, England

SJ   STAN JARZYNSKI
      Department of Primary Industries and Energy

SM   PROFESSOR STUART MACINTYRE
      University of Melbourne

TJV   DR T J VALENTINE
      University of Technology, Sydney

TS   ASSOCIATE PROFESSOR TERRY SMITH
      University of Sydney

WJR   PROFESSOR W J RANKIN
      University of Melbourne

WV   PROFESSOR WRAY VAMPLEW
      De Montfort University, England

To be invited to distil the essence of one's nation is both a privilege and a challenge. To my academic colleagues who shared that challenge, advising on content and authors, to all the contributors, and to the staff of Cambridge University Press I express my thanks.

Australia is the smallest continent, or the largest island, settled as others have been, by waves of immigrants – the ancestors of today's Aboriginal people, the British settlers of the late eighteenth and nineteenth century, the people of varied nationality who came to seek gold, the post-World War II migration from a devastated Europe, refugees from more recent conflicts in Vietnam and Cambodia, arrivals in the last few decades from most countries in Asia and the Middle East, and new settlers from Africa and South America. There is always a trickle of North American migration, while the substantial cross-migration between Australia and New Zealand has been a major influence on both countries.

Australia is a dry continent, despite its lush tropical rainforests. Population density figures, taken for the continent as a whole, suggest sparse settlement. When account is taken of the vast areas of desert, and marginally productive land, we find Australians tend to concentrate in the currently productive areas close to the coast. Many of us love the Australian 'bush' – and long for it when we are overseas; but nevertheless it is usually somewhere we visit, rather than somewhere we live. Similarly, the overseas view of Australians as beachgoers and surfers is an accurate one, but visitors are often surprised at the distances we travel to the beach.

The overseas tourist in Australia is looking to see those things which are 'different' – so we show them our unique fauna such as kangaroos and koalas and maybe a platypus; we fly them to the Northern Territory where they can climb the world's largest monolith and see examples of Aboriginal rock art; and we take them to the Great Barrier Reef to see the coral and the fish.

If you are seeking those distinctive features in this book, you will find them; but you will also find modern Australia and see how it came to be – the Australian Parliament, a Westminster derivative with American modifications; the implications of the federal system for education, health, and transport; and the cultural impact of waves of migration. You will discover that Australia is more than a farm and a quarry – that its contribution to world science has been much larger than its population size might lead you to expect; and you will read of our opera singers, and of our pioneering role, such as in introducing universal adult suffrage.

Within the confines of a single volume, it has not of course been possible to cover all matters affecting the lives of the Australian people. Not all the views expressed in this encyclopedia are those of the editor or of the Press. There are many contributors, selected for their diversity of views. Taking them together, we have shown you our nation.

SUSAN BAMBRICK
La Trobe University
Albury-Wodonga

The physical continent

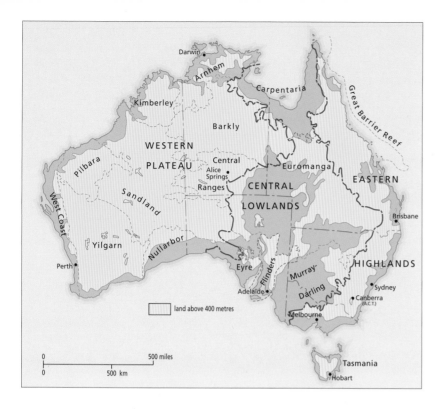

land above 400 metres

0　　　　500 miles
0　　　500 km

Topography

Australia is the lowest, flattest and (excluding Antarctica) the driest continent. Its broad shape has basically been caused by movements of the Earth's crust but most of the detail has been carved by river erosion. These factors, together with the effects of repeated changes of climate and sea level, account for Australia's varied topography today.

The continent has three major physical divisions: the Western Plateau, the Central Lowlands and the broad swell of the Eastern Highlands.

The *Western Plateau* is divided into topographic regions with local names (Yilgarn, Kimberley, Arnhem Land, and so on). Most of these lie on ancient rocks dating back to Precambrian times and have been land for more than 600 million years. Sandland and the Barkly Tableland are underlain by younger (mainly Palaeozoic) rocks, eroded to flat surfaces and largely covered by sand. The limestone Nullarbor Plain was covered by sea 15–20 million years ago, while along the west coast rocks as young as the Pliocene (2–5 million years old) are separated from the plateau by the Darling Fault escarpment.

Much of the centre of Australia is flat, though there are numerous ranges (for example, the Macdonnell and Musgrave Ranges) and some individual mountains of which Uluru (Ayers Rock) in the Northern Territory is the best known (see also p. 57). In South Australia, the Eyre region is a plain but the Flinders area consists geologically of fault blocks that have produced ranges (for example, the Flinders Ranges and Mt Lofty).

The *Central Lowlands*, which stretch from the Gulf of Carpentaria through the Great Artesian Basin to the Murray–Darling Plains, are characterised by thick sedimentary accumulations. As its name suggests, the Great Artesian Basin is made up of water-bearing sedimentary rocks. Water enters the basin in the Eastern Highlands. The central part of the Central Lowlands is the internal drainage basin of Lake Eyre in South Australia, which lies 12 m below sea level. In contrast, the rivers of the Murray–Darling and Carpentaria drainage basins flow to the sea. (See also pp. 15–17.)

The *Eastern Highlands* rise gently from central Australia towards a series of high plateaus: even the highest area, around Mt Kosciusko (2,230 m) in New South Wales, is a plateau. The few younger faults and folds, such as the Lake George Fault near Canberra and the Lapstone Monocline near Sydney, have direct effects on the topography. For most of its length the Great Divide (separating the rivers flowing west from those flowing into the Pacific) runs

Satellite false-colour image of Lake Eyre during a dry period. The white areas are salt pans, and the various shades of blue indicate water of different depths. The surrounding sandy, sparsely vegetated country shows the distinctive pattern of longitudinal dunes. The wind direction, which is predominantly south to north, is shown in the northeast corner of the image where the dunes are building out into one of the lakes from the south.

across remarkably flat country dotted with lakes, and there is in reality not a continuous mountain range although the name Great Dividing Range is widely, but misleadingly, used.

The plateaus of the Eastern Highlands usually terminate on their eastern edge in high escarpments, which together form the Great Escarpment that runs southeastwards from northern Queensland to eastern Victoria. Australia's highest waterfalls – for example, Wollomombi in New South Wales and Wallaman and Tully in Queensland, which are all about 200 m – occur where rivers flow over the Great Escarpment. In Victoria, the old plateau has been dissected into numerous separate High Plains.

THE MOULDING OF THE LANDSCAPE

Volcanoes erupted in eastern Australia throughout the Cenozoic era. Individual volcanoes were often the size of modern Vesuvius, and huge lava plains covered some areas. The older volcanoes are now deeply eroded but the cylindrical fillings (volcanic plugs) that remain provide spectacular scenery at such places as the Glass House Mountains in Queensland and Warrumbungles in New South Wales. Volcanic activity continued into the past 2 million years in Victoria and Queensland, while South Australia boasts the youngest volcano, the 5,000-year-old Mt Gambier. Such younger volcanoes naturally have more recognisably volcanic landforms.

Today, much of Australia is arid or semi-arid. Sand dunes are generally longitudinal, following the dominant wind direction, and most are fixed. Stony deserts or gibber plains (covered with small stones or gibbers) are areas without sand cover that occupy a larger area than the dunefields. Salt lakes, too, occur in many low-lying positions.

Below The Warrumbungle Mountains in northern New South Wales. The two steep-sided hills are the cylindrical remnants of old volcano vents.

Bottom right A gibber plain with stony, silcrete-strewn soil in southwestern Queensland. The deep sands of desert dunes are in the background.

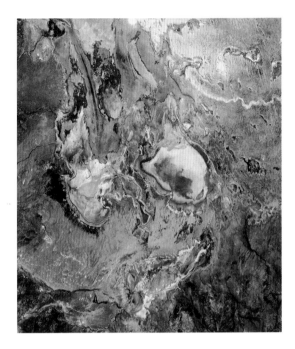

The past few million years were distinguished by ice ages. In Tasmania, there are traces of several phases of glaciation in the Quaternary period, the oldest more than 780,000 years old, and of an Oligocene glaciation about 35 million years ago. However, mainland Australia was affected only during the peak of the last ice age, about 20,000 years ago. Even then, ice only covered 25 km^2 around Mt Kosciusko.

In glacial times, rivers cut down to a sea level more than 100 m lower than it is today. As conditions warmed and the sea level rose once more, the lower valleys were drowned: some now make fine harbours – for example, at Sydney – but others have filled with sediment. Much of Australia's coastal configuration results from the accumulation of sediment on drowned coasts, and in the east there is a characteris-

Australia's maritime setting and external island territories.

The offshore shape of Australia results mainly from the pattern of break-up of Gondwana. Except in New South Wales where the continental shelf is very narrow, it reveals a broad continental shelf bounded by a steeper continental slope. The Queensland coast is bounded by a broad submarine plateau on which the Great Barrier Reef has grown mainly in the past 2 million years (see also pp. 36–41).   CO

Geological structure

tic alternation of rocky headlands and long beaches backed by plains filled with riverine and lagoonal sediments.

The major features of Australian topography are of great age and can be understood only in the context of global tectonics. Australia was once part of the supercontinent Gondwana, and bounded by land to the west, south and east. New oceans appeared to the east and west, and, then, between about 55 and 10 million years ago, the continent drifted across the surface of the globe, moving north from a position adjacent to Antarctica (see also pp. 4–9).

There have been many changes in the climate of Australia in the past, but oddly these have not been due to changing latitude. Even when Australia was close to the South Pole the climate was warm and wet, and this pattern persisted for a long period. During this time much of Australia's characteristic soils were formed (see pp. 12–14). Aridity seems to have set in only after the continent reached its present latitude, and the northern part has probably never been dry. Despite the prevalence of dry conditions today, real aridity is geologically young, with no dunes or salt lakes older than a million years. In contrast, many of the features of the drainage pattern of Australia are ancient: some river courses in the south and east are older than the breakup of Gondwana and the formation of Australia's present continental margins.

Geological timescale.

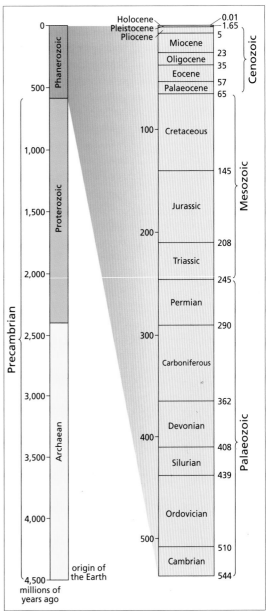

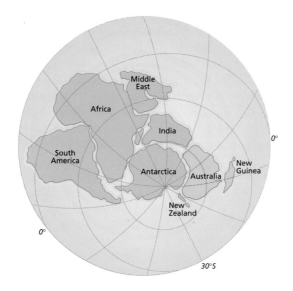

Reconstruction of the supercontinent Gondwana about 270 million years ago, showing Australia in relation to the other southern continents.

Phrases such as 'Earth's oldest continent' and 'the timeless land' convey the impression of a vast mass of land on which nothing of geological significance has happened since time began. In fact, Australia has had a very active geological past, resulting in a physical environment that affects almost every aspect of human life on the continent.

The present structure of Australia can be understood only in terms of this long geological history. An important aspect is that about 160 million years ago, before mid-Jurassic times, Australia was an integral part of a supercontinent called Gondwana. This was a great southern landmass formed of South America, Africa, the Middle East, Madagascar, India, Sri Lanka, Australia, New Zealand and Antarctica. (The name Gondwana means 'land of the Gonds' and is derived from an area of India that was once the ancient kingdom of the Gonds, an aboriginal tribe.)

How long Gondwana had been in existence is not known, but it must have been an entity as far back as the Cambrian period, some 540 million years ago. How the vast landmass was assembled is also unknown, but the constituent parts must have formed independently during the Precambrian and early Palaeozoic. Australia itself was positioned with the eastern and northern edges external, and the southern and western edges internal to the supercontinent.

The external edges had oceanic crustal material added where the proto-Pacific Plate converged on the continent, and the internal edges show rifting where the supercontinent split apart along what are now mid-oceanic ridges. The two areas therefore have quite different structures and histories.

Satellite imagery has revolutionised our capacity to understand the continent physically and economically. We now have a broader frame of reference for studying the relation between geological structure and topography; climate, soils and vegetation; and forests, bedrock and moisture. The images also provide information about the location of mineral resources and the advance of salinisation in agricultural areas.

Satellite false-colour image of part of the large iron-ore mining area of the Pilbara region, Western Australia, looking north. The exposed rocks form part of the Hamersley Basin. Some of the sediments that filled the basin are known as banded iron formations. These show up well as the predominantly blue and green features in the northern part of the image. The sediments have been folded into complex anticlines and synclines. The Ophthalmia Range syncline is the canoe-shaped structure lying across the centre of the image. The Fortescue River and tributaries occupy a large part of the southeastern corner. Their valleys are filled with Tertiary sediments that cover all the older rocks and appear as brownish tints. Their pattern of deposition shows up as a set of lines that resembles contour ploughing. The vegetation in the floors of the river valleys appears as narrow strips of emerald-green.

HOW THE CONTINENT DEVELOPED

The main exposed Precambrian blocks and sedimentary basins, and the fold belts where mountains formed in Precambrian and Palaeozoic times. The Tasman Line marks the division between Precambrian rocks on the west and Cambrian and later rocks (which form the Tasman Fold Belt) on the east.

The earliest rocks in Australia are found in the western half of the continent. They formed as much as 4,200 million years ago and are among the oldest on the Earth. Over millions of years these Precambrian lavas and sediments became deeply buried in the Earth's crust and were transformed by heat and pressure into metamorphic rocks penetrated at depth by masses of granite. Such rock complexes contain much of Australia's reserves of gold, nickel, cobalt and other metals found at such places as Kalgoorlie and Kambalda in Western Australia.

Between these ancient Precambrian centres, or nuclei, are sedimentary basins containing thick iron-rich strata formed during a later phase of continental development. These include the famous iron ore deposits of Hamersley and Mt Newman, which are also in Western Australia.

About 2,000 million years ago zones of melting at the base of the Earth's crust caused rifting, and the resulting rift basins filled with volcanic material and coarse sediments. Subsequent cooling produced broad shallow basins that again filled with sediment. Faulting, folding and shearing of all these rocks, and extensive penetration by bodies of granite, took place about 1,800 million years ago.

Between 1,800 and 1,200 million years ago, still in Precambrian times, some of the ancient lines of weakness were reactivated and the intrusion of further granites occurred. As a result of this sequence of events, vast areas of crust were stabilised and added to the more ancient continental rocks to form the Australian craton or 'shield'. The same events were responsible for the formation of mineral deposits such as those at Mount Isa in Queensland and Broken Hill in New South Wales, from which much of the continent's silver, lead, zinc and copper are mined.

Later, some of these older blocks again split internally or subsided along their margins to produce depressions in which sediments accumulated, some of them still clearly visible in the landscape today. The Macdonnell Ranges, for example, running east–west through the Alice Springs region in the Northern Territory, mark the northern edge of the Amadeus Basin, a downfaulted trough full of sediment, which is more than 10 km thick in places. A scarp slope, of which the Stirling Ranges in Western Australia form a part, represents the faulted western edge of the Yilgarn Block. Not all these breaks

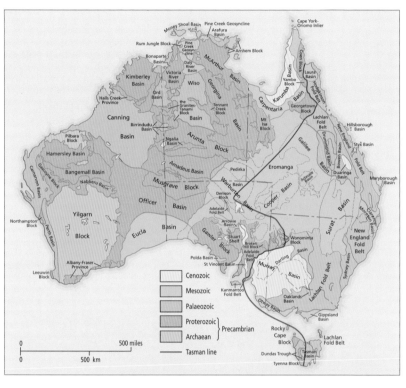

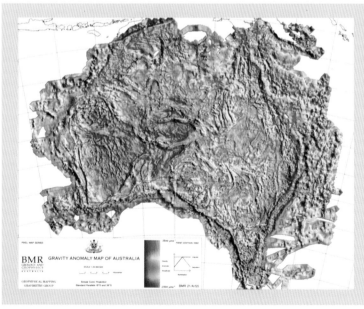

The structure of the Australian continent revealed by a gravity anomaly map. The different colours indicate regional variations in values of gravitational acceleration. The values, measured to an accuracy of one part in a million, differ from a datum. These differences are either positive (greater) or negative (less than the datum value) and depend primarily on variations in the density of material forming the Earth's crust. By contouring these differences over the continent, the shapes of old Precambrian blocks, sedimentary basins and major dislocations are defined. The margins of the continent (shown in red) indicate positive anomalies — the result of rifting.

The western Macdonnell Ranges, west of Alice Springs, are formed of Precambrian rocks that were strongly folded during two main episodes, the first about 550 million and the second about 300 million years ago. The steeply inclined strata have different resistances to erosion.

occurred at the same time; nor were they short-lived. The one along the Macdonnell Ranges was active from 1,000 million to about 300 million years ago.

At about the same time as the faulting along the Macdonnell Ranges line began, the eastern side of the Gawler Block also began to subside. Sandy sediments of great thickness (up to 20 km) accumulated in this subsidence until late in Cambrian times when they were deformed to produce the complex set of folds exposed today in the Flinders Ranges of South Australia (see p. 2).

Near the beginning of the Cambrian, about 540 million years ago, the eastern side of the continent began to grow as volcanic chains of islands and intervening basins formed. This is referred to as the Tasman Fold Belt. It has two components – the western Lachlan Fold Belt (Cambrian–Devonian) and the eastern New England Fold Belt (Devonian–Permian). Strips of sediment and volcanic material, penetrated by granites, today mark the sites of these ancient structures. Masses of material deposited on the ocean floor were transported towards the continental margin and plastered on to the land mass by the movement of the oceanic plate. Rocks of this type are well exposed in the New England Tablelands of New South Wales and the Coastal Belt of Queensland. In Permo-Triassic times, 280–230 million years ago, depressions behind this accreting mass accumulated quantities of sediments rich in plant fossils that became the coal deposits on which much of Australia's prosperity depends.

LATER CONTINENTAL SUBSIDENCE

The extent of the inland sea that covered the Great Artesian Basin and northern Australia in Cretaceous times.

By the beginning of the Mesozoic era, about 240 million years ago, most of the crustal movement had ceased. Australia's subsequent geological history is characterised by regional depressions in a relatively stable continental landmass.

The greatest of these depressions is the Great Artesian Basin, which occupies about a fifth of Australia. This vast basin was partly filled by sediment deposited from streams and lakes associated with a great internal drainage system – rather like the present Lake Eyre drainage in central Australia. These sediments lie on a variety of older rocks that range in age from the Precambrian to the Permian.

During the early Cretaceous (100–120 million years ago) the sea broke through in the Gulf of Carpentaria region and near Maryborough in Queensland to produce a vast inland sea. Variation in the sand content of the sediments deposited both before and after this marine incursion produced interleaving layers of water-bearing strata (aquifers) and impervious deposits. Water under pressure can be tapped using boreholes, and this has enabled pastoral development to succeed in areas of very low rainfall. Other comparable depressed areas are the Eucla Basin (Nullarbor Plain).

In general, the sedimentary rocks filling the basin dip inwards from the edge and, being porous, carry quantities of water underground. In the Great Artesian Basin, this water filters down to great depths because of the thickness of the sedimentary strata, and is trapped there. In the Eucla Basin, it is not trapped because the basin is open to the sea. In the Murray Basin, in contrast, the outlet is so small that underground water builds up. (See also pp. 17–20).

It is important to note that the great plains areas in the eastern and western halves of Australia result from different geological events. In the east, major crustal depressions were filled by sediment scoured off the surrounding uplands, whereas in the west the plains areas were formed by the continued planing off of ancient Precambrian blocks that have continued to rise slowly to maintain an equilibrium position (that is, isostatically).

THE RIFTED MARGINS

The present margins of the continent are the result of plate movements during and after the Jurassic period. About 160 million years ago the western margin was formed by one of the splits that dismem-

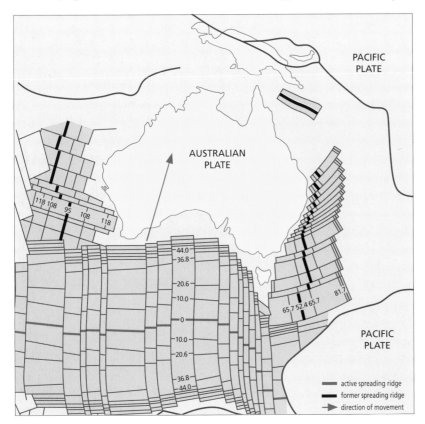

bered the supercontinent Gondwana. Part of southeast Asia, not peninsular India (which was joined to Antarctica to the south), separated from western Australia in a series of complicated movements reflected in the complex arrangement of the sea-floor spreading zones forming the Indian Ocean. The so-called North West Shelf is formed of a series of fault blocks that served first as traps for sediment and then, as crustal movements declined, as a platform on which carbonate sediments were deposited during the Tertiary period. This remarkable sequence of rocks is already proving a valuable source of natural gas and, as drilling technology advances, further resources are bound to be located in the area.

During the late Cretaceous, about 95 million years ago, a rift within the boundaries of the southeastern part of the continent led to New Zealand and the Lord Howe Rise moving off to the east. This explains why the Sydney Basin and other eastern Australian geological elements are abruptly truncated at the present continental shelf. Spreading was more rapid at the southern end of the rift, and the Tasman Sea is hence widest in the south. Rifting along this line had ceased by around 52 million years ago, and the present Pacific Plate margin lies well to the east of Australia, along the line shown on the map below.

Between northeastern Queensland and the present Solomon Islands (not in existence at the time) there was a second short-lived rift between about 65 and 50 million years ago. This produced a deep trench called the Coral Sea Trough. Though initiated much later than the Tasman Sea rift, this terminated at about the same time. The spreading axes of the two rifts are believed to be connected, but substantially offset.

The southern margin of Australia was formed when Antarctica split off along the mid-oceanic ridge shown on the map. These movements were initiated about 100 million years ago, but at first had little impact. The main northwards movements began about 60 million years ago during the Palaeocene. Antarctica seems to have remained almost stationary but the spreading ridge, as well as Australia, moved northwards. This gives a remarkable average rate of movement of the continent of 5–6 cm for each year during the past 65 million years.

This northwards movement has had several consequences. First, the continent has moved through several climatic belts, the histories of which are recorded in the continental sediments. The interior has not always been barren sand dune country. Aridity dates back only to the Pliocene (4–5 million years ago), and even then it was not as severe as at present. The extensive dune systems that cover the central part of the continent date from the Plio-Pleistocene (the past 2 million years) when the continent was approximately in its present position and global climates were fluctuating between cold and dry, warm and wet.

Second, it is well known that certain parts of the Earth's mantle become extremely hot, melting rocks that force their way through the overlying crust. These high-temperature regions are called hot spots. When a crustal plate moves over a hot spot, a linear series of volcanoes forms, the best-known example being the Hawaiian Island chain. Comparable series of hot spots under eastern Australia and in the Tasman Sea have resulted in several volcanic remnants from northern Queensland to Victoria. These

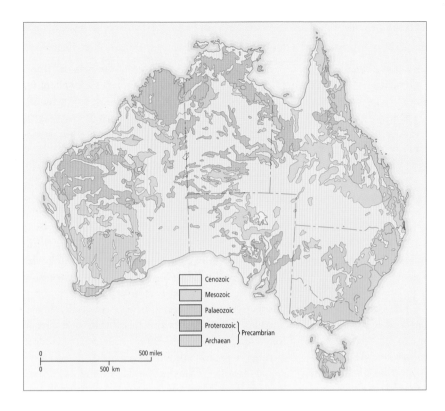

Cenozoic
Mesozoic
Palaeozoic
Proterozoic }
Archaean   } Precambrian

0   500 miles
0   500 km

of slices of more recent rocks heaped up one against the other to form the island's mountainous spine.

Finally, irregularities in the opening between Australia and Antarctica produced the Otway and Gippsland Basins of Victoria. Here the sea advanced and retreated several times over long periods, producing sedimentary wedges and – in the Gippsland Basin in particular – oil and gas sufficient to supply about 60 per cent of Australia's current oil and 27 per cent of its gas productions.   KSWC

Climate

Australia has a relatively harsh and variable climate. Most of the interior is dry; more than three-quarters of the continent receives less than 600 mm of rainfall a year and half the continent less than 300 mm. Northern Australia, however, has heavy monsoonal rains in summer (December–February) and occasionally destructive tropical cyclones. Southern Australia enjoys a generally mild but still highly variable climate with predominantly winter (June–August) rains and frequent spring (September–November) and summer bushfires in the southeastern states.

Climatic records for a few places go back to the early 1800s but the major growth in the network of observing stations took place in the decade or so before the 1908 transfer of responsibility for meteorological observations from the former colonial/state governments to the Commonwealth. The first comprehensive description of the climate of the whole continent was published in 1913.

The present-day networks used for monitoring of

Below   An anthill on the Atherton Tablelands in northeastern Queensland. The fertile soils of the tablelands are based on volcanic rocks. Vulcanism in the Atherton region began about 7 million years ago and continued spasmodically to within the past 500,000 years. In the area are several spectacular crater lakes, among them Lake Barrine.

Right   Part of Lake Eildon in central Victoria, dried up during 1983. This is normally a popular water-skiing resort. Droughts are a regular feature of Australia's climate.

include the spectacular Glass House, Nandewar and Warrumbungle mountains. The hot spot in the Tasman Sea has resulted in a series of flat-topped submarine mountains (called guyots) off the New South Wales coast. In addition, cracks in the crust resulted in the outpouring of thick piles of basalt from the Atherton Tablelands in the north to the Darling Downs in the south of Queensland, the New England Tablelands in the north and the Monaro Tablelands in the south of New South Wales, and the plains of western Victoria. These are some of the most fertile parts of the country.

Third, the northwards movement of Australia brought the stable landmass into contact with curved belts of islands (island arcs) produced along the edge of the Pacific Plate, forming a collision zone in which relatively recent rocks were thrust on to the leading edge of the stable continental rocks. This is well seen in New Guinea, the southern part of which is Australian continent and the northern part is composed

the month-to-month and year-to-year fluctuations of climate and assembly of the national climatic record consist of some 6,000 rainfall observing stations, 500 stations measuring a range of other variables such as temperature, cloudiness, humidity and wind, and 50 upper-air stations measuring temperature, wind and humidity up to a height of 15–20 km.

MAJOR CLIMATIC INFLUENCES

Two of the main global-scale influences on the Australian climate are the descending branch of the so-called Hadley Cell and the ascending branch of the Walker Circulation.

The Hadley Cell is a major north–south overturning in the atmosphere around the Equator. It is ultimately driven by the differences in radiative heating by the sun between the Equator and the poles. The air that ascends in the heated tropics accelerates eastwards as it moves south until the westerly current breaks down into waves and eddies – the familiar meandering jet stream of the upper troposphere, which approximately overlies the surface high-pressure ridge at mid-latitudes.

In the middle of winter (July), the region of tropical ascent migrates into the Northern Hemisphere and the sub-tropical ridge with its series of eastward-moving anticyclones migrates northwards over Australia. Southeasterly to easterly winds predominate over the northern half of the continent and southern Australia is influenced by a general northwesterly to southwesterly flow. In the middle of summer (January), the high-pressure ridge moves southwards and the equatorial trough and northwesterly monsoon winds extend over northern Australia.

The Walker Circulation involves a slow, large-scale east–west overturning along the Equator with its major cell lying across the Pacific. Air ascends in the heavy rainfall region of the warm western Pacific, flows eastwards in the upper troposphere and descends over the cold waters of the eastern Pacific off the desert coasts of Chile and Peru.

WEATHER SYSTEMS

Three major types of daily weather systems contribute to the pattern of Australian climate:

- The eastward-moving, low-pressure systems, with their associated rain-bearing cold fronts, move regularly across southern Australia in the westerlies during the winter
- The 'cut-off' lows to the north of the main belt of westerlies that bring occasional very heavy rains to the southeastern states
- The tropical cyclones that develop over the ocean to the north of Australia between December and April

Tropical cyclones are the most devastating of the weather systems affecting Australia, bringing destructive winds and torrential rains to coastal regions as they move inland. They follow erratic paths and their frequency varies markedly from year to year with, on average, about six cyclones directly affecting the Australian tropical coast annually. Tropical Cyclone Tracy, which struck Darwin on Christmas Day 1974 with a maximum recorded wind gust of 217 km per hour, totally destroyed more than half the buildings in the city and left a death toll of 65 with another 145 people seriously injured.

CLIMATIC PATTERNS

The main features of the Australian climate are evident from the mean annual patterns of rainfall, rain days and temperature. The heavy rainfall across northern Australia and along the eastern tropical coast reflects the influence of the summer monsoon and the effect of the Great Dividing Range on the

Schematic representation of the large-scale controls on the Australian climate. The cross-section of the 10–15-km deep troposphere, shown in exaggerated vertical scale, depicts (left), the mean meridional circulation pattern consisting of the Hadley Cell, the Ferrel Cell and the Antarctic Cell. On the right is a cross-section of the zonally averaged zonal wind with the westerly jet stream dominating the upper troposphere in the middle latitudes. The map (centre) shows a typical daily surface-pressure pattern, with the subtropical high-pressure ridge near its winter location. The cross-section along the Equator (top) shows the main ascending branch of the Walker circulation – a large-scale east–west circulation cell across the tropical Pacific.

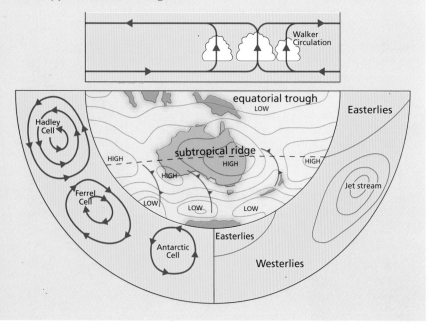

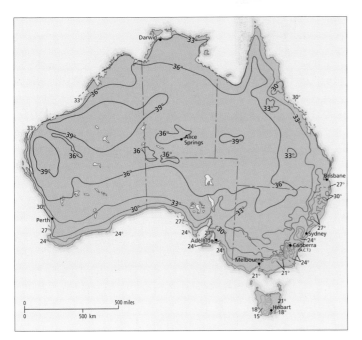

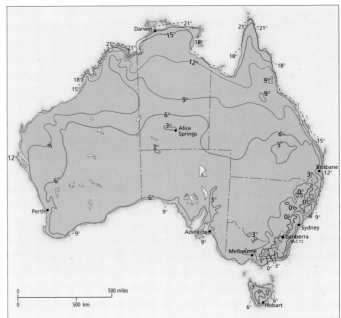

Above left *Average (mean) maximum temperature in January (in °C).*

Above right *Average (mean) minimum temperature in July (in °C).*

Below left *Median annual rainfall (in mm); that is, the amount of rainfall equalled or exceeded in 50 per cent of years.*

Below right *Average (mean) annual number of rain days (a rain day occurs when a daily rainfall of at least 0.2 mm is recorded).*

MEAN RAINFALL AND TEMPERATURE STATISTICS FOR SOME AUSTRALIAN CITIES

City	Rainfall (mm) Jan.	July	Rain days Jan.	July	Max. temp. (°C) Jan.	July	Min. temp (°C) Jan.	July
Cairns	424	28	18	9	31.1	25.5	23.5	17.0
Brisbane	164	57	13	7	29.4	20.4	20.8	9.6
Sydney	102	101	13	11	25.8	15.9	18.4	7.9
Melbourne	47	48	8	15	25.8	13.3	14.0	5.7
Hobart	48	53	11	15	21.5	11.5	11.7	4.4
Canberra	60	39	8	10	27.7	11.1	12.9	−0.3
Adelaide	20	66	4	16	29.5	15.0	16.4	7.3
Perth	8	174	3	18	29.6	17.3	17.7	9.0
Port Hedland	59	10	5	2	36.3	26.8	25.4	11.9
Darwin	409	1	21	0	31.7	30.3	24.7	19.2
Alice Springs	38	17	5	3	35.9	19.4	21.0	4.0

Sources: Australian Bureau of Meteorology, *Climate of Australia* (1989) and *Climatic Averages, Australia* (1989).

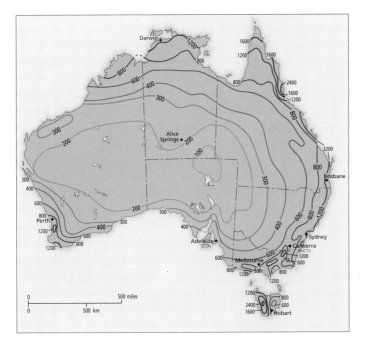

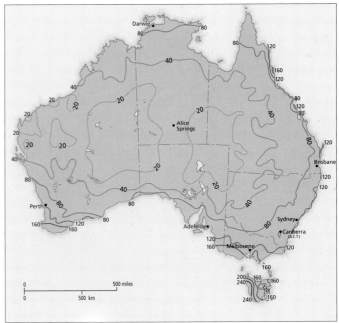

Climatic variability and change

The Australian climate is characterised by very large year-to-year variability, which amply justifies its description as a land of 'droughts and flooding rains'.

The graph shows an 80-year record of year-to-year rainfall anomalies (that is, departures from the long-term mean of around 500 mm) for the Murray–Darling Basin, Australia's largest river system, together with the corresponding anomalies of average maximum temperatures.

The temperature record highlights the large natural variability of climate but shows no sign of the long-term warming trend that is expected to occur as a result of the enhanced greenhouse effect from the continuing build-up of atmospheric carbon dioxide and other trace gases from human activities. Measurements from coastal stations in southeastern Australia reveal a gradual long-term warming trend, but whether this is

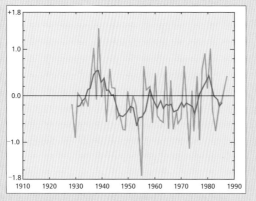

caused by the enhanced greenhouse effect or some natural fluctuation is not yet known. JWZ

Annual rainfall (blue lines) and maximum temperature anomalies (pink lines) and 5-year running means (green and red lines) for the Murray–Darling Basin of inland southeastern Australia.

Queensland in January 1889 and the lowest is −22.2°C at Charlotte Pass in the Australian Alps in July 1945. JWZ

Soils

Australian soils are often described as very old, highly weathered and mostly infertile. This is a broad generalisation but it contains some elements of truth. Soils result from the complex interaction of several factors – climate, organisms, topography, parent material and time. Because there are few if any instances where each of the above factors applies to the same degree, soils everywhere in Australia exist in great variety.

SOIL EVOLUTION

Many soils have formed from older weathered materials on progressively younger surfaces. Some formed on stable surfaces under frequently changing climatic conditions; others developed from older materials redistributed by water and wind. There is little apparent relation between climatic zonation and soil type today in Australia and soil parent materials are more important in determining the soil pattern.

There are many reasons for the diverse and sometimes unexpected range of soils on the continent. For example, in the arid inland, it is not uncommon to find soils that are highly weathered and leached next to soils that are little weathered. Climatic and geomorphic history are important in understanding this type of soil pattern. We now know that geological events dating from the onset of the Cenozoic era (about 65 million years ago) had a significant influence on present-day soil distribution. (See also pp. 4–9.)

The Cenozoic tectonic history of Australia is comparatively low key. No fold mountains developed, nor did extensive rift valleys open up; volcanic activity was largely restricted to a narrow region along the eastern and southeastern coasts; and movement of the Earth's crust consisted mostly of gentle, although significant, uplifts, which are most marked in the southeastern highlands. During much of the Cenozoic, Australia probably had a low relief similar to that of today. A further consequence of this low relief and the continent's latitudinal position is that the glacial periods of the past 2 million years were minor and restricted to the southeastern highlands and Tasmania.

onshore southeasterly winds on the Queensland coast. The region with the highest rainfall is the Queensland coast south of Cairns where Tully has a median annual rainfall of 4,048 mm. The region with the lowest rainfall is around Lake Eyre in South Australia, from where a vast area of low rainfall extends westwards across the continent embracing the Simpson, Gibson and Great Victoria deserts.

Average annual temperatures range from around 28°C on the Kimberley coast in the north of Western Australia to about 4°C in the alpine regions of southeastern Australia. Average daily maximum temperatures range from over 40°C over a large area of the northern interior of Western Australia in summer to around 0°C in the higher parts of the Australian Alps in winter. Average night-time minima range from about 25°C along the northwestern coast in summer to around −6°C in the Alps in winter. The highest recorded temperature is 53.1°C at Cloncurry in

Opposite The broad distribution pattern of Australian soils.

Characteristic soil features

A common element of many Australian landscapes is the iron-rich, mostly hardened material called laterite, ferricrete or duricrust. This is often associated with a mottled red-and-white layer that either underlies the laterite or exists separately, often as a remnant of erosion. This mottled layer may grade downwards to a pale bleached material usually called the pallid zone.

This sequence has long been called the laterite profile, but over large areas of Australia only eroded remnants of it survive. Some of these deeply weathered profiles date at least from the early Cenozoic, some 65 million years ago. Most formed in wetter environments than those in which they occur today, but others appear to be in zones where iron was locally mobilised and redeposited by groundwater.

Because the bleached or iron-mottled zones did not form under similar conditions or at the same time, the old idea of using the laterite profile as a stratigraphic and chronological datum over wide areas of Australia is no longer accepted.

The widespread occurrence in the more arid regions of silicified material called silcrete is also puzzling. This term is usually applied to deposits on or near the surface in which various saprolites (soft, weathered rocks), sediments or soils are cemented by

Erosion of texture-contrast soils near Canberra, ACT. This sheep-rearing land was overgrazed by rabbits when their population reached very high levels in the 1930s and this led to severe erosion by wind and water.

silica, often forming conspicuous landscape features such as flat-topped hills (mesas).

Similarly, much of the stony material on the surface of many of the arid inland areas (the so-called gibber plains) consists of silcrete fragments of various sizes. The precise origin of this material is still uncertain. One theory is that silica cementation occurred during soil formation under stable environmental conditions, perhaps over prolonged periods in landscapes of comparatively low relief at the end of long sedimentary cycles. Most Australian silcretes appear to be of middle to late Tertiary age.

Calcium carbonate accumulations, collectively known as calcrete, are a feature of southern Australia. Most are now thought to be ancient soil features, and much of the carbonate (perhaps largely derived from Miocene marine sediments) has been distributed through the region by wind erosion and deposition during the past 2 million years. In many places today, calcretes form the parent materials for present-day soils.

Evidence of past wind (aeolian) activity is also widespread in less-dry parts of Australia. Some aeolian landforms such as the remains of dunes and crescentic ridges called lunettes, which are now covered in vegetation, may date back to 16,000–20,000 years ago.   RFI

SOIL GROUPS

Australia has six broad groups of soils with the following features:

1 *Shallow stony soils* Gravel or stone throughout the profile, with no horizons and usually of shallow depth.
2 *Deep sands* Usually more than 1 m deep and siliceous, with minimal development of soil profile. Many such soils have formed on aeolian materials (eroded and deposited by wind); others result from the dismembering of old iron-rich weathering profiles.
3 *Sesquioxidic soils* Soils with clay fractions usually dominated by kaolinite and iron oxides. Clay contents usually increase gradually with depth. Many are relict soils and extremely deep.
4 *Cracking clays* Soils with high clay content (50–70 per cent) that swell and shrink greatly on wetting and drying. They have a wide range in depth and usually form on more alkaline parent materials.
5 *Texture-contrast soils* Very diverse soils; characterised by a marked difference in texture between the lighter surface soils and heavier (usually clay)

shallow stony soils	cracking clays
deep sands	texture-contrast soils
sesquioxidic soils	calcareous soils

0   500 miles

0   500 km

subsoils. Many of the latter are dense and very slowly permeable because of their sodic nature.

6 *Calcareous soils* Characterised by soft and/or hard carbonate accumulations throughout the soil; shallow to deep profiles, the latter usually formed on aeolian materials of diverse ages.

Many other soils have formed but these occupy only relatively small areas of the continent. Some widespread world soil types, especially those derived from volcanic ash and Pleistocene glacial deposits, are absent and soils much changed by human activity are rare.

There are, however, several distinctive soil landscape patterns in Australia. First are the soils of the arid zone, many of them acid and strongly weathered – unusual characteristics for such an environment. Second are the cracking clays. Although India and Africa also have large areas of soils of this type, the variety in Australia is much greater. Australia also has a higher proportion of texture-contrast soils than any other continent. These are extremely diverse; they vary in profile depth from about 30 cm to more than 5 m, in the abruptness of increase of their clay component from the surface to the subsoil, in acidity and degree of weathering, and in the erodibility of the subsoils.

LAND USE AND HUMAN SETTLEMENT

Although the regional pattern of different types of land use has been largely determined by climate and, to a lesser extent, by topography, differences in soil nutrients and water availability have generally determined the local areas used for particular crops within the broad climatic regions.

In a generally dry continent such as Australia the optimal use of water for plant crops is paramount. Many areas suffer moisture stress for at least a part of most years, and moisture conservation, which usually involves a fallow period, has long been a feature of Australian agriculture. This has meant, for example, that grain will grow on stored moisture in cracking clays in areas of relatively low and very unreliable rainfall in Queensland and New South Wales. By contrast, in southern Australia wheat growing is possible and indeed favoured on light-textured soils because the winter rains are reliable.

These two examples illustrate the need to consider soil and climatic factors together in almost all forms of land use. This is particularly so in the case of irrigation where excess water (either by rain or inappropriate irrigation) can lead to serious problems such as waterlogging and salinity caused by rising water levels (water tables).

Although Australia has long been regarded as having largely infertile soils, it is more correct to say that large areas are deficient in particular plant nutrients, some areas being highly deficient in many nutrients. The relative importance of these factors depends on whether in today's climate it is possible to improve land use. The reasons for nutrient deficiency invariably lie in the past weathering history of the soils.

The two most widespread deficiencies are phosphorus and nitrogen. In southern Australia, both are countered by the long-established and widespread agricultural use of phosphate fertilisers and pasture legumes. Other deficiencies are common, but usually less widespread. The most significant are sulphur, potassium, and the trace elements molybdenum, copper, zinc and manganese. Some toxicity problems also occur – for example, aluminium and manganese in acid soils, and boron in highly alkaline soils. (See also p. 284.)

Although Australia has always been sparsely inhabited, over much of its area there have been tremendous changes since European settlement some 200 years ago. Before colonisation, Australian soils had neither been cleared of vegetation (other than occasionally by fire) nor cultivated. Human settlement has accordingly had a strong impact in the more favourable climatic zones. Clearing has been coupled with the introduction of exotic livestock, not only cattle, sheep and goats, but also rabbits. These changes, especially those caused by unwise land use, have had harmful effects on many soils.

The chief forms of land degradation are fivefold:

- Erosion by water and wind resulting from the cultivation of erodible soils on steep slopes or in extreme climatic environments, and from the removal of plant cover by excessive grazing; this latter process is often exacerbated by drought.
- Salinity caused by rising water tables as a result of the removal of trees or the excessive use of irrigation water (see also p. 18).
- Acidification largely due to the leaching of nitrates during winter in temperate Australia, a result of the introduction of subterranean clover in cropping and grazing areas.
- Depletion of the original, generally low, reserves of organic matter in many Australian soils, the result of intensive cropping over long periods. This has led to the breakdown of soil structure and the consequent formation of a hard surface crust, a deterioration that inhibits water penetration and the emergence of seedlings.
- Growth of towns. There is a continuing and irreversible loss of land due to urbanisation, a serious problem because of the marked concentration of Australian population centres in the better-watered coastal zone.

RFI

Water resources

SURFACE WATER

I love a sunburnt country
A land of sweeping plains,
Of ragged mountain ranges,
Of droughts and flooding rains

– Dorothea Mackellar [1885–1968]

Australia has a very variable rainfall regime principally because of three factors: its mid-latitude position, its low relief and its oceanic isolation. Its landscape, soils and vegetation combine to transform this varied rainfall pattern into an even more variable and unpredictable sequence of runoff. The average annual runoff is the lowest of all continents.

In most parts of Australia, the ratio of the largest recorded flows to the average monthly and annual flows is very large; indeed, most large rivers have ceased to flow at some time since records began, including the whole Murray–Darling Drainage Division. The Burdekin River in northeastern Queensland, probably the seventh largest river in Australia, ceased to flow most years before a large regulating dam was built. In 1958, seven months after a peak flow rate of 38,500 m³/s – probably the highest flow rate this century – and a flood volume of 15,000 million megalitres it ceased to flow. (A megalitre, ML, is equivalent to 1,000 cm³ and close to the old non-metric measure of an acre-foot; 1 million ML = 1 km³.)

Australian rivers and streams are as unusual in their behaviour as the continent's unique flora and fauna, that likewise are a response to the continent's highly variable rainfall. The rainfall pattern has been termed – only half in jest – a marsupial hydrology.

Demands for water

A coastal and highly concentrated population and localised industry, coupled with a high standard of living, has produced unusual demands and significant local stress on regional water resources. In the future, there is scope for development of the significant water resources of the lightly populated northern part of the continent, although this poses a considerable challenge because of the lack of conventional dam sites.

Australia's highly urbanised population is concentrated, with industry, in five coastal locations centred around Brisbane, Sydney, Melbourne, Adelaide and Perth. Adelaide and Perth already have limited surface water resources. As a result, Perth is increasingly dependent on groundwater – also a limited resource – and Adelaide, which normally draws 40 per cent of its water from the Murray River by pipeline, has to take up to 70 per cent in drought periods.

More than 80 per cent of all water diverted from streams is used for irrigation. Domestic use dominates urban and industrial supplies and in large part is used for gardens. The other important difference from many other developed countries is that most thermal power stations are cooled by sea water or special cooling ponds and not river flows.

Annual runoff

Australia receives on average 420 mm of rain a year, and of this only 48 mm runs off into the surrounding oceans. Antarctica, with 150–200 mm annual precipitation, receives less but it discharges about 160 mm as iceflows. Australia is therefore often described as the driest continent. Almost half of Australia's land surface has no direct discharge to the sea, and a third of this internal region drains into the Lake Eyre system, the lowest point in Australia at 15 m below sea level.

The Murray–Darling Basin is a region of similar size to the Lake Eyre Basin – 106 million ha, one-seventh of Australia – but, unlike Lake Eyre, it discharges to the sea in South Australia with a mean outflow of 12.2 million ML. This volume is, however, less than half the total annual runoff generated in the streams of the basin. The balance is lost by evaporation of floodwaters in the broad, flat, riverine landscapes.

Aerial view of the meandering River Murray on the New South Wales–Victoria border, near Albury. The river is Australia's most important inland waterway and is also a major source of freshwater for irrigation and urban development.

SURFACE WATER RESOURCES OF THE DRAINAGE DIVISIONS

| | Drainage division | Area (km2) | Mean annual runoff | Mean annual outflow | Surface water resource (thousands of megalitres) | | | | | Developed resource |
| | | | | | Major divertible resource | | | | | |
					Fresh	Marginal	Brackish	Saline	Total	
Northeast Coast	I	451,000	83,900	83,900	22,900	0	0	0	22,900	3,540
Southeast Coast	II	274,000	41,900	41,900	14,700	236	113	16	15,100	4,280
Tasmania	III	68,200	52,900	52,900	10,900	0	0	0	10,900	1,020
Murray–Darling	IV	1,060,000	24,300	12,200	12,300	32	0	0	12,400	10,000
South Australian Gulf	V	82,300	877	767	160	71	34	4	269	118
Southwest Coast	VI	315,000	6,670	6,600	1,390	466	849	164	2,870	385
Indian Ocean	VII	519,000	3,960	3,840	235	50	7	4	295	27
Timor Sea	VIII	547,000	80,700	80,700	22,000	0	0	0	22,00	1,980
Gulf of Carpentaria	IX	641,000	92,500	92,500	13,200	0	0	0	13,200	78
Lake Eyre	X	1,170,000	6,310	0	204	0	0	0	204	26
Bulloo–Bancannia	XI	101,000	1,090	0	41	0	0	0	41	0
Western Plateau	XII	2,450,000	1,580	0	102	0	0	0	102	0
Island Territories	XIII	717	n/a	n/a	n/a	n/a	n/a	n/a	n/a	0
	TOTAL	7,680,000	397,000	375,00	98,100	865	1,040	188	100,000	21,500

Source: *Review of Australia's Water Resources and Water Use*, Vol 1 (Australian Government Publishing Service for Australian Water Resources Council, 1985).

Opposite The major rivers and the mean annual runoff of fresh surface water under average seasonal conditions in drainage divisions I–XII.

The table above and the map (p. 17) clearly show the limited wet rim of the continent. The current estimate of divertible freshwater is only a quarter of annual runoff and the currently developed resource is only a fifth of the divertible resource – a twentieth of the annual runoff.

If the total annual runoff is divided by the population, the volume of water available per person is 28 ML. This amount, which is much greater than in most developed countries, is exceeded only by such acknowledged water-rich countries as Canada and New Zealand.

More than 50 per cent of the total runoff, but only one-seventh of the divertible resources, is contained in northern Australia (equatorwards of 20°S) in Drainage Divisions VII, VIII, IX and I. This is a region of low development and even lower population but one with great development potential. It is mostly a region of low relief with insufficient storage opportunities to regulate flow. It is also subject to a summer monsoon with much of the surface runoff generated by occasional very heavy rainfall, associated with tropical cyclones and rain depressions – an irregular and unreliable source of runoff.

Drainage divisions

The most-developed water resource is that of the *Murray–Darling Basin* (Drainage Division IV). The estimated divertible flow, like the discharge, is half the annual runoff and is over 80 per cent developed. The storage capacity now totals 25.4 million ML – greater than the mean annual runoff. The water is used mainly for irrigation, much of it in large public schemes.

The largest dams in Division IV are in the Snowy Mountains region, which also store and divert 1 million ML of water from the coastal Division II (Southeast Coast) to Division IV, while generating, as hydroelectricity, about two-thirds of the potential energy available, and also large amounts of balancing energy using pump-turbine systems. (See also p. 196.)

The *Tasmanian* division (III) has a large supply of surface water, which is regulated by 61 large dams, 55 for hydroelectric purposes. The dams regulate over 60 per cent of the total runoff and store three times the divertible resource (70 per cent of the annual runoff).

The *Northeast Coast* division (I) has the largest divertible resource, of which some 15 per cent is developed. The far northern portion has high rainfall

INTERNATIONAL COMPARISON OF WATER RESOURCES

	Area (106km2)	Population mid-1980 ('000s)	Runoff (109m3)	Volume per person (m3)
Australia	7.7	14.5	400	28,000
Argentina	2.8	27.7	750	27,000
Canada	10.0	24.0	2,300	95,000
Israel	0.02	3.9	0.7	191
Italy	0.3	57.0	160	2,800
Japan	0.4	117.0	540	4,600
South Africa	1.1	29.3	51	1,700
New Zealand	0.3	3.3	393	120,000
USA	9.2	227.0	1,630	7,200

Source: J. A. H. Brown, *Water 2000*, Report No. 1 (Australian Government Publishing Service for Department of Resources and Energy, 1983).

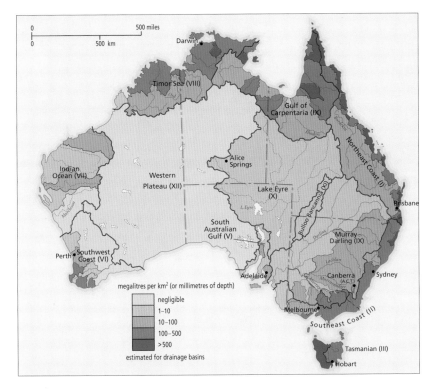

Tumut Pond reservoir, part of the Snowy Mountains hydro-electricity scheme. The diversion of surface runoff from the Snowy Mountains was first mooted in the late nineteenth century for irrigation purposes, but when work started in the 1950s the generation of hydro-electricity had become an equally important objective.

The *South Australian Gulf* division (V) has the smallest water resources of all the divisions that drain to the coast. It is almost fully developed to serve the needs of Adelaide and specialist farming.

The *Southwest Coast* division (VI) covers the southwest corner of the continent. The four basins closest to Perth are fully developed for urban and irrigation supplies. Much of the balance of the runoff is of marginal to saline quality, in part the result of land clearance. There is significant use of groundwater in this division and water appears to be the limiting resource for futher development.

The *Indian Ocean, Timor Sea* and *Gulf of Carpentaria* divisions (VII, VIII and IX) are remarkable for the small proportion of annual flow considered divertible and the even smaller proportion actually used. The single largest regulatory structure is the Ord River Dam and its storage Lake Argyle, which completely regulates the available discharge. However, evaporation and variable flow reduce the divertible resource to 40 per cent of the mean annual runoff of 5.1 million ML.

The *Lake Eyre, Bulloo–Bancannia* and *Western Plateau* divisions (X, XI and XII) do not discharge surface water to the ocean and probably little groundwater. Division X terminates in low-lying Lake Eyre. The lake was thought to receive floodwaters rarely but aerial and satellite observations during the past 20 years confirm irregular but frequent partial fillings. The 1974 flood, when the main lake spilled into South Lake Eyre, was probably the greatest inflow for 500 years. In 1984, an even more unusual but quite local flood spilled South Lake Eyre into the main lake.

Most of the large salt lakes marked on maps of Divisions X, XI and XII are groundwater sinks with only limited inflows from surface water and rainwater accumulations.   PMF

GROUNDWATER

The availability of water has been a major factor in the nature and direction of Australia's development. Groundwater in shallow and deep sedimentary deposits and in rocks is widespread. Although its quantity and quality vary greatly in different parts of the country, it is generally available in many areas where surface water resources are unreliable.

Australia's economically significant pastoral, agricultural and mining industries are all located inland in areas of low and highly variable rainfall and uncertain streamflow. However, many of these areas have large, deep groundwater basins. Additional sources of groundwater are in deposits and in surficial fractured, water-bearing rocks. The water-bearing unconsolidated sediments and rock strata are called

and river flow and this runoff has been partly developed for hydroelectricity. The largest single resource is the Burdekin River, where there is a dam that currently stores 1.75 million ML but could store 8.5 million ML. There is further development in the southern portion where the population is concentrated.

In the *Southeast Coast* division (II), only 35 per cent of the divertible water resources have been developed – mostly around the two metropolitan conurbations of Newcastle–Sydney–Wollongong and Melbourne–Geelong, where the resources are close to full development.

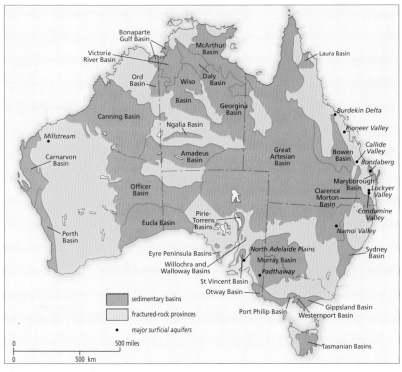

The major sources of groundwater.

Salinity

Salinisation of water supplies is a major problem in Australia, especially of groundwater from surficial and fractured-rock aquifers.

Fresh groundwater (that is, water with less than 1,000 mg/L total dissolved solids or TDS) occurs in about 10 per cent of the surficial aquifers, mainly in fan-shaped alluvial deposits in valleys and coastal river deposits. Brackish water (1,000–14,000 mg/L TDS) is found in about 30 per cent of the surficial aquifers and saline water (more than

14,000 mg/L TDS) in another 30 per cent.

The naturally brackish and saline aquifers are generally shallow and mainly occur inland. The basic cause of most human-induced salinity problems in Australia is the disturbance of groundwater systems by changes in land use, such as clearing land for agriculture and irrigation. Both practices lead to rises of water tables and to salinisation of land, and increased stream salinity.

MAH

Severely salinised soil in the wheatbelt of southwest Western Australia. The green vegetation in the foreground is samphire, one of the few plants able to tolerate the saline conditions. The cause of the salinity is a rising water table after adjacent lands were cleared for wheat growing.

aquifers. Sedimentary basins cover about 65 per cent of the continent and fractured-rock areas about 35 per cent.

More than 60 per cent of the continent's total area of 7.7 million km² is entirely dependent on groundwater; in another 20 per cent, groundwater is the major source of water. Australia's supplies of fresh groundwater could yield an estimated 72,000 million m³ (or 72 million megalitres, ML) a year, of which 14 million ML are divertible; for comparison, the estimate for surface water is 118 million ML. Currently, around 2.7 million ML of groundwater are used each year – about 13 per cent of the total annual supplies of freshwater on the continent. In addition, there are substantial resources of brackish and saline groundwater.

Abstraction of groundwater is highest in the irrigation areas, mainly from aquifers close to the surface. About three-quarters of all water used in Australia is for irrigation. Some 1.7 million ha of land (almost half of which is pasture) is irrigated; 12 per cent of the water used for irrigation is groundwater, almost all derived from private wells.

Groundwater is widely used in the southeastern, eastern and southwestern marginal parts of the continent and is mostly taken from private wells. Altogether, there are around 400,000 waterwells in Australia and these supply about 14 per cent of all water used each year (about 14.6 million ML).

Shallow aquifers

Most surficial aquifers generally consist of sediments derived from older rocks and deposited by rivers and streams. Most of these alluvial sediments are Cenozoic in age and are less than 150 m below the surface. Many of the most highly productive surficial aquifers with good-quality water are alluvial aquifers in river valleys bordering the Great Dividing Range in southeastern Australia and in coastal river valleys, where the groundwater is used for irrigation and urban supplies.

Exploitation of groundwater has, however, significantly changed many of the major surficial aquifers. Overdevelopment is a problem in the Burdekin Delta, Lockyer and Condamine Valleys in Queensland and Namoi Valley in New South Wales, North Adelaide Plains in South Australia, and several other areas. Seasonal and long-term climatic fluctuations, such as droughts of several years' duration, influence some of the shallower aquifers. To combat excessive extraction of groundwater and to prevent the intrusion of saltwater, limitations on groundwater withdrawal have been imposed in the Burdekin Delta and elsewhere, and a recharge scheme implemented.

In the Namoi Valley, 175,000 ML of groundwater are extracted annually from surficial aquifers, mostly for irrigation and to supply urban popula-

The Great Artesian Basin

The Great Artesian Basin occupies an area about a fifth of the size of Australia. It is a confined groundwater basin comprising a multilayered aquifer system. The aquifers occur in quartzose sandstones of continental origin and are confined by low permeability beds of siltstone, mudstone and by marine clayey sediments of middle Triassic to late Cretaceous age (231–65 million years ago).

Discovery of the basin's artesian groundwater resources, around 1880, made settlement possible and led to the establishment of an important livestock industry. The region's population is largely dependent on artesian groundwater. Groundwater from the aquifers in the Lower Cretaceous–Jurassic sequence is of good quality (with generally about 500–1,500 mg/L TDS), dominated by sodium bicarbonate.

In the southwestern part of the basin, the groundwater chemistry is characterised by sodium–chloride–sodium sulphate. The high water temperature, up to 100 °C, is a minor inconvenience for general use, but makes it a geothermal energy source in several places. In most areas of the basin, the water is chemically incompatible with the soils and therefore generally unsuitable for irrigation.

The Great Artesian Basin is up to 3,000 m thick, and forms a large, uplifted synclinal structure (that is, with the sedimentary layers downfolded into a basin shape) exposed along its eastern margin and tilted southwest. Recharge of the aquifers by infiltration of rainfall occurs mainly in the eastern marginal zone, an area of relatively high rainfall.

Large-scale groundwater movement is towards the southern, southwestern and western margins, where natural discharge occurs from many springs, most of which have built up mound-shaped deposits. The flow rate is between 1 and 5 m/year. The length of time the water remains in the aquifers ranges from 10,000 years near the eastern marginal recharge areas to 1.4 million years near the Queensland–South Australia border.

Flowing artesian waterwells have an average depth of 500 m, but one waterwell is known to be 2,136 m deep. Altogether, there are 4,700 wells in the basin that originally flowed but only 3,100 remain flowing. Their accumulated flow is 1,500 ML/day; individual flows exceed 100 L/s. The maximum recorded flow from 1,500 wells was 2,000 ML/day in 1918.

Water from the flowing artesian wells is usually distributed in open earth channels, which are tens of kilometres long, but a piped distribution is being introduced. The Olympic Dam mine and its Roxby Downs town in South Australia are supplied from artesian waterwells in the southern edge of the Great Artesian Basin by a pipeline of 110 km.

There are also 20,000 non-flowing artesian wells. Most are up to several hundred metres deep and are usually equipped with windmill-operated pumps, supplying on average 10 m3/day.

The water levels of the aquifers are still above ground level in most areas of the basin, but development has caused them to drop considerably in some places. In some heavily developed areas, this has caused regional differences of more than 100 m between the 1880s and 1980s. Rapid changes took place during the first half of the century, but conditions have stabilised during the past 35 years. Future (restricted) groundwater withdrawal will produce only minor changes in discharges and pressures according to basin-wide computer-model predictions.

MAH

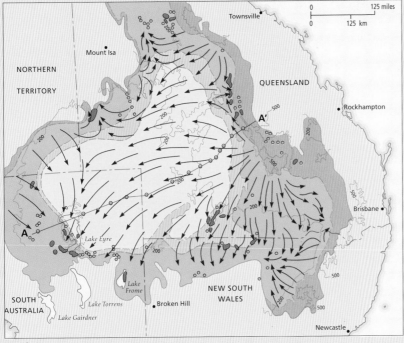

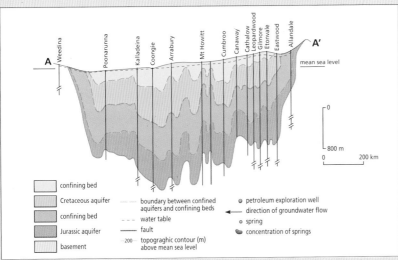

The Great Artesian Basin with its regional groundwaterflow directions and a schematic cross-section from A to A'.

tions. It is one of the most intensely developed groundwater systems in New South Wales. Some wells yield in excess of 200 L/s from alluvial deposits up to 120 m thick.

Many of the coastal valleys in the southeastern part of Australia contain small resources and are partially developed; major development of larger resources of alluvial aquifers has occurred in the Hunter, Mitchell and Latrobe Valleys.

Coastal sand dunes provide significant groundwater sources in parts of Queensland, New South Wales (especially for the town of Newcastle) and Tasmania. Dune sands of the Swan Coastal Plain, overlying the deeper confined aquifers in the Perth Basin, supply 40 per cent of Perth's town water. Total annual withdrawal from the surficial aquifers is 200,000 ML, most of it from uncontrolled private wells used for garden watering, irrigation of market gardens and industrial use. These unconfined, highly permeable, aquifers are highly susceptible to pollution.

Deep aquifers

Several major sedimentary basins underlying large parts of the arid and semi-arid zones of Australia provide significant groundwater resources for land development and settlement in regions of sparse and unreliable surface water. Some 30 per cent of groundwater in Australia is extracted from deep aquifers in the Palaeozoic, Mesozoic and Cenozoic sedimentary sequences in these basins. In some of the basins, the sediments are up to several thousand metres thick.

The best-known groundwater basins include the Great Artesian Basin, and the Murray, Perth, Georgina, Wiso, Daly and Otway Basins. The basins are on a vast scale; for example, the largest, the Great Artesian Basin, covers 1.7 million km^2 and even the smaller Murray Basin extends over 300,000 km^2.

The deep aquifers in these basins consist of sedimentary rocks and are usually tens or hundreds of metres thick. They are hydraulically continuous over large areas, are confined between semipervious layers and form multilayered aquifer systems.

The quality of groundwater in the deeper aquifers is usually better than in the shallow aquifers. Groundwater flows slowly in many of these deep basins and the long and deep flow paths result in very old, and warm to hot water.

Confined aquifers (or pressure aquifers) are bounded from above and below by impervious or semipervious layers, and are artesian. This means that the aquifers are completely filled with groundwater, and that the water level in wells drilled in such aquifers stands above the upper boundary of the aquifers. Flowing artesian wells and springs have water levels that rise above the land surface.

The Murray Basin is a closed groundwater basin with Tertiary sediments of land and sea origin up to 600 m thick. Groundwater is extensively exploited for livestock and irrigation, and increasingly for urban supplies. The basin contains some of the most important agricultural land in Australia. Groundwater yields differ widely, and water quality ranges from fresh to highly saline, with salt content in some areas up to several times that of seawater.

Recharge of the aquifers is from river valleys and alluvial fans draining the higher areas surrounding the basin, especially in the east and south. Regional groundwater movement is towards the central-western part of the basin, and the flow is partly intercepted and drained by the River Murray, which drains most of the inland southeastern region.

The surface-water resources of the River Murray are highly developed, mainly for irrigation, and provide significant supplies for Adelaide and large parts of South Australia. Large-scale clearing of native vegetation has increased recharge, the salinisation of land and the discharge of saline waters. Irrigation has produced large groundwater mounds beneath the irrigated areas and caused waterlogging and salinisation.

Fractured-rock aquifers

Aquifers in fractured rocks (igneous, metamorphic and some sedimentary rocks) provide groundwater from cracks, fractures, joints, cavities and zones of weathering. The yield and quality of the groundwater are often poor but in many arid, mountainous and bare areas these aquifers, which are usually unconfined, may provide the principal supply of water.

One-third of Australia's waterwells are in fractured-rock aquifers. They supply 310,000 ML of water per year or 10 per cent of total groundwater extraction, mainly for pastoral agriculture and domestic use. The population of large areas relies heavily on them. Yields from individual wells are usually small but techniques have been developed to improve them.

Two-thirds of the wells in fractured-rock aquifers occur in the eastern and southern parts of the continent, and they usually provide small yields of good-quality water, particularly in the higher, mountainous parts. Most other wells in fractured-rock aquifers occur in the southwestern region. The quality of groundwater there is generally poor, which is unfortunate as the aquifers underlie an economically important wheat-growing area with a widely dispersed, but relatively high population. Elsewhere in the arid and semi-arid parts of the continent groundwater from fractured rocks provides reliable supplies for livestock, domestic and town water supplies and some mining areas.   MAH

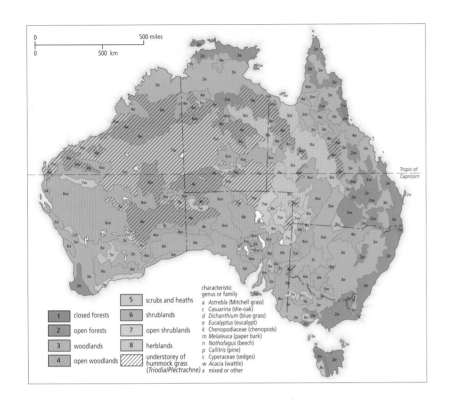

The major groups of natural vegetation.

Legend (map):

1	closed forests	5	scrubs and heaths	
2	open forests	6	shrublands	
3	woodlands	7	open shrublands	
4	open woodlands	8	herblands	

understorey of hummock grass (*Triodia/Plectrachne*)

characteristic genus or family
a *Astrebla* (Mitchell grass)
c *Casuarina* (she-oak)
d *Dichanthium* (blue grass)
e *Eucalyptus* (eucalypt)
k Chenopodiaceae (chenopods)
m *Melaleuca* (paper bark)
n *Nothofagus* (beech)
p *Callitris* (pine)
s Cyperaceae (sedges)
w *Acacia* (wattle)
x mixed or other

Vegetation

VEGETATION PATTERNS

The plant cover of Australia before European settlement is referred to for convenience as natural vegetation. The Aborigines undoubtedly modified the vegetation in many places by the use of fire (see pp. 43–4), but their influence was very different from the later effects of European pastoralism, agriculture and forestry.

The major groupings of the natural vegetation provide a background for considering the changes that led to the vegetation of today. Note that Australian trees and shrubs are predominantly evergreen.

Closed forests (rainforests) have a patchy distribution throughout eastern and northern coastal regions, in places where annual rainfalls are above about 1,200 mm. In warmer climates, the rainforests have a great diversity of plant species and a structural complexity, but in cooler climates they may consist of little more than a layer of trees, dominated by species of southern beech (*Nothofagus*). Some closed forests have been kept as reserves or as managed forests but others have been replaced by pastures or crops, especially sugar cane.

Main picture (below) *Aerial view of the tropical forest canopy in the Bellenden Ker Range, northeastern Queensland. Rainforests occur mainly in the wet coastal regions of eastern and northern Australia.* Top left *Snow gums (*Eucalyptus pauciflora*) in the Snowy Mountains, New South Wales, in winter. Eucalypts are Australia's most widespread tree and live even in cold temperate conditions.* Top right *Drooping she-oak (*Allocasuarina verticillata*) in the Wimmera district of Victoria. She-oaks are common woodland trees in southern Australia.* Bottom left *A species of wattle (*Acacia*) in flower. There are more than 700 species of Acacia in Australia, and the golden wattle is Australia's floral emblem.* Bottom right *The red flowering gum (*Eucalyptus ficifolia*). The Eucalyptus genus has more than 500 species, mostly found in Australia and nowhere else. The flowers are a major source of nectar for bees.*

Open forests are prominent throughout eastern Australia, with lesser areas in the north of the Northern Territory and in southwestern parts of Western Australia. The commonest trees are eucalypts (*Eucalyptus*), followed by wattles (*Acacia*) and cypress pines (*Callitris*). The lower limit of annual rainfall for eucalypt open forests is about 600 mm in temperate regions, but higher in tropical regions; forests dominated by *Acacia* and *Callitris* may occur in areas of lower rainfall. As for rainforests, some open forests are reserves or are managed but others have been replaced by planted trees, especially exotic pines. Other areas have been modified by grazing, or cleared and sown to exotic pastures and crops.

Woodlands are basically attenuated extensions of open forests into regions of lower rainfall, but soil factors may affect their relative distribution. The commonest trees are eucalypts, followed by paperbarks (*Melaleuca*) in the north and wattles and she-oaks (*Casuarina*, including *Allocasuarina*) in the south. Many of these woodlands have been modified by extensive grazing, mainly by beef cattle in the tropics and by sheep in the temperate regions. Large areas of eucalypt woodlands south of the Tropic of Capricorn have been cleared and sown to seasonal crops, especially wheat, in association with native or exotic pastures.

Open woodlands are extensions of the woodlands into habitats that are only marginally suitable for tree growth. The principal trees are *Eucalyptus* and *Acacia*, followed by *Casuarina*, *Melaleuca* and *Callitris*. Some areas of open woodland have been modified by extensive grazing, especially those with a ground layer of palatable low shrubs or grasses. However, many open woodlands on sandy desert soils or shallow stony soils have a ground layer of spiny hummock grasses; much of this country is not grazed.

Scrubs and heaths are dense stands of tall or low shrubs, respectively. They have a patchy distribution, mainly in coastal or near-coastal regions and on infertile soils. There is a wide range of dominant shrubs; the tall shrubs include species of *Acacia*, *Casuarina* and *Eucalyptus*. Some areas remain largely unused, but others, especially those dominated by eucalypts, have been cleared for wheat cropping and grazing.

Shrublands are less-dense stands of tall or low shrubs. Tall shrublands occur on a wide range of soils; the principal genera are *Acacia* and *Eucalyptus*. *Acacia* shrublands (mulga) are widespread in the arid zone of Australia under annual rainfalls ranging to less than 150 mm. *Eucalyptus* shrublands (mallee) are widespread in southern Australia, mostly under annual rainfalls in the range 200–450 mm. In many places, the *Acacia* shrublands have been greatly modified by extensive grazing. Many of the *Eucalyptus* shrublands have been cleared and sown to seasonal crops, especially wheat, in association with native or exotic pastures.

Most of the low shrublands are dominated by members of the family Chenopodiaceae. These chenopod shrublands occur over large areas of southern Australia, largely under annual rainfalls below 250 mm and on calcareous or saline soils. Many have been considerably modified by grazing by sheep or beef cattle.

Open shrublands are extensions of the corresponding shrublands into less-favourable habitats. *Acacia* and *Eucalyptus* open shrublands with ground layers of spiny hummock grasses occupy large areas of sandy desert country. Many open shrublands are not grazed, but some extensive grazing occurs where there is a palatable ground layer.

Hummock grasslands are characterised by the distinctive grasses *Triodia* and *Plectrachne*, both of which are endemic to Australia. Each plant consists of a mass of repeatedly branched stems, bristling with long spine-like leaves. Although hummock grasses are dominant in the ground layer over large areas of Australia, they rarely occur without some sort of upper storey of trees or shrubs, especially the sparse cover of many open woodlands and open shrublands.

Herblands are mostly dominated by grasses or grass-like plants, but there is often a non-grass herbaceous (forb) component, and some herblands are dominated by forbs. Tussock grasslands dominated by species of *Astrebla* (Mitchell grass) and *Dichanthium* (blue grass) occupy large areas of cracking-clay soils in northern and eastern Australia. These grasslands are much favoured for grazing, and in general have proved remarkably persistent. Under annual rainfalls below about 200 mm in southwestern Queensland and northeastern South Australia, and especially on clay soils with stony mantles, herbaceous chenopods are more characteristic than tussock grasses. Large sedges (Cyperaceae) are dominant in some places – for example, on estuarine clay plains along the coast of the Northern Territory and on peat-covered sands in western Tasmania.   JAC

HISTORICAL DEVELOPMENT

The history of Australian vegetation has been reconstructed mainly from fossilised pollen preserved in sedimentary deposits, with additional information provided by remains of leaves and other plant parts. Most of the fossil evidence is from southeastern Australia and there is an almost total lack of information from the northwest.

The early part of the Cenozoic era, some 65–50 million years ago, saw the evolution of an essentially modern rainforest vegetation. This covered most of

Spiny hummock grasslands in the desert areas of the Pilbara region of Western Australia. Triodia *is the dominant grass.*

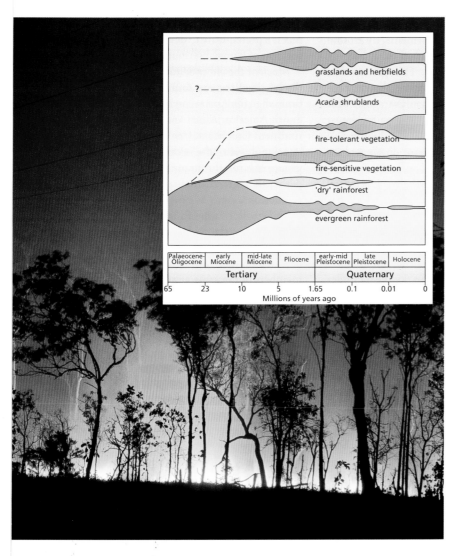

grasslands and herbfields

Acacia shrublands

fire-tolerant vegetation

fire-sensitive vegetation

'dry' rainforest

evergreen rainforest

Palaeocene-Oligocene	early Miocene	mid-late Miocene	Pliocene	early-mid Pleistocene	late Pleistocene	Holocene
Tertiary				Quaternary		

65   23   10   5   1.65   0.1   0.01   0

Millions of years ago

Burning vegetation in the Kakadu National Park, Northern Territory. Forest fires had a significant impact on the development of Australia's vegetation between 15 and 5 million years ago. In the past million years, plant communities have become increasingly more tolerant of frequent fires.

Inset *The relative importance of the major components of the Australian vegetation during the past 65 million years.*

the continent when rainfall levels remained high until the early Miocene, about 20 million years ago. The forests had a rich diversity of species, with prominent representation of southern gymnosperms (Podocarpaceae), myrtles and eucalypts (Myrtaceae), proteas (Proteaceae), olive-berries (Elaeocarpaceae), coachwood (Cunoniaceae), laurels (Lauraceae) and the southern beech (*Nothofagus*). There is evidence also of wet heath characterised by *Banksia*, cord-rush (Restionaceae) and heath (Epacridaceae) that probably occupied poorer soils.

The presence of small amounts of charcoal in the sediments indicates that fires did occur but, because of the moist environment and fire-resistant plants, this factor is unlikely to have had a significant influence on the composition of the vegetation. At this time the vegetation cover was very similar to that in other lands in the Southern Hemisphere, such as New Zealand and southern South America.

The development of a distinctively Australian vegetation pattern dates essentially from the mid–late Miocene (15–10 million years ago) when rainfall and temperatures became lower and more variable and

fires became more frequent and intense. Evergreen rainforest contracted coastwards as the Tertiary period ended. The most-dramatic reduction in extent probably corresponded with a major climatic change to drier conditions about 2.5 million years ago.

The contraction of the rainforest, which also happened in other southern continents at the same time, was accompanied by increased latitudinal sifting of the rainforest flora so that there was a much clearer separation of tropical, subtropical and temperate types. These changes were probably caused by global cooling when the ice cap on Antarctica formed.

A variety of vegetation types evolved to occupy the new, drier environments. They included grasslands and herbfields composed of opportunistic plants that colonised Australia from other continents by long-distance dispersal; communities of plants with hard leathery leaves (sclerophylls) from the edges of the rainforests; and wet-heathland plants that adapted to the drier conditions.

The relatively fire-sensitive trees *Casuarina* and *Callitris* were important components of the canopy of these sclerophyll forests. The scanty evidence from eucalypt-dominated communities suggests that fire was not yet a dominant environmental factor. However, high amounts of pollen from other trees in the family Myrtaceae have been found in Pliocene deposits in central New South Wales, in association with higher levels of charcoal, and this evidence has been interpreted as indicating fire-dependent, wet sclerophyll or tall open forests between 5 and 2 million years ago. *Acacia* was also present, and that may point to the existence of extensive shrublands; the origin of the genus in Australia remains a mystery.

In northern Australia, there was an expansion of drier rainforest types, especially those dominated by pines (*Araucaria*). Some components of these Australian forests may have evolved from rainforest ancestors used to a moister environment. However, as many species are the same as those on other components of the ancient Gondwanan land mass (see p. 5), they may have been ancient communities that simply expanded in response to the return of appropriate conditions.

The past 2 million years have been characterised by marked instability of the vegetation caused by dramatic cyclical fluctuations in climate. The remaining evergreen rainforest was further stressed. Evidence from southeastern Australia indicates that rainforest and sclerophyll vegetation had very restricted distributions within a predominantly steppe vegetation during the cold dry periods of the ice ages.

These colder conditions would have also made it easier for cold-adapted herbaceous plants from overseas to colonise Australia. Probably for the first time

greatest diversity in Australia with 13 of the world's 39 genera.

Of the remaining reptile groups found in Australia, the skinks (Scincidae), pythons (Boidae) and the venomous front-fanged snakes (Elapidae) occur throughout the tropics; the file snakes (Acrochordiae) are Malesian, ranging from Southeast Asia through the Indonesian archipelagos; and the solid-toothed snakes (Colubridae) almost cosmopolitan. The sources of their Australian stocks are still uncertain but are at least partly, if not wholly, Eurasian. All are widespread in Australia except the obviously recent Eurasian file- and solid-toothed snakes, which are limited to comparatively few species around the northern and northeastern coasts. The front-fanged snakes, in contrast, reach their greatest diversity in Australia.

Birds

With some 550 species, Australia's land and freshwater bird fauna is also a particularly diverse vertebrate group, its members occupying a vast array of environments across the continent. There are two major groups: the passerine songbirds (*c.* 305 species) and the non-passerines (*c.* 245 species).

The non-passerines include herons, ducks, birds-of-prey, quail, rails, plovers, pigeons, parrots and cockatoos, cuckoos, owls, frogmouths, nightjars, swifts and kingfishers. The principal non-passerine families are either old endemic groups centred in Australia–New Guinea and probably Gondwanan in origin, or, like the gekkonid lizards, a mix of old endemics and recently immigrant Eurasian genera and species.

Old Australian-centred non-passerine groups are the button-quail (Turnicidae), parrots and cockatoos (Psittaciformes), masked owls (Tytonidae), frog-mouths and owlet-nightjars (Podargidae and Aegothelidae), land kingfishers (Daceloninae) and cuculine cuckoos (Cuculinae). Families in which old endemic and recent immigrant elements are mixed are exemplified by the ducks (Anatidae) and birds of prey (Accipitridae). Among the ducks, such old Gondwanan groups as the whistling ducks (Dendrocygninae), stiff-tailed ducks (Oxyurini) and magpie-goose (*Anseranas*) forage side by side with cosmopolitan dabbling ducks (*Anas*) and swans (*Cygnus*). Among the birds of prey, the endemic buzzard (*Hamirostra*), kite (*Lophoictinia*) and hawk (*Erythrotriorchis*) hunt over the same forests and fields as immigrant Eurasian kites, harriers and goshawks (*Milvus*, *Circus* and *Accipiter*).

The principal Australian songbird families are the:

- eopsaltriine robins (Eopsaltriidae), *c.* 20 species;
- whistlers and monarch flycatchers (Pachycephalidae), *c.* 30 species;
- orthonychine babblers (Orthonychidae, Cinclosomatidae and Pomatostomidae), *c.* 14 species;
- fairy wrens (Maluridae), *c.* 20 species;
- thornbill warblers and pardalotes (Acanthizidae), *c.* 44 species;
- honeyeaters and Australian chats (Meliphagidae and Ephthianuridae), *c.* 70 species;
- grass finches (Ploceidae), *c.* 18 species;
- birds-of-paradise and bowerbirds (Paradisaeidae and Ptilonorhynchidae), *c.* 13 species; and
- woodswallows and butcherbirds (Artamidae and Cracticidae), *c.* 14 species.

Together, these groups include over 80 per cent of all songbirds in the region.

Bottom left *A musk lorikeet* (Glossopsitta concinna). *This blossom-feeding parrot is widespread in eastern Australia.*
Bottom right *The laughing kookaburra* (Dacelo novaeguineae), *the world's largest kingfisher, is endemic to Australia. Its distinctive cackling cry is often heard in the morning in woods and open forests.*

White-naped honeyeater (Melithreptus lunatus) *in southeastern New South Wales. Honeyeaters belong to an old lineage of Australian songbirds.*

Origins of Australian songbirds

Four of the songbird groups – eopsaltriine robins, orthonychine babblers, fairy wrens, and birds-of-paradise and bowerbirds (allowing for isolated member species in the Moluccas and New Zealand) – are endemic to Australia and New Guinea. The remaining five groups (finches excepted) – whistlers and monarch flycatchers, thornbills and pardalotes, honeyeaters and Australian chats, grass finches, woodswallows and butcherbirds – have their centre of diversity in the region and evidently arose there.

Because they resemble Eurasian flycatchers, warblers and finches in form, they have been thought – as indeed have all Australia's songbirds – to have evolved rather recently from immigrant stocks from Eurasia. Current molecular and biochemical research indicates, however, that

- the similarities in form between the Eurasian and the main Australian-centred families of songbirds reflect parallel evolution;
- the Australian-centred families are all more closely related to one another than to any Eurasian family, no matter how much they differ from one another in appearance;
- their lineages are more divergent and so presumably older than any in Eurasia; and
- only the finches among the major families are clearly Eurasian in origin.

The source of the Australian-centred families is not clear; the Australian sector of the supercontinent Gondwana is as likely as any other on present evidence.　　RS

The platypus or duckbill (Ornithorhynchus anatinus), *an egg-laying mammal called a monotreme, is unique to Australia. It lives in freshwater in eastern Queensland and New South Wales and also in Tasmania. It uses its touch-sensitive bill for locating insect larvae on the bottom of rivers and streams.*

Mammals

The small and unusual mammal fauna comprises a clear mix of old Gondwanan and recent Eurasian immigrant stocks. Only four major groups are present: monotremes (Monotremata), marsupials (Marsupialia), bats (Chiroptera) and murid rodents (Muridae). The dingo (Canidae) is excluded, being a descendent of domestic dogs introduced by Aborigines at least 3,000 years ago.

Monotremes and marsupials. Two of the three existing monotreme species are present in Australia – the aquatic duck-billed platypus (*Ornithorhynchus anatinus*) and the spiny, ant-eating short-nosed

echidna (*Tachyglossus aculeatus*). The monotremes are evidently Gondwanan in origin, as, too, are the marsupials (kangaroos, possums, wombats, bandicoots, and the carnivorous marsupial mice and other dasyuroids). They are related to the marsupial opossums (Didelphoidea) of South America in a pattern of distribution characteristic of such an origin. Since their separation from South American stocks, however, marsupials have diversified into 130 species in Australia. All of the Australian families of today are restricted to Australia and New Guinea on the Australian continental plate; most are widespread, although the wombats and koalas are limited to eastern Australia, and possums hardly penetrate the central arid zone where tall trees are sparse. Monotremes, too, are found nowhere else today.

Bats The insect-catching microchiropterans (52 species) are almost certainly Eurasian immigrants but they have spread and diversified across Australia since their arrival. Only five of the world's 14 or so families are represented – the false vampires (Megadermatidae), horseshoe bats (Rhinolophidae), sheathtail bats (Emballonuridae), mastiff bats (Molossidae) and 'ordinary' bats (Vespertilionidae) – and all are more diverse in Africa and Eurasia.

Koala (Phascolarctos cinereus) *photographed in a koala sanctuary on Magnetic Island, off Townsville, Queensland. The koala, a tree-living marsupial (not a bear) that lives only in dry areas of eastern Australia, subsists largely on a few species of eucalypt. It used to be trapped for its fur but is now protected.*

Flying foxes (Pteropus) in subtropical forest, north coast of New South Wales. These large, blossom- and fruit-eating bats gather in large flocks to feed and roost. They wrap their wings tightly around themselves when cold or wet.

New Holland mouse (Pseudomys ovaehollandiae), one of Australia's endemic rodents. All true rats and mice in Australia evolved from species that migrated from Asia via Indonesia within the past few million years.

The other major group of bats in Australia, the fruit- and blossom-feeding megachiropterans (8 species), are members of a single family, Pteropodidae, that ranges from the western Pacific to Africa and is centred in New Guinea. This family includes the largest of all bats, the flying foxes (*Pteropus*), of which there are four species in Australia. All Australian fruitbats are associated with the rainforests of the tropical north and east. Their origin is unclear but, given the family's diversity in New Guinea and adjacent archipelagos, it is possible that megachiropterans evolved from an early stock of bats in the Australasian region.

Rats and mice The murid rodents – true rats and mice – are Eurasian immigrants that probably arrived in Plio-Pleistocene times, within the past 3–5 million years, via the forming Indonesian archipelago. Immigrant stocks arrived not once but probably several times, the first evolving into, among others, the widespread endemic genera of water rats (*Hydromys* and *Xeromys*), mosaic-tailed rats (*Uromys* and *Melomys*), and native and desert hopping mice and rock- and stick-nest rats (for example, *Pseudomys*, *Leggadina*, *Notomys*, *Zyzomys* and *Leporillus*). Last to come was the genus *Rattus* itself, which also spread throughout Australia and has since evolved seven native species.

HISTORICAL DEVELOPMENT

Explanations of the historical development of Australia's old endemic and new immigrant faunas rest on reconstructions of the past environments in which they evolved. According to the fossil record, the ancestral stocks of Australia's old endemic wildlife today were already firmly established by the middle Tertiary period, some 20–40 million years ago. Such a time frame indicates that many if not all were inherited from the southern Mesozoic supercontinent Gondwana, from which the Australian sector did not completely break away until 60–50 million years ago. A warm temperate and rather humid climate prevailed over the continent then. It supported rainforests that survive in pockets on the east coast of Australia, Tasmania and montane New Guinea today (see pp. 21 and 32–4).

Vast lakes in the Great Artesian Basin (see p. 19), through the present Lake Eyre and Murray–Darling Basins, fostered the development of a diverse freshwater bird, reptile and amphibian fauna. Various pelicans, cormorants, ducks, shorebirds, at least three genera of flamingos, myobatrachid frogs and freshwater turtles were present. Remnants of this fauna are still centred there: freckled (*Stictonetta*) and pink-eared (*Malacorhynchus*) ducks, red-kneed (*Erythrogonys*) and black-fronted (*Elseyornis*) dotterels, banded stilts (*Cladorhynchus*) and Australian pratincoles (*Stiltia*). Indeed, despite lying in Australia's arid zone, the Great Artesian Basin is richer today in old endemic freshwater birds than the better watered coasts. Even the ancestor of the plains wanderer (*Pedionomus*) of the Murray–Darling Basin may once have been a Great Artesian shorebird, subsequently becoming adapted to treeless, arid grass-and-herb fields occupied by the plains wanderers of today.

During the past 15 or so million years, as Australia drifted into tropical latitudes towards Eurasia, its climate became drier. This trend culminated in the glacial epochs of the Pleistocene within the past several million years. In Australia, glacial periods were characterised not so much by extreme cold as by great aridity: arid sand dunes crossed the Bass Strait to northern Tasmania while lowered sea levels all but closed land gaps between Australia and Eurasia through the Indonesian archipelago. Australia's plants and animals were severely affected (see Box).

The development of contemporary climatic patterns in Australia – of monsoonal summer rains across the north, Mediterranean winter rains across the south, year-round rain only on the mountain ranges of the east coast, and low erratic rain inland – has had the effect of zoning the flora and fauna concentrically. Pockets of rainforest along the northern and eastern coasts give way to more open eucalypt

Advance of the deserts

The ice ages had four main effects on Australia's flora and fauna:

1. There was widespread extinction among the humid-loving and freshwater vertebrates. In the last phase of aridity, which peaked only 20,000–16,000 years ago, the fossil record shows that Australia lost many of the large animals surviving from the late Tertiary, including a giant monitor, flamingos, several huge eagles and mound-builders (megapodes), giant flightless mihirungs (dromornithids), which were much larger than the emus of today, and giant kangaroos, diprotodonts, marsupial lions and bandicoots among the marsupials.

Drought, fire and the first people in Australia interacted to bring about this massive extinction.

2. The plants and animals of the rain-forests withdrew to refuges in wetter hills and mountains that were then reaching their present form along the east coast of Australia and through central New Guinea. Evidence for this is circumstantial, based on contemporary patterns of distribution: the shared presence in montane New Guinean and Australian east coast rain-forests of members of old endemic stocks, such as microhylid frogs, sooty owls (*Tyto*), king parrots (*Alisterus*), Australian robins (*Heteromyias*), scrubwrens (*Sericornis*), caligavine honeyeaters (*Lichenostomus*), maypole bowerbirds (*Amblyornis*), ringtail possums (*Pseudocheirus*, *Pseudochirops* and *Dactylopsila*) and pygmy possums (*Cercartetus*).

3. In the 'void' left by the retreating humid-adapted faunas and floras, today's aridity-adapted groups spread and diversified. Most if not all apparently evolved and adapted out of ancestral stocks in the retreating rainforests. Eucalypts and acacias came to flourish, and with them such hard-leaved plants as the proteads and tea-tree myrtles.

In their forests, woodlands and heaths, many of the old endemic vertebrate groups diversified as well: southern frogs, the tree frog *Litoria*, the legless lizards, skinks, monitors and front-fanged snakes, bronze-winged pigeons (Peristerinae), broad-tailed parrots (Platycercinae), treecreepers, thornbills and field wrens, honeyeaters, fairy wrens, and butcher birds and woodswallows among birds, and all groups of living marsupials except, to some extent, the possums (Phalangeridae).

4. Through this period, Australia's patchy land-links with Eurasia via the Indonesian archipelago allowed Eurasian stocks to enter and establish themselves wherever environmental change had left openings in habitat.

The grassy understorey of the northern Australian eucalypt woodlands and savannahs, and the saltbush (*Atriplex* and *Maireana*) shrublands of the arid zone probably arose from immigrants in the grass and saltbush families that were able to exploit the monsoonal seasonality and dry saline soils then developing across northern and inland Australia. Few old endemic groups are centred in them: some southern and tree frogs (*Notaden* and *Cyclorana*), diplodactyline geckos, dragons and monitors, comparatively few birds – button quails (*Turnix*), grass wrens (*Amytornis*) and chats (*Ephthianura*) – but moderate numbers of marsupials; also dunnarts (*Sminthopsis*), planigales (*Planigale*), rabbit bandicoots (*Macrotis*), hare wallabies (*Lagorchestes*) and kangaroos (*Macropus*). RS

Red-necked wallaby (Macropus rufogriseus) *carrying her infant in the pouch distinctive of marsupials. Wallabies and kangaroos are widespread in Australia and New Guinea but are found nowhere else today, although marsupials had a much wider distribution in the past.*

Australian faunal divisions

There are five major faunal divisions in Australia today:

1. *Tumbunan zone* (*subtropical rainforests*). This fauna is presently confined to pockets of subtropical and upland rainforest along the eastern seaboard of Australia. Once thought recently immigrant from New Guinea, these subtropical forests appear to hold the remnants of rainforest flora and fauna that were widespread across Australia in mid-Tertiary times; accordingly, this biota has been termed Tumbunan (neo-Melanesian) for ancestor.

It is no longer so rich in vertebrate fauna in Australia, its smaller pockets supporting particularly few species. The high ratio of genera (31) to species (48–50) in birds – and to a lesser extent in marsupials – is a reflection of the antiquity of the fauna and its long history of sifting and extinction.

Significantly, the mammal fauna of the Tumbunan zone is richest in marsupials, the principal Gondwanan component in Australia's mammals. It includes the musky rat-kangaroo (*Hypsiprymnodon*), most primitive of all kangaroos, which commonly moves on four legs instead of two.

2. *Irian zone* (*tropical rainforests, vine thickets and mangroves*). The pockets of Australia's tropical rainforest and mangrove swamps ranged around the north coast of Australia are outliers of the immensely rich lowland tropical rainforest (Irian) flora and fauna of the New Guinea region west to the east Indonesian archipelago. They derive largely from that source when Australia and New Guinea were broadly land-linked at intervals during the past several million years. In Australia, they hold an intricate

mix of species of Tumbunan and tropical Southeast Asian origin.

Although occupying the smallest area of all regional faunas in Australia, the Irian is still as rich or richer than the others, particularly in birds and reptiles, many of which range into the tropical eucalypt woodlands of the Torresian fauna as well.

A feature of Australia's Irian biota is the diversity of bird life in the mangrove swamps (86 species in 35 genera, several of which are restricted only to mangroves). Although mangrove forests are better developed elsewhere in the New Guinea region and the northeastern coast of Australia, the mangrove bird fauna of northwestern Australia, from the Kimberley Division to the Gulf of Carpentaria, is the richest of all. This may be because it derives from a strand fauna that was widespread on the Arafura Plain west from Cape York Peninsula before a rise in sea level at the end of the last ice age flooded the plain.

3. *Torresian zone* (*tropical eucalypt woodlands*). The tropical eucalypt and paperbark (*Melaleuca*) woodlands and forests that shelter and support this fauna sweep broadly across the whole of northern coastal and sub-coastal Australia and south to just beyond the New South Wales–Queensland border. There they mingle with the Bassian biota (below). Inland, they extend south to the northern mulga (*Acacia*)–eucalypt line.

A characteristic of these woodlands is their close understorey of tall annual grasses that grow to 1–2 m high in the summer monsoon and die off during the dry winter. Their dominance affects faunal composition; for example,

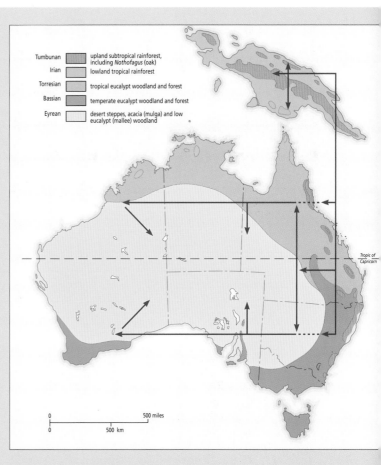

The major geographic components of the vertebrate fauna of Australia and New Guinea. The arrows indicate the apparent spread of the basic stocks of these components, from Tumbunan to Irian and from Tumbunan through Bassian and Torresian to Eyrean.

among birds, seed-eating finches and pigeons predominate over insectivores such as warblers (Acanthizidae) and robins (Eopsaltriidae).

The Torresian fauna contains many species with close relatives in the Bassian fauna. This pattern of geographical replacement reveals, first, that the faunal stocks of Australia's northern (Torresian) and southern (Bassian) eucalypt woodlands have a common origin and, second, that the northern and southern representatives of these stocks have been separated by the present arid zone that developed over the past several million years to evolve largely independently of one another since.

4. *Bassian zone* (*temperate eucalypt forests and heaths*).

The eucalypt forests and heaths of the Bassian faunal zone, with their distinctive drought-adapted (sclerophyll) shrubbery, range patchily around southern coastal and subcoastal Australia. Only in the east do they extend much north of latitude 30°S, following the spine of the Great Dividing Range in pockets north to the Atherton Tableland at 17°S.

Inland, the Bassian biota grades into the flora and fauna of the arid zone through the 'mallee' woodland in the lower Murray Basin, around the South Australian gulfs and through the Western Australian wheat-belt; its inland limit is at the southern mulga (*Acacia*)–eucalypt line there. Its major centre in southeastern Australia is isolated from minor centres in southwestern Australia and Tasmania by the Nullarbor Plain and Bass Strait, respectively.

The Bassian fauna is Australia's richest in frogs (58 species), birds (132 species) and marsupials (47 species), its present broken distribution around the south coast contributing to much recent speciation.

Like the Tumbunan, the Bassian fauna has been penetrated little by immigrant Eurasian stocks from the north. The core stocks of the Bassian fauna are old and seem to have evolved from ancestral stocks in the Tumbunan subtropical rainforests at early stages in the development of Australia's present flora and fauna.

5. *Eyrean zone (arid acacia-chenopod-hummock grassland)*. The Eyrean flora and fauna of Australia's arid zone ranges across the centre of the continent, south and north to the *Acacia* (mulga)–eucalypt lines that mark the beginning of the Bassian and Torresian zones, respectively. Covering almost 70 per cent of the continent, it reaches the west coast on a wide front between Shark Bay and the Eighty-mile Beach–Roebuck Bay area.

Four principal vegetation habitats, each with its own characteristic fauna, clothe the arid zone and its deserts: saltbush (Chenopodiaceae) shrub steppe on hard pan and saline soils in the south; Mitchell (*Astrebla*) tussock grassland on hard pan and gibber plains in the north; spiny hummock grassland (*Triodia*) on stony hills and dunefield deserts; and *Acacia* woodland on shallow soils everywhere.

Despite the vast area covered by the Eyrean fauna, it is rich only in reptiles, almost equalling the Torresian reptile fauna in diversity. Adaptations to withstand drought characterise many Eyrean animals. The two genera of frogs, *Neobatrachus* and *Notaden*, which together include 13 of the 23 Eyrean species, are adept burrowers and secrete cocoons around themselves under ground to survive dry times.

Of reptiles, the dragons (31

species) reach their greatest diversity in the arid zone. The most distinctive of them is the small, heavily spined moloch (*Moloch*), which, with a low metabolic rate, moves extraordinarily slowly over the ground and feeds on

ants; it takes water from the ground to its mouth by capillary action on the surface of its skin.

Eyrean birds have adapted for sustained flight and nomadism to carry them to new waters and sources of food. Examples are the budgerigar (*Melopsittacus undulatus*) and the black and pied honeyeaters (*Certhionyx*), which have lost their outermost primary feathers to narrow and increase the effective length of their wings.

Among mammals, the blind marsupial mole (*Notoryctes typhlops*) has the extraordinary ability of being able to spend most of its life underground; its forelimbs are modified into two flattened claws for digging.

Members of the Eyrean fauna are derived in general from stocks still surviving in both Bassian and Torresian faunas. For example, its grass wrens (*Amytornis*) have apparently evolved from Torresian ancestors, and its flock bronzewing (*Phaps histrionica*) from Bassian stocks. If the Eyrean fauna has been built up by colonisation from outside sources, it has been culled and cut down constantly by extremely arid conditions within.   RS

Budgerigar (Melopsittacus undulatus) in Uluru National Park, Northern Territory. This small parrot is distributed over most of inland Australia. It feeds on grass seeds and flies long distances in search of water and food.

forests and woodlands there and in subcoastal regions around and across the south coast. These in turn grade into acacia (mulga) woodlands, chenopodiaceous steppe, grassland and hummock grass (*Triodia*)-covered dune deserts stretching across the entire inland to the west coast (see p. 21). Such a pattern probably existed through much of the later Tertiary, but it became accentuated during recent times by the fall-off in continental rain, bringing about a great expansion of the central arid zone. The effect of this concentric zoning has been to sift the vertebrate fauna into five distinctive regions – Tumbunan, Irian, Torresian, Bassian and Eyrean (see Box).

THE FAUNA TODAY

Within the concentric faunal zones, the climatic fluctuations of the past several million years created cyclic make-and-break connections around the periphery of the continent. During cold, dry spells, the regional faunas were split and compressed into refugia. For example, although land-linked to the mainland by lowered sea levels then, Tasmania and its wetter forest faunas remained largely cut off by dry heath-covered dunes across the Bass Strait. In the north, the Torresian fauna was broken up and pushed back into refugia in the Pilbara, Kimberley Division, Arnhem Land and Cape York Peninsula. In these refugia, the fauna speciated in isolation. When conditions ameliorated during the warmer, wetter periods between the ice ages (interglacials), the isolated stocks expanded with their habitat and remet, to overlap or, if speciation had not been completed, to interbreed.

In this way, rings of species and subspecies formed around the periphery of the continent. Many of the refugia, such as Arnhem Land and southwestern Australia, are self-evident from the number of endemic forms now present there. Clues to others come from 'faunal barriers', where replacement species and subspecies abut in seemingly unbroken habitat to mark faunal divisions of the past. The most significant of these are the Carpentaria Barrier at the head of the Gulf of Carpentaria, which splits the north Australian Torresian fauna into eastern and western units, the complex Torresian Barrier between the Burdekin and East Normanby Rivers in Queensland, which splits the east Torresian fauna into a northern Cape York Peninsula unit and southern east Queensland unit, and the Eyrean Barrier at the head of Spencer Gulf, South Australia, which splits both southern (Bassian) and inland (Eyrean) faunas into eastern and western units on the southern mainland.

RS

The rainforests and reefs

The tropical rainforests and reefs of northeastern Australia are an international attraction unrivalled anywhere. Both are listed as World Heritage areas (see pp. 52–4). It is becoming increasingly clear that the two environments are intimately connected and need coordinated management for tourism, commerce, recreation and conservation. (See also pp. 35 and 36–41.)

THE TROPICAL RAINFORESTS

The distribution of tropical rainforest and coral reefs in northeastern Queensland. The boundary of the northern section of the Great Barrier Reef Marine Park is shown.

The discontinuous pockets of tropical rainforest along the northeastern coast of Australia are a spectacular but tiny remnant of the ancient Gondwanan forests that once covered the continent (see pp. 22–4).

Today, rainforests probably cover less than 2 million ha (0.2 per cent) of Australia, with some 780,000 ha remaining in northeastern Queensland. This rainforest is confined to a very narrow band close to the coast; most of the remaining vegetation type in northeastern Australia is savannah woodland. Mean annual rainfall for tropical rainforests in northeastern Queensland ranges from about 1,500 mm on the drier margins to some 4,000 mm at Tully and Babinda on the coastal plain and up to 8,000 mm or more on the peaks of the Bellenden Ker Range. Much of the rainfall in this wet tropical zone comes from cyclonic disturbances in the summer months of December–March but it is the rain precipitated on the windward slopes of mountains by the southeast trade winds in the dry season (May–November) that primarily determines the presence or absence of rainforest.

Tropical rainforest occurs on several different geological formations and on a variety of soil types. The Atherton Tableland area is primarily a volcanic landform with deep-red basaltic soils whereas the Bellenden Ker Range includes a mixture of granitic and metamorphic rocks. Within the Rainforest World Heritage Area are several national parks, which include Palmerston National Park (with many walking tracks), Cape Tribulation National Park, Daintree River National Park and Mt Hypipamee National Park. None of the parks is very large but many are surrounded by extensive areas of state forest, some of which has areas of unlogged rainforest.

The complexity of these tropical rainforests is best illustrated by the classes used to describe them by ecologists: 13 major structural types and 17 broad

communities together form a rich mosaic of different plants and animals.

Most of the pristine tropical rainforest occurs in the highest parts of the land where it is protected from all except recreational users by its inaccessibility. The altitude also introduces a much higher rainfall and a distinctly different bioclimatic regime. This upland rainforest contains many species of plants and animals unique to it. Most of the birds that are restricted to this region are upland rainforest species such as the golden bowerbird (*Prionodura newtoniana*), the mountain thornbill (*Acanthiza katherina*) and the tooth-billed catbird (*Ailuroedus dentirostris*). Several mammals are also confined to these forests, including the beautiful diurnal musky rat-kangaroo (*Hypsipyrmnodon moschatus*) and both of the Australian tree-kangaroos (*Dendrolagus* spp.). Numerous frog, reptile and insect species are also found nowhere else.

The feature that characterises the Australian tropical rainforest best is the amazing diversity of species within a relatively small area. For example, there are as many as 119 plant families with 523 genera and over 1,100 species, of which 43 per cent live only in this area. Similarly, the tropical rainforest fauna includes 30 per cent of all Australian marsupial species, 60 per cent of the bat species, 30 per cent of the frog species, 23 per cent of the reptile species, 18 per cent of the bird species and 62 per cent of the butterfly species – all in only 0.1 per cent of the Australian land area.

A pair of birdwing butterflies (Triodes priamus) *mating. The green butterfly is the male. The tropical rainforests harbour a wealth of insect species found nowhere else.*

A white form of lemur-like ringtail possum (Pseudocheirus peregrinus) *in the Mount Lewis rainforest in northeastern Queensland. Ringtail possums are tree-living marsupials with hand-like feet for grasping branches. All are active at night, and have large, protruding eyes.*

For the visitor, this diversity is immediately evident in the vast array of plants and animals encountered during a short walk in the rainforest. Included are such spectacular creatures as the cassowary (*Casuarius casuarius*), the Victoria riflebird (*Ptiloris victoriae*, a bird of paradise), the huge birdwing butterfly (*Troides priamus*) and by spotlight at night very many possums. Among these is the uncommonly sighted white form of the lemur-like ringtail possum (*Pseudocheirus peregrinus*). Within the forest the huge nest mounds of two of the three Australian megapodes attract attention. These ground-nesting birds use the heat of decaying vegetation to incubate their eggs.

Like tropical rainforests elsewhere, there are a large number of plants growing on other plants (epiphytes), such as orchids and ferns, also buttresses on the trunks of many trees, woody lianes, drip-tips on leaves, colourful fungi and patchily distributed plants. In contrast with other vegetation communities, rare species are common and common species rare. These northeastern Australian tropical rainforests harbour the richest assemblage of families of ancient flowering plants known in the world. Examples include the laurels (Lauraceae), custard apples (Annonaceae), banksias and grevilleas (Proteaceae), austrobaileyas (Austrobaileyaceae) and winteras (Winteraceae). Cycads and palms are also extremely well represented, as are ferns and fern allies.

Main picture Lowland rainforest near Babinda on Queensland's coastal plain.

Inset Bracket fungi growing in Wallaman Falls National Park near Ingham in northeastern Queensland. Fungi are a common feature of rainforests.

The ancient plants and animals are descendants of the Gondwanan flora and fauna and there are many examples of peculiar disjunct distributions. For example, the giant stag beetle (*Sphaenognathus queenslandicus*) has its nearest relative in South America. Some leafhoppers are confined to mountain peaks with their nearest relatives in Madagascar and several plants have links to South America.

Another distinctive element of the tropical rainforests is the dawn chorus of birds. Beginning before first light with the pale-yellow robin (*Eopsaltia capito*), each species joins in with its own distinctive song, eventually producing a unique chorus of rich and varied calls.

Giant kauri pine trees (Agathus palmerstonii) in Lake Barrine National Park, Atherton Tablelands, Queensland.

MANAGEMENT OF THE RAINFOREST

Australian Aboriginal communities lived within the tropical rainforests for many millennia before European colonisation and had developed a rich material culture using rainforest products. Their knowledge of plant chemistry was sophisticated and demonstrates an intimate understanding of this environment. Many plants were used for poisons, for medicinal treatment and as food sources. Some of these traditions are practised by several communities who still live in the region.

The modern ecological perspective on tropical rainforest is in sharp contrast with the relatively simple definition used by early European settlers who perceived it as an obstacle to their economic success. Pioneers wrote of 'terrible scrubs' and 'impenetrable jungle' and 'the very worst devil-devil country' when referring to the rainforests of this region and proceeded to cut out the valuable logs such as red cedar and kauri pine and clear the rest for agriculture (see also p. 44). On the coast, the forests were rapidly depleted as the narrow plains were planted to sugar cane. By 1988, the lowland tropical rainforests were virtually extinct, surviving only in a few isolated and small pockets, apart from a very narrow strip in the Cape Tribulation National Park in the northeast. Working from west to east the upland rainforests of the Atherton Tablelands were also cleared, this time for dairying, maize and, more recently, peanuts.

Beginning in about 1874 the tropical rainforests of northeastern Australia were logged for timber. Since 1959 this has been under the direct control of the Queensland Forestry Department. Over the decades the species harvested and the girth limits have varied but in general the logging was conducted on a selective basis, mainly the very largest trees and the few most valuable species. Among the more important timber species are red cedar (*Toona ciliata*), Queensland walnut (*Endiandra palmerstonii*), rose butternut (*Blepharocarya involucrigera*), Queensland maple (*Flindersia brayleana*) and kauri pine (*Agathus palmerstonii*). After World War II, around 200,000 m^3 of timber were logged from these forests every year. This high rate of removal was criticised but the Queensland Forestry Department considered it sound forestry practice to take out the first cut (the timber capital of the forest) before reducing harvest levels to a notional sustained yield. (See also pp. 198–200.)

There has been considerable debate over the maximum sustained yield of these forests but a figure of between 30,000 m^3 and 50,000 m^3 might be close. In the period 1985–88 the permitted harvest was reduced by the Queensland Government from 200,000 cm^3 to less than 60,000 cm^3. The federal government's successful nomination of the area for World Heritage Listing included a complete ban on logging within the listed area. The future management of the rainforests remains uncertain although a joint federal–state authority was established in 1990

The link between the rainforests and reefs along the northeastern coast. The cross-section runs from the Atherton Tablelands area east across the Bellenden Ker Range, over the coastal plain and low coastal range to the coast and out through the islands across the continental shelf to the outer barrier reef (the vertical scale is exaggerated). The bar graph shows mean annual rainfall for selected points along the transect.

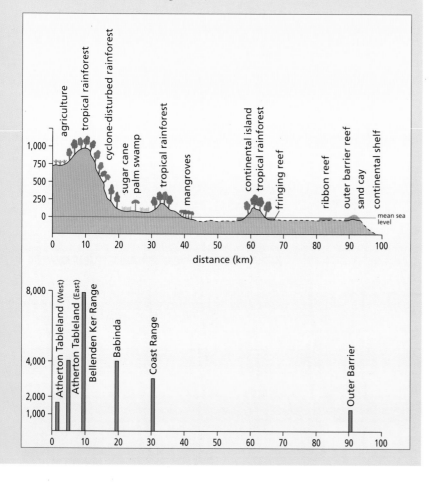

*Mangroves (*Rhizophora stylosa*) in the intertidal coastal zone north of Cairns, Queensland. Although important environmental regulators, mangroves are under threat from developers.*

with the brief to manage the Wet Tropics of Queensland World Heritage Area. In November 1993, a Queensland Government Act finally established an Authority and Board to manage the entire area in an integrated fashion for a variety of uses. Many issues remain, one of the more difficult being how to manage the huge growth in tourists in the rainforests.

REEF AND RAINFOREST INTERACTION

It has only recently been recognised that even so massive a feature as the Great Barrier Reef may be vulnerable to environmental degradation and it has been suggested that mainland management may be responsible for some problems on the reef. A cross-section from the upland rainforests to the outer barrier reefs traverses several other significant ecosystems. Of special importance are the coastal mangrove communities, which are at the centre of much conflict over development plans in the region. Mangroves store nutrients and are believed to have a crucial role in the maintenance of fisheries but many have been cleared for agriculture, for garbage disposal, for tourism development and for mariculture. There is also intensive community debate over the future management of offshore islands and the control of tourism on these.

Much remains to be learned about the biophysical processes that link the reefs and rainforests. An illustration of the complexity can be seen from the mass outbreaks of crown-of-thorns starfish (*Acanthaster planci*) in recent decades. The reefs offshore from the

*Crown-of-thorns starfish (*Acanthaster planci*), a natural enemy of coral polyps growing on the Great Barrier Reef. When the starfish appears in vast numbers it devastates large areas of the reef. It is uncertain whether the mass outbreaks are connected to the runoff of fertilisers from the mainland or are a periodic natural phenomenon.*

Cooktown–Townsville area, which form the major tourist destination, are mainly affected. Some 35 per cent of these reefs are seriously damaged with a further 30 per cent slightly to moderately damaged by the starfish. Recent discoveries by geologists provide evidence that there may have been mass outbreaks of crown-of-thorns starfish long before European settlement of Australia. Other scientists blame human-related activities for the most recent destructive outbreaks.

Adjacent land use does certainly affect the reef region. Erosion from rainfall runoff carries sediments and agricultural chemicals into the marine environment. The consequences of this are poorly understood but it is known that turbidity from high levels of sediment may destroy corals and it seems that excess phosphorus has deleterious effects on certain corals. Large amounts of agricultural chemicals are used in many of the adjacent catchments and attempts are underway to integrate the management of some of the major river catchments.   PSV

The Great Barrier Reef

A reef such as one I now speak of is a thing scarcely known in Europe or indeed anywhere but in these seas.

Joseph Banks on James Cook's voyage of 1770

The Great Barrier Reef is the largest of modern reef systems, occupying the continental shelf of north-eastern Australia for a distance of 2,300 km and over 14 degrees of latitude between the tip of Cape York in the north and Lady Elliott Island in the south. Reef waters exceed 230,000 km² in extent, with almost 9 per cent of the total area covered by reefs or reefal shoals. The reef encompasses 2,900 individual reefs, which include 750 fringing reefs attached to the mainland. The Great Barrier Reef encapsulates an incomparable record of Earth history, sea-level change, oceanography, tectonic change and biological evolution.

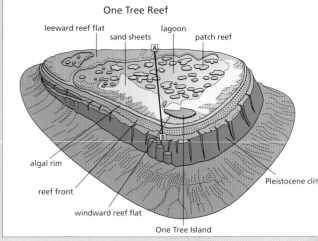

Above *The Great Barrier Reef Marine Park.*

Above right *One Tree Reef in the Capricorn Group of islands in the southern Great Barrier Reef, east of Gladstone. This is a mid-shelf, high-energy, platform reef. The oblique view shows the physical zonation of the modern reef, which is relatively thin (less than 20 m) and sits on top of a Pleistocene limestone pinnacle that represents an earlier period of reef growth. Below The cross-section A—B shows the effect of the earlier shape on the growth of the modern reef. Below right The overhead section shows the relation between the surface zonation and the dominant south-east prevailing weather.*

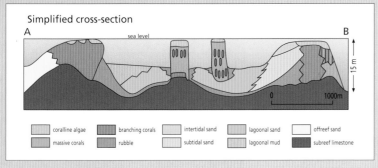

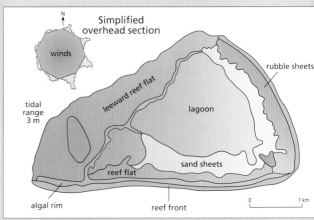

There are major regional differences along the Great Barrier Reef. The northern region forms a narrow shelf no more than 50 km wide and distinguished by ribbon reefs on the edge of the continental shelf to as far south as Cairns. Such ribbon reefs are up to 25 km long but rarely more than 500 m wide and are separated by narrow passes. Behind the ribbon reefs the continental shelf is strewn with large platform reefs up to 25 km across.

Further south, as the continental shelf widens, the Great Barrier Reef occupies only the outer third of the shelf, with reefs forming scattered patches or crescents orientated towards the southeast. There are no ribbon reefs in this central Great Barrier Reef region.

To the south again, the continental shelf widens to around 300 km and the huge reefs of the Pompey and Swain Complexes occupy the outer margin. The southernmost part of the Great Barrier Reef comprises the Capricorn and Bunker Reefs, which form a chain of 22 reefs and 11 shoals. Many of these reefs are covered with vegetation, the best known being Heron Island and One Tree Island.

EVOLUTION OF THE GREAT BARRIER REEF

Individual reefs

The growth of individual reefs is controlled by the substrate, sea-level change (see Box), tidal and wind energy, and accumulation of organic and inorganic sediments.

The effects of substrate are seen on almost all reefs in the Great Barrier Reef, especially those with substrates shallower than 20 m deep. Growth of the reef began during the past 8,000 years on a limestone surface. The high spots of the platform, whether as reef rims or as patch reefs in lagoons, were the first to be colonised by reef organisms.

Energy factors. The Great Barrier Reef has a very high-energy regime and high tidal range and these factors distinguish its constituent reefs from reefs in other parts of the world. The energy effects are manifest in three main ways.

First, the classical zonation seen on the reefs of the Great Barrier Reef of coralline rim, coral flat, sand and rubble flats and lagoon are a consequence of growth in a high-energy situation when sea levels are stable.

Second, the most obvious effect of impinging energy is the sediment on a large part of the reefs. Most of these sediments are derived from the margin and coral flat on the windward side, and are transported backwards across the rim and flat to lower energy leeward environments. Intertidal and sub-

Influence of sea level

Reefs grow when sea levels are high; they die when sea levels fall and expose the coral organisms to the air. A cross-section shows them to have layer-cake or stacked sediments separated by hiatuses (unconformities) that represent periods of erosion when sea levels were low.

During the past 2 million years, growth of individual reefs lasted for some 4,000–14,000 years and were separated by erosion phases of 100,000 years during periods of low sea level. The reefs of the Great Barrier Reef have therefore grown for less than 20 per cent of the time since reef growth was initiated.

The modern Great Barrier Reef started growing between 8,000 and 8,500 years ago, when sea levels rose at the end of the last ice age. Sea level rose rapidly at first (greater than 10 m per 1,000 years) and then stabilised at essentially its present position at 6,200 years ago. PD

tidal sands accumulate at rates of 1.5 m per 1,000 years whereas intertidal rubble and boulder ramparts accumulate at rates of up to 15 m per 1,000 years.

Finally, the development of the organic reef framework is also a consequence of the intensity and distribution of energy. The rates of production of the framework vary between 1 m and 15 m per 1,000 years. The highest rates are in patch reefs and on leeward margins.

As soon as a reef reaches sea level a marked change comes over its growth. Vertical growth is inhibited by sea level and the major growth-propelling factor becomes the physical energy of the system, the consequence of which is as follows:

- The framework on the windward margin changes drastically to low, stubby, branching and encrusting forms; coralline algae encrust the front and top
- Massive production of sediment starts. Subtidal rubble, subtidal sands and intertidal sands develop, all of which are distributed leewards with time as a consequence of the impinging energy

The biological and sedimentary components grow leewards as a function of the high-energy conditions when sea levels are high – that is, the reefs grow landwards. This process could continue until the lagoon fills up, and the reef produces so much sediment that it chokes itself. Usually, however, this stage is not reached because high sea levels have not lasted for a sufficiently long period.

The above mode of growth is repeated as a consequence of successive alternating sea levels (see Box). Growth is episodic: large reef complexes representing successive short periods of accumulation of carbonate sediments (1–15 m per 1,000 years) when sea

Top *Masthead Island, an uninhabited sand cay and its surrounding platform reef off Gladstone in the Capricornia section of the Great Barrier Reef Marine Park.*

Main picture *Aerial view of Wistari Reef, a network of reefs near Heron Island.*

Top right *Staghorn corals* (Acropora) *and white soft coral* (Sarcophyton trocheliophorum) *exposed at low tide on the Great Barrier Reef.*

Bottom left *An example of the varied and colourful underwater life of the Great Barrier Reef. Coral reefs contain a greater variety of plant and animal species than any other habitat except for tropical forests.*

Bottom right *Cardinal fish* (Apopon). *The Great Barrier Reef is home to more than 1,500 species of fish.*

Conservation and tourism

After a much-disputed proposal to mine parts of the Great Barrier Reef for limestone and commercial plans to drill for oil, both federal and state governments joined forces to protect the entire reef. Initially the federal government established a Marine Park covering a vast area (343,800 km²) and embracing some 2,900 reefs along 2,300 km of coast

The Great Barrier Reef Marine Park Authority (GBRMPA) was set up to develop appropriate zoning and management guidelines to protect and control use of the Great Barrier Reef. It is an independent body funded by the federal government but with practical management the responsibility of the Queensland National Parks and Wildlife Service. Management costs are shared equally between the Queensland and federal governments. After establishment of the Marine Park, the entire area was nominated for World Heritage Listing in 1980, and it achieved that status in 1981. (See also pp. 52–4.)

The Great Barrier Reef Marine Park is a vast area, one and a half times as large as Victoria, almost half the area of New South Wales. It is the world's largest and most complex expanse of living coral reefs, encompassing many unique forms of marine life. Throughout the area are almost 3,000 reefs and hundreds of islands and cays.

Most of the offshore islands are National Parks under Queensland government legislation and include such spectacular examples as the virtually wilderness Hinchinbrook Island (39,350 ha) with peaks that tower to over 1,000 m rising almost vertically from rainforest-fringed white sandy beaches. In contrast, Michaelmas Cay (3 ha) rises a few metres above high tide but carries a large and important population of breeding sea birds. In the Whitsunday Islands area, a mixture of private and National Park islands provide a wide range of recreational opportunities for locals and tourists.

Taking the reef as a whole it is estimated that 2.5 million people visit an island or reef each year and in so doing expend around $250 million locally.

Access to the reef is increasing as larger and faster vessels, sea-planes and submersibles become more common. A floating hotel developed some 70 km off Townsville failed for a variety of reasons, but there have been applications for other similar facilities to the GBRMPA. The physical infrastructure has expanded dramatically in the past decade with many pontoons moored on the reef for the use of day visitors. Most tourists see the reefs by glass-bottomed boat, semi-submersible vessel or snorkelling and diving.

Considerable debate continues about the capacity of the reef to sustain continued expansion of various kinds of uses. The federal government recently awarded around $14 million to establish a Cooperative Research Centre (based at James Cook University in Townsville) to study the sustained development of the Great Barrier Reef over the next seven years.

The enormous diversity of corals (more than 400 species), fish (more than 1,500 species) and other marine organisms is evident at almost any offshore reef in the region and equally the brilliant colours of many of the plants and animals, combined with their abundance, guarantees a memorable experience for visitors. At a few locations underwater trails have been developed. A recent development has been

levels are high are separated by no growth during intervening periods of low sea level.

The Great Barrier Reef region

Four interacting processes affected the evolution of the region, and therefore the whole of the Great Barrier Reef Province: rifting, continental drift, sea-level change and subsidence.

The principal physical features of northeastern Australia, of which the continental shelf is one, formed as a consequence of rifting in the late Cretaceous period around 95 million years ago, which juxtaposed deep rift basins, the Queensland and Townsville Troughs, close against the continental edge. Because of this rifting, the northern Great Barrier Reef was from its inception a very narrow reef zone and the distribution and shape of the reefs today reflect this morphology.

This margin formed in high latitudes while Australia was still very close to Antarctica (see pp. 5–9). Since early Cenozoic times, some 50–60 million years ago, Australia has drifted north over a distance of 20 degrees of latitude. Such dramatic plate movements had profound climatic

Hitchinbrook Island, a craggy and colourful uninhabited spot near Tully, is accessible by air from Townsville and by boat from Cardwell. A national park, its many tourist attractions include lush tropical forests, mountains over 1,000 m high and long sandy beaches.

Beach on Whitsunday Island, between Townsville and Mackay. Recreational facilities in the Whitsundays area include scuba diving and trips in glass-bottomed boats and semi-submersible submarines. In some other parts of the Great Barrier Marine Park, recreation and fishing are prohibited.

regular diving at sites where some species aggregate; the best-known example is the assembly of very large potato cod on the ribbon reef northeast from Cooktown, known as the Cod Hole. Here, divers can swim with these gentle fish, which are up to 1.5 m long and weigh more than a person.

Some of the more spectacular sights of the reef are not easy to see. For example, the recently discovered simultaneous mass spawning of hard corals occurs a few nights after the full moon in summer. The corals release bundles of eggs and sperm that float to the surface where they break up and disperse. Night diving to see this incredible event is becoming a popular activity but one available only a few nights each year.

Apart from passive observation the reef region provides a valuable commercial and recreational fishing resource. Fisheries include finned fish, prawns, scallops, lobsters and crabs and are valued at around $40 million of products, involving over 1,000 commercial boats and 2,000 fishermen. Recreational fishing involves about 15,000 boats making an average of some 200,000 trips into the reef region per year. More than three million fish are caught for a total yield of about 6,500 tonnes.

MARINE PARK ZONES

General use 'A'	No restrictions on use except: • no mining • no commercial or scuba spear-fishing
General use 'B'	As for 'A', plus: • no trawling • no vessel more than 500 tonnes
Marine National Park 'A'	Recreation and conservation goals as for General use 'B', plus: • no collecting or spearfishing • fishing with rod or handline only, maximum two hooks
Marine National Park 'B'	Recreation and conservation goals as Marine National Park 'A', plus: • no fishing
Preservation	Preservation in undisturbed state. All activities prohibited except: • scientific research not possible elsewhere

There is also an important game fishery throughout the reef region from bases such as Cairns and Townsville. Yet another commercial activity is the collection of live fish for sale to the aquarium trade and the collection of shells.

The combined demands from tourism, commerce, conservation and recreation have led to the development of zoning plans as a way for the Marine Park Authority to control multiple-use within the region. These zones consist of five classes (see table).

About 75 per cent of the reef area is zoned General Use 'A' with less than 3 per cent in the Marine National Park or Preservation zones. Occasionally, local or periodic restrictions are applied but in general the Great Barrier Reef Marine Park Authority has not limited activities other than mining for most of the reef area.

One of the difficulties for the management agency has been to help people understand the very large difference between the multiple-use nature of the Marine Park and the more conventional preservation attributes of terrestrial National Parks. PSV

changes along the continental shelf of eastern Australia.

Reconstructions of the movement of Australia's continental plate predict that tropical climates first affected the northern tip of northeastern Australia in late early Miocene times and did not affect the region of the southern Great Barrier Reef until the Plio-Pleistocene. Clearly, therefore, the Great Barrier Reef must have formed first in the north and progressively later in the south. This hypothesis is supported by drilling data that show a thick, 1–2-km reef section in the north dating from about 15 million years ago (the early Miocene) and a thin 120-m reef section in the south dating from about 2 million years ago (the Plio-Pleistocene).

Accumulation of thick reef sequences depends on subsidence of the continental margin. The rate of subsidence, together with global sea-level change, determines relative sea level and therefore reef growth. Data from petroleum drill holes in the northern and southern Great Barrier Reef indicate that subsidence affected reef growth 15 million years ago in the Miocene and again in the Pliocene some 4–5 million years ago. PD

The north

Northern Australia, a vast region stretching from the remote Kimberley Plateau of Western Australia through the Top End of the Northern Territory to the tip of Queensland's Cape York, is a land of images.

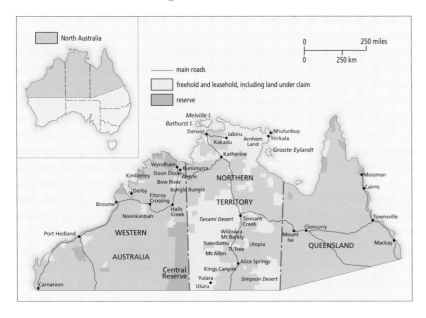

Northern Australia, showing Aboriginal-owned land and reserves.

Argyle Diamond Mine in the Kimberleys, Western Australia. Mining, for a wide variety of minerals, has a major part in the economy of the North.

For most Australians, living in the metropolitan sprawls of Sydney or Melbourne, it is a place to visit but not to live. To them it is a region of vast ranges of red soil, with spiny hummock grassland grazed by huge herds of semi-feral cattle periodically mustered by resilient laconic stockmen; a place where high technology opencast mining is king and where the economic resources of the land are there to be claimed for the national benefit; and an area of extreme isola-tion, where your neighbours live 100 km away, your children's schooling comes via 'School of the Air' (see p. 245) and where masculine interests and activi-ties, in line with the frontier image, are dominant.

However, for northern inhabitants – about 5 per cent of the national population living on approxi-mately half of the continent – the images are some-what different. Like other Australians they are urban-dwellers, with almost 80 per cent living in large towns such as Townsville or Darwin, in mining centres such as Port Hedland, or in smaller service towns such as Broome or Katherine. Many of them are outsiders and see the north through 'colonial' eyes. However, increasingly, people commit them-selves to the northern way of life and believe strongly in its future – unbounded mineral wealth, unlimited attraction for both Australian and overseas investors, and a prime tourist destination.

Still others, the Aborigines who form 10 per cent of the northern population, have different concepts of the north. More than a third of the Aboriginal popu-lation is northern-based and they form 10 per cent of the northern population. Unlike their largely tran-sient non-Aboriginal counterparts, almost half of whom had, in the case of the Northern Territory, migrated inwards from other states in the 5-year period between the censuses of 1981 and 1986, Abor-igines see the north as home – the place of their ancestors and to which they are irrevocably bound. Their acquisition of tenure to over 10 per cent of northern lands makes them a highly significant force in the future of Australia's last frontier.

The issues now emerging from the Northern Ter-ritory include government, tourism and Aboriginal participation in development.

First, the land of beef cattle and mining has become in part the land of government. In 1990, 38 per cent of the Northern Territory's wage-earners worked in public administration, defence and community ser-vice, employed either by Commonwealth, territory or local government agencies; and this sector accounted for almost a quarter of the Territory's Gross Domestic Product. Nearly 80 per cent of the Northern Territory's revenue derived directly from Commonwealth payments from Canberra. The resultant financial dependency of the north on the south is a continual source of friction and frustration.

Second, although only accounting for 6 per cent of Gross Domestic Product and only 9 per cent of waged jobs, tourism is seen as a vital means of breaking this dependency. It is undoubtedly a growth industry. Since 1981, earnings from tourism have quadrupled, and Kakadu National Park, one of the major Top End destinations, received almost six times as many visi-tors in 1990 as in 1982–83. Overseas visitors, primar-ily from the USA, Britain, Japan, Germany and other European countries have come in ever-increasing

Environmental issues

British industry harnessed the energy of steampower a decade before gaolers disembarked their human cargo at Sydney Cove. In one sense, Australia Day 1788 symbolised the dramatic economic and technological transformation of the continent, when stone-using societies of hunters and gatherers succumbed to an Iron Age economy. The invaders were ignorant of the consequences for this fragile ecology of the wanton exploitation of natural resources and the introduction of exotic plants and animals.

ABORIGINES AND COLONISATION

Despite popular imagery, Australia was not virgin territory. Aboriginal people had exploited its diverse ecological niches during the preceding 40 or more millennia, manipulating resources in an intelligent seasonal round in which controlled burning played a major role. Such firing possibly altered some habitats, and some animal species were hunted to extinction – especially after the dingo, an Asian dog, arrived at least 3,000 years ago and became symbiotic with people. Such environmental impacts were limited, however, and because much vegetation is adapted to fire, natural resources proved renewable: human actions never matched the massive contemporary transformations wrought by nature.

Vast environmental fluctuations occurred during the Aboriginal tenancy of this driest of continents. Volcanoes erupted, glaciers grew, shorelines fluctuated as seas fell and then rose more than 130 m, wetlands teeming with life expanded behind their mangrove screens, forests and lakes waxed and waned, rivers once permanent ran intermittently, shifting dunes stabilised and vegetated.

Despite the magnitude of these environmental challenges human persistence and adaptability triumphed as culture was transmitted through some 2,000 generations. Aboriginal identification with clan territories was absolute, so that ancestral events from the distant time known as the Dreaming (see also p. 69) were held responsible for shaping the landscape and endowing its resources, even laying down unalterable routes of communication between places and people. All natural features and resources consequently were connected intimately with spiritual beliefs and rituals. 'Owners' were simply custodians entrusted with the task of managing and transmitting intact their environmental and spiritual inheritance to the succeeding generation. Created in the

Water buffalo in Alligator River, Kakadu National Park, Northern Territory. This park, which is on the World Heritage list, is attracting growing numbers of tourists. A challenge for the future is striking a balance between the demands of tourism and the conservation of fragile environments.

numbers and in 1989–90 accounted for almost 20 per cent of those visiting the Darwin region.

Such growth raises issues for all northerners and, indirectly, for all Australians. Tourist pressure on fragile environments, such as the wetlands of the Alligator River, which are now on the World Heritage list, is of concern to all interested in conservation (see pp. 52–4).

The cultural and environmental emphasis of northern tourism, which promotes unique aspects of the land and its people rather than the facilities offered, poses particular challenges for Aborigines. How are they to participate in the industry, thereby earning significant amounts of privately generated income to free them from heavy dependence on public funding, and also maintain their social and cultural integrity?

Compromises, such as the lease-back of Aboriginal-owned Kakadu to the custodianship of Australian National Parks and Wildlife, the use of uranium royalty money to purchase tourist facilities in the park and the development of an Aboriginal-controlled art and craft industry (see p. 292), seem to provide some of the answers.

Finally, will the tourist boom continue? Or will it stagnate, thus throwing into question the heavy investment by the Northern Territory government in the tourist industry?

Regardless of the future it is clear that the character of the north has irrevocably changed, and that the twenty-first century may generate a very different frontier image from that of the twentieth.   EY

Dreaming, the environment pulsated seasonally and was capable of productive manipulation, but otherwise it was an unchanging constant, proof that before people were, the Dreaming was.

THE ETHOS OF COLONISATION

The new Australians from 1788 were slow to recognise that they possessed a heritage of natural and cultural assets worthy of preservation and careful management. Colonists perceived their duty to be the imposition of law and order on an untamed and unproductive wilderness full of alien creatures. Landscape became a burdensome material resource to be harvested, while government land policy existed to release or to retain it as a means of political and social control. Nobody seriously considered the rights of its previous owners, so the Aborigines were evicted as pests akin to kangaroos, while the vegetation was attacked as the main impediment to progress. The first governor, Arthur Phillip, wryly observed of his new territory that, 'as far as the eye can reach to the westward, the Country is one continued wood'. (See also pp. 86–7.)

The axe bit deeply into trunks of unfamiliar species, in an effort to clear land. The giant cedars along the eastern coastal fringe, felled without any thought for future supplies, provided one of the earliest Australian industries. (So did the seals and whales of coastal waters, hunted to near extinction.) Botanist J. S. Turner observed that even in 1966, 'the wholehearted destruction of the native vegetation is almost a national pastime'. Energetic axemen took a short-cut to opening Gippsland's forest canopy near Melbourne by ringbarking trees. One pioneer recalled that, for decades, their trunks stood 'bleached and white, a monument alike of the great scrub and of the industry that cleared it'.

The ethos of the hardy bushman whose axe and plough tamed the wilderness and made waste lands productive is deeply engrained in national consciousness. The unfortunate consequences of soil erosion, dust storms and abandoned farms are attributed to misfortune and climatic disabilities, rather than to ignorance, mismanagement and cupidity.

PERCEPTIONS OF LANDSCAPE

While some colonists judged Australia's alien environment favourably, the aesthetic sensibilities of many Europeans were repelled by the vastness and character of Australian space. Bernard Smith's perceptive studies of changing taste and attitudes to place show how imported artistic conventions and concepts long obscured real appreciation for Australian landscape. Nostalgic artists adapted local scenery to their imported romantic notions of 'sublime' or picturesque scenery. Justice Barron Field grieved in 1822, that 'there is not a single scene . . . of which a painter could make a landscape, without greatly disguising the true character of the trees'. As the landscape lacked buildings or ruins, it reinforced the notion of wilderness, in which Aborigines constituted part of the fauna.

Persons of sensitivity echoed Field's ambivalence through the first century of British settlement. Field deplored the 'eternal' and 'unpicturesque' eucalypts, while admitting that flora contributed to the

Inset A slow-burning fire in eucalypt woodland, northern Cape York Peninsula. Features that make this typical of deliberate burning by Aborigines include the fire's low temperature and the fact that it mainly destroys low-burning vegetation. Controlled firing promotes the regeneration of grasses and shrubs, which attracts grazing animals such as kangaroos and wallabies, and it also increases visibility for hunting.

Main picture In this recently burnt eucalypt woodland, also in Cape York Peninsula, branches and tree trunks are still smouldering, as the ash layer shows. Such a fire will burn for 2–3 weeks. The vegetation soon recovers.

'healthy' climate. Others voiced feelings of depression, boredom or 'weird melancholy'. Popular author Marcus Clarke (see pp. 311–12), writing in the second half of the nineteenth century, asserted that 'forests are funereal, secret, stern. Their solitude is desolation . . . The very animal life of these frowning hills is either grotesque or ghostly.'

Such environmental attitudes were unlikely to nurture a conservation ethic. Not surprisingly, fauna

acclimatisation societies flourished and individuals introduced rabbits, foxes and birds. The celebrated botanist, Baron Von Mueller, planted blackberry and other future noxious plants, under the erroneous assumption that Australian forests contained no edible plants for the human wayfarer. Zoologist Baldwin Spencer echoed popular sentiment even in 1888. 'There is no scenery in Victoria to speak of', Spencer wrote to an English friend soon after arriv-

Colour symbols of landscape

In early colonial landscape paintings dark green was a prevailing colour, symbolising confining forests. 'What can a painter do with one cold olive-green', Barron Field complained. Late-century impressionist painters shifted their perceptions to a celebration of landscape. Golden vistas, blue hills and purple haze were vibrant evocations of light where previously gloom dominated.

The ethos of these pastoral images, however, was

conservative rather than conservationist. Like contemporary writers Henry Lawson and 'Banjo' Patterson (see p. 311), their pastoral idylls perpetuated human heroism and individuality. The woodcutter, horseman, shearer, even the drover's wife, evoked admiration; the bush or plains provided both the setting and the challenge for their self-reliance.

Significantly, even the celebrated gum-tree scenes by Hans Heysen (1877–1968)

exemplify the wilderness tamed. Cattle, carts and tracks reduce nature to a human, domesticated dimension. It was Heysen, however, who first ventured to the desert fringe and, in the Flinders Ranges, initiated the imagery of the arid frontier.

During the past half century artists have adopted desert landscapes, time-worn rocks, searing heat and isolation as icons, with red as their colour symbol. Kenneth Clark, who claimed Sidney Nolan (see p. 307) as the first artist to portray Australian landscape successfully, enthused that he 'extracted its essences: the red desert, the dead animals, the stranded, 'ridiculous towns'. This latter-day myth of the 'dead heart' replaces both sombre forests and golden summers of pastoral dominance with hostile environments and weatherbeaten people. It is unlikely to promote conservationist sympathy to protect the natural environment.

As most Australians inhabit cities and coasts, industrial pollution and urban sprawl seem more hazardous and real than this fiery world. Besides, it ignores the benign truth that Australian deserts also bloom, that Aboriginal societies subsisted there for millennia before domesticated stock disturbed the ecological balance, and that the cause of many environmental disasters rests with human greed, ignorance or foolhardiness, rather than with capricious nature. DJM

Sand dunes in the Petermann Ranges, Northern Territory. The Martian redness of Central Australia has been commonly depicted by artists.

Prickly pear growing wild at Yelarbon on the Darling Downs, Queensland. This cactus is among several plant and animal species introduced to Australia from other countries that have had serious effects on native habitats.

ing in Melbourne, 'in parts it is pretty but that is all and we can never get beyond the sight of the eternal gum trees: there is not the slightest variation whatever in the foliage for mile after mile: no light and shade for the leaves hang straight down.' Ironically, Spencer soon pioneered the creation of national parks, became a patron of nationalistic impressionist artists and, within three years, deplored 'the mania for ringbarking' eucalypts.

Aesthetics, however, were not the only factor conditioning environmental attitudes. Scientific evaluation of landscape as phenomena, and the experienced hardships and frustrations of simply being there, also contributed. Consider the explorer John Oxley, whose journey along the Lachlan River was obstructed by immense marshes. Forced to abandon his quest for pastures new, he retraced his weary steps across the plains. On 16 July 1817, his sense of exasperation with this disappointing land became evident:

> There is a uniformity in the barren desolateness of this country, which wearies one more than I am able to express. One tree, one soil, one water, and one description of bird, fish, or animal, prevails alike for ten miles, and for one hundred. A variety of wretchedness is at all times preferable to one unvarying cause of pain or distress.

A vulnerable ecology

No other urbanised, industrial country in the Western world is as ecologically vulnerable to human interference as Australia. Floods, droughts and fires recur in almost every region, but there was a deceptive appearance about the landscape if settlers arrived during normal times. In addition, many soils are of low fertility and much tropical land has such a short growing season that grasses possess low nutritive value for European-type land use. Such attractive grasslands, particularly when seen during good seasons, have lured developments that proved ecologically disastrous. Low rainfall is often inadequate to flush out modern chemical pollutants, and salination follows irrigation on what was prime land. Because of the unreliability of rainfall and its great variability in intensity, the removal of the cover and the resulting natural imbalance, may lead to serious erosion. (See also p.14.)

Historical factors compounded the ecological problems. The country was occupied so rapidly by farmers and pastoralists unfamiliar with regional conditions, that they were unable to draw upon generations of conventional lore. Characteristically optimistic, they fell back upon their own experiences learned in their European homelands, which were

totally inappropriate. Exotic grasses and animal species were introduced without prior experiment or controls, so they ran wild. Rabbits, foxes, goats, prickly pear and many pasture grasses have taken a terrible toll of native habitats (see also pp. 273 and 281–2).

A government policy that sought to retain control over lands contributed to environmental degradation. Before 1847, virtually all land was held under lease. This leasehold system has been retained over much of the continent. Lacking security of tenure, however, the occupier is tempted to practise extractive overgrazing. Overstocking was so abused in the Western Lands Division of New South Wales that, by the drought of the 1890s, 15 million sheep were depastured in country capable of sustaining fewer than half that number. Sidney Kidman's rapacious cattle empire straddled the continent early this century, with leasehold properties in marginal grazing country covering an area greater than Tasmania or England. Much of this country is virtual wasteland today.

National parks

Despite an exploitative history of resource development, Australia was prominent in creating park and scenic reserves. A scenic area was proclaimed in Tasmania in 1863 and 5,000 acres (2,023 ha) were reserved in 1866 around Jenolan Caves, New South Wales, six years before the landmark proclamation of Yellowstone Park, USA. The world's first creation of a National Park was declared south of Sydney in 1879, since 1954 named The Royal National Park. The Ku-ring-gai Chase National Park, north of Sydney, followed in 1892. National parks existed in all states by 1916.

NATURE CONSERVATION RESERVES,
DECEMBER 1988*

	Area ('000s ha)	Percentage of state area
Australian Capital Territory	112	46.8
New South Wales	3,812	4.8
Northern Territory	4,000	3.0
Queensland	3,664	2.1
South Australia	11,117	11.3
Tasmania	967	14.2
Victoria	1,823	8.0
Western Australia	15,282	6.0

*In 1993, the national total of terrestrial protected areas was 50,139,421 ha and that for marine protected areas was 39,638,652 ha.

The reasons for establishing these early parks would satisfy few conservationists today. They existed to provide social and recreational amenities, with little basis in moral values or wilderness concepts. The Deed of Grant of the 1879 park empowered its trustees to improve upon nature in various ways. These included the construction of ornamental (exotic) and zoological gardens, racecourses and sports grounds, rifle butts, camping and bathing facilities and public amusements. When New South Wales introduced an Animals Protection Act in that same year, its intention was to protect introduced deer and bird species. The utilitarian tradition persists in the creation of reserves for public amenity.

Commencing in the 1930s, evidence of alarming environmental degradation resulted in the establishment of various Soil or Landscape Conservation Authorities. These bodies also created reserves to protect special economic resources (red gums from overexploitation, rivers from siltation). When economic considerations suit, however, most governments have redrawn park boundaries, so 'National Park' was simply an honorary title in most cases, lacking legal significance.

Tasmania has the greatest area in proportion to its size of any state reserved for parks or scenic reserves, but their existence depends upon the fortunes of industry. Prime timbered areas of both the Mt Field and Hartz Mountains National Parks, for example, were excised during the 1950s. Until 1971, the Board administering all parks and reserves was unincorporated, thereby lacking independent standing. As a section of the Lands and Surveys Department it was subject to that minister's direction whose concerns were not disinterested. An independent Tasmanian Parks and Wildlife Service was created in 1971 as a more appropriate custodian, but the government recently abolished it, re-incorporating it in the Department of Lands. In Queensland, although its natural heritage values are outstanding across a wide environmental range, only 2.02 per cent of its area is reserved for land conservation.

Claims that national parks should be declared on moral or scientific grounds to protect fauna, or for their aesthetic, passive natural beauty, or wilderness values, were voiced in New South Wales and Victoria around the turn of the century. Proponents of the Wilson's Promontory National Park urged that cause. When the [Royal] National Park trustees decided to harvest their timber commercially in 1920, opponents claimed that they were morally obliged to conserve it. Reconciling legitimate recreational requirements with landscape values are major issues today in park management. Recognition of the primacy of scenic and moral criteria in a national park possibly was implicit first in the 1944 Kosciusko State Park Act. This was the first New South Wales park to be permanently reserved and which could be revoked only by a special Act of Parliament.

The case for expediency is easier to argue in the public domain than the preservationist cause. Dam construction, mining or forestry are claimed to increase employment and amenities, including vehicle-access roads, opportunities for powerboats, swimming and fishing, or even scenery conveniently viewed through the windscreen by hurried tourists. Conservationists may be easily portrayed as authoritarian elitist minorities, excluding citizens from 'wilderness', advocating park access only by hardy hikers or canoeists, opposing firearms or the introduction of non-native fish species.

Given Australia's environmental history, it is not surprising that development lobbyists receive much rural support in situations of conflict, or that some urban four-wheel drive vehicle owners demand the right to drive anywhere. It is unfortunate that the conservation movement is largely becoming identified with the urban middle-class with professional skills.

Within recent times conservationists also have added vital utilitarian arguments to their case for maintaining environmental integrity. They stress the need to preserve the wide range of existing genetic stock in order to sustain genetic diversity. This requires the retention of habitats of a size adequate for the long-term maintenance of species. To ensure that a sufficient area is preserved, ecological studies of undisturbed communities are necessary and index areas need to be retained for monitoring the situation in the future. Unfortunately, these cogent arguments also are intellectualist in nature and are unlikely to change public opinion. Even in 1891, Baldwin Spencer regretted that 'the general public have never had much sympathy with what we may call scientific sentiment'.

Until recently Australians have shown a singular lack of concern for another justification for park

Conservation and the international arena

Australia's international role in heritage matters proved positive. In environmental affairs, it has actively participated in the International Union for the Conservation of Nature and Natural Resources (IUCN).

Under UNESCO's Man and the Biosphere programme, 12 Australian biosphere reserves had been declared by 1987.

Australia was the first country to become a party to the Convention on Wetlands of International Importance and Especially as Waterfowl Habitat, 1971. By 1987, 28 wetland areas had been nominated for the Convention.

Australia adheres to the Convention on the Conservation of Antarctic Marine Living Resources and has taken a strong position against commercial whaling and sealing, under the International Convention for the Regulation of Whaling and the Conventions on the Conservation of Antarctic Seals. It proclaimed the Environment Protection (Sea Dumping) Act 1981. The Wildlife Protection (Regulation of Exports and Imports) Act 1982 complies with international obligations under the Convention on International Trade in Endangered Species of Wild Flora and Fauna (CITES). As part of the overall World Conservation Strategy, the government in 1984 endorsed the National Conservation Strategy for Australia.

Australia's contribution to the International Convention concerning the Protection of the World Cultural and Natural Heritage, 1972 (The World Heritage Convention) has been positive internationally and highly controversial at home. Australia was the seventh nation to ratify the Convention in 1974. As a State Party it was elected in 1976 to the World Heritage Committee consisting of 21 and it provided the President at the 1981 meeting. It participated in framing the criteria for inclusion on the World Heritage List. Ten Australian properties had been listed by 1993 (see p. 53).

The Australian Heritage Commission assisted the establishment in 1978 of Australia ICOMOS, a branch of The International Council on Monuments and Sites, a non-governmental organisation associated with UNESCO. Its aim is to conserve places in accordance with the highest standards of scholarship and archaeological, engineering and architectural practice, to safeguard authenticity by first carrying out a conservation analysis, assessing cultural significance and preparing a conservation plan. To assist this process it adapted the ICOMOS Venice Charter (1966) to Australian requirements. This carefully formulated set of guidelines, known as the Burra Charter, has contributed immeasurably to improved conservation standards.

The government complemented this concern for static cultural monuments by ratifying the Convention on the Means of Prohibiting and Preventing the Illicit Import, Export and Transfer of Ownership of Cultural Property.

The 1975 Inquiry on Museums and National Collections found a startling neglect of conservation, for most institutions lacked trained conservators or laboratories. It recommended urgent steps to improve institutional standards and to give priority to training conservators. The government acted promptly to establish a course in Materials Conservation at the Canberra College of Advanced Education (now the University of Canberra), while most state governments upgraded their institutional facilities. The course was later approved as a UNESCO training centre for conservationists from around the Indian and southern Pacific Oceans.

This transformation in conservation standards and facilities represents one of the most significant aspects of recent Australian cultural history, even though there remain daunting areas for action. DJM

Uluru (Ayers Rock). The rock is not only a remarkable site in itself, but is also sacred to the Aborigines, to whom ownership passed in 1985. It is one of Australia's most popular tourist spots and a World Heritage Area.

Alice Springs Telegraph Station. The station, built in 1871 close by the Alice Springs waterhole, was the reason for the town's existence, and the town's name derives from the wife of the supervisor of the construction of the overland telegraph line.

mental or cultural significance were published in 1981. By 1993, there were 10,721 places on the Register. This inventory has no equal in any nation for its comprehensiveness.

This Act hopefully safeguards Commonwealth properties from detrimental actions, but generally its powers are moral rather than legal. Its effectiveness depends upon the passage of complementary heritage legislation by state and territory governments. This has been implemented only to a varying degree in some states.

THE POLITICS OF CONSERVATION

Coincident with the protests associated with the war in Vietnam, environmental groups entered the political arena from the late 1960s in an unprecedented and largely uncoordinated series of protests. Environmental issues, initially on a regional basis but later nationally, were seen by politicians to attract or lose significant numbers of voters. The times spawned environmental action groups, including the Total Environmental Centres, Project Jonah and regional Conservation Councils. The Australian Conservation Foundation played a prominent role in several disputes.

Environmental protection of the quality of urban living lay behind the Sydney green bans (see p. 49). In Victoria, public protests in 1969 supported by *The Age* newspaper, thwarted a scheme to subdivide the ecologically fragile Little Desert. Pollution issues defeated the Clutha coal development in New South

Wales, while major campaigns opposed the loss of wilderness around Myall Lakes. Not all campaigns succeeded, and no amount of effort prevented the loss of Tasmania's Lake Pedder.

Pressures during the mid-1970s ensured that the mining of mineral sands on Fraser Island, Queensland, was banned. The establishment of the Great Barrier Reef Marine Park Authority in 1975 and the exclusion of oil drilling from that region, also owed much to environmentalist pressures. The list of losses remained long, but the tally of wins or compromises grew.

In the past, government-owned (Crown) lands have been considered appropriate for economic exploitation, but competing claims for land use now include acceptance of the economics of passive control. Development and exploitation of non-renewable resources no longer is an automatic process. Governments and commercial interests are learning that sensible and coordinated planning, rather than *ad hoc* decisions, can maintain a proper balance between development and conservation.

The object lesson of public information and cooperation, rather than confrontation, as the way for the future was painfully climaxed in the fight to prevent the damming of the Franklin River Valley in Tasmania (see p. 48), although many developers and some governments have still not accepted that principle. The struggle aroused huge protest rallies in mainland cities and polarised Tasmanians in ways that cut across many personal, party and family allegiances. The election of the Hawke Labor government was assured by the nationwide environmental vote. The Tasmanian government later appealed to the High Court of Australia against the World Heritage Properties Conservation Act 1983, preventing any dam within the Western Tasmania Wilderness National Park World Heritage Area. The High Court ruled by a majority of four to three that constitutional right rested with the external affairs powers of the Commonwealth.

Subsequent years have witnessed the growing professionalism of organised conservation and its greater breadth of perception. The National Trust movement includes landscape considerations as a major factor in historical assessment; the importance of Aboriginal heritage values is more widely appreciated. The natural and cultural heritage of all Australians gradually is becoming an interdependent reality. Although environmental degradation continues apace, the growth of a national conservation ethic was one of the most significant characteristics of a maturer Australian culture as it achieved the bicentenary of European settlement. To sustain this ethic in the face of the economic downturn and mass unemployment in the 1990s will prove a dominant challenge of this decade.   DJM

nations are examined, they would not come up to expectations.

It is possible that some of these areas would be more appropriate as Biosphere Reserves (specially designated areas endorsed as such by UNESCO that contain a relatively pristine core, buffer zones where human impacts are monitored, and rehabilitation zones where the effectiveness of conservation measures can be gauged). Australia already has 12 of these, of which most are national parks and at least two are in World Heritage sites (Uluru and Tasmanian Wilderness).

The Australian federal government has been at pains to point out that, contrary to some assertions, World Heritage listing of an area does not mean that ownership of the area is somehow transferred to the international community, to the United Nations or to any foreign power; nor does World Heritage listing necessarily bar an area from continued economic use (for example, tourism, agriculture or pastoralism) and that, in several cases, such activities continue to take place. Only where development is likely to damage or destroy those characteristics that ensure an area's place on the World Heritage List is such development prevented by legislation. Where certain development cannot continue (as, for example, in parts of the World Heritage areas in Tasmania or North Queensland) structural adjustment assistance has been given.

Australia's National Estate

The National Estate is defined in the Australian Heritage Commission Act of 1975 as 'those places, being components of the natural environment of Australia or the cultural environment of Australia that have aesthetic, historic, scientific or social significance or other special value for future generations as well as for the present community'.

In other words, the National Estate comprises those places or features within Australia, including its Territories, its territorial sea and its continental shelf, that Australians most want to keep, and not historic places or buildings alone: national parks, nature reserves, various habitats for endangered species, natural landscape features and items of geological interest are encompassed, together with Aboriginal sites such as middens, carved rocks and trees, fish traps and cave paintings. Besides various churches, commercial and residential buildings, historic places include shipwrecks, parks and gardens, and structures associated with transport, mining and engineering.

The Australian Heritage Commission, a small Statutory Authority, was established in 1975 to advise the Australian (federal) government on all aspects of the National Estate. One of the Australian Heritage Commission's major functions is the compilation and maintenance of a Register of the National Estate – an inventory of those places defined above.

Besides being a comprehensive list of places in Australia with significant heritage value (and this is determined through the application of certain criteria) the Register's basic purpose is educational – in the broadest sense of the word. It serves to provide detailed information about the natural and cultural history of the nation to all Australians; in particular, to decision-makers who require objective information about places of heritage significance so that due weight may be given to National Estate values before planning decisions and consequent actions are taken.

At 30 June 1993, there were 10,721 places listed in the Register, with 1,576 more nominated places awaiting assessment by specialist technical experts. Various criteria have been developed against which nominated places are assessed (see Box).

However, before a place is included in the Register the Commission must advertise its intentions to include it, and must advise all identifiable owners, and relevant local governments, state governments and federal government departments, to enable any objections to be made. All objections are carefully assessed by technical experts and taken into account before a final decision is made.

The effect of inscribing a place on the Register places a direct legal obligation on federal government ministers, departments and authorities, who are required to ensure that their actions do not adversely affect the National Estate values of places in the Register unless no feasible and prudent alternatives exist – if there are no such alternatives, adverse effects are to be minimised through all reasonable measures.

Apart from this legal obligation, there is no direct legal constraint on owners of private property or on state or local government, caused by entry of that property on the Register. Thus the act of listing a place on the Register of the National Estate does not prevent further development of that place; nor does it permit open or public access.

Of course, information assembled by the Australian Heritage Commission about the National Estate significance of a place entered on the Register may be used by state or local governments to assist those governments in their consideration of the heritage value of that place, as a result of which consideration those governments may decide to impose their own restrictions on the development options available for the place.

In summary, therefore, the general purpose of the Register of the National Estate is, in the words of the Australian Heritage Commission, 'to alert and

Register of the National Estate

Criterion A: *Its importance in the course, or pattern, of Australia's natural and cultural history*

A.1 Importance in the evolution of Australian flora, fauna, landscapes or climate

A.2 Importance in maintaining existing processes or natural systems at the regional or national scale

A.3 Importance in exhibiting unusual richness or diversity of flora, fauna, landscapes or cultural features

A.4 Importance for their association with events, developments or cultural phases which have had a significant role in the human occupation and evolution of the nation, State, region or community

Criterion B: *Its possession of uncommon, rare or endangered aspects of Australia's natural or cultural history*

B.1 Importance for rare, endangered or uncommon flora, fauna, communities, ecosystems, natural landscapes or phenomena, or as wilderness

B.2 Importance in demonstrating a distinctive way of life, custom, process, land use, function or design no longer practised, in danger of being lost, or of exceptional interest

Criterion C: *Its potential to yield information that will contribute to an understanding of Australia's natural or cultural history*

C.1 Importance for information contributing to wider understanding of Australian natural history, by virtue of their use as research sites, teaching sites, type localities, reference or benchmark sites

C.2 Importance for information contributing to a wider understanding of the history of human occupation of Australia

Criterion D: *Its importance in demonstrating the principal characteristics of:*

(I) A class of Australia's natural or cultural places; or

(II) A class of Australia's natural or cultural environments

D.1 Importance in demonstrating the principal characteristics of the range of landscapes, environments, ecosystems, the attributes of which identify them as being characteristic of their class

D.2 Importance in demonstrating the principal characteristics of the range of human activities in the Australian environment (including way of life, philosophy, custom, process, land use, function, design or technique)

Criterion E: *Its importance in exhibiting particular aesthetic characteristics valued by a community or cultural group*

E.1 Importance for a community for aesthetic characteristics held in high esteem or otherwise valued by the community

Criterion F: *Its importance in demonstrating a high degree of creative or technical achievement at a particular period*

F.1 Importance for their technical, creative, design or artistic excellence, innovation or achievement

Criterion G: *Its strong or special associations with a particular community or cultural group for social, cultural or spiritual reasons*

G.1 Importance as places highly valued by a community for reasons of religious, spiritual, cultural, educational or spiritual associations

Criterion H: *Its special association with the life or works of a person, or group of persons, of importance in Australia's natural or cultural history*

H.1 Importance for their close associations with individuals whose activities have been significant within the history of the nation, State or region   SB

---

educate all Australians to the existence of places of national estate significance and to provide an essential reference and a working tool for balancing conservation and development decisions'.

In further recognition of its heritage responsibilities the Australian government supports two funding programmes – the Australian Heritage Grants Programme established and administered by the Australian Heritage Commission, which provides money ($421,000 in 1993–94) for research relating to the identification and evaluation of places of National Estate significance, including the development of standards of conservation practice; and the National Estate Grants Programme, established in 1974 by the federal government and administered jointly, since 1989–90, by the Australian Heritage Commission and appropriate departments in each state and terri-

tory government. The Programme in recent years has provided about $4.5 million annually for projects to assist in the conservation, documentation and presentation of places in or nominated for the Register of the National Estate.

Ideally, a balanced geographical distribution of projects is sought with a reasonable apportionment of grant funds to natural, built and Aboriginal cultural components, and a balanced division among state or territory authorities, local government and non-government (community) organisations. In practice, of course, the allocation of funds in this way is tempered by the quality and quantity of applications in each category received for assessment by the various state heritage committees (or their equivalent) before the transmission of each state's selected projects to the federal minister for approval.

Rock painting, Kakadu National Park, Northern Territory. The park is owned by Aborigines who have leased it back to the Australian National Parks and Wildlife Service. The many Aboriginal occupation sites and their associated rock art have qualified the park for World Heritage listing as a cultural place. The park also meets the criteria for listing as an important natural heritage site.

The number of applications received each year far exceeds the small amount of annual funding available (a little over $0.65 million for each state with smaller amounts for the Northern Territory and the Australian Capital Territory) and thus the selection criteria are strictly applied, hard decisions have to be taken and many otherwise worthy projects may miss out, much to their proponents' disappointment.

This often leads to intensive political lobbying at both the state and federal level, which at times may be out of all proportion to the funding either available or sought, or to the heritage importance of the particular project when considered on a national, as distinct from local, basis.

Such activities can be ameliorated only through a significant increase in the amount of taxpayers' funds available for the Programme which, during the 19 years of its operation, has provided about $60 mil-

lion for around 4,500 projects. These funds, however, are available only for projects associated with properties in the public domain or owned by community organisations, such as the National Trust (see p. 48). A great number of heritage properties in Australia are in private ownership and, until 1993, did not qualify for assistance.

A taxation incentives scheme was introduced in the 1993 Federal Budget to encourage owners of heritage-listed properties to carry out approved conservation work. Private owners of such properties can apply, through a competitive selection process (for the scheme is capped at about $2 million per year), for tax rebates of 20 cents in the dollar, provided the conservation work carried out under the scheme is valued at $10,000 or more. Preference is given to conservation work on heritage places that are visible or accessible to the community. SB

Uluru (Ayers Rock)

Australia's Aboriginal inhabitants have had no need to build great monuments for their sacred ceremonies, as have most other peoples, because they have monumental natural landmarks in abundance. One of these striking landmarks, Uluru, has become world famous as a symbol of the heart of Australia. For the Aborigines of the western desert, Uluru ('great pebble') means much more than a place to visit. To them, it is among the most sacred places in Australia. Nearly every feature of the rock's weather-beaten face has a mythological association.

The springs and caverns at the rock's base are revered as places marking the intersection of invisible paths made by Ancestral Spirit Beings on their wanderings across the land in search of water and food. The tracks of Mala (hare wallaby), Kuniya (harmless carpet snake) and Liru (venomous reptile) all mingle here. Such beliefs are expressed symbolically in the rock paintings preserved in the caves around the rock.

For non-Aboriginal Australians, too, the huge sandstone rock, 9.4 km in circumference, has special significance. Thousands visit the Northern Territory to see Uluru every year, using as their base the modern village of Yulara, built specially for tourists and carefully positioned 20 km away from the rock.

Seeing Uluru at sunset on a calm, clear winter's day changing from salmon pink to brick red and then deep purple, and the reverse at dawn, is the major tourist attraction. For the fittest, there is also the stiff climb up the honeycomb-patterned face – before it gets too hot – to view the flat, sparsely vegetated landscape stretching for miles in all directions. A complete circuit of the rock takes about 4 hours.

The rock is a mere 348 m high but it seems much more because it rises almost vertically from the surrounding plain. The reasons for this are clear. The sediments of which it and the surrounding plain are composed were deposited at the beginning of the Cambrian period (about 540 million years ago) as a sequence of sandstones and conglomerates. These became strongly cemented in the Palaeozoic era when Earth movements upthrust and deformed them. The cementation of the strata was not uniform, and some patches resisted erosion much better than others.

Uluru is one such resistant patch. Today, the component strata of Uluru are very steeply inclined and, because they vary slightly in hardness, the steep strata show up well on the eroding surface of the

The Yulara visitor centre that serves Uluru. It was built several kilometres away so as not to impinge on the splendour of the rock's setting.

rock. The group of 36 dome-shaped rocks called Katatjuta (meaning many heads), or the Olgas (p. 52), 26 km to the west of Uluru, are another such patch of strata of about the same age as Uluru, but these have not been steeply tilted. Their surfaces are scarred by deep chasms formed by erosion along vertical fractures called joints.

It is not known how long these rocks have been exposed to erosion but it must be at least 300 million years. The action of wind, sand blasting and rain water over this long period has shaped the surface of these resistant patches and spread debris around the less-resistant surrounding rocks. This gives the appearance of monoliths arising from the plain.

The first European to climb Uluru was a South Australian surveyor called William Christie Gosse, who discovered the rock in 1873. He renamed it after the South Australian premier Sir Henry Ayers; the original Aboriginal name Uluru is now preferred. The area was first created a national park in 1950. It was then combined with the Olgas under the Northern Territory Parks and Reserves Board in 1958 and reconstituted as Uluru National Park under the National Parks and Wildlife Service in 1977.

In October 1985, ownership of Uluru was restored to the traditional owners, the Yankuntjatjara and Pitjantjatjara people, who leased it back to the federal government for 99 years so that it could continue as a national park. The Aboriginal owners receive a rental and have a key role in managing the park. Many areas sacred to Aborigines are now barred to tourists. In 1977, the park was given International Biosphere Reserve status by UNESCO and in 1987 it was included in the World Heritage List (see pp. 52–4). SEB

The

Aboriginal heritage

Prehistory to 1788

Previous page *Aboriginal camp in Arnhem Land, Northern Territory. Although many Aborigines today are city dwellers, some of the more remote Aboriginal people have maintained their traditional ways of life.*

Australian Aborigines have inhabited the continent for over 40,000 years. During this long period they have mastered major changes in their natural environment: changes in the landforms, especially along coasts subject to the effects of oscillations in sea level during the last ice age, and changes in climate and in vegetation. It is thus not surprising that Aboriginal cultures also have seen significant developments, both through time and regionally, increasingly refining their utilisation of varying environments and resources.

The first inhabitants

It was the discoveries, in the early 1970s, of burials and stone artefacts in shoreline deposits of fossil lakes in western New South Wales that first demonstrated the great antiquity of Australian prehistory. Discoveries elsewhere have since confirmed this timescale.

The earliest human settlers are presumed to have arrived through a series of island-hopping journeys across Indonesia to land on the northern shores of the ancient landmass of Sahul – Australia and New Guinea, which were joined by a land bridge when sea levels were low. There was a low sea level around 50,000 BP (years before present time) when sea journeys would have been at their shortest. Even then, some journeys beyond the range of land visibility were still necessary. Whether such journeys were well planned adventures into the unknown or accidental shipwrecks we shall never know. It is generally presumed that these first immigrants were people adapted to tropical coastal environments with some navigational skills. At some 50,000 BP they were among the earliest of our anatomically modern *Homo sapiens* ancestors.

Aboriginal fossil skeletal remains show great morphological variability up to *c.* 10,000 BP. There is disagreement as to the significance of this variability. Some consider that it reflects two distinct founding populations, who, for a considerable time, maintained their separate genetic identities. Others consider it reflects greater diversity in past populations, possibly due to isolation of intermarrying communities given an overall low population density. It is now clear that some of the morphological variation, such as that from the cemetery of Kow Swamp in the

Murray River Valley, Victoria, was a result of head deformation practices, which would have given the inhabitants of this community a very distinctive appearance. Whatever the eventual outcome of this argument, the identity of Australia's first inhabitants remains poorly defined. Their success in establishing themselves in the diverse regions of the continent subsequently gave rise to very distinctive peoples and cultures.

RECONSTRUCTING THE PAST

At first sight the nature of the evidence for the reconstruction of Aboriginal prehistory may seem scant indeed: it consists largely of stone artefacts, the refuse of meals, mainly in the form of bones and shells, the ashes and charcoal of hearths, and the carved and painted designs which decorate numerous natural rock surfaces (see p. 79). From the recent past, a more diverse range of remains also includes earthen mounds built to raise living activities above waterlogged ground, the stone foundations of wood or bark

Flint tools from Riversleigh in northwestern Queensland. Such tools are the most common Aboriginal artefacts and are found all over Australia.

60

huts, stone arrangements to mark ceremonial bora grounds or other ceremonial locations, and stone-built fishtraps on some coasts and estuaries. Perhaps the most impressive constructions are the extensive systems of weirs and canals built to extend the availability of eels in swamps in western Victoria. Trees scarred by the removal of large sheets of bark for canoe building and others scarred and carved into

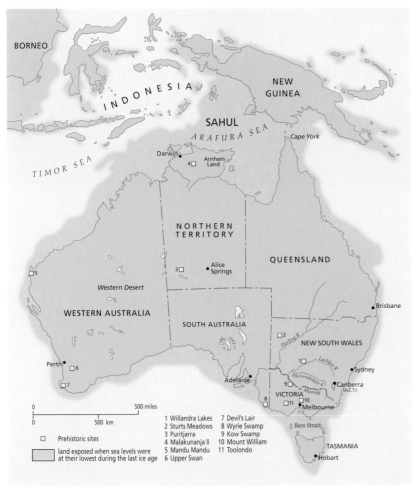

1 Willandra Lakes   7 Devil's Lair
2 Sturts Meadows   8 Wyrie Swamp
3 Puritjarra   9 Kow Swamp
4 Malakananja II   10 Mount William
5 Mandu Mandu   11 Toolondo
6 Upper Swan

☐ Prehistoric sites

land exposed when sea levels were at their lowest during the last ice age

Location of the archaeological sites mentioned in the text.

intricate designs as ceremonial markers are precarious relics, while the unmodified natural features – rocks, waterholes, sandhills, and so on – which give cultural meaning to the land in living Aboriginal society are preserved anonymously in the landscape, invisible to archaeological investigation.

Archaeology has devised and refined a range of techniques to extract information about cultural practices from such unpromising material. The archaeologist needs an understanding if not expertise in many fields, including the natural sciences and ethnography, and it is from the synthesis of such specialist evaluations of the data that past cultural practices and cultural processes may be reconstructed. Thus the nature of our understanding of the prehistoric past will depend on the nature of the evidence preserved, and this differs from site to site, and from period to period.

BEFORE 6,000 YEARS AGO

The early evidence for human colonisation of the continent is difficult to date precisely. In west Arnhem Land artefact-bearing sands in Malakananja II rock shelter have been dated by the thermoluminescence technique to between 60,000 and 45,000 BP while other sites in the region and in northwest Queensland have yielded artefacts in deposits, which, though they cannot be dated, underlie levels of the cold arid peak of the ice age c. 22,000–18,000 years BP by a considerable depth. The southern part of the continent has yielded more certain evidence of human presence by c. 40,000 BP: stone tools on the upper Swan River near Perth are dated to 38,000 BP; in shore deposits of the fossil Willandra lakes in western New South Wales artefacts occur below a 36,000-year level, while in the highlands of southwest Tasmania two sites have been dated to c. 30,000 BP. At this period, although sea levels remained lower than at present, travel to Tasmania would have involved a narrow sea crossing. Mandu Mandu rock shelter on the North West Cape in Western Australia is the only coastal site known with a shell midden dated to between 30,000 and 32,000 BP. Here, the continental shelf is very narrow and the Pleistocene coast, though lower, was not significantly further out than the present coast. Any evidence for coastal settlement elsewhere would now be below sea level.

From the above, it is clear that Aborigines first settled Australia during a period of somewhat less arid conditions than at present. However, it is not until the onset of the severe arid and cooler conditions that peaked around 18,000 BP that a significant number of sites are known. It is likely that the reduction in available surface water caused a more focused settlement, with groups more tightly anchored to reliable water sources. In the arid interior, the first visible trace of human occupation dates from this period at Puritjarra rock shelter near the Cleland Hills, close to an artesian rock hole. The total number of sites, however, remains low, and most contain little archaeological material so that interpretation of cultural practices of this era remains difficult. Most middens on the ancient shores of the Willandra lakes date to the period of decreasing lake levels and increased salinity as the Lachlan River that feeds them diminished and the hinterland began to suffer from aridity. The middens testify to hunting small to medium-sized animals, collecting freshwater mussels and bird eggs, and fishing for golden perch (*Maccullochella macquariensis*) and murray cod (*Plectroplites ambiguus*). When the lakes system dried out completely by c. 16,000 BP the area was abandoned, but in the larger drainage system of the Darling River, foraging continued along the channels of its distributaries, although its overflow lakes were

Aborigines fishing in Rapid Bay, South Australia, c. 1840.

also dry or saline. The now impenetrable rainforests of the Tasmanian southwest were then vegetated by heath and open woodland where rednecked wallaby (*Plectroplites ambiguus*) was an important prey.

Significant discoveries for this era include the treatment of the dead either by inhumation with ochre or by cremation in the Willandra lakes, the use of ochre for unknown purposes from several other localities, and beads made of *Conus* shell from the Mandu Mandu rock shelter and from bone at Devil's Lair rock shelter in southern Western Australia.

As climatic conditions ameliorated at the end of the Pleistocene and in the early Holocene, 10,000–8000 BP, archaeological evidence for human activity increases: there is a gradual extension of people into regions (apparently) unoccupied during the very severe arid conditions. Stone-working technologies do not change significantly, and in general subsistence strategies also tend to remain unspecialised. However, in the Darling River basin there is evidence for the introduction of generalised food grinding or pounding stones, suggestive of increased reliance on plant foods with hard or fibrous tissue such as acacia and other seeds and a range of roots. In southwest Tasmania, the encroaching rainforest caused people to move to the north and southeast of the island where the rich low-latitude coastal resources such as seal and muttonbird were exploited together with fish and shellfish, birds and small terrestrial animals.

It is to this period of readjustment that the first secure evidence of rock art can be dated. Clearly symbolic action such as burial or decoration with beads or ochre dates back to the very beginnings of settlement, but the claiming of places in the landscape by their visual integration into symbolic expression at this time suggests that there were also significant readjustments in socio-territorial relationships.

AFTER 6,000 YEARS AGO

The last rise in sea level reached its present level by *c.*6500 BP. The rising seas invaded coastal plains transforming river valleys into broad inlets and leaving isolated hills as offshore islands. The impact of receding coastlines varied from region to region. On the steeply sloping eastern seaboard, the area of drowned land was not vast, but the indented coastline gave rise to a rich diversity of coastal environments: estuaries, beaches and dunes, near coastal wetlands and the wave-cut rock platforms on rocky headlands. The inhospitable windswept plain of Bass Strait was flooded, Tasmania was cut off from the mainland and remained isolated from later mainland developments. In the north, flooding of the shallow shelf of the Arafura Sea initially led to an extensive loss of land. The flooded lowlands transformed into vast mangrove swamps. The gradual silting up of these swamps eventually gave rise to the luxuriant wetlands of present-day western Arnhem Land by around 1500 BP.

Almost everywhere along the margins of the continent shell middens are the highly visible evidence of Aboriginal adaptation to these new resources of stable and mature coastlines. The nature of adaptations varies according to the ecological conditions and climate, but the exploitation of shellfish and other littoral foods became widespread. However, for reasons that are not well understood, certain coasts, notably in southwestern Australia appear not to have attracted Aboriginal settlement.

In southeastern Australia, coastal camps were most favoured during the summer months, while the stormy weather of the colder winter months depleted offshore fishing and shellfish. However, at all times, a range of hunting and plantfood collecting in the hinterland supplemented the seafood intake. Adaptations included the adoption of shell fishhooks for hook and line fishing from bark canoes by c. 1000 BP. A rapid increase in archaeological remains after c. 3000 BP reflects increased population as a result of the very successful adaptation to the varied resources of the coast and its hinterland.

In Tasmania, seals and the muttonbird (*Puffinus tenuirostris*) provided important foods and particularly a source of fat, which is invaluable in the colder climate. This reliance on fatty foods may explain why from about 3000 BP Tasmanians abandoned fishing, choosing instead to concentrate on sealing and muttonbirding as well as shellfish and hinterland hunting and plantfood gathering.

In the far northern latitudes of monsoonal Australia, seasonality is characterised by wet and dry seasons when the land changes from inundated wetlands to parched scrub and grasslands. The extensive wetlands of Arnhem Land held some food resources all year round, and sustained some of the highest population densities known for hunter-gatherer populations. People tended to forage more widely during the late wet and early dry seasons, when plant and animal foods are at their most abundant. Archaeological data indicates that prior to the full development of the wetlands settlement was more dispersed, probably requiring higher mobility. Shellfish and other resources of the then estuarine river channels were utilised in conjunction with a wide range of animal and plant foods.

Inland, environmental changes after the end of the ice age were less dramatic, except in the eastern highlands, which became inhabited during this period. Certain new food resources became utilised: in the north, a technology for leaching the highly poisonous *Macrozamia* (cycad) nuts gave access to an abundant source of starch which could be prepared in large quantities for major gatherings. In the southern highlands, the Bogong moth (*Agrotis infusa*) played a significant role in seasonal ceremonial gatherings, though its contribution to the overall diet was probably minimal. In the arid zone, food-grinding technology was modified to wet milling, which enables the use of a range of very small seeds such as, for example, *Panicum decompositum* (native millet) or *Portulaca oleracea* (pigweed). The collecting and processing of these tiny seeds into a damper baked on the hot ashes is very labour intensive, but it provides a valuable starch food.

The most striking developments are those of western Victoria, where freshwater swamps provided seasonally rich resources of waterfowl and plantfoods. During spring and summer they also abound in eels which swim out to breeding grounds at sea in autumn to return up the short rivers to the swamps each spring. In several of these swamps a network of channels and weirs was built to extend the eeling resources and control their catch. Between Mt William and Toolondo a canal was dug to join up swamps in adjacent drainage basins, separated by a low rise, thereby considerably extending the availability of eels. These several increased resources enabled the holding of increasingly larger ceremonial gatherings, which also functioned as important foci for exchanges of goods and for other social exchanges.

ARTEFACTS

Another significant change in the archaeological record after c. 6000 BP was the introduction of new stone-working technologies. Throughout the earlier part of Australian prehistory, stone working consisted of removing flakes from a core by the percussion method. Quartzite was the most widely used stone. Flakes were generally fairly large and irregular in shape but provided thin and very sharp cutting edges. These fragile edges could be strengthened by secondary flaking (retouching). A row of short shallow flakes was removed by judicious percussion along part of the edge. In this way a range of cutting, scraping and chiselling tools of varying sizes was manufactured, which functioned primarily for woodworking for the manufacture of hunting weapons, digging sticks and carrying dishes.

Evidence for the wooden implements is scarce indeed. Fragments of worked wood, including boomerangs, were recovered from the waterlogged deposits of Wyrie Swamp in South Australia, dating to 12,000 BP. Otherwise, evidence comes from the very rare paintings which are in a style of sufficient realism to permit the precise identification of subject matter. Such art styles are restricted to some regions of northernmost Australia. Depictions of spears, boomerangs, hafted stone hatchets, string bags and some other implements are attested in the paintings of west Arnhem Land dating back to an estimated 10,000 BP (spearthrowers were developed somewhat later). However, the distribution of these artefacts across the continent may not have been uniform. For instance, although stone hatchets were in use in monsoonal Australia before 20,000 BP, further south they are known only after 6000 BP.

After 6000 BP new types of stone artefacts are added to the existing toolkit. These are smaller and include a number of regularly shaped items such as parallel-sided blades and blades retouched to triangular or trapezoidal forms, small leafshaped points and other forms. The technological advantages of these smaller tools are not easy to assess. Some permit the more effective working of hard woods: for example, the *tula* adze of the arid and semi-arid zones; others appear to be designed for highly specialised projectiles – for instance, the small leaf-shaped points. For most their function remains problematical, although developments in the study of wear on artefacts and of residues, such as wood tissue and blood, are beginning to examine some of these issues.

Many of these small stone tools are made out of microcrystalline siliceous rocks such as chert, chalcedony and also silcrete. The homogeneous texture and hardness of these rocks makes them very suitable stone-working materials. One of the advantages of the smaller tool technology was presumably an ability to exploit the properties of such rocks, which mostly occur as small nodules or pebbles. Their natural occurrence also tends to be very localised. Access to outcrops of these siliceous rocks was therefore important in maintaining this technology. By analogy with recent practices in the Western Desert, it seems likely that they entered the network of exchanged goods. In the Western Desert, the mythological associations of outcrops of such stones also integrate these materials into the ceremonial links between groups. There, their exchange thus also symbolically expresses the bonds between people and certain localities as sanctioned by mythology.

It would be rash to extend this particular picture of trade and political structure from the desert to the entire continent, or necessarily to assume its extension far back in time. It probably developed gradually through varied expressions of social relationships. However, the general principle of mythological validation of land rights was relevant to the exchange of goods from identifiable Dreaming or Dreamtime places (see p. 69). Such a principle has adaptive advantage, particularly in harsh environments, where people may need to call on alliances with neighbours for foraging rights in their lands. Its origin may therefore have considerable antiquity.

Whatever the full implications of the new technology and the exploitation of siliceous stones, after about 2000 BP, their distribution diminishes, and in many areas vein quartz largely replaces these materials. The adoption of vein quartz required technological innovations for the successful flaking of this rather intractable material. Superficially, most quartz artefacts appear crude and irregular by comparison with chert and similar artefacts. The advantage of vein quartz lies in its much wider availability. AR

Population and economy

At the time of European arrival in Australia, Aboriginal people inhabited all parts of the continent and, with one or two exceptions, all of the immediate offshore islands including Tasmania. They lived in environments as diverse as the tropical coasts of the north, the rich riverlands of the southeast and the deserts of the centre. This diversity of habitat, combined with the processes of cultural divergence over time, meant that there were considerable differences in the ways Aboriginal people made a living. However, there were enough significant similarities to speak of an identifiable Aboriginal economy throughout the country.

Aboriginal Australians were traditionally foragers, or hunters and gatherers. Overall their numbers and population densities were low; their technology minimal but efficient, allowing them freedom to move over the land in a regular and patterned way. Although the resources available differed dramatically over the continent, methods of production and distribution were surprisingly similar.

It was ignorance and misunderstanding of the Aboriginal economy that led European observers for many years to relegate other aspects of Aboriginal culture – indeed their standing as human beings – to the lowest levels. A simplicity of tools and a lack of many other material possessions led the colonists to assume similar paucity in Aboriginal worldview and society. Stereotypes of Aboriginal economy quickly developed. These included beliefs that Aborigines led a hand-to-mouth, harsh existence with no leisure; that they wandered aimlessly over the land in pursuit of any barely edible food; that this nomadism manifested itself as a biologically driven 'walkabout instinct'; and, because they did not practise agriculture, a belief that Aborigines failed to alter their environment at all, and as a consequence suffered the vicissitudes of nature, inexorably bound by the pursuit of sustenance. These stereotypes about Aboriginal economy are as enduring as they are mistaken.

It is true that Aboriginal people had relatively few material possessions, did not live in permanent dwellings and did not depend for a living on agricultural endeavour. However, ethnographic and archaeological evidence reveals that overall their standard of living, in terms of nourishment, was at least as high as, for example, most Europeans in the early nineteenth century. Aborigines in most areas of the continent had a wide range of food to choose from. In no area was every potentially edible species eaten. Food preference and cultural practices determined that many items were left untouched in most normal

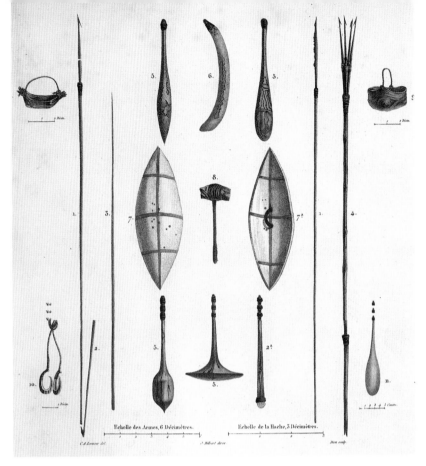

Aboriginal artefacts, from a French drawing, c. 1790. Aboriginal people did not own many possessions, but were well equipped with tools for hunting, fishing and warfare. The middle object in the top row is a boomerang.

seasons. Starvation and malnutrition were generally unknown and the pursuit of food occupied in some areas on average about three days of intermittent work a week, with a great deal of time, at least for men, being devoted to religious and ceremonial matters. A higher value was placed on sociality than on material possessions for their own sake. In their daily subsistence work, people stopped when they had produced enough to fulfil their immediate needs. Goods and resources were not accumulated and surpluses were immediately distributed. Apart from the lack of technology for food storage in most areas, an ethos of sharing ensured that goods and possessions of all kinds were widely available.

External bodies or institutions to enforce law and order were unnecessary as groups, when unable to resolve conflicts themselves, dispersed and went their own ways. Without a big investment in dwellings, capital goods, or indeed in permanent goods of any sort, ease of movement was the order of the day.

The price of this flexibility was nomadism. Yet, this must be seen as a relative concept. Many coastal Aboriginal groups moved only very short distances up and down stretches of beach, usually bringing gathered or hunted food back to central home camps. Even in the most arid parts of the country, Aboriginal movement was regular, covering well-trodden tracks to camps at known and named water sources. Movement was governed not only by subsistence needs but also by socio-territorial rules and by seasonal and cultural exigencies. In all areas, Aboriginal culture was based on affiliation of particular individuals and groups to particular tracts of land: an attachment far more significant and intimate than that generally found in the capitalist West with its view of land as an alienable commodity.

As for agriculture, there were no plants indigenous to Australia that could be domesticated on any scale, and certainly not on the scale necessary to support the permanency of the people needed to provide the labour for such endeavour. In addition, most parts of Australia today are still not capable of sustaining agriculture without the major technology of large-scale irrigation. Similarly, the animals of the Australian continent were unsuitable for domestication. In any case, the issue of the presence of domesticables aside, anthropologists seem certain that the development of agriculture elsewhere in the world stemmed from population and resource crises which did not occur in Australia. Aborigines had reached and were maintaining, at the time of contact (the advent of the Europeans), a reasonable equilibrium with their environment.

However, this is not to say that this meant no change. Aborigines significantly altered their environment over the course of their occupation, primarily through what has been called 'fire-stick farming'. This was the deliberate and planned use of fire for hunting, for improving re-growth of plants, and for clearing undergrowth to improve mobility over the landscape. These practices probably played a major role in the extinction of giant kangaroos and other large marsupials such as the diprotodonts and flightless birds that were larger than the modern emu. Other environment-altering practices reflected the active relationships between land and Aborigines: replanting of yam tops, fostering of plots of particular fruit species through specific seed-disposal practices, food and hunting taboos, which restricted procurement of certain species in certain areas or at particular times, and so on.

REGIONAL VARIATION

Several factors were significant in determining the nature of pre-contact local Aboriginal economies. These included rainfall and local water resources (oceans principally and rivers), topography, vegetation and the history of trade and exchange of both technological and cultural items across Aboriginal Australia. These factors brought about three primary types of Australian economies: coastal, riverine and arid zone. The following sections discuss examples of each.

Northern tropical coast

The Kuku-Yalanji Aborigines lived on the coast of southeastern Cape York Peninsula in far northern Queensland. There, tropical rainforest-clothed mountains slope steeply down to the rocky edges of the ocean. Wide and white sandy beaches punctuated the coastline, facing sporadic smaller coral reefs leading out to the Great Barrier Reef some 40 km offshore. The defining feature of this environment is its high and intense levels of rainfall – up to 3,000 mm a year at some places. This helps create year-round, fast-flowing creeks, deep rivers and thundering waterfalls.

Population reconstruction reveals about 350 Aboriginal people living in an area of some 500 km^2 along the Bloomfield River, on the adjacent coastline and in the immediate hinterland. This gives an average density of one person per 1.43 km^2 – high on the scale of densities in Australia. Occupation patterns were also unusual with semi-permanent camps being the norm. When movement of groups did occur, it was primarily along the reaches of the river and to different places along the beaches. Subsistence activity also focused on the river, its mangrove margins, the beach and its littoral and tidal zones, and the outlying reefs. Hunting activity concentrated on kangaroos, reptiles and small mammals in the nearby open woodland areas and on marine turtles found in the shallow fringing reefs. Vegetable foods and fruits, nuts and berries, all generally collected by women, provided the carbohydrate and vitamin mainstays. Abundant supplies of fish and shellfish were the primary resources which allowed the high population levels and density and the degree of sedentism, as opposed to mobility, found in this area. Sea and rainforest birds and their eggs were also important at different times of the year. At the height of the wet season, for instance, the eggs of the magpie goose (*Anseranas semipalmata*) provided the means for gatherings of hundreds of Aborigines from all over southeastern Cape York Peninsula. This was an opportunity for the trade and exchange of items such as pearlshell, special highly valued resins, and certain material culture articles.

Marked seasonal changes occur in this part of Australia. This had a major effect on the Aboriginal economy. Kuku-Yalanji people classified seasons on the basis of climatic changes (level of rainfall, wind direction, temperature), vegetation changes and the appearance and disappearance of certain major food resources. Five seasons were delineated:

kambar	Late December–March; heavy rainfall period
kabakabada	April–May; light rainfalls
buluriji	June–September; dry weather and cold nights; winds from the southeast
wungariji	October–early November; height of the dry season
jarramali	Late November–early December; thunderstorm time and build-up of the wet season

Kuku-Yalanji people shared with most of the rest of Aboriginal Australia a basic toolkit for subsistence: spears, digging sticks, bark, wooden and string carriers, and stone, bone and tooth scrapers and cutters. Items of material culture and subsistence techniques particular (although not unique) to this area included outrigger canoes, fish stupefacients (chemicals or poisons in certain plants used to stupefy the fish by adding the crushed leaves or roots to the water), bird traps, boiling for cooking, leaching techniques to remove toxic substances from food sources, ritual fighting shields and large double-handed wooden swords, substantial, semi-permanent domed huts, and a degree of food storage (of nuts and some wild yams during the wet season).

Riverine groups of the southeast

The largest populations of inland-dwelling Aborigines – groups such as the Barkindji, Barindji and Wiradjuri – lived in the Murray–Darling River system, which drains the coastal highlands of the southeastern portion of Australia and flows west and south into Victoria and South Australia. This area, some 600,000 km^2, is characterised by thin woodland forests in the east through to grasslands with fringing eucalypt shrubland (mallee) along the rivers. Population densities were highest in the lower regions adjacent to the rivers and lowest in the highland areas. Reconstruction of numbers is difficult, but figures of two to three persons per kilometre of the river for the former and one person per 20 km^2 for the latter seem realistic. Reports of groups of over 600 Aborigines are given for the lower portions of the rivers.

The major feature of Aboriginal economic life in this area was a dependence on the fish, shellfish and waterfowl from the rivers. In fact, for three-quarters of the year, the groups living along the rivers had such an abundance of these resources that they really only must have moved for social or hygiene reasons. The annual cycle of movement, of population groupings and of diet followed the seasonal variations in the river flows and levels. Individual fishing with the use of multiple-prong spears contrasted with cooperative efforts by large groups using nets and weirs. In some areas, stone fish traps were built to catch fish at times of changing river levels. Land animals, such as possums, bandicoots and kangaroo, were hunted and vegetable foods, such as bulrushes, yams and fruits, were gathered. Canoes were used for fishing and for transport. Personal ornamentation was particularly elaborate in the riverine areas. Clothing included possum-skin cloaks, aprons, hats, and necklaces made of hair, string and teeth.

Arid zone of Central Australia

The great desert and semi-desert regions of Central Australia cover almost three million km². Here there is a division between the rocky and better-watered ranges and the lowlands, with their covering of coarse grass and *Acacia* shrubs (mulga). In parts, the latter also include parallel-running red sandhills which stretch for hundreds of kilometres. In the range country, permanent water is normally found only in the gorges made by river courses, while in the lowlands, it exists only in soaks and springs. Rainfall levels throughout Central Australia are very low (600–2,800 mm per year or less) and the rain is extremely intermittent. Seasons are not as clearly delineated as in the north.

In the northwestern region of Central Australia lived the Warlpiri, their territory covering some 40,000 km². Before contact, the Warlpiri numbered some 1,000–1,200, giving an average density of one person per 35 km². Population movement was limited to the gathering together of large groups at major waterholes in good seasons during the autumn and early winter, and the dispersal, in the dry seasons, into small family-based groups that travelled more and further to find food and water. Overall, large distances were covered and mobility was extremely high.

Major food resources included small mammals, lizards, seeds, insects and vegetable foods. Animals were hunted with spears, spearthrowers, throwing sticks and traps and fire was used to drive game. Successful hunting required an intimate knowledge of animal habitat and behaviour. It seems certain that women, gathering vegetable food species such as the yam (*Dioscorea*), the seeds of *Acacia* species and various fruits such as those of the wild tomato (*Solanum*) and the desert banana, provided the bulk of the desert Aboriginal diet. Their contribution was doubtless the most consistent and reliable. Digging sticks and wooden carriers formed the core of women's material culture kit.

Given the relatively basic nature of food-getting technology in the arid zone, it is interesting that there existed a significant repertoire of artefacts unconnected with domestic work. Ceremonial items in this area were particularly elaborate. In fact, it is in the desert regions of Central Australia where ceremonial life in general reached a peak of complexity and flamboyance. Although limited by seasonal abundances of key resources, the most sparse and, to European eyes, barren lands in Australia supported long and impressive ceremonial cycles. This would not have been possible for an economy only barely providing a living for its participants.

Given the radically different environments described above, the surprising thing is the similarity in the Aboriginal societies found in each of them. They shared basically a common material culture –

Hunting provided an important part of Aboriginal diet, even amongst the riverine groups. This engraving of c. 1880 shows a wallaby hunt.

Gathering plants was done by women, who would use digging sticks to unearth roots. Seeds were also commonly gathered, to be baked into cakes. The population remained small enough, and the land sufficiently fertile, for hunting and gathering to provide perfectly adequate food supplies without the Aborigines having to develop agriculture.

at least in those domains concerned with getting a living. The exceptions were those tools and implements used to exploit a resource particular to a specific landform or environmental feature – for instance, canoes and harpoons for turtle-hunting on coastal reefs. Aboriginal groups over the diverse environments also shared reasonably similar forms of land tenure and attachment to land. Perhaps most importantly, Aboriginal social and political relationships relating to resource and food distribution, the division of labour by gender and age, and issues of control of access to land, labour and resources had significant similarities throughout the continent.

The differences in economy and lifestyle which did exist stemmed largely from environmental constraints: differences in the degree of mobility or sedentism; overall population numbers and densities; and the scope or range of social relations (much wider in the desert and very restricted in the coastal areas).

The Aboriginal economy, developed and refined over tens of thousands of years, must be seen as a considerable achievement. With enormous adaptability, economic creativity, and with a simple but efficient technology, Aborigines spread throughout the Australian continent. In the face of a diverse and often hostile environment, Aboriginal people created a living for themselves which allowed for a rich intellectual tradition, an intimacy of involvement and relationship with the land, and a society which demanded a primacy of people over things.   CA

Social organisation

In exploring the traditional Aboriginal social systems, anthropologists have mainly focused upon the remote Aboriginal people least affected by Europeans. However, many Aborigines today live in settled rural and urban areas. Loss of knowledge about original languages, territories, social systems, religion and so on has not precluded a distinctive Aboriginal identity and way of life. Today, about 500,000 people in Australia identify as Aboriginal and since the 1970s there has been an emerging consciousness and expression of an urban Aboriginal identity. In the 1990s these urban and rural Aboriginal people are active politically and culturally, finding modern expressions for their identity in writing, art and social movements.

The considerable literature on Aboriginal social life varies enormously in quality and accuracy. Enthusiastic amateur works and travellers' tales need separating from works based upon committed field investigation, and the date of investigation and writing is a critical factor.

In many early works, there was pervasive influence from crude evolutionism and this can still be encountered in some popular treatments of Aboriginal life. Evolutionism proposed a ladder of pro-

French depiction of Aborigines, c. 1800. Captain Cook considered the Aborigines to be a happy people, without the burdens of care carried by Europeans, but whites soon came to view them as 'primitive' on account of their different social organisation and nomadic lifestyle.

gress among human societies and their cultures, with the lower levels of this ladder seen as closer to the animal world, and furthest from European civilisation. From the earliest European experience in Australia this kind of thinking resulted in Aborigines being labelled as 'primitive'. Being hunters and gatherers, and without the permanent settlements or agricultural practices found elsewhere, they were classified as extreme examples of primitivism, and their small number of material possessions and their mobile lifestyles seemed once to confirm this view (see also p. 64). Nineteenth-century anatomists sought out skeletal and other evidence to complete the picture of the brutish and primitive Aborigine – a living fossil to fit in with the then prevalent view of Australia as a museum of fossil plant and animal species.

Observations of Aboriginal social life throughout the nineteenth and early twentieth century sought to reveal the very origins of European social institutions: law, marriage, the family and religion. Starting with the work of dedicated field ethnographers such as Baldwin Spencer and Francis Gillen in the early 1900s, a picture of considerable social complexity among Aborigines began to emerge. Aboriginal society was revealed to be systematic and organised, relying heavily upon family structures to organise economic, religious and social activity. Anthropology has since focused upon understanding the internal logic of these systems rather than making irrelevant evolutionist comparisons with societies elsewhere.

TERRITORY AND SOCIETY

From the Aboriginal perspective, a geographic territory and its human occupants were spiritually linked through the actions of powerful creative forces. The actions of these ancestral spirits created the landform, generated the animal and plant life within it, and gave rise to the present Aboriginal groups belonging to it. This creative action took place in a mythic past period often referred to in Aboriginal English as the 'Dreaming' or 'Dreamtime', a time when human ancestors, their social organisation, their laws and their technologies were created and authorised for following generations.

Human social groups, their territories and the animal and plant species they contain are intricately linked by religious philosophy and its ceremonial expression (pp. 75–9). Much of the routine of everyday social life is informed and referenced by this cosmological view. Where one camps, how one moves across the landscape, which resources are exploited, how one deals with the vicissitudes of life, are all decided against a background recognition of the presence of powerful spiritual forces continually controlling the world of physical events and objects.

Territory is an essential dimension of any human group existence. Among Aboriginal groups, it is defined primarily by the mythic sites it contains: where the ancestral spirits carried out their activities, or came to rest. Tracing down from the Dreaming, through a father's father and father, a person inherits primary spiritual and exploitative rights and responsibilities to a particular tract of land, and thus the patrilineal group and its estate is the primary territorial unit within which an Aboriginal person orders his or her existence. These land-based groups form local groupings, which in turn can be seen as divisions of a wider regional unit of people and land associated with a particular language. Aboriginal people, therefore, can refer to themselves by a number of varying terms according to their social and geographical situation.

Among the Umpila-speaking people in eastern Cape York Peninsula, for example, there is a term *thampanyu* which refers to the patrilineal estate group, which contains one's primary spiritual sites or *puula* (literally, 'father's father'). Several of these estates and their groups in clusters around a geographic feature – for example, a river mouth – can form a small regional unit, *pama ngaatchimulu* ('people from the one area'). In turn, a number of these clusters make up a continuous strip of coastal territory seen as belonging to the Umpila dialect – the language, its general territory and the people who belong there all being unified by the mythic past. At an even wider level of recognition, Umpila territory combines with other closely related dialect territories along a stretch of coastline to form a province inhabited by the *pama malngkana* ('people of the sandbeach') or *pama kaawaychi* ('eastside people') who recognise social ties through linked mythic tracks, similar dialects, similar economic and social organisation, and a shared intellectual view of the world. A person's 'country' can therefore be defined narrowly or widely, according to the referential context, though a person's authoritative rights socially and territorially diminish with social and geographic distance.

KINSHIP AND DESCENT

Aboriginal people, like many other traditional societies around the world, used principles of kinship and descent to provide critical systems of social organisation. Kinship can be summarised as the establishment and recognition of particular bonds between people through genealogical connection and the parent–child bond. One can trace a kin bond with another by recognition of a common ancestral link. In this way, an individual recognises a wide range of people – traced through both father and mother – as his or her kindred.

While European societies also use these principles to establish particular kindreds for people, kin-based societies differ in their wider application of this system. Aboriginal people, for instance, apply the principle to trace real or putative links to all other known members of a society. This system (classificatory kinship) can therefore be extended to the horizons of the known social world, providing an efficient and practical way of classifying and organising society. It has an elaborate system of kin terms and a body of associated rules to govern behaviour among the many different categories of kin.

The Umpila people of northeastern Cape York Peninsula have, for example, some 23 kin terms and 8 more terms of relatedness applying to in-laws. To this basic nomenclature must be added quite a few additional terms denoting birth order among a set of siblings, and which define the degree of genealogical distance between individuals. In general, where there is a distinctive kin term, there is an associated and distinctive rule of behaviour.

It can be readily appreciated that, with a finite set of kin terms, and a social universe of hundreds of people to apply them to, numerous people are categorised by the same primary kin term. There are, therefore, a number of 'mothers', 'fathers', 'father's mothers', 'elder sister's sons' and so on. To distinguish among these, subsidiary terms are applied which distinguish the degree of genealogical distance. The Umpila, for example, have four such categories, which translate into English as 'actual' or 'blood', 'close', 'middle distance' and 'distant'. This degree of closeness further modifies actual social behaviour towards kin. Behaviour by a man towards an actual (adult) sister, for example, is highly restrained; there is little verbal interaction, and what occurs is highly limited in content by both sides. They are careful not to be alone together, and they are required to avoid physical proximity even in the presence of others. Between distant sisters and brothers, these restraints can be relaxed, though never to the point where sexual interest can be imputed. Similarly, an actual mother's father requires considerable respect from a daughter's son, but with a distant mother's father he may engage in jocular repartee, even to the point of ritualised lewdness and touching the body.

Like all other Aboriginal groups, the Umpila apply the strictest of social rules to actual mothers in-law and fathers in-law. A man must remove himself physically if his mother-in-law approaches, and he may be required to maintain silence in her vicinity. The same situation applies for a woman with respect to her father-in-law. These avoidances are considered respectful, and the breaking of these rules – even unintentionally – requires a compensatory payment of food or other items.

Systems of kin classification ultimately regulate social behaviour. An individual has obligations to kin on the one hand, and expectations from them on the other. Generosity in food, property and social support is the currency of social interaction among members of Aboriginal groups. One is expected to support one's relations in times of trouble, and products from hunting and gathering can be claimed by certain relatives, even given generously to others. It is not unusual for a successful hunter to end up with very little for his own immediate family. But the system is reciprocal: the same hunter will make his own claims from others, or receive generous unrequested gifts in his turn. Kinship therefore provides a charter for the daily routine of life within the Aboriginal camp or settlement, maintaining a social order and an egalitarian system of distribution. Material accumulation by an individual within this type of society is extremely difficult since others have claims upon possessions and products.

Kin principles can be applied to establish particular and restricted descent groups. Here the reference point is a particular ancestor, a remembered living progenitor or a spiritual ancestor from whom a group traces direct descent by a particular principle. Among Aboriginal groups patrilineal descent is the dominant principle, where membership is passed only through males, though both male and female children are inheritors. This is particularly important for establishing primary rights to territory, as discussed earlier. The anthropological concept of the *estate group* refers to this: the group of patrilineally defined people who have a primary responsibility for an estate territory, the locality which contains the group's important ancestral myth sites, and from which they derive special rights and responsibilities with regard to the associated songs and ceremonies.

This area of spiritual responsibility has been distinguished from the economic area by anthropologists. In the annual cycle of resource exploitation, families operated well outside the estates of their male members. While descent establishes the spiritual heartland, wider kin ties through both father and mother mean that an individual can travel and exploit resources in other estates, as part of the annual round of activities. The size of the range varies according to habitat richness. In tropical coastal regions of high seasonal productivity, the range for a family group may be very small, perhaps a matter of a few kilometres, as is the case with the Umpila of northeastern Cape York Peninsula, or the Gidgingali of northeastern Arnhem Land. In the arid interior, where plants and animals are more sparsely distributed, the annual range can be extremely large, with Aboriginal populations widely dispersed for most of the year. The Mardudjara of the Western Desert of Western Australia are a well-known example. Kin-

Social categories

Aboriginal societies are well known for a particular and complex form of descent-based organisation. Here a person's known social universe is divided into either two, four or eight categories, known to anthropologists as *moieties*, *sections* and *sub-sections*. One or another of these categorising systems were found over many Aboriginal societies, and they were important for regulating marriage by prescribing the correct marriage partner and, additionally, categorising those with whom sexual relations would be incestuous.

These categories are usually named, and in the section and sub-section systems, the category names can provide a person's reference name. They do not usually provide a social organisational principle for the everyday life of people: a band or group of people living together will contain a mixture of category representatives. But they are often important in an organisational sense for the placement of people in rituals and in the allocation of labour in ceremonies. While sub-section systems are usually found in Central Australian societies occupying the arid core of the continent, there is no obvious correlation between geographic region and type of system.

Moieties are the simplest form of these systems. Among the Umpila of Cape York Peninsula there are two named categories, *kaapay* and *kuyan*. These words have no direct meaning: they were given by the mythic ancestors who created human social existence. All Umpila people belong to one or another of these moiety categories, as indeed do various surrounding groups.

The basic rule is that I inherit my moiety category in a biological and spiritual sense from my actual father. Thus my category contains all my patrilineal relatives, and the other category contains my matrilineal relatives. The major rule which will be taught to me is that sexual relations with members of my own moiety are incestuous, and I must obtain a spouse from the other category. The rule of cross-cousin marriage accords with this: my spouse will be a mother's brother's child, or a father's sister's child. The Umpila believe that moiety descent has a genealogical quality: it can be seen in the type of hair, body build, bone structure of the face, lines on the hands and so on. Accordingly, adoption of a child is preferentially arranged so that the social father and mother belong to the same categories as the genealogical father and mother.

The Umpila landscape is also divided by moiety, though this territorial division is not exactly the same as the estate division discussed earlier. Several contiguous estates may lie within the one moiety division, but moiety boundaries always align with an estate boundary. For the Umpila, the moiety of a landscape is predictable by its physical features through a complex sensory impression of patterns of light and shade, the angularity of trees and boulders, the slope of hills, and so on.

Section systems contain four categories, best visualised as a moiety system with each moiety section divided into two. Here the marriage rules are more complex, not merely an exchange between two categories. Say, for example, a man of the *Banaga* section takes a wife from the *Garimara* section. Their children become *Milangga* and must marry people from the *Burungu* category. Their children in turn become *Banaga*. As can be seen from this example, the section system groups together relatives from alternate generations. The four sections can of course be logically recombined in different ways to provide either patrilineal moieties, matrilineal moieties or generational levels, and these different combinations may be found in the one society, each being used for ritual or other matters.

Sub-section systems are more elaborate again, with eight categories. This system again follows logical principles in grouping relatives and in creating marriage categories. As with sections, sub-section categories can be recombined to form sections and moieties.

AC

ship and descent provide the structural principles for maintaining an orderly life on a routine basis.

GENDER

It used to be thought that Aboriginal societies were characterised by male decision-making and control, women being mere chattels to be traded for marriage, and providing a serf-like labour base in service to their husbands and other male relatives. This view was in part influenced by careless observation of women's true roles in economic life and the home, and in part by the obvious importance and dominance in the ritual sphere of male secret initiation rites and other ceremonies. It is certainly true that for most of Aboriginal Australia older males were the repository of major mythic and ceremonial knowledge, and were major interpreters of the 'law' as ordained by the ancestral beings. Yet it is simplistic to see women in these societies as only submissive to male control, as a social category without its own gender-specific ritual and knowledge, and lacking any major role in routine decision-making.

Aborigines, like many other kin-based peoples, had a social system markedly differentiating the roles of the sexes. Women's economic roles were sharply distinguished from men's, their responsibilities lying mostly in the gathering of vegetable foods and small game; men were the hunters. As a corollary, women and men had their own separate kits of food-producing tools and their own special technologies and knowledge, including esoteric and secret knowledge of the ancestral spirit forces thought to govern the seasonal production of natural species. Furthermore, the hearth base of a camp is largely a woman's domain, with wives and older women making critical decisions on social arrangement and behaviour. Male–female relations were flexible and subject to change; each party had room to manoeuvre, each had a power base. In the world of myth and ritual, women, in Central Australia at least, had their own secret knowledge base, their own ritual activity, and played an important ritual role in male initiation ceremonies. Women, like men, can in addition express strong and dominant individuality in the everyday life of the social group: they can exert power and influence in the many routine activities involving men and women.

SOCIAL CONTROL

Kinship, descent and gender are major structural attributes of Aboriginal society which both consolidate and differentiate individuals in the social world. Any member of a group is therefore located in a complex matrix of cross-binding relationships which allow an individual life to be pursued, but within the web of rules guiding social behaviour. Life for an individual was mostly lived in small intensive networks of immediate family and kin with periodic gatherings of larger size for ceremonial purposes or seasonal sheltering.

Issues of social conflict are related to the size of social groups. Along the coasts of Cape York Peninsula, the monsoonal season brought people together into wet season camps which might have numbered up to 100 people. The arrival of the dry season saw these camps disperse into smaller family groups which spread along the coast to harvest the plants and animals proliferating after the rains.

Unlike centralised societies, there is no central legal body or enforcing agency among hunter-gatherers, who place heavy reliance instead upon rights and obligations between individuals and their close kin, and those who are in an authoritative or senior position carry much of the responsibility for controlling their junior relations. Dispute settlement operates at the level of the dispute: where it involves immediate family, then members of this category restrain antagonists and use force only when absolutely necessary. Where a dispute operates across family groups, the scale is larger and the potential for serious disruption to life is greater. Here relatives who have responsibilities to both sides, but who are without heavy obligations to one particular group, move in to keep antagonists apart. It may be more

Today, Aborigines live in a variety of contexts – in cities, in communites around country towns and, as here, in traditional rural communites.

acceptable for these peacemakers to receive blows or wounds than for an antagonist. Social control is thus extremely localised.

Disputes and offences also occur further afield. A death in other camps may be attributed to malevolent acts of sorcery by me or my brothers; a wife's family may come seeking vengeance for her death; a man may feel that his family is under threat from another group who have been traditionally seen as enemies and potential murderers. At this point vengeance may be sought by making a 'pay-back' killing: either by ambush or by tricking a victim into a vulnerable position. On occasions, in coastal Cape York Peninsula, traditional enmities between groups would be settled by minor battles fought by spear at arranged locations. Killings from these disputes mean that retaliatory killings are demanded, and in this way conflict between Aboriginal groups could be institutionalised across generations, perhaps even being justified by reference to mythic accounts of conflict between ancestral beings. Death rituals too could involve conflict. The final disposal of the body (perhaps a year or more after death) sometimes demanded a settlement of accounts where sorcery was suspected, and large-scale spear fighting could result.

Where family groups wished to settle a serious dispute, an offender could be required by both sides to undertake an ordeal by standing up to spears thrown at him, or, if this produced no acceptable wound, by offering his thigh to receive spears. The level of homicide in pre-European Aboriginal society is difficult to determine, but it was probably high at certain times and places. Committing incest could result in death, if the degree of incestuous behaviour was serious enough. Transgressions against ritual codes could also bring death.

Aboriginal social life gave people a high degree of autonomy. A male with his wife and children had little dependence upon others for everyday existence, and this autonomy was highly valued. The fact that Aboriginal populations were dispersed into small groups was not so much the result of environmental demands as of a social force which dispersed families quite as much as it brought them together. In arid zones, periods of environmental stress brought people together around water sources, but around the coasts and resource-rich hinterlands people always had the choice of moving away, even if only a small distance. Myth gave an authority to small groups and individuals which could not easily be denied, even though it was underwritten by a wider regional recognition of social ties to distant others. It is this particular balance between group and individual, other and self, the spiritual and the physical, which has given Australian hunter-gatherers their particular social character. Their pursuit of these social values has remained, even when people have

been incarcerated in reserves and subjected to considerable forces of change: it has been an active retention based upon strongly held values, not a passive inability of a supposedly primitive people to acquire the benefits of the dominant European society which now surrounds them.

Today, Aboriginal people live in a wide variety of contexts; many are city dwellers, with a tradition of city living. Others form small communities around country towns, and a significant number still live in their traditional areas within Aboriginal communities. The range of beliefs and behaviour is considerable, yet the concept of an Aboriginal identity can operate strongly in all these locations. In these terms Aboriginal identity (like other ethnic identities) is not something which can be measured from the outside by persistence of cultural traits such as language, ceremony, artefacts or mythic knowledge, but a social phenomenon which distinguishes an in-group from an out-group, and which justifies itself in terms of its own version of history. Yet the remote Aboriginal people who have conservatively kept pre-contact ways continue to provide much inspiration for more urban Aboriginal people. Urban Aboriginal dance, music, literature and art all draw heavily from the more remote groups for symbolic themes, as part of the maintenance of identity and as part of the process of authentication within a wider European society. AC

Language

In Aboriginal tradition, languages were not conceived merely as the historical legacies of human groups. They were formed, consciously and with purpose, during the Dreaming by the Ancestral Beings, who also shaped the known landscape out of a formless mass and created human societies and their values and laws. The languages of the Aborigines had, in their view, thus been in place since the beginning of the world.

The Spirit Beings endowed particular landscapes with particular languages, as part of this process, endowing the people of those lands with the same language. People did not simply speak languages. They were linked to them spiritually, and acquired rights of possession in languages by the principles of Aboriginal Law. People generally inherited the language of their father (and father's father) as their own, in the same way they inherited their land rights. There are, however, exceptions to this rule. Conception and birth in a particular language area would

also sometimes be the basis of someone's language affiliation. Strong association with the mother's family and land would in some areas lead to a primary affiliation with the mother's language rather than with the father's, and so on. In many parts of Australia, especially in remote areas, these rules often still apply.

So-called tribal maps of Australia, which are usually maps of established relationships between languages and particular landscapes, are much closer to being religious, political and legal statements than to being maps of on-the-ground populations of speakers of languages. This is because, while most lands were spiritually associated with a particular language, and most individuals belonged to a particular language-owning group, people of different languages did intermarry and intermingle, and the campsites of one language area would not usually have been used exclusively by the owners of that language.

Most adult Aborigines were bilinguals or multilinguals, often speaking four or five languages or more as a result of interconnections between families in adjacent areas. People of different language groups who lived together regularly tended to speak each others' languages rather than simply all speaking the same language.

Language variability in Aboriginal Australia was significantly a product of relations *among* people, not merely of separations *between* people. It was of course partly a consequence of tens of thousands of years of Aboriginal presence on the Australian continent, and the intense localism of Aboriginal culture. Profound language differences take time to develop, and across a large continent of hunter-gatherers the pattern of interaction was for the most part very restricted in each area. What emerged over the millennia, though, were not separate, monolingual societies but localised, overlapping multilingual groups, who recognised, and lived with, high levels of linguistic difference among their kith and kin.

Aboriginal language variability was certainly very high. Over 200 grammatically and lexically definable Australian languages are known and 500 major local speechforms were recognised – and usually given separate names – by Aborigines during the colonial period. Local dialects would have numbered several thousand in the mid-nineteenth century.

Within particular languages there was also much systematic variation between registers – that is, between socially defined variants of grammar and semantics. For example, in the presence of certain taboo kin such as in-laws or the recently bereaved, a special vocabulary was employed in some languages in order to respect the context in an appropriate way. In some areas an abnormal intonation pattern and voice quality also had to be used in the presence of taboo kin. During sacred ceremonies some groups practised forms of speech that inverted meaning in a complex way, used a mystic speech made up of terms understood only by the initiated, or used a ritual language pronounced with a sound system entirely different from that in everyday use. Aboriginal language, then, was not simply a matter of speaking a language but a complicated procedure by which switching between languages, and between registers within a language, was a normal part of everyday interaction and rested on highly developed social skills. Being multilingual also meant developing good linguistic skills, particularly mimicry. Few neighbouring languages shared exactly identical sound systems.

With some exceptions, Australian sound systems are remarkably similar, perhaps as a result of the traditionally high level of multilingualism. Grammars and vocabularies vary considerably, yet most Aboriginal languages are considered to be genetically related.

Grammar

The highest variation between Australian languages occurs in a broad band from the Kimberley District across to eastern Arnhem Land. These are languages characterised by the extensive use of suffixes and, particularly, prefixes. The rest of the mainland is covered by the 'Pama-Nyungan family' of languages of the entirely agglutinative type which primarily express grammatical cases, moods and tenses by the use of suffixes, in similar ways to Latin, Greek or Sanskrit.

The prefixing (or 'non-Pama-Nyungan') languages, on the other hand, have highly complex verb morphology. Instead of marking subject and object relations by adding subject and object suffixes to the relevant nouns, for example, these languages prefix verbs with complex elements that denote the person, number and gender class (noun class) of subject and object or indirect object. Sometimes this prefix will be a single form, unanalysable into separate components, that refers to a combination of person/number/gender X acting on person/number/gender Y. Again, while many of the suffixing languages have hundreds of unanalysable verbal roots that inflect for tense, aspect and mood, the prefixing languages have very few verbal roots, numbering in the tens rather than in the hundreds. These roots are compounded with different relevant nouns to provide the semantic precision needed. For example, in Kunwinjku, –bu– alone means 'to strike, hit, kill', while –dulu-bu– is 'to pierce', –rayn-bu– is 'to spear', and –jid-bu– is 'to sneeze'.

In Australian languages, grammatical relations are expressed by the internal forms of words, not by the order in which words occur. For this reason, word order is often remarkably free. The same words usually convey the same meaning regardless of what order they are spoken in, so that variation in word order is mainly a matter of emphasis, style and convention.

Aboriginal languages are in no sense 'primitive' or unusually simple, as we can see from the way pronouns are used.

Pronouns commonly occur in both free and bound forms, with the bound forms usually attached to the verb. In Wik-Ngathan of Cape York Peninsula, for example, first person singular accusative is nganha in the free form, and a suffix –nha in the bound form. Most of the languages distinguish dual as well as singular and plural number in pronouns, and many distinguish inclusive and exclusive first person dual and plural forms (that is, 'we-two' and 'we-many' including the addressee, versus 'we-two' and 'we-many' excluding the addressee). A few languages even distinguish 'we-three', 'we-four' as well. In some languages of the Gulf of Carpentaria, non-singular pronouns differ depending on whether the people spoken about are of adjacent generations (for example, parent-child, aunt-nephew), or of the same or alternate generations (for example, siblings, grandparent-grandchild). Many languages in Central Australia and south to the Flinders Ranges employ different sets of pronouns depending on even more complex distinctions between kinds of kinship relations. To speak such languages well, one not only has to master a complicated set of distinctions, one also has to know how all the members of the community are related to one another.

Australian languages vary greatly in grammatical complexity. Those of southeast Arnhem Land, for example, are among the most complex languages in the world, especially with regard to the morphology of verbs. By Australian standards, the Western Desert language (for example, Pitjantjatjara) would be among the simplest, but even then it is no simpler than many other languages such as Bahasa Indonesia.

Vocabularies vary significantly with environments, probably in the range of 5,000–10,000 words. Clearly, in a tropical environment where both marine and mainland species are available, a language must have a wide vocabulary for fish, birds, shells, plants and animals. Coastal material culture was accordingly more plentiful and complex than that of the Western Desert, and required a very much larger vocabulary.

Most Australian languages have only three vowels (although there are quite a few with five or more) while consonants range from 12 to about 20 or so. They have no fricatives or sibilants in most cases (f, v, h, sh, s, z, and so on) and consonant clusters are rarely complex. There are some consonants that are unfamiliar to speakers of most other languages (for example, the interdental and retroflex series). They have no distinctive tones (in the sense of, for example, Chinese) and have a rather even rhythmic structure.

Aboriginal languages thus do not represent major problems for foreign language learners. It is notable, however, that very few Australians, whether of Aboriginal or non-Aboriginal descent, have learned to speak any of these languages well unless brought up to do so. The rapid growth of descriptive grammatical literature and language-learning courses in certain Aboriginal languages has begun to alter this situation, albeit undramatically, since the 1960s.

PS

LANGUAGE TODAY

In traditional Aboriginal culture there was no writing, in the conventional sense. The use of Roman letters to render Aboriginal sounds has been gradually and patchily introduced in Aboriginal schools since the mid-nineteenth century, beginning with missionaries and, since the 1970s, proceeding with government support through some of the remote schools. The success of this bilingual education movement has been variable. It has resulted in a number of people achieving functional literacy in their own languages, but its wider effectiveness has been limited by the fact that a high diversity of languages is spoken by only very small populations in each case, and by the reluctance of many Aboriginal people to regard the achievement of written communication in an Aboriginal language as a high priority.

There has been a dramatic loss of the original Aboriginal languages. In 200 years the 500 or so languages recognised by Aborigines have been largely rendered extinct or reduced to a handful of speakers with incomplete knowledge. In the early days of European conquest Aboriginal populations were reduced from some hundreds of thousands to only about 80,000 by 1900. Moves enforced by government departments and encouraged by most missions concentrated many of the survivors into institutions where some form of pidgin or English was the only viable lingua franca. Use of Aboriginal languages was long suppressed in many schools and until recently was commonly frowned upon by whites in public places.

On top of these factors, abandonment of traditional languages, partly as a means to social acceptance and upward mobility, has been remarkably common and rapid among the Australian Aborigines. Where this abandonment has been in favour of a local Aboriginal lingua franca such as Walmajarri, Kunwinjku or Wik-Mungkan, at least one language in each region is likely to survive into the twenty-first century. Here and there, mostly in the remote north and in western Central Australia, some traditional language variability will survive as well. In many other areas, it is only in a handful of remnant items of Aboriginal vocabulary, in a distinctive pronunciation of English words, and in typically Aboriginal conversational gambits, that Aborigines can be said to continue to practise an Aboriginal form of language.   PS

Mission schools were first established for Aboriginal children in the mid-nineteenth century, and many are still active today, as is this one in Mogumber, Western Australia. Although ways of writing Aboriginal languages in Roman script have been developed and taught, the number of living languages has declined drastically.

Religion

Even though the Aboriginal population in many parts of Australia was decimated through white colonisation, Aboriginal modes of life were transformed, and many groups of Aborigines have adopted and modified Christian beliefs, traditional religions continue to be vigorously practised in many parts of the continent. These religions have common themes, but vary greatly in detail.

CONCEPTIONS OF THE UNIVERSE

Aboriginal conceptions of the universe are essentially animistic. Aborigines envisage the forces and powers underlying everyday phenomena as person-like and believe in a world filled with spirits of various kinds. Ghosts of the dead haunt dense forest, and mischievous sprites inhabit the rocky escarpments. Most important of all are the powerful and dangerous Ancestral Beings, modelled in part on the attributes of humans, and in part on those of other species and phenomena which Europeans think of as inanimate, such as water, rock, fire, the sun or the Milky Way.

Myths relate how these Beings, referred to here as Ancestral Spirit Beings, camped, made love, procreated, quarrelled, fought, foraged and performed ceremonies, just like living human beings. But some also flew like mosquitoes, swam like fish, bit like snakes, and so on. They were often of extraordinary size, in Aboriginal belief, and possessed extraordinary powers, being capable, for example, of travelling for great distances underground, or gouging out great ravines.

The Ancestral Spirit Beings did not create the world out of nothing. The world existed, but the

Beings transformed it. Myths recount the activities of such Spirit Beings in the Dreaming – a creative era which left the social world and its environment in its present state. According to these stories the Ancestral Spirit Beings travelled leaving marks of their activities in the land and waters. For example, an estuary might be described as the path of a giant Crocodile, a mound as Honeybee's camp, and a rock as the transformation of a canoe abandoned by two ancestral women. Some parts of the land may be described as the substance of certain Ancestral Spirit Beings, imbued with their power. For example, a deposit of mica may be described as the Rainbow Serpent's skin, a body of yellow ochre as the fat of the ancestral Kangaroo, and a reddish clay as the flesh of Shark.

Some Ancestral Spirit Beings are believed to remain present, and alive, especially in deep lagoons and waterholes where they went 'inside', or in tidal reaches. For example, in an estuary in northeast Arnhem Land, Mangrove Log Being moves in and out with the tide. Rock, who lies in the form of a reef in the coastal waters, is dangerous if disturbed. There is also a widespread belief in Australia that giant snakes or other serpents, often associated with thunderstorms and rainbows, lie in deep waters. These appear to be associated with sexuality as well as with political power, especially that of men. The sky, too, is an ancestral domain. For example, Moon, in northeast Arnhem Land myth, escaped mortality by going up into the sky. In the southeast there was a predominant belief in a Sky-Being, known as Baiami to the Wuradjeri. In this region, the religious leaders were 'clever-men' who claimed to be able to travel to the sky, to obtain rain, for example, with the aid of quartz crystals.

In Aboriginal belief some of the Beings gave birth to living groups of people. A group's territory often has sites associated with other Spirit Beings as well as the Ancestor, and the group may be linked to several other groups through the travels of the Spirit Beings and by related ceremonies. In some areas a land-holding group with a common set of Ancestral Spirit Beings is clearly defined through descent from the father, although rights and responsibilities are distributed also among a wide network of people with other kin connections to members of the group. In regions such as the Western Desert, groups holding land are much more loosely defined.

Not only were Spirit Beings the ancestors of present human groups, in Aboriginal belief, but they also established the conditions for their continued reproduction. Belief in some kind of conception spirit is common: copulation is not sufficient for a woman to become pregnant. Rather her womb is entered by an entity which originates in a place, often a body of water, where an Ancestral Spirit Being menstruated into the water, or shook pollen or down off the body, or left these entities by some other means. A person has a special attachment to the place of spirit conception, a place that may be, but need not be, in the person's own country. People also tend to identify closely with the Ancestors, especially as they become old. In some Aboriginal religions a person's spirit is believed to return to the waters at death, and in some there is an explicit doctrine of reincarnation.

Aboriginal religions do not look forward to a future state of perfection, or back to a perfect state from which humankind has fallen. Nor are people's actions judged by a Being thought of as perfect, with the good rewarded and the bad punished in a future life. The Ancestral Spirit Beings are conceived of as law-makers, having instituted social rules and ritual practices, only in some cases to break them. But the Beings were not themselves perfect, and do not judge people for adhering, or failing to adhere, to the religious law. People believe that the infraction of a law, such as the prohibition to go into a certain area, may anger an Ancestral Spirit Being, or result in sickness. But it is the prerogative of those with control of a given ritual or place to take action against offenders, with the support of kinsfolk.

It is accepted that all Beings, ancestral and human, have dangerous and anarchic as well as benign and ordered aspects. The passions are not separated off as the source of evil, but taken, rather, as an integral part of existence. Consequently no universal battle between the forces of good and of evil is envisaged. Consistent with this general attitude, Aboriginal people believe that the forces of sorcery can be harnessed in service of religious secrecy and good order. Young novices are threatened with spells should they reveal religious secrets. If a man becomes ill after, say, fighting during a ceremony, then the sickness may be interpreted as punishment by the leaders. Consistent also with this general attitude is the integration of erotic elements into many rituals.

RITUAL

Rituals fulfil many purposes: to dispose of the dead and act as a means of expressing grief; to purify mourners from the effects of a death or from bloodshed; to initiate boys through circumcision and girls through defloration; to reveal religious secrets to novices; to gain access to ancestral power, and control human and non-human resources; to exchange gifts; to settle disputes or substitute for actual fights.

Several of these functions often overlap in the same ceremony. The same songs and dances are often used both in the context of a ceremony and simply for entertainment. The forms used to construct ceremonies, including song-series, dances, sacred designs and objects, are owned by particular groups and sets of groups which cooperate in organising a ceremony.

Many revelatory and other types of ceremony incorporate explicit or implicit sexual symbolism. In some, ritual intercourse is or was practised, often between categories of people for whom sexual intercourse is normally forbidden, rendering the practice all the more powerful. Dances, designs and sacred objects may be implicitly phallic and uterine in form, consistent with a central concern with the continued fertility of people and resources. Some so-called 'increase' ceremonies are explicitly celebrated with the intention of ensuring the reproduction of humans, of food species, or the occurrence of rainfall. Many women's secret ceremonies are concerned with female sexuality and the gaining of power to attract men, and some men's ceremonies are also concerned with 'love magic'.

Aboriginal ceremony is often ritualistic or 'magical' in orientation. People do not attempt to achieve results primarily through discourse with a Spirit Being, as in prayer and supplication – although people do address the spirits. The intention is rather through direct action to harness powers and resources provided, intentionally or unintentionally, by an Ancestral Spirit Being. For example, by touching a sacred object which represents the Being or some aspect of the Being a person believes he or she will get 'power'; or by singing the appropriate songs and performing the appropriate dances representing Rain Being, people believe that they can make it rain when they desire. Nevertheless people will converse with Ancestral Spirit Beings and other spirits, greeting the spirit which resides at a certain waterhole, asking a Being to give them success in hunting, calling on the spirits of the dead not to harm newcomers in their company, or making a gift to the spirit to pacify it, and so on.

Another general quality of ritual action is that some participants identify with the Ancestral Spirit Beings in song, dance and body decoration. Until

their production for the market and for audiences, art, song and dance have been primarily forms of religious expression. Painted designs are applied to objects used in ceremonies, to rock walls, and in the form of body decoration. Two-dimensional designs are also found as sand drawings and sand paintings, which often form part of the setting of a ceremony. These designs represent the traces made by the Being in the landscape, as well, perhaps, as the form of the Being. Designs and objects 'follow', or are regarded as transformations of, the results of ancestral activity.

Songs are also regarded as having first been sung by Ancestral Spirit Beings, handed down from generation to generation, or may be revealed by spirits, in a dream. Dances are mimetic, and with the aid of body painting and objects, performers identify with the Ancestors, and re-enact Ancestral events. In performing the songs and dances the participants act as the Beings, identifying with them.

Such principles underlie not only ritual but also beliefs about sorcery and healing. It is believed that there is a causal connection between a person and a part of the person, such as hair or faeces, even after the part is detached from the whole. A causal relation, not merely a conventional one established through perceived similarity or by a rule, also obtains between a linguistic or visual representation of the person, in Aboriginal belief. Hence action on a part or image of the person harms the person. Conversely, the power of the Ancestral Spirit Being resides in the trace left by the Being, and in a representation of the Being.

The many varieties of religious practices within a particular tradition are integrated through incorporating elements which refer to and 'follow' the Ancestral Spirit Beings. In mortuary ceremonies, songs and dances may be chosen which relate to the group and country of the dead person, or his close relatives' groups and places. They include metaphors of processes of death and decay, such as a song about larvae gnawing through a mangrove log, and symbols of the journey of the soul to the sky or to ancestral land. Close relatives in mourning may be placed under a speech prohibition for a time, as among Warlpiri people and their neighbours, or be obliged to take part in a purification ceremony before re-entering normal, everyday life, as among the Yolngu people of northeast Arnhem Land. Mortuary ceremonies are concerned with the passage of the spirit of the deceased to the ancestral domain, as well as the protection of the living from dangerous spirits of the dead. Since most deaths are attributed ultimately to sorcery, mortuary ceremonies often incorporate a post-mortem to search for a sign of the identity of the supposed killer, and sometimes provide for an ensuing fight.

Mortuary ceremony photographed near Darwin c. 1930. Such ceremonies were conducted both to aid the passage of the spirit of the dead person to the world of the ancestors, and to protect the living from the potentially harmful spirits of the dead.

BURIAL CORROBOREE. N.A.

Initiation ceremony

Bridle Tern is an important Ancestral Spirit Being of the Djambarrpuyngu clan of Buckingham Bay in Arnhem Land. A song tells how the bird suddenly dives down into the sea, catches a fish and rises again into the air. The song, with its dance incorporating a long feathered string representing the bird's line of flight, is performed at a circumcision ceremony. The male dancers encircle the initiand 'capturing' him in the string.

The ceremony here is clearly a symbol of the incorporation of the boy into the domain of men and their religious life, for with circumcision he changes from a 'child' (*yothu*) into a 'bachelor' (*gurrmul*). The ceremony is called in English 'make young-man'.

The same song form is performed also at a funeral, along with the rest of a long series or cycle of songs about the sea. In this context, the song is an image of death and the incorporation of the soul into the ancestral domain. The same falling melody is sung as in the circumcision ceremony, but with connotations of deep grief.

IK

The most elaborate ceremonies are usually male initiation rites and revelatory rites. In an initiation ceremony, a young man undergoes a status change, often accompanied by a physical ordeal such as the pulling out of teeth or facial hair, circumcision (and in some areas later subincision – that is, an incision on the underside of the penis through to the urethra). The content of songs, dances and designs, expressed also in the related myths, often symbolises the separation of boys from their mothers, and their incorporation into the category of adult men. For example, in one type of circumcision ceremony in northeast Arnhem Land the initiands are dressed as women in breast-girdles, but are 'swallowed' by a line of male dancers, who represent the ancestral Python. The initiation of girls in some regions included defloration and a public rite, whereas in other places a girl's puberty rite simply involved segregation at the onset of menstruation, and was a private matter.

In revelatory ceremonies, secret objects, dances, songs and designs are revealed to novices. In some parts of Australia only men have such esoteric ceremonies, and women and children are excluded from secret aspects. In other parts of Australia, men and women both hold esoteric ceremonies; men are excluded from secret women's ceremonies. This revelatory aspect is usually combined with some other function, such as initiation or commemoration of the dead. Religious knowledge and participation is highly valued, for the ceremonies apparently concern the most potent Beings and powers of the universe. The organisation of these ceremonies involves the cooperation of people over a wide region.

Women from mourning ceremony photographed in northern Queensland in the 1930s. Participants in rituals would generally have their bodies painted with intricate patterns. Those on women's bodies were less complex than those on men's.

SYMBOLISM

A striking property of many Aboriginal songs, designs and dances is their rich symbolism. Drawing on the world of animal behaviour, plants, the cycle of the seasons and so on, Aboriginal songs and ceremonies constitute a complex network of meaning. A few simple examples from Arnhem Land demonstrate this well.

Many symbols, including sacred objects and designs, but also song phrases, are multivocal – they have many explicit meanings as well as complex connotations. Interconnection among the meanings of a set of symbols is one way in which a body of religious symbols is integrated, thus giving a person's experience a degree of coherence it would not otherwise have, but also forming an aesthetically engaging whole. For example, in northeast Arnhem Land a certain species of tree stands for the relationship of people to their country as well as to other groups with the same Ancestral Spirit Being. The common name of the tree is used as the proper name of several types of object. These include a tree planted in each clan country by the Ancestral Spirit Being, a cut branch erected in the camp as the focus of a ceremony, and which represents that tree, and the sacred objects which the Ancestral Spirit Being places in the ground and waters. A variety of Ancestral Spirit Beings, each with its characteristic song, design and dances, is associated with the same tree – Goanna climbs the tree, flying Foxes hang in the tree eating fruit, Red-collared Lorikeets fly to the tree, Butcherbird calls from the tree, and so on. The form of a flying Fox hanging in the tree connotes also the basket full of sacred objects, which two ancestral women hung up in a tree and which men stole, in the myth. Both connote fertility in the symbolism of song and dance.

Through connections of these kinds a corpus of songs, ceremonies and designs forms a complex whole in which an infinite number of connections and patterns may be found. If some of the meanings are encoded in abstract designs or obscure song-phrases, and are revealed only to a particular category of people, this is one way of forming a body of secret religious knowledge, an aspect of political control.

RELIGIOUS CONTROL

Until the imposition of state structures, Aborigines had no specialised structures of government such as chiefs or kings, legislatures, courts of law, police, or armies. Yet social life was not anarchic, but ordered. Religious beliefs and practices have a central place in that order, although embedment within a nation-state is undermining both Aboriginal social orders and the role of religions within them.

Customary laws or rules which govern most social activities are believed to have been laid down by the Ancestral Spirit Beings at the beginning of things. Authority relations have a religious basis, especially the relations between old and young. Many activities are treated as religious practices, and so are brought into the same frame of reference and subject to the control of religious leaders. Production and consumption are subject to religious controls through religious taboos, through the religious nature of some major items of technology, and the religious justification of land tenure. Some ceremonies are themselves modes of controlling people. Furthermore, ceremonies themselves are valued resources, the control of which is subject to political competition. In these and other ways, religion is integrated into the whole of social life; it is not a separate institution.

IK

Rock art

The mythological validation of social relations is an important survival strategy of Aboriginal societies which finds symbolic expression in ceremonial gatherings and exchange. That the development of such systems is ancient is suggested by the antiquity of certain exchange networks. Art is a fundamental means of expressing and reinforcing systems of belief, and the arts are widely practised in Aboriginal societies. Only designs painted or pecked out on solid rock survive as evidence of artistic activity in the past, but its occurrence is widespread throughout the continent (see also p. 291).

There are many regional styles of Aboriginal rock art, but some pervasive elements are widespread. Human and animal figures are shown without background or base line, and action is often not depicted. Many of these figures represent mythological events, and are considered to be endowed with the spiritual power of the Ancestral Beings whose images or creations they are.

In Arnhem Land, an elaborate and delicately painted miniature art of men and animals reflects the activities of inland hunters, and is therefore dated to the period preceding the last rise in sea level, possibly as far back as 10,000 years or more. A period of rapid stylistic change leads from this to the contemporary art style in which large colourful figures of animals may be shown with internal organs rendered in intricate designs. The subject matter of this latest art style reflects the environment of the wetlands which became fully established by c. 1500 BP. It is also the style currently employed in bark paintings of the region.

In most of arid inland Australia, more constrained artistic styles pervade, in which a limited range of formal motifs are used: circles, arcs, animal tracks, sinuous lines are pecked or painted on the rocks. Pecked designs are often covered in deep patina and are therefore thought to be ancient. Only at Sturt's Meadow in western New South Wales can they be securely dated to over 10,000 years. An age of up to 30,000 years has recently been claimed for similar rock art in South Australia, but the dating techniques used have been shown to be unreliable. The distribution of these motifs over the rock face appear random, but analyses reveal some regularities in their arrangement, suggestive of meaningful patterning. Paintings in this style are more recent, and motifs include more regular combinations of the simpler elements, as well as some recognisable images of human or other figures. These relate clearly to contemporary art styles of the region in a range of other media.

Aboriginal rock art is often considered to be integral to the original act of creation by the Ancestral Beings, and as such serves to demonstrate the validity of the mythology and of the territorial links between people and their mythological ancestors. People are the custodians of this heritage, responsible for its upkeep sometimes by renovating or adding to the artistic motifs. The sources of the art are considered to lie in the Dreaming itself, and hence to reflect the long unbroken continuity of Aboriginal tradition and history.

AR

Painting of turtle, Obiri Rock, Northern Territory. Rock paintings play an integral part in Aboriginal culture, reinforcing the link between people and the land.

Left Circles inscribed on rock from Wilpena Pound in the Flinders Ranges, South Australia. One theory says that simple carvings such as these could be up to 30,000 years old.

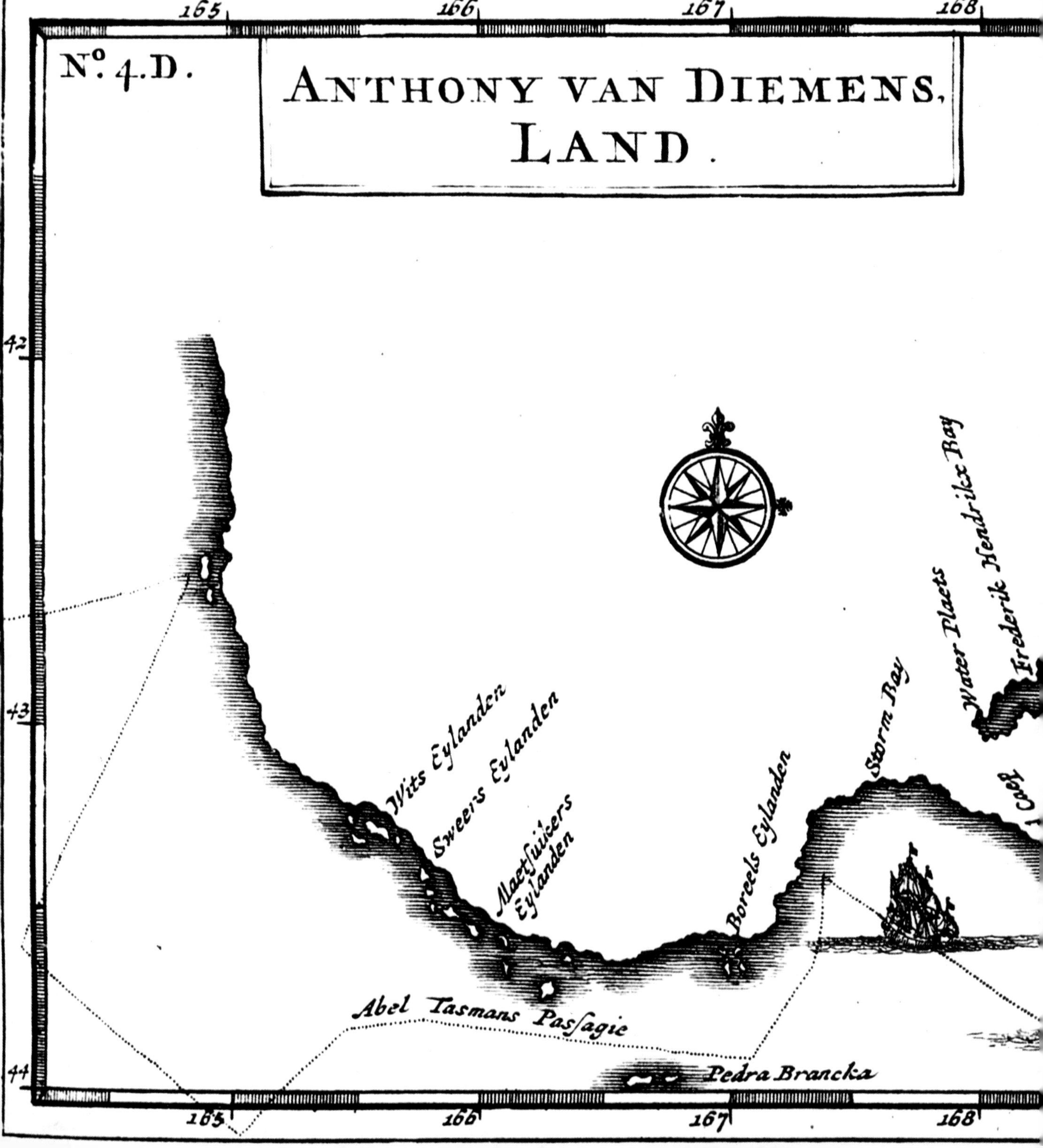

No. 4. D.

ANTHONY VAN DIEMENS, LAND.

Wits Eylanden

Sweers Eylanden

Maetsuikers Eylanden

Boreels Eylanden

Storm Bay

Water Plaets

Frederik Hendriks Bay

1 Cael

Abel Tasmans Passagie

Pedra Brancka

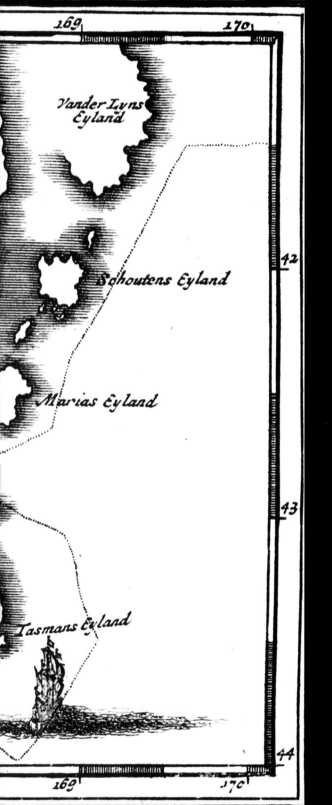

History since European contact

Pre-1770 external contact

Previous page *Abel Tasman named (what is now Tasmania) Anthony Van Diemen's Land on 25 November 1642 in honour of the governor of the Dutch East Indies. This map was reproduced in the Dutch publication 'Oud en nieuw Oost-Indien' of 1724–26.*

The earliest reports made by visitors to the Australian continent are those arising from the voyage of the *Duyfken*. This 'pinnasse' or 'jacht' of the Dutch East India Company left Banten in west Java on 28 November 1605 under the command of Willem Jansz to follow up rumours of gold beyond the Moluccas in the eastern extremities of the Indonesian archipelago.

The *Duyfken* had been one of the first four Dutch ships to come to the east only 10 years before and the 1605 voyage was a continuation of the task of evaluating the trading resources of the whole area. A contemporary chart shows the *Duyfken*'s track along the southern coast of New Guinea, across the western entrance to Torres Strait and some 300 km down the western coast of Cape York Peninsula. One man was killed when a boat was sent to explore the Batavia River and 'finding no good to be done' the *Duyfken* returned to the Company's fort on Banda.

The *Duyfken* was off the Australian coast during the wet season at the beginning of 1606. By a remarkable chance the next change of monsoon brought two Spanish vessels to the same area. These were part of an expedition which had left Peru at the end of 1605 under the command of Pedro Fernandez de Quiros searching for another America in the South Pacific and, more specifically, trying to locate landfalls of earlier expeditions in Melanesia. Becoming separated from Quiros and his visions of New Jerusalem on Espiritu Santo in Vanuatu, Luis Vaez de Torres and Don Diego de Prado y Tovar continued westwards towards New Guinea and, passing to the south through the strait now named after Torres, eventu-

Abel Tasman (1603?–59) with his second wife and his daughter by his first wife, by Jacob Gerritsz Cuyp, 1637. As is indicated by the globe, Tasman was already renowned as a seaman before he first saw Australia in 1642.

ally reached Manila. They may have glimpsed the Australian mainland at the top of Cape York Peninsula in September 1606.

Despite frequent claims, nourished on imagination and abetted by ingenuity, there is no surviving evidence for contacts by European or Asian seafarers with Australia and its Aboriginal inhabitants before 1606. While there probably were accidental landfalls by those driven away by storms on local voyages within the eastern Indonesian archipelago or even from the Pacific, and there was undoubtedly contact across Torres Strait by Papuans, no account of such unremarkable occurrences remains.

Knowledge of global wind systems soon led the Dutch East India Company to adopt a new route from the Cape of Good Hope to Java. Steady westerlies blowing across the southern Indian Ocean provided a rapid passage to the east from where the southeast trade winds carried a ship northwards. Even before the new route was formally approved, Dirk Hartog in the *Eendracht* was blown a little too far to the east and came upon the west coast of Australia. At the end of October 1616 he landed on an offshore island, leaving a pewter plate marked with a record of his visit, and then continued northwards to Java.

Over the next 30 years, Company ships charted most of the Australian coast. In the north, the motive behind the voyages of Jan Carstensz to the Gulf of Carpentaria in 1623 and of Pieter Pieterszoon to Melville Island in 1636 was the search for trade. For the barren west coast, which was frequently sighted by vessels on the regular route to Java, the Company needed reliable charts and on several occasions the directors at home suggested a thorough survey, but local resources were not available. The line of the western coast was much extended in 1627 when Pieter Nuyts passed south of Cape Leeuwin and along the south coast as far as the Nuyts Archipelago in South Australia.

In 1622 an English East India Company ship (the *Trial*) was wrecked in the Montebello Islands. Survivors brought to the Dutch Company's new headquarters at Batavia (Jakarta) not only the unwelcome proof that the secret of the new sailing route was out, but also evidence of its dangers. Seven years later, a major Dutch ship, the *Batavia*, was lost in the low and dangerous islands of Houtman Abrolhos. The saga of the survivors' greed, lust and murder, then the terrible retribution when a rescue vessel arrived from Batavia, fascinated contemporaries as it has modern readers. Although many of the 1,770 Dutch vessels sailing from Europe to Asia in the seventeenth century, and 2,951 in the following century, would have come close to the Australian coast, further losses were not great: the *Vergulde Draek* in 1656, the *Zuytdorp* in 1712 and the *Zeewijk* in 1727.

TASMAN'S DISCOVERIES

This first phase of discovery culminated in the voyages of Abel Janszoon Tasman in 1642–43 and 1644. These expeditions were intended to resolve major geographical issues and to open up the Company's commercial contact with a new section of the area of operation specified in its founding charter. The project began with a plan drawn up by François Jacobszoon Visscher and presented to governor-general Antonio van Diemen at the beginning of 1642. The plan was to sail across the Indian Ocean much further south than the usual route in order to locate, if it existed, the major landmass supposed to lie in southern latitudes. The relationship of this Southland to the known coasts of what was already called New Holland was then to be investigated.

Leaving Batavia on 14 August 1642 in the *Heemskerk* and *Zeehan*, Tasman, with Visscher as pilot-major, first made the Company's fort on Mauritius and then set off southeast. Prevented by bad weather from keeping as far south as their instructions indicated, Tasman came upon the west coast of Tasmania on 24 November and followed it to the south, then east, before anchoring in a sheltered bay. A cursory inspection was enough to show that there was no likelihood of commercial advantage to the Company and, despite signs of their presence, no Aborigines were sighted. Naming the land Van Diemen's Land after his governor-general and other features after members of the Batavia Council, Tasman claimed his discovery for The Netherlands, but there was no reason to stay. Carried offshore by the wind on 5 December, he pressed on eastwards to discover the west coast of New Zealand. Tasman suspected the existence of Cook Strait, but took the South Island at least to be part of a vast continental Southland. By then sailing on to Tonga and eventually north of New Guinea and back to Batavia, he showed that the known coasts of Australia must be separate from the Southland, though that term continued to be used for what was more commonly known as New Holland.

Faced with the southeast monsoon in the Moluccas in the middle of 1643, Tasman had wisely returned to Batavia, but at the change of monsoon early in the next year he and Visscher set out again to resolve some remaining problems. In the *Limmen*, *Zeemeuw* and *Bracq* they followed the southern coast of New Guinea until they crossed the entrance of Torres Strait and came into the Gulf of Carpentaria. Torres' voyage was little known and, although some maps showed a strait, the question of its existence was not of great importance to the interests of the Company. On his previous voyage, Tasman had found nothing to suggest profitable trade in any area which might be approached through such a passage. The achievement of the 1644 voyage was to show the continuity of the coast from Cape York Peninsula, discovered by the *Duyfken* in 1606, to the well-known coast of New Holland in the west. By the middle of the seventeenth century, maps were available throughout the world giving the outline of some two-thirds of the Australian coast and Tasman's track to the south and east set a limit to the possible extent of the land.

FURTHER VOYAGES OF EXPLORATION

Such a large landmass continued to attract occasional visitors and scientific curiosity as the century progressed. In 1688, a wild group of adventurers, including the Englishman, William Dampier, spent over two months careening their ship near the entrance to King Sound in the northwest. They had considerable contact with Aborigines, but could not get them to help with any useful labour. The vivid account Dampier wrote of this and other experiences on a voyage that had taken him around the world earned him command of a voyage with more scientific purposes. In 1699, in the *Roebuck*, he returned to the west coast at Shark Bay where he studied the plants

Early voyages of discovery.

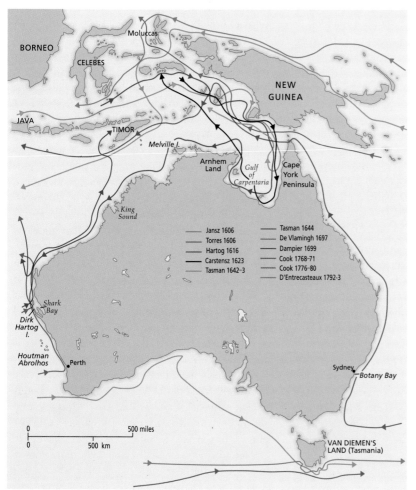

Early voyages of discovery map legend:
— Jansz 1606
— Torres 1606
— Hartog 1616
— Carstensz 1623
— Tasman 1642–3
— Tasman 1644
— De Vlamingh 1697
— Dampier 1699
— Cook 1768–71
— Cook 1776–80
— D'Entrecasteaux 1792–3

The trepang industry

Possibly it was Maarten van Delft's voyage that somehow provided the information that the north coast of Australia had abundant trepang (also called *bêche-de-mer* or sea cucumber). In about 1720, the trade passing through Macassar began to include small quantities of trepang, which, once properly processed, would keep almost indefinitely and could be sold to the Chinese.

The fashion for eating trepang in soups and stews did not have a long history in China, but had arisen about a century before as part of a general enthusiasm for exotic food. Such items were gradually being gathered in from further and further afield. The lack of European interest in consuming or trading in trepang only enhanced the industry's attraction for traders, financiers and seamen in Macassar and soon the port developed as a major centre for the trade – a position it still holds.

Though we know much more about this industry in the nineteenth century when many observers described its operation, by the second half of the eighteenth century getting on for a thousand men were bringing in a large proportion of Macassar's trepang from the grounds on the north coast of Australia. They had not only to collect the animals off the sea bed, but also boil, bury and smoke them on adjacent beaches, as witnessed today by abundant archaeological remains.

Inevitably, the trepangers came into contact with Aborigines and, judging by later evidence, enjoyed mixed relations: misunderstandings, quarrels, violence and bloodshed, but also as Aborigines gradually learned to make themselves understood in the Makasar language and may have supplied a little labour, trust developed and some Aborigines travelled back to Macassar to see a wider world. The substantial profits to be made in the industry, which were carefully apportioned in written contracts, remind us of the sophistication of the trepangers: the practices of Islam were observed and the captains, at least, were literate in the Makasar script. The trepang was, after all, being fed into international trade.

CM

and animals and, searching for water as he coasted northwards, had some brief, unhappy contact with Aborigines. Unimpressed by the land and its people, Dampier planned to reach the east coast by sailing around the north of New Guinea, but despite some important discoveries there, his ship was too weak and the opposing winds too strong for him to press on and he turned away. Dampier's actual exploration in Australia was slight, yet his writing about the land

Dutch–Aboriginal contact

This Dutch observation of Aboriginal life in 1705 comes from the report on van Delft's voyage compiled from journals and crew survivors.

They however possess nothing which is of value themselves, and have neither iron nor anything like mineral ore or metal, but only a stone which is ground and made to serve as a hatchet. They have no habitations, either houses or huts; and feed on fish, which they catch with harpoons of wood, and also by means of nets, putting out to sea in small canoes, made of the bark of trees, which are in themselves so fragile, that it is necessary to strengthen them with cross-beams.

Some of them had marks on their body, apparently cut or carved, which, as it seemed to our people, were looked upon by them as a kind of ornament. They eat sparingly and moderately, whereby they grow up always active and nimble; their diet seems to consist of fish, and a few roots and vegetables, but no birds or wild animals of any kind are used as food, for though animal food exists, and was found by our men in abundance, the natives appeared to be indifferent to it.

According to the notes of the captain of the sloop *Waijer*, from the 14th of June, about five hundred people with women and children, were met on one occasion about two miles inland; at night also they were descried sitting round several fires among the bushes; nothing however was seen in their possession of any value. Our men might also easily have taken and brought over to Batavia with them, two or three of the natives who daily came on board, but the skipper of the *Vossenbosch*, following out his instructions to the letter, would not allow them to be taken without their full consent, either by falsehood or fraud, and as no one understood their language, nothing was to be done in the matter; consequently they remained in their own country.

and its people continues to be read and was, in its time, immensely popular. Even more famous is Swift's parody of such tales of adventure in *Gulliver's Travels* published in 1726. Two of the tales are set near Australia.

Meanwhile there had been further Dutch interest around the turn of the century. In 1694, a major Dutch ship, the *Ridderschap van Holland*, disappeared in the Indian Ocean and this provided the stimulus for a new expedition, partly to search for the missing vessel and partly to chart the west coast of Australia yet more accurately. The undertaking was vigorously promoted by Nicolaas Witsen, a director of the Dutch East India Company and long interested in geographical discoveries.

Three ships – the *Geelvink*, the *Nijptang* and the *Wezeltje* – under the command of Willem de Vlamingh, left Holland in March 1696 and arrived off the Australian coast at the end of the year. Rottnest Island acquired its name from the 'sort of rat as big as a common cat' (the quokka) found there, while the Swan River was so called from the black swans seen on a thorough survey of the site of Perth. Several swans were caught, but died in the tropics before they could be sent back to Europe. Further north, at the beginning of February 1697, a party recovered the pewter plate left by Hartog over 80 years before. De

Vlamingh had a new plate prepared setting out the details of both expeditions and took the earlier plate with him. It eventually reached Holland.

Soon after leaving Dirk Hartog Island, the ships bore away to Batavia. Although the results of Vlamingh's voyage did not meet Witsen's hopes and no reliable trace was found of missing Dutch vessels, the west coast was now securely charted and inspected: there seemed no prospect of gain there and the directors of the Company could not be persuaded to waste money on further disinterested exploration.

On the north coast, however, the position was slightly different. Dampier's books rekindled suspicion of English intentions and in 1704 preparations were begun in Batavia for Dutch expeditions to northern Australia and the north coast of New Guinea, both areas brought into prominence by Dampier. In fact, the voyage to Australia went well to the north of any point reached by the English. Three vessels under the command of Maarten van Delft left Batavia early in 1705 and, after calling at Kupang, proceeded to the north coast of Bathurst and Melville Islands. Unlike most other Dutch captains off the Australian coast, van Delft moved very slowly so that after three months he had reached no further than Bowen Strait in western Arnhem Land. This delay, caused by the onset of the dry season winds and increasing debility and sickness among the crews, meant that there was prolonged contact with Aborigines. The Dutch were able to make a careful assessment of the potential of the land and its people for their interest in trade. The eventual report, which is for us an invaluable ethnographic account, confirmed yet again to the directors of the Company that there was scant hope of profit in this direction.

When the Dutch East India Company representative at Kupang reported in 1751 that a Chinese trader looking for tortoise-shell on the islands to the south had gone further and coasted along the Australian mainland, the Company authorities, ever watching for commercial advantage, requested fuller information. The ensuing correspondence shows that the Company was well aware of the collection in this area of trepang and other maritime products, items of no particular interest to the Company, so it is somewhat surprising that this report led eventually to a final voyage of two ships, the *Rijder* and *Buis*, under Jean Etienne Gonzal in 1756. Although the ships separated at Banda, they both managed to visit the west coast of Cape York Peninsula, a long way from any commercial activity. Two Aborigines were kidnapped and brought back to Batavia, but it is unlikely that they could provide any more promising information than a rapid inspection of the land had revealed. European trade in that era required not only natural resources, but also people and societies organised to present those resources to the Europeans.

COOK'S DISCOVERY

When James Cook and the *Endeavour* entered the Pacific just over a decade after the last Dutch East India Company visit to Australia, his motives were somewhat broader. Having completed his astronomical observations at Tahiti and demonstrated the insularity of New Zealand, which Tasman had thought part of a great southern continent, he turned to charting the east coast of New Holland. Cook's motives were not entirely disinterested as shown by his claiming this coast for the British crown, but the immediate task was simple discovery, completing the outline of the continent as left by Tasman over a century before.

Sailing westwards across the Tasman Sea, Cook intended to begin at the point on the east coast of Tasmania where Tasman had broken off, but probably providentially, the *Endeavour* was blown to the north of Bass Strait so that the first land sighted was the southeastern corner of the continent on 20 April 1770. Sailing quite rapidly along the coast of what is now New South Wales and Queensland with few landings, Cook laid down his chart. Though the stay of a week in Botany Bay was to lead to great consequences, the fullest opportunity to observe the land and its people was at the Endeavour River in north Queensland where the ship was brought for repair after serious damage on a coral reef. Cook was aware of the possibility of passing south of New Guinea and his passage through Torres Strait, the first by Europeans since 1606, connected his survey with previous Dutch discoveries.

This defined the eastern extent of the continent first identified by Tasman's circumnavigation and, despite the scope for much further detailed exploration, especially in the southeast, the familiar outline is easily recognised in Cook's chart. There is also much that is familiar to most Australians in Cook's summary of the land and its Aboriginal inhabitants. Whereas Dampier and most Dutch observers had regretted the absence of societies more like their own, and consequently the lack of opportunity for trade or other assistance, Cook perceived a land whose difficulty and strangeness, while not precluding human occupation, constrained such occupants to noble virtue.

New European interests towards the end of the eighteenth century produced new uses for the land beyond support for its Aboriginal people and fleeting visits by trepangers in the north. In 1773 and 1777, vessels of Cook's second and third voyages called at Adventure Bay in southern Tasmania for wood and water on their way to reaches of the Pacific beyond Tasman's hope. The permanent European settlement established at Port Jackson in 1788 had many contacts with ports of the old trading networks, such as Canton, Calcutta and Batavia, but its central purposes were different. These were to be achieved not only for Britain, but primarily by British settlers, whether voluntary or convict. The land was assumed to be without owners and a community to have been inaugurated only because these purposes were new.

CM

Captain James Cook (1728-79), painted by John Webber in 1776.

Cook's chart of the estuary of the Endeavour River in northern Queensland. Cook stopped here from June to August 1770 to carry out repairs to his ship, The Endeavour on his first exploratory voyage in the southern hemisphere.

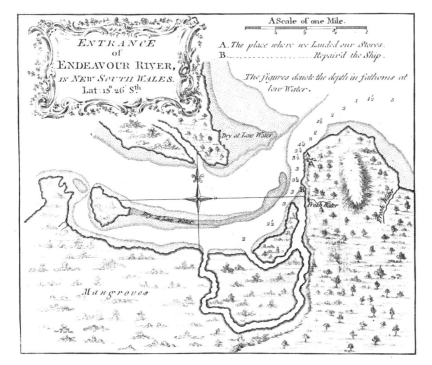

1770–1850

BACKGROUND TO SETTLEMENT

The first of Australia's white colonists landed at Sydney in January 1788, some 18 years after Captain Cook had claimed New South Wales in the name of the crown. The new arrivals were either convicts or their gaolers, but why they came is a matter of dispute. One historian believes that they were the labour force in what was designed as a naval base similar to the Cape of Good Hope and Mauritius. Importance has also been attached to the presence at Norfolk Island of flax and pine trees, both of which were valued by the navy. Botany Bay, it has been claimed, was intended as a plantation where flax plants brought from Norfolk Island could be grown and later made into canvas, sailcloth and rope cable. Another argument is that the sailing of the first fleet

Arthur Phillip (1738–1814), the first governor of New South Wales, portrayed by a later artist as he looked aged around 50.

was influenced by concern lest Britain's longstanding rival, France, establish an outpost which could threaten British interests in the Pacific and Indian Oceans.

Given that Arthur Phillip (naval officer and first governor) was neither instructed to obtain Norfolk Island pines, nor provided with experts needed for the flax industry, it may be doubted whether the desire for these commodities greatly influenced his superiors. The needs of the navy could still be met elsewhere and no concern was expressed when the pines proved useless for masts and flax difficult to produce. Strategic and commercial considerations were conceivably present but so too was concern at the state of Britain's overcrowded gaols. The traditional view that it was essential to find an outlet for convicts, now that the American colonies refused to accept them, still has much to support it. The government had tried to find alternative sites but without success. The gaols and the hulks were overcrowded and there was the danger of an outbreak of disease. New South Wales was believed capable of maintaining white people and it was far enough away to reduce the likelihood of convicts returning to Britain. However much the government may have been influenced by the need to provide a base for shipping or strike a blow at the French, its moves were strongly affected by the domestic embarrassment created by the convict problem.

NEW SOUTH WALES TO 1821

The colony that was established in New South Wales was largely convict in origin and it remained so throughout the early years. Between 1788 and 1821 some 27,658 of these people were landed at Sydney. Their presence necessitated the vesting of considerable powers in the hands of a governor who was responsible not to the colonists, but to his superiors in London.

The penal nature of the colony affected the judicial system which was noteworthy for the absence of trial by jury from either the civil or criminal courts. The fact that the colony was viewed largely as an outlet for convicts also explains the lack of provisions for a monetary system necessitating the use of barter and a variety of other *ad hoc* expedients. To a large extent what made survival itself possible was the willingness of the British government to finance the penal establishment by paying the salaries of troops and officials and purchasing food and clothes for the convicts.

During the years before 1821 only a small part of the vast territory known as New South Wales was occupied by colonists. The outbreak of war in Europe interfered with shipping and increased the demand for manpower at home. On average, less than a thousand convicts were transported each year until hostilities ceased in 1815. Thereafter the rate grew markedly, but by 1821 the colony still contained only about 30,000 people, most of whom lived on the Cumberland Plain between the Blue Mountains and the sea. Men and women under sentence predominated but already the population included numerous emancipists as well as a growing migrant and local-born element. Many of these people engaged in farming or grazing on grants of land that were made available by the government, free of any charge save for a quit rent. Their activities and especially those of the energetic civil officials and officers of the New South Wales Corps, which performed garrison duty between 1791 and 1809, laid the basis for a private enterprise economy. Others contributed to the same end by engaging in the fisheries, in trade and in manufacturing. A variety of industries existed by 1821 and wool was exported in small but increasing quantities.

The presence of private colonists in what was still viewed mainly as a gaol created problems for successive administrators. Arthur Phillip, the first and one of the most outstanding governors, was least affected by these problems because most of his subjects were still under sentence. He depended chiefly on government enterprise and it was to his credit that, despite poor human and physical resources, he had placed the settlement on a secure footing by his departure in December 1792. His successors, John Hunter, P.G. King and William Bligh, who each in turn governed between 1795 and 1808, were like Phillip, naval officers of ability, dedication and integrity. They were confronted, however, by the New South Wales Corps which had gained a hold while its commandants Major Grose and Colonel Paterson successively ruled during the Interregnum of 1792–95. The landed activities of the officers brought great benefit, but by trading, especially in liquor, by exploiting the lower sections of the community and resisting the attempts of the civil authorities to curb their illicit pursuits, they made the colony difficult to govern. Their machinations and especially those of the enterprising but aggressive and authoritarian John Macarthur, contributed to the recall of Hunter and King, and to the overthrow of the irascible, high-handed William Bligh in the Rum Rebellion of January 1808. Matters improved following the recall of the Corps and the arrival of Lachlan Macquarie with his own regiment in 1810. His long era, lasting until 1821, brought stability and economic expansion, but his autocratic ways aroused the resentment of the wealthy, free settlers.

Not least among the causes of friction under Macquarie was his handling of the penal system. None of the early governors was experienced in administering a gaol. The first four were trained at sea, while Macquarie like each of his successors had served in the army. The British government gave only limited guidance and left much to the initiative of the men on the spot. At first, most convicts were employed on public works projects but, as private enterprise expanded, so increasing numbers were assigned to landed settlers and other employers. The well-behaved received a gradation of rewards ranging from full pardons to conditional pardons and tickets of leave. Those who broke the law could be hung, but more commonly were sent to the penal settlement at Newcastle or flogged. Macquarie was criticised for undue leniency, for mixing socially with leading emancipists and for placing them in high positions. Underlying these actions was his belief that the completion of a sentence removed the criminal taint from convicts. Moreover, he considered that since these people were discouraged from returning to Britain, they were entitled to encouragement in New South Wales. Such enlightened opinions were too advanced for the times. Macquarie's policies generated opposition both in the colony and in London where he was unjustly accused of causing costs to increase.

CONVICTS AND SETTLERS 1821–40

The departure of Macquarie heralded a new era in the history of New South Wales. By 1821 little vacant land was available on the Cumberland Plain and settlement was already beginning to move outwards in every direction. This process continued over the next three decades as migrants and convicts poured into the colony in unprecedented numbers pushing the frontiers by 1850 to Port Phillip in the south, beyond Moreton Bay in the north and westward to the limits of good grazing land. The first wave of migrants contained men of capital who were attracted by the prospects of raising wool and the availability of convict labour. Land could also readily be obtained, at first as free grants and later, following the introduction of the Ripon Regulations in 1831, at public auction. Outside the settled districts vacant land was occupied by the squatters – a term initially used of

ex-convicts who often followed criminal pursuits. After 1836, when squatting was officially recognised, the word was applied to respectable graziers who by 1847 had won the right to lease the runs which they had acquired. Their presence contributed to the production of increasing quantities of wool, exports of which expanded at an unprecedented rate.

This expansion was accompanied by the arrival during the 1830s and 1840s of a large influx of migrants whose passages were paid from the land fund and who brought skills rather than capital. Many settled in Sydney stimulating the growth of a city that was already noted for its impressive appearance and range of activities. Originally the headquarters of a gaol it became a leading commercial centre by tapping the resources of the interior and the expanding trade of the Pacific. Its role as the colony's sole port and the centre of government added to its importance and wealth. By 1850 it had developed into a gracious Georgian city full of imposing buildings some of which had been designed in Macquarie's day by the emancipist architect, Francis Greenway (see p. 296). Other townships also took shape in the interior, adding to those such as Parramatta, Windsor and Liverpool which had been founded earlier. They provided services for surrounding parts and serve as a reminder that urban life was important from the earliest days.

One of Greenway's many buildings was the Hyde Park Barracks, constructed in 1819 to house convicts who worked in and around Sydney. Large numbers of these people were to be found in this locality much to the concern of Commissioner Bigge, who arrived in 1819 to conduct an inquiry into colonial affairs. The decision to send him formed part of an attempt by the far-seeing Secretary of State, Earl Bathurst, to obtain information about the various parts of the Empire, so that better policies could be formulated now that peace had returned. In Britain, crime was increasing and there were fears that the threat of transportation had lost its deterrent effect because life for convicts in New South Wales was too easy. Bigge was instructed to inquire into this, to recommend whether or not the colony should continue as a penal settlement and to suggest means by which it could be run more cheaply and effectively. Historians are disagreed as to whether the commissioner was an objective observer, or whether he was unduly influenced by the opinion of his superiors and the friendship he formed with leading free colonists such as John Macarthur. Whatever the case, he conducted his investigations thoroughly and his conclusions, if biased and often unfavourable to Macquarie, were solidly grounded. He recognised that the future lay with wool and recommended the introduction of land policies aimed at encouraging free settlers with capital. He also urged that, in the interests of tighter dis-

Hyde Park Barracks, Sydney, a fine Georgian building designed by Francis Greenway and completed in 1819 to accommodate convicts.

Prisoners at work on Norfolk Island, 1680 km east-north-east of Sydney, c. 1847. One of the severest penal colonies, from 1840 to 1843 it was administered by Captain Alexander Maconochie, who introduced a more enlightened system that sought to rehabilitate rather than merely punish the prisoners. After his recall, harsh discipline was reintroduced.

cipline and as a means of promoting pastoralism, convicts be removed from Sydney and assigned to settlers in the often harsh, isolated conditions of the interior.

Between 1821 and 1840 the convict system was run along lines recommended by Bigge as a means of heightening its deterrent and punitive effect. The privilege of receiving land grants on completion of a sentence was first modified and then removed. Convicts were not permitted to bring property with them and tighter regulations were introduced to control the issuing of tickets of leave and pardons. Discipline was more vigorously enforced and convicts considered unsuitable for private employ were committed to the road gangs where many worked in chains. Those guilty of serious offences against the law were sent to one of the penal settlements, initially at Port Macquarie, then at Moreton Bay and later at Norfolk Island, which became a place of terror. The women were sent to the Female Factory at Parramatta, which operated both as a staging post for those awaiting assignment and an institution for the punishment of offenders. Precisely how the penal system operated at any given stage depended in part upon the individual governor. Sir Thomas Brisbane, who succeeded Macquarie, was a reasonable man whom some accused of devoting undue time to astronomy. Governor Darling gained a reputation for brutality between 1825 and 1831, not least for committing to a road gang two convicted soldiers, Sudds and Thompson, the first of whom died after being placed in chains at a special parade. Richard Bourke, who governed from 1831 to 1838, is normally depicted as a gracious, humane man of liberal beliefs. The labels attached to these two governors, however, are open to question. While Darling was not to blame for Sudds' death and did display a genuine concern for the well-being of the convicts, Bourke, it has been said, was less enlightened and more severe than is sometimes acknowledged.

The convict system operated in New South Wales to the satisfaction of the pastoralists who benefited from the continuous supply of servile labour. In Britain, however, the idea of banishment, which had long been questioned by penal reformers, met increasing opposition for differing reasons during the 1820s and 1830s from Benthamites, evangelicals, humanitarians and Wakefieldians (proponents of the theory of systematic colonisation based on the ideas of the theorist Edward Gibbon Wakefield). The government, too, came to doubt the wisdom of sending convicts now that the colony contained so many free people.

By 1838 it had decided that the present policy should no longer continue. A parliamentary committee, composed mainly of opponents of the system, was appointed to report on the matter. Chaired by and named after the youthful Wakefieldian, William Molesworth, the committee after questioning a range of informed but mostly biased witnesses, recommended the abolition of transportation to New South Wales. In 1840 the government acted accordingly thus ending an era that had brought to the colony over 130,000 forced exiles, male and female.

Once romanticised as being the victims of social and legal injustice, the convicts have come to be viewed mainly as ne'er-do-wells of criminal inclination although this has recently been disputed. Whatever their background they contributed to economic development and many, after completing their sentences, became useful and, in some cases, prosperous members of society. This was even more true of their children, the 'currency' lads and lasses, who earned a reputation for being physically and morally superior to their parents. New South Wales may have been a convict colony in which drunkenness was commonplace. Theft was also rampant, both in the towns and in the bush where gangs of so-called bushrangers preyed on the settlers. Yet, recent studies have indicated that the threat to person and property was considerably less than might have been expected. The existence of opportunities to make a decent living without resort to crime, the presence of growing numbers of free settlers and the existence of a police force helped maintain social order.

VAN DIEMEN'S LAND

Although convict transportation to New South Wales ceased in 1840 it continued to Van Diemen's Land, which had been settled in 1803 following rumours of a French occupation. Developments had paralleled those on the mainland, to the extent that the island attracted free settlers besides serving as an outlet for convicts. Pastoralism, sealing and bay whaling developed and Hobart took shape as a centre for trade and government. The resources of the island, however, were more limited than those of New South Wales and allowed for fewer private settlers. The penal establishment in contrast played a more prominent role and the government resolved in 1838 to continue using it as a convict outlet.

Although the early administrators of the colony included men like Thomas Davey, who were of dubious calibre, their quality improved. Colonel George Arthur, lieutenant governor from 1824 to 1836, was a Tory of great ability who won high praise for the firm but enlightened way in which he handled the convicts. His successor, the humane, liberal-minded, Arctic explorer Sir John Franklin, was also an impressive figure. Not so the ineffective Sir John Eardley-Wilmot who was required during the 1830s to replace assignment by the complicated probation system, the effectiveness of which was reduced by mishandling and economic depression. Its shortcomings reinforced growing opposition to transportation among sections of the free settlers led by John West the Congregational minister and later editor of the *Sydney Morning Herald*. The movement had urban supporters on the mainland who became alarmed when during the 1840s, with the support of pastoralists, the British government attempted to revive transportation by sending selected convicts accompanied by migrants. Mainlanders joined forces with Vandiemenians in an effort to abolish the system. It was only in 1853, after gold had been discovered in eastern Australia and a new government had come to power in Britain, that colonial demands were finally accepted.

WESTERN AND SOUTH AUSTRALIA

Meantime other colonies had been founded on the mainland. Western Australia had been established in 1829 on the initiative of a group of speculators led by Thomas Peel, the son of a wealthy cotton manufacturer. Their scheme for bringing out migrants in return for land, however, was badly conceived and ill-executed. The colony quickly acquired a poor reputation particularly after Edward Gibbon Wakefield used it in his writings as an example of how colonisation should not proceed. The best land fell into the hands of the early arrivals, forcing others into disadvantageous localities. Labour was scarce, agriculture and pastoralism made slow progress and the popula-

View of Port Arthur, Tasmania, in 1860. Port Arthur was a prison-town, intended to provide severe punishment. The convicts there made a variety of goods, built ships and sawed large amounts of timber, and also had to work in the nearby coal mines. At one time it housed 1,200 convicts with a free population of 1,000, many of whom were soldiers.

Warehouses in Salamanca Place, Hobart, built between 1835 and 1860 at a time when Hobart was growing as a trading centre. Hobart had become the capital of Van Diemen's Land, as Tasmania was then called, when the colony was separated from New South Wales in 1825.

tion remained static. Not until after 1850 did matters improve following the decision of the British government to send convicts at the request of some, but not all, sections of the community.

Somewhat greater success followed the settlement of South Australia in 1834. Speculative impulse blended with idealistic motives gave the new colony a unique flavour. The Wakefieldians, who were among its advocates, welcomed the opportunity to implement their ideas on colonisation. Among the migrants who came to the region were men and women anxious to found a colony based on religious and political freedom. These hopes were eventually realised, but not before the colony had experienced setbacks. Authority was divided between Governor Hindmarsh, appointed by the Colonial Office, and Commissioner Fisher who was responsible to a group of commissioners nominated by the South Australian Association. Conflict, exacerbated by clashes of personality, ensued and lasted until October 1838 when a new administrative structure was established and the colony was brought under one man, Governor George Gawler. His policy of promoting economic development by increased expenditure on public works achieved much, as did the steps he took to overcome the backlog in surveying which had previously prevented settlers obtaining farmland. His

spending, however, was too lavish and it was only after his replacement in May 1841 by George Grey and the discovery of deposits of silver, lead and copper that the economy was placed on a secure footing.

VICTORIA

By the middle of the nineteenth century, therefore, four of the Australian colonies were established. Agitation was already under way from the residents of Port Phillip for separation from New South Wales. This region had been settled in the mid-1830s by overlanders from further north and by pastoralists who crossed Bass Strait from Van Diemen's Land. A thriving economy based mostly on the production of meat and wool developed and Melbourne was established as a commercial, social and administrative centre. As settlement expanded so the colonists asserted their own interests which they considered were often overlooked by the government in Sydney. The provision of an administrator, Joseph La Trobe, and representation after 1842 in the New South Wales legislature failed to alleviate discontent. Their claims were eventually heeded by the British government and in 1851 Victoria was established as a separate colony.

NEW SOUTH WALES TO 1850

William Charles Wentworth (1790-1872). From the 1820s to the 1850s he campaigned for self-government for New South Wales. In the political divisions of the time he took the side of the graziers and landowners against urban interests, seeing the future of Australia as lying in its farming.

Separation was only one of a number of political issues that emerged on the Australian continent. In New South Wales the presence of increasing numbers of free and freed colonists had by the 1820s produced vigorous political debate. A group commonly, but in view of its composition, misleadingly labelled emancipist emerged early in the decade. It was dominated not by former convicts but by the local-born William Charles Wentworth, and free migrants such as Sir John Jamison of Regentville who collectively have become known as the Botany Bay Whigs. They drew inspiration from their English counterparts and pressed for representative government and trial by jury using public meetings and the newly formed *Australian* and *Monitor* newspapers to promote their views.

They were opposed by the exclusive faction which was Tory in outlook, composed of wealthy free settlers and led by John Macarthur. Already influential because of their wealth, prestige and friendship with leading figures in London, the exclusives resisted change, arguing that the existing constitution was well suited to a convict colony. Discipline and order were essential and, given the social composition of the population, it was scarcely to be expected that either trial by jury or representative institutions were feasible.

The opinions of the exclusives were supported by the British government which, however, did reform the constitution to meet changing needs. A Legislative Council of between five and seven members, four of whom were officials, was established in 1823. Two years later an Executive Council composed entirely of government officials was created and in 1828 the size of the Legislative Council was increased to 15. All this fell far short of what the emancipists demanded. The Councils were nominated, not elected, and the governor, although expected to heed their advice, could disregard it. Agitation for reform thus continued throughout the 1820s and the 1830s but it was not until 1842, two years after convict transportation ceased, that a representative legislature of 36 members, 24 of whom were elected, was established. Meantime, in response to continued pressure, trial by jury had also been introduced, initially in the civil and later in the criminal court. The process had been gradual, starting in 1823 and being completed by the mid-1830s.

Representative institutions were introduced at a time when new political alignments had emerged. The arrival of increasing numbers of respectable free people reduced the exclusives' opposition to constitutional reform and brought them more into line with the emancipists. This change was helped by the death in 1834 of the intransigent John Macarthur and by

Art and literature pre-1850

Amongst those who came to the colonies before 1850 were people of artistic and literary bent who added a creative dimension to cultural life. Numerous books appeared, beginning with those by the first fleet officers such as Watkin Tench and David Collins. These works and the later publications of visitors and residents contained much information of historical importance and laid the basis for Australian historiography.

There were also works of fiction such as Henry Savery's *Quintus Servinton*, the first novel to be published in Australia (in 1831). Successive waves of new arrivals brought artists including the forgers, Thomas Watling, Joseph Lycett and Thomas Wainewright, followed by free men like Thomas Gill and Conrad Martens.

A succession of versifiers starting with the convict Michael Massey Robinson laid the foundations for Australian poetry, which reached its highest point before 1850 in the publications of the local-born Charles Harpur (see also p. 311).

Literature and art were generally derivative and strongly influenced by European traditions, but their emergence is in itself a comment on the increasing complexity and sophistication of colonial society. Although the ethos was strongly materialist it was by no means exclusively so.

BHF

the fact that both groups were drawn mainly from the graziers and had major economic interests in common. Under the leadership of Wentworth they combined during the 1840s to struggle for a system of government that would make the executive more dependent on the legislature and increase the powers of the legislature over matters of local concern, including land.

The demand for self-government won widespread support during the 1840s but opinion was also divided on political matters. Landed groups dominated the legislature and increasingly they were opposed by urban elements drawn from the new class of migrant whose passages were paid partly out of the land fund after 1831. Together with the merchants and business interests of Sydney they sought a greater voice in political affairs and a more liberal constitution. Their resentment reached a peak when the landed gentry accepted the offer of the British government during the 1840s to renew convict transportation. They were also concerned at the actions of the government in giving way in 1847 to the squatters' demands for greater control over the lands which they had long occupied in the interior.

Religion pre-1850

A piece of old England – the Anglican church of St Leonard's, Southport in southern Tasmania, drawn c. 1850.

All branches of the Christian Church were represented in Australia. Although not established, the Church of England occupied a privileged position in New South Wales until the 1830s when Governor Bourke began treating each of the major denominations equally. It attracted the largest following, over-shadowing the Methodists and Presbyterians, but there was a strong Roman Catholic presence resulting from the high proportion of Irish in the population. Catholic priests were originally excluded on doctrinal grounds and because they were seen as potential troublemakers. Once admitted on a regular basis late in the Macquarie period, however, their influence spread and one of their number, the Benedictine, John Bede Polding received the title bishop even before the Anglican church had placed W. G. Broughton in charge of a see.

The relative position of the different denominations varied from one colony to the next depending in part on the social composition of the population. South Australia, for example, which had been settled by migrants anxious to escape from the hold of the Church of England in Britain, contained a high proportion of what in the mother country were known as nonconformists. In Western Australia clergy were not included among the first colonists and the foundation of the church had to await the arrival of Archdeacon Scott, shipwrecked en route from New South Wales to England. Nevertheless, despite strong secular currents, there as elsewhere religion did play an important part in shaping attitudes.

BHF

Education pre-1850

The first university, that of Sydney, was not established until 1850 but by that stage there existed in each of the colonies a multiplicity of secondary schools, some non-denominational, others church-controlled. They catered, however, for only a small minority of children. More widespread were the elementary schools which in New South Wales were initially run mainly by the Church of England.

During the 1820s a Church and Schools Corporation was established, vested with land and empowered to establish a system of elementary instruction. The policy was not a success and was abandoned under Governor Bourke who endeavoured to introduce a government system based on his experiences in Ireland. Provision was made for all denominations to receive religious instruction, but neither Bourke nor his successors were able to satisfy all groups. Ultimately in 1847 a dual system of state and church schools each under a separate board proved the only way out of a problem arising from strong sectarian feelings.

Similar difficulties arose in other colonies where there was the same trend, varying in points of detail, towards a greater measure of state intervention as a means of providing wider facilities. In the Australian colonies governments were obliged to involve themselves in areas that in Britain remained largely in private hands. Problems arising from distance, the dispersed nature of settlement and limited capital resources were such that little could have been accomplished in fields such as education, health, transport and communications without government help.

BHF

THE AUSTRALIAN COLONIES GOVERNMENT ACT

In no other British colony were divisions so acute or pressures for reform so strong. Nevertheless there was a widespread demand for concessions of the kind introduced in New South Wales in 1842. Similar requests had also been made in other parts of the British Empire and in 1850, as part of an overall policy of reform, the Colonial Office in London introduced the Australian Colonies Government Act. This established representative government in each of the colonies except Van Diemen's Land, which was still receiving convicts, and Western Australia, which had asked for them. It also widened the franchise in New South Wales, redistributed seats to give slightly more say to the towns and separated Victoria from the mother colony. Finally, arising out of Secretary of State Earl Grey's desire to impose a federal structure, partly as a means of preventing intercolonial trade rivalries and customs barriers, provision was made for the New South Wales governor to become governor-general.

Colonial society

By 1851 there had emerged in Australia five colonies whose political institutions were roughly similar and whose histories although different had important points in common. All possessed economies in which primary industry played a major role. All had been founded by Britain and enjoyed the benefits of British law and a system of government that was moving increasingly in the direction of that originating in Westminster.

The bulk of the population, if not born in Britain, were the children of men and women who had come from there. The mixture as between Irish and English varied from one colony to the next, but the overall picture was broadly similar. Whether classes existed in any meaningful sense is open to debate. Certainly there was no aristocracy and nothing to resemble the social structure based partly on birth that existed overseas. It is true that there were gradations of wealth and that the gentry saw themselves as a distinct group whose possession of large estates conferred on them the badge of respectability and a right to rule. Yet there had been no time for rigid divisions to develop. There was a high degree of mobility and considerable opportunities for advancement. Those possessed of entrepreneurial skills and a capacity for hard work rose quickly to a level higher than they could have attained in Britain.

Overall, however, most sections of white society enjoyed a standard of living better than that which prevailed in the country they left behind. Outside Western Australia there was continuous expansion broken only by occasional setbacks such as the depression of the early 1840s in eastern Australia. The demand for labour was strong, employment prospects were good and wages were adequate. Added to all this were the benefits of a climate free from the damp and cold of the northern hemisphere. Men were the most advantaged but the contribution which women made to colonial development was significant. Individuals such as Elizabeth Macarthur, Eliza Darling, Mary Reibey and Caroline Chisholm are among a large group who stand out for their role in advancing the pastoral industry, philanthropy, commerce and the care of migrants. But there were many others active in numerous walks of life.

Life in the colonies, therefore, had considerable attractions for the white settlers. The better-off built attractive residences that were staffed by servants and well-furnished, often with costly imported articles. Dinner parties, picnics, musical entertainments and attendance at race meetings formed a regular part of leisure activities. For those living in the larger capital cities there was the opportunity to attend the occasional play or concert, to visit the museum or to join scientific or philosophical clubs. For the select few there were invitations to Government House, particularly at gala occasions such as the monarch's birthday. At a more popular level there was a variety of pastimes. Sporting activities included cricket, boxing and horse racing, but many spent their free hours drinking and gambling at home or in one of the many public houses for which Sydney in particular was noted.

BHF

1850–1900

The colonists

By the end of the 1850s there were six Australian colonies. Detached from New South Wales were Victoria (1851) and Queensland (1859), their names declaring continuing loyalty to Britain even as they separated from each other. By 1900 colonial reunion was under way. All the colonies, including South Australia (with the Northern Territory), the island colony of Tasmania (Van Diemen's Land to 1855) and hesitant Western Australia voted to federate in 1901 as the Commonwealth of Australia, still firmly within the British empire.

In 1850 much of Australia was recovering from drought and economic depression, but it was on the verge of gold strikes that would vastly increase its wealth and population, especially in Victoria. In 1900, after boom conditions (c. 1860–90) and big finds of gold in the west, the colonists were again faced with drought and depression, both of particular severity.

The colonists appear to have both embraced and rejected their past. Most leading citizens were migrants, mainly British. Many people at all levels remained proudly British, although often disliking aspects of the system they had left. Irish and German settlers had their peculiar difficulties with loyalty to Britain, but any doubts about the English only promoted Australianism, which was where some break with the past appeared. Nevertheless, throughout the century Westminster was the parliament of a 'united' kingdom that included Ireland, and the Australian colonies. were dependent on Britain for

'Aborigines Fighting on the Streets of Sydney', lithograph by John Carmichael, c. 1839. Most European settlers saw Aborigines as an inferior people, a view fuelled by the drastic effects of alcohol.

defence, diplomacy, developmental capital, much of their trade and most of their immigrants, and tied to it by kin, culture and constitutional bonds. They tried to demonstrate their loyalty and worth from time to time: New South Wales sent a small contingent to help in the Sudan in 1885, and all colonies raised forces for the South African war from 1899. Some colonists questioned the appropriateness – or the cost, or even the morality – of these ventures, and few were deeply committed to them, but basic support for the empire was general.

Within Australia conflicting conceptions (seldom mutually understood) of the land, its occupation and use, and of justice and morality, were fundamental to the clash between Europeans and Aborigines. The Europeans recognised some Aboriginal skills, and learnt or used them. In places, at times, they feared the Aborigines, but mostly they saw them as inferior. When Aboriginal numbers quickly declined due to introduced disease and alcohol, the disruption of their lives and sometimes deliberate massacre, it seemed to most newcomers that the Aborigines were giving way to a superior people who could exploit Australia to greater advantage, build up a civilised nation, make a good life for themselves, and help feed and clothe the millions in Europe. Essentially it was seen as a natural process (and, in fact, one invader or another would have come in the nineteenth century). The only hope the Aborigines had was to adapt as best they could to the new world that had burst into their old. When Aborigines, particularly those of mixed blood, were found to be coping and becoming more numerous, official policy was directed at forcibly dispersing them among the Europeans.

It was much the same with the Chinese who began to flood into the goldfields. That they looked different did nothing to help, nor – ironically – did the claim that they brought in disease, but the prime objection was that a European culture, increasingly democratic, was likely to be swamped by an Asian

one, mostly represented by coolies. The free British-Europeans had not come to Australia for that. Some indeed had come only for a temporary visit to make them rich, but most remained as permanent immigrants who were not at all rich. At least they could try to live as well as possible in their kind of society, with luck an improvement on the one they had left, but recognisably Euro-British. The result was a series of actions against the Chinese: abuse and some physical attacks, but more usually legislation aimed at excluding non-white immigrants. The culmination came when the first federal parliament banned Pacific Islanders from Queensland sugarcane fields and restricted all immigration so as to guarantee a 'White Australia' (the Aborigines being ignored). To these Australians a common culture, based on racial homogeneity, was the ideal.

Their own identities and allegiances were mixed enough in themselves. When Australian troops went to war in South Africa they showed both British loyalty and sufficient Australianness to differentiate them from Britons. Even among those for whom the empire bond was strongest, perhaps in the Imperial Federation League, which came to Australia in 1885 and was skewed towards the upper class, there was a will to advance Australia by developing its role within the councils of empire. Some leading Australians, like Alfred Deakin, could reconcile membership of the League with belonging to the Australian Natives Association. That larger body, mainly middle class and most influential in Victoria, was formed in 1871–72, restricted to white males born in Australia, and directed at promoting a national spirit and a strong Australian federation. Yet a hint of anti-monarchical feeling among a few of its early members was soon lost in solid ANA support for the empire. Like most Australians they were both nationalists and empire loyalists. To be themselves they sometimes had to be assertive against Britain, but for survival in a dangerous world they relied on British protection. Duality made sense.

FEDERATION

Colonial regionalism went against a unitary state, but combination was desirable for defence, a common voice and united action on mutual problems, business operations in an increasingly national economy, the initiation of intercolonial tariffs, and the fostering of nascent nationalism. Many voters did not bother to turn out for the referendums on federation, and the so-called majority who voted for it were actually outnumbered by those voting against or not voting at all.

Federation was an innovation with some conservative motives (British links; white Australia), and its

had, but the land was not reserved for the squatters. More and closer settlement by a different class of person occurred and, where appropriate, agriculture emerged beside the pastoral industry.

Poor selectors are alleged to have turned readily to stealing stock; on the other hand, the increasing use of wire fences is said to have made it harder for bushrangers to move freely across country. A more important form of contempt for the law was revealed in the evasions of the land Acts by squatters or speculators and their 'dummies' – men paid to take up temporary selections in order to keep out genuine settlers. Yet if there were few qualms of conscience about such roguery, there were equally few cases of dummies welshing on these legally unenforceable arrangements. Colonial morality may have been selective, but it could be stern.

Productivity on the land was advanced by such local innovations as reaping machines (from a prototype developed in the 1840s), the stump-jump plough (South Australia, 1876), Australian breeds of sheep and cattle dogs, the shearing technique of 'the long blow', shearing machines (in increasing use from the late 1880s), and William Farrer's improved varieties of wheat. Subterranean clover and superphosphate were being tested on a small scale, and it was precisely in that area that most needed to be done.

Soil management was generally inefficient. There were too many poor farmers in both senses: undercapitalised and underskilled. In 20 years (1862–82) the area planted to wheat doubled and doubled again, but the yield per acre fell as the soil became exhausted. More square paddocks were ruthlessly cleared in disregard of nature's curves, hollows and protective cover – a ravaging that can still be seen

Map of Australia of 1893. Despite the opening-up of the land to small-scale settlers since 1860 parts of the north and west of the country had still not been charted.

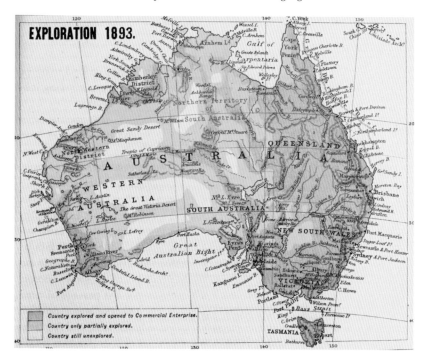

from vantage points in semi-flood conditions. Wide areas were eroded, streams were fouled, and most land quickly deteriorated. Besides sheep, cattle and horses, the settlers introduced much else for practical, sporting or sentimental reasons, or by accident: rabbits, foxes, sparrows, water buffalo, prickly pear, burrs, and so on. The list could be a long one of introduced species that, breeding fast, became terrorists in the land, further endangering it and its unique wildlife. One legacy the nineteenth century bequeathed to the twentieth was the need to repair severe environmental damage.

The drought of 1895–1902 was the worst that white Australia has ever known. It came on top of the economic depression of 1891–94, with its bank crashes, nearly 27 per cent of factory workers unemployed, and – except in Western Australia – a slow recovery. After 20 or 30 years of fast and generally sustained economic growth (despite various slowdowns in some regions and industries), the twin disasters must have left many colonists wondering if their land and commerce were disintegrating. Yet their answers were the usual ones: emigrate (to the golden west or overseas) or, more often, just battle on.

CITY LIFE

By 1871 a quarter of the population lived in the six capital cities (Sydney, Hobart, Perth, Melbourne, Adelaide and Brisbane), and by the time of federation this figure had become a third. Another third lived in towns of some sort; but Australians were not thoroughly urbanised. Many towns were small, most suburban houses were detached, and there was often open country between suburbs. In or near every city were hills, creeks and rivers (even if polluted), bays and beaches, gardens, parklands and sports ovals.

Public transport ran out to the city fringes, and there was the glorious climate. Even urban Australians were not characteristically locked into cramped tenements and industrially fouled air, although every city had some areas of that type. Indeed, man-made filth produced serious epidemics of diseases such as typhoid. Sewerage came early to Adelaide (from 1878), then to Sydney (from 1880), and late to Melbourne: not until the 1890s was a system started there. Even so, space and the open air were the familiar friends of most Australians, and must be considered along with the high 'urbanisation' ratio, the slums and the epidemics.

Australian cities were too new to be classed as historical. Nor were they nineteenth-century manufacturing cities growing up around light industry. They were established as centres from which new lands could be opened up. They were industrialised later, yet were always comparatively large. Little labour was

Bourke Street, Melbourne *by Tom Roberts, c. 1886. The artist's first title for the painting,* Allegro con Brio, *expresses the energy and vigour that could be found in the new cities. The population of Melbourne had nearly reached half a million by the end of the nineteenth century.*

Below right Advertisement for a shipping line based in London, late nineteenth century. The journey time from London to Melbourne was reduced by steam power to six weeks and, with regular sailings, a speedy and reliable postal service was established.

required in the hinterlands they existed to serve, but they needed plenty of labour to service themselves, centrally administer the colonies, and trade staple products. The conveniences and, quite literally, the bright lights were attractive too. These included gas for lighting and cooking, commonplace throughout the period, and the electricity beginning to be used for street lighting, and some commercial purposes.

Sydney and Melbourne each held nearly half a million people at the end of the century. Overall, white Australians increased from 0.4 million to almost 4 million between 1850 and 1900, most of them having been born in the colonies. But the rate of growth slowed. Both immigration and birth rates fell after 1860 – the latter from 42 per thousand to under 28 in the late 1890s. Although Australian living standards remained higher than those of Britain and Europe, they were already dropping below those of the USA before the depressed 1890s reduced them further.

Communications

By the 1890s the world outside had become more accessible to Australia. Under sail, gold-rush immigrants might take 12 weeks to reach Melbourne, but 40 years on mail and travellers to Britain could arrive in about half the time via steamships, the Suez Canal and fast European trains. From the 1880s refrigerated shipping enabled Australian meat, butter and fruit to be exported to Europe.

In 1872 Australia was linked to the world by telegraph, just as many of its own centres had been joined for some years – a development that had helped promote a national economy. (The telephone was in operation by the 1880s, but trunk lines were not opened between capitals until the twentieth century.)

Like the mail, telephone and telegraph services, the railways – after a few early private ventures – were run by the governments, and they expanded from about 20 miles of track in 1855 to nearly 12,000 miles in 1900. The consequences

were enormous: intercolonial travel and trade were less dependent on sea voyages (still risky, though less so than formerly), the coal industry profited, and farming became viable in areas previously too far from markets. Sydney and Melbourne were joined by rail in 1883, although freight and passengers had to change trains at the border because the two colonies had different gauges of track.

From the 1880s trams (horse-drawn, steam or cable) served the cities and their spreading suburbs (although people were still great walkers). The safety bicycle produced a cycling craze by the 1890s and, more than that, the 'bike' was a cheap, convenient means of transport for ordinary people, enlarging the possibilities of pleasure and work for men, women and children, and soon adopted by itinerant workers in the bush.

JB

99

FAMILY LIFE

During the second half of the nineteenth century an increasing number of women were trying to raise the standard of living in their households, and protect their own health, by using contraception: hence the average mother was having perhaps five children at the end of the century compared with an average of seven or more at its mid-point. Those from the urban middle classes led the way in limiting family size, but workers were beginning to catch on. Country women – though tending, like working-class women, to marry young – were slow to adopt contraception. So were the single. Despite Victorian prudery, in places like the goldfields town of Bendigo more than 40 per cent of first births were either illegitimate or too soon after marriage to be 'proper'.

There is mixed evidence about who was marrying

Art and sport 1850–1900

The art galleries and libraries the churchmen did not want open on Sundays were, by 1900, including works produced by Australians. Poetry, verse, short stories and other writing by C. J. Brennan, Henry Lawson, Louisa Lawson, A. B. Paterson, Ada Cambridge and many others were available in book form and in the popular weekly papers. There was complaint too: scholarly Australian books were not sufficiently appreciated, and Sydney scoffed at any book published in Melbourne, and vice versa.

Painters (most notably the so-called Impressionist school of Tom Roberts and his friends) captured Australia's light and promoted aspects of its social ethos, and their work began to be seen in galleries and on exhibition abroad.

Sport, however, had a greater appeal, at least among men. Aborigines were often good at it, and they originated surfing: at Manly in about 1889 the black Tommy Tanna taught whites how to 'catch waves'.

Earlier, and far from the sea, a prosperous white family moved overland from Victoria to Queensland, where their camp was overrun by Aborigines and all 19 Europeans – men, women and children – killed. A broken dray had delayed son Tom, and so one of Australia's top cricketers was saved. A few years later, in 1866, Tom Wills, in a spirit that commands respect, coached and captained an Aboriginal team to play the Melbourne Cricket Club before 10,000 spectators.

In 1900 twice that number watched the grand final of the Victorian Football League, playing the unique Australian Rules game that largely replaced other football in the southern and western colonies. The game had developed from a rudimentary form organised by Tom Wills and H. C. A. Harrison in 1858 to keep Victorian men fit in winter. Alleged to be an adaptation of Gaelic football, it was more likely just a local product. First coded in 1866, it was known until the 1880s as Victorian Rules. It came to be played with an oval ball on an oval field at least twice as large as a Rugby field (Australia had space). Each side – settled finally at 18 men – spread over the whole field, eliminating offside. Scoring was by kicking through upright posts with no cross-bar. It became a fast, rough game, with no scrums but heavy body-contact between players wearing no protective gear, and became characterised by long kicks and high leaps to catch ('mark') the ball, which could not be 'run with' in the normal sense, but had to be kicked, hand-passed by punching, or bounced on the ground every few paces.

Total attendances had been even greater (38,000) for the first test match in 1877, when an Australian cricket eleven beat the English tourists. Confidence was reinforced by the 'ashes' test of 1882 when Australians were victors on English soil. They felt worthy of their sires, and even superior to them.

In the closely settled districts sports of various kinds became one dominant feature of every locality, a focus for community identity, and even a modifier of class and creed – and of colour, sometimes, although whites were uncomfortable about being beaten by blacks. Sport also exacerbated rivalries within local regions and between the Australian Rules colonies and those (New South Wales and Queensland) that settled for Rugby Union. Indeed, an existing rivalry was one of the main factors why Australian Rules was not widely taken up in New South Wales: the Sydneysiders wanted nothing to do with that Melbourne game. Another division was between the wowsers (puritans) and the many gamblers who, collectively and sometimes individually, wagered huge sums on sport.

The most famous horse race in Australia, the Melbourne Cup, was drawing 100,000 people in the 1880s.

JB

The new grandstand, Melbourne cricket ground, from the Australasian Sketcher, *20 January 1877. The new grandstand of brick and stone, with its roof of corrugated iron, was erected by the Melbourne Cricket Club. The upper part seated spectators, the underneath area was intended for a skating rink, refreshment bars and dressing rooms.*

whom. A tendency to marry within one's ethnic group resulted in strongly Irish, or German, or Cornish connections and regions, but overall there was so much marrying out of the group that the trend was towards developing a common Anglo-Australian ethos. Family life was held up as the ideal for all – women and men – and Australian home-ownership was high by world standards and by no means confined to the middle classes. It was an ambition often advanced by membership of a building society. The house might incorporate that Australian invention, the cavity wall (double brick, with space between), and there was usually a garden to provide food and a respectable image, but there remained much drudgery and heavy work for women. It was the era before household appliances lightened their load, and one in which they adhered to the conventions of scrubbing, mangling and starching.

The poorer the family, urban or rural, the more its women and children took any available work that helped survival. It could bind a family together or rack it with tensions – but there were often escape routes from the latter. Country boys might get away and earn good money shearing, and in the cities an increasing range of work was opening up for women (including spinsters) and the young. Sons did not necessarily work under their fathers; place and type of work were frequently switched; and some unskilled jobs – on the new trams, for instance – paid well. Youths might not learn a trade, but they still became handy and independent.

WOMEN

Even in a patriarchal society the position of women in the home was often very high, but their place in public life was normally low. Nevertheless, it was beginning to change. Individuals and small groups were active in the arts, the labour movement, the demand for women's legal and electoral rights, and in promoting the women's cause generally. A few privileged women were entering the professions, and many more women (much less privileged) were being organised from the mid-1880s in the Woman's Christian Temperance Union, with its hundreds of branches throughout the colonies. Its aim was to curb the demon drink for the sake of women, homes and children, but one of its most significant effects was to accustom ordinary women to passing resolutions on public questions and forming deputations to call on ministers of state. Louisa Lawson called her feminist paper the *Dawn,* and the long day of the advancement of women was indeed dawning.

Widows, deserted wives, the sick, aged and unemployed had nothing in the way of pensions. Private and state institutions cared for some of the needy, inside or outside their walls, and government works were sometimes expanded to help the unemployed, but most welfare was ensured by private arrangements. Care by the extended family was common, and so was reliance on friendly societies whose lodges spread throughout the colonies, allowed benefit entitlements to be transferred from place to place, and – unlike the parent bodies in Britain – drew their members from the poorer classes as well as the better off. Half of the adult male workforce in many localities were members of one lodge or another. Even members of the Amalgamated Miners' Association often regarded it 'as a purely accident relief society rather than as a union', leaving funds low for industrial action. When no support was present, the plight of the needy was pitiable indeed.

JB

Sweated female labour, from the Illustrated Australian News, *1890. The Factory and Shops Act forced factories to close at 7 p.m., but employers of women in the garment and other industries gave their workers more work than they could do during the official working day. They were forced to take work home and do several hours of unpaid overtime each evening.*

Education 1850–1900

School classes tended to be large and the regime severe, yet much was gained from an increased schooling. State primary school systems became solidly established: 'free, compulsory and secular' in theory, though none of those things absolutely.

Secondary education remained beyond the hopes of most people unless, as workers, they could gain it at one of the mechanics' institutes or schools of mines. Less ambitious institutes did valuable work in small towns, which is why many places for many years had an 'institute' hall and library. For the highly privileged, including young women, there were the small universities of Sydney (1850), Melbourne

(1853), Adelaide (1874) and Tasmania (1890), although Oxford, Cambridge or some other overseas university was often preferred.

Education thus reflected society's divisions. Social class determined much of it. With the ending of state aid to church schools (mainly between 1872 and 1885, but 1895 in Western Australia), Protestant schools became scarcer and more exclusive.

Ethnic background also influenced schooling: Aborigines were often unwelcome in white schools; Catholics, supporting their schools by their clergy's 'persuasion and compulsion', were

overwhelmingly Irish; and Germans used their own language in their schools.

So emerged the religious divisions. Lutheranism was as important as anything else to the Germans. Catholics and, for example, Methodists (mostly English, and not infrequently Cornish) also developed their own sub-cultures within the common culture. They valued their group fellowship, and joined with or stood apart from the community according to their historical or moral positions. For example, Methodists could readily join in expressions of loyalty to the crown; Catholics not so easily.

JB

Religion 1850–1900

The churches, as well as their schools, lost state aid in this era. (The extremes were 1851 in South Australia and 1895 in Western Australia but aid ended in the other colonies between 1860 and 1870.) That did not worry most churchmen: state aid caused problems, and could be done without. The spate of church-building in the 1880s was proof of this. Through voluntary donations, more, and more impressive, church buildings appeared in city and country than ever before, and they were well attended – especially by the middle classes.

What did worry churchmen was a secularist spirit that seemed likely to challenge Christian values. The state, they

claimed, should still uphold the Christian values endangered by secularist lecturers (appealing to modern science), demands for Sunday entertainments, omission of prayer on public occasions, and too little of the Bible in schools.

The churches also had troubles due to their own divisions, denominational and schismatic, conservative and liberal (the latter adapting to science and 'higher criticism'), and sectarian – especially bitter between Protestant and Catholic. Yet they could also pull together. Some Protestant churches grew more alike; the Methodists were uniting into one denomination; councils of churches were formed from 1889; an interdenominational temperance

crusade was mounted; and there were combined evangelistic missions.

Evangelism did not win many of the unchurched, but it helped to retain adherents. Many of the rigidities of an earlier piety were lost, but attendances kept rising. Towards the turn of the century, on any particular Sunday, the proportions of adults who had attended church, and of children who had gone to Sunday school, were both likely to be around 45 per cent. Whatever that means, it does at least show that Australians had different habits then than in the 1990s, when church attendances were down by more than half, and Sunday schools were insignificant.

JB

1901–1939

THE COMMONWEALTH

On the first day of the twentieth century, the Commonwealth of Australia came into existence. The six colonies, henceforth to be known as states (New South Wales, Queensland, South Australia, Tasmania, Victoria, Western Australia), yielded the Commonwealth a strictly limited range of powers and responsibilities: external affairs, defence, navigation, customs and immigration, postal services, marriage and divorce, and old-age pensions. There was to be free trade between the states but the Commonwealth could make laws for the arbitration of industrial disputes extending across state borders. All residual powers remained with the states, which therefore remained responsible for most acts of government that touched citizens' lives, including education, health, social welfare, law and order and public transport.

The Commonwealth parliament consisted of two chambers: a House of Representatives elected from equal electorates by universal male suffrage (all women could vote in Commonwealth elections after the Franchise Act of 1902) and a Senate based on the same franchise but consisting of equal numbers of senators from each state regardless of population. Constitutional change required the consent of a majority of voters in a majority of states, as well as an absolute majority. A High Court was established to interpret the Constitution and safeguard its provisions.

These arrangements reflected the limits of the impulse that had established the federation. In the aftermath of the severe economic depression of the 1890s, Australians could appreciate the economic benefits of a larger market. Amidst increasing international competition, they felt the need to assert their own national destiny. But their declarations of national sentiment were still qualified by local rivalries and a continuing dependence on the parent country. Australia still relied on Britain for trade and investment. The British monarch was the Australian head of state; the governor-general, who performed the viceregal function in the Commonwealth Constitution, was appointed in Britain. Britain conducted diplomacy and made war on behalf of Australia. Except in constitutional cases between the Commonwealth and the states, appeals from Australian courts were decided in Britain.

Within this imperial framework the Commonwealth and the states embarked on nation building. They created the economic infrastructure by raising loans in the London money market to finance public works. They promoted rural industries and settled new farmers on the land. The Commonwealth levied tariff duties on foreign imports to assist the local manufacturer; the states encouraged immigrants with cheap passages. They pursued pronatalist policies to build up the population and the Commonwealth introduced a maternity benefit in 1912. In public education and public health there was an enlargement of activity, and a national old-age pension was introduced in 1908. Such measures stimulated significant economic growth and the population increased from about 3.8 million in 1901 to about 4.9 million by 1914.

The government was also drawn into a more active involvement in social relations, with new public agencies regulating areas of life that previously had been left to the market, individual preference and moral sanction. The family came to be treated as the primary social unit whose proper functioning was vital to the national interest. New efforts were made to restrict women from participation in the paid workforce, to discourage artificial methods of birth control and to watch over the ways they discharged the responsibilities of motherhood. An associated campaign for moral reform sought to stamp out prostitution, gambling, public consumption of alcohol and juvenile delinquency. Moral reform tapped religious impulses and the pressure groups that urged repression of vice drew their chief support from the middle class. Characteristically, such pressure

Celebrations marking the inauguration of the Commonwealth of Australia, Melbourne. With the Duke of York, the future George V, is the Earl of Hopetoun, the first governor-general of the new Commonwealth. The first Commonwealth Parliament met in Melbourne in May 1901.

Prime ministers of Australia

	Party or parties	Term
Edmund Barton (from 1902, Sir Edmund Barton)		1901–03
Alfred Deakin (*1st time*)	Liberal-Labor	1903–04
John Christian Watson	Labor	1904
George Houston Reid (from 1909, Sir George Houston Reid)		1904–05
Alfred Deakin (*2nd time*)	Liberal-Labor	1905–08
Andrew Fisher (*1st time*)	Labor	1908–09
Alfred Deakin (*3rd time*)	Liberal-Conservative	1909–10
Andrew Fisher (*2nd time*)	Labor	1910–13
Joseph Cook (from 1918, Sir Joseph Cook)	Liberal	1913–14
Andrew Fisher (*3rd time*)	Labor	1914–15
William Morris Hughes (*1st time*)	Labor	1915–16
William Morris Hughes (*2nd time*)	Labor	1916–23
Stanley Melbourne Bruce (from 1947, 1st Viscount Bruce of Melbourne)	Nationalist-Country	1923–29
James Henry Scullin	Labor	1929–32
Joseph Aloysius Lyons	United Australia	1932–39
Earle Page (from 1938, Sir Earle Page)	Country-United Australia	1939
Robert Gordon Menzies (*1st time*)	United Australia	1939–40
Robert Gordon Menzies (*2nd time*)	United Australia-Country	1940–41
Arthur William Fadden	Country-United Australia	1941
John Curtin	Labor	1941–45
Francis Michael Forde	Labor	1945
Joseph Benedict Chifley	Labor	1945–49
Robert Gordon Menzies (from 1963, Sir Robert Gordon Menzies) (*3rd time*)	Liberal-Country	1949–66
Harold Holt	Liberal-Country	1966–67
John McEwen (from 1971, Sir John McEwen)	Liberal-Country	1967–68
John Grey Gorton (from 1977, Sir John Grey Gorton)	Liberal-Country	1968–71
William McMahon (from 1977, Sir William McMahon)	Liberal-Country	1971–72
Gough Whitlam	Labor	1972–75
Malcolm Fraser	Liberal-National Country	1975–83
Robert Hawke	Labor	1983–91
Paul Keating	Labor	1991–

Alfred Deakin (1856-1919) by Frederick McCubbin, 1914. Deakin was prime minister three times during the first ten years of the Commonwealth.

groups attributed immorality to lack of restraint, which was a failure of individual will, and lack of discipline, which was a failure of parental nurture. However, they also deprecated the evil effects of urban and industrial conditions, which presented temptations to the weak and gave them the money and opportunity to indulge them. The desire to regulate and control the consequences of industrialism therefore sometimes resulted in a concern to reform economic life. Here it intersected with the discontent of wage-earners.

THE LABOR PARTY

In the depression of the 1890s there had been widespread unemployment and distress. The trade unions had been defeated by the combined strength of the employers and the government in major disputes in the mining, pastoral and transport industries. The defeated workers established their own political party, the Labor Party, to redress the balance and make good their losses. The Australian Labor Party achieved rapid success at both federal and state levels of politics, so that by 1914 Labor had experienced office (albeit briefly in some cases) in the Commonwealth and all six states.

The initiative was held in the early Commonwealth parliaments by protectionist liberals, led until 1903 by Edmund Barton and then by Alfred Deakin; they held office with Labor support and introduced most of the significant reform measures. But Labor soon became the largest party and Deakin was forced by 1909 to join with his former opponents, the conservative free traders, in a Fusion of the non-Labor forces. From 1910 to 1913 Labor held a majority and built on the policies that the liberals had begun. The most important of these were arbitration and new protection. The Commonwealth (in 1904) and most of the states created arbitration courts to settle industrial disputes without recourse to strikes and lockouts. Deakin declared the principles of new protection in 1906: protection of local industry in the past had merely made it possible for employers to pay decent wages to Australian workers; new protection would guarantee Australian living standards by requiring that local employers who wished to enjoy the benefits of the tariff paid their employees a 'fair and reasonable' wage. The task of determining the meaning of a fair and reasonable wage fell on the Commonwealth Arbitration Court. Its president, H. B. Higgins, declared in 1907 that such a wage ought to keep a man, his wife and children in frugal comfort. While the High Court overturned the legislation on which this decision was based, Higgins continued to use the principle of the 'basic wage', as it became known, in future industrial awards and it was also adopted by the states. By the end of World War I, the great majority of Australian workers were covered by arbitration awards that embodied a basic wage regularly adjusted for price changes.

By formally recognising trade unions, arbitration assisted their rapid spread throughout the Australian workforce, so that by 1914 it was more highly unionised than the workforce of any other country. The Australian Labor Party embraced arbitration and maintenance of men's employment so that they could be breadwinners became the basis of social policy, overshadowing alternative methods of improving living standards through public provision of services. In this period of working-class mobilisation, however, there was considerable impatience with arbitration and its constraints on more militant workgroups as well as with the failure of Labor governments to bring about more substantial improvements. From 1909 to the outbreak of World War I, a series of strikes and lockouts punctuated the industrial peace.

WILLIAM MORRIS HUGHES

When Britain declared war on Germany in August 1914, the Australians accepted that they too were at war. An expeditionary force quickly occupied German New Guinea. In November 1914 a first contingent of the Australian Imperial Force, specially recruited for service abroad, sailed with a New Zealand contingent to Egypt, from where they took part in the 1915 attack on the Dardanelles and later in the cavalry campaign that drove Turkish forces out of Egypt and Palestine. The main Australian force was transferred at the end of 1915 to the Western Front, and was engaged there until victory was secured in 1918. During World War I 331,000 Australians enlisted in the armed forces, 63,000 lost their lives and another 152,000 were wounded, a remarkably high casualty rate that reflected the High Command's use of the Australians as shock troops.

The number of casualties strained the strength of the Australian Imperial Force and the number of volunteers fell away by 1916 as the initial enthusiasm

The White Australia Policy

One of the first measures of the Commonwealth parliament was the passage of the Immigration Restriction Act in 1901. In what became known as the White Australia Policy, a dictation test was used to deny entry to non-Caucasian immigrants, and the Pacific island labourers who had been brought to Australia by Queensland sugar planters were repatriated.

Aborigines were denied entitlement to Commonwealth pensions, and the states imposed more systematic restrictions on them. The institutionalisation of racism reflected the increased unease of white Australians. Compulsory military training was introduced in 1910 and military expenditure increased to build up the Australian navy.

SM

for the war gave way to doubts and misgivings. The Labor prime minister, William Morris Hughes, campaigned for conscription but the majority of his party opposed it. After the narrow defeat of the first conscription referendum in October 1916, he was expelled from the Labor Party and formed the Nationalist Party from the anti-Labor forces and the ex-Labor conscriptionists. A second referendum in December 1917 again rejected conscription, although earlier in the year Hughes had played on the electorate's fears to win a general election.

He singled out sections of Australian society and accused them of disloyalty – those of German or Austrian descent, he harried and interned; Catholics, who were mostly of Irish origin and accordingly sympathetic to the Irish nationalist uprising that began in 1916, he vilified; and working-class radicals, for whom the Russian Revolution of 1917 came as a clarion call, he repressed. The upsurge of radical unrest coincided with discontent among wage-earners, whose income failed to keep pace with the cost of living in a period of shortages and inflation. A wave of strikes continued until 1920. These wartime divisions ran deep and the long-term result of the war was to shift the orientation of Australian nationalism. Hitherto nationalism had a progressive or radical inflection, seeking an end to dependence and therefore antagonistic to Anglophile conservatism. The wartime sacrifices and the formation of ex-servicemen's organisations completed the formation of a new and more popular conservative nationalism, affirming the existing order and deeply suspicious of dissent.

Hughes exploited these feelings at the Paris Peace Conference where he insisted on separate Australian representation, scorned the idealistic liberalism of the United States President Woodrow Wilson, and insisted on Australian and New Zealand control of the southwest Pacific. Henceforth the Australian prime minister communicated with London directly rather than through the governor-general and the Dominion Office, and Australia maintained its own representation at the League of Nations. Rather than abandoning the imperial relationship, however, the intention was to make Britain more aware of Australian needs. Thus, while Australia complained when Britain took its support for granted during confrontation with Turkey in 1922, it repeatedly urged Britain to build its military presence in the Far East. When the British parliament enacted the Statute of Westminster in 1926 to recognise the full constitutional competence of the dominions, Australia did not ratify the statute.

POST-WAR ECONOMY

The framework of post-war economic development reflected this alignment. Australia embarked on further expansion and diversification of the rural industries, employing British capital to finance new settlement schemes for ex-servicemen and British migrants. Tariff protection was still provided for the manufacturing sector, which consolidated the heavy industrial base that had been established during World War I; but Australian imports were favoured with a reduced imperial tariff. In return, Australia sought British markets for its new range and volume of primary products. These arrangements were designed to reconcile the interests of urban businessmen (who dominated the Nationalist Party) and the farmers (who had established their own Country Party). A new prime minister, Stanley Melbourne Bruce, replaced Hughes in 1922. He summarised the strategy at an Imperial Conference in the following year with the slogan of 'men, money and markets'.

Bruce's strategy brought renewed growth during the first part of the 1920s. Agricultural output expanded. There was a substantial increase of population in the cities, and both Sydney and Melbourne attained a population of more than one million during the decade. The spread of the main cities created new belts of suburbs, with the single-storey bungalow on a quarter-acre block replacing the inner-city terrace as the dominant urban style, and a corresponding weakening of close-knit communities for the privatised concerns of house and garden. The motor car competed with older forms of public transport – by the end of the decade there were 571,000 cars on Australian roads. Greater mobility allowed new forms of consumption and leisure, notably the cinema and the mass-spectator sports such as football, racing and cricket. The first radio station began

transmission in 1924 and by 1929 there were 300,000 radio licences. The new medium also fostered the growth of advertising, and built markets for a new range of consumer products. Thus there was substantial growth in the electrical, chemical, metal fabrication and construction industries. In 1927 the Duke of York opened Parliament House in the federal capital of Canberra, whose bush setting and modern civic design symbolised the dominant values of the era, just as the British dignitary affirmed the imperial ties.

The prosperity of the decade depended on circumstances beyond Australian control. As the economies that had been damaged by the war rebuilt their productive capacity, and as other agricultural producers increased their output, Australian rural producers encountered stiffer competition. The problem weighed most heavily on those farmers who had been put on the land by the post-war settlement schemes. Undercapitalised, burdened by debt repayments, handicapped by a high cost-structure and often located on marginal land, many suffered acute hardship. As export earnings stagnated, overseas lenders became more reluctant to finance further Australian borrowing. In 1927 the Commonwealth established a Loan Council to coordinate its borrowing requirements with those of the states, and impose some control over the public debt.

After a British Economic Mission investigated Australia and reported critically on its economic policy, the Commonwealth Government sought to reduce wage costs. It had already instructed the Commonwealth Arbitration Court that in fixing the basic wage it was to consider the economic effects rather than simply make increases to compensate for higher prices, and it had created additional powers to enforce awards and punish recalcitrant unions. In two major industries – maritime transport and timber – the court's reduction of working conditions triggered violent, prolonged and costly disputes that were further inflamed by penal sanctions against the unions. In another industry – coal – it was the owners who locked the men out when they would not agree to wage reductions, yet the government withdrew prosecution of a leading coalowner. While in every case the workers were eventually driven back to work, the Commonwealth Government decided that because of constitutional limitations on its arbitration jurisdiction, it would hand responsibility back to the states. When this proposal was defeated in the House of Representatives, Bruce called an election. It was won by the Labor Party.

Labor took office at the end of 1929, just as the economic difficulties turned into a depression of unprecedented severity. Already the prices of Australia's chief export commodities, wool and wheat, had fallen; after the collapse of the New York stock

The opening of Parliament House in Canberra, 1927. Built as a temporary structure, it was not replaced until 1988.

exchange in October 1929 paralysed the financial institutions of the world economy, commodity prices tumbled further. Foreign loan sources dried up and the reduction in overseas earnings made the servicing of existing debts extremely difficult. At first, the new government led by James Scullin sought to avoid contraction of the domestic economy. It encouraged farmers to maintain production with the promise of price guarantees; it further increased tariff levels to protect manufacturers; and while it pruned some items of expenditure, it continued to regard public works as the appropriate means of maintaining employment.

This strategy could not be maintained. First, the government lacked a majority in the Senate and was therefore unable to implement some of its measures. Second, it had little control over finance and was unable even to determine the policy of its own Commonwealth Bank. Since the Commonwealth suffered a considerable reduction of revenue, it relied on the banks to finance its expenditure. Third, the inability to meet overseas commitments forced it to ask Britain to defer debt repayment. The Bank of England sent one of its senior officials, Sir Otto Niemeyer, to Australia in 1930.

Following Niemeyer's severe strictures, the Commonwealth and state governments pledged to balance their budgets and reduce expenditure. One section of the Labor Party resisted the social consequences of the drastic reductions required to achieve a balanced budget, but by 1931 control was slipping from their hands. Early in that year, the banks devalued the Australian currency and the Commonwealth Arbitration Court imposed a 10 per cent cut in wages. By May 1931 these Labor critics had to accept a package of additional economies known as the Premiers' Plan: all public expenditure, including social welfare expenditure, was cut and there was a reduction of interest rates on domestic debts. By this time

the Labor Party had suffered defections from both its left and right wings. The right wing, led by the cabinet minister J.A. Lyons, defected because the government resisted capitulating to economic orthodoxy. The left wing, led by the New South Wales premier J.T. Lang, broke away because the government did eventually succumb to that orthodoxy. Lang pursued an increasingly demagogic path after refusing to meet interest payments to London on the state debt, until 1932 when he was dismissed by the state governor. Lyons joined with the Nationalists to form the United Australia Party.

THE DEPRESSION

The depression created social turmoil and political instability. Responsibility for assisting the unemployed rested with the state governments and at first they provided only meagre handouts of food. By the winter of 1930 every Australian city had witnessed large-scale demonstrations by the unemployed; the states developed new forms of relief, including labour camps, designed to keep them off the streets. Among conservative sections of Australian society there was a response, including the formation of public bodies and secret armies dedicated to the protection of property and the defence of God, King and Empire. While these right-wing organisations claimed to uphold constitutional government, they were strident in criticism of the Labor government. The prospect of Australia defaulting on its financial obligations caused them acute anxiety; so, too, did the appointment on the insistence of the Scullin government of the first Australian governor-general, Sir Isaac Isaacs, who took office in 1931. While some, such as the New Guard, took on an increasingly fascist appearance, the most influential of them all, the All for Australia League, directed its efforts into the establishment of the United Australia Party and helped it to defeat the Labor government at the end of 1931.

Recovery from the depression began in 1933, but its impact was felt in public life right through the decade and it cast a shadow over the memories of the generation who lived through it. While few escaped its effects, it fell most heavily on the unemployed. Nearly 30 per cent of the workforce was unemployed in the winter of 1932, and most Australians probably had some experience of failure to find work. The level of public support, either in direct provision of sustenance or in the various relief work schemes that were devised, generally kept the unemployed from starvation, but many suffered from lack of adequate nutrition, clothing, housing and medical care. Every city had its shanty town where those who had been evicted from their homes lived in packing cases or

him. And the youngest boy kept looking at him and he'd say, 'You don't own this house.' He went around saying everything belonged to his mother.

Australians serving overseas, particularly in the army, earned outstanding reputations. Their battle rolls include honours from Gallipoli, France, the Middle East, North Africa, Greece, Malaya, Papua, New Guinea and Borneo.

In both wars civilians were active in persuading men to volunteer and sending them away, collecting funds and comforts for troops in Australia and abroad, taking up work left by men enlisting, and welcoming home casualties or returning servicemen. In World War I only the long lists of casualties, the

War fever captured in a patriotic poster from World War I.

AUSTRALIA FOR EVER !

immense effort volunteers put into war work and propaganda, about 4,500 internments, and the bitter conscription debates of 1916–17 distinguished war from peace. World War II moved closer to home, especially from 1942: there was rationing and black marketeering, the appearance of European refugees, prisoners of war, and vast numbers of American servicemen, air-raid trenches and shelters, gas-driven cars, appeals for rubber, aluminium and camouflage nets, austerity fashions, smaller newspapers and restricted entertainment. The wireless and the Japanese brought war near. Nonetheless, unlike people in Europe and Asia, some Australians could still live as though at peace, and some managed more comfortably than they had during the Great Depression.

Australia fought the world wars in order to maintain traditional links and/or defensive alliances with a powerful, white, English-speaking ally. It fought World War I as a member of the British Empire, being automatically taken as included in Britain's declaration of war on Germany on 4 August 1914, and in Britain's assent to the armistice of 11 November 1918. As part of the Empire Australia signed the Versailles peace treaty of 28 June 1919, and entered World War II by declaring war on Germany on 3 September 1939. It followed Britain and the USA in declaring war on Japan on 8 December 1941, and in accepting the surrender of Germany on 8 May 1945 and of Japan on 2 September 1945. Although Australia seemed more independent internationally in 1945 than in 1914, the effect of the world wars was to lock it into the foreign policy preoccupation it developed before 1901: to attach itself to a European power which might protect it from any threat emerging from its Asian neighbours. The world wars allowed Australia to keep its ties with Europe, and to defy its geographical place in Asia.

WORLD WAR I

When the Great War began in August 1914, Australia's population was nearly 5 million. By the armistice 416,809 Australians, about 16.4 per cent of the white male population and probably about half those eligible, had enlisted in the Australian Imperial Force (AIF) and 4,225 Australians served with the Royal Australian Navy. The Australian Flying Corps, of four squadrons, was formed by transfers from the AIF. About 331,000 AIF troops embarked for service abroad, mostly in France: 63,000 died, and another 152,000 were wounded or injured. About 65 per cent of those who embarked were thus made casualties by the war: about 2,000 returned men were permanently hospitalised, 90,389 were receiving disability pensions in 1920, and about 50,000 were in hospital in 1939.

The Anzac tradition

At dawn on Sunday 25 April 1915 the Australian and New Zealand Army Corps (ANZAC) began landing at a small cove on the Gallipoli peninsula, in Turkey. Instead of the gently sloping ground they expected, they confronted scrub-covered cliffs and an increasingly stubborn Turkish defence. By nightfall about 13,000 Australians and about 4,000 New Zealanders were ashore, and in furious fighting they had won a toehold on the clifftops. That day set the standards of Australia's fighting services: soon it would be called Anzac Bay, and the place Anzac Cove.

The Turks won the campaign: Anzac was evacuated on 19 and 20 December 1915. Perhaps 50,000 Australians fought there; 8,418 died and 19,441 were wounded.

The landing at Anzac was immediately and widely hailed as making Australia both a nation and a partner to Empire: by 1916 Anzac Day was being celebrated, and since the late 1920s it has remained Australia's most important national holiday. It honours all Australia's servicemen and women, in all wars.

To be a returned soldier became a special distinction, and in almost every community in the country after 1915 honour boards and war memorials honoured and remembered those who fell or those who served. In a land which had erected very few monuments before 1914, these memorials literally changed the landscape of Australia, fusing both the land and the nation with the tradition of Anzac.

BG

WORLD WAR II

Women watching the departure of their loved ones in the Australian Imperial Force advance party early in World War II, December 1939.

By September 1939 Australia's population was about 7 million. By 1945 about 976,000 Australians, including 915,000 men, equivalent to 13.1 per cent of the white male population and again probably about half those eligible, had enlisted in the armed services.

About 691,000 men and 36,000 women served in either the Second AIF or the Australian Military Forces, about 190,000 men and 18,000 women in the Royal Australian Air Force, and about 34,000 men and 6,600 women in the Royal Australian Navy. Of these 37,500 died, and about 60,000 were wounded or injured. Most of these casualties were suffered among the 397,000 people who served overseas: the casualty rate was equivalent to 24.5 per cent of those who embarked. This was a much lower rate than during World War I, although many more Australians were taken prisoner in 1939–45 (28,756) than in 1914–18 (4,044), while among Australian aircrew in Bomber Command over Europe casualties exceeded 50 per cent. In 1947, 54,249 World War II veterans were receiving disability pensions, and 4,660 were classified permanently unemployable in 1948.

World War II confirmed the tradition of Anzac as the dominant expression of Australian nationality. Men enlisted conscious of the standards set by the First AIF, and by 1945 they had added a host of battle

The Australian War Memorial in Canberra. It was opened during World War II, on 11 November 1941. Building commenced in 1934. In 1968-71 it was extended, and remodelled in 1984.

honours to the pantheon of Anzac. To the Great War memorials were added new sets of names, and hundreds of suburbs and communities dedicated parks, schools, halls and swimming pools to those who served or fell. On 11 November 1941 the Australian War Memorial opened in Canberra: it is the largest and most popular monument in Australia, and one of the largest of its kind in the world. The official war histories, 15 volumes for 1914–18 and 22 for 1939–45, easily remain Australia's largest historical enterprises, while the Returned Services League (RSL), founded in 1916, by 1946 had 374,000 members, and was among the most effective pressure groups in Australia.

LEGACY OF WAR

The strength of the Anzac tradition and the influence of the RSL grew from the enormous impact the world wars had on those Australians who experienced them. In both wars the terrible legacy of lives maimed or cut short, women widowed young, and hopes blighted, cast shadows over almost every Australian. 'I will remember him all my life', a returned soldier declared in 1988 of a mate killed in New Guinea in 1942. He voiced the loss several generations of Australians felt. The wars were literally too immense for the survivors to forget them, and perhaps the most dramatic changes they made to Australia were those people felt personally.

The political consequences of these feelings varied. After 1918 the Labor Party, split by the issue of conscription, had no say in national policy, and the dominant political note was a sense of post-war exhaustion, and a determination to keep Australia safe by maintaining the nation's alliances, by securing former German colonies in the Pacific, and by emphasising caution and stability.

World War II ended with Labor in government,

and a national mood of hope and confidence, of determination to rebuild, of shedding colonies, and of promoting change. As early as 1943 the Commonwealth Government began planning for post-war reconstruction, including industrialisation, full employment, the Snowy Mountains (hydroelectricity) Scheme, and the expansion of education. After both wars, however, the sense of being a small, vulnerable nation persisted, and large-scale white immigration was encouraged in part to build up Australia's population for defence purposes.

GOVERNMENT CONTROL

Whereas Australians believed that the wars were fought in defence of democracy and civilisation, and that in war Australian individualism has been most distinctly displayed, in fact the wars vastly strengthened the control of governments over citizens.

One obvious effect of the wars was the rapid extension of government control over individuals. Regulations under the War Precaution Acts of World War I and the National Security Acts of World War II considerably restricted individual liberties of speech and action in the cause of wartime security, and after both wars governments extended many of these wartime controls into peacetime.

In 1914–18 the Commonwealth Government intervened in several areas formerly left to private enterprise, notably in signing export price agreements for primary products with the British government, controlling the price of sugar, and establishing the Australian Commonwealth Shipping Line. The government also moved strongly into recruiting, internment of aliens and people of enemy descent, repatriation, and land settlement, but it failed to control domestic prices for basic foodstuffs, groceries, clothing and rent, and it still left much to voluntary effort, notably in respect to recruiting and war comforts.

Government control was carried much further in World War II, particularly by the federal Labor government after October 1941. The state entered into a close supervision of almost every aspect of Australian life, especially via price control, rationing, and manpower supervision.

In January 1942, for example, the government established the Manpower Directorate, from July 1942 called the Manpower Priorities Board, which decided priorities of manpower needs, and channelled the labour of men and women to meet these. From October 1943 'the Manpower' even began transferring men from the armed services and war-related industries, chiefly back to food growing. By May 1945 the Board had discharged over 100,000 men from the army, and transferred a similar number of men and women from war production work to transport services and food, housing, coal and timber production.

Public acceptance of this widening government control is suggested by the conscription question. During the 1914–18 war plebiscites on conscription provoked the most bitter debate in Australian history, with 'No' votes of 51.6 per cent on 28 October 1916 and 53.8 per cent on 20 December 1917 narrowly defeating government proposals to introduce it. Yet in July 1942 conscripts defended the Australian territory of Papua from the advancing Japanese, and the government met relatively little opposition when in February 1943 it legislated to allow conscripts to be sent to fight anywhere in the South West Pacific.

WARTIME ECONOMY

The wars boosted Australian economic activity, particularly in the industrial sector, although they did not end the dominance of primary production (food and wool) in the country's export earnings. In both wars Allied policy identified Australia as a major food supplier: the chief beneficiary of this was probably the Australian wheat industry.

In 1915, to boost Allied food production, the Commonwealth guaranteed a minimum payment for wheat, and in 1916 the British government pre-purchased Australia's entire wartime output. The 1915–16 crop jumped over sevenfold on the 1914–15 total, and the value of wheat exports rose from £900,000 in 1915 to £22.6 million in 1920. The British government also pre-purchased Australia's entire wartime production of meat (in February 1915), wool (November 1916) and butter and cheese (1917) at above pre-war prices, thus underwriting the value of Australia's chief exports. Wool's export earnings, for example, leaped from £22.1 million in 1915 to £50.5 million in 1920, although by then wartime shipping shortages had created huge stockpiles of wool, wheat and butter, and these were to depress prices during the 1920s.

Primary production was less significant to Australia's export earnings during World War II. Government crop quotas and increased food processing within Australia saw wheat export values fall from £20.9 million in 1938 to £8.7 million in 1939 and £9.8 million in 1945. Wool's export earnings rose from £42.6 million in 1939 to £49.4 million in 1945, but this was still less than in 1920. Nonetheless export earnings from wool, wheat and flour alone were 49 per cent of all export earnings in 1915–18 and 43 per cent of them in 1939–45, and primary production largely fuelled increases in total export values of 244 per cent in 1914–18 and 164 per cent in 1939–45.

At the same time the wars reinforced (rather than caused) the steady industrialisation of the Australian economy after 1900. Pig iron production, for example, rose from 76,500 tonnes in 1914 to 211,140 tonnes in 1918, an increase of 176 per cent; it rose a further 434 per cent to 1,127,000 tonnes in 1939, reached a wartime peak of 1,589,160 tonnes in 1942, and stood at 1,140,360 tonnes in 1945, a wartime increase of 1.2 per cent. The gross domestic product of manufacturing appears to have risen more significantly between the wars than during them, while the number of people employed in manufacturing fell by a fifth in 1914–18, more than doubled in 1918–39, rose by a third in 1939–45 and rose by three-quarters in 1945–70. While wartime controls gave government experience in directing the economy, particularly after 1941, it may be that the significance of the wars themselves in the industrialisation of Australia has been exaggerated.

EMPLOYMENT

Unemployment was not necessarily relieved by wartime conditions. Whereas in 1914–18 there was no significant change in unemployment, and an increase from 1921, from 1941 there was a sharp fall in unemployment, and only a slight increase from 1946. In 1985 the economist N. G. Butlin estimated unemployment as percentages for the workforce as shown in the table.

UNEMPLOYMENT AS PERCENTAGES
FOR THE WORKFORCE, 1914–50

1914	3.27	1939	8.76
1918	4.39	1943	0.95
1920	3.39	1945	1.19
1922	6.11	1950	1.75

Again, the low percentages for World War II may derive from wartime manpower controls and the experience gained from them, rather than from industrialisation. In both wars wage rates improved: the basic wage became almost universal between 1915 and 1918, while real wages reached record levels in 1942–43.

Women got most wartime work opportunities as voluntary workers. The major patriotic fund organisations – the Red Cross and the Australian Comforts Fund – were staffed largely by women volunteers. The Red Cross sent overseas supplies valued at £3.6 million in 1914–18, including 10.5 million cigarettes and 1.16 million pairs of socks, while 400,000 Red Cross workers dispatched supplies valued at about £9 million in 1939–45. The Comforts Fund, among many other gifts, sent 1.5 million pairs of socks during 1914–18 and over 3 million pairs during 1939–45.

City girls filling and sewing chaff bags on a farm in Armidale, New South Wales. Women were widely employed in World War II, especially as voluntary workers.

The wars did not significantly increase the proportion of women in the paid workforce, at least not in civilian occupations. Only about 1850 women served in the armed services during the 1914–18 war, as army nurses; 60,600 women served in 1939–45. Women also took jobs created by wartime factories or vacated by men enlisting, but this had little or no enduring significance. In the manufacturing sector, for example, 88,000 women were employed in 1918 and 214,600 in 1945, but during both wars the number of women workers in manufacturing actually grew more slowly than during most neighbouring peacetime periods.

The five-year intervals beginning 1909, 1914 and 1919 saw percentage increases in the number of women workers of 19.1, 8.4 and 16.9; the seven-year intervals beginning 1932, 1939 and 1946 saw percentage increases of 34.5, 29 and 16.6. In all sectors, in neither war were there significant increases in women as a percentage of the workforce (indeed women formed 21.8 per cent of the workforce in 1901, and 25.3 per cent in 1982), or in working women as a percentage of women aged between 15 and 65. Perhaps the biggest change was during World War II, when 76,900 women, or 62 per cent of the 1939 workforce, quit domestic service for other kinds of work. Most never went back.

Aborigines volunteered to serve in both wars, frequently in the hope of bettering the peacetime condition of their people. The armed services kept no records of enlistments on the basis of race, but perhaps 500 Aborigines joined the First AIF, and perhaps 2,000 the Second, while small numbers joined the navy and the air force. In World War II one Aborigine was promoted to officer rank, and at least one became a fighter pilot. In addition Aboriginal and Torres Strait Islander labour and reconnaissance units performed valuable service in northern Australia in 1942–45. Islanders enlisted at twice the rate of white Australians – 850 served in the war. After 1945 the RSL supported the claims of Aboriginal and Islander ex-servicemen for better treatment, but neither these men nor their people benefited from their war effort.

Even servicemen who survived the wars to return sound in mind and body were not well rewarded. After the armistice in 1918 AIF soldiers in Britain were offered a wide variety of training courses to help them adjust to civil life, but most of these were short-term, while the troops awaited ships to take them home. Servicemen from World War II could receive much more generous educational assistance, including support during university and college courses, apprenticeships, and on the job re-training.

The most extensive and probably the most popular form of assistance offered was soldier settlement – the settling of a man and his family on his own farm. By 1948 over 35,000 World War I veterans and 2,113 World War II veterans had got farms; there were 9,099 World War II soldier settlers in 1961. But soldier settlement was the old state-run closer settlement schemes on slightly more generous terms, and, like closer settlement, soldier settlement led to many failures. By 1948 roughly two-thirds of the 1914–18 war veterans had abandoned or transferred their farms, while in the 1980s 1939–45 war men were still quitting war service blocks too small to be viable.

WAR DEBT

Against such doubtful gains, the wars inflicted significant costs and losses on Australia, and not only in casualties and suffering. Australia's war debt was £377 million in 1920, £831 million in 1934, £1,491.7 million for World War II in 1949, and £893 million for World War II in 1961.

More importantly the wars entrenched a conservative outlook in Australian society. Against a greater sense of national purpose can be set still strident demands for conformity, a continued sense of being threatened, and a prolonged dependence on a larger ally. Against a greater horror of war can be set the landslide vote at the 1966 federal elections in favour of sending troops to Vietnam. Against the many technical and material changes the wars generated can be set the twentieth-century conviction that progress itself is essentially material. Against the achievement and pride of the Anzac tradition can be set the creation of national ideals which look back rather than forward. Australia gained little from the world wars.

BG

Australia since 1945

Australians responded to the end of World War II with a mixture of relief, pride and optimism. The German surrender in May 1945 provoked some celebration, but it was not until the dropping of the atomic bombs on Hiroshima and Nagasaki in early August that people awoke to the possibility that the war would soon end. Japan's surrender was finally confirmed in a radio broadcast by the prime minister, 'Ben' Chifley, on 15 August 1945.

The announcement provoked an outpouring of 'peace delirium' right across the country. The streets of almost every city and town were turned over to spontaneous celebration with dancing, singing, flag waving and sometimes riotous behaviour. After six years of war and nearly four years of home-front austerity the cathartic-like response to victory was understandable.

It was also the case that Australians had much to be proud of: with a population of only 7 million the country had contributed 2.5 million servicemen and women to the war effort, their fighting men and women had won battle honours in almost every major theatre of the world war, the young nation had withstood the first direct attacks on its own territory, and the civilian population had displayed a maturity and single-minded determination which, in the dark months of 1942, had allowed the nation's economy quickly to be placed on a total war footing and halt the Japanese drive south.

Australians were very conscious of the fact that their victory was the result of a national effort and that civilian Australians had as much to be proud of as those in the armed forces. One of the benefits of the war was a sharp decline in the nation's overseas indebtedness. With victory achieved, the nation's thoughts turned to winning the peace.

THE CHIFLEY GOVERNMENT (1945–49)

Australia greeted peace with a new prime minister. Joseph Benedict Chifley had succeeded to that office in July 1945 following the death of the wartime leader, John Curtin. The son of a blacksmith, 'Ben' Chifley was a one-time engine driver and trade union official who, like many working-class Australians of his generation, had enjoyed little formal education. Despite this, however, he had shown himself to be an able treasurer under Curtin and his easy-going style hid a shrewd intellect and determined personality.

J. B. Chifley, prime minister 1945–49, speaking at Adaminaby, New South Wales, two months before losing the 1949 election.

Chifley assumed office with a full programme of post-war reconstruction (for which as treasurer he had been largely responsible) already in place. It had five main aims: the maintenance of full employment, securing reliable markets for the nation's primary produce, the expansion of manufacturing industries, improved educational opportunities for the young, and population growth which would be boosted by a combination of natural increase and a government-sponsored immigration programme. The detailed planning bore fruit when, at short notice, the nation had to deal with the speedy demobilisation of the armed services, the return of its prisoners of war and the reconstruction of a civilian economy. That there was so little disruption was testimony to the careful preparations.

Of all the schemes and policy initiatives connected with post-war reconstruction, the one that captured the imagination of Australians was the Snowy Mountains Hydro-electric Scheme. The concept of turning the rivers back inland had long been a dream in Australia, one of the driest continents on earth. In 1949 work commenced to divert water from the Snowy River inland to power a succession of hydro-electricity generating stations before flowing into the Murray and Murrumbidgee rivers where it would be used for irrigation. Although a great engineering achievement, in the long run the Scheme has had unforeseen environmental consequences with increased soil salinity in the areas it serves (see also p. 196).

Less immediate in their impact, but more important in terms of the future shape of Australian society, were the plans to stimulate population growth. Like most western nations, Australia experienced a rise in the birth rate after 1945. The post-war 'baby boom' in Australia, however, resulted neither from government initiatives, nor from women having more children: it was caused by proportionally more women marrying and by their starting and completing their families earlier in the marriage. In 1947 the birth rate climbed above 3 per 1,000 for the first time since 1923 and remained high (peaking at 3.58 per 1,000 in 1961) for the next two decades.

The other factor in population growth was the post-war immigration programme. Traditionally Labor had been opposed to large-scale immigration and the Chifley government's initiative in sponsoring it represented a radical departure for the ALP. Australia's experience of World War II had caused the change of heart. In a variation on the 'populate or perish' argument, there was a general recognition that Australia could defend itself only if it had a population large enough to provide the manpower for essential war production. In his August 1945 White Paper, the minister for immigration, Arthur Calwell, sought to reassure Australians that the immigrants chosen would blend in well with the existing population: they would all be white, predominantly British, and young (it was believed that children would cause the least disruption to the economy). As it happened, the Australian government's fears about maintaining full employment in the immediate post-war years, a reluctance on the part of Britain to encourage emigration, a concern over the reception of non-British migrants and a shortage of ships all combined to delay the scheme's implementation. It was not until 1947 that the first immigrants arrived, displaced persons from war-torn Europe. (See also pp. 225–7)

Australia's foreign policy during the immediate post-war period was steered by the mercurial and independent-minded foreign minister, Dr Herbert Vere Evatt. 'Doc' Evatt had spent the war forging a much more independent and enterprising foreign policy than had ever been the case before, and this approach continued after the war. Evatt, for instance, refused to bow to pressure and allow the USA to keep a military base on Manus Island, which Australia controlled as part of the mandated territory of New Guinea.

Australia's independent stance is best illustrated, however, by its roles in creating the modern United Nations and helping secure independence for the Dutch East Indies. At the foundation conference of the UN in San Francisco in 1945, Evatt strove to curb the influence of the great powers with permanent seats on the Security Council and to enhance the authority of the General Assembly, where all nations were represented. Australia did not get everything it sought, but it achieved more than any other middle-ranking power in successfully sponsoring amendments to the UN Charter. The result was that Australia, rather than Canada or South Africa, came to be seen as the leading Commonwealth country in this period. The respect accorded to Australia was given official recognition in San Francisco when Evatt was elected as the first president of the UN General Assembly.

Australia's sympathy towards the decolonisation movement in Asia also marked a break with the past. The Chifley government was very supportive of those Indonesian nationalists who refused to accept the reimposition of Dutch colonial rule after 1945. The Indonesians even nominated Australia to represent them on the UN committee which was set up to resolve the issue. Unfortunately the talks broke down and two years of civil war followed before the Dutch finally agreed to independence. Australia's support for Indonesian nationalism did not find favour in London and Washington, but it did earn goodwill from other nations in the region.

Australia's regional interests and the global concerns of its allies did not always find an easy resolu-

tion. It suited the USA, who were mindful of the growing cold war in Europe and feared the growth of communism in Asia, to make an anti-Communist ally of the defeated Japanese. The Australian government, however, was reluctant to accede to the USA's desire to impose a generous peace treaty on Japan. It was not until the USA agreed to a tripartite defence agreement between Australia, New Zealand and the USA (ANZUS), that would ensure mutual protection against a re-militarised Japan, that Canberra (by this time Chifley and the ALP were out of office) finally agreed to sign the peace treaty with Japan.

Although the ALP had won a clear victory in the September 1946 election (the first time Labor had won two successive federal elections), the Chifley government was constantly frustrated in its attempts to implement social and political reforms by a combination of powerful vested interests and restrictive interpretations placed on Australia's Constitution by the High Court. When towards the end of the war the government established a free medicine list, doctors in Victoria mounted a successful High Court challenge which had the effect of throwing into doubt the power of the federal government to legislate in the area of social services and pensions. It was to be the first of a string of successful legal challenges to federal government legislation in the areas of health, air transport and banking. The solution, of course, was

Bank nationalisation

In 1945 the Chifley government legislated to reform the banking sector. The Commonwealth Bank Act made that federally-owned institution the nation's central bank, and replaced the Bank's board with a single governor directly responsible to the federal treasurer; the Banking Act extended wartime measures giving the Commonwealth Bank power to control interest rates and the flow of money. The Banking Act also included provisions compelling federal, state and local governments (and their instrumentalities) to use government-owned banks.

In 1947 the High Court ruled this part of the Banking Act unconstitutional. Fearful that all its banking legislation was now under threat, the federal government announced that it would carry out what had been official Labor policy since 1934 and nationalise all banks. In an atmosphere of mounting crisis, legislation was passed and then immediately challenged before the High Court.

In 1948 the High Court ruled that nationalisation was beyond the powers of the federal government, a view which was confirmed a year later by the privy council.

JWK

Coalminers stand by as troops move in with bulldozers and excavators at an open-pit mine in New South Wales. The two-month-long strike in 1949 was to have a critical effect on the Labor government's public standing.

to hold a referendum amending the Constitution. Unfortunately for the Chifley government, the Australian electorate has traditionally rejected referenda questions that do not have all-party support. Between 1944 and 1948 the government sought constitutional amendments to give it increased powers in no less than 18 separate areas. All but one, giving it powers to legislate in the areas of social services and pensions (and for which there was all-party support), were lost.

Australians enjoyed boom conditions in the immediate post-war years. Wool and wheat earned high prices and manufacturing industries were at full production. Rather than the unemployment the government had feared, the demand for labour was so strong that female factory employment in the late 1940s equalled that of World War II. The booming economy made a welcome change from the rigours of war and depression; it also helped raise public expectations. Increasingly Australians became impatient with the Chifley government as chronic shortages in building materials, housing and consumer goods denied them the immediate material benefits of prosperity. The fact that wartime petrol rationing continued and that inflation was running at the then unheard-of annual rate of 10 per cent, only added to voter unease.

To add to the government's difficulties in what was to be an election year, a bitter strike broke out in the troublesome coalmining industry in June 1949. The Communist-led miners' union refused to obey return to work orders and for two months the country endured severe power shortages, with over half a million people thrown out of work. Inevitably the Chifley government shared in the blame for the dispute, even though it had moved quickly to enact

Sir Robert Menzies.

emergency legislation and even ordered troops into the mines to restore essential supplies. When in December 1949 voters went to the polls, the Liberal and Country parties were able to use this strike, together with the bank nationalisation dispute, consumer shortages, high inflation and petrol rationing to create a picture of a government out of touch with the aspirations of ordinary Australians. In a closely fought campaign a Liberal and Country Party coalition led by Robert Menzies emerged victorious.

THE MENZIES YEARS (1949–66)

The success of Robert Gordon Menzies in 1949 marked one of the most astonishing comebacks in Australian political history. Forced to resign as prime minister and leader of the United Australian Party in 1941, Menzies used his years on the opposition backbench to refine his own political philosophy and build a new political party. Portraying itself as representing neither big business nor big labour, the 'new' Liberal Party looked to the interests of 'the forgotten people', the middle class. It quickly swallowed up the largely discredited UAP and in concert with the Country Party offered a viable alternative to Labor.

Menzies was to remain prime minister for the next 16 years. His hold on power, however, was not as secure as it appears in retrospect. In federal elections in 1954 and 1961 the ALP actually received a greater proportion of the first preference votes (50.03 per cent in 1954) than the Liberal and Country parties combined. Menzies owed his record term in office to a mixture of good fortune and good management. He was fortunate to come to power at a time when Labor's post-war economic reforms were just starting to bear fruit. A strong domestic economy combined with record commodity prices helped Menzies through the first few years, although there was a minor slump following a drop in wool prices at the end of the Korean war. The growth in manufacturing was particularly marked, with Australian industry producing a whole range of goods, such as cars and consumer durables, that had previously been imported. Annual factory production in Australia rose from £489 million in 1949 to £1,843 million in 1959.

COMMUNIST PARTY DISSOLUTION BILL

Menzies was fortunate to face an opposition wracked by internal divisions, ineffective leadership and declining morale. Menzies did not create these difficulties for the ALP but he certainly exploited them.

One of his promises in the 1949 election campaign had been to introduce legislation outlawing the Com-

munist Party. Whether Menzies believed the Communist Party constituted a real threat to the nation is a moot point: he knew any attempt to ban the CP would expose divisions within the ALP.

Legislation banning the CP was passed by parliament (a divided ALP caucus was directed by the federal executive not to oppose the bill) in October 1950. It was almost immediately declared unconstitutional following a successful appeal to the High Court in which 'Doc' Evatt, deputy leader of the ALP, appeared on behalf of the plaintiffs.

Although Evatt insisted that he had acted in a private capacity, it seemed to many people that the ALP was aligning itself with communism. Certainly Menzies was able to exploit the ALP's disarray with a hastily-called general election.

With his mandate renewed, Menzies then held a referendum to grant the government power to ban the Communist Party. Evatt, who had become ALP leader following the death of Chifley, ran a brilliant campaign and against all predictions secured a majority No vote, albeit by the barest of margins, 50.48 per cent.

THE PETROV AFFAIR

Just prior to the 1954 election Menzies was informed that Vladimir Petrov, a Russian diplomat and self-confessed MVD spy, had defected, bringing with him evidence of a 'spy ring' in Australia. With the economy undergoing a severe downturn, the affair was a godsend for the coalition government. Although Menzies resisted overplaying his hand, his coalition partners were not nearly so scrupulous and in an atmosphere of mounting rumour about Labor involvement the government scraped home (despite a majority of voters favouring the ALP). There is no doubt that the Petrov affair secured electoral victory for Menzies, although he did not engineer the defection as some have suggested.

Following the Petrov revelations, a Royal Commission was established to investigate espionage in Australia. The Commission did not produce any evidence that warranted bringing charges against anyone, but it did succeed in sullying the reputation of a succession of journalists, trade unionists, communists and ALP members who were called before it to give evidence. Evatt insisted on representing two of his own staff members who were named in evidence, but his increasingly erratic behaviour and inability to distance himself from the events saw the commissioners eventually ban him from further appearances. The pressure of events was taking its toll on Evatt. When in October 1955 he addressed federal parliament on the subject of the final report of the Petrov Royal Commission, Evatt announced that

Evdokia Alexeyevna Petrova, the wife of Vladimir Petrov, a Russian diplomat and spy who defected in April 1954, being forced on to a Moscow-bound plane by Russian guards at Sydney airport. She was later released when the plane landed at Darwin and her guards were disarmed. The defection and Petrov's unmasking of a spy ring in Australia led to the Soviet Union's breaking off diplomatic relations with Australia on 25 April 1954 (not resumed until 4 June 1959).

he had written to Molotov, the Soviet foreign minister, who had replied that the Petrov documents were forgeries. Although he remained as opposition leader until early 1960, Evatt was never a serious challenge to Menzies again.

The Petrov affair was also the final catalyst for a split in ALP ranks. Evatt's appearance before the Commission outraged many ALP anti-Communists, while other party members thought the mostly Catholic anti-Communist faction were disloyal for being directed by outside organisations. After six months of accusation and counter accusation the 'Groupers' were expelled from the Party by order of its federal conference meeting in Hobart in March 1955.

At first, the 'Split' was largely confined to Victoria and it was not until 1956 that a small number of New South Wales 'Groupers' left the ALP. In Queensland the 'Split', which in that state resulted more from feuding between trade union and parliamentary members of the Party than it did from ideological divisions, was delayed until April 1957 when the ALP Premier, Vince Gair, and most of his ministers were expelled by the Party's state executive. The breakaway groups in the various states later joined together as the Democratic Labor Party. Their fierce opposition to the ALP caused the defeat of at least one state ALP government (in Victoria in June 1955), and helped keep the ALP out of power federally for the next decade and a half.

Menzies' leadership style

Menzies' dominance of Australian politics in the 1950s was not just due to the misfortunes which struck the ALP, however, as it also owed much to his skills as a politician. An important innovation in the constitution of the Liberal Party was the inclusion of provisions ensuring female representation on state executives. Realising that women were usually more conservative in their voting habits than men, Menzies was careful to emphasise issues and policies which concerned women. His use of the 'Communist bogy' was masterful: trotted out before each election, it brought the opposition into disarray and scared the more impressionable voters back to supporting the coalition. Menzies was also helped in this tactic by the fact that many of the recent immigrants to Australia were refugees from Eastern Europe who harboured deep fears of communism.

Nor were Menzies' skills as a public speaker insubstantial. Although he was not a charismatic orator, he was a talented debater and a forceful speaker. Menzies retained many of the characteristics of the leading barrister which once he had been: with his clear, strong baritone voice, ability to speak without notes,

and imposing presence, he liked to play the role of the clear-thinking advocate who was willing to share a joke with the jury (of voters). His usual tactic at political meetings was not to prepare a set speech, but to provoke interjections and rely on his quick wit and dry humour to score points off his opponents. Menzies' arrogant bearing infuriated his enemies (and some of his colleagues as well), but there is no doubt that the image he presented came to epitomise that of an Australian prime minister.

Menzies, a genial father figure to many voters, could also be quite ruthless in his private political dealings. Aware of the divisions which had wracked the UAP when he had been leader, he kept a firm hand on his own party and strove constantly to maintain the coalition with the Country Party which was so essential to electoral victory. Potential rivals and people he crossed swords with, such as Percy Spender, Richard Casey and Paul Hasluck, were effectively but quietly removed from the political scene.

Standard of living

At the end of World War II there had been a severe shortage of housing. This was not really relieved until the end of the 1950s. Over half the houses being constructed in New South Wales in 1952, for instance, were being put up by owner-builders. People would buy a block of land, and then over a number of years build their own home. Often half the house would be built first and occupied while the rest was slowly completed. Despite the shortages, home ownership increased dramatically. In 1947, 39.7 per cent of the dwellings in Sydney were either owned or being purchased by the occupier. In 1954 it was 59.6 per cent and in 1961, 71 per cent. The boom in home ownership contributed to the dramatic growth and distinctive form of Australia's cities. In 1947, half the population of Australia (3.8 million) lived in the capital cities, by 1971 the proportion was nearly two-thirds (7.6 million). The single-storey, three-bedroomed house and lawn, built on a quarter-acre block, in a sprawling suburb, has been much criticised by intellectuals who see it as evidence of the mindless conformity of Australians. In fact the typical suburban home is evidence, not of dullness, but of the fundamental equality of Australian society.

Allied to the growth in suburbia was a consumer revolution. In 1948 there was one motor vehicle for every 10 Australians, by 1960 one for every four, and ownership of a car had become the norm for Australian families. Similarly, refrigerators, electric washing machines, vacuum cleaners, and a whole range of kitchen appliances became commonplace in Australian homes in the 1950s. Television provides

Above *Evidence of conformity or of a fundamentally democratic mentality? Sprawling suburban development in Melbourne.*

Right *Consumerism grew vigorously during the 1950s' boom. Advertisement for a washing machine from* The Australian Home Beautiful, *1955.*

the best example, however. Four years after transmission began in Melbourne and Sydney in 1956 (and long before anyone outside a capital city could receive a television signal), one-third of Australia's homes had a television set.

In subtle but very perceptible ways the products of modern consumer society changed the way Aus-

tralians lived and thought about themselves. The car, telephone and television set allowed the distinctive Australian suburbs to grow. Cars and refrigerators (and the fact that more mothers than ever before were in full-time paid employment) altered the way people did their shopping. Weekly visits to the regional shopping centre and supermarket replaced the need to buy perishables from the corner store or have regular weekly shopping outings to the city stores. Increased prosperity, combined with the baby boom, also gave birth to a whole new sub-culture, that of the teenager.

Youth culture

The young in Australia, as elsewhere in the western world, were specifically targeted by commercial interests for the first time in the 1950s.

Cheap, mass-produced plastic toys became available for the first time, fads such as the 'yo-yo' and 'hoola-hoop' were devised and sophisticated forms of cross-promotion, with a product tie-in between films, comic books and merchandise targeting the young. Adolescents were a particular focus of attention. By pandering to an adolescent's desire to establish a unique identity, record companies, soft-drink manufacturers and clothing makers encouraged the creation of a distinctive youth sub-culture, which they could exploit.

The teenage phenomenon was something which shocked many older Australians. There was a perception that teenagers were out of control, and that their behaviour verged on the criminal. Attention focused on one teenage sub-cult in particular, the bodgies and widgies, who with their distinctive fashion in clothes and fondness of Rock and Roll came to epitomise the delinquent teenager.

Despite the fact that there is no evidence to suggest teenage crime was actually increasing, concerned citizens responded to the phenomenon with fear and panic. They blamed neglectful parents, the lack of discipline in society or the breakdown of the family. In fact they blamed everything but the real causes, the demographic factors which had suddenly produced comparatively large numbers of teenagers and the commercial interests which had helped fashion them.

Post-war immigration

Between 1947 and 1983, close to 3 million immigrants (two-thirds of whom were non-British) arrived and settled in Australia. This massive influx has irrevocably changed the ethnic basis of the Australian population. (See also pp. 225–7).

Early widgie, depicted on a magazine cover in 1951. With the onset of Rock and Roll widgies and the similar cult of 'bodgies' came to be regarded less tolerantly by middle Australia and were widely seen as an alarming manifestation of deliquency. However, there is no evidence of an increase in teenage crime during their heyday.

In 1947 the population stood at 7.6 million, and with 97 per cent either born in Australia or the British Isles no one would have questioned its domination by Anglo-Celts. In 1988 it was 16 million, 53 per cent of whom have at least one non-Anglo-Celtic ancestor.

The change produced some tensions (especially in the early 1950s), but what is really notable is the apparent ease with which non-Anglo-Celtic immigrants have been assimilated into Australian society.

A high proportion of these 'new Australians' were Catholic, helping to raise this denomination's proportion of the population from 20.7 per cent in 1947 to 27 per cent in 1991. Because most of these new Catholic immigrants were non-Irish, it also helped weaken the centuries-old Irish puritanism which had dominated the Catholic Church in Australia.

INTERNATIONAL AFFAIRS

Menzies' first foreign minister, Percy Spender, continued 'Doc' Evatt's policy of being a friend to Asia. At a meeting of Commonwealth foreign ministers at Colombo in 1950, it was Spender who suggested the outlines of a scheme which would assist the development of decolonising nations and stop communist expansion. Known as the Colombo Plan, it was eventually adopted by every nation in South and South-east Asia, together with Australia, Canada, New Zealand, the UK, the USA and Japan.

The scheme provided for the more industrialised nations to provide financial, technical and professional help to the less-developed countries. In the first six years of the scheme, Australia gave more, per head of population, than any other nation. The Colombo Aid money was never enough, of course, but the psychological impact should not be underestimated and further enhanced Australia's standing in Asia. The scheme also helped break down (among educators and students at least) racist sentiment in Australia. In the early 1950s, 10 per cent of those studying in Australian universities were Colombo Plan students from Asia.

As the Colombo Plan was getting underway the stage was also being set for the gradual disassembling of Australia's independent post-war foreign policy. Over the course of the 1950s there was a gradual shift of emphasis from developmental aid and non-military treaties, to defence aid and military pacts, which slowly drew Australia into the USA defence alliance. Australia's signing of the ANZUS treaty, in July 1951, marked the beginning of the process. This treaty, to which successive governments (of all political persuasions) have adhered, forms the basis of Australia's defence alliance with the USA. This is despite the fact that ANZUS does not guarantee military intervention by the USA if Australia were attacked: it merely states that an attack in the Pacific area on any one of the three signatory nations would endanger the peace and safety of the other two and that they would act to meet the threat in accordance with their constitutional processes. (In 1985 the USA suspended its treaty obligations to New Zealand after the Lange Labor government announced that visits by nuclear-armed ships were no longer welcome.)

Within six months of Menzies coming to power, the Cold War in Europe became a 'hot war' in Asia. Australia was the first nation to commit troops to the conflict in support of USA actions in Korea. Menzies characterised the conflict as the beginning of a third world war. The fighting lasted for three years and cost 281 Australian lives. Then in 1955, on the eve of Malayan independence, Australia sent troops under the Australia, New Zealand and Malaya (ANZAM) regional defence pact to help control communist insurgency in Malaya. It was the first occasion on which Australian troops had been stationed abroad during peace time.

The French defeat in Indo-China in 1954 convinced the Australian government (and other nations in the region) that a defence pact which was much wider in scope than ANZUS and ANZAM was needed to contain communism. The South-East Asia Treaty Organisation (SEATO) was the result, a collective defence pact drawing together world powers, like the USA, the UK and France, regional powers like Australia and New Zealand, and emerging nations like Pakistan, the Philippines and Thailand.

Not all the countries in the region supported the creation of SEATO, however, and India, Malaya, Burma and Indonesia attacked the agreement for strengthening the hand of neo-colonialism. SEATO would later be used to justify USA and Australian intervention in Vietnam.

Despite the Menzies government's concern over communist expansion, military spending had only a low priority. Annual defence expenditure in Australia declined from 4.9 per cent of GDP in 1953 to 2.5 per cent in 1964. It is true that a scheme for 18-year-old males to undergo 3–6 months' military training was introduced in 1951, but this was abandoned eight years later on the grounds that modern warfare no longer required large numbers of partially trained soldiers.

The government's policy was, in effect, to rely on others to defend Australia. Menzies agreed, in 1950, that Britain could test nuclear weapons on Australian soil and use the Woomera, South Australia, rocket range (a joint UK–Australia weapons research facility established in 1947) to develop the Blue Streak missile. With Britain's gradual withdrawal west of Suez, however, the Australian government increasingly focused its defence thinking on the USA. America was encouraged to commit troops to Indo-China and, beginning with North-West Cape in 1963, the Australian government signed agreements allowing USA communications and satellite control bases to be built in Australia. By encouraging powerful allies to maintain a presence in the region it was believed Australia could shelter under their defence umbrella.

In April 1965 Menzies announced that a battalion of Australian combat troops was to be sent to assist the government of South Vietnam. He stated that this was in response to a request from the South Vietnamese government. What he did not say was that the Australian government had suggested to the USA that such a request be sent. Thirty military 'advisers' had been sent to Vietnam in July 1962 and by 1965 this number had grown to 100. However, to commit even a single combat battalion (just over a thousand men) the government had had to introduce conscription six months earlier; otherwise the rundown Army of the day would not have been able to support even this number in the field.

THE LIBERALS IN DECLINE (1966–72)

In January 1966 Menzies announced his retirement from political life. At 71 he had been prime minister for a total of 18 years and had held office continually for a record 16 years. He was succeeded by his loyal deputy Harold Holt. Menzies' departure caused no perceptible change in government policy. The Liberal and Country parties viewed themselves as the natural parties of government and saw little reason for self-questioning. Gradually, however, an increasing brittleness in coalition unity, and a growing lack of direction, became apparent.

Under Holt, Australia was brought even more firmly under the USA defence umbrella. Following representations from the USA, the government announced in March 1966 that the size of its force in Vietnam would be trebled to 4,500 and would include conscripts. By October 1967 the Australian commitment had reached its peak of 8,000. Unlike his predecessor, Holt took Asia and Asian affairs seriously, but his sycophantic behaviour towards the USA was something that rankled with many Australians. On a visit to Washington in June 1966, Holt used President Johnson's election slogan to declare that Australia would go 'all the way with LBJ' in Vietnam. And when Johnson visited Australia in October (the first visit by a serving USA president), Holt fawned over his guest, basking in the reflected applause from the cheering crowds. Although there were some antiwar protests during the visit, it was clear that most Australians felt warmly towards Johnson and fully supported both the war and conscription. This was made clear in December 1966 when a federal election, fought substantially over the issue of conscription, resulted in a record first preference vote for the Liberal and Country parties. Holt's term as prime minister was short-lived, however: in December 1967 he disappeared while swimming in heavy surf at Portsea in Victoria.

The treasurer and deputy leader of the Liberal Party, William McMahon, was expected to succeed Holt, but a bitter leadership squabble broke out within the coalition. The acting prime minister and leader of the Country Party, John McEwen, who had been feuding with McMahon for some time, announced that his party would not participate in a coalition government led by McMahon. No fewer than six candidates declared their candidacy, with John Grey Gorton, Liberal leader in the Senate, eventually emerging victorious.

The loss of direction within the Liberal Party, which had become apparent in the last year of Holt's leadership, intensified under Gorton. Disillusionment and a lack of cohesion found increasing public expression in criticism of the leader. Gorton's larrikin streak, combined with a readiness to ride roughshod over cabinet and pursue a strongly centralist line with the states, scandalised many of his colleagues. Liberal unity was not helped either by a massive swing against the government in the October 1969 federal election. Dissatisfaction with Gorton's leadership reached a climax in January 1971 when the minister for defence, Malcolm Fraser,

Above *Lyndon Baines Johnson in Australia in 1966, the first serving American president to visit the country. Prime Minister Harold Holt, to the left of the president, made the most of his association with Johnson's popularity.*

Right *Poster of the 1966 election, which was partly fought on the issue of conscription. Most Australians at the time being in favour of supporting the American troops in Vietnam, the ruling Liberal and Country parties were returned comfortably.*

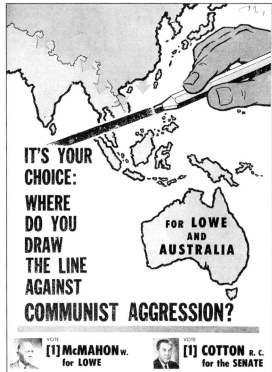

IT'S YOUR CHOICE: WHERE DO YOU DRAW THE LINE AGAINST COMMUNIST AGGRESSION?

FOR LOWE AND AUSTRALIA

VOTE [1] McMAHON W. for LOWE

VOTE [1] COTTON R.C. for the SENATE

resigned stating Gorton was unfit to be prime minister. A Liberal Party meeting vote resulted in a tie and Gorton used his casting vote to decide the issue against himself. The party then elected William McMahon as its leader.

VIETNAM

The quagmire of Vietnam was contributing to the Liberals' growing disunity and lack of direction. When it was first announced that Australian troops would be sent to Vietnam, in April 1965, most people accepted it as necessary. Certainly the next morning there was almost unanimous press support. The only major newspaper to oppose the move was the *Australian*, which headlined its editorial 'THE WAR THAT CAN'T BE WON'. Over the course of the next few years these words were to prove all too prophetic.

At first, Australian troops served with the USA Army's Air Cavalry operating out of Bien Hoa. It was not a success: the Australians did not like USA Army tactics, were appalled by the Americans' acceptance of high casualty rates, and resented being under foreign command. When the size of the contingent was increased to 4,500, in May 1966, the Australians were able to take responsibility for their own area and operate under their own command structure. They established a task force base at Nui Dat, in Phuoc Tuy Province to the southeast of Saigon. The Australian public were constantly told (and the Army and Defence Department apparently believed) that they were in South Vietnam to fight communist infiltrators from North Vietnam. In fact, the troops in Phuoc Tuy faced well-organised, locally supported, communist guerrilla groups and the occasional North Vietnamese mainforce units that could also contain locals. It was never made clear to the Australians what their primary role was; whether it was to fight the mainforce North Vietnamese, or to engage in counter-guerrilla and pacification actions against smaller local units. The roles were not necessarily compatible and the Australian task force lacked the manpower to carry out both duties without the help of USA or South Vietnamese forces. Given their different priorities and command structures, cooperation from their allies was not always forthcoming. The Dat Do Hai minefield illustrated the sort of problem the task force faced. This minefield had been laid by the Australians between two villages, to stop infiltration along the coastline, and the Saigon government had agreed to provide the troops necessary to protect it. This the local commanders were unwilling or unable to do and at night guerrillas were able to infiltrate the minefield, deactivate mines and carry them away to reuse as protection for their own bases.

Apart from their military duties, the Australian forces also undertook a Civil Action Programme in Vietnam. Financed out of SEATO aid money, the aim was 'to win the support of the [local] people' for the government of South Vietnam, and to establish 'goodwill towards the Australian forces in general'. At its height, Civil Action involved 8 per cent of task force personnel in schemes to repair roads and bridges, erect village markets, provide water, and give health, education and public welfare assistance to the locals. As with the task force's military activities, however, local cooperation was not always forthcoming and this tended to lessen the impact of the programme.

Within two months of establishing their task force base at Nui Dat, the Australian army had its first and only major clash of the war when on 18 August 1966 a patrolling company of 6 Royal Australian Regiment made contact with a North Vietnamese force of battalion strength. In the ensuing battle at Long Tan, 245 enemy were killed and at least 500 wounded, for the cost of 18 Australian dead and 21 wounded. Battles like Long Tan did not characterise the conflict for Australians, however. The Vietnam war for the ordinary Australian soldier usually meant long and painstaking patrols in the jungle, with the constant risk of injury from mines and booby traps, and only very occasional clashes with the enemy. The monetary cost of the conflict to Australia was an estimated half a billion dollars. The social cost was 496 killed, 2,398 wounded and a divided nation.

At home, attitudes to the war fell into three distinct phases. Prior to 1968, most Australians accepted that it was necessary for their troops to be in Vietnam to contain communism. They were also reassured by government claims that Australia's allies were winning the war. It was conscription, rather than the war, which was the subject of most public debate at first. The national service scheme, which Menzies announced in November 1964, required all 20-year-old males to register for a ballot to determine whether they were called-up for two years' military service. Unlike earlier peacetime training schemes,

however, it was selective (the odds of being balloted were 1 in 10), allowed fewer exemptions (although tertiary students could have their call-up deferred), had a much longer length of service, and permitted the use of national servicemen overseas. Although there was some unease about the overseas service provisions, initially conscription proved popular with voters. It did not, however, enjoy the approbation of the young, particularly university students, who became increasingly vocal in their opposition to conscription and the war.

In 1968 the first major public doubts about the war began to emerge. The slowly growing list of Australian casualties (particularly of conscripts) had caused concern for some time. But it was the Tet Offensive, of February 1968, which was the real turning point. Australians were shocked to have the hollowness of the allies' repeated claims of victory so easily exposed by the Vietcong thrust. Henceforth the whole rationale of Australia's involvement in Vietnam would be seriously questioned. There were renewed doubts about the fairness of conscription, the legitimacy of the South Vietnamese regime, the morality of USA bombing of North Vietnam, and whether by sending troops Australia was really helping the people of Vietnam at all. All Australians were affected in some way by the public airing of such doubts. Families were torn apart as teenage sons and daughters argued with parents, while in turn the parents struggled to reconcile concern for their son's life with the loyalty they were expected to give to the government and nation. In August 1969 public opinion polls showed that for the first time a majority of Australians were opposed to the continuation of the war.

From the middle of 1969 onwards, anti-Vietnam war sentiment dominated public opinion. More and more young men refused to register for national service or obey call-up notices, and people who had never protested before (or since) were increasingly moved to take part in anti-war demonstrations. These street marches, which had been growing in size and frequency since 1968, eventually evolved into the 'Moratoria', a series of coordinated national demonstrations designed to bring the centres of all Australia's cities to a standstill for a few minutes of silent protest. In the last and biggest 'Moratorium' in June 1971, an estimated 1 million Australians took part. Faced with such massive and growing opposition the federal government's problem was how to extract itself from the conflict while still managing to save political face. In November 1969, the newly elected USA president, Richard Nixon, announced a policy of Vietnamisation. USA ground troops were to be gradually replaced by South Vietnamese soldiers, while bombing was stepped up in order to force the North to the negotiating table. Such a policy also

Demonstration against the Vietnam War, Melbourne, 1970. By the end of the 1960s public opinion had turned round and the dominant feeling was anti-war.

The Vietnam legacy

The Vietnam war left deep scars on Australian society that have not yet entirely healed. Many of the 46,852 Australians (17,424 of them national servicemen) who served in Vietnam still resent not being accorded the respect and honour they believe are their due. Certainly some are still bitter about the shame they were made to feel for fighting in what ultimately proved an unpopular war.

In 1987 the process of public reconciliation began when an emotional and highly successful 'welcome home' march was staged in Sydney for Australia's Vietnam veterans. In 1992 the Vietnam Memorial in Canberra, honouring the 496 Australian servicemen who died, was unveiled. Once again the warm public welcome accorded to the estimated 70,000 veterans and relatives who attended did much to relieve some of the bitterness that many veterans still feel.

The Vietnam experience also had the effect of causing Australians (in the short term at least) to turn their backs on Asia. Interest in the study of Asian languages, culture and history declined at schools and tertiary institutions for some time, and Australian companies tended to overlook business opportunities in the newly industrialised countries of Asia in favour of pursuing markets in Europe and North America.

JWK

offered the opportunity for Australia to start withdrawing troops. Beginning in November 1970 the size of the task force was reduced for the first time. By the end of 1971 only the 'advisers' and a few others remained to be finally withdrawn after the ALP achieved office in December 1972.

Paralleling the Liberal and Country parties' slow decline in the late 1960s was the gradual resurgence of the Australian Labor Party. Arthur Calwell had taken over as parliamentary leader of the ALP on Evatt's retirement in 1960. With his Irish Catholic ancestry, lower-middle-class background, and firm adherence to the reformist ideals of the ALP, Calwell epitomised old Labor. The ALP's massive loss in the 1966 election, which had largely been fought over the issue of conscription, deeply hurt Calwell and in February 1967 he stepped down. The new leader, Edward Gough Whitlam, was determined to avoid the public airing of internal divisions which had previously harmed the ALP. One of his first tasks was to wrestle control of party policy-making away from the ALP machine and make the federal conference and federal executive more representative of the party rank and file. Next came the task of winning party backing for a reform programme which could build on his victory over the party machine.

In the 1969 federal election the ALP achieved important gains, although the coalition under Gorton still managed to hang on to office. The ALP's more responsible image with Whitlam as leader was one factor. Another, of course, was growing public disquiet about the Vietnam war. It is only in retrospect that the ALP's position appears to have been one of total opposition to the war. Paradoxically the Liberal and Country parties' attempts over many years to portray the ALP as disloyal for not giving total support to Australia's involvement in Vietnam, worked against the government in 1969. But probably the most crucial factor of all was the ALP's changing support base. Under Whitlam's leadership the Labor Party ceased to portray itself simply as the party of the industrial working class. Instead it emphasised its moderate position on most issues and aimed to appeal directly to middle Australia – white-collar employees – as well as to the young and a growing band of intellectuals disillusioned with the conservative political parties.

THE 1960S

In the 1960s Australia experienced what amounted to a cultural revolution. In the space of a couple of years, Australians threw off their conservative (and conformist) image and became much more tolerant towards those who were different, or had different standards of public or private behaviour. The most obvious examples of this growing sophistication were to be found in the areas of immigration policy and censorship. Important immigration reforms had already been introduced in the 1950s – such as allowing some non-Europeans to become citizens and abolishing the dictation test – but a restrictive immigration policy based on race had remained in force. Following pressure from immigration reform groups the ALP removed the 'White Australia' policy from its platform in 1966, and, in the first major debate on immigration since federation, federal parliament abandoned all immigration restrictions based on race (see p. 105). Changes to moral standards were equally dramatic. In the early 1960s Australians endured one of the most restrictive censorship regimes in the Western world. Increasingly, however, the public demanded to read, see and hear whatever they wished. Belated recognition of changing public attitudes came with the federal government's appointment of the liberal-minded Don Chipp to the sensitive post of minister for customs in October 1969.

Most of this pressure for change came from the young. The affluence and economic security of the 1960s gave the generation of 'baby boomers' the freedom to challenge many of the beliefs and values of their parents, especially their sexual morality. By the end of the 1960s no taboo seemed beyond challenge: sex before marriage, child rearing for unmarried couples, homosexuality. The introduction of oral contraception for women helped facilitate the change by making promiscuity safer as far as the risk of falling pregnant was concerned. By the end of the decade 40 per cent of women of childbearing age in Australia were using the Pill. In the middle of the 1960s the marriage rate, which had risen in the 1940s, once again began to decline. The churches, which might have been expected to stand fast against such dramatic changes in public morality, were themselves in a state of flux. Church attendances and participation rates, especially amongst Protestants, were in decline, and the pronouncements of the Second Vatican Council led to a freeing up of attitudes among Catholics, with greater openness in their Church.

Improving standards of education also affected community attitudes. Prior to World War II few Australian children continued their education beyond the minimum leaving age of 14, and fewer still benefited from a university education. After 1945 much higher educational standards were gradually introduced for school leavers, and there was a dramatic growth in tertiary education. University enrolments grew from 30,630 in 1950 to 53,391 in 1960, and on to 116,778 in 1970. There was also a general opening up of Australian society to outside ideas as television and jet travel helped break down distances and integrated Australian culture more closely with that of the rest of the world.

The greater freedom and openness enjoyed by Australians in the 1960s had its greatest impact on women. Traditionally Australian society had been intensely masculine and patriarchal, structured so as to deny women full social equality with men. A few women's organisations existed, but they tended to be either genteel service organisations like the YWCA and the Country Women's Association, or sectional pressure groups such as the Australian Federation of University Women. Issues like equal pay and health policies for women were occasionally raised for public debate, but there was no real attempt to mobilise women, who themselves tended not to question their role in society. The world-wide women's liberation movement of the late 1960s and early 1970s changed this picture radically. The growing band of young university-educated Australian women (their numbers grew sixfold to 36,000 between 1950 and 1970) were particularly receptive to the movement's ideas. The experience of university had shown that they could compete equally with men, and the 1960s student protest movement had attuned them to the irony of their own situation: that while advocating the rights to self-determination and

equality for other races they were still being denied full equality in their own society. Although initially ridiculed by the media, the ideas articulated by the 'second-wave feminists' – particularly critiques of gender roles and domestic life – helped change community attitudes towards women's role in society. It became acceptable for married women to engage in full-time paid employment. The proportion of women in the workforce rose from 22.8 per cent in 1954 to 31.7 per cent in 1971, and in 1971 married women accounted for 56.8 per cent of the female workforce. Certainly one of the unforeseen consequences of the women's liberation movement is that by the 1980s the two-income family had become the norm in Australia.

Black Australia also began to reassert itself in the 1960s. There were two aspects to this growth in Aboriginal protest, a greater concern shown by white Australians towards the indigenous population, and a cultural and political revival among Aborigines themselves. The growing white disquiet found legislative recognition in the overwhelming success of a 1967 referendum. The Liberal and Country Party government had asked voters to amend the Constitution so Aborigines could henceforth be counted in the Census and to give the federal parliament the power to legislate in their concerns. The referendum was widely interpreted as giving Aborigines full citizenship rights and the electorate gave a record vote (90.77 per cent) in favour of the amendments. The size of the Yes vote should not be seen simply as an expression of 'goodwill' towards the Aborigines, however: an affirmative vote did not threaten the *status quo* and an analysis of the No vote shows that rural Australia was far from whole-hearted in its support.

Paralleling the changing attitudes of urban white Australians towards black Australians was a cultural and political revival among Aborigines themselves. Beginning in the late 1950s, there had been moves by non-traditional and urban Aborigines to create or revive their own welfare organisations (see pp. 142–3).

The 1960s also saw an escalation in protests by traditional Aborigines. In 1963 people at the Yirrkala Reserve in the Northern Territory petitioned federal parliament over the excision of 150 square miles (390 km²) of what they thought of as their land for bauxite mining. In a landmark decision a Federal Parliamentary Select Committee recommended compensation. In 1965 Aborigines who lived and worked on the Wave Hill cattle station in the Northern Territory staged their own protest. The Australian Workers Union had asked the Federal Arbitration Commission to extend the basic wage to all Aboriginal workers. The Commission agreed, but delayed implementation of the new award until 1968. The

Gurindji workers at Wave Hill cattle station, who had long complained about their low wages ($6 a week, plus flour and sugar), walked off in protest. Their demands soon shifted from wages to land rights, however, when they requested that station land around Wattie Creek, a traditional camp site, be returned to their control. After two years of protest the federal government agreed to give the Gurindji title to 10 square miles (26 km²) of land surrounding Wattie Creek, while the cattle station owners retained their lease over the other 6,000 square miles (1,554 km²). The symbolic importance of the Yirrkala and Wattie Creek victories should not be underestimated, however. They marked the first time a federal government had recognised an Aboriginal land claim.

WHITLAM AND FRASER (1972–83)

On 2 December 1972 Australian electors went to the polls. After 23 years of continuous conservative rule federally, opinion polls suggested a narrow win for the ALP. The Labor Party, with its popular leader, Gough Whitlam, at the fore, ran a brilliant campaign, mixing show-biz and statesmanship, with a promise for much-needed reform; its slogan, 'It's Time', seemed to capture the mood of the electorate. The Liberal–Country Party coalition, on the other hand, stumbled in the lead-up to the election, and appeared tired and dispirited. McMahon, the prime minister, certainly failed to inspire voters. In the closing days of the campaign the coalition resorted to mud-slinging, claiming an ALP government would be a tool of the trade union movement and would open the floodgates to pornography. The scare tactics failed and the

Gough Whitlam, speaking at a rally in Melbourne in 1972.

ALP won a narrow victory (49.6 per cent of the primary vote compared with the LCP's 41.48 per cent). The result translated into a nine-seat majority for Labor in the House of Representatives, but a hung Senate with five Democratic Labor Party senators (the party that formed out of the ALP split in the 1950s) holding the balance of power.

Whitlam, the new prime minister, was one of a new breed of Labor politicians. The son of a senior Commonwealth public servant, educated at private and government schools, an arts/law graduate of the University of Sydney, and married to the daughter of a distinguished New South Wales judge, he was thoroughly middle class in background and upbringing. Although regarded as a 'silvertail' by old-time Labor men, Whitlam's social background, and intellectual and cultural interests, were not much dissimilar to the younger, affluent and more highly educated voters who swung to support Labor in the late 1960s and early 1970s. Blessed with intelligence and wit, fluent in speech, Whitlam had a commanding presence. He was 6 feet 4 inches (193 cm) and his voice was deep and resonant. As opposition leader he dominated parliament and established a clear ascendancy over the McMahon government in the lead-up to the election.

The ALP was elected to office on a platform of reform and Whitlam wasted no time in initiating change. Three days after the election (and before the final declaration of all the polls) Whitlam and his deputy, Lance Barnard, were sworn in as a special two-man ministry. They announced an immediate end to conscription, the release of gaoled draft dodgers and the dropping of all pending prosecutions under the National Service Act, the opening of diplomatic relations with Communist China, and the re-opening of the Arbitration Commission case into equal pay for women. When, two weeks later, the full ministry was sworn in, the pace of change picked up still further: the Australian dollar was revalued, immigration changes announced, the imperial honours system abolished, new guidelines for unemployment benefits formulated and military aid to South Vietnam abolished. Added to which, three of the new ministers criticised Nixon's resumption of the bombing of North Vietnam, which aggrieved the US government. And all this within a month of the election.

After nearly a quarter of a century of conservative rule the rapidity of change under Labor exhilarated some and terrified others. During the 18-month life of the first Whitlam ministry an unprecedented number of bills were presented to parliament. There did not appear to be any activity of government that would escape reform. In new areas like urban development, the arts, the environment and government administration – as well as in more traditional ones

Demonstration in 1975 in Melbourne against the government of Malcolm Fraser, appointed by the governor-general Sir John Kerr after he dismissed Whitlam's government. Although feelings ran high against this action, Fraser won the subsequent federal election.

government was to recognise itself, and then convince the electorate, that the 'long boom' conditions were gone forever and that a major overhaul of the economy was required.

FRASER 1975–83

On 13 December 1975, the Liberal and Country parties won 53 per cent of the primary vote and the largest majority of seats of any government since federation: 91 to 36. The new prime minister, John Malcolm Fraser, had the reputation of being an extreme right-winger. Tall and disdainful in appearance, this wealthy grazier and scion of the Victorian establishment had once told reporters that 'life was not meant to be easy'. Heeding Machiavelli's advice that it was better for a ruler to be feared than loved, he had shown a ruthless determination and displayed nerves of steel in the weeks leading up to the dismissal of the Whitlam government. The legacy of those events would remain to haunt him, however, and despite continuing election victories in December 1977 and October 1980 he never quite laid to rest the charge that he had originally obtained office by underhand means.

The person who carried the greatest burden of guilt for the manner of Whitlam's dismissal, however, was the governor-general. Subjected to a constant barrage of derision and protest whenever he appeared in public, the strain took its toll and Kerr's behaviour became increasingly erratic. While presenting the prizes at the conclusion of Australia's premier horse race, the Melbourne Cup, in November 1977, he appeared to be intoxicated and was jeered by the crowd. A month later Kerr resigned as governor-general. Subsequent holders of the office have had to work extremely hard to rehabilitate the governor-generalship in the eyes of many Australians.

Fraser quickly established a reputation for break-

ing election promises. For example, his promises that the government would maintain Medibank, the Prices Justification Tribunal, support wage indexation and introduce a permanent scheme of tax indexation were all broken over the life of the government. The explanation for the list of broken promises was, that the economy demanded cuts in government expenditure. What infuriated the government's critics was that those being asked to make sacrifices were invariably the unemployed and welfare recipients, while the rural sector benefited from a restoration of the superphosphate bounty, and new subsidies for cattle producers and dairy farmers.

FRASER'S NEW FEDERALISM

Despite Fraser's reputation as an arch conservative he was responsible for attempting a number of important reforms in government administration.

Fraser's New Federalism, for instance, attempted to simplify the financial relationship between the federal and state governments. The scheme promised the biggest change to federal–state relations since the uniform income-tax agreements of World War II. The states were asked to accept a fixed share of federal revenue in return for having the power to levy their own taxes and charges returned to them.

In the end little came of New Federalism, however, after the states accused the federal government of simply trying to transfer some of its responsibilities on to them.

More successful were constitutional amendments ensuring the convention for filling casual Senate vacancies was henceforth adhered to, the creation of an office of Commonwealth Ombudsman and the passing of a Federal Freedom of Information Act. The Fraser government also showed itself to have a social conscience and to be attuned to environmental issues, with the passing of the first Aboriginal Land Rights Act, its actions to save Fraser Island off the Queensland coast from wholesale sand mining, and its commissioning of a pioneering environmental inquiry into uranium mining in the Northern Territory.

Fraser's liberalism was most forcefully expressed in foreign policy. The coalition government continued the tradition established by Whitlam of maintaining friendly relations with China. Furthermore, Fraser's abhorrence of racism led him to do something without precedent by a conservative Australian prime minister, and that was to become a champion of black Africa.

At the Commonwealth Heads of Government Meeting in 1979 Fraser played a pivotal role in solving the Rhodesian question and ensuring black majority rule for the renamed Zimbabwe.

Malcolm Fraser, on the right, listening to a speech by Robert Mugabe at the Commonwealth Heads of Government meeting in 1979. Fraser played a key part at this conference in solving the Rhodesia problem and ushering in majority rule for the renamed Zimbabwe.

THE ECONOMY

It was not all plain sailing for Fraser's government and again it was the economy which caused most concern. The recession continued and, following a record devaluation of the Australian dollar in November 1976, even higher interest rates, a credit squeeze and further cuts in government expenditure were announced to counter inflation. Of particular concern to the government was a significant drop in budgeted tax receipts in 1976–77. It was to be the first indication that increasing numbers of Australian companies were exploiting loopholes in an effort to minimise tax. Outlawing tax avoidance became a major political challenge for Fraser.

In August 1982 a Royal Commission originally set up to investigate corruption in the Ship Painters' and Dockers' Union released a report detailing a network of tax fraud, corruption, drug smuggling and illegal arms dealing in Australia. In all, 1,412 companies, many involving prominent members of the Liberal Party, had evaded millions of dollars in tax. Although Fraser tried to deal firmly with the issue by introducing retrospective legislation to recover the lost money, he encountered opposition from sections of his own party. Even watered-down anti-tax avoidance legislation was passed only with ALP support as some government members crossed the floor.

The gradually worsening economy affected social attitudes. The 1970s had begun with many young Australians appearing to reject the materialism of their parents. For a short time 'dropping out' and going 'back to nature' enjoyed a vogue. Such lifestyles, however, were very much the product of affluent times, and as Australia's economic position slowly worsened, getting a job became the major priority for most young people. For low achievers in their teens the harsher economic climate proved devastating. As unemployment grew, school leavers found it increasingly difficult to break into the workforce. By 1982 one in five Australian teenagers aged between 15 and 19 was unemployed. Despite repeated government attempts to improve job prospects for the young a sub-culture of youth unemployment emerged in 1980s Australia.

Fraser's political style was to keep his opponents continually off balance. He did this partly by turning speculation about early elections, and early elections themselves, into something of a political art form. In December 1977 and again in October 1980 Fraser called snap polls at least 12 months before they were due in order to take advantage of favourable political circumstances. The tactic eventually led to his own undoing, however, when in February 1983 he called a snap election for March to take advantage of leadership wrangling within the ALP. The tactic backfired when, on the same day, the opposition leader, Bill Hayden, was persuaded to voluntarily step aside and allow the challenger, Bob Hawke, to take his place. The speed and ease with which Labor changed leaders caught Fraser completely wrong-footed for once.

With unemployment running at over 8 per cent, high inflation and a wage freeze beginning to bite, it was no surprise that the first opinion polls showed Labor ahead. The government also suffered from its refusal to force the state government of Tasmania to back down over plans to dam the Franklin River in a wilderness area of that state (see p. 48). Eager to regain the initiative, Fraser began by attacking Hawke's character, claiming he was 'too unstable' to be prime minister. As the ALP leader had long been one of the most popular figures in Australian public life, this only helped draw the electors' attention to Fraser's own deficiencies and low public rating.

difficult issues, such as a tax summit in 1985, failed, but the 'Accord' of 1983 survives 10 years later.

During the life of the Hawke government (1983-91) the economy and its management came to dominate political debate in Australia. The treasurer, Paul Keating, induced the Cabinet and caucus to abandon many long-cherished Labor beliefs and the Hawke government embraced economic rationalism, floating the currency, deregulating financial markets and easing restrictions on foreign investment. Keating's authority in economic matters was so great that he was even able to persuade his colleagues to accept fiscal restraints that resulted in a series of balanced or surplus federal budgets between 1987 and 1990. Although the government's economic reforms and preparedness to reduce budget expenditure earned applause from the business community (and for a time made Keating the darling of the financial markets), there were some who questioned whether such policies benefited ordinary working men and women, the ALP's traditional supporters. Three successive, but narrow, election victories in December 1984, July 1987 and March 1990, with Labor losing support in working-class strongholds, suggested that traditional party allegiances were changing.

Things began well enough for the Hawke government: the drought of 1980-83 broke, Australia emerged from recession, and inflation and unemployment fell steadily. The economy boomed with three years of strong economic growth. The traditional Australian problem of economic growth encouraging imports soon asserted itself however. With world commodity prices remaining depressed, the already shaky balance of payments position worsened. The government's response was threefold: push up interest rates to slow the importation of consumer goods, contain wage pressures, and attempt to restructure the economy to make the country less dependent on its traditional commodity exports. Despite the high interest rates (home loans peaked at 17.5 per cent in July 1989), and a fall in the value of the dollar (dropping 30 per cent in 1985), Australia's overseas debt continued to grow. In May 1986 Keating warned that Australia risked becoming a 'banana republic'. Such candid comments not only typified the realism that had entered economic debate, they also indicated the frustration felt by a government attempting to rectify structural deficiencies in the economy that should have been addressed 20 years previously.

Deregulation of the financial markets, strong economic growth and a booming stockmarket, provided the right conditions for a new generation of speculators and take-over specialists to prosper in Australia. The spectacular rise, and audacity, of such new business entrepreneurs as Alan Bond and Christopher Skase not only provided entertainment for the Aus-

tralian public, but also epitomised the recklessness of Australian business practice in the 1980s. This lack of prudence extended to a number of leading Australian financial institutions (both private and state-government owned) which were caught up in the speculators' rush. The world stockmarket crash of October 1987 marked the beginning of the end for many of the high-flyers. By the 1990s most of their business empires had collapsed and the government-owned banks of Victoria and South Australia face such severe loses that it will take years for the states' finances to recover.

Slowing down an overheated domestic economy, reducing the trade deficit and lowering overseas debt became the main aims of the government from 1986 onwards. The problem was how to ensure that the economy could make a soft landing. In 1990 unemployment began to rise as Australia slid into recession. At first, treasurer Keating was undaunted, claiming it was the recession Australia 'had to have'. A subsequent downturn in the world economy, however, ensured that Australia's recession would last longer and be more painful than anyone anticipated. By 1993 unemployment had reached 11 per cent with over a million Australians out of work. Nor did the recession provide any relief for Australia's growing overseas debt, which by June 1993 had reach $150 billion.

KEATING'S LEADERSHIP

In May 1991 the long-simmering tensions between Hawke and Keating surfaced publicly. Hawke was accused of reneging on a secret promise to step aside as prime minister before the next election to allow Keating to take over. In a subsequent leadership challenge Hawke won the caucus vote and Keating, the government's most effective parliamentary performer and the man most commentators credited with being the dominant intellectual force in Cabinet, retired to the backbench. Six months of instability, declining government popularity and blundering by Hawke's choice as replacement treasurer, John Kerin, followed. When a second leadership challenge was mounted in December 1991, Keating emerged victorious. Hawke, electorally the most successful ALP prime minister in Australia's history, became the first Labor Prime Minister ever to be defeated in a leadership challenge.

Paul John Keating had been involved with Labor politics all his adult life. Born in the working-class western suburbs of Sydney, he had joined the ALP on the eve of his fifteenth birthday, entered federal parliament at the age of 25, been the youngest person ever appointed as a federal Labor minister (in 1975, aged 31), and in May 1991 became the longest-serving federal Labor treasurer in history. Three decades of involvement in Labor politics had honed Keating's skills: his sharp wit, scornful invective and colourful language made him the favourite of the government benches during parliamentary question time. A man of cultivated tastes, he was privately contemptuous of the Australian obsession with sport; Keating nevertheless made a point of becoming a supporter of Collingwood, the quintessentially working-class Australian Rules Football club, while positioning himself to challenge for the prime ministership in 1990.

Keating's task, in preparing the Labor government for the election due in 1993, was a daunting one. Growing unemployment, the worsening recession, and the fact that the opposition was led by a former professor of economics, Dr John Hewson, ensured that the economy would be the main election issue. In November 1991 the Liberal and National Party opposition announced 'Fightback', one of the most far-reaching programmes for economic reform ever seen in Australia. Its cornerstone was the lowering of income tax by means of a substitute goods and ser-

Paul Keating, who took over as ALP leader and as prime minister from Bob Hawke in December 1991 after a prolonged power struggle. He went on to win the 1993 election, despite trailing in the opinion polls throughout the campaign.

Australia and the monarchy

Before World War II few Australians questioned their nation's relationship with the British monarchy. Sentiment and tradition, economics and the law (Australians were British subjects, whose head of state was the British monarch) combined to make the Crown a revered institution in Australia.

When Elizabeth II made the first visit by a reigning British monarch to Australia in 1954, she received a rapturous reception. Huge and joyous crowds followed the young Queen's every move and upwards of 7 million people (out of a population of 9 million) confessed to having viewed the royal visitors at least once. Subsequent royal tours have not attracted anything like the same degree of public enthusiasm.

The decline in royalist sentiment was a gradual process and had less to do with the monarchy *per se*, than with Australia's changing relationship with Britain. Australia's defence realignment towards the USA (accentuated by Britain's decline as a world power after 1945), Britain's reorientation towards Europe, and the declining importance of trade between the two nations, all combined to make Australia and Britain increasingly irrelevant to one another. (In 1938 the UK took 55 per cent of Australia's exports and supplied 41 per cent of imports; in 1991 the UK took 3 per cent of exports and supplied 7 per cent of imports.) Even the sentimental attachment that many Australians had towards 'home' was weakened by the impact of post-war European immigration and, more recently, Asian immigration.

With the substance of the relationship impugned in this way, it was inevitable that the symbols of Australia's connection with Britain would also face challenge. It was the first federal Labor government in more than two decades, the Whitlam government (1972–75), that took the initiative. Appeals to the Privy Council were abandoned, imperial honours replaced by the Order of Australia, attempts made to have reference to the monarchy removed from Australia's pledge of allegiance, 'Advance Australia Fair' adopted as Australia's anthem, and the title 'Queen of Australia' bestowed upon Elizabeth II.

The Fraser government (1975–83) restored 'God Save the Queen' and imperial honours, but this was reversed in turn by the Hawke government (1983–91).

The catalyst for serious public discussion about whether Australia should become a republic was the dismissal of the Whitlam government by the monarch's representative in Australia, the governor-general, in November 1975. Twelve months after the sacking, a public opinion poll found 47 per cent of those surveyed were in favour of Australia becoming a republic.

Despite significant public support for a republic (particularly amongst young Australians), for a decade or more after the dismissal the ALP shied away from the issue, leaving it to the press and committees of prominent citizens to debate. It was the approaching centenary of federation and the possibility of achieving cross-party support that placed republicanism back on the mainstream political agenda in Australia.

In June 1991 Hawke told the Constitutional Centenary Conference, established by his government to advise on constitutional reform, that it was inevitable Australia would become a republic. The ALP subsequently adopted this as part of its federal platform. Debate over a republic again accelerated after Keating took over as Prime Minister. In January 1992 Keating spoke in favour of a new flag without 'the flag of another country in its corner' and when visiting Japan in March 1992 said that Australia's future lay in shedding its attachments to Britain and aligning its economy more closely with Asia and the Pacific. Since the March 1993 election, Keating has discussed Australia becoming a republic before 2001.

Recent adverse publicity about the behaviour of some younger members of the British royal family has not strengthened the republican case, so much as weakened that of supporters of a constitutional monarchy., In 1993 opinion polls indicated for the first time that a majority of Australians favour Australia becoming a republic.

JWK

Aboriginal settlement at Wybalenna on Flinders Island, 1847. The first mission stations set up to attract Aborigines were failures.

invasion; the younger children could not remember when there were no white people in their country. But this second phase of mission stations gave the Aborigines a chance to re-group. Though the people had fewer living areas to choose from, a few decades of living among the whites had given them greater skills. They were self-confident among themselves, many were hard-working and competent; where there was sufficient land, they were self-sufficient. When in later years they were driven from the missions as state governments withdrew leases or grants, the years on the stations were looked back on as a golden age where there had been land, supplies, food, work, schools, churches and order in daily life.

The effect of this second phase (1860–90) of mission stations in southern Australia was rather different from that intended by its sponsors. The people found strength in numbers, they shared a common culture. The stations brought a new awareness to residents who presumably before 1788 had thought of themselves as members of family groups rather than as 'Aborigines'. Large numbers of people assembled from diverse areas on to small reserves, united by common experiences and a dislike of patronising managers, began to feel a shared Aboriginality against a common aggressor rather than the family loyalties by which they had previously been united.

The children of the missions were not as effectively won for Europeanism as the missionaries imagined. The decline in the performance of larger ceremonies such as initiation did not necessarily mean a decline in Aboriginal self-concepts. Ceremonies mattered to the old people, of course, some of whom held out fiercely against missionary teaching;

but the uninitiated children continued to identify as Aboriginal. Though they had not known pre-invasion life, they knew they were Aborigines because their parents raised them as Aboriginal, and because the whites treated them as Aboriginal.

Their grandchildren and great-grandchildren include the Victorian Kooris (Aborigines) of today. Though very few are of the full-descent or speak a Victorian language, most are fiercely proud of their identity. They realise that a literate, articulate Aboriginal need be little more Europeanised in beliefs, feelings and intuitions than a tribalised person.

THE ENTRY OF THE STATE

The period of church-controlled mission stations merged in Victoria with the creation of the Board for the Protection of the Aborigines in 1860. The other southern states followed, and the re-entry of government into Aboriginal affairs marks a turning-point in the history of race relations.

It was the motivation of governments which had changed. For the first 60 or 70 years of settlement (and very much longer in outlying areas) it had been assumed that the Aborigines of the full-descent were declining into extinction and that it was only a matter of time before none survived. One of the purposes of the missions at this time, in fact, was to protect the apparently poor remainder from further oppression, a function which became known in the twentieth century as 'smoothing the dying pillow'. But by 1860 it was apparent in the rural regions of Victoria that the people of part-Aboriginal descent were not only continuing to identify as Aborigines, but their numbers were increasing.

It is a sad commentary on the perceptions of white Australians that, as soon as it became apparent that the Aborigines had been saved from extinction, they began to adopt methods to control the population and prevent its increase. One apparently simple method of control was to drive the 'half-castes', whom the whites persisted in regarding as people quite distinct from 'full-bloods', into the white community. Victoria was the first to enact legislation: the Aborigines Act of 1886 allowed only 'full-bloods' and 'half-castes' over 34 years of age to remain on the reserves which now, in the foreseeable future, could be closed; meanwhile the expelled Aborigines would be forced into the general community and eventually disappear. Other states introduced similar legislation within 20 years: the policy of dispersal (for such it was rather than its official title of Protection) became the goal of all but one of the southern states by 1910. The exception was Tasmania, which refused to concede that its part-Aboriginal survivors were Aborigines at all.

Among the whites there were at least two conflicting forces. Aborigines must be dispersed, yet their merging must not be allowed to upset the citizens of the country towns. The cross-purposes of the state administrations may be seen in the differing definitions of Aboriginality. No state allowed Aborigines to drink alcohol, and for this purpose 'Aborigines' were defined in the various Liquor Acts as people of any recognisable degree of Aboriginal descent. In contrast the purpose of all the turn-of-the-century Aborigines Protection Acts (Victoria 1886, Western Australia 1905, New South Wales 1909, South Australia 1911) was to close the reserves and merge the Aborigines with the whites, so here the looser definition of 'half-blood' was utilised. Thus in New South Wales a 'half-caste' Aboriginal man who did not receive rations was not an Aboriginal under the Aborigines Protection Act and could be expelled from his home and birthplace on a reserve; the same man was defined as an Aboriginal under the Liquor Act and could be expelled from a hotel for being Aboriginal! Through carelessness and indifference as much as conscious policy at this time, the white legislatures were moving to define the indigenous people out of existence.

The period 1886–1918, therefore, was a period of greater oppression for Aborigines who had been allowed to live in comparative seclusion for many years. Now another white pressure group added itself to the twin pincers of Protection Board and rural townspeople. The farmers' demands to release the land currently occupied by the reserves coincided with the political pressures to expel the residents to stop the Aboriginal population increasing. But the townsfolk were the first to complain when the Aborigines, expelled and with nowhere to go, began to gather outside the fringes of the towns. Hundreds of Aboriginal families now faced a decade of homelessness as they wandered from one to another of the old

Semi-westernised but poverty-stricken Aboriginal women photographed in c. 1881.

living areas, moved on in turn by the police sergeant or health inspector at the orders of the local mayor.

The state governments, instead of choosing humane and rational solutions, took the easiest way out. Reserves were kept open, but people expelled from them; fringe-dwellers about the towns were hurried on – to new reserves in areas where the whites were not yet complaining. The results were twofold: one, in New South Wales, was an expensive administrative muddle for the authorities who were busy closing down reserves while opening new ones to house the same people expelled from the first. The other was the new experience for many Aborigines, especially in Western Australia, of being driven from many smaller reserves to reside on a single, large one presided over by a manager with an immense power to control daily life. The infamous Moore River Settlement of Western Australia, established in 1916, was one example of the catastrophic shift in state policy in this period. A regulation of doubtful legality allowed the compulsory transfer of people from fringe camps or reserves to the settlement which at one point held over 1,300 people. Hundreds of *nyoongars* (as southwestern Aborigines call themselves) still hold bitter memories of forced marches and humiliations carried out half a century ago.

THE NORTH

At the turn of the century different policies towards Aborigines were pursued in the Northern Territory (at this time governed by South Australia) and Queensland. One reason for this difference lay in the much larger proportion of Aborigines to whites; another was the frontier-like conditions which still prevailed in the more remote areas. While the southern states were opting, though uncertainly, for merging, the Northern Territory and Queensland governments believed that the solution lay in large undeveloped reserves in which the people could be protected from exploitation. An Aborigines Act of 1897 led to the establishment in Queensland of half a dozen large reserves and many smaller ones. Unlike the southern Aborigines, the definitions of whom were framed for different purposes, in Queensland almost everyone of Aboriginal descent could be classed as an Aborigine, confined to a reserve and kept there compulsorily.

After the Commonwealth Government assumed control of the Northern Territory in 1911, there was greater concern for the survival of the 'full-bloods'. Baldwin Spencer, the chief protector of Aborigines, recommended in 1913 the establishment of what later became a standard administrative tool: reserves of up to 1,000 square miles where tribal Aborigines could follow traditional modes of life, but within which they could be taught the elements of European civilisation. Though there was confusion about the ultimate fate of the reserves, the idea that Northern Territory, and to a lesser extent, Queensland Aborigines were fundamentally different from southerners, persisted for many years. Queensland's legislation was held for some years as a model of protection. At the first conference for Commonwealth and state Aboriginal authorities in 1937, it was decreed that the fate of all 'caste' Aborigines was to be merged with the whites: the Northern Territory and Queensland 'full-bloods' were exempted.

In the south the administrators drifted towards ever-greater bureaucratic control. Reserve closures failed because the Aborigines refused to leave and because the white townsfolk objected to the resulting fringe-camps. Now to the policy of dispersal of men and women was added a second element, the removal of Aboriginal children from their families and communities to be raised in institutions by white authorities.

CHILD-REMOVAL

The rationale of child-removal, up to 1850, had been based on the belief that children could be raised as Christians and members of the industrial working classes. Then the hiatus in white control left families in peace for some three or four decades until the authorities, recognising the rapid growth in the self-identifying population, reassessed child-removal as a new method of social engineering.

By 1911 all the state Acts permitted the removal of children. New South Wales established two institutions, at Cootamundra and Kinchela. Victoria followed a different policy of mixing the children in white (Child Welfare) institutions or adopting them. At Moore River (Western Australia), Colebrook (South Australia), the Half-Caste Institution (Alice Springs) and Catholic institutions at Melville Island (Northern Territory) children were socialised into white society and their links with their own culture, as far as possible, broken. In Queensland children of part-descent were liable to be removed and transported to Palm Island. Only the full-descent children of the north, imprisoned within the large reserves, were comparatively safe from separation at this time. It is difficult to calculate how many children were removed, but the proportion of one child in three in the 1920s may not be inaccurate.

Separation affected not only the children but their descendants. A child removed who did not return, and who bore four children who did not identify as Aboriginal, was an effective loss to her community, over 25 years, of five people. Over a period of 100 years, the total losses to Aborigines resulting from

Kindergarten for part-Aboriginal children at Palm Island near Townsville, northern Queensland, c. 1930. Palm Island was a base for children of mixed descent who were taken by state authorities from Aboriginal homes and settlements. The removal of very young children in particular had a permanently deleterious effect on the Aboriginal population.

the nationwide policy of child-removal have represented, in 1988, as many again as the current self-identifying Aboriginal population.

Many children in time returned to their communities, but only those taken at an age when they could remember where they had come from. Some returned with skills and abilities which those who remained on the reserves did not possess. Because they had spent their lives among white people, they had confidence in dealing with them. Experience had given them a wider view, or they had seen alternatives to oppression and exploitation. Many became leaders of community organisations and some of national Aboriginal concerns. Aborigines raised apart from their communities include Charles Perkins, until 1988 secretary of the Federal Department of Aboriginal Affairs, since 1994 chair of the Aboriginal and Torres Strait Islander Committee (ATSIC), Lois O'Donoghue, the former chair of ATSIC, and Rob Riley, a former chairman of the National Aboriginal Conference.

RESERVE CONDITIONS

World War I interrupted the administration of the new Protection Acts, but the 1920s, when the processes of dispersal were working most efficiently, was one of the worst periods for Aborigines since 1788. Probably at least half the Aborigines in settled Australia were uprooted from their homes; thousands of children were removed. In Queensland the 'protective' legislation which kept communities together on the reserves became progressively harsher as new regulations were introduced. Managers had the right to search residents, confiscate or

sell property, read mail, control bank accounts, language, recreation, entry and exit permits. By the onset of the depression the features of Aboriginal administration were, in Queensland, the harsh and worsening reserve conditions. In New South Wales, South Australia, Western Australia and Victoria there operated two policies, mutually exclusive, of closing reserves in answer to one set of criteria, and opening new ones in answer to another. The chief feature of the Northern Territory was the employment of Aborigines on cattle-stations as 'ringers' (cattle-men and women) or domestic servants on wages and conditions little different from slavery.

The depression brought new pressures onto the embattled communities. Unemployment hit Aborigines particularly hard: not only were they the first put off work, they then found that they were not eligible for the 'dole'. Men who as a result of state policies had been driven from the reserves into the workforce a few years before had now to apply to the Aboriginal authorities for food relief, which was set at a much lower rate than for Europeans. As 'bag-towns' (temporary makeshift camps) proliferated outside country towns, local authorities increased pressure in forcing Aborigines back to the reserves. The run-down houses had not adequately contained the previous populations, but now they were swollen by hundreds of new arrivals, few of whom wanted to be there.

This period was also marked by a series of harsh amendments to the Aboriginal Acts of many of the states. Western Australia widened the definition of Aboriginal over whom controls could be exerted; South Australia introduced new regulations restricting miscegenation; New South Wales in 1936 allowed the removal of any Aboriginal person to a designated area (that is, a reserve). The states followed each other in seeking ways, not as 30 years before, to drive Aborigines from the reserves, but to force them back on to them. If the 1920s was the period when Aboriginal morale reached its lowest point since the invasion, the 1930s were the nadir of oppression of human rights. Effectively in several states it had become a criminal offence to be Aboriginal, since a declaration as such could cause the person named to be immediately transported to a reserve and kept there indefinitely.

ABORIGINAL PROTESTS

The 1930s are also a different kind of turning point. Probably it was the very harsh and worsening conditions, and the fact that Aborigines were now mixing more freely with one another on the big reserves, which caused the protests which had been a trickle in the 1920s to become a torrent. In 1932 Bill Cooper of Cumeroogunga established the Australian Aborigines League. John Patten and Bill Ferguson in 1938 put together the newspaper Abo Call which demanded the abolition of the New South Wales Aborigines Protection Board. Pearl Gibbs and Margaret Tucker demanded that Aborigines be allowed to leave the reserves when they wished. There were public meetings to which for the first time only Aborigines were invited. A 'Day of Mourning' was marked on the sesquicentenary of the invasion. World War II robbed the movement of its momentum. The most significant outcome, though obscured

at the time, was an Aboriginal self-confidence which grew throughout the decade, a confidence in the power to change unjust laws, to attract the press, to win minor victories against the protectors.

The same process of self-confidence repeated itself, especially in the north, during 1939–45. Hundreds of Aborigines, accustomed only to pastoral station life, were trained as soldiers or non-combatants in army camps (p. 114). They were well fed, paid a regular cash wage and treated more or less the same as the regular soldiers. By the end of the war probably more than half the Northern Territory adults in contact with the whites had seen an alternative to the appalling infant death rate, brutal treatment and starvation rations of the pastoral stations.

One of the earliest exponents of post-war self-confidence was Fred Waters in Darwin. In 1951 he organised a strike at the Bagot compound against the poor food and conditions. Without laying formal charges, the Welfare Branch of the Northern Territory government whisked Waters away to the other end of the Territory and the ensuing publicity caused a number of concerned white people to think more deeply about the conditions under which Aborigines were forced to live, as well as their future status within the whole community.

TWO DECADES OF WHITE AND BLACK COOPERATION

The two decades following the 1939–45 war were characterised by joint organisations of black and

A 'Day of Mourning' held in January 1938 on the 150th anniversary of what the Aborigines characterised as 'the whiteman's seizure of our country'. Only Aborigines were invited to attend this protest against their treatment at the hands of whites. Aboriginal militancy had been growing during the 1930s.

Charles Perkins, Aborigine who led the Freedom Ride of 1965 through various towns in New South Wales notorious for their treatment of Aborigines, and who later became secretary of the Federal Department of Aboriginal Affairs. In 1994 he became chair of the Aboriginal and Torres Strait Islander Committee.

white people which formed the principal pressure groups upon governments. One of the earliest was the strike, in May 1946, of Aboriginal cattlemen in the Pilbara (Western Australia) led by a white man, Don McLeod, and two Aboriginal men, Dooley Bin-Bin and Clancy McKenna.

More common in this period were the various Aborigines Progress and Advancement Leagues. In the 1950s almost all were managed by whites; the period's end was signified by the mostly successful Aboriginal attempts to take over the management of these organisations.

The best known of the joint organisations was the Federal Council for the Advancement of Aboriginal and Torres Strait Islanders, formed in 1957 by the impetus of South Australian, New South Wales and Victorian Advancement Leagues. Though its generally left-wing tone effectively kept it outside the white establishment, FCAATSI achieved significant successes in the 1960s.

One of its most successful actions was its contribution to the campaign to force Northern Territory cattle-station bosses to pay their Aboriginal stockmen a minimum wage from 1965. Another was its participation in the 1967 referendum campaign, which by amendment to the federal Constitution enabled Aborigines to vote and the federal government to assume a concurrent power with the states to legislate in Aboriginal affairs (see also pp.126–7).

A further result of the 1967 record vote in favour of constitutional change was the establishment of the Council of Aboriginal Affairs, and the appointment of a minister in charge of Aboriginal Affairs. Two subsequent government initiatives were the establishment of the Australian Institute of Aboriginal Studies (1968) and the Aboriginal Arts Board (1973).

There were two different kinds of issues with which FCAATSI and the many Aboriginal Advancement groups were concerned. One, broadly, was civil rights – the right of Aborigines to attend white schools, own property, buy land, drink in hotels and generally to integrate into white society. The other was a revival of a separate cultural identity. One impetus ran towards white society, the other away from it, but because Aborigines suffered both a denial of civil rights and the right to cultural identity the two issues were intertwined.

It was the events of the late 1960s which polarised the supporters of the joint organisations by making the distinction clearer. As some civil rights in certain states were granted, younger Aborigines demanded a recognition of their own leadership, particularly in policy making. The resulting splits to a large extent ended the two decades of cooperation.

In 1969 Oodgeroo Noonuccal (Kath Walker) attended an overseas conference on indigenous peoples and returned convinced that Aboriginal and Islander people must control their own organisations. The following year a motion was put at the FCAATSI annual conference that only Aborigines and Islanders should serve on the executive committee. The motion was lost, but a splinter group, formed mainly of Aborigines dissatisfied with the white control of the joint organisations, left FCAATSI to form the National Tribal Council. Though the council's life was short, many of the office bearers such as Oodgeroo Noonuccal, Bruce McGuiness, Denis Walker and Charles Perkins were Aborigines who would, without the joint cooperation of the whites, greatly influence Aboriginal affairs in the 1970s.

Perkins had also been involved in another pressure group which, while affiliated with FCAATSI, remained to an extent apart. This was the student movement whose role in Aboriginal affairs, though short, was decisive. In 1965 Perkins led a group of 30 students through a number of New South Wales towns notorious for their ill-treatment of Aborigines. They picketed clubs, shops and amenities available only to whites, and when violence erupted, the national press highlighted the conditions of the towns as well as the actions of the students. The Freedom Ride, as it became known, was important not only for its achievements but for the way in which they had been won. Students used the tools of demonstration – protest, placard, confrontation and publicity. Younger Aboriginal radicals such as Paul Coe had been to university themselves; their training enabled them to see what sometimes had not been apparent to long-time workers in the organisations still controlled by the whites.

THE ABORIGINAL TENT EMBASSY

The 1970s can be recognised as a turning point in which Aborigines began to gain control of their internal affairs. By 1972 all the surviving Advancement Leagues were under Aboriginal control while other autonomous organisations like the Aboriginal Legal Services and the Aboriginal and Islander Medical Services evolved with little white input. Other Aboriginal initiatives included the Aboriginal Sports Foundation (1969), Aboriginal Hostels (1973) and the Outstation movement (middle 1970s) which involved hundreds of Aborigines moving from government settlements back into traditional homelands.

In 1971 the McMahon Liberal–Country Party government still offered no relief from the assimilationist policies of the past which, in particular, opposed the granting of land rights on any grounds but economic. Nor did there appear any prospect that land rights on the basis of earlier occupation might be achieved through the courts after the rejection, by

Protesting against the submersion of their traditional culture and rights, four young Aborigines erected a tent in the grounds of Parliament House, Canberra, dubbing it the 'Aboriginal Embassy'. The protest, on Australia Day 1972, gained such widespread support that it unexpectedly lasted for a year.

Mr Justice Blackburn of some Yirrkala (Northern Territory) people's claim that their lands had been unlawfully invaded. Blackburn ruled that Aboriginal land tenure was not recognisable as private property, which implied that no Aborigines had an inviolable right to traditional land. McMahon, in a speech on Australia Day 1972, confirmed that his government ruled out land rights based on traditional association. The same day a tent was erected outside Parliament House and the Aboriginal Tent Embassy established.

Using methods learned in student demonstrations rather than in the white-dominated organisations, the Aborigines proceeded to embarrass the national government. Amidst critical media comment, the police demolished the 'Embassy' in July, but by then two new factors had emerged. One was the electorally damaging publicity surrounding not only the government's handling of the 'Embassy' but its attitude to Aboriginal affairs generally, the other was the Aborigines' demonstrated ability to organise coordinated national demonstrations and deputations.

The Whitlam government had promised much support, including land rights, and the first nine months of Labor administration of the Aboriginal portfolio are remembered as a time of considerable largess. One significant novelty was the creation of the National Aboriginal Consultative Committee. The name itself indicated the government's wariness in allowing the Aborigines too much – or any – responsibility, and much of the short life of the

NACC was spent in wrangles about the scope and limits of its powers. The Labor government ended in 1975 with the NACC in disarray, an Act to override the Queensland government's Aborigines Act unused, and the Northern Territory Land Rights Bill incomplete. Though much remained unaccomplished the Labor government had made lasting changes. Perhaps the most symbolic was the return of traditional land to a Gurindji (Northern Territory) leader, Vincent Lingiari, in August 1975.

THE 1980s

The Fraser administration, in spite of National Party opposition, continued Labor's direction and introduced legislation (The Land Rights (Northern Territory) Act 1976) which created the Central and Northern Land Councils and allowed claims to be entered over certain areas including existing reserves and unalienated crown land. In 1977 the NACC was reconstituted as the National Aboriginal Conference which still, however, lacked any real executive or policy-making function. A significant innovation was the Aboriginal Development Commission in 1980. The various government-sponsored bureaus of land acquisition and economic enterprise were combined under a very free charter which gave the all-Aboriginal commissioners powers to act without direct ministerial interference.

After a promising start, relations between the

Conference began to deteriorate. The dangers to the government of a constitutionally non-responsible body of senior Aboriginal spokespeople with ready access to the press became more apparent when Labor began negotiations to implement a policy of national uniform land rights. Relations worsened as pressures from the state governments and the Australian Mining Industry Council drove the government steadily further from the minimum demands of Aboriginal pressure groups. These now included the major regional organisations like the land councils and legal services. The legislation proposal was abandoned in 1986, which surprised and disheartened many white Labor supporters as well as Aborigines.

By 1988 some of the trends which had been apparent since the 1950s had come to fruition. Land councils, housing associations, co-ops, cultural associations and child-care organisations were all indications that regional management was almost entirely in Aboriginal hands. The organisation Link-Up was established to help people removed from their communities to come home. But the failure of National Land Rights and Makaratta (treaty) proposals indicated that nationally Aborigines had little more power than before. Self-management rather than self-determination seemed to be the goal of the Hawke Labor government. The Aboriginal and Torres Strait Islander Commission was intended to draw together the executive, advisory and policy making functions of many government and non-government Aboriginal organisations.

INTO THE 1990s

By 1992 it was apparent that the Aborigines, largely through their own efforts had arrived as a major irritant to white governments, which still were reluctant to recognise that nothing short of a major re-negotiation with Aboriginal leaders would satisfy them. A treaty promised by Hawke had failed to materialise and the federal government's Council for Aboriginal Reconciliation had not yet produced any recommendations. Prime Minister Keating seemed more ready than Hawke to recognise claims based on indigenous rights rather than equality of citizenship. The most significant advance was the Mabo Judgement, by which, in 1992, the High Court of Australia recognised that the people of Murray Island, in Torres Strait, held and continued to hold Native Title to their land. Though there were many obscure and complicating factors, it appeared possible that mainland Aborigines might now be able to argue their claim for Native Title in relation to areas of crown land held by the states and Commonwealth.

Late in 1993 the federal government, accepting many of the implications of the Mabo Judgement, introduced the Native Title Act which recognised the continuing existence of Native Title in areas of land or water; it appeared that title might be claimable in all areas except where it had been specifically extinguished. To circumvent long and expensive litigation, Tribunals were established to determine the eligibility of Native Title claim, and the claims of others. PR

Maralinga, sculpture by Lin Onus, 1990. Maralinga, South Australia, was used as an atomic testing ground by the British government during the 1950s. In 1985 a Royal Commission found that these tests had harmful effects on the Aborigines who lived in the area. In common with other drives to assert Aboriginal rights, an Aboriginal-led movement has attempted to force the British government to clean up the site.

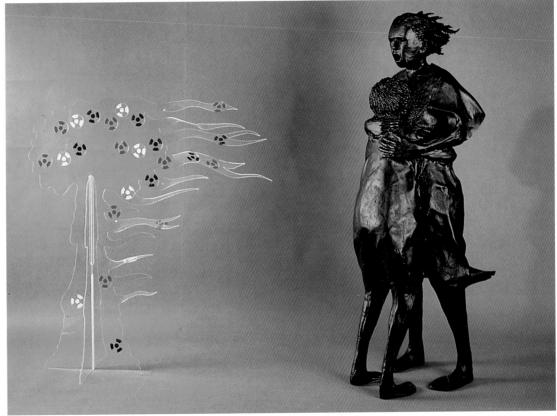

Government

Political parties

The basic character of the Australian political party system has been unchanged for over 70 years, and many of its characteristics date from about 1910. In that year, Australian voters were confronted with a choice between the Australian Labor Party (ALP) and a Liberal party. Over the next 30 years the Liberal Party underwent a number of changes of name and structure before reverting to the title Liberal Party of Australia in 1945. But for most Australians, the essential party choice has remained between the ALP and a Liberal party from 1910 to the present time.

A modification occurred around 1920 (the date varied from state to state) with the formation of what became known as the Country Party. However, within a few years it became clear that this party would in nearly all cases operate in some kind of alliance with the Liberal Party; so that the choice remained one between the ALP and one or more non-Labor parties. The latter often differed among themselves, but hardly ever to the point of ceasing to be a non-Labor alliance. The essential duality of the party system remained.

During the 1970s (the year again varied from state to state) the Country Party changed its name to National, so indicating a wish to become more broadly based and to seek support in the major cities as well as in rural areas and country towns. It has had little success in this direction. So, just as the major division between Labor and non-Labor could be said to date from 1910, even the modification of that situation, under which much of the country sector of the non-Labor side formed a separate party, has survived for almost as long a period.

This type of situation is not unique to Australia. In most other countries with a record of consistently democratic government there has been a similar freezing of the party system since the 1920s. Nevertheless, it is noteworthy that the basic political choice has remained unchanged in a nation which has experienced such fundamental transformations in economy, ethnic composition and other respects.

From time to time since the 1920s there have been suggestions that this system of parties has become outdated and can be expected to change in some direction more appropriate to a changing society. The most obvious form of such a change would be the appearance of one or more new parties, to replace or to supplement the time-honoured two-and-a-half party system of the ALP on one side and the Liberal and National parties on the other. In the past, it has usually been suggested that it is the ALP which is outdated and likely to be replaced or at least reduced to minor importance. Less was heard of this during the 1980s, when in fact the ALP was electorally dominant. More attention was given to the largest minor party of the decade, the Australian Democrats, which can take support from both Liberals and Labor. The Australian Democrats reached a peak at the 1990 election, when they polled 11 per cent of the formal votes for the House of Representatives, but this declined to 4 per cent in 1993. The Democrats had appealed for support partly on environmental issues, but this did not prevent the appearance of a separate Green Party, which had some success in Western Australia in 1993. It has sometimes been suggested that greater emphasis on environmental and related issues may produce a basic change in Australian politics.

While such changes are not impossible, history suggests that we should be cautious in predicting any such fundamental change in the number and strength of major Australian parties. The fact that the existing parties have survived with so little apparent change is an indication of their success in adapting to a rapidly changing nation. These general comments and warnings are a necessary background to consideration of the individual parties.

THE AUSTRALIAN LABOR PARTY

The ALP is the oldest of the Australian parties, having been formed at the time of federation (1901) from Labor parties founded in the various colonies in 1890 and the following years. Since at least 1910 it has been the largest single party in terms of electoral support although until recently it has rarely polled more than the combined total of the Liberal and National parties.

Labor's success in winning five successive federal elections since between 1983 and 1993, apparently securing office until at least 1996, is unprecedented in the party's history. Its best previous record was to win two successive federal elections and to remain in office from 1941 to 1949. Its recent success owes

Simon Crean, president of the Australian Council of Trade Unions 1985-90 and subsequently made minister for primary industries and energy by Paul Keating, and later minister for employment, education and training. Moves such as this typify the strong links between the Australian Labor Party and the trade unions.

much to its Accord with the trade unions (see below); and also to discord within its principal rival, the Liberal Party.

The ALP, like similar parties in Britain, New Zealand and a few other countries, has the unusual characteristic of being partly composed of trade unions. That is, trade unions not only give it support, including financial support, but actually form part of its membership, through affiliation. In all states the affiliated trade unions comprise a majority of the party's governing body, variously called the state convention, conference or council. These state bodies in turn choose most of the members of the National Conference and National Executive, although the National Conference also includes the party's federal and state parliamentary leaders.

The ALP's organisation has changed significantly since the 1970s, this being one example of the powers of adaptation which have enabled it, like the other major parties, to survive in greatly changed conditions and to resist the intrusion of new parties. For many years, from the 1920s to the 1960s, the ALP retained outdated principles of organisation – and, for this reason among others, was rarely in office. Its organisation was concentrated at the state level, although federal politics became increasingly the dominant field. It was not until 1964 that the party even had a full-time national secretary. All states were equally represented on its National Conference and Executive and these bodies were seen largely as instruments to control the federal Labor members of parliament, supposedly in the name of the party rank and file but actually to give power to trade union and other factional leaders in the states. Such an apparent domination of the people's elected representatives was unpopular with the voters and could be exploited by Labor's opponents.

The National Conference, which until 1969 had only 36 members, in 1990 had 101. State representation varies according to population, from 23 for New South Wales to eight for Tasmania. The state and federal parliamentary leaders, who also form part of the Conference, can at least ensure that the Conference is aware of the likely electoral consequences of its decisions.

The National Conference normally meets only biennially. The National Executive, chosen by the Conference, retains more of the old pattern. It has two representatives of each state (and one from each of the two territories) plus the four federal parliamentary leaders (the leader and deputy leader from each house of parliament). The Executive, which meets twice yearly, can be a powerful body but the old principle of subordination of members of parliament to the extra-parliamentary machine has nevertheless almost disappeared.

The relationship between the party and trade unions, which is the most distinctive characteristic of the ALP and of other Labor parties, has developed in some unexpected ways. This relationship was often seen as old-fashioned and outdated by developments in both the party and the unions. Only about 55 per cent of Australia's trade unionists belong to unions which are affiliated with the ALP and this proportion has tended to fall. This is because few unions of white-collar workers, especially those in the public sector, have affiliated. In Australia, as in other countries, it is now less true that political allegiance is determined by occupation, so that even many members of blue-collar unions vote for other parties. There have been very few new union affiliations during the last 50 years.

On the other hand, there has been a marked tendency for unions to join the Australian Council of Trade Unions (ACTU). All unions with more than 10,000 members, and many smaller ones, belong to the ACTU. And since the late 1970s, especially since the election of the Hawke federal government in March 1983, there have been unprecedented close relations between the party (including that government) and the ACTU. This has been shown by an Accord between the party and the ACTU adopted just before the 1983 election, and setting out in some detail the economic and social policies which a Labor government would adopt, in return for a disciplined and restrained attitude to wage increases by the unions. Though the detailed content of the Accord was only partly realised and the document itself soon became outdated, the term has come to symbolise this close and (for Australia) novel relationship between party and unions. Between 1983 and 1993 there were seven such agreements. Whereas the original Accord dealt with a variety of social policies, its real importance was its effect on wages and the later agreements, up to 'Accord Mark 7' in 1993, have been frankly concerned only with wage policy and with other policies, in the field of taxation and social welfare, which are relevant to wage levels. The breakdown of this relationship between the ACTU and successive Labor governments has often been predicted but the relationship has proved remarkably durable, even during a time when the value of wages has fallen.

Although there has recently been a period during which the union connection with the ALP has strengthened, this has not been by means of the party's formal structure but through relations with the ACTU, which, in a formal sense, is quite unrelated to the party. Large and powerful unions, through the ACTU, can influence a Labor federal government, whether or not they are actually affiliated with the party. Much the same is true of the relations between unions and Labor governments at the state level, through the ACTU's state branches, which in most states are called Trades and Labour Councils.

Nearly all blue-collar unions nevertheless remain affiliated with the party. One motive for doing so may be that this gives their members, and especially their leaders, advantages in seeking endorsement as Labor parliamentary candidates. Especially at the federal level, people from a blue-collar or working-class background would have almost disappeared from the parliamentary Labor parties (which tend to be dominated by former white-collar workers, together with some from a business or professional background) had it not been for those who have reached parliament by way of positions in blue-collar unions.

Since 1989, the ACTU has conducted a strong campaign for the amalgamation of unions. Its aim was to reduce the number of unions at the federal level to about 20 by the end of 1993. Although this was over-ambitious, many amalgamations have taken place. The declared intention has been to produce unions, each of which covers one industry, but political and other disagreements between union leaders are producing a less-tidy result. One consequence of these amalgamations may be to increase the proportion of unionists in ALP-affiliated unions. This is because of the absorption of non-affiliated unions by larger unions that are already affiliated.

Another development of recent years has been the formal recognition of factions within the party, including at the parliamentary level. Factionalism has a long history in the ALP but in the past was always denounced as leading to disunity and defeat. Now there are recognised factions in the federal and most state parliamentary parties and in the extra-parliamentary organisation, with recognised leaders, regular meetings and more or less fixed membership.

In the federal parliamentary party there are (in order of size) a Labor Unity (or Right) faction; a Left faction; and a Centre Left faction; together with a few members who decline to belong to any of these groupings.

The justification given for this institutionalising of factions is that in practice it limits rather than encourages disunity in the party. The factions provide mechanisms by which different sections of the party can seek agreement and compromise without public antagonism. Such antagonism may escalate into serious divisions which in the past have marked the ALP's history and helped bring about many of its defeats. This development of formal factions seems unique to the ALP among the world's Labor parties but shows every sign of permanence.

To what extent do such factions exist because of different views of what the party should be trying to achieve? More broadly, what are the ALP's objectives? Like other Labor parties, it is sometimes called 'socialist' – especially by its opponents! The party's Objectives describe it as 'a democratic socialist party', having 'the objective of the democratic socialisation of industry, production, distribution and exchange, to the extent necessary to eliminate exploitation and other anti-social features in these fields'. However, it has been clear for many years that the party will not seek to bring any large section of the economy under public ownership. Indeed, more recent interest has been in the extent to which Labor governments will privatise existing businesses which have long been publicly owned.

Complete or partial privatisation has already occurred in the airline and banking industries and is likely to spread to telecommunications and other industries. Although the Left is opposed to privatisation in principle, it has not seriously attempted to resist these developments and certainly does not demand any large-scale extension of public ownership. The Left faction is likely to look more critically at consequences for Australia of the alliance with the USA, but it does not seriously propose a non-aligned Australia; it is more concerned with the interests of the very poor and disadvantaged, but its differences with the Right on such matters are, at most, differences of degree. If differences between Left and Right factions are so uncertain it is not surprising that those between either and the Centre Left faction (where the latter exists) are still more indefinite.

In short, the remarkable acceptance of formal factions within the ALP reflects a diminution, not an aggravation, of real policy differences within the party. Since there are no fundamental disagreements, there is seen to be a need to prevent minor ones, and also disputes over personal advancement, building up into serious disruption. In that respect, the system has so far been a success.

THE LIBERAL PARTY OF AUSTRALIA

The Liberal Party enjoyed a long period of success after its re-foundation in 1945, being the major party in federal government (in coalition with the Country, or later the National, Party) from 1949 to 1983, except for 1972–75. Though its record in state politics varied widely it was generally successful at this level also, especially in Victoria where it held office alone from 1955 to 1982. The 1980s were a time of failure, the party in 1989 being in opposition in the federal parliament and in all but one state (New South Wales). Although its fortunes did not turn in the federal sphere, they did in the states. By 1994 it was in power in all states except Queensland.

Despite its title, the party can fairly be described as conservative and some of its leaders have been happy to describe it as such – a notable change from earlier times when no major Australian party would have dared to use such a term of itself. It has many of the characteristics of conservative parties elsewhere. That is, it has a large membership, most of which is not expected to be active; it emphasises the importance and ultimate autonomy of its parliamentary members in determining the party's policies, while providing mechanisms for others to play an essentially advisory role in policy matters; it is unambiguously supportive of a capitalist economy and the American alliance; and it has the support of most sections of the business community but has no formal ties to business organisations. Its extra-parliamentary organisation is concentrated at the state level and it supports the principle of federalism, usually (although not invariably) opposing attempts to augment federal power at the expense of the states. In most of these respects, differences between the Liberal Party and the ALP have tended to become less clear during the past 20 years.

At the state level, Liberal organisation varies much more than is the case in the ALP. However, there is always a widespread network of local branches, which form councils at the level of state and federal electorates. There may be regional councils covering wider areas; and there will be a much more important and larger state council, where much of the discussion of policies will take place. The state councils elect state executives and also choose the eight delegates from each state which make up the federal council, which meets annually and has important administrative and financial functions. The council elects a federal executive with 13 members and there is also a large (by Australian standards), well-established and effective federal secretariat.

Despite its emphasis on the states, therefore, the Liberal Party has a larger and more constantly active federal organisation than the ALP. This has been because it has in the past been able to raise more

Andrew Peacock, leader of the Liberal Party from 1983 to 1985 and then again from 1989 to 1990, the leadership having changed on both occasions following election defeats by Bob Hawke's Australian Labor Party.

funds to maintain such organisations and has tended to be made up of people with more time and money to devote to the party. However, these differences between the two parties, like many others, have become less clear.

All organisations tend to lose patience with unsuccessful leaders, but the Liberal Party is particularly likely to replace those who fail to win elections. Thus in 1985 Andrew Peacock was replaced as federal leader by John Howard, after a creditable, but ultimately unsuccessful, performance at the federal election in 1984; Howard was in turn replaced by Peacock in 1989, having failed to win the election in 1987. Peacock in turn resigned as leader following the party's electoral defeat in 1990, and was replaced by John Hewson who, in turn, was replaced by Alexander Downer in 1994. Also in 1989, Jeff Kennett was defeated as Victorian parliamentary leader, having failed to win office at two successive elections. (He was, however, re-elected leader in 1991 and became state premier in 1992.) The party's long record of success in federal and Victorian politics prior to the 1980s no doubt helps to explain this intolerance of apparent failures of leadership in more difficult times.

If the parliamentary membership of the ALP is made up principally of former white-collar and professional employees, with smaller numbers of former lawyers, medical practitioners and union officials, the parliamentary Liberal parties illustrate important variations on these themes rather than totally different patterns. The proportions of 'higher' or self-employed professionals – barristers, solicitors

State party leaders can enjoy considerable power. Sir Johannes Bjelke-Petersen, photographed here with his wife Lady Florence, herself a senator, was controversial Country Party premier of Queensland from 1968 to 1987. (The Country Party changed its name to the National Party in 1982.)

and medical practitioners – are higher; those of white-collar employees are much lower; and there are many more company directors and executives, who might be said to be the Liberal equivalents of the ALP's union officials. But, of course, the company directors do not have, or need, the equivalent of the ALP's system of affiliated unions to help them reach parliament.

The Liberal Party also includes at all levels, including the parliamentary levels, significant proportions of farmers, which leads us to consider the mixed success of the party that initially saw itself as the representative of farmers and of rural communities more generally – the National Party.

THE NATIONAL PARTY OF AUSTRALIA

The National Party began as a loose alliance of state Country parties. It has always been the least centralised of parties and illustrated this by gradually changing its name from Country to National in different states. It revealed its uncertainty as to title and expectations by calling itself the National Country Party at the federal level from 1975 to 1982.

The party is a major political force in Queensland and New South Wales. It is weaker in Victoria and Western Australia and hardly exists in South Australia and Tasmania. It has local importance in the Northern Territory, as the major element in a combined National and Liberal Party (the Country Liberal Party). In the 1993 election for the House of Representatives, the party secured 7 per cent of the votes. This was made up of 15 per cent in Queens-

land; 45 per cent in the Northern Territory; 10 per cent in New South Wales; 0.2 per cent in Western Australia; 5 per cent in Victoria; and 0.3 per cent in South Australia. It contested no seats in Tasmania.

The party's greater success in Queensland reflects both the more decentralised population of that state and the fact that the party has built up an exceptionally strong organisation there, the latter being aided by the existence of a heavily slanted electoral system which has enabled it to be the major governing party at the state level (in coalition with the Liberal Party from 1957 to 1983); and, from 1983 to 1989 when a Labor government came to power, to have won a majority of seats in the state parliament in its own right and to have governed alone. In other states and at the federal level, the best the Nationals can hope to do is to form the smaller section of a coalition with the Liberal Party, as was the case in New South Wales after 1988.

Despite these limitations, the party has a large rank-and-file membership – about the same size as that of the much more extensive Liberal Party. While this membership is very largely made up of farmers the party depends for much of its electoral support, and draws many of its parliamentary representatives, from the country townspeople. Its electoral support has been more stable than those of the other major parties, but its existence has often seemed problematical.

The great variation in National Party support between states, and its failure to establish itself effectively in some, indicate the absence of clearly defined nationwide support. It has been further threatened by the relative decline – in many places, an absolute decline – in the rural population; and also by a widespread public rejection of the principle that the rural electorates should have fewer voters than urban or metropolitan electorates, a principle on which much of the party's earlier success depended. Such a principle now applies only in state politics and only in Western Australia (where the party is in any case ineffective). The additional weight given to the rural vote in Queensland state politics, where the National Party had been most successful, was drastically modified after the ALP won office in 1989.

The ideology and policies of the National Party may be seen as variants of those of the Liberal Party, though such a description might be rejected by National leaders. The party is emphatically conservative, sounding even more hostile to socialism (and, when this was something of an issue in Australian politics, to communism) than the Liberals. It also appears more conservative on a variety of social issues. On the issue of a possible Australian republic (see p. 135), which was given prominence by the ALP after the 1993 federal election, it is safe to say that the clearest opposition among the major parties will come from the National Party. Its traditional reason for existence has been a claimed need to protect the special interests of the rural minority, including rural industry. In the past, the latter objective involved support for government regulation of the marketing of primary products, often derided by its opponents as a 'socialist' policy. During recent years, when the Liberal Party (and even the ALP) has sought extensive deregulation of the economy, this could have produced serious conflict between these parties, and disrupted the cooperation which they have usually shown. It seems likely that this will be resolved by the general acquiescence of the National Party in considerable deregulation of these marketing processes.

It can be seen from this brief summary why there is considerable doubt as to the long-term future of the National Party as an independent organisation. The general stability of its support over a long period, and the more general durability of the Australian party system over 70 years, serve as warnings against too hasty predictions of its disappearance, which would take the form of merging with the Liberal Party. However, the demonstrated failure of the party to become national either in the sense of extending to all states or of establishing itself in the state capital cities, together with the apparent weakening of its commitment to defend the systems of public regulation of the marketing of primary produce, suggest that the arguments for its survival are becoming weaker. It was notable that in 1989 its newly elected federal leader, Charles Blunt, himself predicted that a further re-election of the federal Labor government would probably be followed by a merger of the Liberal and National parties. Blunt lost his own parliamentary seat in the 1990 election and was replaced as leader by Tim Fischer. After another ALP victory in 1993 there was again talk of a possible merger among Liberals but the National Party leaders showed no enthusiasm for the idea. Nevertheless, it was the first time that a leader of the party had made such a prediction, even conditionally, and reflects the dubious future of the party itself, though not necessarily of the interests and the policies which it has fostered.

THE AUSTRALIAN DEMOCRATS AND OTHERS

The Australian Democrats were during the 1980s contenders for the position of a new major player in the Australian party system.

Founded in 1977, the Democrats, like other minor parties and groupings, owe almost all to the existence of proportional representation systems of voting for upper houses of parliament and especially for the

federal Senate. In 1987, the Democrats secured about the same total vote for the House of Representatives (6 per cent) as the National Party; but whereas the Nationals won 19 House of Representatives seats, the Democrats won none. This was because the Democrats' support was spread relatively evenly across states and regions; whereas the Nationals' support was far more concentrated, in both state and regional terms. Democrat candidates for the Senate polled only slightly better than Democrat candidates for the House (7.6 per cent); but they won two Senate seats in South Australia and one in every other state. These seven senators, together with three others outside the major parties, held the balance between the ALP senators on the one side and the Liberal and National senators on the other and so were able, as long as government and opposition members in fact opposed each other, to determine what legislation was enacted. The Democrats have continued to hold this position in the Senate largely because they polled well in 1990. Five of their senators then elected will hold their seats until 1996. In 1993, they polled more weakly and only two new Democrat senators were elected.

The origins of the Democrats in the late 1970s were complex. The party was formed by a dissident Liberal, Don Chipp, who had failed to secure appointment to the non-Labor ministry of Malcolm Fraser in 1976; but it secured support and membership from a mixed body of voters and most of its members of the federal parliament (all of whom have been elected to the Senate) had not previously been prominent in politics. Its position on policy matters could be described as falling between the major parties in some respects while seeking to outdo them all in others. It is clearly not a socialist party, even in the vague sense in which the ALP sometimes applies that term to itself. On the other hand, it has been generally favourable to social welfare policies. It has shown an interest in questions of environmental protection and quality of life, though it has so far failed to secure the solid support of those who have been most active in these fields. It has been definitely opposed to the mining and export of uranium and is more neutralist in its policy stances on foreign policy than the ALP and even more so than the Liberal and National parties.

The Democrats have tried without success to win seats in the House of Representatives. At the 1990 election their leader, Senator Janine Haines, who had replaced Chipp as leader in 1986, unsuccessfully contested a House of Representatives seat and then retired from politics. The Democrats have had a much higher proportion of women leaders than the larger parties. Three of its five leaders, including the present leader Senator Cheryl Kernot, have been women.

Janine Haines, leader of the Australian Democrats from 1986 to 1990. Minority parties like the Democrats have traditionally been better represented in upper houses of parliament, both state and federal, than in lower ones, because of the system of proportional representation used to elect upper house members.

A further indication of a certain public dissatisfaction with all the major parties, but also an indication of the Democrats' failure to mobilise much of this dissatisfaction, has been the success of other alternative candidates at Senate elections. Some of those elected since 1987 had policies which at least overlapped with those of the Democrats but apparently regarded the Democrats as unsatisfactory. These included a senator from the Nuclear Disarmament Party, from New South Wales, and one from the 'Vallentine Peace Group' (Jo Vallentine was the successful candidate) from Western Australia. The current senators from Western Australia include two from the Greens (WA).

It is also worth mentioning the remaining senator, Brian Harradine, an Independent senator for Tasmania since 1975. In an earlier era, Senator Harradine was a member of the ALP. His position is not easily defined in terms of the larger parties but his strong personal following in Tasmania appears to have secured him at least 20 years in the Senate.

Another significant development, in 1989, was the formation of a Tasmanian Labor government which held office until 1992 because of the support of a group of five members of the state House of Assembly calling themselves Green Independents but who may be regarded as another new party. The election of these members was an indication of the increased salience of environmental questions in Australian politics. In this sense it might be seen as a prelude to the appearance of an Australia-wide Green party, like those of Germany, Sweden and elsewhere. It is certainly of interest that this group should have been formed as such, rather than joining the Democrats. However, Tasmania has the only Australian parliament for which elections for the lower house are conducted under a proportional representation system. It was thus relatively easy for a new party to win widespread support to win seats; certainly easier than would be the case in the federal House of Representatives or in the lower house of any other state. The alliance with the Greens was not a success for the ALP in Tasmania, the state Labor government being defeated by the Liberals in 1992.

AND THE FUTURE?

The major Australian political parties are all among the country's older institutions and, at least in the case of the ALP, are facing their second century of life. Many feel, understandably, that they are, or at any rate ought to be outdated, and in some respects they are. Many people are looking for alternatives and sometimes finding them. But this is not a new situation and none of the newer parties or groups looks assured of success.

The old parties, for better or worse, have quietly discarded much that has ceased to be useful to them. Labor has discarded socialism, in fact if not in name; that is, it no longer seeks to bring at least some of the more important sectors of the economy under public ownership. The Liberal Party has lessened its attachment, in any case symbolic, to residual special ties with Britain; and it can no longer make use of a supposed 'communist menace'.

This does not mean that such parties have nothing further to dispute. They still disagree about the fundamentals of economic policy. The old question of the proper role and powers of trade unions, the fundamental question for the Labor Party and hardly less important for its opponents, has revived in a modern form, to give new validity to the old division between Labor and non-Labor. Despite the increased salience of environmental decisions and policies, the most central political question for Australia for the rest of this century and beyond may be whether trade unionism is to be fostered as an important partner of governments – as in much of Western Europe – or pushed into an increasingly marginal social role – as in much of the rest of the world. That is a question worthy to remain central to a democratic political system; and the 'old' Australian party system is in most respects well placed to deal with it and to turn the country in one direction or the other.   DR

Australian federalism

Nearly a century after the inauguration of the Australian federation in 1901, the federal system may appear stable and conservative. The Constitution as then adopted remains almost unchanged. Forty-two attempts to change it by referendum of the voters, put forward at one time or another by all political parties, have produced only eight changes, some of them technical and uncontroversial. The Labor Party, which at one stage sought the replacement of federalism by a unitary system, has long since drawn back from what seemed a hopeless prospect. It has, however, in the 1990s, set up a committee to investigate the possiblility of Australia becoming a republic. This would involve alteration to the Constitution, particularly those sections relating to the Queen's representative, the governor-general.

The non-Labor parties have often opposed the extension of Commonwealth powers, partly because they have sought to preserve the powers of the states and partly because, especially as regards economic regulation, the Commonwealth is the only effective instrument of government power. To exclude the Commonwealth from such areas therefore limits the powers of government in general. But non-Labor federal governments may sometimes welcome increased Commonwealth powers for their own purposes.

It is safe to say that the principal changes to the real powers of the commonwealth ever since federation have come not from changes to the wording of the Constitution but from changing interpretations by the country's highest court, the High Court of Australia. There have been several phases of the High Court's record of constitutional interpretation. To simplify these, it could be said that the Court tended to restrain the Commonwealth until 1920; took a broader view of Commonwealth powers from then until about 1945; again tended to restrict the Commonwealth until the 1970s; and, more recently, has again tended to broaden its interpretation of Commonwealth powers, a process which appears to be continuing.

The Court has not overtly displayed political or ideological bias. One of its most famous past judges, Sir Owen Dixon, advocated 'strict and complete legalism' as the basis of its judgments. But he and other judges conceded that in the broader sense any court interpreting the Constitution must also be 'political' and the Court has recently been more clearly swayed by considerations of government efficiency and efficacy. By the standards of the United States Supreme Court it has exercised restraint in matters which could otherwise be determined by parliaments; this being due partly to the fact that the Australian Constitution, unlike that of the USA, includes no Bill of Rights aimed at shielding citizens from the powers of legislatures in general. Nevertheless, the Court has recently become a much more pervasive factor in Australian government.

Some recent cases illustrate this trend. In 1983, the *Tasmanian Dam Case* ((1983) 158 CLR 1) supported Commonwealth legislation preventing the Tasmanian government from constructing a particular hydroelectric dam (see pp. 48 and 51), in part because of obligations to protect the environment which the Commonwealth had entered into by international agreements under its 'external affairs' power. Other aspects of this decision suggested that there were also other sections of the Constitution which could enable the Commonwealth to act in areas that had previously been seen as coming solely within the powers of the states.

In the same year, the *Social Welfare Union Case* ((1983) 153 CLR 415) gave the Commonwealth and its instruments (now, in particular, the Australian Industrial Relations Commission) power to involve themselves in a great range of industrial disputes, a power which had previously been subject to many arbitrary limitations.

In 1988, the Court in *Cole* v. *Whitfield* ((1988) 78 ALR 42) gave a new, simpler and less-restrictive interpretation to one of the great constitutional bugbears, section 92, which says that ' trade commerce and intercourse between the states . . . shall be absolutely free'. The Court held that this section was intended only to prevent the erection of protectionist barriers to interstate trade and was not relevant to other purposes (including the invalidation of an attempt to nationalise banking) for which it had been used in the past.

If the increase in federal power through judicial review of the Constitution has progressed rapidly during recent years, another aspect of federal domination, control over state finances, has been much more consistent. Since World War II, the Commonwealth has been able to limit the real autonomy of the states through its power to grant them funds upon specified conditions; and its domination of the Loan Council, which controls governmental borrowings (see also pp. 159–60).

Despite these developments, the states are far from being wholly subordinate or mere instruments of the federal government. It remains the case that the states directly determine most public spending and together employ more than twice as many people as the Commonwealth. For electoral reasons, if for no others, federal governments are reluctant to engage in unnecessary confrontations with the states. At all

Parliament House, Canberra. This new Parliament House replaced the original building in 1988, following an international competition won by the firm of Mitchell Giurgola.

in Tasmania, which was guaranteed a minimum of five members under the Constitution, remain somewhat smaller than elsewhere. The Senate, as in the USA, has the same number of members for each state, irrespective of population. At present there are 76 senators; 12 from each state and a further two from each territory.

The powers of the Senate under the Constitution are formidable and include the power to reject (and not merely to delay) any legislation. The Constitution itself provides means for resolving a deadlock between the two houses, including a double dissolution in which both must face re-election. This procedure has been followed, successfully enough, on several occasions and it is one which inevitably involves considerable delay.

This situation can lead to a crisis if, as in 1975, the Senate rejects budgetary legislation required to maintain the work of government, which cannot wait on the delay of many months involved in the normal procedures aimed at resolving deadlocks. The governor-general resolved this situation by dismissing the Labor government of Gough Whitlam and installing a caretaker government headed by the Liberal Malcolm Fraser, which immediately dissolved parliament and proceeded to an election, at which it was returned with a large majority. The bitterness which this crisis produced lasted at least until the election of the next Labor government, over seven years later.

The Role of Parliament

In Australia, as elsewhere, there have been many complaints that parliament has declined in importance, due to the discipline exercised by the political parties, which largely removes the prospect that parliamentary deliberation may affect whether legislation succeeds or fails or even whether its content is changed in any significant respect.

A similar, and related, argument suggests that the domination of parliament by the ministry, and especially by a few senior ministers or simply by the prime minister, has largely vitiated the role of parliament.

In the Australian federal parliament, unlike that of Britain, such domination by the ministry is both symbolised and assisted by the fact that the offices of the ministers and their staffs are situated in Parliament House itself.

There is no doubt that such arguments have much force. It can, however, be pointed out that these are not new developments. They have been true for at least the last half-century and in some respects for a much longer period.

Yet parliament has rightly been regarded as a central, if not the central, institution of government; and it is likely to remain so.   DR

There is no legal reason why a similar situation should not arise at some future time.

MINISTRIES AND CABINETS

Australian ministries follow a common pattern derived from Britain, with the federal ministry being more complex as well as more important than those of the states and territories.

In each case the ministry is composed of members of parliament, headed by, and usually dominated by, the prime minister (Commonwealth), premier (state) or chief minister (territory). Other than in the federal government, the ministries are quite small, usually comprising no more than 12 ministers, all of whom comprise the cabinet.

In 1956 the federal ministry, then numbering 19, was divided into a cabinet of 12 and a group of 7 other ministers (the 'outer ministry'). These 'outer' ministers were consulted over matters which were their particular responsibility but were not involved in the government's overall policy and practice. This division between cabinet and outer ministers has now become a settled practice in federal politics, whichever party is in office. In 1993, there was a federal cabinet of 19 members with an additional outer ministry of 14.

The functions of cabinet, federal or state, include consideration and approval of legislation; overall questions of policy, especially if they involve large expenditure or are likely to be controversial; and the appointment of judges and of a small number of officers at the head of the public services and other governmental authorities. Cabinets are usually divided into a number of committees which give special consideration to particular subject areas.

The prime minister (or the equivalent in the states and territories) is normally by far the most powerful member of the ministry, though this power varies in details with the personality of the holder and those of his subordinates. In a non-Labor government, the prime minister has the power to choose and to remove other ministers.

A Labor prime minister or premier must accept the ministry which is chosen by a ballot of the Labor members of parliament (caucus); but may decide what portfolios are held by each and, in the case of a prime minister, which ministers are members of cabinet. The prime minister determines what is discussed by the cabinet. Although wise to avoid antagonising a majority of ministerial colleagues, it is only in very exceptional circumstances that an attempt has been made to bring down a prime minister or premier while in office.

The cabinet, whether federal or state, is the determinant of the government's policies.   DR

Financing federalism

Five-dollar notes being minted. Convention has it that the lowest denomination note bears the monarch's head.

The Treasury Building, Canberra. The federal government raises income tax revenue; the states raise revenue such as payroll tax, land tax, and various charges.

The 1901 Australian Constitution granted powers of taxation to both the Commonwealth (federal) and state governments, except that customs and excise duties were exclusive to the Commonwealth. Federal jurisdiction was largely restricted to international or interstate activities such as defence, foreign affairs, trade, communications, citizenship and the currency. The federal parliament had powers with respect to banking and insurance, invalid and old-age pensions, and industrial disputes extending beyond the limits of any one state. The states retained general responsibility for law and order, health, education, social and community services, transport, and urban and industrial development. Local government played a subservient role concerned largely with roads and property services such as refuse disposal. The Commonwealth could make grants to the states on its own terms and conditions.

From 1928 the Australian Loan Council, which consisted of the chief ministers of the Commonwealth and the states, exercised joint federal/state control over all government borrowing except federal borrowing for defence purposes. In 1942, however, the federal government used wartime powers to centralise and standardise income tax, previously the principal source of state revenues, making general-purpose grants to the states in recompense. This monopoly was retained after the war, and effective control over the Loan Council passed to the federal government. Further constitutional changes in 1946 extended the range of social service benefits which the federal government could provide.

Increasingly after World War II the federal government used its financial strength to make not only general-purpose grants to the states but also payments specifically earmarked for purposes such as education, health, transport and urban services. Its financial domination was soon complete. What had started as a highly decentralised system of taxation and public expenditure had become one of the most highly centralised systems in the world.

Today, the federal government collects about 79 per cent of all taxes, with state and local taxes accounting for about 17.5 per cent and 3.5 per cent, respectively. About one-quarter of the federal budget represents payments to state and local governments, and about one-third payments of benefits to individuals. After allowing for interest and other transfer payments, only about one-fifth remains for outlays on goods and services; the budget is thus essentially an elaborate mechanism for the redistribution of revenue within the public sector and between that sector and the private sector.   RLM

159

Fiscal federalism

The principal elements in Australian fiscal federalism may be summarised as follows:

(a) *Taxation.* Compared with the overlapping of taxes that occurs in most federal countries, Australia has achieved a substantial degree of tax separation, with the Commonwealth having control over all income taxes, customs and excise duties, and sales taxes. The states rely mainly on pay-roll taxes, stamp duties, gambling and liquor taxes, motor taxes and business licence fees, with land revenue and mining royalties also being important sources of revenue. Local government taxes consist almost wholly of rates on land or real property.

(b) *General-purpose grants.* Under the arrangement by which the federal government collects all income taxes, the Commonwealth makes unconditional grants from general revenue to the states and the territories, amounting to about one-quarter of the states' recurrent revenues.

Determined on a formula basis between World War II and 1975–76 and as a proportion of Commonwealth tax collections between 1976–77 and 1984–85, the total amount of general-revenue grants is now determined by the Commonwealth from year to year on an *ad hoc* basis. General-revenue grants are also paid to the states and the Northern Territory for distribution to local governments.

(c) *Fiscal equalisation.* General-revenue grants are distributed among the states and the territories on the basis of assessments by the Commonwealth Grants Commission which are designed to equalise fiscal capacities – that is, to give each state the capacity to provide comparable services if it also imposes comparable taxes and charges. But the level and pattern of services and taxes are left to each state to determine for itself.

Both revenues and expenditures are subject to equalisation. The Commission's assessed relativities in the most recent review imply that New South Wales and Victoria should receive about 16 and 19 per cent less than an equal *per capita* distribution respectively, and that the other states should receive varying proportions ranging from 8 per cent more than an equal *per capita* distribution for Queensland to 45 per cent more for Tasmania and nearly 367 per cent more for the Northern Territory.

The distribution of local government grants in each state is determined on a somewhat similar basis by a State Grants Commission, established for the purpose in accordance with commonwealth and state legislation.

(d) *Specific-purpose payments.* The Commonwealth makes specific-purpose payments, for both recurrent and capital purposes, amounting in total to about two-thirds of its general-purpose payments. The distribution of most of the major specific-purpose grants is taken into account by the Commonwealth Grants Commission in its assessment of general-revenue grant relativities.

Apart from the local government grants, the most important payments to the states are for education, health, housing and roads. Although these have the effect of relieving state budgets and do not usually incorporate matching conditions, through these payments the Commonwealth has increasingly involved itself in the formulation and implementation of programmes in what are essentially state spending responsibilities.

(e) *Loan Council programmes.* Since World War II, the Commonwealth, through its domination of the Loan Council and its income-tax monopoly, has controlled the amounts and terms of borrowing by state governments and has progressively reduced the size of loan programmes. During recent years, however, there has been a substantial relaxation of controls over borrowing by states, semi-government (public enterprise) bodies and local government. This followed the exploitation of non-conventional sources of finance by the states and the deregulation of private sector financial markets. In the case of the states, the Commonwealth through the Loan Council first adopted a system of global limits over the total amount of borrowing, while leaving the individual states free to determine the pattern, terms and conditions of borrowing; there were continuing restrictions over overseas borrowing. More recently, procedures have been introduced which relate Loan Council allocations to approved state overall budget results adjusted for a number of other transactions which have the characteristics of borrowings. The new procedures are designed to enhance the role of the financial markets while ensuring that allocations are consistent with macroeconomic fiscal policy objectives.

As a result of these arrangements, the pattern of Australian fiscal federalism is determined very largely by decisions of the commonwealth government. Through its highly developed fiscal equalisation arrangements, Australia has achieved a greater degree of horizontal fiscal balance and equality among state and local governments than any other federal country. At the same time, however, a chronic mismatch of financing and spending decisions at all levels of government has resulted in Australia becoming an extreme case of vertical fiscal imbalance. In all levels taxes and other own-source revenues are chronically out of balance with expenditure responsibilities.

RLM

The legal system

Australia is a federal democracy with power divided between six states and a shared Commonwealth. Each state's authority is confined within its own boundaries while the Commonwealth Government extends over the whole continent.

The legal system in each of the states is based on the common law of England. The parliaments, courts, judges, magistrates and lawyers all resemble their English counterparts, and some of the laws now in force have their roots in court decisions made in the twelfth century on the basis of medieval social custom.

A MEDIEVAL ROOT

Australia is a 'common-law' country. This means that today's law is an evolutionary offshoot of 'the common law' of England (as it is, for example, in all parts of the USA except Louisiana and every province in Canada except Quebec). In particular, case law (judge-made law) is a significant source of law alongside legislation.

Mace and Speaker's chair in the House of Representatives.

Case law made up the bulk of the system Australia inherited from England. Although ordinances made by England's early kings provided some legislated law, medieval judges decided cases mainly on the basis of customary rules and principles of justice. It was largely to decisions in previous cases that they looked for the authority to declare that particular rules or principles had legal force. This resulted in the doctrine of precedent: the law as identified by a properly constituted court in an earlier case, unless overruled by a higher court, can and normally must be applied by a court hearing a similar case later.

Because the king applied medieval case law and such legislation as there was to the whole of England, replacing a previous diversity of local customary laws, the system that resulted was called, as a whole, the common law. Confusingly, however, the phrase 'common law' often refers to case law only (for example, in 'common-law rights' established through centuries-old legal precedent, as opposed to 'statutory rights' created at a stroke by various Acts of parliament).

In the sixteenth century, the law of England was extended to Wales, but Scotland has retained much of its own legal system. As parliament developed, the law of England and Wales incorporated more legislation, and by the end of the seventeenth century the doctrine of parliamentary supremacy over the courts was firmly established: rules which owe their existence to case law can be changed by statute. However, Parliament did not in fact legislate on most matters already provided for by precedent, and case law continued to be the predominant source of law well into the twentieth century. In other types of system, custom and legal precedent do not have as much weight, and the law is more thoroughly codified through legislation (Article 371 of the French Civil Code, for instance, goes so far as to state formally: 'At all ages a child should honour and respect its father and mother.') CC

Makaratta: A Treaty with the Aborigines

British colonies in Australia made no treaties with Aborigines akin to the Indian treaties made in many parts of the USA and Canada. Undertakings were made by the Australian government to negotiate such a compact, sometimes referred to by the Aboriginal title of *Makaratta*. Nothing, however, has come of this. The Commonwealth parliament has passed a Resolution acknowledging both the Aborigines' status as the continent's prior occupants and their right to self-determination (though 'within the Australian State').

Aborigines have outstanding claims for land rights, greater self-management, acceptance of the applicability of tribal law, and preservation of Aboriginal culture and traditional sacred sites.

In 1992 the High Court overturned long-held legal doctrine by declaring that the common law of Australia recognised that the rights and interests in land held by the indigenous inhabitants under their traditional laws and customs survived the establishment of British sovereignty. Federal legislation which came into force in 1994 set up tribunals to hear claims to Native Title (see p. 145). Claims can only be made in respect of unalienated state or territory crown land. The Western Australian parliament purported to enact legislation inconsistent with the Commonwealth legislation and conferring fewer rights on Aborigines. The dispute awaited resolution by the High Court.

J-PLF

No Bill of Rights

Unlike the USA (and since 1982 Canada) Australia has no Bill of Rights. Most of the framers of the Constitution believed such legislation was not in the spirit of majoritarian democracy and the British notion of the supremacy of parliament. Some regarded constitutionally entrenched rights as needed only by countries where liberalism was not strongly rooted.

There was also what today would appear as the darker side of this attitude. A clause providing for equal protection of the laws was rejected because of fears that it would invalidate colonial laws that discriminated against Asians and Africans.

There are a few constitutional rights in relation to Commonwealth and, to a lesser extent, state legislation (see p. 164–5), but these are rather limited. Australia has ratified the two 1966 United Nations Covenants on Human Rights and the 1965 Convention on the Elimination of All Forms of Racial Discrimination (implemented through the Racial Discrimination Act of 1975). This removes all legislative discrimination against Aborigines and any other racial group, but it is undeniable that racial prejudices continue to make Aborigines the victims of *de facto* discrimination by some officials and law-enforcement agents.

In 1992 the High Court of Australia held that there were some rights implied in the Constitution by virtue of its provisions for representative government. It was on this ground that the Court held invalid a federal Act prohibiting the broadcasting of political advertisements during election campaigns, but making provision for 'free time' to be given by broadcasters to parties and candidates. Freedom of communication was held to be a vital ingredient of representative government. It seems likely that, to some degree, other rights will be similarly regarded, such as those of movement and assembly.

AUSTRALIAN OFFSHOOTS

The first settlers of a British colony take with them the law of England so far as it is applicable to local conditions at the time of settlement. As the eastern colonies of Australia were initially penal settlements there was doubt as to the date from which English law applied. These doubts were settled by the Australian Courts Act, an 1828 statute of the British parliament. It provided that all case law and legislation in force in England on 25 July 1828 should be applied to the colonies of New South Wales (which then included Victoria and Queensland) and Van Diemen's Land (now Tasmania). Western Australia received the common law on its formation in 1829, South Australia on its formation in 1836.

Unlike Wales, the colonies were not incorporated into the English legal system. Each colony was a new and distinct system. Its further development depended partly on statutes expressly enacted for it by the British parliament. (Other British statutes enacted after the colony's receipt of the common law did not apply). Delegated legislation, such as the ordinances of the colony's governor, was another source of law, and so was case law – local courts and the Privy Council in London had to interpret the common law in its new setting. The colonies' own legislatures also made laws, a task which they gradually took over from the British parliament.

By the end of the nineteenth century, each colony was a self-governing democracy. Although the colony's governor was responsible to the British government in matters deemed to be of imperial concern – such as defence, foreign affairs and merchant shipping – in all other matters the governor was bound by the advice of the colony's own government, which required the confidence of its parliament in order to hold office.

Until federation, relations between the Australian colonies were similar to those between foreign countries. The federation of the colonies was the result of 10 years of negotiation by colonial delegates at a series of conferences and conventions between 1890 and 1899. The chief motives for union were a desire to put an end to inter-colonial trade wars and the establishment of a common market, fear of foreign invasion and a belief that a united Australia would have more influence in the shaping of imperial policy. The draft constitution that was negotiated was approved by the electors of the six colonies at referendums before being sent to the British government with a petition for its enactment.

The Constitution which is contained in the Commonwealth of Australia. Constitution Act 1900 (UK) came into force on 1 January 1901 when the colonies became states of the new Commonwealth.

As a result of a series of Imperial Conferences between the world wars culminating in the Statute of Westminster 1931 (UK) the British Dominions (which included Australia) were recognised as having equal status with the United Kingdom in all aspects of their domestic and external affairs. The Statute of Westminster was adopted by the Australian parliament in 1942, to operate retrospectively from 3 September 1939. It gave the Commonwealth parliament power to override any British statutes, other than the Constitution. The Australian States, however, did not have this power until the enactment of the Australia Acts 1986 by the British and Australian parliaments. This legislation also formally terminated the power of the United Kingdom to make law for Australia.

A lock up at Elphinstone, east of Castlemaine, Victoria, c. 1890.

Australia's remaining constitutional link with Britain is the fact that the two countries share the same (mainly ceremonial) head of state in the person of the Queen. There is current debate whether a hereditary head of state, who is furthermore not resident, is appropriate for Australia (see p. 135). If the Australian Commonwealth abandons the monarchy, there is a question whether states which are opposed to this change will be able to retain the role the Queen has in their own state constitutions. LRZ

PARLIAMENTARY GOVERNMENT

The Constitution vests the Commonwealth's legislative power in a bicameral (two-chamber) parliament (pp. 156–8), consisting of the Senate (upper house) and the House of Representatives (lower house). Executive power, which the Constitution vests in the Queen, is exercisable by the governor-general, who is appointed by the Queen on the advice of the Australian prime minister. As in Britain, the power of the Crown is in fact exercised by the prime minister and the rest of the cabinet. They remain in office only so long as they are supported by a majority in the lower house.

The system in the states is parallel, with a state governor fulfilling a figurehead role on behalf of the Queen. Real executive power is exercised by a government of parliamentary ministers requiring support from the lower house in the state parliament. (Only in Queensland is the state parliament unicameral.)

The Commonwealth Senate is elected, and its powers more closely resemble those of the American Senate than those of the unelected British House of Lords. In 1900, the smaller colonies would federate only if the Senate were given an equal number of representatives from each state and made strong enough to counterbalance the House of Representatives. (With its seats allocated on the basis of population, they feared that the House of Representatives would allow the large states – New South Wales and Queensland – to dominate.) With some comparatively minor exceptions, the Senate was given equal powers with the House of Representatives.

Australia's combination of the British institution of parliamentary government and American institution of a strong upper house with equal representation of the states helped produce a constitutional crisis in 1975, when the Senate refused to pass appropriation Bills to enable the government to carry on. Controversially, the governor-general exercised a residual power to intervene in a substantive way in the affairs of state by dismissing the prime minister, in order to break the deadlock.

INDEPENDENT COURTS

The appointment of judges is the responsibility of the executive (the cabinet) in each jurisdiction. Once they are appointed, it is a fundamental principle that judges should be independent of executive direction or control, an aspect of the American doctrine of separation of powers that has been adopted in the Australian Constitution. In order to secure their independence, federal judges can be removed only by the governor-general acting on an address from both houses of parliament on grounds of proved misbehaviour or incapacity. The rules for the removal of judges of the states and territories vary, but in all cases removal is difficult.

Australian courts are organised in a series of hierarchical structures reflecting the nine major geographical jurisdictions in the federation: the Commonwealth, the six states, the Australian Capital Territory (the city of Canberra) and the Northern Territory. In addition, three offshore territories – Norfolk Island, Christmas Island and the Cocos (Keeling) Islands have their own separate courts.

The High Court of Australia is the most superior, and it is the ultimate court of appeal in the federal and all of the state systems. Below it, in the federal hierarchy, are the Federal Court of Australia, the Industrial Relations Court and the Family Court of Australia. In each state's system there is a Supreme Court. Below it are intermediate courts commonly called District or County Courts, and below them are Magistrates Courts, Local Courts or Courts of Petty Sessions. In New South Wales and Queensland, a separate division of the Supreme Court is the Court of Appeal.

The state Supreme Court deals with both state and federal matters and hears appeals from lower courts. Appeals on federal matters from state Supreme Courts usually go to the Full Court of the Federal Court (single-judge sittings of the Court hear cases that have not been heard before). Appeals may be taken from the Federal Court to full sittings of the High Court. Appeals may also be taken from a state Supreme Court directly to the High Court. Nearly all appeals to the High Court require special leave.

In 1988 a system of cross-vesting of jurisdiction was adopted to overcome problems which had arisen where a particular court, such as the Family Court, could deal with only part of a litigant's case. The system allows federal courts to deal with matters previously within the exclusive jurisdiction of state courts, and it gives state courts jurisdiction over matters previously reserved for federal courts or the courts of other states. Courts have a discretion to decline this extended jurisdiction where it would be inappropriate. CC

Top Edgar John Azzopardi with documentation amassed during his single-handed campaign against what he claimed were corrupt elements in the New South Wales police force. In 1969 a collision with a police car triggered his 'crusade'; in 1993 he and his wife were awarded $70,000 by the New South Wales Victims' Compensation Tribunal after a Commission finding that a series of threatening telephone calls to the Azzopardi house were made from a local police station.

Bottom The Aboriginal barrister Bob Bellear was admitted to the New South Wales Bar in 1979. He became co-founder of the Aboriginal Housing Company in Redfern, Sydney, and in 1987 was counsel assisting the Royal Commission into Aboriginal deaths in custody.

REDRESS AGAINST MALADMINISTRATION

So far as federal law is concerned Australia has moved further than any other common-law country to improve the citizen's rights of redress in case of unjust decisions by government officials. The system includes judicial review, an Administrative Appeals Tribunal, and an ombudsman.

Judicial review of administrative decisions made by officials of the Commonwealth can be sought in the Federal Court and the High Court. Review is similar to that in the courts of other common-law countries in that the court cannot substitute a new decision for the one under review – it can only review the legality of the decision. However, since passage of the Administrative Decisions (Judicial Review) Act in 1977, the courts have been rigorous in cutting down excesses of discretionary power. Procedural fairness is insisted on. A decision will also be held to be invalid if all relevant considerations have not been taken into account, that is, if the decision-maker does not have regard to all relevant up-to-date information.

Unlike the courts, the Administrative Appeals Tribunal, created in 1975, has power to review the merits of decisions and substitute a different decision. Its decisions can be appealed to the Federal Court on questions of law.

Amending the Constitution

Australia's Constitution has proved very difficult to amend. Proposed amendments have, in most cases, to be passed by an absolute majority in both houses in the Commonwealth parliament and then submitted to a referendum of the people. The amendment is affirmed if it is approved by a majority of the electorate voting throughout Australia and, additionally, by a majority in a majority (currently four) of the states. This provision was adopted from the Swiss constitution.

Although dozens of proposals have been put to the people, they have approved only eight amendments. These amendments have added only two new subjects of power to the Commonwealth's list, namely a variety of social service benefits (in 1946) and the Aboriginal people (in 1967). No proposal has ever passed that did not have the support of both the government and opposition parties. Even when such joint support has been forthcoming (which is rare) it has not always guaranteed success. However, the powers exercised by the state and Commonwealth governments today are very different from what they were in the early days of the twentieth century, or even 20 years ago. In the absence of formal statutory amendment, government powers have been modified through case law arising out of judicial decisions.   LRZ

The ombudsman cannot overturn a decision, and cannot review decisions made by ministers or judges, but can recommend financial recompense for negligent advice and recommend that decisions which are unjust or otherwise wrong be revised. This office, created in 1976, is not restricted as much as a court regarding the material on which a finding can be based, and it can take up the cases of people who are unfamiliar with the law without requiring them to be parties to an action.

The Freedom of Information Act and the related Archives Act also contribute to making government more open and responsive. Some states have also made provisions for improved administrative review and freedom of information.   RB

STATE AND COMMONWEALTH POWERS

Under the Australian Constitution the Commonwealth parliament is given power to legislate with respect to specific matters only. The most important subjects are trade and commerce with other countries and among the states, all forms of taxation, defence, external affairs, immigration, social security, postal and broadcasting services, marriage and divorce, and a variety of commercial and financial subjects, including banking and insurance, patents, trade marks and copyright, trading and financial corporations and negotiable instruments. Its exercise of these powers, furthermore, is explicitly limited by a number of provisions in the Constitution: for example, the Commonwealth Government can acquire property only on 'just terms'; it cannot establish any religion, interfere with the free expression of any religion or impose a religious test as a qualification for any office; laws of taxation and commerce cannot discriminate against or grant any preference to states or parts of states.

The Constitution does not give states any enumerated powers and explicitly restricts only a few: they have no power to raise armies; they cannot levy cus-

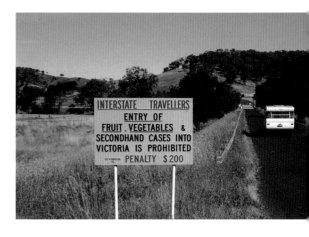

toms and excise duties (the courts have interpreted this to include sales and purchase taxes); they are forbidden to discriminate against non-alien residents of the other states. Otherwise, the states retain the powers they had before federation, including most topics that are subjects of commonwealth power. However, if a valid law of the commonwealth parliament is inconsistent with a state law, the former prevails to the extent of the inconsistency.

The validity of a state law does not usually depend on the subject matter of the law, but a federal law will be upheld only if the commonwealth has a specific power to legislate on the matter.   LRZ

EXPANDING COMMONWEALTH POWER

In the list of powers granted to the Commonwealth, there is no mention of most areas of the law that affect the day-to-day life of the citizen – for example, there is no mention of industrial production, mining, agriculture, land use, environmental law, criminal law, local government, labour relations, education or housing. Prima facie, therefore, these may be regarded as within the exclusive power of the states. However, as a result of judicial interpretation of the Constitution and the financial might of the Commonwealth, federal control in many of these areas is extensive.

Control of much manufacturing and financial activities is now regarded as authorised by the Commonwealth's power with respect to trading and financial corporations when conducted by companies (as distinct from individuals and partnerships). Unlike the commerce power, this power is not confined to interstate and overseas trade.

A wider area of potential control is now available to the Commonwealth parliament as a result of a High Court decision in 1983 holding that the power with respect to 'external affairs' authorises the Commonwealth parliament to give effect to any international treaty on any subject to which Australia is a party. This has enabled the Commonwealth by entering into treaties to regulate matters that otherwise would be within the exclusive power of the states, including racial discrimination and the protection of natural and cultural heritage.

Courts have followed the principle that a grant of power gives the grantee authority to do all things that are reasonably necessary to fulfil the object of the power. On this principle they have, for example, upheld the Commonwealth's right to control air navigation within states on the ground that this is necessary in order to control trade and commerce between states and with other countries.

Another principle that has helped to extend federal

A roadsign on the Victoria–New South Wales border, reminding travellers entering Victoria of trading laws.

power is that, where a law operates directly on a subject of federal power, the political reason for using the power is irrelevant to the validity of using it. The court upheld the right of the Commonwealth to refuse export licences to a company planning to mine minerals on an island off Queensland, even though the Commonwealth's political object was to protect the environment of the island, a matter over which it has no direct power.

The Constitution grants to the Commonwealth the power to give financial assistance to any state on such terms and conditions as it thinks fit. The Commonwealth has used this power to induce states to use or refrain from using their own powers. Universities are for the most part created by state law, but the Commonwealth fully finances all of them and has considerable influence and *de facto* control.

Since World War II only the Commonwealth Government has levied income tax, from which it makes grants to the state governments (pp. 159–60). Most of the grant money is given unconditionally as general revenue, but grants for specific purposes in the areas of housing, hospitals, road construction, etc. may have detailed conditions attached, including close supervision by Commonwealth officials. The states retain the constitutional right to levy income tax and they have the right to refuse conditional federal grants, but they rarely do so.

Political sentiment sets limits to what the Commonwealth government feels it can do to override state laws and policies. In 1986 it reversed its policy of national land rights for Aborigines largely because of pressure from some state governments.   LRZ

THE COMMON MARKET

One of the chief reasons for federation of the Australian colonies was the establishment of free trade among the states and a common tariff policy in relation to other countries. This was achieved by the Constitution, in section 92, declaring that trade, commerce and intercourse among the states shall be absolutely free, and by giving the Commonwealth the exclusive power to levy customs and excise duties and to grant bounties on the production and export of goods.

The requirement of 'absolutely free' interstate trade gave rise to much disagreement and scores of High Court and Privy Council cases which upset major policies of many governments in the Commonwealth and the states. In 1988, however, a unanimous court overruled most of the earlier cases and held that the provision was aimed solely at laws which discriminated against interstate trade with the purpose or effect of protecting the trade or industry of a state against that of another.   LRZ

The Economy

The economy 1788–1890

European settlement of Australia before 1890 is largely the story of the transformation of a continent through the discovery and exploitation of resources yielding products valuable in international trade.

In 1788, Australia was inhabited by Aboriginal hunters and gatherers whose last contact with other cultures had been in the remote past. The new British colony was a tiny and isolated collection of convicts and their keepers ruled by a naval officer, Arthur Phillip (see also p. 86).

A century later, the remnants of the Aboriginal population were scattered in the interior, while the colonists had turned the continent to new uses and had grown rich. Successful participation in an expanding international economy underpinned the growth of a free and prosperous colonial society.

The incentives arising out of Australia's resources persuaded people to settle in a strange land and lured capital halfway around the globe. Together, exports and capital inflow paid for imports on a scale that made goods available in quantities and in a variety that could not have been achieved from local production because of the limited economic specialisation possible with a small population.

In the nineteenth century, this overseas orientation was overwhelmingly towards Britain: all but a few of the settlers came from Britain and Ireland, most Australian trade was with Britain, and Britain provided nearly all the overseas capital invested in Australia in this period.

THE CONVICT ECONOMY

The decision to found a penal colony on the east coast of Australia was taken at a time when the British government knew nothing of the resources the new land might contain. So large a continent was thought likely to have much of value, but for the moment the absence of known resources and Australia's distance from trade routes were important to the success of the penal venture. It was hoped that the settlement would eventually be self-supporting. Convicts were to produce food on government farms and clothing in government factories as well as making roads and buildings.

The private sector was to be largely independent of the gaol and to consist mainly of convicts whose terms had expired. Official policy seems to have favoured the development of subsistence farming on smallholdings granted by the local administration. Government farming failed, however, and the government was forced to buy grain from private farmers.

This trade encouraged the early development of an exchange economy and allowed private access to funds with which to buy imports. Government purchases were paid for by the issue of receipts that circulated as a local currency and could be consolidated into Treasury Bills drawn on London. The trading system allowed the concentration of wealth and foreign exchange in a few hands, as did the manipulation of public power for private gain by officers and others. The conflicts inherent in this situation generated a series of clashes between the administration and the officer traders, culminating in the Rum Rebellion of 1808.

Convict labour was important to the private sector, both through direct employment on terms that amounted to the public subsidy of private activity and indirectly through the use of convicts on government construction projects.

Previous page Wheat, Australia's most important crop, grown in all states. Highly efficient in agriculture, Australia is the third largest exporter of wheat in the world. An average farm produces enough food and fibre to meet the needs of 300 people.

View of Hobart Town from the Windmill, Van Diemen's Land by John Black Henderson, c. 1855. The whalers in the harbour are a reminder that Hobart, Tasmania, was developed as a base for South Sea whaling.

The Aboriginal population suffered a catastrophic decline which began almost immediately the penal settlement was established (see p. 137). The population balance was disturbed when Aborigines were exposed to diseases against which they had few biological defences. Initially, the main killer was smallpox, which may have come through the penal colony at Botany Bay or may have come from the north, where Macassan fishermen sometimes landed. Venereal disease, measles and respiratory infections clearly originated from the white population and killed large numbers of Aborigines (see also pp. 228–9). Deliberate killing of Aborigines was common but appears to have been a lesser cause of population decline. High mortality, ill health and venereal disease also affected fertility. The speed and extent of the Aboriginal depopulation diminished the capacity to resist white settlement, and the spread of the pastoral industry through southeastern Australia that was to occur after 1820 prevented any possible restoration to pre-contact size of the Aboriginal population.

THE PASTORAL ECONOMY

Though the initial efforts of the colonists focused on agriculture and the raising of livestock to feed themselves and the convicts, it was recognised that sources of export income would have to be found if the colony were to prosper in the long run.

The convenience of Sydney and Hobart as ports for sealers and whalers operating in the southern oceans provided the first significant opportunity for export growth. Sealing and whaling were well established by the 1820s and continued to expand until the depletion of the herds and a fall in world demand brought the collapse of the industry in the 1840s. Whaling helped to stimulate shipbuilding, fostered the local carrying and provisioning trade, and encouraged urbanisation. The industry was also the first to employ only free labour. This early prominence, however, did not give whaling a central role in the transition to a rapidly growing free economy. A substantial shift towards economic growth based on the exploitation of overseas demand for the products of abundant local resources did not begin until fine wool production developed in the 1820s and was not decisive until the late 1830s, by which time the dynamic element in export growth lay primarily with the wool industry.

The first attempts to produce wool for export around 1800 were confined to a few coastal locations, for nothing was known of the grazing resources of the interior of southeastern Australia until after the crossing of the Blue Mountains in 1813. Once the crossing had been made, exploration proceeded

apace. Much of it was carried forward by the pastoralists themselves as the flocks spread inland.

Wool faced a large prospective export market, and the discovery of the grazing lands provided the means of achieving a rapid and prolonged expansion in output. Wool exports overtook whaling exports in the early 1830s and later in the decade also exceeded the foreign-exchange earnings derived from sales to the government store and from British expenditure on the penal establishment. Free immigrants now came in large numbers (see also pp. 222–3), and private capital flowed in to seek profits from the pastoral boom.

Economic expansion was interrupted by depression in the early 1840s. Low wool prices and a reduction in capital inflow resulted from changed economic conditions in Britain. The depression in Australia, however, was not wholly a response to external economic forces. The pastoral boom lasted for several years after wool prices began to fall in 1836. The drying up of capital imports was delayed until after 1840 and was influenced by falling profit opportunities in the pastoral industry as well as by the state of the British capital market. The fall in pastoral profits was due partly to lower wool prices, caused by changes in the British wool market, and partly to difficulties internal to the industry. The course of the depression in Australia was also influenced by pressure on the local administration's budget caused by the mismanagement of its finances.

The depression brought distress and ruin to many, but pastoral growth soon resumed. Expansion was slower than in the 1830s but was nonetheless impressive, the industry tripling in size between 1840 and 1850. During this period Australia came to supply around half of Britain's wool imports, displacing Spain and Germany as principal suppliers. Successful competition in the British market was possible because wool's high value in relation to its bulk meant that transport charges were only a small part of total costs, even with the slow and expensive transport links then in existence.

Australian economic development destroyed the convict system. In the 1820s and 1830s the emphasis of British policy began to shift towards the fostering of a free society and economy and away from the protection of Britain's narrow interest in the maintenance of convict transportation. Transportation to New South Wales ceased in 1840, though Tasmania continued to receive convicts until the 1850s and Western Australia, which had begun as a free colony, took transported British convicts from 1850 until the 1860s. The colony of South Australia was free of transported convicts from the start. On the rest of mainland southeastern Australia, convicts were a small and diminishing proportion of the population by 1850.

By this time, the colonists had been given a good deal of political independence from London and were on the verge of gaining substantially complete self-government. Economic growth also brought congenial institutions, including the vigorous development of a money and banking system appropriate to a pastoral export economy.

In 1850 the colonists enjoyed high living standards as a result of their own productive efforts and in spite of the withdrawal of British government expenditure that had financed much early consumption.

Though the exploitation of natural resources allowed rapid export growth, and though exports were essential to economic growth and the emergence of high living standards, the degree of economic specialisation arising from international trade should not be exaggerated. Most economic activity was still directed towards the domestic market. The pastoral industry produced meat for local consumption as well as wool for export. Non-pastoral agriculture produced as much in value terms as the pastoral industry, and all its product was sold locally. With population growing rapidly, a high proportion of productive effort was necessarily used in building and construction.

Station Pier, Port Melbourne, in the 1860s. The gold rushes of the previous decade saw the influx of thousands of immigrants, and Melbourne's river wharfs developed in response, to become the focal point of Australia's coastal and overseas shipping.

Urban activity was important, and nearly 30 per cent of the population lived in the main port cities. Manufacturing was negligible, but there was a great deal of employment in commercial, financial and transport activity and in domestic service. It is estimated that in 1846–50 the pastoral industry accounted for 15 per cent of gross domestic product. Agriculture and the mining of copper and small amounts of coal accounted for 22 per cent, manufacturing and private construction for 9 per cent, public service and construction for 4 per cent, and private services made up the remaining 50 per cent of gross domestic product in this period.

By 1850, 15 million sheep were spread over the southeast and Tasmania. Australia's emergence as an important supplier in the British wool market now meant that the previous high rate of growth of Australian output could not be expected to continue far into the future. When Australia entered the market, her tiny output could grow much faster than overall market demand and still have a negligible impact on wool prices. Once Australia had become a major supplier, however, the further growth of Australian output would itself begin to affect prices and hence the profitability of further expansion.

ECONOMIC GROWTH AND STRUCTURE 1860–90

The gold rushes brought an increase in the scale of the economy which allowed the emergence of a more complex economic structure in later decades. Largely, this concerned growth in the domestic sector.

Population growth fell sharply from an average of around 9 per cent a year during 1800–60 to 3.4 per cent between 1860 and 1890, by which time the population had reached 3.5 million. Immigration was now less important than natural increase as a source of population growth (see also pp. 222–5).

Export growth slowed even more dramatically. Exports had risen faster than population until the mid-1850s. Now export growth began to lag behind population, particularly in value terms.

With the domestic sector, the quantity of production is a basic determinant of living standards. With exports, however, it is the total value of production that matters, because this is what limits the long-run capacity to buy imports. The value of Australian exports rose at 2.6 per cent a year between 1861–65 and 1871–75, but at only 0.6 per cent a year between 1871–75 and 1886–90. Annual exports per person fell from £15 in 1861–65 to £9 in 1886–90. While this overstates the extent of the fall in the quantity of imports per person that was paid for by exports (because import prices were falling), it is certain that the ability to finance imports from export earnings was seriously reduced.

Part of the explanation for the decline in Australian export growth in this period is that the great rise in exports in the 1850s had come from the exploitation of a non-renewable resource. Once the limits to the expansion of goldmining had been reached, there was no stabilisation of gold output at a high level but a fall in output as reserves were depleted. A crucial underpinning of the existing level

Gold diggings at the junction of the Two Creeks, near Ophir, New South Wales, 1851. Ophir was the centre of Australia's first gold rush, following the discovery of the metal in the year of this print. The name given to the town is taken from an ancient Middle Eastern city fabled for its gold.

The Gold Rushes

The economic situation changed dramatically with the discovery of alluvial gold near Bathurst in New South Wales in1851. This sparked a series of rich finds, mainly in Victoria, which transformed Australian export capacity. The initial exploitation of the goldfields was extraordinarily rapid, the volume of production reaching twin peaks in 1853 and 1856.

The surge in exports encouraged a re-orientation of non-gold activity towards the domestic market. Pastoral production was drawn away from wool exports and towards the supply of meat for local consumption. The growth of local demand stimulated service activity and the manufacture of products for which import competition was ruled out by Australia's distance from overseas sources of supply. Where imports were possible, however, Australian production suffered because the domestic inflation brought on by the sudden rise in exports raised production costs relative to import prices. Imports soon arrived in quantity in response to the rise in Australian purchasing power.

The population response to the gold discoveries was equally rapid. Immigration boomed, the population doubled in five years, and the share of Victoria in the Australian total climbed steeply. This, however, was not the beginning of a new long-run phase of faster population growth. On average, Australia's non-Aboriginal population doubled every eight years between 1800 and 1850. The gold discoveries extended the early phase of rapid population growth and in the process took the population to 1 million in 1858, a size that would not otherwise have been reached until later in the century.

The easily worked gold deposits were soon depleted. Though new discoveries were made in the period 1860–90, none matched the finds of the 1850s. As the surface deposits dwindled, gold production declined and gold mining changed its character, digging and panning by independent miners giving way to deep-lead mining by companies. The mining sector became more diversified. Copper and coal production continued to grow, tin production began, and the discovery of silver, lead, and zinc at Broken Hill in New South Wales in the 1880s marked a new and important stage in mining development.

Overall, however, the growth in the production of other minerals did not fully offset the decline in gold, with the result that the total output from mining was somewhat smaller in 1890 than it had been in the mid-1850s.

RVJ

of exports was being removed. In consequence, even the maintenance of total exports at the level of the late 1850s required a substantial growth in non-gold exports.

A renewed growth in wool exports was the means by which some export growth was achieved after 1860. Wool exports had stagnated in the 1850s, and Australia's share in the expanding British market for imported wool had fallen. After 1860, however, high export prices, a falling rate of growth in the local demand for meat, and easier labour supplies than during the gold rushes brought a period of rapid growth in wool output. In contrast with earlier expansions in the industry, this phase of pastoral growth was associated with high investment.

The capital requirements of the wool industry before the 1850s had been minimal, the major physical assets being the sheep themselves. Fixed structures had been few and primitive. The implementation of a new pastoral technology brought

The official opening at Albury, New South Wales, of the Great Southern Railway on 2 February 1881. Two years later the extension of the route to Melbourne was completed, but passengers had to change trains at Albury because the tracks of the two states were of different gauges.

expenditure on wool washpools in the 1860s, on water conservation in the 1880s and, most important of all, on fencing throughout the period from the 1860s to 1890.

This pastoral investment was highly productive before about 1875 and was financed largely from the resources and profits of the industry itself. Sheep numbers rose from 20 million in 1860 to 50 million in 1875, representing annual growth of 6 per cent. Wool exports grew even faster at a rate of over 10 per cent a year in both value and volume in this period.

Important changes took place in the wool industry from the middle of the 1870s. Investment rose further. This investment, however, was now increasingly financed by overseas borrowing, and it failed to stimulate a commensurate increase in wool output. Indeed, the rate of growth in the quantity of wool produced fell to around 4 per cent a year during 1875–90. Wool prices also fell so that the annual growth in wool proceeds was reduced to about 2 per cent.

The reduced productivity was due to the movement of the pastoral frontier into the arid inland. By 1890 the industry had expanded into areas incapable of sustaining sheep in the long run. Sheep numbers briefly exceeded 100 million in the early 1890s before being drastically reduced by drought. There were also market limits to expansion. The fall in wool prices was itself due partly to the growth in Australian supplies, and a faster growth in physical output would have accelerated the price decline.

Real gross domestic product grew at 4.7 per cent a year between 1860 and 1890. Product per head grew at 1.2 per cent a year, about equal to the British rate but only half the rate of *per capita* growth in the United States. Australian income per head had been exceptionally high at the end of the gold rushes, perhaps the highest in the world. By 1890, Australian superiority in this respect had been much reduced because of the faster *per capita* growth experienced in the USA.

The period 1860–90 is remarkable for the absence of major depressions and for the way in which gross domestic product continued to grow in the face of a marked slowing in export growth. Investment in the Australian economy also began to rise in the second half of the 1870s. Much of the investment boom was financed by overseas borrowing.

Overseas funds poured into the pastoral industry and into the hands of the colonial governments for spending on railway construction. Indirectly, capital imports also stimulated the other main avenue of investment, house building, by lowering interest rates. Australian capital formation at this time was a labour-intensive process involving simple structures, basic building materials and simple equipment. Capital inflow made high investment possible by financing imports of consumer goods, which freed labour for use in the construction industry.

High overseas borrowing led to a rapid rise in amount of income due overseas. This came to pose a serious threat to the stability of the Australian economy because the investment of the 1880s did not produce much export growth. The slow growth in pastoral exports has already been discussed. Investment in railways made inland transport cheaper but may not have had much effect on export capacity in the short run. Even without railways, land transport costs were only a small part of the total production costs of wool, while the policy of building lines to serve existing traffic flows meant that many areas were reasonably fully exploited by pastoralists before the railway arrived. In the long run, railway building stimulated export diversification by reducing transport costs for commodities such as wheat but this effect was not important before 1890. The slow growth in exports meant that income due overseas rose from 20 per cent of export income in the late 1870s to nearly 40 per cent of exports in the late 1880s. By this time, overseas borrowing was equal to about 70 per cent of export income. The Australian economy had become very vulnerable.

The developing economic structure reinforced the already distinctive pattern of Australian urbanisation. The capital cities held 33 per cent of the population in 1891. Other towns, some of them tiny inland settlements, held a further 23 per cent of the population, and rural areas held the remaining 44 per cent. Australia remained more heavily urbanised than other regions of recent settlement.

The economy 1890–1945

The year of Australia's centenary of white settlement, 1888, was one marked by high extravagance. In the streets, the Jubilee of Queen Victoria's reign was still being celebrated with gala exhibitions, pageants and brilliant illuminations.

In the economy, Australian and British investors joined in a furious speculation in suburban land and housing and in shares, especially those of mining and finance companies. Assisting the spree, trading banks' advances to their customers soared, having already doubled over the previous seven years, while the banks kept lower reserves relative to their deposit liabilities. For the economy it was an era of dangerous living, in more ways than one. Pastoral activity had been pushed hard to its natural limits, given the existing technology. Profitability of the industry started to decline after 1883 and, with time, so must the inducement to invest. Moreover, the economy was now more exposed to the depressive effects of any downturn in overseas demand for wool on account of the previous growth of the export sector.

Public investment, fattened on the savings of British bondholders, had also risen to very high levels in the 1880s, as, too, had the dizzy height from which the economy could fall if the prop of capital inflow was removed. Interest on borrowings had to be delivered to Britons and these commitments were multiplying far more rapidly than the means of payment generated by the initial public investment. Much public investment was ill-conceived and wasteful; some of it was certainly pork barrelling by politicians – aimed to fetch votes at elections – rather than predicated on careful assessment of economic benefits.

Patterns of preceding economic change – that is in pastoral expansion, public investment and house building, all of which by the late 1880s had the overly sweet smell of fruit beyond its prime – created conditions in which growth was not sustainable. A downturn in the British trade cycle combined with a liquidity crisis arising from the insolvency of Baring, a leading financial house, in November 1890 and the loss of British investors' fortunes in Argentinian securities, depressed Australian export prices and incomes and militated against capital inflow. But by then the Australian undercurrents sweeping the economy towards depression were already strong.

In the first 40 years of the twentieth century many important changes occurred in the economic lives of Australians. The jobs in which they worked and the mix of goods and services that Australians produced

Differences in economic structure go far towards explaining this. Only 25 per cent of the Australian workforce was engaged directly in agricultural and pastoral activity in 1890, compared with about 40 per cent in the USA and other new countries. The small share of employment accounted for by the agricultural sector was due partly to the high labour productivity of Australian rural activity. This in turn reflected the relative unimportance in Australia of subsistence agriculture. Agricultural and pastoral output was overwhelmingly for sale, much of it for export. The absence of large numbers of small farmers operating on the fringe of the market system contributed substantially to the high level of urban development. Also important was the high level of employment in services, itself partly a reflection of high income per head and the high level of commercial activity in the port cities.

A further distinctive feature of the period after 1860 was the direct participation of government in the economy on a large scale. After the coming of self-government, the colonial governments quickly became active entrepreneurs and investors. Governments were responsible for 39 per cent of domestic investment and raised 58 per cent of direct overseas borrowings in the period 1861–90. Much of this public investment was used to provide valuable infrastructure, particularly railways.

Investment plans, however, were made in an era of easy credit and loose budgetary constraint. Some of the railway building of the 1880s was wasteful, at least in the short run, and the high level of capital formation financed by overseas borrowing raised the amount of income payable overseas and raised the local cost structure by raising the demand for labour. Governments also spent large amounts on programmes of assisted immigration, especially in Queensland.   RVJ

changed. Also, the pace at which the economy expanded in these years ebbed and flowed. Recovery from the 1890s depression was muted by serious drought at the turn of the century. Further recovery was turned around by production losses during World War I and drought just after it. Rapid output growth in the first half of the Roaring Twenties gave way to negligible growth in the second half of that decade and then to the Great Depression of the early 1930s. The year 1932 saw possibly as many as one-third of Australia's workers without jobs. Thereafter a recovery set in, with World War II ushering in still further growth. To live through these years was to watch the economic tide surge, recede and begin its roll again. Market forces were partly responsible for this rhythm but the lives of Australians were also importantly affected by the economic policies adopted by governments.

WORK AND OUTPUT

At federation in 1901 Australia had a European population of 3.7 million. Of these, 1.5 million or 40 per cent were in the workforce. On the eve of World War II the population numbered 7 million, 43 per cent of whom were working or actively seeking employ-

ment. Most of Australia's workers bore little resemblance to those described in the colourful bush ballads of Henry Lawson, Breaker Morant and others. Even at federation only one-third of Australia's workforce were engaged in the primary industries (24 per cent in agriculture, dairying and pastoral pursuits, 10 per cent in mining). By the beginning of the 1920s there were as many factory jobs in towns as there were jobs on farms and stations. This trend was to accelerate. By 1947 28 per cent of Australia's workers were in manufacturing (the secondary sector) compared with just 15 per cent in agriculture, dairying and pastoral pursuits. Most Australians worked in the service or tertiary sector, in building and construction, in providing transport services, in commerce – for instance, in shops and banks – and in other service areas, notably as public servants, domestic servants in middle-class homes, especially before World War I, and as hotel workers. Most of these jobs kept Australians in the towns and cities.

The jobs at which Australians worked were broadly reflected in the types of goods and services – gross domestic product (GDP) – which were produced. The most important change in the mix of output was the increasing share of manufacturing in GDP and the diminishing share of the primary

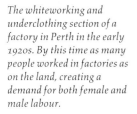

The whiteworking and underclothing section of a factory in Perth in the early 1920s. By this time as many people worked in factories as on the land, creating a demand for both female and male labour.

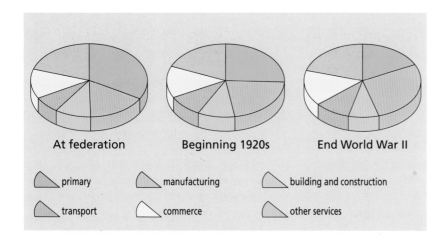

At federation   Beginning 1920s   End World War II

primary · manufacturing · building and construction
transport · commerce · other services

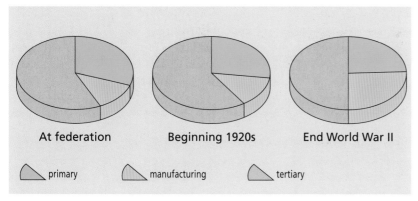

At federation   Beginning 1920s   End World War II

primary · manufacturing · tertiary

Above top *The workforce in 1901, the early 1920s and 1947.*

Above bottom
The increasing share of manufacturing industry in the gross domestic product between 1901 and 1947.

STRUCTURAL CHANGE

Yet while it is clear that this was not a period of sustained economic growth in *per capita* terms, it was nonetheless a period of increasing diversity in the goods produced and the inputs used to produce them. Such changes helped set the style if not the pace of future growth. Moreover, the years after 1907 to the onset of the Great Depression of the 1930s saw Australia attain one of the highest population growth rates in the West and this was something that Australian governments actively sought.

Manufacturing was becoming increasingly important, the primary sector less so. But this is not the full story. For within both sectors the range of output was increasing. In the primary sector the depressed wool prices of the early 1890s hastened diversification of rural land use. Interest in the possibilities of refrigerated cargoes led to the establishment of new export industries centred on meat and dairy products. From 1896 wheat growing also expanded greatly, acreage under wheat for grain rising from 5.5 million acres (2.2 million ha) in 1900 to 15 million acres (6 million ha) in 1930. This was facilitated by technical advances, both biological (new wheat strains) and mechanical, which permitted wheat farming to spread into arid lands. Governments promoted rural diversification and closer settlement by building railway branches and roads through the wheat belts and diffusing technical knowledge to the new farmers. Irrigation and dry block settlement schemes were extended and governments also paid bounties on the export of many rural products to promote their production.

Up to 1914 manufacturing had largely centred on the processing of primary products and the maintenance of transport, especially railways. The wartime rupturing of trade, however, speeded up the potential

sector. The most marked change occurred during the late 1930s and in the war years: manufacturing accounted for 12 per cent of GDP in 1901, 14 per cent in 1921, 19 per cent in 1939 and 27 per cent in 1947.

The real level of GDP per inhabitant is often taken as a guide to a country's standard of living. The rate at which Australia's real GDP per head advanced in the first 40 years of this century repeatedly faltered. Rises were almost totally offset by falls, so much so that real GDP per head of population in 1939 was no higher than at the outbreak of World War I. Similarly, the real level of GDP per head attained in 1914 was only slightly greater than that of 1889. Overall, Australian per capita output grew sluggishly, at an average annual rate of around 1 per cent per annum, which has led economic historians to dub these years as ones of relative economic stagnation.

Right *Gross domestic product per head of population 1889–1945 (£s in 1911 prices).*

Far right *Woollen Mills in Castlemaine, Victoria, in the 1920s. Manufacturing of textiles increased after World War I, stimulating small-scale as well as larger enterprises.*

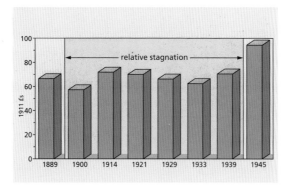

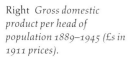

for diversification of output. The war transformed the market prospects for BHP (Broken Hill Proprietary Company Limited, formed 1885) pig iron and steel and encouraged many new forms of heavy and light engineering, textiles and basic chemical manufacture. The early 1920s saw the rise of new consumer durables (the car, new chemical and electrical goods and housing styles). It was in the early 1920s, too, that the federal government increased tariffs on imports from overseas with the aim of protecting war-born industries and of providing job opportunities for an increasing population.

Governments were also active in other areas. They provided urban infrastructure in the 1910s and 1920s: water supply and sewerage, street improvement, roads, public buildings, the telephone, electricity and the electrification of urban transport services. This public investment helped buoy the demand for urban labour and provided jobs.

EXTERNAL TRANSACTIONS

International transactions were of great importance to the Australian economy. Around 15–20 per cent of GDP was exported. The biggest buyer was Britain who took half of Australia's exports. Wool accounted for 50 per cent of the goods shipped, the balance largely comprising wheat, flour, hides, dairy products and meat. Metal manufactures, including machinery, were the single most important import followed closely by clothing, textiles and footwear. In most years the import bill exceeded export receipts. This did not cause balance of payment problems, at least while British investors were prepared to lend their savings to Australians. Much of this capital inflow from Britain took the form of fixed interest loans to governments, especially the states. Much of it financed branch railways, country irrigation projects and the urban infrastructure mentioned above.

The role of migration in building the population 1890–1945.

Britain was not only Australia's biggest trading partner and supplier of capital for Australian development, but was also the main source of migrants. While natural increase was the main contributor to Australia's population, the rate of net migration played a major role just before World War I and again in the 1920s. Between 1901 and 1930 the total increase amounted to 2.7 million with net migration being responsible for about 30 per cent of this expansion. Three-quarters of the net arrivals came from Britain, mostly from the industrial counties of England. As with capital, Australian governments actively courted this inflow. The most direct method was by offering assisted passages. More roundabout means included the tariff and public works in country and town which created jobs and more prosperous conditions than otherwise for labour. Some governments, notably Western Australia in conjunction with Britain under the Empire Settlement Act of 1922, dangled the lure of land settlement, albeit the schemes turned out to be dismal failures, as were the experiments with soldier settlement (see p. 114).

GOVERNMENT AND THE ECONOMY

Australia's purposes in seeking additional population were defence and development. The first was insurance against aggression or eastern overflow from Japan and China (the term 'yellow peril' was in vogue). Norman Lindsay's Bulletin cartoon of 1911 well depicts Australians' fears. As for the second, development meant the quantitative expansion of output and jobs. It meant adding to Australia more producers, more consumers, more taxpayers. Development was seen as needing government initiative, action to develop resources by bringing from Britain people and capital, by building railways, irrigation schemes, other public works and increasingly by supporting manufacturing through the tariff. The Australian dream was of an ever-expanding, prosperous, white and secure oasis in the south. Development would breed prosperity. Relatedly, wages were to be directly protected via a system of wage awards, the seminal decision being the Harvester Judgement of 1907.

Government initiatives proved to be a mixed blessing. Certainly, they helped draw immigrants to Australia's shores and supported the much-desired larger population. But they also harboured dangers. The tariff reduced the degree of openness of the economy and impaired, along with initiatives in wage fixing, the international competitiveness of Australia's exports, reducing trade and misallocating resources. An increasing share of resources was shunted into lower yielding activities – from wool into closer settlement and an increasingly uncompetitive manufacturing industry.

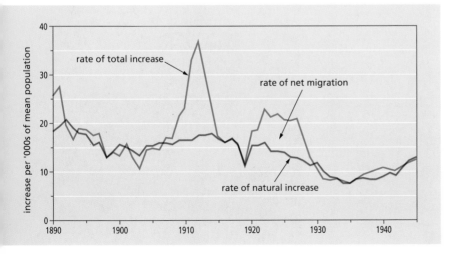

Sleeping at His Homework *by Norman Lindsay. A notorious cartoon published in the* Bulletin *on 19 January 1911 that encapsulated white Australians' fears of being overwhelmed or attacked by Asians from China and Japan.*

The Producer's Burden, *cartoon from 1932. Taxation and tariffs were increased in an attempt to remedy the slump. Although the policies were unpopular they did help with recovery.*

Nor were the foreign borrowings used wisely. There was no careful choice among projects and returns from public infrastructure and rural development were low and slow in coming. The problems this raised were twofold. First, while the states continued their borrowing spree in London, so interest and dividend payments owing abroad rose alarmingly, up to the value of 30 per cent of Australia's total exports. Second, British financial circles started to react and as early as 1927 questioned Australia's public borrowing, advising British investors to think twice. Any cut-back in capital inflow would have severe repercussions for domestic employment and the balance of payments. Australia was headed for economic difficulties before Wall Street announced her crisis to the world in the closing months of 1929.

The Great Depression of 1929–32 was worldwide. The downturn in the USA (of which the Wall Street crash was a signal) and Europe was transmitted to Australia through reduced export prices and volumes which reduced Australia's income and increased the country's balance of trade deficit (export prices declined 23 per cent in 1929–30). Sources of foreign lending around the world dried up at this time. Internal problems described in the preceding paragraph compounded the effects of the collapse of the world economy, making the depression in Australia unusually deep.

Unemployment and falling income produced considerable social disruption and hardship. For many Australian families the land of plenty suddenly became one of soup queues, rabbit stew and bread and dripping. Governments now adopted new policies,

not in the name of development but of recovery. At the end of 1929 the assisted-immigration programme was closed down and, but for a trickle of orphans and urban urchins, remained so until 1938–39. In 1930 and 1931 the Labor government stepped up the level of the tariff. A real wage reduction of 10 per cent was ordered by the federal court in January 1931 and the Australian pound was devalued by about 20 per cent relative to sterling. Under the terms of the Premiers' Plan of 1931 government expenditure was to be cut by 20 per cent, interest rates reduced and taxation increased. While the cuts in government spending worked to increase unemployment, on balance these policies aided recovery. In particular, the devaluation and reduced wage costs increased Australia's exporters' competitiveness; for manufacturing, which seems to have led the recovery, wage cuts reduced costs and import competition was mitigated by the devaluation and higher tariff (though the latter further misallocated resources). Australia, however, did not lead the world economy in recovery, to some extent it had to await it.

In terms of the unemployment rate and real GDP per head, the recovery was barely complete at the outbreak of World War II. Considerable economic expansion and rapid industrialisation occurred thereafter as Australia switched her manufacturing resources to wartime production. DP

The economy since 1945

The Australian people emerged from World War II determined to create a better society than that which had entered the war. It was to be a society which banished the spectres of pre-war unemployment and poverty. In their place would be full employment, the creation of a welfare state and greater material prosperity with rising standards of consumption.

It was, nevertheless, a society facing serious economic problems. Though Australia had suffered little war-time damage to its physical assets, one-fifth of its workforce awaited demobilisation and the economy, which was still geared to total war, required major reconstruction if it was to return successfully to peace-time activity. Many parts of the economy were ill-equipped to meet the competitive challenges which peace-time would bring. Domestic transport was largely dependent upon a railway system in which a mixture of narrow, standard and broad gauges prevented easy interstate rail transportation. Vast tracts of land were subject to soil erosion, loss of fertility and rabbit plagues; farm equipment was scarce and electricity was available to very few rural communities. In the manufacturing sector, in spite of much progress since the 1920s, many industries had developed no further than the assembly stage of production whilst domestic supplies of basic products like steel and coal were still extremely limited.

Apart from the immediate problem of the transition to a peace-time economy, three economic problems dominated the attention of Australian governments and economists. First, with the service people demobilised, how could lasting full employment be guaranteed? Second, once peace-time trade relations were restored, how could the economy be insulated from large fluctuations in world demand for Australian products and from competition from foreign imports of manufactured goods? Last, how could the continued growth of Australia's population be ensured?

Federal government solutions to these problems emphasised their preoccupation with full employment and combined to give government an increasingly dominant role in the Australian economy. They also resulted in what one historian has described as the two major idiosyncracies of Australian economic development since 1945: the rapid growth of the country's stock of labour and capital, and the sluggish growth of its foreign trade.

FULL-EMPLOYMENT POLICY

As in all Western democracies at the end of World War II Australians considered the question of full employment to be the outstanding post-war economic problem. It was, however, a problem with some contradictory features. Apart from the immediate problem of returning 600,000 service personnel back to civilian employment, there were fears that a brief post-war boom marked by inflation and labour shortages would be followed by prolonged depression and unemployment.

The Australian government relied on three main mechanisms to achieve full employment. The first was to establish a stable world demand for Australian trade products by encouraging other countries to adopt a full-employment policy similar to that favoured by Australia. To this end, Australian representatives embarked on a vigorous diplomatic effort to have included in every major international agreement a reference to the importance of full employment as an objective of national and international economic policy. These efforts gathered world support for the full-employment principle which, by mid-1945, had been officially adopted by Great Britain and the USA and had been included in the objectives of the United Nations' Charter. The second was the use of public expenditure to support aggregate domestic demand at a level capable of maintaining a fully employed economy. This policy, enshrined in the white paper, *Full Employment in Australia*, was tabled in Parliament and acceded to by all parties in May 1945. The third was to retain, at least in the short run, price and other direct controls

Workroom in a department store in Adelaide in the 1950s. Post-war governments pursued a full-employment policy, which produced a rate of unemployment that remained below 2.5 per cent from the mid-1950s to the mid-1970s.

in the domestic economy.

The outcome of these policies was that within two years of the war ending the armed forces were demobilised without the expected slump materialising: demand and employment remained high though prices did rise sharply. The onset of war in Korea in 1950 gave a further upward thrust to prices by sharply lifting world demand for Australian wool. Government attempts to control the boom, and the collapse in wool prices at the end of the war, produced a period of acute instability in the economy and for several months unemployment rose sharply. However, a worldwide boom, which was to last into the 1970s, was already under way and helped the Australian economy to mend quickly. By the end of 1954 unemployment had fallen back to less than 3 per cent; thereafter, it rarely exceeded 2.5 per cent of the workforce until 1975.

LABOUR SUPPLIES

It has already been noted that a major idiosyncracy of Australian economic development since 1945 is its high rate of labour-force growth. This growth was determined in the main part by the high rate of growth of the Australian population, which regularly exceeded 2 per cent per year between 1946 and 1970. This is an unusually high rate of increase among developed nations where population growth rates have commonly not exceeded 1 per cent per year since 1945. Equally striking is the contribution of immigration to that growth. Since 1945 there are few countries of the world in which immigration has played such a large role in population increase as Australia where, in some years, as much as half and rarely less than one-third of the total population growth was due to immigration.

The contribution of the migrant programme to Australian economic growth was immense. From the beginning of the assisted-immigration scheme until the early 1960s, when children of the post-war baby boom began to swell the natural supply of new entrants into the labour force, migrant workers contributed, in some years, up to 80 per cent of the increase in the male labour force. Migrants were an especially important source of labour to the manufacturing and building sectors where they also provided large supplies of essential skills. The great public works construction projects like the Snowy Mountains Hydro-electric Scheme were largely built with migrant labour. Migrants contributed greatly to the growth of rapidly developing industrial centres such as Wollongong and Port Kembla in New South Wales and Elizabeth in South Australia. High rates of population growth fed by migrant inflows acted as a major stimulus to the Australian economy, helping to maintain the demand for housing space, public and other utilities and for consumer goods well into the 1960s. The growing population allowed greater variety in means for enjoying life, a variety which was enormously enriched by the post-war migration inflow of European and other non-English-speaking peoples. Their arrival changed and enriched Australia's culture, skills and view of the world more completely than at any time since European settlement in 1788. (See also pp. 225–7).

INVESTMENT AND CAPITAL IMPORTS

As with population, investment in Australia increased sharply after World War II, more than doubling pre-war rates of investment. Much of this additional investment went into building private housing and into the social infrastructure required by Australia's rapidly growing population. The greater part, however, went into the expansion of productive assets. In the 25 years following World War II private investment into agriculture, manufacturing, commerce, and (in the late 1960s) into mining surged forward, expanding Australian export industries and manufacturing industries.

Though Australians financed the greater part of this investment from their own savings, large amounts of private capital flowed into Australian industries and commerce from abroad attracted by high returns and by the desire of foreign manufacturers to get around Australian tariffs and import controls. One consequence of the high level of foreign investment is that industries such as petrochemicals, pharmaceuticals and motor vehicles became wholly or largely foreign owned or controlled by the 1960s. Another consequence was that Australian technology was greatly enhanced by foreign know-how which accompanied the foreign capital.

A new feature appeared in foreign investment in the mid-1960s: for 20 years following 1945 foreign capital largely consisted of direct investment into plant and equipment, but from 1965 onward, portfolio investment grew rapidly, overtaking all other forms of foreign investment in Australia. In the view of many observers, this development added a new and possibly undesirable source of instability to the economy without contributing significantly to its development.

TRADE AND EXPORTS

Except for a brief period in the early 1950s Australian trade has lagged behind the rate of growth of the gross national product. This experience contrasts

179

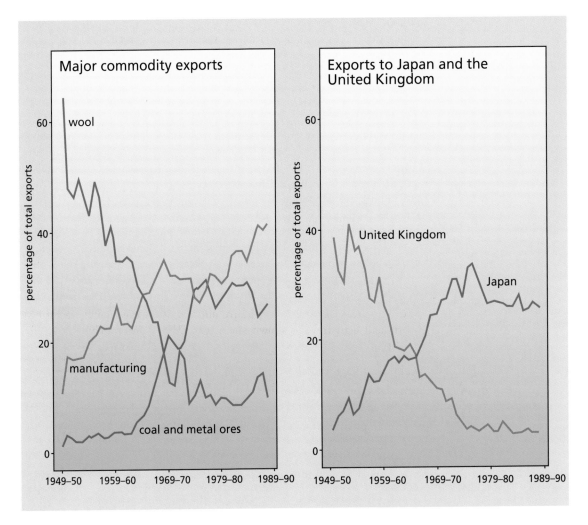

Major commodity exports

wool

manufacturing

coal and metal ores

percentage of total exports

60

40

20

0

1949–50   1959–60   1969–70   1979–80   1989–90

Exports to Japan and the
United Kingdom

United Kingdom

Japan

percentage of total exports

60

40

20

0

1949–50   1959–60   1969–70   1979–80   1989–90

Left *Major commodity exports (percentage of total exports).* Right *Exports to Japan and the United Kingdom (percentage of total exports).*

with that of most other advanced countries where trade has increased notably faster than production since 1945. In part, the tendency of trade to lag behind production is a well-recognised tendency among recently settled countries with rapidly growing populations.

In Australia, however, additional factors hindered the economy's trade performance after 1945. First, Australian exports mainly consisted of primary commodities such as wool, wheat, coal and metal ores. Except for a brief period between 1945 and 1952, world demand for these commodities has grown more slowly than world income. Second, the growth of protectionist policies in Europe and the USA has led to a severe decline in many of the traditional markets for Australian agricultural commodities. Third, Australian post-war trade policy has been avowedly protectionist. Until the early 1960s declining terms of trade, balance of payments problems and fear that foreign competition would adversely affect her domestic manufacturing industries led Australian governments to impose high tariffs and other controls on most imported goods.

Though many controls were lifted in the 1960s, Australia's effective rates of protection remained

among the highest of the world's advanced industrial nations. Such protection has not only helped to slow the growth of imports into Australia, it has also inhibited the growth of an export-oriented manufacturing sector.

Fortunately, the depressing features of Australia's trade have been offset by important advances in the export trades themselves. Traditional export industries have made great increases in productivity since 1945. Major advances in large-scale farming technology, soil conservation and fertility improvement programmes, eradication of rabbits and advances in livestock and arable husbandry have made Australian agriculture one of the most cost-efficient in the world. Australian mining projects are highly capital intensive and cost-efficient. It is notable, also, that where there have been major successes in manufacturing exports, the industries concerned have usually produced high-technology goods with low levels of domestic protection, and have relied on the comparative advantages bestowed by a highly literate and skilled workforce.

Another major development since 1945 has been the redirection of Australia's trade from Britain and Europe to the Pacific/Asia region where rapid economic growth – especially by Japan – has yielded new markets for Australia. A related change has been the rapid growth of mineral exports since the mid-1960s. Although this growth has helped to offset the decline in agricultural exports, it has been a mixed blessing for Australia. On the one hand, minerals helped to lift the value of Australian exports and exchange rates at the end of the 1960s; on the other, one of the main exchange-rate consequences of the mineral boom, with its associated capital inflows, was severe damage to the Australian manufacturing sector's ability to compete in foreign markets, and to compete against increasingly cheaper manufactured imports.

GOVERNMENT AND THE ECONOMY

As in other Western nations, the proportion of gross domestic product and of the workforce directed to government activities has grown since 1945. The commitment to full employment has involved Australian governments in adopting the full range of macro-economic controls adopted elsewhere in the West. In addition, the desire to protect its manufacturing industries and to develop its export industries has encouraged Australian governments to intervene in the economy – especially through tariff and other forms of protection – much more extensively than appears in other advanced economies. Similarly, Australian governments continue to operate many public enterprises including most natural monopolies such as railways, electricity supply, postal and telecommunications, as well as retaining some interest in the Commonwealth Bank and former government airlines, which compete with private institutions.

Each of these developments has led economists to characterise Australia as a big-government, 'rent-seeking' society in which individuals and groups try to gain economic benefits through government employment, welfare payments or by obtaining favourable government decisions, rather than by devoting their energies to income generation and the production of real goods and services. Whilst such characterisations help to highlight areas for concern in the Australian economy since 1945, they fit Australia less well than many other OECD countries. Thus, public-sector employment, the best measure of big government, grew by only 1 per cent (from 19 per cent to 20 per cent of the labour force) between 1945 and 1975. This is the lowest rate among OECD countries and, in spite of a more rapid increase after 1975, public-sector employment in 1987 at 25 per cent of the workforce was still well below the average for that group of countries. These figures indicate how European concepts of big government do not transfer well to Australia, except perhaps in the sense that the term 'big government' may be used to mean extensive regulation by government in ways that do not require substantial labour inputs.

OCCUPATIONS

Slow growth of export markets for Australia's rural products and the growth of farming productivity resulted in a steady decline in agricultural employment from 16 per cent of the workforce in 1947 to 5 per cent in 1992.

Manufacturing, on the other hand, supported by a growing home market and an improving trade performance, maintained its share of employment at about 27 per cent of the workforce until the mid-1960s. Thereafter, however, adverse exchange-rate consequences of the mineral boom discussed earlier, caused manufacturing employment to contract to 23 per cent by 1975 without any compensatory increase in employment appearing within the mineral sector itself (mining has occupied about 2 per cent of the workforce throughout the period 1947 to 1992). Since 1975 the manufacturing sector has continued to decline as an employer of labour and in 1992 employed only 14 per cent of the total Australian workforce.

In employment (structural) terms the economy has depended increasingly on the growth of its service sector. In 1947 this sector employed 45 per cent of the workforce and by 1975 the proportion had grown to 70 per cent. Services have continued to expand and today employ 79 per cent of the workforce. (It should be noted that construction, which is included with services throughout this section, occupied between 7 per cent and 10 per cent of the workforce between 1950 and 1992.) As noted earlier the growth of the service sector, at least until after 1975, was not a product of the growth of government employment. The faster growth which appears to have occurred after 1975 is somewhat misleading. That growth is partly a statistical illusion created by the growth of unemployment in the non-government sectors after 1975, and only partly a consequence of real growth in public-sector employment. The main reason for the growth of the service sector has thus been the growth in real incomes, and the rising skills and education levels of the Australian workforce. Together, they have created a rapid growth in demand for personal and commercial services in Australia and for export, trends that reflect the growing sophistication and post-industrial features of the Australian economy.

For nearly 30 years following World War II Australians enjoyed a kind of economic golden age with high growth rates, improving living standards and low rates of unemployment and inflation.

Assembly line General Motors–Holden's Dandenong plant, Melbourne. Federal government policy from 1984 to rationalise the motor vehicle industry, primarily through the abolition of import tariffs, led to the closure of several factories and the shedding of thousands of jobs. In 1992 General Motors-Holden and Toyota formed a joint-venture company.

One area of lasting concern, however, was in the area of trade. Whilst the overall balance of payments improved during the 1950s and 1960s, the improvement was based upon a strong inflow of foreign capital rather than any improvement in export performance.

Over the same period Australia's terms of trade fell by almost 40 per cent. Since Australia commonly carries a large deficit on invisible account, the outcome of the continuing failure to increase export earnings was a continuing deficit on the current account. It is this deficit which accounts for the persistence of Australia's policy of high tariff protection, in spite of its self-defeating consequences for industrial development.

DEPRESSION AND RECONSTRUCTION SINCE 1975

As with so many other advanced industrial nations, the last 18 years or so have been years of uncertainty and anxiety about Australia's future. Much of this uncertainty and anxiety arises from Australia's underlying balance of payments problems.

These appeared to have been resolved in the late 1960s when the minerals boom attracted large amounts of foreign capital and yielded a vast new export potential. However, when the boom collapsed following the fall in oil prices shock at the end of 1973, capital imports slumped and the current account deteriorated sharply.

For a time the trade position remained viable with the help of large downward adjustments in the value of the dollar, and an improvement was even experienced at the beginning of the 1980s when the second increase in oil prices provided powerful incentives for the exploitation of Australia's vast energy resources. In response, Australians borrowed large amounts of foreign capital to develop these resources.

Then, almost as soon as the projects were under way, world trade moved into deep depression leaving the Australian economy with large overseas debts, contracting export markets and a further sharp decline in the terms of trade. Together, these events pushed Australia into a deteriorating round of trade deficits and rising debt-servicing problems which saw foreign interest payments increase from nearly $2.5 billion or 34 per cent of the current account deficit in 1983 to $13.2 billion (82 per cent of the deficit) in 1991.

Another lasting anxiety has been the coincidence of low rates of economic growth and high rates of inflation and unemployment which settled on to the economy in the mid-1970s. Since 1975 unemployment has rarely fallen below 5 per cent of the workforce; inflation rates, though falling in recent years,

have generally been well above those of Australia's trading partners, and average growth rates remain significantly below those achieved in the 1950s and 1960s. Efforts to deal with these problems in the 1970s and early 1980s were at best half-hearted and at worst resulted in rapidly growing government budgetary deficits, high interest rates and deteriorating balance of payments.

The federal Labor government, in power since March 1983, responded to these challenges in two main directions: first by allowing greater play of market forces to encourage and improve the efficiency and competitive strength of Australian industries; and, second, by maintaining tight control over aggregate demand and wage increases. The first direction involved the government in reassessing and, to some extent, abandoning long-cherished Labor policies. The second has required the government to rely heavily upon the goodwill and support of the trade unions and wage-earners.

The Labor government thus began dismantling and reducing elaborate tariff and other protective structures around key industries; it deregulated the financial system and allowed exchange rates greater freedom to respond to changes in the balance of payments. Currently, the government is considering

extending the process of deregulation into other sectors such as transport and telecommunications, and has begun to privatise public enterprises such as Qantas and the Commonwealth Bank. Major advances have been made in tax reform and in the reform of the public service and higher education. Key industries like motor vehicle manufacture and steel production have been encouraged and assisted to restructure in ways that will increase their world competitive position. Many of these policies were resisted by traditionally minded sections of the government's party and by other interests who see in them threats to established privileges and occupations. Nevertheless, significant advances have been made on most issues, freeing-up large areas of industry's ability to respond to outside competition.

Demand and wage control, however, have had to bear the greater part of the immediate problems of balance of payments correction. This is because of the high propensity among Australians to import in the event of a rise in their incomes. Fortunately, demand restriction has complemented another of the government's principal aims, that of reducing its budgetary deficit. In practice, this has meant that governments have been involved in unpopular restrictions on expenditure whilst maintaining revenue levels, though with such success that large federal budgetary surpluses were achieved between 1986 and 1989. On the income side, wage restraint has been made to bear an unusually heavy burden. Wage controls have resulted in average real incomes of Australian workers stagnating for nearly 10 years. Whether this restraint will continue is one of the most important questions presently facing the Australian government.

In spite of the advances made, Australia's current account deficit continued to deteriorate. In July 1989 the annual deficit stood at $22 billion, or 6.3 per cent of gross domestic product, with 25 per cent of Australia's export earnings going to pay foreign interest payments alone. Concern over this problem forced the government to restrict money supplies, driving interest rates up to record levels. The resulting slow down in the economy had the effect of reducing the growth of imports and thereby improving Australia's current account. It also caused unemployment to rise from 5.4 per cent in November 1989 to 11.1 per cent in early 1993.

Against this background Australia's prime minister, Paul Keating, called a federal election for 13 March 1993. In the ensuing campaign, attention focused almost exclusively on policies of the opposition Liberal Party which advocated more privatisation of the health services, deregulation of the labour market, and the introduction of a broad-based consumption tax. In the event, Australian voters were unwilling to accept these reforms and in a surprising result re-elected Labor to power for another three years. Although this is seen by many commentators as a rejection of some areas of reform, the general process of reforming the economy initiated at the beginning of the 1980s will continue, though how far and how fast is perhaps the most important single question presently facing the Australian government and the Australian people.   HMB

Manufacturing industry

In a world context Australian manufacturing is unique. The market it serves – a population of some 17.8 million people – is small for an advanced industrialised economy, and Australia is geographically isolated from its major foreign suppliers and customers. The population is also heavily concentrated in five mainland capital cities separated by considerable distances: Brisbane, Sydney, Melbourne, Adelaide and Perth. These factors, combined with a fragmented internal transport system, have resulted in dispersed production in many industries, and small-scale, inefficient plants.

Manufacturing inefficiency has been exacerbated by the attempts over the years of state governments to develop their local manufacturing base. To boost employment, all have offered substantial financial inducements to firms – especially foreign multinationals – to set up operations within their respective states. Such operations have tended to be small-scale, in terms of international standards.

At the federal level, efforts by successive governments for decades to support domestic production and maintain full employment by erecting tariff and non-tariff barriers to trade have further encouraged the diversification and inefficiency of Australian manufacturing. Historically, the highest levels of assistance were received by Australia's notoriously inefficient automobile, textiles, clothing and footwear industries.

However, significant micro-economic reforms in the 1980s have led to marked reductions in all kinds of trade barriers and other types of industry protection and assistance. As a consequence, efficiency levels have improved markedly throughout most industries, as old plants have been closed, labour productivity has improved, and firms have upgraded their technology so as to be internationally competitive.

Company Size

Not surprisingly, companies are small by international standards. In 1993, the largest company in Australia was The Broken Hill Proprietary Company Limited, a highly diversified iron and steel, and oil and gas producer, with annual sales of $16,680 million. The fiftieth largest company enjoyed sales of $2,506 million, the one hundredth largest sales of $1,381 million, and the two hundredth largest sales of $627 million.

Only one of the top 10 companies (BHP, the largest) was classified as being in the manufacturing sector of the economy, and even then it has substantial interests in mining, oil and gas and other natural resources. The other nine largest companies operated in retailing (four), banking (two), insurance, telecommunications and publishing/media.

After BHP, the next largest manufacturing firm was Foster's Brewing ($10,201 million), ranked as the eleventh largest firm. Then followed the highly diversified producer BTR Nylex (eighteenth, $6,076 million); building materials producer Pioneer International (twentieth, $5,356 million); diversified paper products producer Amcor (twenty

second, $5,171 million); food producer Goodman Fielder (twenty-fourth, $4,709 million); building materials and sugar producer CSR (twenty-fifth, $4,699 million); oil and chemicals producer Shell (twenty-sixth, $4,634 million); and Boral, another building materials producer (twenty-seventh, $4,306 million).

The generally small size of Australian manufacturing is emphasised by the fact that at the factory level, only 54 per cent of manufacturing employment was in plants employing 100 or more people, a level that is very low compared with the USA, the UK and Canada.

Notable also is the existence in many industries (particularly services) in Australia of statutory corporations owned wholly or partly by federal and state governments. Telecom (fifth) and the Commonwealth Bank (fourteenth) were among the country's top companies in 1993, with Qantas coming in at twenty-seventh. In addition, there are state banks, insurance and superannuation commissions, and rail, electricity supply, water and gambling authorities which rank in the top 100 Australian firms by sales. In fact 21 of the largest 100 companies in

Australia in 1993 were owned wholly or partly by either the federal or state governments.

Even Australia's largest firms look small by American standards. In 1992, General Motors, the largest company in the USA had sales of $US 132,775 million, greater than those of BHP by a factor of more than eight (and even then not allowing for exchange rate differences). BHP would have ranked only at position 24 in the USA.

In 1992 not a single Australian company ranked among the world's top 50 industrial corporations, and only 9 made *Fortune* magazine's 1992 list of the top 500 global industrial firms. The USA topped the list with 161 firms; Japan boasted 128 companies on the list, Britain 40, Germany 32 and France 30. Next were Sweden 14, then Australia and Switzerland each with 9 and Canada with 8. On this international list, BHP would have been in position 125.

DKR

An important player now on the international scene, the airline Qantas (which merged with the domestic carrier Australian Airlines in 1993) had modest beginnings, this office in Longreach, Queensland, being its second headquarters.

CONCENTRATION

Though modestly sized, Australian industries are in ownership terms highly concentrated. In the 1970s and 1980s many large companies expanded both internally and externally via takeovers. Diversification into new industries and vertical integration into both raw material supplies and distribution were common. Mergers were fuelled by several factors: a less-protectionist stance on the part of successive federal governments; encouragement from the Australian Industries Assistance Commission for companies to expand to enhance operating efficiency and improve international competitiveness; and the absence of effective antitrust legislation regulating takeovers.

Among Australia's most highly concentrated industries are biscuits, tobacco, cotton ginning, hardwood woodchips, batteries, chemical fertilisers, corrugated fibreboard containers, pulp, paper and paperboard, and felt and felt products. Across a whole range of industries, however, the diversification and vertical integration strategies of large conglomerates over the last 20 years have given them a central role in the Australian economy.

DIVERSIFICATION

Manufacturing companies have also expanded steadily overseas and into other sectors of the economy. Firms in the relatively most concentrated industries – rubber products, butter, cheese, pulp, paper and paperboards, soap and other detergents, pumps and compressors, steel pipes and tubes – have tended to diversify most actively. More circumscribed have been footwear, clothing, pesticides, iron and steel casting, fabricated structural steel, furniture, printing, and petroleum refining: generally (but not entirely) smaller scale, less technically progressive industries, geared more to local markets. Historically, such industries have been protected from foreign competition by tariffs or import quotas, and sell bulky, relatively low-value products carrying high transport costs.

Australian manufacturing industries which have received the most diversification by firms located in other industries include a wide range of food industries, chemical-based industries, and metal casting, forging and extruding industries. Expansion here has been into closely related industries using similar manufacturing techniques, and in many cases reflects an element of vertical integration. In poultry, bread, raw sugar and beer there has been much less inbound diversification because of an entrenched small number of existing firms with strong brand images, or the need to invest heavily in specialised production equipment.

FOREIGN INVESTMENT

Direct foreign investment is highest in industries where large multinationals are operating under conditions of rapid technological change, and where transport costs and tariffs have made it attractive for a foreign firm to develop the Australian market from within. Industries that are more than half foreign-owned include motor vehicles, non-ferrous metals (especially aluminium), and batteries; pesticides; soap and other detergents; cosmetics and toilet preparations; pharmaceuticals and veterinary products; radio, television and audio equipment; and animal and bird food, tobacco, confectionery, and vegetable products. Companies that are foreign-owned tend to be more profitable than their Australian counterparts.

PERFORMANCE

The productivity and efficiency of Australian manufacturing industry has always been constrained by its geographic isolation, the limited local market, and high levels of tariff protection. Nearly all domestic industries operate at what would in the USA be considered well below the minimum efficient scale, even though production is substantially more concentrated than in the USA. Economies of scale at plant level have been difficult to achieve. Leading firms in many industries operate more, smaller plants than might appear to be optimal because of transport requirements and the need to co-ordinate supply across a geographically fragmented market. They tend as a result to be scarcely more productive or profitable than their smaller rivals.

Australian manufacturing industry has sought to combat the problem of its fragmented domestic market by adapting production technology to small-scale operation, and concentrating investment in small-scale, non-capital intensive areas. As a consequence of the high market concentration/small firm size scenario, the link between profitability and concentration is significantly less marked than in other countries. Until the mid-1970s, the relatively small number of industrial companies in Australia and the absence of effective legal prohibitions on price-fixing, meant that prices were often determined in consultation with rivals. The costs of small-scale production and low levels of labour productivity meant, however, that excessive monopoly profits never followed. Even today, it seems unlikely that attempts to improve resource allocation by reducing levels of industrial concentration would increase efficiency. Initiatives in the 1980s encouraged mergers, reflecting an acute awareness by the federal government that Australian companies must grow in size to prosper in the global market place, although a change in this policy emerged in 1993 when new antitrust legislation was passed which made it more difficult for mergers to take place. The belief now in Australia is that firms will only succeed in international markets if they learn to compete successfully at home.   DKR

Agriculture

Two hundred years ago Australia was a land without agriculture. Today, agriculture is the nation's largest and most diverse industry and Australia occupies a place in the front-rank of global agriculture as one of the world's leading producers of food and natural fibres. The average Australian farm produces enough food and fibre to meet the needs of 300 human beings so that Australia sustains its own population of 17.8 million and also 35 million people overseas.

In 1992–93 the value of Australia's agricultural production totalled around $22 billion with over $17 billion, or nearly 80 per cent, derived from exports and the balance sold on the domestic market. Australia is the world's largest exporter of wool, the second largest exporter of meat, the third largest exporter of wheat and a major international supplier of sugar, dairy produce, fruits, cotton, rice, grains and seeds, and dryland farming technology. By the mid-1990s, 'new' farm industries are expected to provide in total about $4 billion revenue annually. The relatively new industries include production of cashmere and angora mohair from goats and possibly commercial wool production from llama and alpaca; production of exotic poultry and game; and the recent establishment of tea, coffee and cocoa plantations.

Live sheep being loaded on to a ship at Portland, Victoria, an important port for the export of both wool and sheep. Although agriculture is a major earner of foreign revenue, its percentage of the overall value of national exports has fallen from around 80 per cent in the early 1950s to below 40 per cent.

Australia's achievements in agriculture have occurred in the face of harsh climatic and other natural conditions. The area of the Australian continent is about the same as the USA (excluding Alaska and Hawaii) and larger than the whole of western Europe. Australia's landmass is flat, compared with most countries. However, Australia overall is the driest continent in the world. Moreover, rainfall variability in Australia is greater than world average variability for all but a narrow belt of southern and southwestern Australia (see pp. 9–12). Unreliable rainfall and recurrent droughts have thus been a hazard since the beginning of farming in Australia.

Less than two-thirds (about 510 million hectares) of Australia's vast land mass is suitable either for grazing or arable agriculture. The majority of its soils are shallow, infertile and fairly fragile, derived from ancient, weathered material (pp. 12–14). Over 70 per cent of Australia's total area is covered by desert or semi-arid zone soils and to a lesser extent by shallow stony soils on mountainous country. Only a very small proportion is intensively farmed. About 17 million hectares are devoted to broadacre (extensive livestock and crop production) and intensive crop production and a further 26 million hectares have been sown to improved pastures. The remainder of the land used for commercial agriculture, around 467 million hectares, consists chiefly of grazing the natural vegetation.

The relative importance of agriculture in the Australian economy continues to evolve in a manner which follows the evolution of the rural sector in all developed countries. The contribution of agriculture to national export earnings has declined from around 80 per cent in the early 1950s to a little under 40 per cent currently. Even more dramatic has been the fall in agriculture's direct contribution towards gross national product from 20 per cent in the mid-1950s to around 4 per cent today. The decline in the relative importance of agriculture in Australia was accelerated by the influence of the mineral boom. It should be noted, however, that when account is taken of the upstream and downstream impact of agriculture on the economy, the total farming, farm input and food industries account for over 20 per cent of national economic activity.

AUSTRALIA'S FARMS AND LABOUR

Australia has 125,000 farms, which range in size from grazing enterprises extending over a million hectares or more, to horticultural farms as small as 1 hectare or less. Thirty years ago Australia had over 200,000 farms. The reduction in farm numbers and increased farm size have been brought about by adjustments to world and domestic economic condi-

Cotton harvest at Milguy, New South Wales. Modern technology has considerably reduced the numbers of people employed on the land.

tions and the adoption of new farming technology.

Over 90 per cent of Australian farms are family farms managed and operated by the owner, usually with some family labour. Only 5 per cent of farms are corporate farms operated as public or private companies. Over two-thirds of Australia's farming enterprises are in the major grazing industries of sheep and cattle and in grain growing. Many of these farms are mixed grain–livestock or sheep–cattle farms. The other major farming enterprises, which taken together comprise a little under one-third of total farm holdings, are dairying, horticultural production, and sugarcane growing.

In 1989–90, 416,000 people were directly employed on farms, or 5.4 per cent of the Australian workforce. Over two-thirds of these people were members of farm-family partnerships, sole owner-operators, or unpaid family helpers, and a little less than one-third were employees on wages. A notable feature of the farm workforce in recent years has been a near doubling of the number of women who are employed on farms to 110,000. This trend is partly attributable to economic pressures which have led to members of family partnerships taking off-farm employment. Moreover, technology has reduced the need for heavy labour and there is also an increasing recognition that women are able to supply the skills required for modern agricultural production.

The use of labour-saving technology has resulted in a decline of almost 100,000 people employed on farms since the early 1950s. However, the increasing reliance of agriculture upon modern technology and services has generated a proportional increase in employment in off-farm sectors servicing agriculture and in contracting of on-farm services.

The system of linkages and markets associated with the food and fibre sector as a whole is now commonly referred to as agribusiness. It includes the farm production sector, the input supply sector and the marketing sector – comprising farmers, suppliers of farm inputs, produce marketing agents and fibre processors, wholesalers, retailers and consumers – with the finance and transport sectors operating throughout the system. Agribusiness employs around 1.4 million people or about 20 per cent of the total workforce. Without counting the transport and finance sectors, it accounts for over 20 per cent of gross national product, and contributes to the economy an annual value-added in the vicinity of $30 billion.

PRODUCTIVITY

A key factor in the history of agriculture in Australia has been the ability to compete on world markets. The first sale of Australian wool by auction in England in 1821 showed an ability to produce wool of superior quality to that generally available in Europe and was the beginning of the highly successful development of Australia's wool industry. The later development of refrigerated transport stimulated the production of commodities such as dairy products and meat. In the early days, Australia's preferential access to the UK market first as a member country of the British Empire and subsequently as part of the Commonwealth was important to the prosperity of Australian farming.

In the first half of the twentieth century intensification of rural production was part of the policy of population expansion. After World War II, increasing pressure was placed on Australian agriculture by events at home and abroad. At home, during the 1950s and 1960s, there was increasing protection of domestic manufacturing industries which adversely affected the competitiveness of Australian agriculture. Australia's loss of preferential access to the UK market when the UK joined the European Economic Community in 1973 was a major blow to a number of Australia's rural industries. During the 1970s and 1980s, increasing protection of agriculture in developed economies overseas made it more difficult for Australian agriculture to compete on world markets.

From the 1950s through the 1980s, these international and domestic factors have contributed to a downward trend of 2 to 3 per cent a year in Australian farmers' terms of trade. Between 1960 and 1992 the ratio of prices received by farmers to input costs fell by a half. In the face of this long-term cost-price squeeze, agricultural production in Australia has continued to rise and rural industries have steadily become more technologically advanced.

The key to the ongoing efficiency of Australian agriculture has been the ability to adapt to changing market circumstances and a sustained growth in productivity. The resilience of Australian agriculture in the face of a changing and often unstable world market, and a fickle nature, is explained in large part by the multi-product nature of most rural enterprises. For example, unlike most other parts of the world where a cereal grower usually devotes land exclusively to crop production, the Australian wheat farmer is also typically a sheep farmer. By adapting their product mix Australian farmers are able to cushion themselves against some of the more severe movements in product prices and costs.

For the three decades up to 1986 the productivity growth for agriculture was 2.7 per cent a year, compared with 2.0 per cent for manufacturing and a little over 1 per cent for the economy as a whole. Furthermore, in Australia, the growth in productivity of agriculture relative to that in manufacturing and other industries has been higher than in most other developed countries. Hence, Australian farmers have been able to continue competing with non-farm industries for resources in Australia, despite rising agricultural protectionism overseas.

Although a continuation of on-farm productivity growth is important for the ongoing prosperity of Australian agriculture there appears to be scope for substantial productivity improvements beyond the farm-gate, particularly in the handling, transport and marketing of rural products. For example, a Royal Commission into Grain Storage, Handling and Transport concluded in 1988 that the adoption of changes to existing arrangements could reduce costs to grain growers by about $10 per tonne. Productivity improvements in the handling and marketing of rural products will be achieved if government policy leads to greater competition in the marketing process and adoption of technological innovation in handling and marketing.

RESEARCH AND INNOVATION

The future competitiveness of Australian agriculture in a world market will require sustained increases in productivity, which in turn is critically dependent upon research and innovation. Unlike research in many other areas, the opportunities to import useful agricultural research and innovations from overseas are limited. Australia has a biophysical environment with many characteristics that are specific to agricultural production in Australia.

The year of federation of the Commonwealth of Australia, 1901, was perhaps the lowest point of Australia's agriculture. Wheat yields had plummeted, pastures were deteriorating and livestock numbers were declining alarmingly. There was a catastrophic

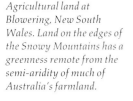

Agricultural land at Blowering, New South Wales. Land on the edges of the Snowy Mountains has a greenness remote from the semi-aridity of much of Australia's farmland.

fall in sheep numbers from 100 million to 54 million in the drought years between 1893 and 1902. The factors that lifted agriculture from this plight were innovations and a better understanding of the inputs and management required for successful farming.

Valuable innovations, initially made by farmers and pastoralists, were supplemented and then progressively superseded by contributions from the departments of agriculture and the agricultural colleges, the first of which were founded towards the close of the last century. In 1920 the Faculty of Agriculture at the University of Sydney was established and a similar Faculty was established at the University of Melbourne shortly thereafter. The Waite Agricultural Research Institute was founded in South Australia in 1924, and the Council for Scientific and Industrial Research – since 1949 the Commonwealth Scientific and Industrial Research Organization (CSIRO) – in 1926. The federal and state governments have a long history of providing funds for rural research and development aimed at increasing the rate of technological progress both on-farm and beyond the farm-gate. Government research funding has been increasingly complemented with Rural Industry Research Funds, derived from compulsory levies on farm produce, and private enterprise research centred in the chemicals and food and fibre processing industries.

Almost all Australian soils were found to be deficient in phosphorus and nitrogen and many were also lacking in one or more trace elements such as molybdenum and copper. One of the greatest advances in Australian agriculture has been the pasture improvement which came with the development of sown pasture plants of a number of annual legumes, notably subterranean clover and various medicks. These plants were selected by Australian scientists from the Mediterranean Basin, although they had not been used in the region or elsewhere as sown pastures. The sowing of improved pastures, with nutrients from superphosphate – commonly with a trace element added – and nitrogen contributed from the legumes raised soil productivity enormously. Over most of the extensive tablelands, pasture improvement enabled a fourfold increase in production. It is estimated to have contributed almost half of the huge increase in stock numbers in the 20 years to 1970. The balance is attributed to an array of factors including control of rabbits by myxomatosis, disease control, fodder conservation, fencing and better flock management.

Throughout the history of agriculture in Australia, fluctuation in rainfall, and the consequent soil moisture available for crop and pasture growth, has been the major factor influencing yield variability. In 1901 William Farrer released the most notable of his new wheat varieties, 'Federation', and within a few

years almost the entire Australian wheat plantings were of locally bred strains. The advent of a legume-based improved pasture in the rotation served to maintain soil fertility and grain yields as well as enabling increased sheep numbers. Subsequent developments in plant breeding and mechanical cultivation have helped increase production under dry conditions. In the wheat industry, semi-dwarf varieties with a short growing season, stubble retention and minimum tillage techniques have substantially increased wheat production under conditions of low soil moisture.

Some of the other more notable agricultural innovations and advances in Australia include the development of the pure-bred merino sheep which accounts for 75 per cent of the nation's sheep flock of

162 million; the early mechanical innovations such as the stripper harvester and the stump-jump plough; the spectacular biological control of the prickly-pear cactus; control of rabbits by myxomatosis; the selective breeding of strains of crops and livestock better adapted to Australian conditions; and greatly improved systems of preservation and transportation of agricultural commodities.

In recent years, experts are claiming that the technological sophistication of rural industries is being underestimated by Australians. They argue convincingly that a continuing strong programme of rural research is vital for the future of the nation's agriculture. Research into blowfly strike and internal and external parasites promises to reduce significantly the present costs incurred by sheep farmers, which account for over $7,000 each, per year, in lost production and treatment costs. Work on biological control of pests and weeds is anticipated to have considerable benefits and advances in genetic engineering are expected to have a substantial impact on animal and plant breeding.

Merino rams being inspected. Three-quarters of Australia's sheep flock are merinos kept for wool, which accounts for about a tenth of Australia's exports. Modern merinos are the product of years of breeding from stock originally brought from South Africa and England and then cross-bred with Saxon, Silesian, French and American merinos.

THE INTERNATIONAL ENVIRONMENT

The key international factors influencing the world demand for agricultural commodities are population growth, economic growth and the way in which economic growth and income is distributed in the world economy. On the supply side, the agricultural and trade policies of the major producers and consumers of agricultural commodities, such as the USA, the European Community, Japan, Russia and China, play a central role in determining not only world production but also trade patterns.

World population growth is expected to continue to decelerate over the next decade and is expected to have only a small effect on the demand for food and agricultural fibres. The rate of world economic growth exerts a major influence on growth of demand for agricultural commodities. A change in the rate of world economic growth of one to two percentage points can cause a 10 per cent change in the average level of world agricultural prices.

The world pattern of income distribution is another important factor influencing demand for agricultural commodities. Consumers in developing countries spend more of any extra income on food than do consumers in developed countries. Many developing countries experienced substantial rises in incomes during the 1970s, largely because of increased revenue from high oil prices. This led to a substantial expansion in agricultural imports by these countries. In contrast, in the early 1980s, developing countries suffered from high world interest rates and consequent serious external debt problems. In this period, income was transferred back to the developed countries and this income redistribution had a negative effect on the growth in demand for agricultural products, which was exacerbated by the world economic recession of the early 1980s.

Japan is by far Australia's major agricultural trading partner, accounting for 21 per cent of all farm exports in 1988–89. The second most important importer of Australia's farm produce is the USA, consuming a little under 9 per cent of Australia's exports. The most significant other markets are Russia, the People's Republic of China, Saudi Arabia and Egypt. Only one European nation – Italy – ranks among Australia's top 10 agricultural export markets. This fact highlights the dramatic nature of the changing pattern of export markets. Twenty years ago almost two-thirds of Australia's farm exports were consigned to the UK and Europe.

Over the next decade, food demand in the Southeast Asian region is expected to increase at an annual rate of 4 per cent while only a 2 per cent annual increase in Asian food production is anticipated. Australia's geographic location means that it is ideally situated to supply a large part of the anticipated growing Asian market, but there is likely to be strong competition for this market from other countries including New Zealand, South America, the USA and Canada.

FOREIGN TRADE

In recent years, there have been changes in attitudes towards agricultural protection and a growing awareness within the international community of the economic costs of protection and the problems of international trade arising from domestic support policies. The apparent change in attitudes has been associated with a number of factors such as the buildup of large world surpluses of agricultural commodities in the early 1980s (which were subsequently later stockpiled or dumped on world markets at subsidised prices) and increasing evidence that domestic policies in a number of countries were not meeting their objectives. The Australian Bureau of Agricultural and Resource Economics has played a significant educational role in this regard at both the national level and internationally.

In most OECD countries and the newly industrialised Asian countries domestic food prices are set at levels well above world prices. Protection levels are particularly high in Japan, the European Community, and the newly industrialised countries, such as South Korea. And in recent years the USA has engaged in trade-wars with the European Community through its Export Enhancement Program (EEP) to the detriment of Australian and New Zealand farmers. The general effect of protectionist policies in these countries is to lower world trading prices since domestic production is usually stimulated and domestic consumption constrained. Another important effect of policies, such as the European Community's Common Agricultural Policy, is that they cause much of the variability in world commodity prices. That is to say, people, not nature, are responsible for much of the fluctuation in world prices.

It has been estimated that the net benefits to Australia from the phasing out of agricultural protection on a multilateral basis would be over $A3 billion. Liberalisation of the European Community grain and meat markets alone would result in real net incomes of Australian farmers increasing on average by over 11 per cent. For the European Community and Japan the gains from multilateral trading liberalisation would be about $A30 billion for each country.

At the launching of the Uruguay Round of GATT (General Agreement on Tariffs and Trade) trade negotiations in September 1986 agriculture was given a prominent place on the agenda for the first time in 40 years. Most of the trade liberalisation in earlier rounds of negotiations under GATT has been of manufactured products and Australia has felt that it has received little specific benefit from this liberalisation. In 1986–87, Australia took the lead in organising the 'Cairns' Group' which held their first meeting at Cairns, in Queensland. The Cairns' Group is comprised of 14 food exporting countries, including both developed and developing countries, that claim not to subsidise their agricultural sectors to any significant extent. The Group recognised that any comprehensive long-term framework for agricultural policy reform would take many years to negotiate and implement and they accordingly placed particular emphasis on action in the short-term as part of a multistage process of policy change.

Australia has two clear objectives. First, to achieve agreement under GATT for a reduction in support levels of policies that distort agricultural trade and, second, to encourage the adoption of policies that attain domestic objectives, but have less-disruptive effects on trade than the policies currently in place. Benefits can be obtained from even a small reduction in agricultural protection. For example, a 10 per cent multilateral reduction in agricultural support is estimated to give an economic gain of $US 3.3 billion to the world as a whole. It is also possible to design domestic policies which have less-disruptive trade effects. It is estimated that a change in policy in the six major developed agricultural producing and trading countries whereby protection to farmers was maintained while their consumer food markets were opened to international trade, would provide net benefits to all six countries. The benefits to Australia alone would amount to $US 1.5 billion.

The Uruguay Round of trade negotiations was the most wide-ranging ever undertaken under the auspices of GATT. It is likely to represent the last opportunity for a considerable time for the problems of world agricultural trade to be resolved on a multilateral basis. If the negotiations on agriculture fail, there is a danger that disillusionment with GATT could lead to major developed countries and regions forging bilateral trade agreements which would be to the detriment of smaller trading nations such as Australia and New Zealand. Some progress has been made towards a reduction in the levels of agricultural protection in some important countries. In Japan, for example, protection measures for a number of commodities such as rice, milk and beef have been reduced while the European Community has extended their system of agricultural supply control measures to a wider range of products, including grain cereals. The People's Republic of China and Russia have embarked on fairly major reforms of their agricultural policies. The general aim of the Chinese reform programme has been to open the agricultural sector, and the economy generally, to world market forces.

The biggest potential stumbling block to major progress in the removal of agricultural trade barriers is the different views on long-term agricultural reform held by the European Community and the USA. After six years of negotiations it is still unclear whether or not the Uruguay Round of GATT will achieve substantial trade liberalisation for agricultural products.

DOMESTIC POLICIES

In the 1930s and 1940s home-consumption price schemes were introduced in a number of Australian rural industries. The aim of these schemes was to set domestic prices so that exports of commodities would effectively be subsidised when world prices were low. In the two decades or so after World War II the general thrust of agricultural policy was to encourage the expansion of production with the objective of improving Australia's balance of payments under a fixed exchange-rate regime. In addition to various direct incentives to farmers – most notably income-tax concessions and input subsidies – water resource and land development schemes were undertaken by government.

In the 1970s, policy emphasis turned to rural reconstruction schemes which were introduced to assist adjustment of low-income farmers, beginning with the Dairy Farms Reconstruction Scheme. As a consequence of the restructuring of the dairy industry and innovation which took place in the 15 years up to 1980, there was a doubling of milk production per farm and a 40 per cent increase in the production per cow. The removal of all barriers to trans-Tasman trade in dairy products from July 1990 under the Closer Economic Relations Trade Agreement with New Zealand (pp. 217–19) placed further pressure on the industry to adjust.

The focus of agricultural price policy moved away from price stabilisation-support measures towards the more limited objective of reducing the uncertainty faced by farmers from possible large price declines. Price underwriting schemes were introduced in a number of rural industries. Another notable development in the 1970s and early 1980s was the increasing attention given by farmer groups to assistance given to other industries and the enhanced understanding of intersectoral and macro-economic issues. This was in part stimulated by the mining boom in the late 1960s and early 1970s, which had a substantial impact upon agriculture as a result of the rise in the value of the Australian dollar associated with the additional foreign exchange that the new mineral wealth earned. The effect upon the agricultural sector of the new mining activity was estimated to be equivalent to a doubling in the tariff protection given to the manufacturing sector.

In the 1970s there was a substantial debate on the idea of tariff compensation, the argument being that while substantial protection existed for import-competing manufacturing industries economic efficiency would be improved by increasing assistance to agriculture and other export industries. However, government policy gradually moved towards an objective of reducing protection levels throughout the economy and within the farm sector the aim over recent years has been to encourage farmers to respond to changing economic conditions, rather than attempting to protect and shield agriculture from the forces of change.

The farm sector as a whole would receive a substantial net benefit from a reduction in assistance to all industries, although a few rural industries that are highly protected would be disadvantaged. Removal of protection and subsidisation measures to all sectors of the economy could lead to an increase in real net returns to agriculture of around 7 per cent, or average savings of around $5,000 on each farm in 1988–89. An Economic Statement in May 1988 announced reductions in assistance to manufacturing and rural industries to be phased in over the period to 1992. Net gains of around $470 million annually are likely to accrue to the rural sector, an average of $2,700 on each farm, as a result of these reductions.

In the 1980s there was a focus on the major macroeconomic forces exerting an influence on the performance of the rural sector: currency exchange rates, interest rates, wages and inflation. The progressive deregulation of the Australian financial system, particularly after 1983, was a striking development. Two very important changes for the farm sector have been the floating of the exchange rate and the removal of most of the interest-rate controls formerly imposed on the banking sector.

THE NATURAL-RESOURCE BASE

The size and quality of Australia's natural-resource base is now recognised as being a most important factor in influencing the future productivity and prosperity of agriculture. The 1980s was a period in which emerging environmental and natural resource constraints to expanding production became very evident. Moreover, it was a period in which Australian governments were forced to become involved in resolving an increasing number of conflicts between different groups of land users.

Problems of conservation are, of course, not new in Australia. As early as the 1890s, the severe droughts of that period starkly showed the dangers inherent in exceeding resource and environmental limits to production. While most Australian farmers can now handle normal seasonal droughts, the old man droughts where seasonal rains fail, and then fail again and perhaps again, still have devastating effects on livestock numbers and crop production. The practice of bare fallow in the 1930s, though giving an immediate improvement in crop yields, led to serious loss of soil structure and consequent severe windswept and water-induced erosion. Largely in response to these events, the first Australian soil-conservation service was formed in New South Wales in 1938 and similar agencies were established in all states soon after. Today, problems of land

Irrigation of cotton fields, Bourke, New South Wales. Significant irrigation of land was first carried out in Australia in the 1870s. State governments promoted irrigation schemes in the next decade in reaction to Australia's recurring droughts.

degradation in the form of soil erosion, loss of soil structure, salinisation induced by irrigation, dryland salinisation, soil acidification, and residues and runoff from fertilisers and chemicals pose important constraints to expanding agricultural production.

Since European settlement in Australia, there has been much political and public advocacy of irrigation schemes. Since World War II, the area of irrigated land has risen from around 0.5 million hectares to 1.6 million hectares, approximately 7 per cent of the total area under crops. Over two-thirds of the total area irrigated lies within the Murray–Murrumbidgee–Darling River Basin, the waters of which were increased when the Snowy Mountains Scheme was completed (p. 196). The basin is one of Australia's most productive agricultural areas accounting for about one-third of Australia's total agricultural produce. The irrigated lands are the backbone of a number of industries – most notably, canned fruits, cotton, dried vine fruits and rice. Irrigation water is also used for pastures, cereals, vegetables and fodder crops such as lucerne.

It is now estimated that nearly 100,000 hectares of irrigated land in the basin show signs of salinisation and that salinisation and water logging are causing a loss in production of around $80 million each year.

The clearing of deep-rooted natural vegetation and its replacement by shallow-rooted crops or pastures is the major cause of dryland salinity. Approximately 3 per cent of Australia's agricultural area is affected by dryland salting with Victoria and Western Australia being the most badly affected states. Soil acidification is a quite separate problem that is associated with the use of superphosphate over periods of many years, particularly on pastures containing subterranean clover. Acidification affects about 20 million hectares of land used for grazing on improved pastures and cropping in southeastern and western Australia.

With the benefit of hindsight, one can point to many costly mistakes in agricultural policy generally and in government policies that relate specifically to conservation issues. Today, federal and state governments are aware of the environmental problems surrounding rural land and water use and of the challenges posed for decision makers. Undoubtedly, this awareness was heightened in 1989 when an environmental group obtained 18 per cent of all votes in one state election. In 1986 the Australian Soil Conservation Council was formed and a major initiative of the Council was the formation of the National Soil Conservation Strategy. In recent years the Bureau of Rural Resources and the National Resource Information Centre have been established, and a Resource Assessment Commission formed in 1989.

Natural-resource management is a difficult task because uncertainty is at times pervasive and because

the use of the market mechanism alone to retain efficient resources use is precluded due to externalities and the often common property characteristics associated with natural resources. The guiding principle for government policy should be to formulate policies which allow for flexibility to changing circumstances and that induce individual decision makers to take account of the full social cost of their actions. The predicted global warming, expected to result from greenhouse effects, provides an extreme example of a common problem that transcends national boundaries. Human behaviour may now significantly affect world climate and it could greatly change present environmental constraints on agriculture.   AHC

The minerals and energy sector

MINERALS

Mount Newman iron ore mine, Western Australia. Mining is today one of Australia's largest industries, but one that is especially prone to the effects of international recession.

The gold boom of the 1850s with its influx of population and investment transformed the image of at least some of the Australian colonies; and the gold boom of the 1890s repeated the process, if less dramatically.

The minerals boom of the 1960s, and subsequent periods of expansion, have also brought major structural change to the Australian economy; and this expansion occurred over a wide range of minerals.

In the period 1970–92, the index of gross product in mining rose from 48 to 180; in contrast, over a substantial part of the period, was the weak growth of the manufacturing and agricultural sectors. In 1992–93 exports of resources accounted for close to half of Australia's export earnings.

VALUE OF EXPORTS OF SELECTED MINERAL COMMODITIES, 1992–3

Commodity	$million
Crude oil	1,852
Liquid natural gas	1,051
Alumina	2,333
Aluminium	1,723
Coking coal	4,542
Steaming coal	2,981
Gold	4,302
Iron ore	2,895
Lead	407
Mineral sands (Titanium minerals)	534
Nickel	645
Zinc	1,020
Copper	790

Source: *Australian Mining Industry Council.*

Such development was heavily dependent on the overseas market. For example, the boom of the 1960s in iron ore, coal, bauxite and nickel was based largely on the Japanese economy. The vulnerability of Australian prosperity to Japanese demand was summed up in the much-publicised political statement, 'If the Japanese economy sneezes, Australia catches cold.'

Japan's unwillingness to become too heavily dependent on a single source of supply for industrial raw materials limited market opportunities for Australia; and structural changes in the Japanese economy from the 1970s – in response to the energy crisis – slowed market growth further and sent Australia to strengthen her marketing efforts in other areas (for example, in Korea, Taiwan and more recently China).

European and North American markets are also, of course, served for specific minerals, but transport costs are a significant factor. The reduction in transport costs for bulk minerals from the 1960s onwards was an important catalyst in Australia's development of her mineral industry over the last three decades.

Since the 1960s, the energy sector has increased in importance in the resources sector, with petroleum discoveries, with the oil price increases of the 1970s, and with substantial increases in coal production and exports to a world trying to reduce its dependence on oil. By the early 1980s, the energy sector accounted for over half the value added in the resource industries.

The industry has achieved mastery in a wide range of technologies associated with exploration – satellite imagery and geophysical equipment; with mining – abrasion resistance and blasting techniques; and processing – continuous smelting and flotation (see also pp. 279–80).

Pricing

The relative importance of Australia as a producer and exporter of a number of mineral commodities would suggest a significant Australian influence on world prices. While Australia has certainly had some market power in the mineral sands industry, it has not been able, in major export industries such as coal and iron ore, to influence prices in Australia's favour as much as hoped for. A number of attempts have been made by the federal government to coordinate the negotiations of individual producers with overseas purchasers who – in the case of Japan in particular – often successfully present a united front.

While the contribution of the minerals and energy sector to exports, and foreign capital inflow associated with resource development, assisted in maintaining a relatively strong exchange rate in the 1970s and early 1980s, falling resource and agricultural prices contributed to the major real depreciation of the Australian dollar in the second half of the 1980s and again in the period 1992 to mid-1993.

Taxation and government charges

Until the 1972 advent of the Australian Labor Party government at the federal level, the mining industry enjoyed a tax position which was not unfavourable compared with other sectors. Since that time, it has faced an increasing tax burden brought about in part by the political perception of it as a highly profitable industry which can be taxed without political consequences.

This is not necessarily true in the longer term, as a more restrictive tax regime can be expected to reduce investment levels. It is for this reason that the federal government has for some sections of the industry – for example, oil production – introduced resource rent taxes (on total profitability), which in theory are so structured as to minimise their impact on investment decisions and patterns of production. State governments, however, continue to charge royalties, and to levy rail-freight charges (on state rail systems) considerably in excess of not only cost, but also of rates charged to other users.

Foreign investment

The mineral boom of the 1960s was financed by a combination of domestic and foreign capital and the high degree of foreign ownership and control gave rise to nationalistic concerns and attempts by government in the 1970s to limit foreign ownership to 50 per cent of any project.

Continuing investment in the 1970s and 1980s also had a very significant overseas component. The international nature of the mining industry, and its inherent risks, the restricted nature of the Australian capital market and Australia's chronic balance of payments problems all contributed to the high degree of foreign ownership.

Another factor which should not be underestimated was the need to gain access to foreign markets – for example, for Australian bauxite and alumina.

Low profitability in some parts of the resources sector in the 1980s brought with it a fall in the interest of foreign investors. Pressure on the Australian dollar in the late 1980s has brought once again acceptance of foreign capital and major investment off-shore by Australian resource companies has brought a changing public perception of the foreign investment issue.

Access to minerals

Mineral access has been restricted in the name of environmental protection, and also as a consequence of the granting of Aboriginal land rights. The Australian Mining Industry Council estimates that one-quarter of Australia's land surface is now either severely restricted or closed to new exploration or mining activity. The 1993 Land Tenure Map of the Australian Surveying Land Information Group (AUSLIG) indicates that 14.2 per cent of the nation's area is under Aboriginal control and 6.6 per cent is comprised of national parks, reserves and other conservation areas. Other restrictions include urban areas and coastal zones and restrictions on state and Commonwealth land.

The High Court's Mabo decision of June 1992 recognised a form of land title, Native Title, to have existed in Australia at the time of European settlement. The legislative impact of the Mabo decision led to discussion of State rights versus Commonwealth powers. The federal Native Title Act met particular resistance from Western Australia as it was perceived as having potential to restrict mining companies from operating in a large proportion of the state. One result of recent moves has certainly been a resurgence in mineral exploration in Victoria, which is thought to be less subject to restrictions on access.

Coal Mine at Goonyella, Queensland. Coal deposts were discovered early by white settlers, in 1796 near Newcastle, New South Wales.

MINING WORKFORCE

At March 1993, around 92,500 people were employed in the mining industry – 19,800 in New South Wales mainly in the labour-intensive coal industry; 21,300 in Western Australia (predominantly in the iron ore industry) and 21,500 in Queensland, of whom 8,400 are in the coal industry.

Western Australia and Queensland in particular are seen as the resource-rich states, followed by New South Wales and Victoria with its Bass Strait oil- and gas-fields.

South Australia and the Northern Territory, although they are both mineral producers, have not been able to develop and export their uranium resources to the full because of government policy.

Smelting and refinery operations employed an additional 65,000 people in 1987–88, but probably only about 59,000 in 1991–92 – a fall in the workforce of about 9 per cent in five years.

ENERGY

Electricity

The provision of electricity is usually the responsibility of public authorities rather than of private corporations.

Queensland and New South Wales are well endowed with black coal, including steaming coal suitable for electricity generation. Victoria depends on brown coal from her major deposits in Gippsland, east of Melbourne. South Australia and Western

The Snowy Mountains Scheme

The Snowy Mountains Scheme, centred as its name suggests on the Alpine region of the Great Dividing Range, impounds the waters of the Snowy River, which would otherwise flow swiftly to the coast, and diverts them, together with the waters of the upper Murrumbidgee River, westwards through tunnels beneath the mountains to the Murray and Murrumbidgee Rivers. In their journey to the irrigation storages, the waters drop 800 m. There are seven power stations in all, with a total generating capacity of 3,740,000 kw. The additional irrigation water supplied annually is 2,380,000 megalitres.

No charge is made for water, either as an input resource used by the Snowy Mountains Scheme, or as one of its outputs. The entire cost of the works is met by charges for the electricity supplied to New South Wales, Victoria and the Australian Capital Territory. The scheme's flexibility reflects the need to conserve water in the Australian context. Two-way flow tunnels enable water to be diverted to storage when river flows are in excess of power station needs. The 1,500 MW Tumut 3 power station incorporates a pumped storage facility, enabling water that loses elevation in response to peak power demands to be pumped back to higher storage during low-load periods, using power from the thermal stations.

Construction of the scheme took 25 years and was completed in 1974. The scheme was constructed by the Snowy Mountains Hydroelectric Authority, but is maintained and operated under the direction of the Snowy Mountains Council as a joint Commonwealth–NSW–Victoria venture. In the early 1990s, major refurbishment of the two underground powerstations, Tumut 1 and Tumut 2, was undertaken.   SB

Turbine hall, Murray 1 power station in the Snowy Mountains. The Snowy Mountains Scheme had a dual purpose: to generate electricity by hydroelectric means and to divert water from the mountains for irrigation. Murray 1, opened in July 1968, is one of seven power stations in the Scheme, the last of which began operation in 1972.

Australia use natural gas among other fuels. There is no nuclear power generation in Australia, although uranium is produced for export. Diesel oil is used for power generation in remote locations, but electricity so produced is expensive by Australian standards.

Solar power is used in appropriate applications – for example, in remote communities and for powering remote communications equipment. With the number of hours of sunshine in Australia, solar heating for both commercial and domestic hot water is practicable and popular.

Tasmania, with its high rainfall and mountainous southwest, is heavily dependent upon hydroelectricity, although plans for further developments in the wilderness area met with environmental opposition which was successful in preventing development of the Franklin/Gordon dams (see p. 48).

Hydroelectricity is also important in meeting the peak load and emergency needs of the populous southeastern corner of the continent, through an imaginative scheme which provides not only power, but also water for irrigation of the drier inland areas.

Petroleum

Since the discovery of the Bass Strait oilfield in the 1960s, Australia has enjoyed a high degree of self-sufficiency in petroleum production, although as Bass Strait crude oil is light, she has still had to depend on overseas supplies for the heavier fractions. The degree of self-sufficiency is expected to decline in the late 1990s.

Estimates by the Australian Bureau of Agricultural and Resource Economics in 1993 suggest that Australian crude oil production will meet around 50 to 70 per cent of Australian consumption in the year 2000, depending on the success rate in exploration. Experience in the 1970s and 1980s has been that the date of expected decline in self-sufficiency has been continually extended as new supplies have been discovered and developed, and it is possible that further discoveries may improve the position. Those who remember back to the balance of payments problems faced when Australia imported all her petroleum requirements are particularly anxious that the policy climate for petroleum exploration should remain sufficiently encouraging to ensure geologically prospective areas are fully explored.

In 1987, the Federal Government passed the Petroleum Resource Rent Tax Assessment Act. This Act was amended in 1991 to enable exploration expenditures in lapsed projects and relinquished permits to be transferable and exploration expenditure incurred on or after 1 July 1990 to be transferable to the new owner in the case of the farmout of a whole interest in a project. International industry analysts have generally praised the PRRT as one of the most attractive fiscal regimes in the international arena.

Natural gas is supplied to Melbourne from the Bass Strait field, while Adelaide, Sydney and Canberra are supplied from the Moomba fields in Central Australia. Darwin is supplied from the Palm Valley and Mereenie fields in Central Australia. Brisbane and Gladstone receive their gas supplies from the Surat Basin fields in Queensland and Perth is supplied from fields in the Perth Basin and from the North Rankin field. A new project linking the Cooper Basin fields in Queensland to the Moomba pipeline will allow Queensland gas to be supplied to South Australia.

As in other countries, considerable research has been done on coal liquefaction (both black and brown coal); the possibility of commercial-scale liquefaction of central Queensland's oil shales has also been studied. The use of plant material to eke out liquid fuel supplies is not significant overall, but occurs in specialised uses; for example, the use of bagasse (sugar cane waste) at sugar mills. The use of ethanol/petroleum fuel mixes is also being encouraged on environmental grounds.   SB

Commercial fishing boats in the harbour at Portland, Victoria. Despite Australia's vast coastline, fishing is not a major industry, in part due to the low levels of fishstocks around the continent.

The fishing industry

The Australian commercial fishing industry was ranked fifth among the nation's rural industries in 1991–92 after wool, cattle, wheat and dairy products, with a gross value of production of $1,290 million.

The Australian fishing zone (AFZ) of 200 nautical miles was proclaimed on 1 November 1979 replacing the 12-mile declared fishing zone. Australia has one of the longest coastlines of any country in the world and, since 1979, has had a large fishing zone of almost 9 million km², about the size of its land area. Yet the fishing sector is not a large component of the Australian economy either in terms of employment or value of production. Australia's fishery production of 221,000 tonnes in 1991–92 represented only 0.2 per cent of total world production. The basic conditions for the type of rich fishing grounds that occur in the Northern Hemisphere do not occur in Australian waters. The barren nature of the Australian continent and consequent low runoff, the lack of nutrient-rich currents and the narrow continental shelf in many areas contribute to poor productivity.

There are some 3,000 known species of fish and at least an equal number of crustacean and mollusc species inhabiting Australian waters. Despite this, fewer than 400 of these are commercially exploited.

Approximately 25,000 people work in the catching and processing sectors of the industry, providing a major source of revenue for many coastal towns.

About 9,000 boats operate in the industry, most of which are less than 21 m in length.

The industry is not greatly affected by international trade problems and is lightly assisted by governments. The main problems are associated with the common-property nature of the resource, protecting stocks and restraining fishing effort in major fisheries while at the same time not preventing gains in economic efficiency or development of new fisheries.

TRADE

The pattern of Australia's seafood trade shows marked differences between the nature of the export and domestic sectors.

The export sector is dominated by high-value products (notably prawns, rock lobsters, scallops, abalone and pearls) while imports consist largely of fresh, chilled or frozen fish, prawns and canned goods.

The total value of fisheries' exports was $979 million in 1991–92, Japan and the USA being major markets. Imports are sourced from more than 70 countries and were valued at $509 million in that year.

AQUACULTURE

Although most forms of aquaculture can be considered to be in their infancy in Australia, a remarkable surge of interest, investment and growth has occurred in many types of aquatic farms over the last decade.

Australia has enjoyed a relatively long history of success in the farming of Sydney rock oysters. More recently, there has been commercial cultivation of the Pacific oyster, blue mussel, rainbow trout and Atlantic salmon. The economic viability of prawn farming is still to be proved. There has been successful rearing of barramundi, a popular local fish, and both recreational and commercial stocks are being replenished. Goldfish farming is proving a success. Freshwater crayfish farming is developing, as well as commercial production of some algae.

Research is continuing into hatchery rearing of species such as abalone, scallops, giant clams, flat and pearl oysters.

MANAGEMENT

Under Australian legislation, Commonwealth and state governments are responsible for the conservation and optimum utilisation of fish resources. Since the early 1980s it has become obvious that many fisheries resources of the AFZ were at, or nearing, full exploitation and were vulnerable to depletion by overfishing.

The level of fishing effort exerted by the fleet has increased rapidly over the last 15 years and it is generally considered that there is an excess of fishermen and excess fishing capacity in the industry. As a consequence, the Australian government has introduced a series of management regimes aimed at achieving the continued existence of adequate, self-sustaining stocks of marine resources which are able to support a strong, stable, fully viable and internationally competitive fishing industry.

Management plans are based on an allocation of fishing rights to a select number of fishermen, or by a limit on the catch of fish. Other measures include seasonal and area closures, size limits on gear, boats and fish landed and gear and equipment regulations. Close government/industry liaison is a feature of the formulation of all new fisheries management plans.

FOREIGN FISHING

Australia allows foreign fleets to operate in fisheries that are not fully exploited by Australians and are not likely to be in the near future. Foreign fishermen can operate in the AFZ only if they are licensed to do so and comply with terms and conditions of access determined by Australia. Japanese (tuna), Taiwanese (fish trawling), Thai (fish trawling) and Korean (squid) fishermen have operated for various periods in the AFZ.

A number of fish stocks migrate through the AFZ, the high seas and fishing zones of neighbouring countries, requiring programmes for international research, conservation and management. Australia engages in a variety of cooperative programmes with regional countries bilaterally or through shared membership in international fisheries organisations.   SJ

Pine plantation in the Otway Range, western Victoria. Timber has been harvested from the hillsides since the mid-nineteenth century, and pine plantations were first established in the 1930s.

Forestry

THE NATURAL FORESTS

The natural forests of Australia cover 41.3 million hectares (5.4 per cent) of the continent. Apart from the 34.9 million hectares of eucalypts (of remarkable diversity and range of productivities), there are tropical and subtropical rainforests (2 million hectares) and savannah woodlands (64 million hectares) but these are no longer commonly used commercially for timber production. (See also pp. 21–2.)

Approximately 12.5 million hectares (30 per cent) of the native forests are permanently reserved as State Forests, primarily managed for timber production in association with catchment protection, recreation and wildlife conservation. Another 12 per cent is reserved as National Parks (under state, not national, jurisdiction) in which logging is not permitted (see also pp. 46–8). Private landowners hold 11 million hectares (26 per cent) of all native forests, but little is known about their productivity and management, even though they have traditionally supplied up to half the total timber production in some states, notably Tasmania and Queensland.

The natural forests, both state and private, traditionally supplied most of Australia's production of timber, for example, even in 1985: 4.84 million cubic metres of sawlogs (31 per cent of the total timber harvest) and 5.22 million tonnes of pulpwood (33 per cent). By 1990, only 20 per cent of the total harvest was sawlogs from the natural forests. The balance is from the rapidly expanding plantations of softwoods.

Production and consumption

Australia's major fisheries are prawns ($226 million), rock lobster ($340 million), abalone ($91 million), tuna ($114 million), fin fish ($264 million), scallops ($48 million) and oysters ($43 million).

Australia has minimal commercial fishing in inland waters because of the general lack of suitable river systems. The main inland fisheries comprising golden perch, Murray cod and European carp, are based on the Murray–Darling Rivers and their tributaries.

Although consumption of fish and seafood is relatively low at around 17.3 kg per person per year imports contribute about 60 per cent of that total consumption.   SJ

THE PINE PLANTATION PROGRAM

Because of traditional preferences for coniferous timbers and the very limited extent of natural softwoods, experiments with conifer plantations began in the 1880s. By the 1920s, all states had Forest Services, each with an active pine afforestation programme. In the 1960s, a national plantation programme was created to establish a resource base to supply new industries, and to augment the natural forests which would be virtually exhausted by the year 2000.

The primary goal of the Pine Program was to achieve national (or in some cases, state) self-sufficiency in most wood products by the year 2000. Throughout this century, Australia has imported approximately 25 per cent of all sawn timber used (softwoods from the USA, Canada and New Zealand), one-third of the woodpulp and one-third of the paper consumed (from Europe, North America and New Zealand). The self-sufficiency doctrine was justified on the basis of national defence, potential savings in foreign exchange, and employment creation in rural areas. This afforestation drive was rarely justified on any economic efficiency grounds, and questions of marketing and the competitiveness of Australian forest-processing industries were not addressed rigorously until after 1980.

Pine plantations

There are now over 1 million hectares of man-made plantations in Australia.

Since 1965, the rate of establishment of new plantations has consistently been 35–38,000 hectares per year, of which 90–95 per cent has been with Pinus species, – P. radiata in southern Australia and P. caribea and P. elliottii in Queensland.

Approximately 70 per cent of all these plantations are owned by state Forest Services, about 28 per cent by large, private, forest industry companies, and less than 2 per cent by individuals and farmers.

Between 1964 and 1975 states received concessional loans from the Commonwealth Treasury to assist plantation development, but numerous schemes to assist or promote afforestation by the private sector have been of very doubtful efficacy.

Although the average productivity of Australian pine plantations (16–20 m^3 per hectare per year) is quite high by world standards and in comparison with natural forests (1–4 m^3 per hectare per year pine tree-farming has not been considered a commercially viable land use. The major reason for this, and deterrent to private-sector afforestation, is that log prices were generally quite low, by international standards, being derived basically from the historical prices paid by small, inefficient industries utilising natural forests which had cost very little to produce. RNB

ESTIMATED REMOVAL FROM AUSTRALIAN FORESTS IN 1990–91

Hardwood	m^3 (million)	%
Pulpwood	6,801,000	34
Sawlogs	4,061,000	20
Softwood		
Pulpwood	4,954,000	25
Sawlogs	4,110,000	21
Total	19,926,000	100

THE ANNUAL CONSUMPTION OF FOREST PRODUCTS, 1985–91

Sawn timber	1985–86 m^3 (million)	1990–91 m^3 (million)
Eucalypt	1,653,000	1,401,000
Other native species	160,000	129,000
Pine	1,144,000	1,292,000
Imported softwoods	935,000	1,064,000
Imported hardwoods	242,000	171,000
Total	4,113,000	4,057,000
Papers	(tonnes)	(tonnes)
Eucalypt-based	1,200,000	1,380,000
Pine-based	480,000	580,000
(Net) imports	700,000	550,000
Total	2,380,000	2,510,000

FOREST INDUSTRIES

The sawmilling industry based on the natural forests is generally small (typically less than 10,000 m^3 per year of logs), scattered, labour-intensive, family-operated businesses. However, there has been a steady process of amalgamation, as a few large companies buy out the sawmill licences and associated quota allocations of state logs. Yet it is doubtful whether there are in fact any significant economies of scale in hardwood sawmilling, because of the extremely heterogeneous and defective (hollow or crooked) nature of the logs, in most regions. Furthermore, the natural forests rarely produce large volumes of wood in one location, and markets are very widely dispersed, presenting very serious logistical/transportation problems in operating large mills based on natural forests.

The new softwood sawmilling industry is very different, consisting of a small number of multinational companies operating very large and capital-intensive mills (with, for example, an intake of 200–250,000 m^3 per year of logs, capital of $25 million and 25–30 employees).

These mills are continuously supplied with very large volumes of uniformly good-quality logs, from nearby plantations, at quite low extraction and transport costs. This is a similar structure to the capital-intensive sectors of pulp and paper, and reconstituted panel products. The changing resource base and international market pressures are altering the size, structure, location, capital intensity and ownership of Australia's forest industries.

EXPORTS

Woodchip plant in Eden, New South Wales. More eucalypt is exported as woodchip than as sawn timber.

The major export of forest products is eucalypt woodchips, principally to Japan, of 4.5 million tonnes, valued at approximately $250 million per year. Exports of eucalypt sawn timber average 32,000 m3 (1 per cent of domestic production) worth $18 million per year. Although Australia imports 710,000 tonnes of papers, there are exports of 87,000 tonnes (of particular grades/types in which Australia is competitive) worth $75 million per year.

EMPLOYMENT

The forestry sector, broadly defined, employs approximately 1.8 per cent of the national labour force. Total employment in all segments of the sector has been steadily declining for the past 30 years at a rate of 2 per cent per year, even though production, consumption, exports, and value of production have steadily increased. This is the obvious result of the restructuring of the processing and harvesting industries, as well as the technological change common to all Australian industries during this period.

POLICY ISSUES

Two major interrelated policy issues will determine the future of the Australian forestry sector – conservation and competitiveness. There is strong conservationist pressure for the cessation of logging on most publicly owned native forests. The Australian Conservation Foundation (ACF) is demanding a moratorium on logging, and argues that future forest industries in Australia should be smaller than at present, and use exclusively logs (preferably of Australian species) which have been grown in plantations established on previously cleared, marginal farmlands.

The ACF has argued that natural forests are intrinsically too valuable, as water catchments, for recreation, for wildlife habitat and as landscapes, to be destroyed by logging to supply forest products which either are not required or can be more economically imported from other countries. The opposite perspective is presented by the forest industry companies and trade unions, who see the rapidly expanding resource of fast-growing exotic pines as the key to major efficiency gains and industrial expansion.

The Forest Industries Growth Plan envisages a manifold increase in sawmilling and pulp/paper capacity, which would make Australia a major exporter of forest products, and asserts that this is only conditional upon further increases in the plantation programme and the continued logging of native forests.

There is insufficient evidence to establish clearly the economic viability of such new industries – in fact there are strong grounds to doubt their viability. Despite a series of long-running governmental inquiries since 1979, a series of political decisions are still to be made, weighing up the relative merits of environmental conservation and industrialisation–employment–foreign exchange earnings – a dilemma hardly unique to Australia's forestry sector. RNB

EMPLOYMENT IN THE FORESTRY SECTOR, 1986 AND 1989–90

		1986	1989–90
Forestry	Professionals	1,200	1,100
	Others	12,400	11,100
Industries	Sawmills	18,400	14,200
	Plywood/panels	5,300	5,600
	Joinery	15,000	13,800
	Others	9,600	9,100
	Pulp and paper mills		7,900
	Containers	10,600	9,000
	Other paper products	4,200	4,400
Total employment		85,000	76,200

Transport

Transport systems, external and internal, are of great importance to Australia. Australia is a major trading nation exporting agricultural and mineral commodities in large volumes. Hence the economic significance attached to efficient handling of bulk commodities overland, through the ports, and over long sea hauls to remote markets in North America, Europe and East Asia.

The internal geography of Australia also places unusual demands upon transport. Population, consumer markets and secondary industry are heavily concentrated in and around the six capital cities of the Australian states (all of which are seaports) and in the newer federal capital. Within a country of continental size these conurbations lie much further apart than do the cities of Europe and the USA. In some cases transportation from producer to user within Australia can be more costly than shipping merchandise in from overseas, with adverse implications for the nation's industrial development.

In these circumstances the issue of improved efficiency in transportation has been taken up by federal and state governments.

SHIPPING

Australia is a major trading nation, with 99 per cent by volume of its international trade carried by sea. On a cargo–distance basis Australia's seaborne transport task is the fifth largest in the world. In addition, large volumes of cargo are carried by sea as part of Australia's domestic trade, with total coastal freight flows in 1991–92 equalling 43.7 million tonnes and 96.4 billion tonne kilometres.

Australia's major export commodities are minerals and farm products. Most of Australia's seaborne imports are carried by liner shipping services, although some bulk cargoes, such as petroleum, are also imported. The most important coastal cargoes are also bulk commodities.

Australia's international bulk trade is characterised by the export of coal, iron ore and wheat. Although relatively energy self-sufficient, Australia does import a substantial volume of crude oil and petroleum products. Australia's international container trade is characterised by the importation of manufactured goods such as machinery, telecommunications equipment and office machines. These goods are imported primarily from the EC, Japan and the USA. On the export side Australia's containers largely carry primary products such as frozen meat to the USA and Japan, seafood to Japan, fruit and vegetables to the EC and dairy products to southwest Asia. Wool, Australia's second largest export, by value, is also carried in containers.

The only domestic general cargo trade of significance is between the island state of Tasmania and the mainland. The Commonwealth Government subsidises the shipping of eligible domestic non-bulk cargoes between Tasmania and the mainland under the Tasmanian Freight Equalisation Scheme. This scheme makes payments to Tasmanian shippers to compensate for the higher costs of sea carriage incurred by them compared to the land transport costs paid by shippers in all other states.

On 30 June 1992, the Australian trading fleet consisted of 76 ships of a total of 3.3 million deadweight tonnes. Most ships operate in coastal trades although some operate in both coastal and international trades. Australian ships carry about 3 per cent of Australia's international cargoes when measured by volume and 5.3 per cent when measured by value. About 26 ships are dedicated to international trading. The size of the fleet in ship numbers has declined in recent years, from a peak of 109 in 1984 to 76 in 1992, reflecting the introduction of newer, larger ships.

Shipping in Australia is predominantly privately owned and receives no operating subsidies from the Commonwealth Government. The Commonwealth owns the Australian National Line (ANL) which operates 14 ships in coastal and international trades. ANL is expected to operate in a commercial manner and returned a profit from 1983–84 to 1990–91.

MAJOR SEABORNE EXPORTS AND IMPORTS, BY VALUE AND VOLUME IN AUSTRALIA, 1990–91

	Tonnes (thousand)	$ (million)
Imports	na	
Road vehicles		4,368
Machinery		4,083
Crude oil and petroleum products		2,990
Textiles		1,534
Electrical machinery		1,366
Paper products		1,128
Clothing and footwear		1,008
All imports		35,101
Exports		
Coal	72,339	3,665
Wool and textiles	9,374	3,564
Non-ferrous metals	1,720	3,347
Meat products	1,071	3,033
Metal ores and scrap	60,324	2,945
Crude oil and petroleum products	9,705	2,561
Cereals	15,692	2,411
All exports	304,202	42,956

na   Volume figures for imports not available.
Note   Some commodity volumes and values are confidential and are not included in the above table under individual commodities but are included in the import/export totals.
Source: Australian Bureau of Statistics, *Catalogue No. 9206.0.*

Waterfront

The improvements in efficiency in the shipping industry have been comple-mented by similar policies directed at achieving reform of Australia's water-front industries. Initially these policies were directed at the traditional port services, such as the stevedoring, towage, and pilotage. Now the focus of gov-ernment policy has moved to encompass the port as a transport system, from the cargo owner's warehouse to the port's sea boundary.

In the mid-1980s the Webber Task Force (1986) and the inter-State Commis-sion investigated the waterfront industry. This led to the establishment of the Waterfront Industry Reform Authority (WIRA) in 1989 to oversee reforms in the stevedoring industry. The federal government instituted a three-year reform programme in November 1989, with the central feature being the introduction of enterprise agreements and reduction in labour costs. In order to reduce sur-plus labour, $413 million was outlaid in early retirement and redundancy packages, the federal government providing $165 million with the balance funded by a special levy on the shipping industry – the main beneficiaries of improvements in waterfront performance.

Between November 1989 and October 1992 the reform process achieved many important results, such as a 57 per cent reduction in the stevedore labour force from 8,872 to 3,818, while containers handled per man shift increased by 130 per cent. According to WIRA, reduced workforce and faster turnround lead to savings of at least $300 million per annum.

State governments also participated in waterfront reform, by redefining the role and functions of their port authorities. For example, the NSW Maritime Services Board has been restructured with a significant workforce reduction being the benefit. In many other instances port authorities have handed over some non-core activities to private enterprise and introduced measures to increase inter-port competition. Overall the number of port authority employ-ees throughout all of Australia decreased by 41 per cent between 1985 and 1992 with the great bulk of reductions occurring in the years 1990–92. BTCE

However, in both 1991–92 and 1992–93 it recorded post-tax losses of $9 million and $8 million respec-tively. The Western Australian state government also operates a small shipping service known as the Western Australian Coastal Shipping Commission which trades as Stateships. The Tasmanian govern-ment just recently replaced the *Abel Tasman* with the more modern *Spirit of Tasmania* on the Bass Strait trade.

Australian domestic shipping trades, in common with most countries, are largely restricted to Aus-tralian flagged and crewed ships. When an appropri-ate Australian registered ship is not available to carry domestic cargo around Australia, a foreign registered ship may be used after either a single voyage or con-tinuous voyage permit has been obtained from the Commonwealth Department of Transport.

Over the last 10 years the Commonwealth Gov-ernment has been encouraging the shipping industry to improve its efficiency and competitiveness. These moves are directed at achieving cost savings for domestic industries relying on shipping and enabling Australian shipping to compete for a greater share of overseas trade.

The government has fostered industry agree-ments on major cost factors such as crew levels and work practices aboard ships. As a complement to these agreements it has offered incentives in the form of taxation concessions and capital grants to shipowners introducing more efficient ships. These policies led to the introduction into the Australian fleet of 34 vessels in the period 1987–93.

RAILWAYS

Public railways have operated in Australia since 1854. The six colonies constructed their railways independently using different gauges because of percieved advantages for their individual pur poses. When federation of the six states into the

AUSTRALIAN COASTAL FREIGHT TASK, BY MAJOR COMMODITY, 1991–92		
Commodity	Tonnes (million)	Tonne-kilometres (thousand million)
Iron ore	7.4	33.2
Bauxite/alumina	9.1	20.3
Petroleum oil	7.7	17.5
Petroleum products	5.9	9.2
Other cargo	13.6	16.2
Total	43.7	96.4

Source: *Department of Transport and Communications, Sea Transport Statistics, Coastal Freight, 1991-92, (Canberra, 1993)*

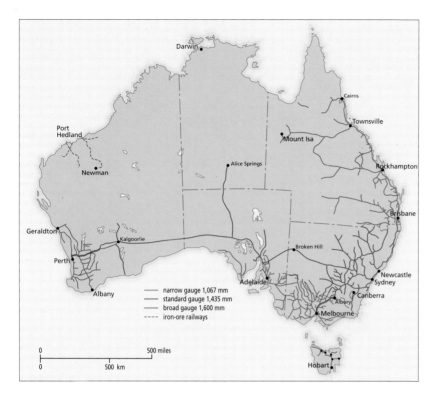

The public railway systems, and some private railways. The private railways are the iron-ore railways, and the short line in Tasmania running southwest from the northern coast.

standard gauge of 1,435 mm, Victoria's railways were entirely a broad gauge of 1,600 mm, Queensland, Western Australia and Tasmania had a narrow gauge of 1,067 mm, while South Australia had both narrow- and broad-gauge railways. When federation of the six colonies into the Commonwealth of Australia took place in 1901, each state government retained responsibility for maintaining its own railways. The Commonwealth also built a trans-Australian railway to link Western Australia to the eastern states; it came into service in 1917 and was operated by the Australian National Railways Commission. In the early 1970s, a Commonwealth offer to take over all the state railways was accepted by Tasmania and South Australia and their systems transferred to the Australian National Railways Commission (although South Australia retained control of urban rail services in Adelaide).

Commonwealth of Australia took place in 1901, each state government retained responsibility for maintaining its own railways. The states were formerly independent colonies and as an indirect result of railways having been constructed before federation, different rail gauges were adopted in different states.

Railways in New South Wales developed on the

Since federation considerable progress has been made in overcoming the problems caused by the variety of gauges with a number of projects being conducted with a view to standardising the gauge to the 1,435 mm standard on the major mainland trunk routes. The longest of these is the 3,961 km Sydney–Perth line, incorporating one straight section of 500 km, the longest straight track in the world. In January 1970 the first freight train crossed the continent without a change of gauge. All inter-capital rail links are now standard gauge, apart from the direct Adelaide to Melbourne link which is still a 1,600 mm gauge line.

Far left Container vessel in Sydney Harbour. In common with the worldwide trend, Australia's international shipping fleet has moved in recent years to fewer, larger vessels.

Left The Indian-Pacific train in the Blue Mountains near Sydney.

THE RAIL SYSTEMS OF AUSTRALIA – KEY STATISTICS (1990 – 91)

System	Route Length (km)	Net tonnes carried (million)	Passenger journeys Surburban (million)	Country [a] (million)
Government-owned:				
Australian National	6,612	13.2	–	0.3
State Rail Authority (New South Wales)	9,810	58.3	243.8	2.3
Public Transport Corporation (Victoria)	5,179	9.7	106.8	6.2
Queensland Railways	10,015	83.0	42.1	0.9
State Transport Authority of South Australia (Western Australia)	–	–	8.0	–
Westrail	5,554	24.4	8.0	0.3
Privately-owned:				
Iron-ore railways (Western Australia and South Australia)	1,393	113.6	–	–
Sugar mill tramways (Queensland)	3,501	22.2	–	–
Coal railways (Victoria and New South Wales)	78	7.9	–	–
Other railways (various states)	197	14.3	–	–

[a] Includes double counting where a journey involves more than one system
Source: Australian Bureau of Statistics, *Year Book Australia, 1994.*

The seven government owned railways systems are operated by:

- Australian National Railways Commission (owned by the Commonwealth Government and operating as Australian National (AN))
- State Rail Authority (SRA) of New South Wales
- Public Transport Corporation (PTC) of Victoria (operating V/Line and the urban 'Met')
- Queensland Railways (QR)
- Western Australian Government Railways Commission (Westrail)
- State Transport Authority of South Australia
- National Rail Corporation (NRC).

In September 1991 the National Rail Corporation was established by the Commonwealth Government in association with the state governments of New South Wales and Victoria as a company with each government holding equity. The main function of the organisation is to operate the interstate rail freight network on a commercial basis in line with international best practice.

The Commonwealth Government has announced a major upgrading of the national rail network to provide a complete standard gauge mainline link from Brisbane to Perth with connections to various ports. This work will complement other investment by the NRC to improve rail terminals and rolling-stock.

The upgrading of the rail network will take place on both state and Commonwealth owned sections of the network. The works being undertaken include the conversion of the Melbourne–Adelaide link to standard gauge, upgrading of the Melbourne–Brisbane corridor to improve the reliability of transit times and allow the operation of longer trains, Melbourne terminal improvements and port access, and standard gauge connections to the ports of Brisbane and Adelaide.

Following the creation of the NRC, Australian National's role is to operate:

- South Australia and Tasmania intra-state services
- three interstate passenger services, namely the Indian Pacific, the Ghan and the Overlander.

Under the newly introduced concept of 'single corridor management', these services will be operated by AN alone, whereas previously two or three systems were involved.

Government non-urban railways are used predominantly to carry bulk freight such as wheat and coal to coastal ports for export, as well as non-bulk container cargoes. Over the three-year period from 1990–91 to 1992–93, total freight carried averaged 179.2 million tonnes per year with bulk freight averaging 150.9 million tonnes and non-bulk 28.3 million tonnes per year respectively.

Country passenger rail services operate in all states except Tasmania and South Australia. Urban passenger rail services are operated by SRA in Sydney, Newcastle and Wollongong, while Metrail operates in Melbourne, QR in Brisbane, the State Transport Authority in Adelaide and Transperth in Perth.

A number of private freight railways operate in Australia. The largest of these are the specialist iron-ore carriers, Hamersley Iron Ore Railways, Mt Newman Railroad, Robe River Railroad and Goldsworthy Railway. These are all located in the remote northwest Pilbara region of Western Australia. Over the three-year period from 1990–91 to 1992–93 an average of 112.5 million tonnes of ore were transported each year by these private railway systems.

Queensland's sugar-mill tramways regularly carry over 20 million tonnes annually of raw sugar and cane. In 1992–93, 26 million tonnes were transported. Several other smaller private railways in various states concentrate on minerals and general freight and tourist services.

ROAD TRANSPORT

On a per capita basis Australia supports one of the most extensive road systems in the world. The total length of all roads open to the general public at June 1992 was 816,000 km, of which some 291,000 km or 36 per cent were sealed with a bitumen or concrete

The major roads.

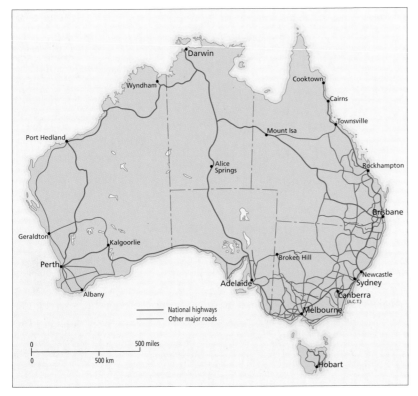

National highways
Other major roads

0   500 miles

0   500 km

ROAD LENGTHS OPEN FOR GENERAL TRAFFIC, 30 JUNE

Surface of roads	NSW 1990	Vic 1990	Qld 1992	SA 1990	('ooo km) WA 1992	Tas 1992	NT 1992	ACT 1990	Australia
Bitumen or concrete	77.8	68.4	59.6	24.3	43.1	9.5	5.8	2.4	291.0
Gravel/other improved	64.6	48.3	48.4	-	46.0	13.0	6.6	0.2	227.0
Formed only	32.4	23.6	49.4	70.6	36.3	0.2	5.2	-	217.7
Cleared only	20.6	21.0	16.7	-	17.7	1.9	2.8	-	80.7
Total	195.4	161.3	174.1	94.9	143.1	24.6	20.4	2.6	816.4

Source: Australian Bureau of Statistics, *Year Book Australia, 1994.*

NUMBER OF MOTOR VEHICLES ON REGISTER, 30 JUNE

Type of vehicle	1988	1989	('ooo) 1990	1991	1992	1993
Passenger vehicles	7,244	7,442	7,672	7,734	7,913	8,050
Light commercials	1,205	1,247	1,280	1,438	1,510	1,549
Rigid trucks	576	601	618	335	379	389
Articulated trucks	51.2	51.3	50.8	51.1	50.7	51
Other trucks	52.4	52.3	55.9	42	48.5	46.8
Buses	92.8	96.2	99.2	49.4	52.7	54.9
Motor cycles	323	317	304	285	292	292
Total	9,544	9,807	10,080	9,934	10,246	10,433

Note   Since 1991 data not strictly comparable with earlier year levels.
Source: Australian Bureau of Statistics, *1991–92 Motor Vehicle Registrations, Australia. Catalogue No. 9303.0.*

MOTOR VEHICLE ACTIVITY LEVELS, YEAR TO 30 SEPTEMBER 1991.

Type of vehicle	Total kilometres (billions)	Average kilometres ('ooo)	Total Tonne-km (millions)	Average Tonne-km ('ooo)	Total Tonnes (millions)	Average Load (tonnes)
Passenger vehicles	114.3	14.3	–	–	–	–
Motor cycles	1.6	5.7	–	–	–	–
Light commercials	22.8	16.9	4,752	6.1	133	0.44
Rigid trucks	6.1	18.5	20,547	68.3	506	4.07
Articulated trucks	4.0	76.0	62,906	1,240.5	391	19.24
Other truck types	0.2	14.2	–	–	–	–
Buses	1.4	33.3	–	–	–	–
Total	150.4	14.9	88,205	78.1	1,030	2.25

Source: Australian Bureau of Statistics, *Survey of Motor Vehicle Use, Australia, 1991, Catalogue No. 9208.*

surface. Total travel for various vehicle types amounted to over 151,000 million vehicle kilometres in the 12 months to end September 1991, a decrease of 1.8 per cent over the corresponding period in 1988. About one-third of the total distance travelled was for business purposes, just under one-quarter was attributed to travel to and from work and 43 per cent for private purposes. Passenger vehicles accounted for three-quarters of the total distance travelled; freight vehicles accounting for the bulk of the remainder (21.8 per cent) while motor cycles accounted for 1.1 per cent and buses 0.9 per cent.

The dominance of private car travel is very marked with around 60 per cent of non-urban passenger-km performed by cars, surpassing all other modes of passenger movement. After cars, bus or coach travel accounts for around 12 per cent of total passenger travel with the level increasing over the past decade partly in response to a deregulation of non-urban bus travel during the 1980s.

Road funding

ROAD EXPENDITURE BY LEVEL OF GOVERNMENT ($m Actual Expenditure)

Government	86–87	87–88	88–89	89–90	90–91	91–92	92–93
Commonwealth	1,290	1,294	1,302	1,352	1,587	1,358	1,824
State	1,483	1,478	1,833	2,217	2,647	2,836	na
Local	1,399	1,442	1,472	1,687	1,790	1,815	na
Total	4,172	4,214	4,607	5,256	6,024	6,009	na

na   not available.
Source: Australian Bureau of Statistics, *Government Finance Statistics, unpublished information.*
Commonwealth Budget Statements.

Over the five-year period from 1988–89 to 1992–93 expenditure on roads in Australia by all levels of government has averaged $5.6 billion annually. Although the states have primary responsibility under the Australian Constitution for road funding, the Commonwealth Government has, since 1926, provided funds to the states and territories through 'specific purpose payments' ('tied' grants), to assist the states in meeting expenditures for purposes designated by the Commonwealth.

Since 1974 the Commonwealth Government has assumed financial responsibility for construction and maintenance of the National Highway System (NHS). Commonwealth grants have also been provided to state and local governments to supplement their road-funding programmes. Under the Commonwealth Government's Australian Land Transport Development Program over the three-year period from 1990–91 to 1992–93 a total of $4.8 billion was outlaid on roads. This included expenditure on engineering improvements at locations with a poor safety record ('black spots') and for urban public transport projects. Smaller outlays included payments for road safety and land transport research and the repayment to the states and territories of registration fees for interstate commercial vehicles under the Federal Interstate Registration Scheme.

From 1994 the federal government's responsibility for road funding will be confined to the construction and maintenance of the NHS.

It is noteworthy that the federal and state governments support:

- road safety research
- uniformity between the states of vehicle and traffic regulations
- vehicle design rules for safety and emissions
- control of truck-driver shifts and rest periods
- a uniform basis for truck registration charges.

Revenue from road users is derived largely from Commonwealth excise on petroleum products, and also from state vehicle registration and other state charges. In New South Wales and Queensland, some road expenditure costs are recovered by the limited use of road tolls. In 1991–92 and 1992–93 some $99.8 million was collected in these states.

Road safety

The marked decline in road fatalities in Australia over the last 21 years from 3,422 in 1972 to 1,977 in 1992 is of particular significance given that over this same time period the number of motor vehicles on the road has more than doubled to over 10 million along with a corresponding increase in total vehicle kilometres travelled.

The decline in fatalities as well as serious injury can be attributed to a number of important legislative initiatives as well as improved vehicle design and better roads and traffic management. Of particular significance in reducing fatalities and serious injury were the compulsory seat belt laws enacted by the states and territories from 1970 to 1972. In addition, the series of Australian Design Rules (ADRs) introduced from 1970 onwards ensure progressively greater protection for occupants in the event of a collision or a roll-over.

Opposite top Road train in Western Australia. In some sparsely populated regions the permitted vehicle length is sufficient to allow the operation of road trains. In general, large and articulated trucks are increasingly favoured for long-distance haulage, and by the late 1980s annual road freight movement had passed 90 billion tonne kilometres.

Opposite bottom Sydney (Kingsford-Smith) Airport. There is an international airport at each of Australia's state capitals, Kingsford-Smith handling most passenger traffic. The international terminal here is shown at the top left.

COMPARATIVE STATISTICS ON ROAD FATALITIES, 1982–92.

State	Persons killed		Fatalities per 10,000 vehicles		Fatalities per 100,000 population	
	1982	1992	1982	1992	1982	1992
NSW	1,253	652	4.5	2.0	23.6	10.9
Vic	709	396	3.3	1.5	17.8	8.8
Qld	602	416	4.2	2.2	24.8	13.6
SA	270	165	3.6	1.8	20.3	11.3
WA	236	200	2.9	1.8	17.6	12.0
Tas	96	74	4.0	2.4	22.3	15.4
NT	60	54	10.3	6.4	46.0	31.3
ACT	26	20	2.3	1.2	11.2	6.7
Australia	3,252	1,977	3.9	1.9	21.4	11.2

Source: *Federal Office of Road Safety, Road Fatality Statistics, Australia, Annual Report 1992.*

accomplishes almost half of Australia's total road freight movement. The use of B-Doubles is more common in the longer interstate routes.

AIR TRANSPORT

As a large island continent with a widely dispersed population, Australia is heavily dependent on air transport. Over 99 per cent of international travellers are carried by air, and air is the predominant form of long-distance public transport for domestic passengers.

Airports and airways

There are seven major international airports: Adelaide, Brisbane, Cairns, Darwin, Melbourne, Perth and Sydney. A further eight airports are designated as restricted international airports where customs facilities are made available to flights with prior approval only. As at mid-1994, the Federal Airports Corporation, a government-owned business enterprise, owned and operated 22 airports which accounted for over 87 per cent of air passenger movements in Australia during the 12 months to June 1993. In mid-1994, privatisation of FAC airports was under consideration.

A major programme for developing airport facilities is being undertaken to ensure that airport infrastructure is adequate to underpin the growth of the aviation industry. Major capital works during 1992–93 included a parallel runway at Sydney (scheduled to open in late 1994), and expansion and development of the international terminals at Sydney, Melbourne, Brisbane and Adelaide. Construction of a new airport 46 km west of Sydney's central business district also commenced in 1993. Sydney West Airport is scheduled to be open for international operation prior to the Sydney Olympic Games in the year 2000.

Responsibility for airways systems including air traffic control, flight advisory services, and aeronautical communications is vested in the Civil Aviation Authority (CAA), a self-funded government enterprise. The CAA also administers aviation safety standards, including air crew and aircraft licensing.

In December 1991 the CAA commenced a modernisation programme for Airspace Management and Air Traffic Services based on standards set by the International Civil Aviation Organisation. A major contract to develop The Australian Advanced Air Traffic System was awarded to Thomson Radar (Australia) Corporation in December 1993.

International air services

The rapid economic expansion in Asia over recent years has been reflected in the growth of international air transport in the region. The growth of

ROAD FREIGHT

The road freight sector in Australia is amongst the most efficient in the world. Over the years the freight task transported by road has increased substantially, almost doubling over the last decade to over 90 billion tonne kilometres. Of this nearly 80 per cent comprises non-bulk commodities. The growing demand for door-to-door delivery has helped the road freight industry capture an increasing share of the non-bulk freight task from rail.

Interstate trucking accounts for around 30 per cent of the road freight task, with over 95 per cent of long-distance road freight being hauled on articulated trucks. The most common of these trucks consists of a three-axle prime mover with a triaxle trailer, which

billion calls were made in 1992–93.

Satellite space-based facilities are used to serve certain remote locations and for some international traffic. These services are provided using the domestic satellite system and access to the INTELSAT and INMARSAT global satellite networks. Australia is a major user of the INTELSAT system and is a significant investor in the global submarine cable network. The domestic satellite system also provides radio and television broadcasting, relay and transmission services.

The Australian telecommunications industry has changed significantly in recent years following a programme of reforms initiated by the government in 1988. The Telecommunications Act 1991 provides the general regulatory framework for the provision of telecommunications facilities and services in Australia and there is also complementary legislation covering specific issues. The government has made specific provision for various social objectives such as the provision of universal service. Post-1997 arrangements for the industry will be determined after a government review.

In February 1992 the government-owned monopoly carriers, Telecom (domestic services) and OTC (international services), were merged to form AOTC which was subsequently renamed Telstra. As the holder of a general carrier licence and a mobile carrier licence, Telstra is able to operate a full range of telecommunications facilities. It pro-

vides local, trunk, international, mobile and various other services. In 1992–93, Telstra employed 70,600 people and earned revenue of almost $12.7 billion.

The government-owned domestic satellite operator AUSSAT was sold in early 1992 to Optus Communications Ltd as part of the process of establishing network competition in the form of a transitional duopoly. Optus holds a general carrier licence and a mobile carrier licence. It commenced mobile, trunk and international services during 1992 and will continue to roll out its network and services over the period to 1997. An interconnection agreement with Telstra currently enables Optus to access a large proportion of the Australian population. In 1992–93, Optus employed 2,300 people and earned revenue of $300 million.

There are various other companies providing telecommunications services in Australia. Vodafone, the third mobile carrier, commenced services in October 1993. Service providers resell capacity purchased from the general carriers, and supply additional services, in specialist market niches. There are also providers of value-added services such as email and electronic data interchange.

AUSTEL, an independent statutory body, has overall responsibility for the economic and technical regulation of the Australian telecommunications industry. Its major functions include the promotion of fair and efficient market competition within the

Selection of stamps from the bicentennial year, 1988, showing Australian values: the family, outdoor life, sport, and the continuing but now less prominent link with the British monarchy.

industry and the protection of the public interest and consumers. AUSTEL also manages the numbering of national telecommunications services and reports on competitive safeguards and carrier performance. In addition, it has responsibility for the licensing of telecommunications carriers and service providers, technical regulation and the setting of technical standards, and administration of the universal service levy.

Other government bodies with a role in the telecommunications industry include the Trade Practices Commission, the Telecommunications Industry Development Authority and the Telecommunications Industry Ombudsman.

POST

The government-owned Australian Postal Corporation (more commonly, Australia Post) runs Australia's domestic and international postal services. It was corporatised in 1989, when a commercial charter and board were put in place. Economically, it is required to provide an efficient, low-cost postal service that covers its expenses and funds at least half of its capital expenditure from trading revenue. Socially, it is required to provide a universal postal service at a uniform price throughout Australia.

Although parcel and courier services are open to competition, Australia Post has enjoyed an effective monopoly in respect of letters. In late 1993 the government announced its intent to institute a managed approach to the introduction of further competition for Australia Post beginning in mid-1994.

In 1992–93 Australia Post handled 4,166 million articles through some 4,200 post offices and agencies.

BROADCASTING

Australian broadcasting is divided into three sectors: national, which is government-funded; commercial, which is supported by advertising; and community, which is maintained by sponsorship announcements and community support. The community broadcasting sector also receives some government funding through the Community Broadcasting Foundation. The commercial broadcasting industry is regulated by the Australian Broadcasting Authority (ABA), which controls licensing and service planning, and imposes content regulations on the community and commercial broadcasters.

National broadcasting

National broadcasting is in the hands of the Australian Broadcasting Corporation (ABC) and the Special Broadcasting Service (SBS). Both are accountable to parliament but editorially independent. ABC, the larger network, was formed in 1932. It provides a television network and four radio networks, with statutory responsibilities to broadcast in every major region and to remote areas through AUSSAT. It also provides international services through Radio Australia and Australian Television International. SBS, established in 1978, runs a television and two radio services geared specifically to multicultural and multilingual programming; services are broadcast in the state capital cities, in Canberra, Newcastle, Wollongong and to several regions in New South Wales, Victoria, Tasmania and Queensland.

Commercial television

Commercial broadcasting television services were provided by 45 stations operating throughout Australia in 1991–92. Sydney, Melbourne, Perth, Brisbane and Adelaide have three competing commercial television services. Since 1988–89 the federal government has implemented a policy of providing, in regional areas of the eastern states, a range of programmes similar to that available to city viewers. A similar policy is to be implemented in Tasmania in 1994. Until the advent of the domestic satellite system in 1985, remote areas of Australia had no access to television.

Commercial radio stations

Commercial radio stations generate material locally but are primarily reliant on networking for programmes like news bulletins. As at 30 June 1992, 152 commercial radio services were operational in Australia. Of these, 39 were located in state capital cities and 113 in other centres. Over the past 10 years there has been an increase in the number of FM services available in the capital cities and some other major cities. FM services are gradually being established in regional areas.

Community radio

Community radio was inaugurated in 1975. Diverse needs and interests are catered for, the intention being to make radio accessible to the community and allow local organisations to control their own broadcasts. Licences for community services are granted in three areas, community, radio for the print handicapped and special interest. Educational, specialist music, ethnic, Aboriginal and religious services are most prevalent.

Community television

Community television is still in its formative stages in Australia. Trials for community services were undertaken during the 1980s. In 1993, the ABA granted licences for community services to groups in Sydney, Melbourne, Adelaide and Brisbane.

A dealing room in the National Australia Bank, amongst the largest of Australia's trading banks.

from making such loans. When the restrictions were removed, the banks moved rapidly into the market (for example, issuing a credit card, Bankcard, in 1974). Finance companies reacted by diversifying into wholesale finance. They have come under a great deal of competitive pressure since financial deregulation in the early 1980s

Merchant banks have also come under considerable competitive pressure, but they continue to play a role in wholesale finance. These institutions grew strongly when banks were prevented from paying interest on very short-term deposits, successfully attracting large-denomination deposits to lend to business. Today they provide expert advice in areas such as mergers and acquisitions, equity floats and offshore capital raising.

Long-term savings institutions such as superannuation funds and collective investment vehicles such as equity trusts, property trusts, fixed interest and cash management trusts attract savings from small investors. These funds are aggregated and invested in local and overseas assets such as shares, property, mortgages and money market or fixed interest securities. Superannuation has been given substantial taxation advantages by the government and funds under management have been growing rapidly.

FINANCIAL MARKETS

The major players in Australia's financial markets are financial institutions, businesses, households and overseas investors. The seven principal markets are closely related. Participants move from one to another and are often active in all seven.

- The *cash market* deals in very short-term deposits and loans
- The *short-term money market* deals in bank bills, promissory notes and negotiable certificates of deposit with a maturity below one year
- The *deposit market* deals in deposits with financial institutions. These include deposits which can be drawn on by cheque, term and savings deposits, and certificates of deposit
- The *loans market* deals in consumer and business loans, and housing mortgages
- The *intercompany market* effects direct financial transactions between businesses
- The *fixed-interest market* deals in federal government securities with a term greater than one year, and in state and local government securities
- The *equity market* deals in company shares

These financial markets are linked to offshore financial markets through the foreign-exchange market, where Australian dollars can be converted into foreign currencies and vice versa. The demand for foreign currency arises from importers while the supply comes from exporters and overseas borrowers. Overseas borrowing plays an important role in the Australian financial system because domestic savings are not large enough to meet the needs of government and business borrowers.

MONETARY POLICY

The Reserve Bank of Australia implements the government's monetary policy by varying interest rates in the cash markets. The Bank sets cash interest rates and supplies the financial system with an amount of cash consistent with this interest rate. The Bank does this by changing the amount of cash in the financial system through open-market operations, the buying or selling of government securities or foreign currency. For example, a sale of government securities or foreign currency takes cash out of the financial system and forces cash interest rates up.

The objectives of monetary policy are determined by the government's economic policy objectives. Interest rates are the only flexible policy instrument available to the government and they are changed to meet whatever appears to be the most pressing economic problem at the time. Thus, interest rates were increased to support the sliding Australian dollar in 1985, eased in 1987 to stimulate the economy and offset the effects of the October 1987 stock market crash, increased in 1988 to slow the economy and to reduce the current account deficit and reduced from 1990 on to stimulate an economy in deep recession. The reliance on interest rates to achieve economic policy objectives has induced wide fluctuations in them and this has in turn created some instability in the financial system. TJV

International economic relations

There have been dramatic changes in the factors affecting Australia's trading patterns and international economic relations in the years since the end of World War II. Chief among these were the dismantling of the Commonwealth Preference, whereby commonwealth countries gave each others' products reduced tariff rates, and the creation of the European Community, which produced impediments to trade with European countries, large-scale immigration, the Korean and Vietnam wars, the rise of Japan to prominence in world manufacturing and trade; recently the emergence of Korea, Taiwan and other Asian countries as manufacturers and exporters and the oil-price shocks of the 1970s.

Trends in international trade

The conventional view of Australia as a country whose income is significantly generated by international trade is somewhat misleading. In 1991, 22 per cent of Australia's gross domestic product (GDP) was generated by exports, compared with 11 per cent in

A farmer dumps wheat outside the United States Embassy in Canberra in protest against subsidised grain sales to the former USSR. Australian rural interests have been threatened by sales of American produce to Yemen, Pakistan, and other markets in Asia.

the USA, 41 per cent in Switzerland and 68 per cent in the Netherlands. The 'degree of openness' is not particularly high when measured against countries such as the Netherlands and Switzerland, in part at least because Australia has no land borders and so does not have the ready trade which they can afford. This has the disadvantage that the transport costs to many markets are high.

The apparent advantage that Australia would seem to be relatively insulated from world fluctuations is offset by the fact that a substantial proportion of exports comprise rural and resource-based commodities, whose prices can fluctuate substantially.

At the end of the 1940s Australia's international commerce was still dominated by the UK, but by the end of the 1980s the UK had become in many respects a relatively insignificant trading partner. In 1949–50

Foreign Investment in Australia (%)			
	UK	Japan	USA
1949–50	77.4	–	15.3
1985–86	4.6	9.2	16.0
1988–89	6.8	11.8	16.8

over half of Australia's imports came from the UK and nearly 40 per cent of exports were sent there. Further, at the time most of the flow of foreign investment in Australia was provided by the UK.

Realignment of world trade in part due to the creation of the European Common Market and the rise of Japan as an economic power meant that by 1991–92 both exports to and imports from the UK had become a small share of total trade. Only 7 per cent of foreign investment was provided by the UK in 1988–89 when 17 per cent came from the USA and 12 per cent from Japan. In the main, it also has been Japan and the USA which have supplanted the UK as a trading partner. Now about a quarter of Australia's exports go to Japan and 12 per cent to the USA, while each accounts for a fifth of her imports. Trade with other Asian countries, while still small, is growing rapidly and must hold enormous potential for future growth. For instance, exports to ASEAN countries accounted for 8 per cent in 1984–85 and 13 per cent of total exports in 1991–92.

There have been far-reaching changes in the composition of exports. Australia's reliance on wool and rural exports in the early post-war years is well known. Exports of textile fibres were half of total exports, and rural products 80 per cent in 1951–52. By 1988–89 the figures had declined to 10 per cent and 30 per cent, respectively, as exports of minerals and manufactures grew in significance. The 1960s were periods of high investment and rapid growth in mineral exploitation, as a result of which exports of coal and ores rose from 6 per cent to 24 per cent of total exports between 1951–52 and 1986–87. The other major change has been the rise in exports of manufactured goods. Over the period in question other exports (including manufactured products) increased from 15 per cent to 47 per cent.

By contrast, there have not been great shifts in the composition of Australia's imports. In 1991 manufactured products such as chemicals, textiles, metals, metal manufactures and transport equipment accounted for the major part of merchandise imports, which were nearly 76 per cent of total imports.

Three further aspects of Australia's long-term international economic situation are of considerable interest. The first concerns the 'terms of trade'. The data above firmly establish Australia's role as a primary- and minerals-based resource exporter with a growing contribution from manufactured exports. In the last 20 or so years a great deal of public discussion of natural resources and related questions of population growth and environmental issues has given the impression that resource-based products could well be in short supply on world markets. The prices Australia receives for her exports compared to the prices paid for imports do not reflect such a scarcity. Apart from some isolated surges in export prices, such as during the Korean and Vietnam wars, the terms of trade have pursued a downward trend. The message of the graph is that now a given quantity of exports purchases only half the quantity of imports that it did in 1948.

The second issue is the degree of protection afforded to Australian industry, particularly those sectors competing with imports. While rates of protection (tariffs, subsidies, quantitative restrictions on imports) are still high they have been moving down significantly. Thus the average effective rate of assistance (which is net assistance allowing for direct as well as indirect effects of tariffs, etc.) to the manufacturing sector has fallen from 36 per cent in 1969–70 to 19 per cent in 1986–87. These figures measure the percentage by which on average prices to firms are effectively raised by various forms of protection.

STATE OF THE CURRENT ACCOUNT

In the first half of the 1980s the authorities became concerned about increases then taking place in Australia's current-account deficit and the foreign indebtedness it generates. The current-account balance measures a country's receipts from exports and other income earned abroad less payments for imports and income earned by foreigners in Australia. In the figure, Australia's current-account balance and the goods and services balance (exports less imports) are expressed as percentages of GDP in order to illustrate their scale relative to total economic activity. When the current account is in deficit it can be shown that private investment exceeds private saving and/or public expenditure exceeds taxation receipts (a fiscal deficit); that is, there is net borrowing from abroad.

It can be seen from the graph that the current account has been in deficit for most of the time since World War II. Indeed, Australia has traditionally been a 'capital importing' country, borrowing from abroad to finance either private investment or public spending in excess of that which can be financed from private saving or taxation. At the end of the 1970s the deficit increased beyond its average level by several percentage points as a percentage of GDP. Was this due to a rise in profitable and worthwhile private or public investment opportunities, or was it perhaps caused by wasteful public spending? Would the extra foreign indebtedness it generated be a problem for economic management? If it were a problem, what should be done about it? Depending on the answers to these questions the deficits could be good or bad for the country.

The initial reaction of the authorities was to attempt to reduce the current-account deficit by tightening monetary policy (raising interest rates). The higher interest rates led to a slowdown in economic activity in 1986–87 and some decrease in the deficit, but following the stock market crash of October 1987 interest rates were reduced. The next move was to cut public spending and increase taxation turning the fiscal deficit into surpluses for four years from 1987–88. However, a coincidental rise in private investment meant that this budget deficit cutting did not generate a corresponding fall in the current-account deficit. The monetary authorities again tried high interest rates through 1988–89, the

Terms of trade 1947–1992.

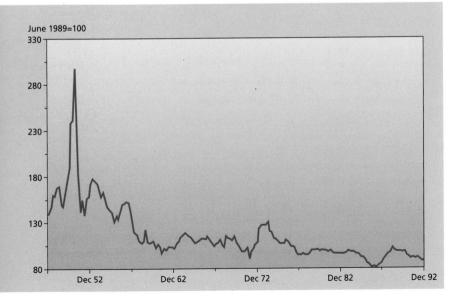

June 1989=100

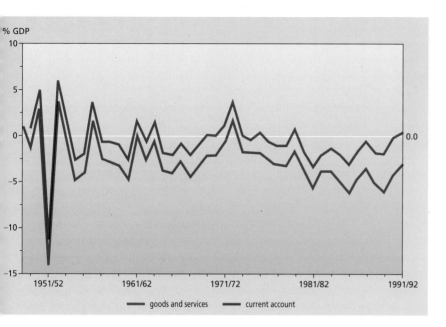

% GDP

goods and services — current account

Goods and services and current-account balances shown as percentages of gross domestic product.

result being that the economy went into the worst recession since the 1930s. Eventually, the current-account deficit fell, though the depressed state of the economy must account for much of the decrease.

For a variety of reasons, not the least being the devastation of the 1990–92 recession, it has come to be widely accepted in Australia that tight monetary policy is not an appropriate response to larger than usual current-account deficits. With market-determined exchange rates and minimal restrictions on borrowing from abroad, current-account deficits generated by high levels of private investment must be presumed to reflect high rates of profit, which attract foreign lending. The profitability of enterprises is the criterion which will give foreign lenders confidence that interest and dividend obligations are liable to be met. Domestic residents benefit from the further incomes (wages, rents, etc.) which the foreign investment produces. Policy action is then needed only to correct distortions in the investment/saving, borrowing or trade processes or when government budget deficits are regarded as excessive. Moreover, any distortions need to be corrected at their source. For example, do Australia's tax laws discourage private saving?

The goods and services and the current-account balances fluctuate with the level of activity. For instance, the current-account deficit fell during the 1982–83, 1987 and 1990–92 recessions. Further, there appears to have been a tendency for the goods and services deficit to fall through the 1980s and it was in surplus during the recession. It is too early to say whether this is explained solely by the severity of the 1990-92 recession or results from longer-run forces. Nor can anyone be sure how long the high rates of investment which have been supporting the deficit will last.   JDP

Trade relations

New Zealand

Trade between Australia and New Zealand is governed by the Australia New Zealand Closer Economic Relations Trade Agreement (ANZCERTA). This agreement came into effect in 1983. It replaced the New Zealand Australia Free Trade Agreement, 1966 (NAFTA). ANZCERTA is a free trade agreement. It contained a plan and schedule for the elimination of tariffs and other restrictions on 'substantially all' trade between Australia and New Zealand as required by Article XXIV of the General Agreement on Tariffs and Trade. Australia and New Zealand are both Contracting Parties to GATT as this international agreement governing international trade is known.

ANZCERTA has been negotiated in two phases. The first was in 1981–82; the second, leading to significant amplification of the agreement, in 1988.

ANZCERTA 1983

This agreement declared Australia and New Zealand (excluding the Cook and Tokelau Islands) to be a free-trade area (Article 2).

There were numerous annexes to this agreement. They provided for special treatment for a wide variety of products of industries which made cases to the governments for exceptions to the full rigour of Articles 4 (the progressive reduction of tariffs to zero) and 5 (the phasing out of quantitative restrictions and tariff quotas). These included a wide variety of products such as carpets, iron and steel, furniture, household appliances, motor vehicles and their components and, as with most free-trade areas and customs unions, several agricultural products including wheat, sugar, wine and dairy products.

The commitment to free trade was unequivocal but was hedged with all manner of special arrangements which could have remained substantially in effect until at least 1995. Provision was made (Article 22) for ANZCERTA to be reviewed in 1988 and, even in 1983, it seemed likely that by then the governments would be hard to convince that exceptions should be allowed to persist through to the mid-1990s.

The New Zealand prime minister, David Lange (on the left), shakes hands with his Australian counterpart, Bob Hawke, after conclusion of the review of the ANZCERTA free-trade agreement between the two countries in August 1988.

ANZCERTA 1988

The review of the agreement was initiated by the two prime ministers, Bob Hawke for Australia and David Lange for New Zealand, in November 1987. It was completed during the first half of 1988 and the agreement was formally amended by the prime ministers on 18 August 1988.

The result was that the agreement was amended by a Protocol on Acceleration of Free Trade in Goods and a Determination on Export Restrictions. These documents basically gave effect to a decision to remove virtually all impediments in the way of establishing a single trans-Tasman market by 1 July 1990.

In the hitherto vexed area of agriculture, there was an Exchange of Letters on Trans-Tasman Trade in Dairy Products and a Protocol on Harmonisation of Quarantine Administrative Barriers. That means that after some 25 years of often difficult negotiations the farming communities in both countries have been persuaded that protective barriers are no longer needed between the two countries.

Perhaps the most important of the 1988 understandings is the Protocol on Trade in Services. It brings services, or non-merchandise transactions, such as travel, insurance, banking, advertising and consultancies, within the scope of ANZCERTA on the basis of rules which are relatively clear. It remains to be seen, however, whether they will lead to the elimination of discriminatory practices enforced by professional associations and other vocational groups such as trade unions. Growth of transactions in the non-merchandise aspects of the economic association between Australia and New Zealand have been very encouraging.

Merchandise trade between the two countries has flourished since 1966, when NAFTA came into force. That agreement and ANZCERTA have done much to change the attitudes both of politicians and business. Trade has grown rapidly as the table shows.

In 1991–92 Australia was New Zealand's largest market, taking 19 per cent of total exports (for comparison, Japan took 16 per cent and the USA 13 per cent of New Zealand's exports). Australia was also ranked first in the statistics of suppliers of imports to New Zealand in that year, with 22 per cent (USA and Japan were second and third with 18 per cent and 15 per cent, respectively).

Trade with Australia is now fundamental for New Zealand's export-oriented economy. Not only is it the major partner in merchandise trade, it is important in non-merchandise earnings. Indeed, a specific objective of ANZCERTA is to stimulate earnings from exports of services between the two countries.

This is indicative of the success of NAFTA/ANZCERTA from New Zealand's point of view. While Australia has gained in absolute terms, its overall performance after over twenty-five years could be described as consolidation in the face of tough competition from Japan, other newly industrialised countries in Asia, the European Community and the USA.

New Zealand's export performance in the Australian market has been encouraging from its point of view. The sequence of negotiations and the progressive reduction of import and financial restrictions has changed attitudes in both business and commerce. The ANZCERTA arrangements have won public acceptance in both countries.

ANZCERTA 1988 should further encourage the growth of trade and service transactions between the two countries. Nevertheless, both countries are oriented to the international market and are not seeking to achieve self-sufficiency in the ANZCERTA area. They compete with each other, notably in meat and dairy products and in some manufactured goods.

The success of the Australia–New Zealand free trade area may best be measured, in the future, by an examination of the extent to which it has helped both partners to increase exports of elaborately transformed manufactures (as distinct from processed raw materials) as well as the agricultural and mineral products they produce so efficiently.

ANZCERTA has changed the nature of the trading relationship between Australia and New Zealand. The process of harmonising business law, and integrating important sectors such as air transport is under way. From a trading point of view Australia and New Zealand may be seen in 10 years' time as a single trading entity, as the European Community is

AUSTRALIA–NEW ZEALAND MERCHANDISE TRADE			
years ending 30 June	exports to New Zealand ($NZ millions)	imports from New Zealand ($NZ millions)	ratio Australia: New Zealand
1969–70	81	193	2.4 : 1
1974–75	168	536	3.2 : 1
1979–80	605	945	1.6 : 1
1984–85	1,767	2,337	1.3 : 1
1989–90	2,750	3,257	1.2 : 1
1991–92	3,188	3,428	1.1 : 1

increasingly regarded. As a joint ministerial statement released after the review of the agreement in 1993 put it:

> We have consolidated work already under way as a result of the 1988 CER Review . . . and updated or amended areas of the Agreement . . . The CER Rules of Origin . . . have been made more predictable and transparent.
>
> . . . there has been a substantial liberalization of bilateral trade in services since 1988. In 1992, Australia removed its banking inscription and New Zealand removed its broadcasting inscriptions . . .
>
> We are pleased to note the important step forward our Governments have taken by agreeing to create a single trans-Tasman aviation market. This will bring increased competition with benefits to consumers and the economies of both countries . . .
>
> In response to the views of business, our governments agreed that tax should be on the Review agenda. We have discussed technical aspects of trans-Tasman tax, including equity taxation, with a view to reducing any specific tax impediments to trade and investment . . .
>
> This Review is not an end point. It is a further step in a relationship that will continue to evolve in response to developments in Australia and New Zealand and in the wider world . . .
>
> In developing CER we remain committed to the goal of improving the capacity of our economies to participate effectively and competitively in the dynamic Asia–Pacific region and in the global economy.

AB

CHINA

In recent years Australia's exports to the Northeast Asian economies have accounted for around 44 per cent of total exports.

Of this group Japan is the most important, accounting for about a quarter of the total exports and for about two-thirds of the group total. China accounts for about 3 per cent of Australian total exports, a similar order of magnitude to exports to the 'other two Chinas', Taiwan and Hong Kong. In 1990–91 the value of exports to China reached $1.3 billion.

Australian imports from China account for about 3 per cent of total imports, valued in 1990–91 at $1.5 million. There was a substantial trade balance in favour of Australia which has been reversed. Imports have grown faster than exports from about 1 per cent of total imports in 1977–78 to 3 per cent in 1990–91.

Exports to China have tended to vary widely. This reflects their domination by agricultural products. In 1990–91 wool accounted for about 17 per cent of Australian exports to China, and wheat for about 23 per cent. Other major export items were metal ores (17 per cent), non-ferrous metal (2 per cent) and coal (2 per cent). Australia's steel exports to China are also expected to grow rapidly. This group of resource-based products accounts for about 60 per cent of Australian exports to China. The variability in exports reflects both changes in export availability in Australia and the impact of the process of reform in China on demand.

Australian imports from China are dominated by textiles and clothing, which account for nearly 38 per cent of the total. The next largest items are machinery (6 per cent), electronics (4 per cent) and food (3 per cent).

The pattern of trade between the two economies is complementary. Australia is relatively well endowed with natural resources, the products of which are in demand in a rapidly industrialising country like China. In turn, China's exports reflect its competitiveness in labour-intensive products, such as textiles, clothing and some machinery.

Further rapid economic growth in China will increase the level of demand and raise the importance of China in Australian trade. It could do this much faster than for the other Northeast Asian economies because of China's size and scale of export demands. One factor influencing the rate of growth in China will be the growth in China's exports to the rest of the world, which will in turn depend on the access to markets for China's products. Australia has a keen interest therefore in China's international trade performance.

Another issue of mutual interest to both economies is the security of supply as perceived by China in the procurement of materials for industrialisation. This is likely to be a major issue for China, again because of the potential scale of its purchases in world markets. One method of alleviating this concern is to invest in industries supplying the materials in the source country. China has major investments in Australia, some in iron ore mines in Western Australia, and another is a share of an aluminium smelter in Victoria. Investments in coal mines are also being discussed.

Australia is also an investor in China. Projects include a large number related to agricultural production or the processing of agricultural products. These effectively transfer technology from Australia to China. Other investments are in labourintensive industries and some tourist projects. This type of two-way investment is likely to continue as a feature of the economic relationship between the two countries. CF

Society

Population

Previous page *A crowded surf beach on the shores of Bass Strait at Torquay, Victoria. The fine climate, sand, surf and open space of Australia has formed a society that values the outdoor life.*

Australia ranks sixth among the world's 174 nations in land area, and 44th in population numbers(17.8 million in 1992). Although the size of the continent is equivalent to the landmass of the USA (excluding Alaska and Hawaii) its total population amounts only to that of New York City. In 1988, at the bicentennial of European settlement, over 16 million people lived in Australia, compared with just under 3 million in

Spectators at a rodeo at Mount Isa in Queensland. The Aboriginal population of Australia is now reckoned to be about a quarter of a million, but this figure includes people of mixed race.

1888, and 1,030 Europeans and at least 300,000 Aborigines in January 1788. The discrepancy between population and area creates an illusion that Australia is an empty continent, still to be populated. This apparent emptiness, however, is explained by the fact that Australia is the most arid continent, and only about one-fifth of the land – along parts of the coast – can support more than sparse settlement.

The nature of the physical environment goes far towards explaining the size and distribution of Australia's population, and its high level of urbanisation. Furthermore, that European settlement is so recent accounts for other major features of the country's population, including its relative youth, and high growth rate – compared with the populations of other industrialised countries – and the continuing importance of immigration.

The outdoor, physical and beer-drinking Australian male of popular tradition, although not representative, is still a reality.

GROWTH

Since 1788, more than a third of Australia's population growth has been due directly to immigration, but its contribution has varied greatly over time. During the pioneering stages of European settlement – until the end of the 1850s gold rushes – immigration was the mainstay of population growth. Initially, most of the arrivals were convicts and their keepers, but from the 1830s assisted immigration became essential to the populating of Australia (see also pp. 88–9). Because of labour shortages and the high cost of passages from Britain, colonies undertook to meet part or all of immigrants' travel expenses. For about 150 years, this assisted immigration was like a tap which was turned on in boom and shut off in recession.

Distance from Britain also led to recruitment of labour from South Sea Islands, especially for work on the cotton and sugar plantations of Queensland and northern New South Wales. Under labouring contracts, about 57,000 'Kanakas', from island groups such as Vanuatu and the Solomons, were brought to Australia during the second half of the nineteenth century.

A man from the Indian subcontinent in Victoria Market, Melbourne. As the level of European immigration has declined in recent years, that of Asian immigration has increased. There were, for example, 5,000 more people born in India living in Australia in 1991 than in 1990.

Spectators at the Northcote Festival, Melbourne. Many young Australians are of non-English speaking backgrounds.

During the gold rushes of the 1850s (see also pp. 94–5) Australia's total population passed 1 million. Australia was by then better known and over the remainder of the century assisted immigration became relatively less important. During the economic recession of the 1890s, the rate of population growth fell to the lowest level hitherto recorded as immigration all but ceased and natural increase faltered. Even the 1890s gold rush to Western Australia did little to restore population growth; internal migration, rather than movement from overseas, was the main demographic response, and most of the influx originated from regions of high unemployment, especially in Victoria and South Australia.

During the first half of the twentieth century, the rate of population growth continued to fluctuate as immigration waxed and waned and as marriage and birth rates varied in response to economic conditions. Before the outbreak of World War I, the annual rate of population growth was about 2 per cent, but the war marked the start of a period of almost 30 years during which this growth could not be maintained. The war necessitated a virtual suspension of immigration, and although movement resumed in the 1920s the Great Depression intervened and brought assisted arrivals virtually to a halt from 1931 to 1937. More so than before the birth rate responded to the impact of recession as many couples postponed or curtailed family formation. For the only time in Australia's history the annual rate of population growth fell below 1 per cent.

Not until after World War II did national population growth become a major issue in government policy. In 1945, Australia was a small nation of only 7.4 million, and population issues loomed large after the Japanese surrender. The reasons for fostering growth amounted to much more than a desire to strengthen the country militarily after the recent threat of Japanese invasion: the domestic labour force in the post-war period was insufficient to power industrialisation and make up the leeway in housing construction and national development projects. The accelerated decline of the birth rate in the 1930s had exacerbated the problem since its legacy after the war was an unusually low number of school leavers entering the labour force. In 1945, the government launched a programme to increase Australia's population by 1 per cent a year through immigration, and thereby achieve a total annual growth rate of 2 per cent.

Promotion of population growth in Australia remained an objective of government policy for more than 25 years after World War II and immigration was long sustained, on average, at levels about sufficient to achieve the 1 per cent target. Another, completely unexpected, boost to population growth in the late 1940s and 1950s was the baby boom. This came about not only through catching up of family formation delayed by the war, but also through a sustained marriage boom which saw record numbers marrying and having children.

Rapid growth and economic expansion dominated the quarter century after World War II. Without passage assistance, immigration to Australia would have

POPULATION GROWTH IN AUSTRALIA SINCE 1790

Year	Total ('000s)	Annual growth rate (%)	Year	Total ('000s)	Annual growth rate (%)
1790	2				
1800	5	9.6	1900	3,765	1.8
1810	12	9.1	1910	4,425	1.6
1820	34	11.0	1920	5,411	2.0
1830	70	7.5	1930	6,501	1.9
1840	190	10.5	1940	7,078	0.9
1850	405	7.9	1950	8,307	1.6
1860	1,146	11.0	1960	10,392	2.3
1870	1,648	3.7	1970	12,663	2.0
1880	2,232	3.1	1980	14,726	1.5
1890	3,151	3.5	1985	15,901	1.4
			1990	17,169	1.5

Totals estimated as at 31 December. Aborigines included from 1970. The figure for 1987 is an estimate of the resident population.
Sources: D. T. Rowland, 'Population Growth and Distribution', in United Nations, *Population of Australia*, ESCAP, p. 16 (Bangkok, 1982)
Australian Bureau of Statistics, *Australian Demographic Statistics*, March Quarter 1988, Australian Bureau of Statistics Catalogue No. 3101.0 (Canberra, 1988)
Jing Shu and Siew Ean Khoo, *Australia's Population Trends and Prospects 1992*, Bureau of Immigration Research, Australian Government Publishing Service (Canberra, 1993)

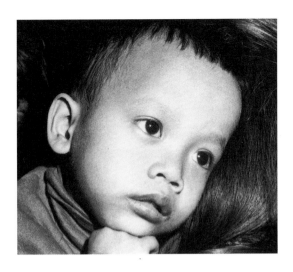

Four-year-old Cambodian boy being taken to new parents in Australia in 1976. Abolition in 1973 of the previous pro-European policy on immigration was followed by a commitment to take in refugees from the war-torn areas of Indo-China.

the movement from the UK and Eire. Southern European migration entailed a further broadening of the origins of European migration, although the majority came without government assistance and relied on relatives to sponsor them and assist in finding employment and accommodation.

The process whereby compatriots encourage and assist with the migration of others has been called 'chain migration'; this is most typical of people from rural backgrounds and has contributed to the high levels of residential concentration of southern Europeans in Australian cities. During the 1960s, the volume of migration to Australia soared to a record level as the success of the migration programme was evidenced in the ability of the economy and the community to absorb great numbers of immigrants from diverse origins.

Another major policy change in immigration resulted in the lifting of restrictions on non-Europeans. In the 1950s and 1960s, small numbers of non-Europeans were admitted, provided that they had skills and qualifications needed in Australia. By embarking on this course, albeit in a token way initially, Australia was following a trend in international migration towards a weakening of racial barriers and an emphasis in immigration policies on occupational skills rather than national origins. Despite the allowance for immigration of small numbers of well-educated non-Europeans, racial discrimination continued in Australian immigration policies, provoking criticism from the press and politicians, especially in Africa and Asia.

The main step in removing restrictions on non-European immigration did not occur until 1973, when the Whitlam government adopted a policy of non-discrimination on the grounds of race, colour or nationality in the selection of immigrants (see also pp. 236–7. Despite the extent of this change, the policy has received bipartisan support. In the late 1970s, the Fraser government affirmed its responsibility to assist refugees, and began admitting tens of thousands of Indo-Chinese, together with smaller numbers of refugees from other regions. A final change, which made the non-discriminatory policy more effective, was the broadening of criteria for family reunion. Admission requirements still reflect Australian social mores and law such as the unacceptability of polygamous marriages. But since the late 1970s, Australian residents have been able to sponsor the migration of non-dependent children, parents and siblings in addition to close dependent relatives (spouses, dependent children and aged parents). Refugee movements, together with an emphasis on family reunion in the immigration programme, created a large-scale wave of Asian migration in the 1980s; this marked a radical departure from the belief that national unity and social harmony were necessarily founded on cultural and racial homogeneity (see also pp. 266–7).

In the 1980s, the lack of long-range objectives for immigration led to marked variations in the annual intake of settlers. When the government abandoned population growth as an objective for immigration, economic migration – the notion that immigration could be used to enhance Australia's economic development – also became less influential.

From the 1970s, the Australian economy was considered unlikely to benefit from a continued large inflow of the large numbers of unskilled workers who had been so important to industrialisation and resource development in previous decades. Thus the objectives of immigration in the 1970s and 1980s gave more emphasis to humanitarian and social considerations – especially assisting Asian refugees and facilitating family reunion by enabling settlers to sponsor the immigration of relatives.

Unrestricted migration of New Zealanders, who do not require a visa to enter Australia, also accounted for a substantial proportion of immigrant arrivals during this time. Yet towards the end of the 1980s, government interest in economic migration revived; there was then much interest in the view that immigrants with occupational skills and capital for investment could bring substantial economic benefits to the country, and efforts were made to increase their numbers in the settler intake. Migration reached record levels in 1988-89, but has since dropped substantially.

In the post-war period, departures have offset many of the gains from overseas. Charles Price, a prominent writer on Australian immigration, has shown that departure is a normal characteristic of any large-scale immigration and only refugees, or others in jeopardy in their home country, have low departure rates and rapid uptake of Australian citizenship. Price estimated that Australia lost almost 22 per cent of the settlers who arrived between 1947 and 1983, for reasons such as dissatisfaction, family responsibilities, better prospects overseas and an original intention to leave eventually, despite arriving as a permanent settler.

BIRTH RATE

Even as early as the 1880s, the birth rate had dropped in Australia as couples sought to limit the size of their families. In a young country where the need for population growth seemed self-evident, the decline of the birth rate caused consternation and raised uncertainty about the future. The economic crisis of the 1890s added impetus to the fall and provoked Australia's first forebodings of population decline. The prospect of population decline was to surface again amid the marked drop in the birth rate during the 1930s and the 1970s, but the 1890s experience provoked especially fervent discussion because the causes of change were unknown and occasioned wild speculations about national decadence.

Until the last quarter of the nineteenth century, married women in Australia bore an average of more than six children. From the 1880s, average family size declined rapidly and the norm of two or three children was already typical among women who had their children before World War II. Thus in a span of only 50 years, from the 1880s to the 1930s, the transition occurred from the large to the small family norm. Urbanisation and industrialisation created the social context for the change, and by the 1880s events such as the introduction of compulsory schooling initiated the decline. It has been argued that the introduction of compulsory schooling in Australia during the 1870s and 1880s made large families an economic liability – for example, by restricting children's time to work or help their parents – and a hindrance to

providing an advantaged upbringing for children. Methods of contraception became more available and more widely known around this time as well; while contraception provided the means to achieve family size goals, it did not provide the motivation to limit fertility and was not a cause of change in itself.

Every generation born since the start of the twentieth century has had an average family size of between two and three children. The lowest figure recorded so far was for women born in the early 1900s, whose child-bearing was unusually restricted as a result of the Great Depression and World War II. By contrast, in the post-war period the baby boom years, from 1946 to 1961, saw a temporary departure from the long-term trend towards the two-child family. A baby boom had been anticipated after the war as demobilisation brought a rush of delayed marriages. Yet, unexpectedly, the boom continued, and lasted right through the 1950s. This second phase of the boom was due mainly to a marriage revolution: much higher proportions of people were marrying and having children. The high level of post-war immigration also contributed to the baby boom, since it added to the numbers in the main ages of family formation.

After 1961, the birth rate declined again, with only one interruption, and has been at a very low ebb since 1976. Many changes have brought the birth rate to this low level including: (1) a decline in the proportions marrying; (2) an increase in childlessness within marriage; (3) greater resort to abortion and sterilisation; (4) secularisation, which has encouraged a break with long-standing traditions about starting a family, and greater emphasis on individual self-fulfilment. In the 1980s, the changing position of women in society, shown in their rising educational attainment and employment, indicated that motherhood and domestic duties have ceased to be all-consuming roles for Australian women. Social scientists anticipate that the birth rate will remain low in the 1990s, for similar reasons.

DEATH RATE

Throughout much of the nineteenth century, 1 in 10 infants died in their first year, compared with less than 1 in 100 in 1992. The high death toll in infancy and childhood meant that in the nineteenth century the average life span was only about 50 years. Greater life expectancy has resulted mostly from the prevention of diseases which once caused high mortality among children and young adults.

Infant survival has improved with changes in child care and nutrition, together with control over communicable diseases such as diphtheria, typhus, typhoid and poliomyelitis. Among young adults,

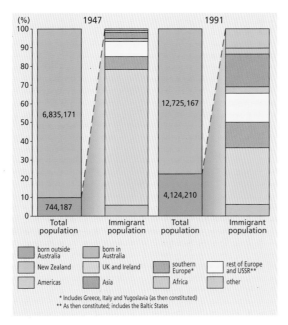

Countries of birth recorded in the Census of 1947 and 1991.

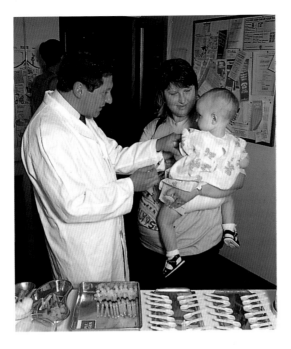

Improvements in child care and immunisation improved life expectancy at birth for males from 51 in 1900 to 73.9 in 1990 and for females from 55 in 1900 to 80 in 1990.

improvements in living conditions and medical procedures have appreciably reduced death from childbirth and infectious diseases, including tuberculosis. Similarly, tuberculosis has ceased to be a major cause

of death in middle and later life, but heart disease and cancer have taken a greater toll as a rising proportion of deaths has occurred at advanced ages.

During the 1950s and 1960s, the death rates of the elderly remained unchanged, especially for men, suggesting that a final plateau had been reached in their life expectancy. Since about 1971, however, there have been notable declines in death rates at all older ages, mainly because of a reduction in deaths from heart disease. Medical progress, along with an emphasis on healthier diet, less smoking, and more exercise have contributed to this change.

Overall, the decline of mortality since the late nineteenth century is attributable to two main causes: improvements in standards of living (including better nutrition, housing and sanitation) and medical interventions. The contribution of medical science has included not only immunisation and treatment of diseases but also extending knowledge of, and education in, the prevention of ill health; many improvements in environmental conditions and lifestyles have flowed from the latter. Changes in death rates continue – even at the oldest ages – but they now represent relatively modest additions to life expectancy. Future gains could depend less on medical science and more on education about risk reduction, in relation to diet, exercise, smoking, drinking, driving, drug addiction and the new threat of AIDS (acquired immune deficiency syndrome).

Population structure and ageing

The age structure of a population provides both a synopsis of its history and an indication of its future development: for example, the impact of past events affecting births, deaths and migration is often preserved in the differing sizes of age groups, and future inbuilt variations in the numbers entering school, commencing work or retiring can be read from the age structure.

In 1881 Australia had a young age structure with 39 per cent aged 0 to 14 years and 2.4 per cent aged 65 and over. In 1991, Australia still had a relatively young age profile compared with those of other industrialised countries: 22.4 per cent were aged 0 to 14 years in 1991, 11.3 per cent were 65 years and over and the shape of the pyramid remained broadly triangular, whereas 'old' age structures, such as that projected for Australia in 2031, are rectangular with similar proportions in most age groups.

Despite the fairly youthful triangular form of the 1991 age structure, the population had been ageing for most of the previous hundred years. The one exception was during the baby boom, when the rise in the birth rate temporarily reversed the ageing process by increasing the proportion of children in the population. A fall in the birth rate is the most influential factor in population ageing because smaller families lead to a lower representation of children and, hence, to a higher representation of people of working age and older.

The changing representation of different age groups in the population influences the size of the labour force relative to the numbers of children and retired people and affects the demand for goods, amenities and services – such as maternity hospitals, education facilities, housing and nursing homes.

The future holds substantial changes in these areas as the ageing of the population continues and the large baby boom generation (born 1946–61) advances into middle age and later life. The movement of bigger generations into older ages is itself a force for population increase – one which will make zero population growth in Australia an impossibility before the second quarter of the twenty-first century.   DTR

ABORIGINAL POPULATION

In 1975, the Report of the National Population Inquiry said of Aboriginal Australians: 'They probably have the highest growth rate, the highest birth rate, the highest death rate, the worst health and housing, and the lowest educational, occupational, economic, social and legal status of any identifiable section of the Australian population.' For 150 years after the foundation of European settlement the Aboriginal population suffered a drastic decline. Their original numbers will never be known accurately: a commonly quoted estimate is 300,000 in 1788, but modern archaeological evidence suggests that 750,000 was a possibility. Demographer Leonard Smith estimated that, by 1921, Aboriginal numbers had fallen to less than 61,000 through a combination of disasters including the ravages of epidemic diseases such as smallpox, venereal diseases causing sterility and proneness to abortion and other diseases related to confinement in unhygienic living conditions. Added to this were the effects of killings by early European settlers, social disruption and malnourishment and starvation resulting from the destruction of native plants and animals in the course of pastoral development.

The Notallwotall tribe of north Queensland in 1900. No one knows for certain the size of the Aboriginal population at the outset of European settlement, but it may have been as high as three-quarters of a million.

Subsequent demographic recovery brought Aboriginal numbers to more than 100,000 in 1971 and 265,378 at the 1991 Census – still far below the suggested 1788 figure. In 1991 the figures showed that about two-thirds of the Aborigines were enumerated in urban areas, and much of the dramatic rise in numbers during the 1970s and 1980s was due to more urban residents of Aboriginal and Torres Strait Islander origin identifying themselves as such. The population defined as Aboriginal consists not only of full-bloods but also of persons of mixed descent, including some of less than half Aboriginal origin.

Statements about the health and mortality of the contemporary Aboriginal population, however, mainly refer to Aborigines in rural areas, where there is a high representation of people of predominantly Aboriginal descent, whose way of life is quite different from that of modern, urban Australia. During the early 1980s, Aborigines in non-urban Australia had an expectation of life at birth of no more than 55 years. This figure was well below the 71 years for males and 78 years for females in the total population of Australia, because of the high mortality of Aboriginal infants and adults. Health programmes have made considerable progress in improving child survival but, in the late 1980s, the risk of death in infancy and early childhood remained higher for Aborigines than for the rest of the population (see also pp 238–9).

The excessive number of deaths of Aboriginal infants is associated particularly with low birth weight and gastro-intestinal and respiratory infections, which stem from inadequacies in diet, housing, sanitation and health care in the pre-natal and post-natal periods. The work of demographers such as Alan Gray has shown that Aboriginal adults also have exceptionally high death rates in middle age – 'much higher than in any national population anywhere' – again because of exceptional health risks in their environment. The high death rate is mostly due to circulatory diseases, especially ischaemic heart disease, together with injuries, poisoning and respiratory diseases. Alcohol abuse is a contributing factor in many deaths and, unlike infant mortality, the problem of high adult mortality is not necessarily solved by improvements in health services.

The recent transition from high to low birth rate has been a feature of both rural and urban Aboriginal life. This national trend has been facilitated in rural areas and small towns through Aboriginal health programmes which have increased access to family planning. The average Aboriginal family size fell from six children, in the late 1960s, to about three in the late 1970s, reflecting changing attitudes to the costs and benefits of children. While this change might be interpreted as a sign of greater acceptance of certain Western values, diversity remains an overriding feature of the Aboriginal population. Although only a small population, comprising 1.4 per cent of the Australian total, the Aboriginal population is now as varied as any group in Australia in terms of place of residence, occupation, income, religion, language, intermarriage, descent and degree of participation in the wider society.   DTR

Language

Although the Australian Constitution does not provide for a *de jure* official language, English is the national language, which fulfils most of the functions of an official language.

ABORIGINAL LANGUAGES

Of the 150 Aboriginal languages still spoken, about 100 are used by only a small number of speakers and are most likely to be extinct within a generation or two. The remaining 50 are spoken by a few hundred or, in a few cases, a few thousand. The most widely used include Warlpiri, Aranda (Central Australia), and Pitjantjatjara (South and Central Australia). Genocide, assimilationist pressure and detribalisation have led to rapid language shift and the death of about 50 Aboriginal languages since the European colonisation of Australia. At the same time, a number of English-based Aboriginal creoles have developed, which are replacing traditional languages over an extensive part of northern Australia. There are also Aboriginal varieties of English used by monolingual fringe Aborigines and, in certain functions, by speakers of Aboriginal languages and creoles (Kriol). In the 1991 Census 44,327 people were recorded as using one or more Aboriginal languages at home.

AUSTRALIAN ENGLISH

There is a distinct Australian national variety of English which probably originated as a combination of (mainly southeastern) English regional dialects used by those migrating, or transported, to the Australian colonies.

Australian English differs from its British and American counterparts in vocabulary, phonology and grammar. Contrast Australian *footpath* with British *pavement* and American *sidewalk*; Australian (American) *truck*, with British *lorry*; Australian (British) *petrol* with American *gas(oline)*.

Examples of characteristically Australian words are *homestead* (main residence on a large farm), *brick-veneer* (a house whose external walls consist of a timber framework and a single layer of non-structural brickwork), *home unit* (one of a number of apartments in the same building, owned under a separate title), *chook pen* (fowl enclosure), *migrant* (immigrant) and *paddock* (enclosed piece of land). Among Australian idioms are: *do your block* (become angry), *hear it on the bush telegraph* (hear a rumour), and *shout someone a drink* (treat someone to a drink).

There are *diminutive* formations ending in *-o*: for example, *garbo* (garbage collector) and *milko* (milkman). These are also applied to names: for example, *Johnno* and *Kenso* (from *John* and *Kensington*).

In phonology, there is a continuum from broad Australian to cultivated Australian, the social variety closest to standard British English. In the middle is general Australian, the variety used by the majority of the population. The variation is most apparent in vowel sounds, such as those in *main* and *bowl*. The broad variety forms are closer to Standard British [main] and [bʌul] *mine* and *bowel*.

The social factors determining the use of the varieties of Australian English are: sex (females tend more towards the cultivated and less towards the broad variety than males), social class, level of education and type of school. (People who attended non-government schools are more likely to speak cultivated Australian than those from government schools.) There is little regional variation in phonology in comparison with Britain or North America, but more than was previously assumed. For instance, Sydney speakers tend to pronounce *castle* with an [a:] (as in *bar*), while in Melbourne [æ:] as in *bat* predominates. In *dance*, the [a:] is far more usual in Adelaide, and the [æ:] in Brisbane.

In grammar, standard Australian English tends to follow British norms, but there are non-standard past tenses *come*, *done* and *run*. (For example, 'when

Multilingual signs in Melbourne. Twelve languages other than English are spoken at home by more than 50,000 Australians. In 1990 government funding assisted over 500 community organisations speaking 49 languages to maintain their cultural links.

we were away, a big fire *come* down and killed all the trees'.)

In vocabulary there are also some variations between the states. A corner shop is a *milk bar* in Victoria and New South Wales, but a *deli* in South Australia. A pork sausage is a *fritz* in South Australia, *a pork German* in Victoria, and *a devon* in New South Wales, while a suitcase is a *port* in Queensland and northern New South Wales.

In communicating, Australians tend to be informal and stress solidarity rather than power. So firstnames are used to address people regardless of age, status and gender.

The Australian education systems generally promote reading and writing at the expense of the spoken word. The Australian English vocabulary is codified in the *Macquarie Dictionary*, which treats all items used in Australia as standard and marks distinctively British and American ones. The Australian Broadcasting Corporation has a Committee on Spoken English which makes decisions on the questionable pronunciations.

COMMUNITY LANGUAGES

There are about a hundred languages other than English used in Australia which were transplanted through immigration. Such languages have been used in Australia since early in the history of white settlement – in nineteenth-century cities, on the goldfields, where there was a fairly rapid turnover of languages, and in rural German-speaking enclaves, in South Australia and western Victoria. In these settlements, German was maintained for three to six generations.

The mass immigration programme launched in 1947 led to a marked change in Australia's population composition and ultimately the policy of multiculturalism. The recognition of Australia's linguistic resources and needs, associated with a new national identity, is reflected in policies supportive of community languages (so called since 1975 to stress their legitimacy in Australian society) in education, radio, TV, libraries and interpreting/translating.

According to the 1991 Census 14.8 per cent of the population speak a language other than English at home. There are 12 community languages used at home by over 50,000 speakers (in rank order) Italian, Greek, Chinese, Croatian|Serbian, Arabic, German, Vietnamese, Spanish, Polish, Macedonian, Filipino languages, and Maltese. The numbers would be considerably higher for some languages if non-home domains were considered. Melbourne is Australia's most multilingual city.

The 1991 Census showed a variation in shift from *home* use of the first language to English by the first generation from 3 per cent among Mandarin speakers from Taiwan to 57 per cent among Dutch. Language shift tends to be highest in the 25–34 age group and lowest among the elderly of the first generation. It increases markedly in the second generation.

Community languages have undergone changes to adapt to the needs of the new environment. This includes use of English vocabulary (for example, *beach, gum tree, chemist, high school*) and the transference of English meanings to words in the first language (for example, Italian fattoria (farm) being used to mean 'factory'). However, there is much variation between individuals and between families or communities. Some community languages are experiencing structural change (such as loss of case and verb endings, generalisation of one definite article, and a change in word order).

LANGUAGE POLICY

In 1982 the federal government initiated an inquiry into the need for a national policy on languages. It addressed such areas as: the teaching of English as a first, second and foreign language, adult illiteracy, Aboriginal languages, language needs of people with communication handicaps, teaching languages other than English, language needs in overseas relationships and translating/interpreting.

The subsequent report (1984) and a government document outlining a National Policy on Languages (1987) established four guiding principles: competence in English, maintenance and development of languages other than English, provision of services in languages other than English and opportunities for learning second languages. These are incorporated into the Australian Language and Literacy Policy (1991), which emphasises English literacy more than the National Policy on Languages.

In recent years, much emphasis has been placed on training in the languages of Australia's major Asian trading partners, especially Japanese and Chinese, while retaining other aspects of the policy. The states themselves have been active in developing complementary language policies, especially in education. Several (for example, Victoria and South Australia) are gradually making a second language part of the normal education of all school children.

Features of linguistic pluralism in Australia are a telephone interpreter service, the teaching of a diversity of languages at primary and secondary levels, multilingual radio stations, a multilingual TV network (using English subtitles), and widespread public library facilities in languages other than English. The language policy is served by a National Languages and Literacy Institute.   MC

Values

The British took nothing of Aboriginal ideals or values when they settled on the eastern seaboard and penetrated the hazardous interior. Australia's predominantly European constellation of values derives from the standards and expectations held by those segments of British society which transferred to the distant continent and dealt with the exigencies of survival and exploitation. Such values have translated the needs and demands of immigrant peoples who later came looking for security and opportunity. They have been promulgated in Australian law-making, enforced by regulation, celebrated in national art and literature and researched and reviewed by social scientists.

The British brought ideas and hopes fostered by philosophies current in late eighteenth-century Europe. The revolutionary cry of liberty, equality, fraternity inspired settlers in many parts of the New World, and Thomas Paine's *The Rights of Man* (1791–2) distilled the more fervid ideals of English people. In Australia these ideas and values were construed as political freedom, material opportunity and the comradeship necessary for survival in the alien and unpredictable environment. It was a male idiom, but it served well as a means of expressing an emerging nationalism.

A less-heroic philosophy, Benthamite utilitarianism (based on the social and political teaching in England of Jeremy Bentham (1748–1832)), influenced English reformists and also Australian political and administrative arrangements. Its emphasis on 'the greatest happiness for the greatest number' tempered the rugged individualism typical of colonial Australia. Notwithstanding, attitudes to land were exploitive and to society instrumental. Overseas investment drove the economy. Primary production and expansion of exports were paramount. This has not changed.

Australians maintain an ingrained respect for material and utilitarian values. 'The Australian Dream' of owning a house on its defined plot of land tells of the primacy given to material security and personal wealth. Three out of four adults own their own home (usually mortgaged for the first 20 years). Home ownership increases with age such that 85 per cent of people over 40 years live in their own home. When Australians are asked to list their goals in life, security takes first place for most. Good family life comes second. Prosperity, excitement, importance and status are much less desired.

In 200 years of European settlement the state has always been central to economic, political and social life. The early necessity for government's involvement in everything became a habit. Australians expect government to provide the answers. Australian insistence on egalitarianism necessitated authoritative regulation to ensure that social, political and economic equality was maintained. Equality and authority were obverse sides of the same coin and its value dominated Australian political thought.

Australians have created legends that celebrate popular ideals and values. A persistent account portrays the archetypal Australian committed to egalitarianism, mateship, toughness, scepticism and fair play. Participation in the major wars of the twentieth century reinforced the legend celebrated in the Anzac 'digger'. The model of the tough, resourceful, sardonic 'Aussie' battler simplifies a national ethos which is far more sophisticated and subtle than the populist picture permits. The image ignores the extent to which cleavages associated with the multiple

dimensions of sex, class and race and the vagaries of Australian multiculturalism cut across the revered mosaic.

Hedonism comes naturally in Australia where a warm, balmy climate fosters delight in the senses. Australians revel in sunlight and colour, surf and sand, good food, wine and beer. The body should be beautiful and it is very important. A pervasive national image, carried on billboards throughout this century, has been the tall, blond, bronzed surf lifesaver. In wartime, the hero wears a slouch hat and his initiative, bravery and wry sense of humour inspired the Anzac legend. In the *Crocodile Dundee* films of the 1980s Paul Hogan played a contemporary version of the tough Australian bushman with dry humour that has international appeal, but there are less-flattering stereotypes emphasising an anti-intellectual, beer-swilling, slothful sensualism.

Hedonism links easily with enthusiasm for leisure. Standard hours of work are relatively low. Under award regulations the average Australian works 35–37 hours a week and takes an annual holiday of 4–6 weeks. The weekend, especially the long weekend, is a highly valued institution and recognised as such in legal argument and judicial decision about working conditions. Employees are compensated with substantial pay-loadings for weekend work.

Paradoxically a national enthusiasm for leisure is countered by general satisfaction with work. The Australian Values Surveys in 1983 and 1989 found 85 per cent of workers content with their job and of those expressing negative feelings most owned simply to having mixed feelings about it. Work satisfaction increases with age; teenage workers are most likely to be discontented and people in their forties most contented at work. Trade unionism and rights to industrial action are strongly endorsed. But trade unions, whose influence is often seen to be too great, are regarded with ambivalence and suspicion. Australians' political and industrial values are sharply divided by class and labour-market situations.

Sport figures significantly in the depiction of Australian values. Fine climate, open space and an egalitarian readiness to admit almost everyone to participation have helped produce a nation where sport and sporting prowess matter very much (see pp. 341–51).

Although most Australians live in cities on the rim of the continent, they hold to a vision of the bush as the essential Australia. The imaginations of artists and writers and ordinary people have been captured by the unique strangeness and vastness of the inland. The terror of the early European settlers, who fared badly in this driest of continents, has given way to fierce pride and joy in the often terrible landscape. Australians live in the cities, but, in holidaytime, they travel into the bush as a sort of pilgrimage. The camping trip, the days of bush-walking into the mountains, the long journeys in four-wheel-drive vehicles into The Centre, the two-week excursions of schoolchildren, all celebrate the awe and reverence that the ancient land evokes.

The Australians' love of the bush has been only slowly turned to conventional environmental concern. White settlement was exploitive, but, until recently, little thought was given to possible aesthetic damage. The fragility of some strange and lovely areas urgently needs protection to save sea or land or wildlife. Environmental values are now endorsed strongly and widely enough to activate the major political parties (see pp. 148–54).

Australian egalitarianism and endorsement of mateship have not prevented overt racism surfacing on many occasions (see pp. 266–7). Although the White Australia policy of earlier times has long been discarded, the sentiments survive. The strong European immigration that commenced after 1945 is now being amplified by immigrants from Asia and the Pacific. The heterogeneity of Australian society (by 1991 about one-quarter of Australians were born overseas) gives racism a dangerous and divisive potential. Authorities argue anxiously about its extent. The truth of these contentions is hard to determine; Australians answer survey questions about preferred friends and neighbours with careful tolerance. Antipathy intensifies with apprehension about new arrivals competing for employment and access to resources like housing and education.

Class in Australia is not unimportant, but class divisions appear more blurred and negotiable than in nations with a longer history. Wealth and income weigh heavily in determining class superiority, but the way these are gained counts strongly too.

Above *Walkers in the Australian Alps, Victoria. The Australian love of the outdoor life is coupled with a fascination with and pride in the country's sparsely populated, rugged interior.*

Opposite *Houses and backyards in the Sydney suburbs. Ownership of a detached house with its own land is the Australian norm.*

Prestige attaches to positions of authority and influence; the professions, the land, business and industry entail higher social standing, to which Australians are quite sensitive. Despite widespread anti-intellectualism, education is valued as the way to advance income and status. Relatively high rates of social mobility point to the permeability of class lines. This more than any other feature of Australian life preserves the faith in egalitarianism, despite income and wealth differentials that are as wide as those of any capitalist economy.

Australian values current in an earlier time can be readily drawn from paintings and sculptures, stories and histories, drama and songs that extol and review political and social culture. Portents of changes occurring are harder to identify, but there are new heroes and fresh images. Captains of industry, tough and resilient, are now as significant as sporting champions. Winning is now important and defeats, in sport or business, are best forgotten. Prejudices of race and sex and culture are under siege and nationalism encircles a multiplicity of peoples.   AD

233

Rural–Urban differences

There is no clear cultural division between the metropolitan centres and everywhere else in Australia. Some rural towns have non-agricultural economic bases. Some display cultural traditions which have been brought by international migrants. All are part of Australian society. The cultural differences to be found between rural and urban Australia stem from the differences between agricultural and non-agricultural society.

The distinctively rural aspect of Australian society is associated with family farm agriculture and the social relationships which have grown with settlement based upon it. The family farming culture consists of values and beliefs related to the nature of the farming enterprise, the role of the family and relationships and differences between country and city. Agriculture is carried out almost entirely by small businesses, the majority of which are family partnerships. Farms often remain in families across generations, but seldom do so over more than three generations. Entry into farming usually occurs by way of farm upbringing, over three-quarters of male farmers being sons of farmers.

Farming is a desired occupation in terms of local rural community status. The term 'farmer' is often used to encompass the occupations of both farmer and grazier. Graziers derive income from grazing sheep and cattle rather than cultivation of crops. Graziers have traditionally been accorded higher social status, but where conditions are suitable, many farmers combine both activities. The farming community has a delicate relationship of interdependence with the towns which have grown with farming. Farmers look upon town businesses as dependent on them. Townspeople look upon farmers as wealthy and propertied, but they know that their own businesses are vulnerable when economic conditions for farming are bad. Conflict sometimes arises when townspeople feel that farmers are putting their own interests above others in the community, but such manifestations of the tension in the town and farm community relationship are very rare.

Values attached to the farming lifestyle and the role of the family in it, sometimes generalised as agrarianism, have contributed to the maintenance of this agricultural system. Farming is seen not only as a good lifestyle but as an ennobling vocation, in that it consists of honest hard work in a situation in which self-reliance is essential and enterprise is rewarded. Farming produces many of the essentials of life for urban as well as rural people, and in Australia it provides a traditionally very important contribution to economic prosperity by way of production for export.

Agrarianism has many facets, some of which are not uniquely rural but have maintained particular characteristics in the farming situation. The farmer has traditionally been assumed to be male, but his wife is also expected to be hard-working and resourceful in farm work, as well as domestic tasks. A growing number of women operate farms in their own right. Others have taken on different occupations or businesses to supplement farm income. The traditional patriarchal view of farm women as homemakers and child-minders may be basically similar in country and city, but for farm women the reality of work at home has been different.

The value placed on self-reliance is not unique to rural enterprise, but in farming it has a special meaning. Despite improvements in transport, many farms remain remote from town and city services. Farm families sometimes have to manage alone or with the help of friends and neighbours in situations in which urban dwellers would call on professional or other services. Farm families' places of living are also places of work, and the nature and quality of farm work are visible. Neighbours are in a sense also colleagues. When combined with opportunities for cooperation among farms, this makes for farm neighbouring relationships which are different from those of town and city. Despite distances between farmhouses, neighbouring is potentially more intense and potentially but not, as is sometimes assumed, necessarily, more satisfying.

Agrarianism is associated with conservatism. Rural Australia is a bastion of the conservative political parties. Australia has, in the National (formerly Country) Party, one of very few rural-based political parties in the world (see pp. 152–3). This political response is associated with, and perhaps dependent upon, countrymindedness: a set of beliefs about the value of country living, which, although related to the value placed upon hard work, family life, private enterprise and self-reliance among farm families, is often generalised into a common defence of the country against encroachment by city-based government and business, and what are seen to be undesirable features of urban lifestyles such as immorality and political radicalism. Countrymindedness has done much to bind rural Australia politically. Country people have seen the populations of many towns with economies based on service to agriculture decline in absolute terms since World War II, while the largest towns and the major urban centres have grown.

Sometimes the city appears openly hostile. Farmers have been told that some of their farm practices are harmful to their own land and livestock. They

A bush fire reaching Elanora Heights, a northern Sydney suburb, January 1994. Bush fires are a threat to both rural and urban life. In late 1993 and early 1994 bush fires in New South Wales burned out of control and spread to the suburbs of Sydney. Over 100 homes were destroyed and many more were damaged. Thousands of hectares of bush and parkland were burnt, and 4 people died.

have heard demands from urban-based environmentalist groups for expansion of national parks, which may not only consume agricultural land, but could also harbour animals which may become a threat to crops and livestock. Environmentalism has added another dimension to countrymindedness.

Agrarianism and countrymindedness create tensions for country people. While they want to retain the country lifestyle and values for their children, they know that city education and careers offer potential for relatively high income, which appears increasingly unlikely on the farm. While they value hard work and self-reliance, they envy the facilities and associated comfortable lifestyle of the cities. And while they see themselves as the backbone of the

Australian economy, they see their share of exports having declined and the future for their international markets appearing bleak.

Some of the distinctive aspects of agrarian culture are under threat as family farmers experience economic difficulties. Since the early 1970s, the economic condition of Australian agriculture has declined as its terms of trade have deteriorated and governments have been unwilling to provide compensating support. The number of family farms is decreasing, and among those people remaining in farming, about one-third undertake off-farm work. Farm families are finding that the opportunities to pursue their ideals of individual enterprise in the traditional way are diminishing. IG

Multiculturalism

It could be said that the history of Australia is a history of migration. Notwithstanding issues associated with Australia's first migrants, the Aborigines, who arrived some 40,000 or more years ago, migration issues have been recurring ingredients in Australia's social and political history from the arrival of the First Fleet in 1788 to the more recent waves of refugees from Indo-China (see also p. 226). More specifically, the policy of multiculturalism and the significance of ethnic distinctiveness are two important, closely related aspects of that history.

Ethnic distinctiveness is a term often used by demographers to characterise the diversity of origins of the Australian population. Using the term this way one could say, for example, that almost a quarter of the Australian population was born overseas and that close to 40 per cent are migrants or children of migrants.

Sociologists generally view ethnic distinctiveness to be synonymous with terms such as ethnicity, ethnic identity and cultural identity, which characterise individuals' and groups' maintenance of cultural ties. The more typical ties are those of language, religion, locality and history. Groups which organise around such ties are referred to as ethnic groups, which number several thousand in Australia. There is, for example, the Alliance Française – a group dedicated not only to maintenance but also to promotion of the French language; the separate Ukrainian Catholic and Orthodox churches and ethnic schools; and a variety of Welsh and Scottish groups which maintain the significance of particular histories and regional origins in the UK. There are also groups which combine more than one cultural tie, such as Vietnamese Buddhist associations and Vietnamese Chinese groups.

However, not all groups have such obvious cultural ties. There are, for example, Italian, Aboriginal or migrant groups which are active in promoting their members' interests but for whom the common tie of being Italian, Aborigine or migrant is somewhat artificial in terms of longstanding *cultural* ties. That is, in each case the recognition of a common link with other Italians, Aborigines or migrants is a product of recent and local circumstances and is not an indication of how those people have historically approached their culture and organised their lives.

In Italy, for example, Italians do not have significant attachments to a pervasive Italian culture but, rather, organise their lives around smaller regional and even smaller village or *paese* groups. In Australia, Italians often organise as Italians to achieve common political ends. COASIT, for example, is an organisation which assists Italians and their families in the welfare area. Similarly, at the parish level of the Australian Catholic Church, Italian committees protect the interests of Italian Catholics. At the same time, those same Italians organise socially around their regional and sub-regional ties by belonging to groups identifying with areas such as Friuli, Abruzzi and Veneto.

So we have two types of ethnic group in Australia – those which spring from attachment to significant cultural ties and those which arise more from local, political circumstances. Some ethnic groups straddle both categories, which means that it is not always possible to say that a particular ethnic group is either/or in terms of its origins. From this preamble we can now turn to some of the important issues of the policy of multiculturalism.

E. G. Whitlam, prime minister 1972–75, has been given credit for shifting ground and changing direction towards an official policy of multiculturalism. How he saw this policy is reflected in his statement:

> We do not want migrants to feel that they have to erase their own characteristics and imitate and adopt completely the behaviour of existing Australian society. We want to see that society enriched by cross fertilisation that will result from migrants retaining their own heritage.

The Whitlam government's policy made a sharp break with previous thinking, which assumed migrants' eventual conformity to the Australian cultural model or, at least, the inevitable withering of migrant culture. Although a new approach was initiated by the Whitlam era, the success of this policy has been questioned. Why is this so? Two related factors are worth noting.

Ukrainian Orthodox church in Essendon, Melbourne. Places of worship often provide a focus for individual ethnic groups.

First, the term multiculturalism means different things to different people. In some quarters it denotes the diversity of origins of the Australian population, a usage we could call demographic multiculturalism. This viewpoint is found mainly in educational organisations and is indicated by terms such as cultural mosaic and multicultural nature when referring to the migrant presence in Australian schools.

Others see multiculturalism as referring to the valuing of cultural diversity only so long as it does not threaten the existing unity and welfare of the whole society. Various government circles display this thinking with their stress on the value of a cohesive society and Australian ways of doing things. We could call this usage holistic multiculturalism.

A third, less-common form of multiculturalism emphasises the role of political processes in Australian ethnic relations in which migrant groups are legitimate interest groups. These groups mobilise to increase migrants' social participation and equality. In many parishes of the Australian Catholic Church, for example, Italians' political organisation has been motivated by the interests of Italian Catholics as *Italians* rather than concern for the parish as a whole.

These three conceptions of multiculturalism have often overlapped in that more than one strand can be identified in a given discussion. This has resulted in an inconsistency which arises when the three principles of a successful multicultural society – cultural identity, equality of opportunity and access, and social cohesion – are examined closely. These principles are often presented as if their coexistence is unproblematical. However, it is not possible for migrants to maintain their cultural identity or ethnicity, have equal access to the opportunity structure and, at the same time, not threaten the unity and cohesion of the nation. Currently, the more migrants attempt to achieve equality by setting up separate structures, such as ethnic schools and welfare agencies, the more they remove themselves from the wider arena in which decisions about distribution of resources are made. These actions prejudice their attaining equality of opportunity and access and are viewed by Angloceltic Australians as undermining social cohesion and unity of the nation.

To reconcile this inconsistency, it is necessary to accept that ethnic relations are political relations and that there is a necessary role of conflict and, possibly, a perceived threat to social cohesion. Accepting the role of conflict means that current thinking about multiculturalism must change if it is to have any semblance of what is actually happening in the world. Until then it remains merely a varied parade of ideas, a many-faceted ideology.   FL

Health

The health of the people of Australia is a product of a number of interacting factors: the demographic characteristics of the population; the social origins and

Crowd at a parade in Melbourne. Infant mortality in Australia is low and life expectancy high, especially amongst immigrants, who, on average, enjoy better health than those born in Australia.

economic circumstances of different groups; the quality, nature and funding of medical institutions and services; and national and local approaches to illness prevention and health promotion.

THE HEALTH PROFILE

Like most other urban, industrial societies, Australia has low birth and death rates. In 1990, the expectation of life at birth was 80 years for females and nearly 74 years for males, and these figures have been rising throughout the century. On the criterion of longevity, then, Australia is a fairly healthy country, similar to Norway and Italy, and better than the USA, Great Britain and New Zealand.

The most common causes of death are heart disease and stroke, and cancer. Overall infant mortality is low by international standards. Among children and young adults, most deaths result from accidents, particularly motor vehicle accidents. By the early 1990s, AIDS had not yet become a major source of mortality in Australia, suggesting that Australia's vigorous and prompt efforts in prevention are yielding health dividends.

Although most Australians can expect to have long lives, surveys of the population suggest that long life is not always healthy life. Rates of both acute and chronic illness are high enough to suggest that health – at least according to the World Health Organization's definition of complete mental and physical well-being – is more the exception than the rule. In the typical fortnight, the majority of the population experience at least one illness. Rates of illness, especially chronic illness, are higher for older people: 96 per cent of people over the age of 75 have an illness, and they are also likely to have several health problems rather than just one. For that reason, Australia can anticipate a greater burden of ill health as the population ages with increasing longevity and low birth rates.

Age is the first and most obvious health differential, and one that is so nearly universal as to appear natural, although international variations in sickness rates and longevity show that even this basic differential can be influenced by social, political and economic variables. Other health differentials are more obviously the consequence of social arrangements.

For example, Aboriginal Australians suffer substantially higher mortality at all ages than any other group of Australians despite improvement in Aboriginal death rates during recent decades. Infant mortality among Aborigines is more like that in Third-World countries than it is like the rest of Australia, standing at three times the national average. Maternal mortality is about five times the non-Aboriginal level and among adult men aged 35–44, the death rate is 11 times that of the total male rate. The incidence of preventable, disabling conditions such as trachoma-induced blindness, alcoholism and sexually transmitted diseases is many times higher than in the rest of the population.

Despite difficulties of access, rates of hospitalisation among Aborigines are higher than the national average, and hospitalisations of Aboriginal children are at five times the rate for other children because Aboriginal children are especially vulnerable to middle-ear and respiratory infections, diarrhoeal disease and parasites; and the consequences of these infections are much more serious than they are for the rest of the population. For example, three times as many Aboriginal as non-Aboriginal children suffer hearing loss as a result of middle-ear infections. In addition, Aborigines have a disproportionately high incidence of such chronic conditions as hypertensive disease, diabetes and tuberculosis.

Although little is known about the health of the Aboriginal population before European settlement, it is certain that the present profile of ill health can be substantially attributed to the loss of access to land and the destruction of traditional nomadic ways of life, as well as to the importation of diseases such as leprosy and syphilis by the early British settlers.

A dramatic contrast is presented by the health of Australia's most recent arrivals. With the exception of refugees, the foreign-born, particularly migrants of southern European origin, often enjoy superior health compared to people born in Australia. This pattern results in part from the fact that prospective migrants are screened on health criteria before they are admitted. However, the longer they live in the country, the more migrant health comes to resemble that of people born in Australia, and the children and grandchildren of migrants have usually lost much or all of their health advantage. Epidemiologists are studying with interest the gradual deterioration in the health of the foreign born, comparing them with people remaining in their country of origin, in the hope that such comparisons will help shed light on risk factors that arise from people's way of life.

Whatever their ethnic origins, Australians with good education, white-collar jobs and comparatively high incomes enjoy better health than their counterparts with less education, blue-collar jobs and lower incomes. These contrasts are similar to health differentials recorded in the USA and the UK, but they do not accord with the image of Australia as a classless society, and official health statistics are still not recorded in a way that would permit researchers to monitor these gradients easily. However, recent Commonwealth Government policy initiatives have given priority to reducing inequalities in health.

Class differences in mortality are evident at all ages: people who earn high salaries in professional occupations are less likely than poorer Australians to die prematurely, and children's mortality patterns parallel those of their parents. A similar differential prevails for illnesses: the better their incomes, the fewer illnesses Australians experience. Another comparison which echoes overseas findings is that women experience more illness and rely more heavily on medical goods and services than men do. Among both men and women, people outside the labour force are more likely than those in paid work to report illness.

Unlike Third World countries where malnutrition and poor living conditions make killers of common infectious illnesses, most non-Aboriginal Australians experience acute illnesses as unpleasant and temporarily disabling but self-limiting problems (for example, headaches, colds and flu and gastric upsets) which can usually be managed by simple over-the-counter remedies and bed rest. Diseases that rarely afflict people in the developing world form a significant portion of the burden of illness in Australia. Chronic conditions such as diabetes, elevated blood pressure, heart disease, asthma and arthritis require long-term management if their disabling consequences are to be minimised. Over half the population suffers from a chronic condition.

The Royal Flying Doctor Service of Australia

The Royal Flying Doctor Service of Australia first took to the air in Queensland in May 1928. Founded by the Rev. John Flynn, the Service now covers over 6 million km² and visits over 5,000 field clinics from 13 bases. It employs a staff of 312, uses 37 aircraft and attends over 150,000 patients a year.

The Service provides free aeromedical emergency and comprehensive health-care services to people who live, work and travel in Australia's remote outback. Its annual operating expenditure is over $30 million of which two-thirds is government funded, the remainder being provided by donation.

Services include carrying emergency and elective patients, holding regular field clinics that may be held in the shade of an aircraft wing, and home radio or telephone consultations with trained medical staff. RFDS also provides its radio communication services for the School of the Air (p. 245)

Over 2,500 medical chests containing an extensive range of supplies are provided at particularly remote outposts across the country, such as isolated pastoral properties, remote mining sites, Aboriginal out-stations, and lighthouses. Patients can then be diagnosed and treated by radio consultation at any hour of the day or night.

A new primary health-care philosophy, promoting healthy living, extends the role of the RFDS in illness prevention. A more culturally sensitive approach to Aboriginal health-care, through consultation with indigenous authorities, has also been adopted.   BH

Patient with a broken neck being transported by the Royal Flying Doctor Service. Founded in 1928 by a Presbyterian minister, the service provides medical care to people living in isolated settlements far from the coastal towns and cities.

MEDICAL CARE

Most primary medical care is delivered by private general practitioners and specialists who work on a fee-for-service basis, although some salaried doctors are employed in hospitals and clinics. By contrast, nurses – the largest segment of the medical workforce – are salaried, as are most physiotherapists, occupational therapists and nutritionists. Dentists, optometrists and pharmacists are mostly self-employed.

On average about 40 per cent of people with an illness consult a health worker (usually a doctor) about it over a two-week period, and just over 1 per cent of sick people have an episode in hospital. A system of public and private hospitals provides 5.3 beds per thousand population, proportionally more than in either the UK or the USA. About 80 per cent of these beds are in public hospitals which absorb a large portion of the government health dollar. Indeed, over half of total public and private recurrent expenditure goes on institutional services which include nursing homes, ambulance services and blood transfusion units as well as hospitals.

Funding for medical goods and services comes from a mixture of public and private sources, with about three-quarters of total expenditure coming from Commonwealth and state governments. The six states and the two territories are responsible for the provision of most medical services, running the public hospital system and community health centres. The Commonwealth does not generally provide services, but since 1942 it has held the power to raise revenue through income tax, and it therefore carries major responsibility for financing medical care.

A universal public medical insurance scheme, Medicare, partly funded by a 1.4 per cent levy on income, pays for individual hospital and medical services. Doctors can bill Medicare directly and receive 85 per cent of an established common fee, or they charge the patient who then recovers a rebate from Medicare and must pay the difference between the Medicare rebate and the doctor's fee.

Individuals and families may also insure themselves privately to help pay for services not covered by Medicare. People on government pensions and benefits are issued with a health care card which entitles them to have the doctor bill Medicare direct, so that they pay nothing at the time of service. The Commonwealth also funds medical care by subsidising the cost of drugs through a Pharmaceutical Benefits Scheme which provides a selected list of prescription medicines for a dispensing fee (currently about $16). Other prescription drugs and all over-the-counter remedies are paid for entirely by patients. The 'user pays' principle also applies to care delivered by practitioners other than doctors – for example, dentistry, private counselling or home midwifery services – and also for alternative therapies such as naturopathy or acupuncture.

ILLNESS PREVENTION AND HEALTH PROMOTION

Although not currently big budget items like treatment-oriented medicine, the prevention of illness and promotion of good health are recognised to be both more personally appealing and (in the long run) more cost-effective means to better health for the population. Most of the long-term reduction in premature death has been accomplished by improvements in the standard of living, such as better diet and housing, and by public health measures, such as vaccination, sewerage systems and safe water supplies. The challenge now is to achieve a similar reduction in premature disability; that is, to diminish the burden of chronic, degenerative conditions which detract from the quality of long life. If this can be accomplished, it will also bring some further reduction in premature mortality from sources such as accidents, cancer and heart disease.

Some risk factors, such as smoking, can be addressed by health education aimed at changing individual behaviour patterns. Because smoking is a preventable cause of death, it has been the target of vigorous health education campaigns, although such campaigns are not nearly as well resourced as tobacco advertising and industry lobbying. Until recently, most smoking cessation programmes were aimed at middle-class white men, although cigarette marketing targets the young. Recent comparisons suggest that the smoking rates are about the same for both sexes among young people.

The emphasis on lifestyles as major contributors to ill health in modern societies encourages a focus on individuals as responsible for their own health problems. Such an orientation ignores, however, the part played by the physical, economic and social environment in constraining individual health choices and in shaping the health of the population. What appears to be a personal choice often turns out to be a consequence of access to resources. A variety of economic and social factors exert powerful influence on the way of life of sectors of the population, and hence shape opportunities for personal illness prevention behaviours.

Some environmental sources of disease, such as atmospheric lead or other air pollution, cannot be controlled by individuals: they require the involvement of manufacturing and commercial sectors, and regulation and monitoring by governments. To take an example, the Commonwealth Government is setting fairly stringent standards for the use of chlorofluorocarbons which are thought to damage the ozone layer, an appropriate initiative for a nation with high rates of skin cancer. Such interventions have been referred to as ecological prevention, and according to many estimates, they may be the most significant forms of illness prevention available.

Workplace exposure to such hazards as cotton or coal dust, asbestos fibrils or toxic chemicals must be eliminated, but many industries have been reluctant to undertake the necessary changes, despite the high cost in lost work days and in compensation. Several Australian states (New South Wales, South Australia and Victoria) have comprehensive occupational health and safety legislation, and the Commonwealth Government has established a National Occupational Health and Safety Commission to liaise between unions, employers and the federal government on occupational health matters.

A potential bridge between curative medicine and illness prevention is community health, implemented in Australia through a system of government-funded community health centres initiated during the early 1970s. Although financial support for the centres has been minimal, particularly in the economic stringencies of the 1980s and 1990s, the centres employ a variety of health workers who provide a wide range of health education and community development programmes as well as some basic primary care. That is, they are designed to build on traditional medical practice, using it as a point of contact to generate opportunities for the kinds of personal and social interventions that can actively reduce the burden of disorder rather than simply fixing problems once they occur. The philosophy behind community health is to change the fundamental sources of illness and injury – sources in people's way of life, in their working conditions, and in their social and physical environment.

Pressure is strong to continue to invest mostly in individually oriented, high-technology curative medicine. For example, Australia is known internationally for its work on reproductive technology, particularly artificial conception. Because of low success rates and the expense of procedures, it is estimated that each baby eventually born as a result of *in vitro* fertilisation has cost over $40,000 before birth. Critics of such investment observe that very little is being spent on measures to prevent the infertility that gives rise to the need for *in vitro* fertilisation in the first place.

Similar comparisons can be drawn between the amount of money invested in expensive medical machinery which could be spent on occupational safety inspections, building basic Aboriginal maternity and health facilities, supporting independent living for the disabled or staffing metropolitan community health centres.

Important to future health will be decisions about a wide range of social and economic matters: agricultural and manufacturing systems, social security and public services probably have as much bearing on the health of the nation as explicit arrangements for medical care or health promotion.

The health of the Australian population in the twenty-first century will be a product of varied and complex individual and collective choices, only a few of which will have been defined as being about health when they were made. The remoteness of health causes from their consequences makes the task of planning for a healthy future all the more challenging.   DHB

Skin cancer

The incidence of skin cancer in Australia is higher than in any other country, varying from 2 to 4 times the rate in the United States and Great Britain to 10 times or more the rate in Japan. Skin cancer incidence rates in Australia continue to double around every 10 years. Each year, over 150,000 people require treatment and, on average, 1,000 die due to these tumours.

Melanoma is the most lethal but least common at around 2–3 per cent of all skin cancers, and is responsible for 80 per cent of the deaths that occur each year. Squamous cell carcinoma, 10–15 per cent of all skin cancers, is the second most common with around 30,000 people requiring treatment and about 200 deaths annually. Finally the most common but rarely lethal, basal cell carcinoma, affects around 120,000 people each year.

Recent education programmes, such as Slip!(on a shirt) Slop!(on a suncreen) Slap!(on a hat), have led to deep tans going out of fashion, and protective clothing and sunscreens being used regularly. These changes will not be reflected in skin cancer incidence rates for another 30 to 40 years. Today's high rates are due mainly to sunlight exposure received over the last 40 to 50 years.

While ozone depletion is relatively small and is not responsible for the present high rates of skin cancer, the possibility of increased ultraviolet radiation in future is a cause for concern.   RM

Alcohol and drugs

Anti-drunkenness poster aimed at young Aborigines, produced by the Drug Offensive, a national campaign begun in 1985.

In April 1985 the Commonwealth Government launched its National Campaign Against Drug Abuse (NCADA) emphasising both illicit drugs (for example, heroin, cocaine and cannabis) and licit drugs (alcohol and tobacco). Throughout Australia alcohol and drug (a & d) agencies expanded. In 1987 two academic research centres were established. Community and school programmes outside the umbrella of a & d agencies were initiated. Television and radio advertising has been prominent and law enforcement agencies generously funded. The campaign has enabled a & d agencies to expand existing programmes and introduce new projects, including ones that minimise the demand for drugs. For example, a distinctively decorated bus toured Castlemaine, Daylesford and Malmesbury in Victoria as part of a programme aimed at the young unemployed. Again in Victoria, by late 1987, 26 schools had a Peer Support Program operating and a further 20 were about to enrol. In the ACT a similar Teenagers Teaching Teenagers programme was launched, and continues in secondary schools.

The *Life Education Centre* production, established in Sydney in 1979 and recently introduced into primary schools is popular. The visual production aims to reduce future drug use by generating in children an appreciation of and respect for the body. Its major weakness has been the 'one-off' experience. Teachers are now developing work books for it, within the curriculum.

By mid-1988 an estimated 700,000 Victorian school students had seen the FM Theatre Company production *On The Rocks*. Here a popular troupe of young actors dance and sing their way through issues of social concern to young children. The ACT Skylark puppet show *Inside Story* has been researched, shown to be effective and is being introduced into primary schools on a national level. This *Inside Story* takes Pippa for a magical trip inside her own body where she examines her thoughts, emotions and feelings. She learns how alcohol and tobacco can harm that magic. The kindergarten version *Tiny Pods and Silver Wings* has been combined with *Inside Story* in video form and supplied by the Commonwealth to all state education bodies. The impact on schools located in the poorer communities, where many teenagers involved in the drug scene come from, remains unknown. The independent task force that is evaluating the first six years of NCADA may provide an answer.

The *per capita* consumption (pcc) of alcohol rose rapidly in the 1950s and 1960s and peaked in 1978. Since then it has fallen by 23 per cent. Drinking habits of many have changed. Consumption of wine has increased steadily while beer has fallen. Low-alcohol beers now constitute 22 per cent of all alcohol consumed. Binge drinking has become common among the 12–17-year-olds and many boys and girls in this age group drink to unsafe levels. Despite the drop in pcc, alcohol is the major problem-causing drug. The medical and social morbidity costs of alcohol are high. The hidden crimes of domestic violence and incest are understated as is absenteeism.

While the overall tobacco consumption has fallen in the past decade by 23 per cent, it has increased slightly for women. This increase is reflected in the rising number of tobacco-related deaths in women, early menopause, excessive facial hair and underweight frail babies. In terms of death, health morbidity and other costs, alcohol and tobacco far outweigh the costs from other drugs.

The fear, expressed in 1984, that cocaine would sweep through the Australian illicit drug scene has not been realised. Heroin remains the preferred drug for 'shooting up'. Amphetamines are popular and cannabis is widely used both by intravenous drug users and others. How widespread cannabis use is remains conjectural. Seizures off the coast valued at $10 million or more dollars show that an international group is operating.

In phase two of NCADA a wide variety of TV and other advertisements directed attention to the harmful consequences of specific drugs, such as heroin in 1987 and alcohol as used by adolescents in 1988.

COMMUNITY ATTITUDES

Patterns of acceptable drug use change with time. Current practices range from *laissez faire* to prohibitionist, with alcohol being relatively uncontrolled compared to the ban placed on heroin, cocaine and cannabis.

These proscription practices bear poor relationship to health consequences of drug use. For example, over the past five years alcohol and tobacco, jointly, have been responsible for 96 per cent of drug deaths in Australia while death from cannabis use has not been recorded. However, cannabis remains an illicit drug and costly in terms of police and court action. Research into the question as to what benefits people obtain from drug use, despite the harm inflicted, remains haphazard.

SMOKING LEGISLATION

In 1987 Victoria introduced the Tobacco Bill. This bans the advertising of cigarettes/smoking in cinemas and on billboards. It also bans sponsorship by the tobacco industry of many sporting and cultural events. An extra tobacco franchise was imposed and, with this money, a Foundation was funded to take over the promotion of sporting and cultural bodies deprived of financial support previously available through sponsorship. It is estimated that $23 million dollars will be available for distribution. South Australia introduced similar legislation in April 1988 and Western Australia intends to do likewise. New South Wales has so far declined.

DRUG USERS AND AIDS

Among injecting drug users (IDUs) the realities of recognising that prohibition has failed to stem the tide of illicit drug use and that abstinence is a goal seldom reached in treatment centres has led to the promotion of the Minimisation of Harm concept for drug users. The need to contain the spread of AIDS (and hepatitis B and C) among IDUs has fortified the acceptance of this minimisation concept. The two principal factors leading to the spread of the AIDS virus, HIV, and to hepatitis B and C are drug injection and sexual activity. For drug injectors the frequency of both injection and needle sharing, and the size of the needle-sharing pool are crucial.

The encouragement of the heroin substitute methadone, in Australia, together with the introduction of needle-sharing schemes (started in 1987), have promoted the minimisation concept. There is growing evidence that methadone users inject less frequently, share needles less often and have fewer sharing partners, with the result that they are less at risk from HIV.

There is, however, a high association between IDU and prostitution. Continuing reports of high levels of sexually transmitted diseases among prostitutes emphasise the mutual risk of HIV spread to IDU and prostitute. These reports are consistent with the idea that unsafe sex is being practised. Such practices are more likely following the intake of alcohol, benzodiazepines and other drugs, the use of these being common among IDUs. KP

Streetwize comic, 1992. Sydney-based Streetwize Comics publish literature dealing with health, legal and other issues of special concern to the young. Funded by various government departments on a project basis they offer practical advice in an easily understood form. This issue on AIDS had to be reprinted because of heavy demand.

Education

Formal schooling was established in Australia about 25 years after European settlement in 1788. Its early expansion was largely stimulated and controlled by religious and private organisations rather than by the various colonial governments of the time.

During the last three decades of the nineteenth century, separate education Acts were adopted by each of the colonial governments which endorsed the provision of free, compulsory and secular elementary education, controlled and funded by the governments themselves. Subsidies to private educational efforts were discontinued, although religious organisations, mainly the Anglican and Roman Catholic churches, continued to be active in the provision of schooling in which religious instruction played a major role. When federation occurred in 1901, education was left as a state responsibility, with no significant role being given to the Commonwealth Government. This arrangement went virtually unchanged until after World War II.

Although each state exercised responsibility for its own educational system, there emerged a remarkable homogeneity across states in educational structures. By World War II, schooling was compulsory in most states from age 6 to 15, except for Tasmania where it was compulsory until age 16. Primary schooling included grades 1 to 6/7 (from ages 6 to 12/13), and secondary schooling included grades 7/8 to 12 (ages 13/14 to 18). Most young people received two or three years of secondary schooling, but the completion of secondary school was attained by less than half of any age cohort. Until recently, secondary school completion was seen as an avenue for tertiary studies, and the later years of secondary school were highly selective and the curriculum academically oriented and specialised.

Melbourne Church of England Grammar School. The main providers of education in the colonies' early years, the Anglican and Roman Catholic churches still run many schools today.

FUNDING

Government primary and secondary schools are funded primarily by the states, although the Commonwealth Government provides some supplementary funding, recently about 11 per cent.

Like primary and secondary schooling, tertiary education was originally the responsibility of the states. However, in the early 1970s the Commonwealth Government began to assume greater financial and policy control over the tertiary sector through the Commonwealth Tertiary Education Commission (CTEC), and by 1991 about 74 per cent of university funding was provided by the government. TAFE funding remains largely the responsibility of the states, with about 25 per cent of resources being provided by the Commonwealth. Private initiatives at the university level are beginning, with several institutions already operational. The scope, impact and relationship of private establishments with those funded by the government remains uncertain.

TYPES

A feature of Australian education has been its dual structure at the primary and secondary levels. The existence of government and private schools has been an accepted characteristic of the system in recent years. By 1987 about 26 per cent of primary and secondary students attended non-government schools, 80 per cent of which were linked to the Roman Catholic church. The states and the Commonwealth

Tertiary education

Following a period of growth and restructuring during the late 1980s, Australian tertiary education in 1993 consisted of two divisions: universities and their affiliated colleges (higher education), and institutions of Technical and Further Education (TAFE).

In 1993 there were 37 universities which enrolled about 577,00 students, or 23 per cent of all post-secondary enrolments; the remaining enrolments were in TAFE colleges, of which there were 884.

In 1993 about 12.3 per cent of the labour force held degrees, of which 60 per cent were male and 40 per cent were female. By comparison, in 1982 only 9 per cent of the labour force held degrees, of which 64 per cent were male and 36 per cent were female. Since 1987 female participation in higher education has exceeded that for males; in 1991 female participation rates were 52 per thousand in the 17 – 64 -year-old population compared to 44 per thousand for males.

In 1993 there were 42,571 overseas students in Australian universities, or 7.2 per cent of the student population. They were enrolled mainly in business, engineering and science courses.

LJS

School of the Air

The School of the Air educates students, mostly between the ages of 4$\frac{1}{2}$ (pre-school) and 12/13 (Year 7), who live in remote areas in the Australian outback. It operates out of centres in Western Australia, Queensland, New South Wales, South Australia and the Northern Territory.

The first, and perhaps most publicised, is the Alice Springs School of the Air in the Northern Territory; it was officially opened on 8 June 1951. Servicing an area of 1.3 million square miles (3.37 million km^2) and extending across the borders of Western Australia, Queensland and South Australia, the school in 1993 has around 140 students, of which the furthest is over 1,000 km from Alice Springs. There are 14 teachers and 8 support staff, funded mainly by the Northern Territory Department of Education and supplemented with voluntary fees from parents. Lessons are conducted using transceivers (two-way radios), television sets, video recorders, cassette recorders, and lap-top computers. These can be hired from the school for a modest fee.

Class sizes range from 8 to 18 students, and each class collectively spends up to 30 minutes on the radio each day. Students also spend a 10-minute private session with their teacher once a week. These radio sessions complement correspondence lessons which take five to six hours of students' time each day, five days a week. These lessons are prepared by teachers at the Alice Springs school and are supervised by an adult, usually a parent, in the students' homes. Library materials from Alice Springs are available. Teachers also travel thousands of kilometres every year to visit each student in his or her outback home.

The School of the Air provides an innovative and important educational opportunity for isolated children, who can then continue their secondary education at a large number of boarding-schools in many country towns and the capital cities.

LJS

In Australia's vast hinterland, stations (very large farms or ranches), can be hundreds of miles from the nearest town or city. The School of the Air provides education for children far removed from the nearest school.

Government have increasingly provided funds to non-government schools on an individual needs basis. By 1992 about 56 per cent of the funds for non-government schools were provided by government sources, primarily the Commonwealth. The provision of government funds to non-government, largely church-related schools, has been and continues to be a contentious issue in Australian education.

The 1970s and 1980s were years of rapid change for Australian education. Several trends have occurred which have significantly affected the characteristics and processes of the system. Perhaps the most notable for Australian schooling has been the increasing number of pupils staying on. In 1968, before rapid expansion occurred, only 25 per cent of young people remained in the system to Year 12. By 1970 this figure increased to 29.3 per cent, and by 1980 to 34.5 per cent. By 1993, retention to Year 12 had reached 76.6 per cent. This rapid increase has meant that secondary schooling has become less academically oriented, more comprehensive and less oriented to entry exclusively into tertiary study.

In 1983 the Australian Labor government embarked upon a policy of encouraging more pupils to attend Year 12. The retention figures quoted previously suggest that this programme has met with success. In 1987, the same government explored measures to achieve the dual goals of equality through wider access to tertiary studies, and greater efficiency. By 1988 this programme had been implemented, with the result that the binary system has been gradually dismantled through the merging of colleges of advanced education (CAEs) and universities. The funding of the new unified system is linked to performance profiles of universities based on enrolments, teaching workloads and research productivity.

TESTING AND CURRICULUM

There is no national examination system in Australia. Most states have their own examination procedures for admission to tertiary institutions. The Australian Scholastic Aptitude Test (ASAT) is widely used as part of this assessment.

In April 1989 the Australian Education Council (AEC) issued a statement, *The Hobart Declaration on Schooling*, in which national goals and structures for cooperation between schools, states, territories and the Commonwealth were agreed upon. This statement has provided the foundation for the development of learning profiles for eight curriculum areas: the arts, English, health and physical education, languages other than English (LOTE), mathematics, science, studies of society and environment, and technology.

The completion of these profiles during 1993 was an important development in national curriculum activities, particularly for the standardisation of teaching and learning in the eight areas, and for national reporting on student achievement. For each learning area there are consultants who focus on equity issues for gender, Aboriginal and Torres Strait Islander students, English as a second language (ESL) students, and special education students.

In spite of recent changes, the structure of Australian schooling remains intact. The Australian educational system at the primary and secondary levels remains highly centralised at the state level, with minimal funding coming from the Commonwealth. The university sector has been almost entirely centralised at the Commonwealth level, which provides most funds through its Department of Employment, Education and Training. With more young people completing secondary education, this will affect changes at both secondary and tertiary levels as Australian education makes the transition from elite schooling at the upper levels to mass schooling at the secondary level, and possibly to the tertiary level as well.   LJS

Roman Catholic St Patrick's Cathedral in Melbourne, built between 1858 and 1897, except for the spires, which were added in 1936. At 27.3 per cent of the population in 1991 the total number of Catholics had passed that of Anglicans.

Religion

In Aboriginal Australia religion pervaded all aspects of life. The land was sacred, and tribal ritual and imagery were infused with religious symbolism. The Aboriginal Dreaming (see pp. 75–9) told of a sacred heroic time which, although infinitely remote, has ordered the way of life thereafter. The Dreaming survives in traditional Aboriginal communities despite the secularism widespread elsewhere in Australia.

British Christianity came in the minds of the colony's early military administrators and their criminal charges. This religion was stern, punitive and linked to law and order. The churches followed the spread of population and successfully demanded from government land, church building assistance, aid to denominational schools and legislative reinforcement of religiously inspired morality. Governments assisted church and school building until the last decades of the nineteenth century when legislation ended the building subsidies and created an education system that was 'free, secular and compulsory'.

Consequent questions of state aid for non-government schools provoked the longest series of political battles between secular and religious interests in Australian history. Despite the Australian Constitution separating church and state, successive federal governments have provided financial aid to denominational schools. In 1992 over one-quarter of Australian children attended independent schools. Denominational schools give powerful witness to the influence of religion in national life.

Three current questions dominate religious debate. The first from the altered status of women, demands female ordination. Some protestant denominations recognise female priesthood claims, the Anglican general synod since December 1992.

Yet to contemplate it are the more patriarchal – catholicism, Greek orthodoxy and orthodox Judaism. The second question arises from technology aiding human reproduction, with religious protagonists debating the ethics and legal safeguards for human rights and responsibilities. Question three arises from religion's traditional concern with sexual morality; the AIDS epidemic uncovers the many faces of religion, from condemnation to care.

While Australia has no established church, religion and religious leadership are closely linked to social status, culture and national origins. Presbyterians and Anglicans were largely upper class with church leadership drawn from Scotland and England. The middle classes tended to follow nonconformist faiths bringing church leaders from similar Welsh or English origins.

A disproportionate number of convicts and much of the working class were Irish catholic, long dominated by an Irish episcopate and priesthood. Culture, class and religion deepened antagonisms brought from Britain. Denominational rivalries erupted frequently between protestants and catholics, who responded by isolationism and rejection of the larger society. They built their own schools, hospitals, orphanages and welfare organisations, only recently relaxing their costly suspicion of protestant and secular influences.

Anti-Semitism also marred the national reputation for fairness and tolerance. Australian Jews, consistently 0.4 per cent of the population, form a cohesive community holding to traditional moral and intellectual values, most apparent in their significant representation in universities, business and professions.

Bitter sectarianism evident in earlier social history has now been quelled by realisation of the widening diversity of new and immigrant religions, deepening ecumenism stimulated by common challenges and by secularisation apparent in all highly industrialised nations.

Enclaves of other world religions, Buddhism, Hinduism and, especially, Islam reflect present ethnic diversity. Immigrants who brought their religious leaders with their religion from the home country sustain the integrity of religion and culture. European immigrants who anticipated finding a welcome in established Australian churches familiar to them from the old country were often disappointed. Australian institutions have not been adept at meeting the needs of non-English immigrants and the churches are no exception.

Structural changes and shifting allegiances are altering the demography of religious life. The 1977 merger of Methodists, Presbyterians and Congregationalists produced the Uniting Church, to which 8.2 per cent of Australians claim allegiance. The con-

Church attendance

Church attendance improved throughout the nineteenth century, a trend due in part to growth of towns and rural centres and building and staffing of churches.

In 1901 regular church attendance distinguished 60–80 per cent of Methodists, 30–55 per cent of Roman Catholics and 17 per cent of Anglicans.

Reliable estimates of church attendance do not occur again for 50 years.

The high point of recent decades was reached during the stable 1950s with 19 per cent of Anglicans, 21 per cent of Presbyterians, 33 per cent of Methodists and 75 per cent of Roman Catholics attending church regularly.

The Morgan Gallup polls in the following decades chart the decline. In 1981, only 12 per cent of Anglicans, 37 per cent of Romans Catholics and 8 per cent of Presbyterians attended church regularly, but 34 per cent of the newly amalgamated Uniting Church did so.

These surveys of larger denominations ignore diverse new sects which claim strong, lively congregations.   AD

tentious decision to amalgamate was rejected by about one-third of Presbyterians, now only 4.3 per cent of the population.

Membership of the Anglican Church, previously the largest in the country, declined from 39 per cent in 1933 to 23.9 per cent in 1991. Roman Catholicism (27.3 per cent of the population) is now the biggest denomination.

Declining congregations of the major denominations have been offset by the growth of pentecostalist movements and the appearance of new fundamentalist faiths. Both inspire strong emotional commitment to a celebratory religion. They attract a predominantly young, middle-class congregation for whom religious commitment is a major factor. Only the Pentecostalist Church was separately listed (0.9 per cent of the population) in the 1991 Census. The notable growth of the others was evident in the doubling of the residual Christian category during the 20 years from the mid-1960s to mid-1980s, but in 1991 the largely fundamentalist 'other Christian' religions had fallen back to 2 per cent of the population.

Increasing numbers declare they have no religion or decline to nominate any. The tiny 0.1 per cent with no religion in 1901 increased slowly, then rapidly to almost 7 per cent in 1971 and 12.9 per cent in 1991. The proportion not answering the Census question on religion had grown to 10.2 per cent in 1991.

The 1983 and 1989 Australian Values Studies showed about 20 per cent of adults attending weekly religious services. Only 33 per cent of Australians

RELIGIOUS DENOMINATIONS 1901–91: NUMBER OF ADHERENTS ('000'S)

Denomination		1901	1933	1961	1971	1981	1991
Anglican		1497	2565	3668	3953	3810	4018
	(%)	40	39	35	31	26	23.9
Baptist		89	106	150	175	190	279
	(%)	2.3	1.6	1.4	1.4	1.3	1.7
Brethren			10	15	22	21	
	(%)		0.1	0.1	0.2	0.2	
Catholic		855	1300	3036	3443	3786	4606
	(%)	22	19	25	27	26	27.3
Church of Christ		24	63	96	97	89	78
	(%)	0.6	0.9	0.9	0.8	0.6	0.5
Congregational		74	65	74	68	23	
	(%)	2	1	0.8	0.5	0.2	
Jehovah's Witnesses					35	51	74
	(%)				0.3	0.4	0.4
Lutheran		75	60	160	196	200	250
	(%)	2	1	1.5	1.5	1.4	1.5
Methodist		504	684	1124	1099	491	
	(%)	13	10	10	8.6	3.4	
Orthodox				154	338	421	475
	(%)			1.5	2.7	3	2.8
Pentecostal						72	150
	(%)					0.5	0.9
Presbyterian		426	713	976	1028	638	732
	(%)	11	11	9	8	4.4	4.3
Salvation Army		31	31	51	66	72	71
	(%)	0.8	0.5	0.5	0.5	0.5	0.4
Seventh Day Adventist		3	13	31	42	47	
	(%)	0.1	0.2	0.3	0.3	0.3	
Uniting						712	1387
	(%)					5	8.2
Other Christian		115	128	234	223	473	339
	(%)	3	2	2	3.2	3.2	2
Total Christian		3696	5741	9308	10990	11133	12465
	(%)	98	86	89	86	76	
Buddhist						35	13.9
	(%)					0.2	0.8
Hebrew		15	24	59	62	62	74
	(%)	0.4	0.4	0.6	0.5	0.4	0.4
Muslim					22	76	147
	(%)				0.2	0.5	0.9
No Religion		6	15	37	856	1577	2176
	(%)	0.1	0.2	0.4	6.7	10.8	12.9
No Reply		56	849	1103	781	1595	1712
	(%)	1.5	12.8	10	6.1	10.9	10.2

Percentage totals only approximate to 100% because of rounding denomination percentage. Population totals for each denomination are rounded to the nearest 1,000. Totals for all Christians in each year are based on exact figures counted in the census.

pray relatively often and 33 per cent, again, are at least sometimes aware of a God-like presence in their life.

The same surveys found religious belief more prevalent than practice. Of Australians 85 per cent believed in God, 73 per cent in a soul, 60 per cent in life after death. Those Commandments concerned with respect for the rights of others remain a powerful moral force, but those concerned with duty to God, including keeping the Sabbath holy, are precepts accepted by about half and put into practice by one-quarter of Australians questioned.

Secularisation, understood as decline in religious commitment, occurred in traditionally secular Australia. But, it has not taken on the alarming dimensions assumed elsewhere, because belonging to a church has never been socially important: Australia has always been a secular society. AD

The media

Media ownership and control in Australia is the subject of lively debate. The main media have traditionally been owned by a small number of commercial interests, which have effectively dominated sources of news and information. In late 1992 the Labor government's new Broadcasting Services Act came into force. The new legislation substantially de-regulated broadcasting, allowing the introduction of new broadcast services, including subscription television and 'narrowcast' services (tailored for limited specialised audiences), and reduced the licensing functions of the regulator. However, it maintained restrictions on ownership of broadcast television and radio.

The Act limits foreign ownership of broadcast media (to a maximum of 20 per cent for commercial television, and 35 per cent for the new satellite pay television licences); and restricts the concentration of media ownership in two ways. No-one is allowed to control a television licence which broadcasts to more than 75 per cent of the Australian population, or to control more than two radio stations in the same licence area. There are also complex cross-media ownership rules, which are designed to separate control of commercial radio and television stations broadcasting in the same area, and newspapers which circulate in that area.

These regulations allow television networks to cover the populations of Australia's five largest markets (Sydney, Melbourne, Brisbane, Adelaide and Perth), so long as they do not control a radio station or a newspaper in any of those cities. There is one five-city network, and two three-city networks. Satellite pay television (expected to start by late 1994) will be a national service, with up to ten channels.

The media environment in Australia is particularly dynamic in the mid-1990s, with the introduction of pay television, and new broadcasting technologies, such as cable and microwave to the home. Since 1986 there have also been substantial changes of ownership in commercial television, and takeovers and closures of major metropolitan newspapers.

Unless otherwise specified, the information below is current at September 1993.

TELEVISION

Television in Australia is either national broadcasting (government funded) through the Australian Broadcasting Corporation (ABC) and Special Broadcasting Service (SBS), or commercial (funded by advertising). Subscription television (funded directly by subscription fees) and community television (not-for-profit television, funded by sponsorship) are being introduced. SBS is a unique multicultural television channel, with foreign language programmes subtitled in English, as well as English language programming. It is partly funded through commercial sponsorship. There are approximately 26 metropolitan and 25 regional television stations. Commercial regional stations draw on the three metropolitan networks, Channels 7, 9 and 10, for news and general programming (see also pp 211–12).

One of the more interesting developments in recent years was the grant of a Remote Commercial Television Service licence to Imparja Television, controlled by an Aboriginal group in Central Australia. The first community television class licence was issued in 1993, to provide community and educational programmes through a non-profit organisation.

NEWSPAPERS

Newspapers at the national and metropolitan levels are largely in the hands of two owners: Rupert Murdoch's News Limited and the Fairfax Group (25 per cent owned by Conrad Black). In 1993, Murdoch owned 66 per cent of the print media by circulation and Fairfax 22 per cent.

Murdoch owns one of the two national newspapers, *The Australian* (circulation 150,000) and many of the largest metropolitan daily papers, including *The Daily Telegraph Mirror* (circulation 443,000) in Sydney and *The Herald-Sun* (circulation 571,000) in Melbourne. As the titles indicate, most of these morning papers have absorbed their evening stablemates in the last few years. His Sydney-based weekly *The Sunday Telegraph Mirror* has a circulation of 695,000.

The Fairfax Group owns the second national newspaper, *The Australian Financial Review* (circulation 77,000) and major metropolitan daily newspapers, including *The Sydney Morning Herald* (circulation

A newsagency in Elwood, a southeastern suburb of Melbourne. There are two national newspapers in Australia (The Australian and The Australian Financial Review) as well as many specialist and regional newspapers.

Foreign ownership

In April 1993 Conrad Black, a London-based Canadian publisher, increased his stake in the Fairfax Group from 15 per cent to 25 per cent, after a review of government policy limiting foreign ownership in the print media. The Foreign Investment Review Board (FIRB) is required to examine all investment proposals in the media sector, and make recommendations to the Treasurer. Legislation prevents foreigners having a controlling interest in a commercial television licence, but the level of ownership and/or control in the print media is a matter of policy rather than legislation.

In mid-December 1993 a Senate committee decided to inquire into the circumstances in which government decisions had been taken in 1991 and 1993 to increase the percentage of foriegn ownership of newspapers, and whether there had been any political influence in those decisions. This followed a statement by Conrad Black (in his memoirs *Conrad Black – A Life in Progress*) that he had been promised consideration of his claim for his stake to be lifted to 35 per cent after the March 1993 election.   HM

263,000) and Melbourne's *The Age* (circulation 235,000). The Fairfax Sunday paper *The Sun Herald* has a circulation of 609,000, mainly in Sydney.

Australians are quite well served by specialist and regional newspapers. In 1988 there were about 638 mainstream regional and metropolitan newspapers, including suburban free papers supported by advertising, and approximately 93 ethnic newspapers, including 3 dailies.

MAGAZINES

There are over 800 magazines in Australia, representing a diversity of interest and ownership. However, the largest slice of the mass-circulation magazines is owned by Kerry Packer's Australian Consolidated Press. Packer (who also owns the Channel 9 network, and 10.5 per cent of the Fairfax Group) owns 46 per cent of the circulation of the top 30 magazines; Rupert Murdoch's News Limited owns 23 per cent, and his nephew Matt Handbury owns another 9 per cent; Time Warner has 4 per cent of the circulation of the top 30 magazines.

Packer's main titles include *The Bulletin*, a weekly news and general interest magazine (circulation 105,000); *The Australian Women's Weekly*, a monthly magazine with a circulation of 1,097,000; and other large-circulation women's magazines such as *Cleo*, *Cosmopolitan*, and *Woman's Day*, a weekly magazine with a circulation of 1,092,000. News Limited's women's magazine *New Idea* is their largest seller, with a circulation of 892,000, followed by *TV Week* (circulation 504,000) which is in fact owned jointly with Packer (March 1994 figures).

In the early 1990s several new entrants, including Australian editions of US Magazines such as *Sports Illustrated* and *The National Inquirer*, tried for a foothold in the market; but the only apparent stayer is another women's magazine *Who Weekly*, published by Time Warner. The women's market is very hotly contested, with Consolidated Press launching yet another title in 1993.

RADIO

There are three national ABC radio stations in Australia, Radio National, JJJ (non-commercial FM youth music network) and ABC Classic FM. In metropolitan areas, there are 18 AM and 19 FM commercial stations as well as 112 regional commercial AM and FM stations (December 1991 figures). The ABC also has an extensive network of 48 regional stations, and an AM station in each metropolitan area. Community broadcasting in metropolitan and regional areas accounts for 112 stations, mainly FM. Some of these stations provide multilingual ethnic broadcasting, as does SBS Radio in six cities, mainly on the east coast. Aboriginal radio is thriving; the Central Australian Aboriginal Media Association (CAAMA) controls Radio 8KINFM in the Northern Territory, and there are Aboriginal-run radio stations in the Kimberley, and on Thursday Island, among other places in northern Australia.

The ABC also operates an international shortwave and satellite radio service, broadcasting 24 hours a day in English, and another 24 hours a day in eight languages to Asia and the Pacific area.

The broadcasting legislation introduced in late 1992 allows special purpose and limited audience 'narrowcast' broadcasters to start services with a minimum of formality, and dozens have started operations. Typical applications are tourist information radio stations, and similar niche markets. One of the main objectives of the new legislation is to encourage greatly expanded numbers of radio services, exploiting new technologies and meeting information and entertainment needs (see also p. 211).

CENSORSHIP AND REGULATION

Censorship in Australia is fairly limited and principles of self-regulation operate. There are two main media regulatory bodies in Australia: the Australian Broadcasting Authority (ABA), which is responsible for overseeing self-regulatory codes drawn up by the commercial and community broadcasters, reviewing complaints, and determining standards for children's television programmes and levels of Australian content on commercial televion; and the Australian Press Council (APC), which is an autonomous body established in 1976 with a balanced representation from the industry and the public and an independent chairperson. It deals with complaints and monitors laws, government and community activities that may threaten principles of press freedom.

There are other regulatory bodies such as the Office of Film and Literature Classification and the Media Entertainment and Arts Alliance, with an established Code of Ethics. A Senate Joint Select Committee has been in operation since the late 1980s, considering censorship of videos, video and computer games, and electronic services (such as dial-up telephone services) concerning explicit sex and violence, especially where scenes show the denigration of women.

All visual media have guidelines to viewing; the television categories are General Exhibition (G); Parental Guidance (PG); Mature (M) – age 15 plus: Mature Adult (MA). Television licensees may not broadcast Restricted (R) – age 18 plus – material unless it has been modified, and are prohibited from broadcasting X-rated material. The classification system for interactive video games and computer games is similar, but more restricted in all categories.

BC/HM

Occupations

Historically, the share of Australian GDP gained through agriculture has been high (see pp 168–73. This share has decreased in recent years although it remains high in comparison with other OECD countries. Agricultural production is capital intensive, covering large areas, and it is carried out on large-scale units employing a rural proletariat (wool); or in family farms on large acreages (wheat and dairying).

Manufacturing did not develop in Australia until the 1890s. Prior to this the need for goods was met by trade from Britain. The increased need for labour, caused by the growth in the manufacturing sector during the twentieth century has been met by waves of immigration (see pp. 225–7). The workforce is therefore highly diverse in terms of social characteristics and educational backgrounds. Over the last 20 years the proportion of the workforce employed in white-collar occupations has increased, and the proportion of workers employed in manual occupations has declined.

The Australian workforce consists of approximately 8.5 million workers; 5.9 million of whom work full time. In spite of the large mining and agricultural sectors, 85 per cent of all jobs are located in urban areas. In 1991, 9.4 per cent of the workforce were unemployed (see pp. 254–5). By early 1993 this figure was 11.1 per cent.

Wages are largely determined by awards made at either the state or federal level, though over-award payments are frequently made at plant level. The Australian Conciliation and Arbitration Commission (now called the Australian Industrial Relations Commission) established the principle in 1969 that equal payments should be made to all people who performed equal work. In 1972, this was extended to 'equal pay for work of equal value'. However, these determinations have not resulted in different social groups earning equal wages. For example, women in the Australian workforce earn less than men on average: adult females earn 85 per cent of the average adult male wage.

THE PRIVATE AND PUBLIC SECTORS

Public sector employees are in local government, state government or the Commonwealth Government. A large proportion of public sector employees are employed at the state level (66 per cent in 1992). This reflects state government responsibility for education, health and police. Public sector employment has declined as a proportion of total employment, falling from 30.6 per cent to 29.3 per cent in the five years to March 1992.

EMPLOYMENT CONDITIONS

In Australia, the standard working week is central to the awards made through arbitration. A working week of 35–40 hours is generally accepted as standard, with overtime payable if longer hours are worked. About 40 per cent of those in employment work between 35 and 40 hours per week, and 42.5 per cent work longer than 40 hours. Some 17.5 per cent work part time.

As in most other OECD countries the length of the working week declined in the first half of the twentieth century from 49 hours per week in 1900 to 40 hours per week in 1950. Since then reduced working hours have been won largely in the form of holidays. Most workers are entitled to 10 paid public holidays per year and 5 days sick leave as well as 4 weeks paid annual leave.

About 10 per cent of the workforce are employed in casual jobs. This means that they are paid a higher hourly rate instead of receiving paid leave entitlements. They have no security of tenure. Women make up 63 per cent of casual labour, in contrast to the 34 per cent of permanent employees who are women.

Aboriginal workers at a cattle station at Petermann, Northern Territory. Aboriginal workers are predominantly employed in rural jobs.

SEGMENTATION

Changes in the labour market have affected some groups more than others. This is due to segmentation: the concentration of individuals sharing particular personal or social characteristics into certain industries and occupations. Australian labour market segmentation is high compared to other OECD countries.

Women

Over the past decade, the number of women in work has risen by about 20 per cent. As a result the female share of total employment has risen from 35 per cent in 1977 to 42 per cent in 1991. Most of this increase is due to an increase in demand in those occupations which employ a high proportion of married women working part time.

In 1991 over half of all employed women were concentrated into two major occupational categories: clerks and sales personnel, and personal service workers (54.8 per cent). This compares with only 16.2 per cent of the male workforce in such jobs. Within the major occupational categories segmentation also occurs. More than 98 per cent of engineers and building professionals are male. In contrast, 65 per cent of teachers are female. Teachers account for 48 per cent of all female professionals but only 17 per cent of male professionals (see also pp. 265–6).

Class at Nepabunna school, South Australia. Women's share of the total work force is approaching half, but concentration is uneven from occupation to occupation. Teaching is one that is dominated by women, who fill around two-thirds of all teaching jobs.

Aborigines

There are about 140,000 Aboriginal people of working age in Australia. Around 47 per cent of the Aboriginal population live in communities with fewer than 1000 people, approximately 27 per cent on Aboriginal land or on Aboriginal-owned pastoral properties. The geographic dispersion of Aboriginal people outside urban centres, caused by invasion and displacement, has resulted in a concentration of Aboriginal people in pastoral, horticultural and mining sectors of the economy.

Unemployment among Aboriginal people tends to be higher than for the population as a whole, especially outside the cities and for women and young people. Aboriginal people are under-represented among managers and administrators and in professional jobs, and over-represented in the labourers and related workers category (see also pp. 264–5).

Young People

Teenage and young adult male employment has fallen consistently since 1966 and part-time work has become more common. The expansion of white-collar jobs has worked particularly to the advantage of young females, whose employment is concentrated in these areas. With the decline in manufacturing more young male school leavers may join them in the future.

Immigrants

Immigrants, especially non-English speaking immigrants, are particularly concentrated in manual work (see pp. 266–7). Since the beginning of the recession in 1983, the unemployment rate for non-English speakers has also increased faster than for English speakers. The effect is most pronounced for workers from Italy, Greece, the former Yugoslavia, Poland and Malta. CR

Child care

Child care has emerged as a major social and political issue of the 1990s. The increase in the number of women who combine paid work outside the home with responsibility for young children is one of the major reasons for this (see also pp. 265–6).

The workforce participation rates of mothers of young children have increased rapidly in recent decades. Around 45 per cent of mothers of children below school age and almost two-thirds of mothers of children at primary school have paid jobs. Child care services are also needed in order to allow parents to have time to study, to undertake training courses or simply to have a break from child-rearing responsibilities. While services which cater for pre-school-aged children receive most of the attention in public debate there is also a concerted lobby for services which provide after-school and vacation activities for young children of school age.

Historically, in Australia, group care for children outside the home has been the preserve of voluntary and philanthropic organisations. The Kindergarten Union of New South Wales was formed in 1895 and similar bodies were formed in all states within two decades. The Kindergarten Unions focused their energies on providing services for working-class children in the congested industrial suburbs of the major capital cities. Their aim was to instil middle-class attitudes and values into these children and to remove them from the 'vicious' influences of their own environment. Kindergartens were not intended to relieve mothers of the responsibility for the day-to-day care of their children and a clear distinction was drawn between kindergarten services (which only operated for very limited hours) and child care centres which served the needs of working parents. This dichotomy exists to the present day.

In 1972 the federal government entered the children's services arena with the passage of the Child Care Act. This Act, introduced in the last weeks of the McMahon Liberal–Country Party government, enabled capital and recurrent grants to be paid to non-profit organisations providing child care; funding did not commence until the Whitlam government (1972–75) came to office. Child care proved to be a highly contentious issue under Whitlam. Traditional organisations (such as the various Kinder-

garten Unions) saw the availability of federal funds as a just reward for decades of effort and believed that they should have the major say in determining the types of services funded. By contrast, the Labor government was far more sympathetic to the aspirations of feminist groups and community development advocates, who saw child care as a vehicle for social change. These groups demanded services managed by parents rather than professionals and attempted to develop a range of approaches to service provision which were outside the traditional mould. There were problems, too, with several state governments which resented Labor's method of directly funding local community groups and bypassing the states.

Under the Fraser (Liberal – National) government (1975–83) Commonwealth expenditure on child care was wound back considerably and increased emphasis given to the view that families (that is, women) should provide child care themselves or purchase it on the market. Strong efforts were made to identify child care as a welfare service for the needy, rather than a normal community provision. When services were provided by the Commonwealth an emphasis was placed on low-cost options such as family day care (where women care for small groups of children in their own homes) rather than child care centres which involve capital construction costs and the employment of staff who have to be paid award wages. Although there was strong opposition to this approach from community groups and women's organisations, who regarded family day care as exploitative and not necessarily in the best interests of the children, this policy direction remained the major thrust under Fraser.

Following the election of the Hawke Labor government in 1983 and the reorientation of federal politics around labour market and labour movement issues, the debate about child care provision changed markedly. So, too, did federal government priorities. The expansion of services was considerable. At the beginning of 1993, the federal government was providing assistance to almost 200,000 child care places (compared with 46,000 a decade earlier). The majority of these places are in centres, not family day care schemes. However, fees have escalated and the means test for subsidies excludes virtually all families with two full-time income earners. Despite this, the government has promoted child care as an adjunct to its employment policies. It has introduced access guidelines which give first priority to parents who are in the workforce or training or studying with a view to obtaining employment. It has also introduced tax concessions and special arrangements designed to encourage private employers to enter into partnership with the government to provide child care for employees – particularly women employees in low-paid industries.

Pre-school centre in Elsternwick, Melbourne. Pressure for child-care facilities is great, as a third of mothers of pre-school children have regular employment.

In a highly controversial move, the Hawke government decided that from the beginning of 1991, children attending private (for-profit) child care centres as well as those using community-based services, were eligible for Commonwealth Government fee subsidies.

The considerable increase in public expenditure in child care services over recent years has not gone without challenge. Both within and outside the Labor party there are vociferous critics of the direction of government policy. However, while reductions in the level of financial support for child care services could well occur, any wholesale winding back of commitment in this area is unlikely in the foreseeable future. Publicly funded child care services are widely acknowledged as a basic prerequisite for the well-being of parents and children in modern society. DB

Unemployment

THE MEASURE OF UNEMPLOYMENT

There are three major sources of unemployment statistics covering recent decades. The Commonwealth Employment Service (CES) issues figures on the number of people registered as wanting work, and the Department of Social Security (DSS) provides figures on the number of people receiving unemployment benefits. Both sets of figures are byproducts of administrative procedures not initially designed to provide estimates of the unemployment rate. A third data set is provided by the Labour Force Survey carried out by the Australian Bureau of Statistics (ABS). Being designed for the purpose it is generally regarded as providing the most authoritative unemployment figures.

The ABS survey is based on a multistage sample covering about three-fifths of 1 per cent of all dwellings. Approximately 31,000 dwellings are surveyed in this way each month. The labour force definitions used conform closely to international standards. People are classified as employed if they have done at least one hour of paid work in the relevant week. Thus those who have worked for only two or three hours and who may be registered for work with the CES and legitimately drawing unemployment benefits would not be counted as unemployed by the ABS.

To be counted as unemployed respondents must not only have been without any paid work, but must also satisfy two further conditions:

- They must have looked actively for work in the four weeks preceding the relevant week – for example, by writing job applications or consulting CES notice boards, and
- They must have been available to start work in the relevant week.

Respondents who say they want work but are not actively looking for work, perhaps because they believe there is none available and have therefore become discouraged, are not counted as unemployed. Likewise, a respondent who wants work and may indeed be actively looking for work, but who has made other arrangements for the week in question (e.g. is taking a training course or a holiday) and is therefore not immediately available for work, will also not be counted as unemployed. The result of these definitions is that a large number of people without work but wanting work are excluded from the official figures. Estimates are that these so-called hidden unemployed are at least as numerous as the officially unemployed. Thus the actual number of people wanting work is at least twice the official figure.

In addition to its series on the numbers registered as looking for work, the CES maintains figures on the numbers of job vacancies of which it has been notified. One measure of the seriousness of the unemployment problem is thus to compare the number of registered jobseekers with the number of vacancies. In the September quarter of 1983, one of the worst years in recent decades, there were 43 jobseekers for every registered vacancy.

WHO ARE THE UNEMPLOYED?

Women normally have had higher rates of recorded unemployment in Australia, although somewhat inexplicably the gap disappeared quite suddenly in 1983. There is, however, substantially more hidden unemployment among women than men. Women continue, therefore, to experience higher overall unemployment rates (see also p. 252).

Younger age groups experience higher levels of unemployment with the rate for 15 to 19-year-olds rising to almost 23 per cent in 1983 before dropping back to 19 per cent in 1986. Those over 55 have the lowest rates at around 5 per cent in recent years. This figure does not, however, give a true indication of the seriousness of the problem for older workers, for the average duration of unemployment in the oldest age

Commonwealth Employment Service office in Melbourne. In common with the rest of the industrialised world unemployment in Australia increased substantially in the early 1990s.

group is over a year. For the youngest group it is less than six months.

Unemployment is highest among the least educated and least skilled sections of the workforce. It is higher among the overseas born than among those born in Australia, the worst-affected groups being the Lebanese and Vietnamese whose rates in 1986 were around 25 per cent. Worst of all, the unemployment rate among Australian Aborigines in 1986 was 35 per cent, almost five times the figure for non-Aboriginals (see pp. 264–5).

The regions experiencing the worst unemployment are the heavy industrial areas of Wollongong and Newcastle in New South Wales and western Adelaide in South Australia. All these areas have been affected by the general contraction which has occurred in the manufacturing sector in recent years.

GOVERNMENT RESPONSES

Prior to World War II, unemployment relief was provided by state governments or by charitable organisations. It took the form of either food handouts, for those who could show need, or wages (usually at below-award rates), for the performance of government-provided relief work. In 1945 the federal government took over responsibility for the problem and introduced the Commonwealth Unemployment Benefit, as part of a new package of social security legislation. The Benefit is today administered by the Department of Social Security. One of the eligibility criteria for the receipt of Benefit from the DSS is that the recipient be registered with the CES as wanting work.

Benefits are generally below the wages paid in even the poorest paid employment. The single adult rate is about 30 per cent of average weekly earnings net of tax while the rate for a married person with four children is about 70 per cent of net average weekly earnings. The unemployment benefit for single people has generally also been below the level of the old-age pension.

EXPLANATIONS OF UNEMPLOYMENT

The rise in unemployment which began after 1974 was part of a world-wide trend, triggered by the four-fold rise in the price of oil agreed to by OPEC. However, the Australian debate as to the causes of the problem has tended to focus on more local explanations.

One theory, common in popular thinking but absent from serious writing, is that young people have been too pampered and are now work-shy, choosing to live on unemployment benefits rather than work. On this view the unemployed are regarded as 'dole bludgers' ('dole' refers to the unemployment benefit; 'bludger' is a colloquial term meaning someone who shirks responsibilities).

The theory heard most often from economists is that wage levels in Australia are too high. Such writers note that the most dramatic rises in unemployment corresponded with substantial increases in wages paid to Australian workers.

Another explanation, popularised in Australia by a former federal government minister, Barry Jones, in a best-selling book, *Sleepers, Wake!*, is that the rise in unemployment is due to technological change (industrial robots, office computers, and so on) and that Australia will never again experience full employment.

A further line of argument, which focuses specifically on the long-term decline of the manufacturing sector, is that Australian capital has been moving offshore to take advantage of cheap labour available in neighbouring Asian countries.

POLICY OPTIONS

Full employment remains, in theory, a government objective and politicians invariably interpret each new set of unemployment figures in this light. However, a good deal of government policy is based on different assumptions. As the number of unemployed grows, so does the duration of unemployment. Furthermore, long periods of unemployment destroy workers' confidence in their ability to find work and even to perform adequately if they do find work. Thus, recent years have seen a number of government initiatives, aimed specifically at the long-term unemployed, offering training or other transitional programmes designed to help them back into the workforce.

Older workers who have experienced long-term unemployment are probably beyond this kind of help. They may have become effectively unemployable. It has been suggested that in such cases the requirement that people continue to look for work in order to be eligible for unemployment benefits be waived.

The reasoning here is that if society can no longer provide jobs for all its members, it makes little sense to require its least-employable members to continue a futile search for work in order to be eligible for income support. This kind of development has been foreshadowed by Barry Jones and others who argue that as we move towards an era in which work is a scarce resource, the link between work and income will have to be broken and every citizen provided with a guaranteed income, regardless of status in the labour force .   AH

The trade unions

A number of working men's associations were formed or re-formed in the building and metal trades and in the printing industry. These new organisations can properly be considered trade unions. Their memberships were largely confined to craftsmen and they sought to regulate the supply of skilled labour, to raise wages, to improve working conditions and to shorten hours of work. In 1856 some associations in both Sydney and Melbourne, led by the building trades, won an eight-hour day, an achievement without precedent in Britain, Europe or the USA (see also pp.96–7).

As the easily won gold began to peter out, company mining largely replaced small-scale prospecting. By the end of the 1850s, wages in urban areas were down to something like pre-gold rush levels. There were further reductions in the 1860s and some unions lost the eight-hour day. But unionism was now firmly established.

A union of coalminers was operating in the Hunter Valley north of Sydney by the early 1860s. By the 1870s there was a goldminers' union in Victoria, and in Sydney there were unions of seamen and of metal workers' assistants. Sydney unions formed a Trades and Labour Council in 1871 to coordinate policy on matters of common interest and the Melbourne Trades Hall Committee began to assume similar functions in 1879. Central bodies were formed in the other colonies during the next 10 years. The first intercolonial union conference met in 1879, the second in 1884, and there were to be four more before 1890. In 1883, following a strike of tailoresses, women workers began organising a union in Melbourne's clothing trades.

In the 1880s the organisation of the unskilled proceeded more rapidly. Waterside workers, builders' labourers, railway and tramway workers had formed unions by 1885. In 1886, a number of shearers' unions were established in the three eastern colonies and in South Australia. Three of these unions amalgamated early in 1887, and, by 1890, the Amalgamated Shearers' Union (ASU) had more than 20,000 members, most of them in New South Wales. The Queensland shearers had their own union and there was also a union of rural labourers in that colony.

Of the 71 unions in existence in New South Wales in 1891, 12 were formed between 1882 and 1885 and 42 after 1886. This growth rate, however, tends to hide the instability of colonial unionism. The seasonal nature of the pastoral industry, a major bearer of economic growth in the period 1860 to 1890, helped create a large pool of casual labour in both rural and urban areas. Transport, waterside, seamen and shearers' unions all experienced difficulty, at various times, in holding their organisations together and in pursuing union claims. Fluctuating employment levels also affected unions in the manu-

Trade union banners in a parade in Melbourne, 1990. Trade union membership was high in Australia in the 1970s and 1980s, with around 55 per cent of all wage and salary earners belonging to a union. By 1990 this had fallen to 40 per cent.

THE RISE OF UNIONS

The first attempts to form combinations of working men in Australia were reported in 1831, just five years after free immigrants began arriving in New South Wales in increasing numbers. By 1850, some 20 societies had been formed in Sydney and 12 in Melbourne. Not all survived, and most appeared to be less concerned with improving wages and working conditions than with providing some security for their members against illness and injury. But appearances were deceptive. Despite the repeal in 1824 of the Combination Acts (originating in Britain and adopted in New South Wales, these Acts prohibited workers from forming unions and taking strike action), the legal status of working men's associations remained uncertain. A friendly society façade was a form of insurance against harassment by the state. Some societies, nevertheless, devised ways to bring pressure on employers, and most were prominent in the agitation to end convict transportation, which, for free working men and women, was a living standards issue.

The discovery of gold in New South Wales and Victoria in the early 1850s had a profound impact on the labour market. Thousands of workers were drawn to the diggings, while the wealth produced stimulated urban development and manufacturing.

facturing sector. Manufacturing, although expanding, was continually handicapped by a small local market and a flow of imports from technologically more advanced foreign competitors. The resulting jobbing shop environment meant that even skilled tradesmen could not expect continuous employment. In slack periods most unions in the manufacturing sector lost members and struggled to sustain a commitment to their rules and objectives. The coalminers' unions, too, found that the small local market greatly weakened their bargaining position.

The manufacturing environment encouraged contract work and, as contractors sought ways to cut costs, craftsmen were quickly forced to come to terms with semi-skilled and process workers. Moreover, in pursuit of their goals they were frequently militant and aggressive. The unskilled workers' unions, on the other hand, were seldom as militant. Shearers and waterside workers, for example, faced an awkward dilemma: they had to avoid industrial conflict during periods of seasonal unemployment, but this necessity meant, in effect, that they could strike only when the intermittently employed casual worker had the opportunity to make good wages. The ASU's problems in this regard were compounded by piece rates and bonuses.

Strike defeats

A severe economic depression, which was affecting rural and urban industries by early 1891, aggravated the union movement's weaknesses and contributed to a series of strike defeats. The maritime strike of 1890, the biggest industrial dispute in nineteenth-century Australia, the shearers' strike in the first half of 1891 and the Broken Hill miners' strike in 1892, were all costly reverses. The ASU claimed a victory over the pastoralists in 1894, but a dramatic drop in membership in the 1895 season left it greatly weakened and its fortunes declined steadily in the next four years. While each of these strikes had its own distinct cause, all, to some extent, were fought over the refusal of employers to recognise unionism.

In May 1890 a port blockade of non-union shorn wool brought Queensland's pastoralists to the conference table. Employers believed they had witnessed the harbinger of a concerted union challenge to their right to manage. A few months later, when maritime workers in Adelaide and Sydney struck in support of ships' officers, who were seeking to affiliate with Labour Councils, an intercolonial combination of waterfront and pastoral employers was quickly formed. Commercial and financial interests gave it their enthusiastic support. The strike spread to all waterfront unions, to transport workers, to miners and, for one week, to shearers in New South Wales, but the employers stood firm.

The combined pastoralists' associations then issued their own shearing agreement. When shearing began in the 1891 season, the shearers' unions had little option but to fight for their right to be consulted. The Broken Hill strike and the ASU's strike in 1894 both resulted from employers abandoning negotiated agreements which still had a year to run.

The maritime strike of 1890 is a key event in the history of labour politics. There had been desultory talk about political action in trade union circles in the late 1880s and some Labor candidates had stood for parliament in Queensland in 1889. But in all the eastern colonies, and particularly in New South Wales, the strike defeat gave the question greater urgency. A decisive argument stemmed from the manner in which the governments of New South Wales and

Mass meetings at Flinders Park, Melbourne, in 1890 during a labour and shipping strike. The strike was the largest in nineteenth-century Australia, but nevertheless was defeated.

Victoria had backed employers. Unionists were now more easily persuaded that labour needed to capture the power of the state if social reform were to become a reality. In New South Wales the Trades and Labour Council hastily assembled a group of candidates to contest elections early in 1891. They won 35 seats.

All colonies, except Western Australia, had Labor members of parliament before 1900, and a Labor government actually held office in Queensland for a week during 1899. But it was the New South Wales party which set the example for others. It went through a period of consolidation after its initial success, and its electoral fortunes waned. Yet throughout the 1890s it maintained a strong presence in the New South Wales parliament. No government could be formed without its support. It exploited this crucial position to bargain for social reforms, including old-age pensions, and the procedures it developed to discipline its parliamentarians were to contribute significantly to the development of the modern Australian party system. By 1904 it was the official opposition.

Arbitration

The strike defeats also gave a boost to demands for compulsory arbitration and for larger and more effective forms of combined union organisation. The latter materialised as the Australasian Federation of Labour, but the depression rendered it stillborn. More success attended the former. New South Wales, Victorian and Western Australian governments had introduced differing forms of compulsory arbitration by 1901 and a Commonwealth system was introduced in 1904.

Reflection on the strikes and on the distress caused by the depression also made socialism, both parliamentary and utopian, more popular. With unemployment reaching unprecedented heights, it became more plausible to argue that capitalism had run its course and that a better form of social organisation would evolve, or would have to be created. But the socialists' momentum did not last, partly because they were not united and partly because their ideas were viewed with suspicion by the pragmatic leaders of the Labor parties. By 1900, the socialists, European migrants prominent among them, had become critics of a Labor Party leadership devoted to a cautious election-oriented reformism.

The 1890s ended with a severe drought which cut Australian sheep numbers by more than a third (see also p. 98). This second economic catastrophe led to diversification in rural areas and to attempts to stimulate manufacturing. Both federal and state governments took part in the process, promoting closer settlement in an effort to hasten the development of wheat, sugar and dairying industries. The results of their efforts were to help change the face of rural society and of rural work relations. The huge pastoral properties of the nineteenth century gradually disappeared. There were more family farms and consequently more well-populated districts which were largely capable of meeting their own labour needs, sometimes even in the periods of peak demand. The ASU amalgamated with the Queensland Shearers' Union in 1904 to form the Australian Workers' Union, but the AWU was not as militant as its predecessors and its adherence to arbitration, which grew more steadfast as it expanded into other industries and became enmeshed in labour politics, added to the forces which were dampening down conflict in rural industrial relations. The focus of union and political labour activity became increasingly urban from the early 1900s onwards.

Under the stimulus of the newly formed arbitration systems unionism grew apace. By 1910, Australia had become the most highly unionised country in the world, and, by 1921, 53 per cent of all wage and salary earners were unionised. The popularity of the federal Court of Conciliation and Arbitration under its second president, H. B. Higgins, encouraged unions to establish federal associations. The requirements for registration with arbitration courts brought organisational and structural change to many unions which, together with their common interest in arbitration, further reduced the appropriateness of the craft union/new union dichotomy.

Labor parties, too, developed rapidly. Labor candidates contested the first election for the Commonwealth parliament in 1901 and subsequently Labor members, backed by a group of reformist liberals, formed minority governments in 1904 and 1908. In 1910 the world's first labour governments to win parliamentary majorities took office in the Commonwealth and in the states of New South Wales and South Australia. The Commonwealth Government introduced some notable measures in the next three years, including a maternity bonus, a workers' compensation system and a Commonwealth Bank. The record of Labor electoral success continued until 1916 (Western Australia had a Labor government by 1911 and Queensland by 1915), when the Labor Party as a whole split on the question of compulsory overseas military service. It lost office in the Commonwealth and in New South Wales as a result.

The decision by H. B. Higgins, in 1907, to award a basic or minimum wage sufficient for 'the normal needs of the average employee . . . in a civilised community' was the single most important contribution made by the arbitration system to union growth, particularly among the unskilled. Only unionists working under federal awards received Higgins' wage, but the state courts followed the federal court's example and for some 50 years it was the practice for arbitra-

Henry Bournes Higgins (1851–1929), attorney-general in the Labor government of 1904 and president of the Court of Conciliation and Arbitration from 1907 to 1921. He established a minimum wage for male workers in a judgment of 1907, and did much to establish the role of arbitration in industrial disputes.

tion tribunals to award a basic rate and, then, if unions could justify their claims, a margin for skill or a special loading for arduous or dirty work. But Higgins considered an average employee in a civilised community to be a married man with three children, and the emphasis on a male breadwinner that developed from his 1907 award reinforced the economic and gender-based pressures within the labour market, which obliged women to work for wages about half the basic wage. The sexual division of labour in industry, commerce and the public service was further reinforced as a result.

Arbitration, however, did not create a working man's paradise. Higgins' basic wage underestimated living costs and state basic wages were lower than the federal wage. In 1911, when Higgins decided to adjust his wage to allow for changes in the real value of money, he had only the most rudimentary index at his disposal. Moreover, notions of justice notwithstanding, tribunals tacitly accepted that they should not award more than the market place had already allowed. That was not always enough to permit a 'civilised' existence. A protectionist tariff was introduced in 1902 and revised upwards in 1908 and 1920, but the nineteenth-century problems of overseas competition and a small local market continued to dog manufacturing and to hinder attempts to establish heavy industry. Thus, apart from the war years, unemployment was high throughout the period 1900 to 1921, at least by later twentieth-century standards, and it sustained a downward pressure on wages, especially for the unskilled, which was reflected in tribunal determinations. To add to their problems, some unskilled unions had difficulty obtaining an award because the legal procedures involved were protracted and costly. Most had difficulty in enforcing award conditions across their respective industries.

Frustration with arbitration was a common ingredient in a number of bitter strikes before World War I, and when inflation began to erode living standards after 1914, dissatisfaction increased. Coalminers in New South Wales struck successfully for higher wages in 1916 and in the following year a dispute in a railway workshop precipitated what was virtually a general strike in that state. Unions wanted arbitration, but they were far from happy with the long delays in over-crowded courts, the caution and conservatism of judges and the constant changing of rules and procedures as the High Court interpreted the meaning of notions like dispute. Even Higgins fell from grace when he refused to hear the claims of unions involved in the 1917 strike.

Some contemporary European commentators described the early Australian Labor parties as pace-setters for twentieth-century democracies. They were greatly impressed by Labor's social welfare

policies, which they attributed to a nationalistic desire to create a collectivist society free from the inequality and poverty of Britain and Europe.

Individualism

However, individualism was the prevailing ideology of colonial Australia. As in other newly settled countries, many immigrants and native-born hoped to obtain security and independence through a small business or farm. The Labor parties won considerable support by endorsing policies designed to help realise these ambitions. When viewed from such a perspective, their achievements lose much of their novelty, particularly, too, when it is acknowledged that New Zealand liberal governments anticipated much of the legislation which earned Australia its reputation for progressiveness.

Similarly, Australian unions, despite their early development, were not especially militant or powerful. Strike defeats greatly outnumbered strike victories in the period 1890 to 1921. In a sense, too, arbitration hid the unions' true worth for it eased the task of winning and consolidating memberships. While unionists became relatively more plentiful, it is by no means certain that Australian unions became stronger. Indeed, in their struggle to discipline their memberships, to sustain themselves during economic fluctuations and to wring concessions from Labor governments, their experiences provide more close parallels than differences with the history of unionism in Britain and Europe.   JM

TRADE UNIONS TODAY

Trade unions have a major impact upon Australian politics. They have visibility and influence through links with the Australian Labor Party (ALP), through the arbitration system, through direct industrial action and by lobbying governments.

The ALP was set up by Australian unions in order to gain a political voice after the severe and often unsuccessful industrial conflict of the 1880s and 1890s. About 60 per cent of Australian unionists belong to unions affiliated with the ALP.

Wages tribunals had been set up before federation. In 1901 the Australian Constitution gave the federal government the following power: 'Conciliation and arbitration for the prevention and settlement of industrial disputes extending beyond the limits of any one state' (section 51 (XXXV)). Then the Conciliation and Arbitration Act 1904 set up the federal conciliation and arbitration machinery.

Unions may engage in strikes and other forms of direct industrial action which give the unions involved high visibility and indeed notoriety, but not necessarily influence. In fact, the use of the strike weapon may constitute a sign of lack of influence. The existence of the so-called penal clauses has in turn led to major conflict between unions, employers and governments.

Working with a Labor government has often been an advantage but can have its own complications. Trade unions may lobby state and federal governments, which may be done by individual unions but more often it is done through the major peak organisations.

Capital cities and some provincial centres have Trades and Labour Councils (TLCs), sometimes known as Trades Hall Councils (THCs). The Australian Council of Trade Unions (ACTU), formed in 1927, is the federal peak organisation of all its affiliates who join via the metropolitan TLC (or equivalent). It is important to realise that not all unions are affiliated to TLCs. For many years the large and powerful rural-based Australian Workers' Union (AWU) stayed outside. Most non-manual unions were reluctant to identify themselves too closely with the blue-collar-dominated ACTU. Their objections have melted away and one by one the white-collar public-sector unions have affiliated with the metropolitan Labour Councils. Until the late 1970s most such unions were affiliated to specific peak organisations. The two major groupings, ACSPA (Australian Council of Salaried and Professional Associations) and CAGEO (Council of Australian Government Employee Organisations) dissolved into the ACTU in 1979 and 1981, respectively.

Most white-collar public-sector unions have held back from the next logical step – namely, affiliation with the ALP. Some have given other assistance to

On a national day of protest in November 1992, Victorian demonstrators march against industrial policies of the newly elected state government, in particular the abolition of holiday leave loadings and weekend penalty rates, and a proposed Industrial Relations bill.

the ALP. At a state level the Public Service Association (PSA) of New South Wales, for example, has a long history of surveying the parties and candidates at election times and of rating the results. This often meant that the New South Wales PSA had given *de facto* electoral support to the ALP. More recently in 1982 the Victorian Branch of the Teachers' Federation gave substantial financial support to the Victorian Labor Party led by John Cain in tacit exchange for favours.

Affiliation with the ALP is a significant step which most blue-collar and few white-collar unions (depending upon one's definition) have taken. It is a landmark, as is the first strike.

Australia used to be one of the most highly unionised countries in the world in the 1970s and 1980s. About 55 per cent of wage and salary earners were members. By 1990 this had fallen to 40 per cent. The overall percentage changed only moderately from 1970 to 1984 but its occupational nature changed dramatically. The changing occupational character of Australian trade unionism is indicated by those large unions which had the highest rate of growth in the period 1976–1983. Of the top 10 the Federated Miscellaneous Workers' Union and the Transport Workers' Union were the only non-white-collar unions and teachers and public-sector clerical workers' unions were predominant.

The ACTU and other sections of the trade union movement have long wished to have fewer unions, and more unions organised on an industry basis. It has been argued that the arbitration system itself, which requires the registration of unions, has encouraged the proliferation of unions. In 1990, however, Commonwealth legislation was passed designed to ensure a minimum size of 10,000 members.

It is important to realise that Australian trade unions do not constitute a monolith. They are probably more coherent and cohesive than are their employer counterparts but have their industrial and political differences. They do share one feature. They are primarily reactors rather than initiators. Unions need to respond to the economic conditions, the views of government and of the various industrial tribunals and, last but not least, the actions of management.

The arbitration system provides an arena within which conflicts between labour and capital are mediated. In order for matters to come before the federal arbitration system there has to have been a 'dispute' 'extending beyond the limits of any one state'. The High Court's interpretation of these matters has been very broad and so-called paper disputes occur. The Court had traditionally taken a narrow view of the definition of what constituted an 'industrial' dispute. This changed in 1983 when the High Court declared that social welfare workers, covered by the Australian Social Welfare Union, were engaged in an 'industry' and hence were eligible for federal registration.

In Australia industrial relations cover what happens within the arbitration system and within 'collective bargaining' (which, unlike arbitration, does not involve a third party). Governments have tried to influence wage levels but often they have been unsuccessful. The arbitration system is relatively autonomous. Furthermore, with collective bargaining governments have even less influence over the outcome. Yet wages policy can help undermine a federal government. MJS

Equal opportunity legislation

During the early 1970s pressure began to build up from newly mobilised sections of society such as Aborigines, women and ethnic minorities for Australian governments to pass anti-discrimination legislation (see also pp. 263–7).

The first real progress came during the Whitlam period. In 1973 Australia ratified International Labour Organisation (ILO) Convention 111 and National and State Committees on Discrimination in Employment and Occupation were set up. In 1975 the Commonwealth Government passed the Racial Discrimination Act, which was implemented energetically by the Commissioner for Community Relations, Al Grassby.

Much of the lobbying for anti-discrimination legislation came from the Women's Electoral Lobby (WEL) formed in 1972. WEL was bitterly disappointed that the 1975 Act did not cover discrimination on the ground of sex. However, before the end of International Women's Year the South Australian Sex Discrimination Act 1975 was passed. The New South Wales government followed with the Anti-Discrimination Act 1977 and the Victorian government with the Equal Opportunity Act 1977.

During the late 1970s the Australian Labor Party was made aware of the need to develop systematic policies to gain women's votes, which had disproportionately gone to the non-Labor parties. Anti-discrimination and equal opportunity legislation became central to Labor's electoral campaigns. Early experience showed that complaint-based legislation was not sufficient to combat the widespread disadvantage experienced by women in employment. In 1980 the New South Wales Labor government became the first to introduce the legislative requirement for written equal employment opportunity (EEO) programmes. Public sector agencies were required to take positive steps to identify and remove barriers to equal opportunity for women and members of specified groups.

With some exceptions, the term EEO rather than affirmative action (AA) is used in Australia. The term affirmative action has been associated with the numerical employment quotas sometimes imposed

Women workers sorting apricots at a cannery in Goulburn, Victoria, in 1981. The previous year the New South Wales government enacted legislation enforcing equality of opportunity in response to widespread discrimination against women workers.

in the USA by federal courts when employers have been found guilty of discriminatory practices. Courts have no role in Australian EEO or AA programmes, and there is no possibility of court-imposed quotas. Australian EEO and AA legislation explicitly entrenches the merit principle and numerical performance indicators are used only to measure whether women and designated groups are moving closer to the success rates characteristic of the organisation.

Labor victories in Victoria and South Australia in 1982 and in Western Australia in 1983 led to the introduction of new or stronger legislation. All three states passed Equal Opportunity Acts in 1984 and introduced or strengthened EEO programmes in the public sector.

At the Commonwealth level the new Labor government ratified the UN Convention on the Elimination of All Forms of Discrimination Against Women in 1983. The Sex Discrimination Act 1984 did not include EEO provisions, although it did allow, in

accordance with the Convention, for special measures to promote equality. Cooperative arrangements were developed whereby State Equal Opportunity Commissions handled complaints under both Commonwealth and state legislations. The same year saw the passage of the Public Service Reform Act 1984, which introduced the requirement in the Australian Public Service for written EEO programmes directed at women, Aborigines, migrants from non-English-speaking backgrounds and their children, and people with disabilities.

In 1986 the Hawke government finally passed, after vociferous opposition, the Affirmative Action (Equal Employment Opportunity for Women) Act. The term affirmative action was here retained, despite being a political liability. This important Act was the first to introduce the requirement for written AA (EEO) programmes into private-sector employment in Australia. It applies to companies (and now to voluntary organisations) with more than 100 employees as well as to all institutions of higher education.

One criticism made by WEL and by the Australian Council of Trade Unions (ACTU) was that it did not include sanctions, apart from the naming in parliament of employers who failed to provide a report. In 1988 the Victorian government announced that it would not give assistance and contracts to employers who were named and the Commonwealth followed suit in 1992. Nonetheless, concerns about effectiveness remain, particularly in view of increased casualisation in the service sector of the economy.

More recent Commonwealth legislation has included the Equal Employment Opportunity (Commonwealth Authorities) Act 1987. Although this contained no new elements, the opposition decided to oppose it, giving rise to a dramatic revolt. The shadow minister for the status of women, Senator Peter Baume, resigned from the front bench and a quarter of the Liberal senators crossed the floor to vote with the government.

The election of a Labor government in Queensland in 1989 led to the passage of the Queensland Anti-Discrimination Act 1991, but in Tasmania opposition from the Legislative Council and the defeat of the Labor government in 1992 meant the lapsing of the Tasmanian Anti-Discrimination Bill. With the passage of the ACT Discrimination Act 1991 and the Northern Territory Anti-Discrimination Act 1992, Tasmania remains the only State or Territory where complainants are wholly dependent on Commonwealth anti-discrimination legislation (which excludes state employees from its coverage).

In 1990 the Hawke government ratified International Labour Organisation Convention 156 on equal opportunities for workers with family responsibilities. State and territory governments have begun incorporating the ground of family or carer responsibilities into their anti-discrimination legislation. So far, the Commonwealth has only taken the more limited step of prohibiting dismissal from employment on this ground.

Other recent developments in Australian anti-discrimination legislation have included coverage of industrial awards, strengthening of provisions relating to HIV/AIDS discrimination and the introduction in some jurisdictions of a prohibition on age discrimination and/or racial vilification.   MS

Socio-economic inequality

Australia is a society which boasts an egalitarian ethos. This has arisen largely because its initial European settlers were convicts and soldiers and the later settlers were immigrants who came with hopes of improving their social and economic position. There is no rigid status order and social mobility is considerable.

INCOME

However, despite this egalitarian ethos there still exists considerable socio-economic inequality. There are significant inequalities in the distribution of income and wealth, a situation promoted by the virtual lack of any form of wealth tax.

The inequality is even more marked in the distribution of wealth. It has been shown by various studies that the top 1 per cent of adult individuals own approximately 25 per cent of personal wealth and the top 10 per cent of Australians own 60 per cent. At the other end of the spectrum there are 2 million Australians living below the poverty line including 700,000 children.

In recent years the inequalities have increased as governments have adopted policies aimed at reducing labour costs and effecting a redistribution from wages to profits. The net worth of the very wealthy has increased at a much greater rate than the total wealth of all Australians.

Changes to social security arrangements in the 1980s brought tighter targeting of benefits coupled with higher payments. The effect has been to protect the position of the poorest but leave lower to middle-income earners worse off. Particularly adversely

affected have been married couple families with two or more children, single people aged 15–64 and married couples with no dependants whose head was aged under 65.

Unemployment (see pp. 254–5) remains the dominant cause of poverty while the cost of housing is the major pressure on the poor. Unemployment, at one stage reduced to 5.9 per cent from the 10.1 per cent in 1983, rose again and by the start of 1993 had reached a post-war record figure of 11.1 per cent.

Australian governments vary in their approaches to socio-economic inequality. The Australian Labor Party (ALP) was set up by the union movement in 1891 in order to represent workers' interests in the national parliament. The Australian working class organised trade unions throughout the 1860s and 1870s but unionism became a mass phenomenon from the late 1880s. In the 1890s unionists experienced defeats in strikes which convinced them that industrial action alone was insufficient to secure the economic and social gains for which they had been striving (see also pp. 257–8). When the ALP has been in government it has pursued labourist rather than socialist policies.

The unions won from governments (state and federal) a system of conciliation and arbitration that enabled either capital or labour to refer a dispute to an arbitral body which was able to make a judgement having the force of law. Labor governments in particular set up the framework of a welfare state but in its long period of rule (1949–72) the coalition continued to govern in the same vein. For much of the period since federation, however, government has been by various non-Labor parties, all of which have espoused individualist and anti-socialist policies, and have, since 1921, had the support of rural-based parties.

The Hawke and Keating Labor governments came to office having agreed to a prices and incomes Accord with the Australian Council of Trade Unions (ACTU). Although the Accord re-legitimised the role of unions at a time when they were under attack domestically and in other English-speaking countries, most notably Britain, the real level of wages declined throughout the 1980s and the level of profits for business again reached the high levels of the late 1960s.

The Hawke government shelved its proposals for a wealth inquiry. The prime minister's pledge to 'eradicate child poverty by 1990' was not realistic. However, in the 1990s Labor introduced substantial increases for childcare and for payments for families with children. The Keating government's election platform extended this further. The aim was to divert resources to families with children so that by 1990 no such family would have an income below the poverty line.

Aboriginal mother and children. Aborigines are subject to higher unemployment, lower life expectancy, worse health and a higher birth rate than the rest of the population.

ABORIGINES

Aboriginal and Torres Strait Islander Australians (1.5 per cent of the population) are the most impoverished group. Less than half of Aboriginal people of working age (15 years and over) are in the workforce (that is, in jobs or seeking jobs), compared to 62 per cent for the total population. In 1986, it was estimated that 35 per cent of these were unemployed although preliminary 1991 Census data suggests an improvement since then. The majority of Aborigines who are employed are to be found in the lower skilled and lower paying jobs. Aboriginal unemployment is at least five times the national average. Aboriginal incomes (on average) are only half the levels enjoyed by other Australians.

For generations Aborigines were subjected to policies which segregated them on reserves and missions but in the 1950s there was a policy turnabout to assimilate them into the wider population. After much lobbying by Aboriginal activists (particularly the Federal Council for the Advancement of Aborigines and Torres Strait Islanders) and their supporters, the discriminatory legislation which segregated and controlled them was dismantled throughout the 1960s. They gained the right to vote (1962) and in 1967 a referendum which gave the Australian government concurrent power with the states to legislate for Aborigines was passed by an overwhelming majority of Australian voters (90.77 per cent).

In 1972 the Whitlam Labor government was elected after 23 years of Liberal Party–Country Party coalition rule. It introduced pluralistic policies in Aboriginal affairs which acknowledged the unique status of Aborigines and Torres Strait Islanders as the indigenous peoples of Australia. It instituted a policy of self-determination, set up the Woodward Royal Commission into the question of land rights, upgraded the Office of Aboriginal Affairs to full ministerial status, set up an elected advisory body, the National Aboriginal Consultative Committee, and funded Aboriginal-run legal, medical and other service organisations.

The Fraser coalition government (1975–83) enacted a modified version of the Whitlam government's proposed land rights legislation and broadly continued policies of a pluralist nature although it titled its main policy thrust 'self-management'(see also pp. 144–5).

Throughout the 1980s Aboriginal activists lobbied for their people to be recognised as a sovereign nation, for land rights to be extended to all their communities where feasible and for compensation to be paid where such return is impractical. Since the enactment of the Aboriginal Land Rights (Northern Territory) Act 1976 and other legislation at the state level which granted land rights in various forms, interests opposed to land rights, such as mining and pastoral capital, some sections of the Liberal and National parties, and some fundamentalist Christian groups, have lobbied against land rights and positive discrimination for Aborigines.

In the face of this lobby (and its success in turning public opinion against land rights), in 1985 the

Hawke Labor government withdrew from its commitment to enact national land rights legislation. However, in June 1992 the High Court of Australia recognised continuing Native Title to land under common law for the people of Murray Island in Torres Strait (the Mabo Judgement). This decision has been hailed by many Aboriginal and Torres Strait Islander groups as a landmark one, which recognises that Australia was not, in law, unoccupied at the time of European settlement and which provides another avenue for them to have their prior ownership of certain 'unalienated' areas of land recognised. The Keating government passed tha Native Title Act 1993 to enable such claims to be made. (See also p.145.)

Throughout 1986 and subsequently, the Committee to Defend Black Rights publicised the number of Aboriginal men dying in prison and police custody. In mid-1987 the Hawke government set up the Royal Commission into Aboriginal Deaths in Custody and this, followed by the debate occasioned by the Bicentennial in 1988, would appear to have influenced the Australian public to be more sympathetically disposed towards Aboriginal arguments about the injustice of their situation. Despite this, because of the size of their population, they are likely to continue to experience the problems of an entrapped minority, an internal colony. Nevertheless, they are determined in their resistance to this colonial status and have continued to engage in the politics of embarrassment both at home and abroad and have forged enduring links with other indigenous peoples.

SEXISM

Gender stereotyping has also been a significant source of inequality in Australian society. White women gained the vote in some states as early as 1894 (South Australia) and the Franchise Act of 1902 gave them the right to vote in national elections.

This achievement was largely a result of the activities of the Woman's Christian Temperance Union and the Women's Suffrage Leagues. During the early years of this century Australia led the world as a pioneer of women's political rights.

Throughout the post-World War II period many married women entered the workforce. In the 1960s some women became politically active when they joined the anti-Vietnam war protest movement. They were also influenced by women's movements in other Western countries to set up a Women's Liberation Movement in the early 1970s. They demanded equal pay, equal status with men before the law and the right to control their own fertility.

As mentioned previously the Whitlam Labor government was responsive to lobbying by the Women's Liberation Movement, the Women's Action Committee and, in particular, the Women's Electoral Lobby (WEL). Under this government equal pay was granted, women's advisory structures were set up and women's health and other service centres were funded.

Throughout the mid-1970s anti-feminist groups such as Women Who Want to be Women and Right to Life organisations lobbied the Fraser coalition government and the public to return to support for a traditional woman's role which gave priority to child care and domestic duties, left the public sphere to men and a few childless women or ones who had raised their families, and left control over women's bodies in the hands of the medical profession. The main efforts of the women's movement during this period were aimed at maintaining the achievements of the Whitlam period and infiltrating the political parties, the unions, public office and the bureaucracy.

After the Hawke government came to power there were a number of symbolic achievements for women, notably the enactment of the Sex Discrimination Act 1984 and the Affirmative Action (Equal Opportunity for Women) Act 1986. This legislation was sponsored by the feminist Minister for Education and Youth Affairs, and Minister Assisting the Prime Minister on the Status of Women (1983–88), Senator Susan Ryan. She held a portfolio with Cabinet ranking but, because of her opposition to policies based on the then fashionable economic rationalist theories which influenced a number of key ministers in the Hawke government, she was seen as uncooperative and, after the 1987 elections, she was moved to the position of Special Minister of State, Minister Assisting the Prime Minister the Status of Women and for the Bicentenary and Minister assisting the Minister for Community Services and Health. Without a department to run her influence in the govern-

Senator Susan Ryan, who was Minister for Education and Youth Affairs, and Minister Assisting the Prime Minister on the Status of Women in Bob Hawke's government, 1983-8. During this time she sponsored two important anti-sex discrimination acts.

ment was reduced. Presumably feeling she had achieved all she could hope to in such an economic and political climate she left political life for a career in publishing.

In many ways Senator Ryan was a trail blazer in her own right and also the most visible representative of a group of women in her party who worked unstintingly for equal rights for women in all spheres of Australian life. Her career spanned a period during which the numbers of women in public office at the national and state level expanded significantly. Prior to the 1993 election, there were 29 women in the national parliament, including 19 in the Senate (25 per cent) and 10 (7 per cent) in the House of Representatives. Although this figure represents a considerable improvement over the last two decades it constitutes only 13 per cent of the total number of members.

Despite the fact that there has been considerable energy expended by anti-feminist groups, equal rights for Australian women appear to be a lasting achievement at the formal level. In the last decade payments to low-income families, extension of superannuation coverage to most workers, increases in child care, and the introduction of a child maintenance support scheme have been of particular significance for women in weaker socio-economic positions (see pp. 252–4). The Keating government plans to strengthen and extend the previously mentioned Sex Discrimination and Affirmative Action acts to 'further advance women's equality and freedom from sexual harrassment'.

A major issue for women remains unemployment. The 1980s saw a significant increase in the number of women in the workforce, especially in part-time work and service industries, the major growth area of the economy (see p. 252). While state funding for child care has increased since 1990, studies still suggest that few men have come to share child care and domestic duties equally with their spouses, the working mother continues to have two jobs, one in the paid workforce and an unpaid one at home. Many opt for part-time work as a solution. Most of those who work full time are disadvantaged by the continuing sex-segregated nature of the labour market and the option to work overtime or devote themselves to their careers to the degree necessary to ensure promotion is not available. Therefore, in fact, Australian women's incomes remain lower than those of men. Even those in full-time non-managerial employment earn only 85 per cent of male earnings. Further, domestic violence and violence by men against women in the public domain is a daily occurrence.

Despite a significant number of positive changes which make it possible for many Australian women in the 1990s to do things their mothers could not,

patriarchal sex roles and associated aggressive male behaviour are still barriers which loom large on the horizon of a woman seeking to assert her equal rights.

RACISM

Any overview of social inequality in Australia must consider the further issue of immigration. Racism, ethnocentrism and the struggle between labour and capital have set much of the pattern of immigration debate and policy throughout Australia's history.

From the introduction of the first Australian scheme for mass immigration (which was begun in New South Wales in 1832 with government assistance towards payment of the passages for working-class immigrants) there has been an ongoing conflict between Australian workers and immigrant competitors. Employers looking for a plentiful supply of cheap labour have supported assisted immigration.

Trade unions, and Australian-born workers generally, however, have wanted to keep out cheap labour which would undermine the conditions they have won through union activity. Soon after the colonies obtained the power to legislate on immigration (as part of the Australian Colonies Government Act 1850), legislation imposing immigration restrictions was passed, and after 1850 voluntary migration began to overshadow assisted immigration for the first time.

The immigrants who have been perceived as the greatest threat have been Asians because they were physically and culturally distinctive, and industrially docile. However, the immigrants who have actually always been most competitive with Australian-born workers for jobs are the British but since they are 'not visible' they have not been subjected to racist and ethnocentric policies and social attitudes.

Historian Humphrey McQueen says that with the gold rushes 'negative contempt' for Asian 'coolies' turned to 'positive hatred' and anti-Chinese riots occurred on many goldfields; for example, Hanging Rock (1852), Bendigo (1854), Buckland River (1857) and Lambing Flat (1861). Chinese immigration restriction acts were passed in Victoria (where, in mid-1850, one adult male in five was Chinese) in 1855 and New South Wales in 1861. Anti-Asian sentiment crystallised and the Immigration Restriction Act of 1901 (federal legislation) effectively banned Asian labour. This Act, which came to be known as the 'White Australia Policy', was, in part, the successful culmination of the efforts of the labour movement but also reflected hostility to competition by small-scale businessmen, such as those in the furnishing trades, who resented Chinese competitors (see also pp. 225–7).

Restaurants and shops in a Melbourne street. Modern Australia is a multicultural society.

These restrictions coincided with similar measures in North America, and fears of the Japanese in the Pacific. They also followed the winding up of most assisted British immigration and accompanied a period of depression and increased working-class unrest in the 1890s. Australian fears of the 'yellow hordes' continued to be fuelled by popular reaction to the military exploits of the Japanese, especially their bombing of Pearl Harbor (1941). Further, conservative politicians made much of the twofold threat (political and racial) of Communist China until the Whitlam Labor government recognised the People's Republic of China in 1972.

The White Australia Policy earned Australia international condemnation throughout the 1950s and 1960s and the coalition governments began to dismantle it quietly, a process completed when the Whitlam government came to power.

In the post-World War II period there was a large influx of predominantly European immigrants (between 1947 and 1972 Australia received a net gain

of 2.4 million immigrants). As with Aborigines during this period, the policy was one of assimilation. Immigrants to Australia were expected to assimilate as quickly as possible but, because this is very difficult to do and because many thought the cultures of their countries of origin could enrich what they perceived to be the somewhat narrow British culture inherited by most Australians, they found the expectation that they assimilate to be offensive.

By the early 1970s the voting power of these groups was recognised by the major political parties. Because they came from diverse backgrounds it was difficult for the Australian political parties to devise a policy which would sufficiently aggregate their interests to attract a large ethnic vote.

One answer to this was the policy of multiculturalism (see pp. 236–7) . After its introduction by the Whitlam government both major parties adopted it and it continued more or less unchallenged until historian Geoffrey Blainey and others began to complain that, in particular, the influx of Asians throughout the 1970s (especially after the fall of Saigon) and 1980s, and the policy of multiculturalism in general, were undermining the Australian way of life. They forewarned of increasing racial hostility. Some conservative politicians questioned the policy of multiculturalism and argued that it was necessary to take measures to 'control the ethnic mix' in Australia by taking fewer Asian immigrants. However, this has united otherwise disparate and sometimes antagonistic ethnic groups in defence of the policy and of the government's family reunion programme. The majority of the Australian electorate would appear to be more multicultural in outlook than such politicians as they have been consistently defeated at the polls.

In summary, then, Australia is a multicultural nation, it is considerably more egalitarian than many other societies and social mobility is achieved by many via their education and occupations, but socio-economic inequalities are still significant in all spheres of life, and gender and racial stereotyping are still facts of life although they are less salient than they were two decades ago.

Progress on measures aimed at elimination of inequality has been achieved largely by interest groups and social movements exerting pressure on political parties and governments, particularly Labor governments. Moreover, without sympathetic government action empowerment of women and racial and ethnic minorities was unlikely to have occurred. In the main, the labour movement too has chosen to rely on a government-sponsored conciliation and arbitration system to achieve improvements in workers' lifestyles and life chances. Therefore, all these achievements remain vulnerable to action by future governments.   CJ

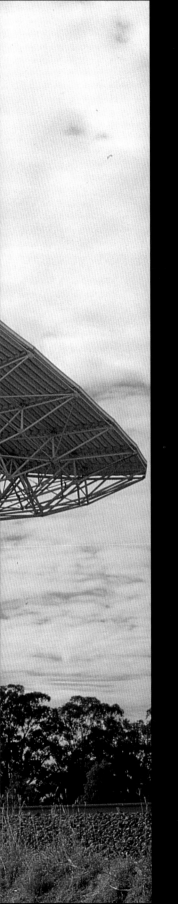

Science
and
technology

The origin and development of science

PATRONAGE

From the beginning of European settlement Australia was visualised as an emporium of nature, a source of material and insight for the development of science in Europe. Early explorations of the continent were closely associated with scientific investigations, from James Cook and Nicolas Baudin to George Caley, who enlisted the help of the Aboriginal people in his collecting work, and Ferdinand Bauer, sent out from England by Joseph Banks (1743–1820), a scientific worker on Cook's *Endeavour* voyage of 1769–70. Bauer had invested £10,000 in the trip and had then returned to take up the directorship of the botanical gardens at Kew and was elected to the presidency of the Royal Society in 1778.

From settlement to the mid-nineteenth century, Australian science was dominated by imperial and viceregal patronage, was focused on collection and observation and was influenced by individuals who had little intention of settling permanently within the peculiar environ which they so closely studied.

Science was constrained because in each colony numbers were small, facilities for research or experiment were very limited and the inspiration from purely theoretical discourse was weak. The small coteries of individuals interested in science hence relied on the encouragement of such patrons as Joseph Banks, W. J. Hooker (1785–1865) and Sir Richard Owen (1804–92) in Britain or upon the moral and financial support of colonial bureaucrats such as Sir Thomas Brisbane, governor of New South Wales 1821–25, John Hunter, governor of New South Wales 1795–1800, and Sir John Franklin, governor of Tasmania 1837–43.

SCIENTIFIC INSTITUTIONS

The demographic impact of the gold discoveries in New South Wales and Victoria dominated colonial life after 1851 and led to the emergence of a more sustained colonial science. Particularly in Victoria, the larger bureaucracy, the increase in the number of professionals and the fast growth of the major cities led to the emergence of scientific institutions.

The earlier, small scientific societies, agricultural societies, botanic gardens and observatories gave way to a variety of more permanent forums. Philosophical societies, later to become Royal Societies, were founded in Adelaide (1853), Victoria (1854), New South Wales (1856) and Queensland (1859). Geological surveys focusing on mineralogy were founded in Victoria in 1852, and Tasmania in 1859. The surveys as a whole did not achieve permanent status until the 1870s and 1880s, when work extended to encompass the whole range of geology, mineralogy, petrography and palaeontology.

However, it was the foundation of the colonial universities on the London model (Sydney 1852, Melbourne 1855, Adelaide 1874) which provided a research and teaching backbone to the Australian scientific enterprise. From the time they were founded the universities concentrated on science and provided a regular basis for the more general scientific activity of such leading figures as the museum builder Frederick McCoy (1817–99) in Melbourne, Ralph Tate (1840–91) in Adelaide and Archibald Liversidge (1846–1927) in Sydney.

The status of Australasian science was indubitably raised by the research programmes mounted within

The Australian Museum, Sydney. Founded in 1827 as the Colonial Museum, it was Australia's first museum, and boasts a fine natural history collection.

the universities. The most important of these included Horace Lamb's research programme in hydrostatics in Adelaide, D. O. Masson's work on the constitution of atoms in Melbourne, J. T. Wilson's research on the anatomy and evolutionary relationships of marsupials in Sydney, E. H. Rennie's work in organic chemistry in Adelaide and William Bragg's investigations in radioactivity in Adelaide. Bragg was later awarded a Nobel Prize for his X-ray analysis of crystal structures (1925).

Outside the universities, science in the colonies became increasingly utilitarian and specialised – for example, the formation of several acclimatisation societies throughout the colonies in the 1860s and 1870s (see pp. 44–6). Science remained dependent on official favour, either through the appointment of experts to bureaucratic employment or consultancy, or through the granting of money and land to scientific institutions. The emergence of general museums in the 1850s and of economic and mining museums in the 1870s and 1880s owed much to official support.

SCIENCE AND THE ECONOMY

Throughout the nineteenth century there was little recognition of any great divorce between science and its applications (technology). Most of the active scientific investigators taught or discussed the links between investigation and mechanism, chemical applications, agriculture, mining and mineralogy. Thus the Victorian industrial chemist J. C. Newbery (1843–91), scientific superintendent of the Industrial and Technological Museum, offered courses of instruction in chemistry, metallurgy and telegraphy, just as Archibald Liversidge, Professor of Geology and Mineralogy in Sydney, influenced the collections of the Sydney Technological Museum.

A good early example of the practical focus of science was the Victorian Board of Science, established in 1858 to examine inventions and claims on the government made by scientists as well as to advise policy makers on mineral deposits and potentials for mining. The membership of the Board included Victorian scientists such as Frederick McCoy, the botanist Ferdinand von Mueller (1825–96), and the director of the Victorian Geological Survey, Alfred Selwyn (1824–1902), alongside civil service and political nominees.

During the 1870s and 1880s the link between scientific expertise and the needs of economic development was forged in the area of scientific and technical instruction. Political awareness was evidenced in the Technological Commission in Melbourne (1869) and the Technological Conference in Sydney in 1879, the latter stimulating the formation of the Technical

Education Board. Chairs of engineering were established at the University of Melbourne in 1882 and the University of Sydney in 1884, and a rash of agricultural and mining colleges emerged during the 1880s and 1890s, most of which employed individuals engaged in scientific and technical research and investigation.

By the turn of the century New South Wales alone was spending over £100,000 annually on such training facilities, 13,000 students were enrolled in some form of technical education and many more were associated less formally in such bodies as Mechanics' Institutes, financed, at least partially, from colonial coffers. By World War I a great many scientifically informed students had emerged from the universities; of the 4,700 or so degrees awarded by Sydney University prior to the end of 1915, over 40 per cent were in the fields of science and medicine.

This is not to say that the new technologies invented in Australia arose directly out of science, but rather that during the last two decades of the nineteenth century a scientific and technical culture appears to have developed which served to nurture a spirit of informed, practical investigation. Earlier Australian inventions (John Ridley's stripper or the stump jump plough) may have owed little to formal knowledge, but several of the later nineteenth-century inventions do seem to have developed from a knowledge of scientific theory and its applications. Australia certainly boasted a sturdy tradition, from Thomas Mort's food preservation and refrigeration,

The Australasian Association for the Advancement of Science

The AAAS first met in Sydney in 1888 with a subscribed membership of 820.

From as early as 1879 Archibald Liversidge had advocated a peripatetic, annual national science forum modelled on the British Association for the Advancement of Science, founded in 1831. The AAAS was expected to nationalise the colonial scientific enterprise and to raise the status of natural science in the eyes of the colonial populations.

Six thousand circulars were sent out to members of scientific societies, and 38 such societies were approached for direct support. After 100 years of European settlement, Australia now had its own, continent-wide forum for scientific reportage and debate.

By 1888 Australian science had moved a long way from its original location within small coteries, but it was still reliant for its inspiration upon established British models. In this, science was not out of line with other elements of Australian life.

II

H. V. McKay's harvester, Henry Sutton's series of electrical applications (including an early television), to Lawrence Hargrave's work on powered flight or William Farrer's investigations into scientific wheat breeding. More generally, during the 1880s Australia seems to have freed itself from its former great reliance on Britain as a source of new technologies.

PHASES OF DEVELOPMENT

Before 1851 Australian science was small-scale, subject to the problems posed by distance and lack of resources, and dependent upon the fluctuating presence of a few key activists. From then until the 1880s science became institutionalised and located within larger urban networks and universities, most of which owed something to official financial support.

From the 1880s to World War I, Australian science began to benefit from its own training facilities as graduates emerged from universities and colleges, and successful research programmes raised its status both at home and within a wider, international context. Now that there was greater popular support for science and a degree of commercial utility, the stage was set for the emergence of a larger, national scientific enterprise, epitomised by the foundation of the Commonwealth Institute of Science and Industry in 1916.

II

Geology and biology

Aborigines have inhabited the vast continent of Australia for more than 40,000 years and have an intimate relationship with the land (see pp. 64–5). Practical knowledge of the whereabouts of water and suitable stone for implements, the location of fruits and medicinal plants, and the habits of various animals meant they built up a basic understanding of some aspects of geology and biology.

Legends linking floods and droughts with the Dreaming added a philosophical element to Aboriginal ideas about the origin of the land. The attitudes of the European settlers who came in 1788 were also initially practical, learning the locations of suitable sites for water, clay, lime and stone, the properties of various woods and the edibility of certain plants and animals.

European settlement was preceded by numerous visiting expeditions with naturalists, who, although they had an eye for the possibility of wealth from natural sources, were also concerned with broader philosophical and scientific matters, trying to fit new data into accepted schemes of classification, or to modify long-accepted theories. These expeditions took back to Europe evidence of previously unknown plants and animals which excited the taxonomists and theorists. How did the eucalypts, the banksias and the marsupial and monotreme mammals fit accepted classifications?

The years of exploration and early settlement were ones in which descriptive natural history reached its zenith and most of the work on Australian flora and fauna was essentially descriptive. However, some studies in comparative anatomy and in reproductive physiology were carried out in Europe on specimens of platypuses and kangaroos to determine their taxonomic status. The Australian animals appeared more unusual than the plants to European eyes, and the earliest illustrations of these animals are often exaggerated or distorted compared with the general accuracy of the flora illustrations, as can be seen in the drawings of Sydney Parkinson (1745–71) for Joseph Banks.

Study of living Australian organisms from the late eighteenth to the mid-nineteenth century coincided with the developing research in vertebrate palaeontology and palaeobotany overseas, and Australian fossil finds caused excitement because they, too, seemed to indicate a past history of life which was not the same as that in Europe.

The understanding of Australia's geology was more difficult to achieve than the understanding of biology. Only when skilled geologists could explore large tracts of country and study relationships between various rock masses could there be any real comprehension, which began with the coordinated mapping of large tracts of Australia in the second half of the nineteenth century, when official geological surveys were set up in the various colonies. Few Europeans sought to tap the vast store of knowledge about these matters held by the Aborigines. It would have been a difficult task because of cultural and linguistic differences, although Aboriginal help was frequently sought in locating water and plant foods and suitable routes through unknown country.

The contribution of Australian work to the fields of biology and geology during the early European period, though scarcely science as we now know it, was to establish wider recognition by European naturalists of a more extensive biological environment than had been previously known, and acknowledgement of geological and biological conditions which did not fit previously accepted ideas.

The strange fauna, different plants and apparent different ages (compared with Europe) for many fossils and coal deposits suggested a geology out-of-step

THE KANGOOROO.

A kangaroo depicted in The Voyage of Governor Phillip to Botany Bay *(1789). The engraving was based primarily on a drawing by John White, the surgeon with the First Fleet. In* White's Journal of a Voyage to New South Wales, *published two years later, the posture of the kangaroo was corrected. The first Europeans in Australia were prone to distort the stranger features of the continent's fauna, and to depict other features as if belonging to familiar European animals.*

with that of the Northern Hemisphere. This contributed greatly to the recognition that ideas of universal consistency in geological events could not be sustained. Ludwig Leichhardt (1813–1848?) in particular warned against expecting uniformity of the geological history of Australia with that of Europe, and P. E. Strzelecki (1797–1873), popularly known in Australia for naming the highest peak in the Australian highlands Mt Kosciusko, after his fellow countryman, although originally expecting uniformity, came to recognise it could not be so. These matters, which perplexed Charles Darwin when he visited Australia in 1836, and also later interested the naturalist and traveller Alfred Russel Wallace, contributed in some part to the development of the theory of evolution by natural selection, which Darwin and Wallace published in a joint paper in 1858.

While the first inkling of the vast late Palaeozoic glaciation came from work in India, Australian evidence gathered by the geologists A. R. Selwyn (1824–1902), R. Daintree (1832–78), T. W. Edgeworth David (1858–1934), C. A. Süssmilch (1875–1946) and others reinforced this idea and helped to establish its validity. Evidence of this widespread (largely Southern Hemisphere) event was important in the development of the concept of the supercontinent Gondwana and the consequent interest in continental drift (see pp. 4–9), which reached a high point in Australia in the 1920s.

From the late 1800s biological contributions in Australia assumed a more applied character with the important work on wheat breeding by William Farrer, continuing interest in sheep-wool refinements and the study of plant oils and other substances, such as timber, by J. H. Maiden and R. T. Baker. However, important fundamental research on zoogeography and anthropology was being undertaken by W. Baldwin Spencer, and the work of J. T. Wilson and his colleagues J. P. Hill and C. J. Martin on marsupial and monotreme anatomy in an evolutionary context was widely acclaimed. Later came efforts to eradicate the problems caused by the earlier rash of acclimatisation societies and other bodies, which imported willy-nilly cacti, lantana, blackberry, rabbits, foxes, deer, water-buffalo, ostriches and camels. By this time it was realised that the native animals and plants were those which had evolved and adapted to survive on poor soils, and subject to recurrent drought and periodic fire.

Contributions to biology and geology continued to increase following the establishment of Commonwealth-funded research bodies in the 1920s. The work was directed towards trade and industry and there was little incentive, encouragement or opportunity to engage in fundamental research. Nevertheless, some original work of general significance was done by these bodies and other organisations before World War II.

MODELS OF THE LANDSCAPE

In geology, the study of old landscapes was of considerable significance. W. G. Woolnough explained the development of the vast hardened ('duricrust') surfaces, mainly of Western Australia, and recognised their variations in different climatic zones. W. R. Browne in these years used his field-mapping to point out fundamental relationships between granite batholiths and the history of fold-belt deformation. In the same period W. J. Dakin's research in marine zoology achieved world-wide recognition.

The emphasis has been on studies of arid and tropical regions, including the unique Great Barrier Reef (pp. 36–41) and Antarctic environments (pp. 284–7), and the use of satellites to record the wanderings of camels in the interior, the behaviour of crocodiles in northern rivers, the depredations of the coral reefs by the crown-of-thorns starfish and the breeding of seals.

The past 20 years have seen the beginning of attempts to view the biological resources of Australia on a continental scale. The changes in flora and fauna during and following the Pleistocene epoch (in which glaciation played only a minor part in Australia) are being unearthed in studies at various localities. They show evidence of marsupial and other large animals living in a fertile, well-watered interior very different

Aerial photography

The use of aerial photography and its geological interpretation, pioneered as a research technique by W. G. Woolnough and by the Western Mining Corporation in the 1930s in the search for oil and mineral deposits, was furthered by work during and following World War II.

More recently, satellite imagery as a tool for geological and biological research in deeply weathered terrains has been widely developed. H. J. Harrington and others at the Australian Geological Survey Organisation have been among the first to use digital terrain modelling techniques to study the topography and underlying gravity characteristics of the continent.

DFB

Lungfish (Neoceratodus forsteri), the only living Australian representative of an ancient group of bony fish that made its first appearance some 400 million years ago. Only a handful of related species survive – in Africa and South America. Its most remarkable feature is the single lung, modified from an air-bladder. This is used as a supplement to the gills to obtain oxygen when the rivers in southeastern Queensland, where it lives, are reduced to pools in dry periods.

from today's arid environment. The period of habitation by Aboriginal peoples is also being extended by evidence found in these studies, and it may be that the extinction of many creatures and introduction of others was the result of activity by Aborigines.

The relative antiquity of much of the landscape of Australia, hinted at by earlier geologists, is being confirmed by many recent studies. Mountain-building during the past 65 million years, which produced many of the mountain ranges of the world (Alps, Andes, Himalayas and the Southern Alps of New Zealand), was of minor significance in Australia, and the succeeding Pleistocene glaciation, which left a layer of loose debris over much of northern Europe, northern Asia and North America, was significant in Australia mostly for causing considerable lowerings of sea level: thus rivers were rejuvenated and cut deep valleys in an otherwise nearly stable landscape.

Geologists and geomorphologists have realised that European and North American models of landscape formation are inadequate, and Australian ideas are also now being applied to other parts of the world.

Our understanding of the so-called 'lucky country', the world's flattest and driest, moving inexorably northwards at some 7 cm each year, owes much to the efforts of geologists and biologists, and the lessons learnt on this island continent have contributed widely to human well-being.

THE OLDEST ROCKS

The ancient nature of the continental surface has become well established and the oldest rocks of the continent have proved to be important to science, yielding secrets about the formation of continents and mineral deposits. The Precambrian rocks are widespread, particularly in the western half of the landmass (p. 9). In some places they are well exposed and they have been painstakingly mapped, mainly since the late 1940s. This work, carried out by the Australian Geological Survey Organisation, state geological surveys, university and company geologists, has built up perhaps the world's most complete record of the Proterozoic era (between 2,500 and 600 million years ago). These rocks are the hosts for some of the world's largest and best-studied ore deposits, such as Broken Hill and Mount Isa and the more-recently discovered Olympic Dam ore body, Roxby Downs, South Australia.

The beautifully preserved, unique, soft-bodied fossils found in Precambrian rocks at Ediacara in South Australia by R. C. Sprigg in 1947 were the first to give the world an inkling of the life which teemed in the ancient oceans some 650 million years ago. In Victoria the oldest known land plant, *Baragwanathia*, has been found in rocks of Silurian age. The next youngest period, the Devonian, has yielded in eastern Australia and Antarctica numerous fossil fishes, among them being examples of lungfishes. Descendants of these were found living in the Burnett and Mary Rivers in central Queensland in the 1870s and caused a sensation in scientific circles. In northwestern Australia the Devonian rocks contain perfectly preserved examples of coral reefs which have attracted the attention of the international geological community.

The Imperial Geophysical Experimental Survey (1928–30) attempted to apply established overseas techniques to the study of known and potential ore bodies in Australia. It showed that these techniques were often unsuitable or needed considerable modification for Australian conditions, because the deeply weathered surface rocks were unlike the fresh rocks in Canada or elsewhere, for which the techniques were designed. Since that time Australian geophysicists have developed new techniques in the search for ore bodies beneath the weathered zone, and for coal, oil, gas and underground water. DFB

Radioastronomy

Astronomy, traditionally based on optical observations, underwent a revolution in the second half of the twentieth century when observations were made using the strong radio waves naturally emitted by celestial bodies and detectable by instruments on the Earth. A complementary image of the Universe emerged, rich in new information on its fundamental nature.

Born a neglected infant in the 1930s, radioastronomy broke into vigorous adolescence as soon as World War II ended when the technology was ripe; and it fell to Australia, perhaps more than any other country in the world, to guide the new science through its formative years. The action was centred on the Radiophysics Division of CSIR (later the CSIRO – Commonwealth Scientific and Industrial Research Organization) in Sydney which had been engaged in wartime radar research. E. G. ('Taffy') Brown was its chief, and the radioastronomical research was led by Joe Pawsey, the undisputed father of Australian radioastronomy.

Early discoveries in the late 1940s were made with demobilised military radar sets supplemented by improvised laboratory equipment. First came J. G. Bolton's discovery (1947–48) of radio stars, one cor-

responding to a known object (the Crab Nebula), in our own galaxy, the Milky Way, and others to external galaxies. New results of a revolutionary nature on the Moon, Sun, our galaxy and radio stars poured forth from different members of Pawsey's versatile group. With these discoveries radioastronomy came of age and for the first time Australia had been the parent of a new science. The International Union of Radio Science recognised these achievements by holding its 1952 General Assembly in Sydney, the first international scientific conference ever held in Australia.

The subsequent history of radioastronomy in Australia, as elsewhere, depended critically on the technological acumen required to design low-cost radio telescopes of very large effective aperture. Because radio waves are hundreds of thousands of times longer than light waves, the apertures of radio telescopes need to be correspondingly larger to produce images of comparable sharpness. In the 1950s and 1960s Australian radioastronomers became known for their ingenuity in developing unorthodox radio telescopes, such as the Mills Cross.

The best known of Australia's radio telescopes of the period was a different kind of instrument, the 64-m steerable dish at Parkes in New South Wales. Commissioned in 1961 it soon produced a string of discoveries, and remained the most powerful instrument of its kind for many years. In 1962 the Parkes Telescope obtained an accurate position for a quasi-stellar object, or quasar, which led to its identification as a distant and extremely luminous object. The identification of quasars continued to be an important part of the work at Parkes for many years. A major project of its early days was a new catalogue of radio sources, completed in 1969. Another large-scale project was mapping the southern part of our galaxy, and our two closest neighbouring galaxies, the Large and Small Magellanic Clouds, through observations of the 21-cm radio waves emitted by neutral hydrogen gas. The detail in these maps transformed ideas about the structure of our galaxy and the Clouds.

Radioastronomy programmes outside CSIRO, at the universities of Tasmania and Sydney, were also greatly expanded in the 1960s. The Tasmanian work concentrated on long radio waves (up to 300 m) coming from sources such as Jupiter and the Milky Way. The University of Sydney operated two instruments, both interferometers. One of these, the Molonglo Cross (operating at a wavelength of 73 cm), had a large collecting area and high resolving power, and proved to be an excellent instrument for radio source surveys. It was also used for large-scale surveys of the southern Galaxy, as well as searches for pulsars and supernova remnants. 1978 saw its conversion to the Molonglo Observatory Synthesis Telescope (MOST).

Parkes Telescope in western New South Wales. This radio telescope put Australia in the first rank of world astronomy in the 1960s.

Scientific instrumentation

There are now more than 400 companies in the Australian scientific instrument industry, most of them small but together employing some 20,000 people. In the past decade this industry has made excellent progress. Exports have increased at the rate of 20 per cent per annum and its overall growth has been twice that of the manufacturing industry as a whole.

Before World War II Australia was almost entirely dependent on imports for the supply of scientific instrumentation. The exigencies of that war necessitated the production in Australia of many types of munitions, including instruments required for optical and radio methods of observation and communication, and for the rapidly broadening applications of radar methods for such purposes as navigation, detection and distance measuring.

By the end of the war Australia was supplying not only its own armed forces with all their requirements for optical instruments but also many required by the Allied Forces and by the civilian population. It was a noteworthy achievement considering that the project necessitated the development of methods for the first production in Australia of optical glass. It is surprising and unfortunate that this wartime experience had little influence on the post-war development and production of optical instruments in Australia.

TELESCOPES
AND RADAR EQUIPMENT

By contrast, the wartime experience in the general area of radiophysics led to a lasting and profound influence on the post-war development of science and technology in Australia. Many of those involved in wartime radar developments led the CSIR (later the CSIRO – Commonwealth Scientific and Industrial Research Organization) Division of Radiophysics into the new field of radioastronomy, in which Australia became and remains a world leader (see pp. 275–7). Much of their success was due to the development of a wide range of radio telescopes of novel design, including the famous Parkes 64-m dish, commissioned in 1961. This dish has been continually updated and is now one of the array of telescopes which constitute the Australia Telescope, constructed as a Bicentenary project and commissioned by the Australian prime minister in 1988.

Australian researches in radioastronomy have resulted in notable contributions to astronomy, physics and cosmology. They are also of increasing significance to various branches of Australian industry. The Australia Telescope, costing $50 million, has an Australian content exceeding 80 per cent. It has provided the 25 industrial firms involved in its construction with invaluable experience of a large-scale, high-precision, high-tech project involving the design of advance antennae relevant to satellite communication and the use of Very Large Scale Integration (VLSI) chips for signal processing.

The Interscan microwave aircraft-landing system was developed by CSIRO radioastronomers, who adapted their methods of locating objects in space to aircraft navigation. The Interscan system has been adopted by the International Civil Aviation Organization and Australia now has the opportunity to compete with overseas organisations for its share of the large market which is expected to develop in the next decade.

THREE INVENTIONS

There was no appreciable commercial production of scientific instruments in Australia until the early 1960s. There were, however, three Australian inventions which resulted in substantial production by overseas instrument manufacturers.

The first was the double-pass spectrometer invented in the CSIRO Division of Chemical Physics in 1949. The invention was a simple attachment which almost doubled the optical performance of the spectrometer and virtually eliminated signals caused by scattered radiation. It proved particularly useful in infrared spectrometers, where the scattered radiation can be extremely large. Such spectrometers were produced in the USA under licence to CSIRO from 1952 until 1972 and earned substantial royalties.

In 1958 the flame-ionisation detector was developed in the ICI Research Laboratories in Melbourne. This was a device for use with gas chromatography, which is a widely used method of isolating and determining the concentrations of the various components in organic gaseous vapours. It improved the detection limits by factors up to 10,000 and still occupies a central place in gas chromatography. It earned substantial royalties during the life of the patent.

An entirely new instrument, the sequenator, was developed at St Vincent's Hospital, Melbourne. It automatically determines the amino-acid code of proteins or peptides. This instrument, and its improved descendants, are now used worldwide but Australia reaps no economic benefits. This was largely because the instrument was the brain-child of a high-principled Australian-Swede, the late Pehr Olaf Edman, who believed that scientific discoveries belonged to the world and should not be patented.

SPECTROSCOPIC INSTRUMENTS

The first scientific instrument invented and produced in Australia in large quantities over an extended period is the atomic absorption spectrometer, developed in the CSIRO Division of Chemical Physics in 1952 and used for determining the elements in a chemical substance.

It is now manufactured in Australia, the USA, England, Germany, Japan, China and Taiwan. Current world production is valued at some $220 million per year. Australia's production, which began in 1958, is second only to that of the USA.

The success of this instrument has led to the production in Australia of other spectroscopic instruments. There are now two Australian companies making absorption spectrometers and one making atomic-emission instruments. A small company produces the atomic spectral lamps for use in atomic absorption spectrometry.

The Australian spectroscopic instrument industry employs more than 1,000 people, and its output is in the range of $80–$100 million per year. More than 80 per cent of this output is exported.

MEDICAL INSTRUMENTS

Another major segment of Australia's scientific instrument industry is medical instrumentation. Australia's implantable cardiac pacemakers are now in quantity production and sold worldwide. Ultrasonic body scanners and the bionic ear are also exported widely. There is also an increasing production of medical laser products, such as lasers for use in surgery, ophthalmology and acupuncture.

MINERAL INVESTIGATION

As befits a country rich in mineral deposits, Australia has developed, via CSIRO and companies working with it, many instruments designed for exploration, typification and quality control in the mineral industry. They include SIROTEM, a large-scale electromagnetic exploration device; COALSCAN, which measures ash in coal on a conveyor belt; and numerous remote-scanning (satellite) instruments.

An interesting recent development is the demand from overseas for duplicates of large scientific instruments developed at universities as part of the research programme. For example, Melbourne University Physics Department developed Particle Induced X-Ray Equipment (PIXE) which produces a micro-image of the mineral specimen and identifies its atoms in various parts of the image. Six duplicates of the Melbourne instrument have now been made

by the university for overseas customers. Similarly, the Sensitive High-Resolution Ion Micro Probe (SHRIMP) developed by the Australian National University Earth Science Department can determine the isotope ratios of elements from specific regions of a mineral specimen. Duplicates have been made for research laboratories overseas.   CKC/AW

Metallurgy

Australia is an important metal-producing country and its metallurgists have made a major contribution to the science and technology of metal production. Metals are produced from ores in a series of steps involving, respectively, size reduction to liberate valuable minerals, concentration of the minerals, chemical reaction to form the metal and refining of the metal. Australia has a history of research and development as well as technical innovation in all these areas, extending over 100 years.

FROTH FLOTATION

There can be no doubt that the greatest single contribution has been the process of froth flotation. The modern process, in which mineral particles in water attach to gas bubbles and rise to the surface in a froth, was developed in Australia by C. V. Potter (1901) and modified by G. D. Delprat (1902–03). It was first successfully used at Broken Hill in the first years of this century and then rapidly spread throughout the world where it is now used universally to concentrate sulphide and, to a lesser extent, oxide minerals. In 1912, at Broken Hill, F. Lyster introduced the first true differential flotation process for the selective flotation of zinc sulphide.

SMELTING

Another early development, though one that was less widely adopted, was pyritic smelting and semi-pyritic smelting of copper ores in a blast furnace. Though previously attempted in the USA, it was first performed successfully at Mt Lyell, Tasmania, by R. C. Sticht in 1896; the last furnace ceased operation there only in 1969. The process enabled impure copper material (matte) to be produced using the heat of oxidation of pyrite (iron sulphide) to provide all or most of the heat required.

Pioneering work in zinc-fuming was done by F. H. Evans at the Cockle Creek works of the Sulphide Corporation in 1906–08. This led to the modern process for injecting carbonaceous reductants through nozzles called tuyères into a slag bath; this was subsequently commercialised in the USA.

Continuous disilverising of lead bullion using zinc as a collector was developed at the Broken Hill Associated Smelters, in Port Pirie, South Australia, by G. K. Williams in 1932. It remains an efficient process today. In 1947, Williams suggested using up-draught rather than down-draught sintering (which was the practice of the day) for preparing lead concentrates for blast-furnace smelting, his idea being that the gas could be collected for acid production and at the same time the problem of lead-fall in the windboxes would be overcome. Up-draught sintering was implemented and it proved to be so successful that it remains the standard practice today.

A process for removing iron from partially reduced ilmenite (iron titanium oxide) by 'rusting' to produce synthetic rutile (titanium dioxide) was developed by R. G. Becher in 1961 in the Western Australian Government Laboratories; the process has been used commercially at Capel, Western Australia, since 1968 and, more recently, at several other locations. An alternative, known as the Murso Process, was developed by H. N. Sinha of the CSIRO in the early 1970s. Though technically superior in some respects, it has not yet found commercial application.

The intense bath-smelting process SIROSMELT was developed in the CSIRO in the 1970s. This novel process involves combusting a fuel below the surface in a slag bath using an air-cooled lance. It has been commercialised by Mount Isa Mines Ltd, which operates large copper and lead plants, and by Ausmelt Pty Ltd. Other plants have been built in the USA, Korea and India and others are planned or under construction; it is likely that SIROSMELT will make a major impact on non-ferrous smelting in the decades to come.

Considerable savings in energy usage for crushing and grinding of ores have been achieved over the past 25 years as a result of studies on the breakage of minerals and the development of complex computer models to simulate the behaviour of crushing and grinding plants. The studies have led to improved flowsheet designs and computer control systems. The Julius Kruttschnitt Mineral Research Centre in the University of Queensland and the CSIRO have been at the forefront of this work.

WJR

Immunology and disease

The immune system of higher vertebrates such as ourselves is a complex, multicellular system that has developed through evolution to detect and eliminate threats to health and life. An essential and extraordinary property of the system is its ability to respond to the unpredictable, because the spectrum of foreign structures (termed antigens) of harmful infectious agents is potentially infinite.

For more than 40 years Australian scientists have made outstanding contributions to the science of the immune system, or immunology. These began with the enunciation in 1949 of the concept of immunological tolerance by the Australian physician and virologist Frank Macfarlane Burnet (1899–1985), for which he shared the 1960 Nobel Prize for medicine with the British zoologist Peter Medawar.

We now know that the immune system achieves its extraordinary versatility by generating a very large number of cells (lymphocytes), each of which expresses on its surface a single type of antigen-binding site (receptor), with the total repertoire of types in the lymphocyte population covering a virtually infinite spectrum of antigens.

When a given antigen structure binds to a lymphocyte receptor, the cell is stimulated to proliferate for several days, thus producing an expanded number of progeny cells of the same type (clonal selection and expansion). These cells also differentiate to become capable of mediating various effector mechanisms, which leads to elimination of the infection; some of them survive for many years, thus providing 'immunological memory' and conferring specific resistance or immunity to reinfection.

Right Sir Frank Macfarlane Burnet (1899–1985), pioneering immunologist and joint winner of the Nobel Prize for medicine in 1960.

Smallpox and its eradication

Smallpox has never been endemic in Australia, although there were extensive outbreaks among the Aborigines of the eastern half of Australia in 1789–90 and in 1829–31, and in the centre and the west in 1860–61. Numerous ships arrived in Australian ports with smallpox on board between 1820 and 1950, but the only extensive outbreak after a breach in the quarantine system was the mild form of smallpox, variola minor, in New South Wales in 1914–17.

The Australian scientist Frank Fenner was deeply involved in the World Health Organization's successful global smallpox eradication programme, which began in 1967. After winning international recognition for his work on the pox virus that causes myxomatosis (the disease of rabbits) and on the genetics of vaccinia virus, Fenner was enlisted by the World Health Organization in 1969 to give advice on technical aspects of the programme.

Subsequently he was appointed Chairman of the Global Commission for the Certification of Smallpox Eradication and senior author of the official history of the programme. For this work he shared the 1988 Japan Prize for Preventive Medicine with the two full-time officers of the World Health Organization most involved with the programme.

RVB/FF

If the destructive forces of the immune system are unleashed against normal self-components, potentially serious, autoimmune diseases result. Therefore, the imposition and maintenance of self-tolerance is essential. Macfarlane Burnet's clonal selection theory, which he formulated in 1957, offered an explanation of how the immune system develops the ability to distinguish between 'self' and 'non-self'.

Other key Australian discoveries include the demonstration of the immunological role of the thymus gland by Jacques Miller in 1960 and the elucidation of the interaction between lymphocytes and major histocompatibility (transplantation) antigens by Peter Doherty and Rolf Zinkernagel in 1973.

During the past 25 years two Australian institutions have established international reputations for their work in various aspects of immunology: the Walter and Eliza Hall Institute for Medical Research in Melbourne and the John Curtin School of Medical Research in Canberra.

RVB/FF

Agricultural science

BIOLOGICAL CONTROL

The Australian flora and fauna evolved during a long period of isolation, and in many groups are very different from those elsewhere. Introduced animals and plants sometimes found conditions very suitable and several have become serious pests. Not infrequently they arrived without their complement of parasites and predators, and so some were potential candidates for biological control. Very early success (1920s) with the control of the prickly pear (a cactus) by the introduced moth *Cactoblastis* gave a tremendous boost to the concept and, to many people, unreal expectations for the procedure. Many subsequent attempts have now been made, and Australian biologists have been pioneers in a number of areas.

The first instance of a parasitic rust, or plant disease, being used as a biological control agent was the rust of skeleton weed, a serious pest in wheat because

Lake Moondarra, near Mount Isa, Queensland, before and after clearance of Salvinia molesta, *an infesting aquatic weed. The weed was destroyed by introducing a small beetle.*

control, and its introduction undoubtedly represents one of the major developments in Australian agriculture.

Very useful control of *Salvinia* and several other aquatic weeds has been effected by introduced insect predators, and some of these agents have subsequently been of value to other countries – as for example, *Salvinia* in Papua New Guinea, Sri Lanka, Malaysia, Zambia and other countries in Asia and Africa. In Australia, this control has been successful throughout most of Queensland.

The biological control of some introduced insect pests has been effective, but fewer innovative developments have resulted from these studies. However, one highly original instance of biological control deserves special mention and that is the introduction of dung beetles, mainly from South Africa. Native Australian insects were ill-adapted to the large dung pads of domestic cattle. These pads can render a large area of pasture unproductive and also provide a breeding place for fly pests. A large number of dung beetles, mainly scarabs, have been introduced to deal with the problem over a wide range of environmental conditions. Some species of dung beetle failed to establish, but many have helped to re-establish a biological cycle, resulting in improved soil fertility and a reduction in fly breeding places.

MD

NITROGEN FIXATION

Infertility in Australian soils is frequently the result of nitrogen deficiency. Since the 1940s, Australian researchers have been in the forefront of world studies to overcome this deficiency by utilising leguminous plants, which form nitrogen-fixing nodules on their roots – a symbiotic relationship with rod-shaped bacteria called rhizobia that are able to fix atmospheric nitrogen. There is strong collaboration between research workers in Australia and overseas, especially in developing countries of the Pacific region, Africa and South America.

Nodulated legumes add 1–2 million tonnes of nitrogen to Australian soils and crops each year. Subterranean clover (*Trifolium subterraneum*) and lucerne (*Medicago sativa*) in the temperate regions and various stylos (*Stylosanthes* spp.) and siratro (*Macroptilium atropurpureum*) in the tropical and sub-tropical regions are the principal pasture legumes. They are the nutritional backbone of the sheep and cattle pastoral industries and provide nitrogen to build up soil fertility for subsequent cereal and oilseed crops.

Since 1970, grain legumes such as soya beans, lupins, field peas and faba (broad) beans have become important agricultural commodities in Australia; as

of its tendency to clog the harvesting machines. The pest came from southern Europe and a great deal of testing to ensure that the rust was specific to skeleton weed was carried out in southern France before permission was given by quarantine authorities for its release in Australia. The rust was in fact remarkably specific, and it spread across the country with unexpected rapidity, resulting in the control of one strain of the weed.

Another example of both host specificity and rapid spread came from the introduction of the myxoma virus to control the European rabbit. This introduction was a momentous one for Australia, because the rabbit had become a pest of major importance over most of the southern areas, and was in the late 1940s virtually uncontrollable. By the mid-1950s hundreds of millions of rabbits had died of myxomatosis, and plant growth and wool production had increased dramatically. In later years, less-virulent strains of virus had become common and the rabbits had developed some genetic resistance, so that by the 1980s they were again abundant in some places during some seasons. However, the virus is still exerting significant

Wool technology

Australia has long enjoyed a reputation for the production of fine wools. It is not surprising, therefore, to find that considerable effort has been put into research to secure the use of wool against the intrusion of synthetic fibres into textile production.

Among the many advances in this field two stand out – the Self-Twist Spinner and the Siroset method of permanent pleating of wool fabric. The self-twist spinner is a device that produces a yarn in which the twist alternates over short intervals. The process enables the spindles to move at great speeds without breaking the yarn. Indeed, the machine can work at speeds more than 120 times faster than conventional spindles, and produces a yarn that is in every way as versatile as the standard yarn.

This was the first major change in spinning technology since Hargreaves introduced the spinning jenny in 1764, thus taking the textile industry out of the cottages and into factories. Unlike that revolution, which produced drudgery for masses of workers, the new spinner made possible good working conditions in air-conditioned environments with one operator attending several instruments. Instruments of this type are now standard throughout the developed world.

Wool has always been a desirable fabric whether it be used for rough rustic garments or for high fashion. In the quality clothes industry, its biggest problem was that it would not hold a crease without continual pressing. Artificial fibres could be made that would produce a fabric that would hold permanent creases.

As a result of research with various blends of wool and artificial fibres, and special treatment of the wool itself, it has been possible to make a textile that has all the desirable properties of wool and all the utility properties of synthetics. In addition, other work at the CSIRO has reduced the combustibility and shrinkage of woollen fabrics to such an extent that they are now very safe and economical for use in blankets and children's wear.

KSWC

Automatic winding machinery at a Warrnambool textile mill in Victoria. With the large amounts of wool it produces, Australia has been active in finding methods of processing yarn that keep wool competitive in world markets.

well as contributing to their own nitrogen requirements they contribute nitrogen for subsequent non-leguminous crops and provide a break in disease cycles. Nitrogen fixation associated with the utilisation of energy from the breakdown of crop residues can also contribute to the nitrogen pool of soil, and research is in progress, especially with sugar-cane trash in Queensland, to maximise the nitrogen input through appropriate management and technology of the leguminous stubble.

The basis of the early experimental work was the production of inoculants containing rhizobia, matched to the legumes to be sown, and the development of protocols to ensure the quality of the commercial inoculant. Novel inoculation strategies, designed to introduce a high number of bacteria, have been responsible for many of the derived benefits. Inoculation of seed as it is augered (transferred) from storage bins, the use of a liquid spray into furrows below the seed at sowing and the inclusion of adhesive into commercial peat inoculant to enhance inoc-ulant cover on seed are some examples of improved inoculant technology.

Molecular biology techniques have provided an understanding of the nature of the unique symbiotic relationship between rhizobia and legumes. Biochemical and physiological approaches have been used to study the chemical processes of biological nitrogen fixation, and the role of haemoglobin in the nodules as a modulator of the essential supply of oxygen into the oxygen-sensitive root environment.

Novel techniques, such as the measurement of ureides (urea derivatives) in plant sap and, in the CSIRO Division of Plant Industry, the refinement of the measurement of nitrogen-15 (natural abundance) by mass spectroscopy, have been developed to determine the amount of nitrogen fixed in leguminous crops, pastures and trees. This work is providing useful insights into measurement methodology and is leading to the development of agronomic strategies to maximise nitrogen fixation and the utilisation of the products of fixation.   AG

Trace elements

Australia's ancient soils have undergone several cycles of weathering and leaching, and so are generally lower in plant nutrients than many soils from other countries.

The necessity to add nitrogen and phosphorus and other major plant nutrients was recognised quite early, but often these supplements did not overcome the problems of nutrient deficiency. It was not surprising therefore that Australian scientists were in the forefront of developments in the detection of the importance of minor elements.

Copper, zinc, molybdenum, boron and cobalt and other deficiencies have been recognised, and in many places agricultural production has been made possible by the addition of quite small amounts of one or more of the deficient elements.

One example is in an area of South Australia previously known as the Ninety Mile Desert. Over 2 million ha, which earlier had supported one sheep to 8 ha, can now support five sheep per hectare following the addition of quite small amounts (about 8 kg/ha) of zinc and copper.

A similar requirement was found in an area of about 1 million ha of the coastal plain near Esperance, Western Australia. Well-watered, but previously worthless land was made productive by the addition of zinc and copper, but, there, superphosphate was needed as well.

Molybdenum was found to be deficient in many parts of eastern Australia. This discovery was particularly important because this element is essential for the proper nodulation of legumes like subterranean clover, which are needed for the production of efficient pastures over vast areas (see pp. 282–3). As little as a few grams per hectare were effective and last for several years.

These results were spectacular, but more remarkable was the finding that cobalt was essential to animals. This was first discovered by Australian agriculturists about 1934. However, it was not until the mid-1950s that a way of providing the minute doses required by the cellulose-digesting microorganisms in the rumen of sheep and cattle was developed. This involved depositing a pellet containing cobalt in the rumen, together with a piece of roughened steel rod to erode the pellet slowly – a simple but very effective procedure. It is now known, from work done elsewhere, that cobalt is part of the molecule of vitamin B_{12}. This discovery has had far-reaching consequences in human as well as animal nutrition.

MD

Sheep grazing on the area now known as Coonalpyn Downs, near Keith, South Australia. This area used to be called the Ninety Mile Desert until it was discovered in the 1950s that the land could be made fertile by the addition of modest quantities of zinc and copper.

Antarctica

Australian scientific associations with Antarctica commenced almost at the time the frozen continent was discovered. They can be grouped as follows:

- an early, passive phase, covering most of the nineteenth century, when Australia was a staging post at the beginning or end of voyages for foreign expeditions;
- a middle phase, roughly 1895–1931, when Australians were actively involved in the 'heroic era' of Antarctic exploration either in foreign or Australian parties; and
- the modern phase, post-World War II, when Australia commenced continuous involvement in all aspects of Antarctic affairs, using scientific endeavour as the instrument of credibility.

The earliest known association was in 1810 when Frederick Hasselburgh departed Sydney and discovered Macquarie Island lying about halfway between Tasmania and the Antarctic Circle, which led to the rapid establishment of a large commercial fur-sealing enterprise.

EXPEDITIONS

The peak mid-nineteenth-century activity was during the years 1839–41 when major scientific expeditions of Charles Wilkes (USA), Dumont d'Urville (France) and James Ross (UK) used Australia as a departure point. The Wilkes expedition was the first to refer to the 'Antarctic continent', and it conducted a programme which included charting, geology and biology. Dumont d'Urville led an expedition of discovery

The Antarctic *in Antarctica in 1895. This was Australia's first Antarctic expedition, and one of those on board was to be the first man to set foot on the Antarctic mainland. Australia has played a large part in Antarctic exploration and scientific investigation ever since.*

and incorporated much science in the 32 volumes of results. The Ross expedition was interested in charting, but also in phenomena relating to the magnetic pole and Antarctic botany and zoology. Among its major activities were the discovery of Mt Erebus (an active volcano) and the inland and inaccessible position of the South Magnetic Pole.

HMS *Challenger* later used Australia as a departure point during its global circumnavigation, during which it laid the foundation of oceanography.

Henryk Bull led the *Antarctic* expedition from Melbourne on 26 September 1894. This was the first Australian Antarctic expedition. The object was to revitalise Antarctic whaling on a scientific basis. Included was Carsten Borchgrevink, a Norwegian immigrant to Australia. This expedition set the stage for all later Australian Antarctic activity.

Borchgrevink is commonly credited with being the first man to set foot on the Antarctic mainland. He also recovered lichens. The *Antarctic* expedition inspired Borchgrevink to organise the *Southern Cross* expedition which left Hobart on 19 December 1898 to winter over at Cape Adare. Among its scientists was the Australian-born physicist Louis Bernacchi. Ten people wintered over in 1899. They made geological and biological collections and produced maps. The 1899–1900 summer was used for exploration in the region. The party crossed the Antarctic Circle homeward bound on 28 February 1900. The expedition was the forerunner of those normally seen as part of the 'heroic era'. Bernacchi was a member – again as physicist – of Robert Falcon Scott's *Discovery* expedition in 1901–04.

Douglas Mawson, T. W. Edgeworth David and Alistair Forbes Mackay accompanied Sir Ernest Shackleton's 1907–09 *Nimrod* expedition in which the Australian contribution was very important. Edgeworth David led the first ascent (at age 50) of Mt Erebus (3,794 m) and the trio then trudged westwards, making the first direct observation of the South Magnetic Pole. This was an expedition with a high scientific component.

Scott's last expedition (with the Australians Frank Debenham and Griffith Taylor) passed through Melbourne *en route* to New Zealand, its final stopping-off point. Mawson had been invited but decided to organise his own venture, the 1911–14 Australasian Antarctic Expedition, the best known of all Australian Antarctic adventures. This visited Macquarie Island to establish a radio relay station on the way south. After Macquarie Island the expedition sailed to Commonwealth Bay, where it spent two winters. The Commonwealth Bay party conducted geological, meteorological and geophysical studies, including an identification of the South Magnetic Pole by Eric Webb. The expedition also established, under Frank Wild, a western base, some 2,400 km west of Commonwealth Bay. This party did coastal exploration, discovered a meteorite and reached the extinct volcano of Gaussberg. While Mawson was on his journey, the South Pole was reached by Amundsen and Scott and thus his successful, non-controversial expedition has been overshadowed. On his return to Australia, Mawson laboured successfully to have Macquarie Island established as a conservation area.

This expedition was the first Antarctic journey to be dominated by scientific objectives. Early programmes had a scientific component but were mainly exploratory. From this time on Antarctic activities became more scientific in design.

The first use of an aeroplane in Antarctica was by the Australian Sir Hubert Wilkins late in 1928 during the Shackleton expedition over the northern part of the Antarctic Peninsula. The value of flight came in reconnaissance, aerial photography and in covering great distances quickly, often over otherwise impassable areas.

The Australian programme of most lasting significance was Mawson's British, Australian and New Zealand Antarctic Research Expedition (BANZARE) of the summers of 1929–30 and 1930–31. The expedition's aim was to claim territory. The land that was claimed was ceded to Australia in 1933 and Australia formally established the Australian Antarctic Territory in 1936. The territory, on a sector basis, represents 42 per cent of Antarctica and consists of two components – a large sector between longitudes 45°E and 136°E and a smaller eastern sector between longitudes 142°E and 160°E. The two are separated by Terre Adélie. This expedition marked the commencement of serious Australian government intervention, through territorial claims, in Antarctica.

Following World War II, Australia became involved in Antarctica at government level. An Antarctic Division was established with Phillip Law as its first director. It built a station at Macquarie Island in the 1947–48 summer. In that season, a station was established on Heard Island and this continued until 1953–54 when it was closed to allow a move to Mawson on the Antarctic mainland. This has been occupied continuously since and is the longest continuously occupied Antarctic mainland station. Davis was opened in 1957 and Wilkes (built for the USA during International Geophysical Year) was taken over in 1958 and rebuilt at Casey in 1969.

RESEARCH PROGRAMMES

Australia has made major contributions to international Antarctic science. Pioneering geoscience involved mapping and scientific study of the Prince Charles Mountains in the 1960s and the 1970s. Enderby Land, west of Mawson, has been identified

Top right Australian base on Macquarie Island about halfway between Tasmania and the Antarctic Circle. An earlier base on the island was the first one devoted to Antarctic exploration established by an Australian government agency.

Below right A member of a newly discovered and important group of algae called the Parmales abundant in Antarctic seas and a significant food source for some of the zooplankton. The cell wall of the alga, named Triparma columnacea, contains silica. The bar scale is equivalent to a length of 1/1,000 mm.

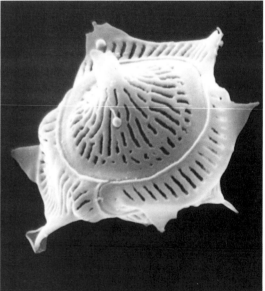

as perhaps the best-preserved ancient terrain on the Earth's surface with rocks up to 4,000 million years old. The Prince Charles Mountains have now been reoccupied and are currently being restudied.

Upper-atmosphere physics, the study of events in the range 70–250 km above the Earth, has taken advantage of the locations of Australian stations to show that auroral events in the Northern and Southern hemispheres are simultaneous and that the

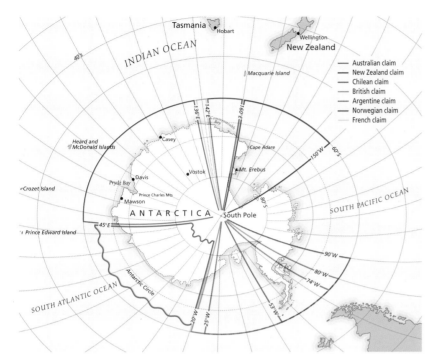

Territorial claims to Antarctica. Australia has an active research programme based at its scientific stations at Casey, Davis and Mawson.

aurora australis is part of an oval structure in the polar regions. This has since been verified by satellite observations.

In 1979, Australia became involved in internationally coordinated marine biology programmes, initially BIOMASS (Biological Investigation of Marine Antarctic Systems and Stocks), under the umbrella of the Scientific Committee on Antarctic Research (SCAR), but subsequently CCAMLR (Convention for the Conservation of Antarctic Marine Living Resources), a convention developed under the Antarctic Treaty and with its headquarters in Hobart, Tasmania.

The Antarctic Treaty

The greatest event in Antarctic history was, without doubt, the Antarctic role in the International Geophysical Year (IGY) in 1957–58.

Twelve nations, including the seven claimants of Antarctic territory (Argentina, Australia, Chile, France, New Zealand, Norway and UK) cooperated in using Antarctica as a giant laboratory. Science had been the basis for establishing IGY stations and after its success the countries involved decided that the successful cooperation should continue.

This led to the Antarctic Treaty which came into effect in 1961. Australia, to meet its obligations, conducts a large science programme on a year-round basis.

The Australian Antarctic Division has conducted continuous programmes in physics and glaciology and, in recent years, in biology (terrestrial and marine). The Australian Geological Survey Organisation (AGSO) carries out the government geoscience, and the Bureau of Meteorology, the meteorological programmes.

The contributions of government agencies are augmented (and often overshadowed) by those of Australian universities and other research institutions in many disciplines.

PGQ

The re-supply ship MV *Nella Dan* (lost during 1987) was modified for marine science and a decision was made to build, in Australia, an Antarctic research/passenger vessel. Australian marine biology/oceanography programmes are concentrated in the Prydz Bay region.

The marine biology programme has been successful in documenting broadly the oceanographic conditions in Prydz Bay, in making major contributions to understanding the life cycle of krill (*Euphausia superba*) and in defining a new order of polar microalgae – the Parmales. These studies will provide the basis for future directions in Australian Antarctic marine biology.

The programme by terrestrial biologists has identified hitherto undescribed bacteria, and organisms whose affinities are still not understood, in lakes of the Vestfold Hills, and has produced a mass of monitoring data now becoming of great value as environmental science evolves.

Australian glaciologists have conducted their programme as part of IAGP (International Antarctic Glaciological Program) in an attempt to answer questions related to the characteristics and history of the East Antarctic ice cap. Shallow drilling and measurements made during tractor traverses suggest that the ice cap is neither growing nor shrinking, and that the loss by icebergs and by wind ablation is matched by precipitation. This result is critical because the greenhouse effect has to be monitored as the world atmosphere changes and warms.

As Antarctic ice accumulates it traps bubbles of air and thus the ice preserves a record of the atmosphere over long periods of time. Drilling by Soviet Scientists at Vostok in the Australian Antarctic Territory has provided data on the change in composition of the atmosphere and world climate over the last 160,000 years.

Plans are now drawn up and equipment is being built for the Australian programme to drill through the Antarctic ice at its thickest point (almost 4.8 km) during the 1990s. This work will establish changes over 0.5–1.0 million years, the only place on our planet where this can be done with precision. A programme on Law Dome drilled to bedrock – a depth of over 1,200 m – and showed the suitability of the drilling equipment for deep drilling.

Medical research on people in isolation has been a continuing component of Australian activity and the results are now becoming of great value as humanity begins long traverses in space.

Important future trends in Antarctic science involve more marine science from the new vessel – *Aurora Australia* – and Australia's contribution to studies of global change, especially those under the umbrella of the International Geosphere–Biosphere Program (IGBP). The Antarctic component will be coordinated by SCAR.

PGQ

Culture
and the arts

Aboriginal art

Traditional religious art

Like Aboriginal oral history, the visual arts illustrate and record a monumental timespan. Over 40,000 years, Aborigines expressed their intellectual and religious attitudes to the land and the meaning of life through elaborate art and ceremony.

A rich oral mythology expressed in ceremonial life is at the very centre of Aboriginal culture. Essentially, all tribal groups believe that their ancestral spirits entered Australia in the creation time, or the Dreaming, when the landscape was partly formed. Some, such as the giant serpents, came from beneath the ground. As they moved, they created ridges and valleys and behind them rivers flowed into the sea. Many Aborigines also believe that the creation ancestors filled and fashioned the cosmos, becoming the sun, moon, stars and planets.

Each clan claimed tracts of land by virtue of descent from the spiritual ancestors. Certain people had the duty of guarding sacred sites, visiting and retouching art, conducting ceremonies at special places, or clearing unwanted vegetation from sacred rocks and trees.

The exceptionally strong relationship with ancestral heroes and with the landscape forms the basis of all Aboriginal art. Dance, song, ceremony and material arts all combine to form a unified whole, a complete artistic network that articulates the landscape and the Dreaming.

Above *Dendroglyph, or tree carving, depicted c. 1890. Trees carved by Aborigines are found in New South Wales and southeastern Queensland.*

Right *Boulders in the Devil's Marbles National Park, Tennant Creek, Northern Territory. The Devil's Marbles are known as Karlukarlu to the Kaytej people who live around them, and feature in their stories of the Dreaming.*

Symbolism

Representational art showing human and animal forms exists beside abstract symbols. Essentially, the symbols can be used for a number of purposes, and members of different groups understand each other's symbols to varying degrees.

The Walpiri-Pintubi communities of the western desert region create magnificent ground designs from plant down, ochre and clay. These are patterns showing the land, as well as events of the creation era. A range of symbols is used, including arcs, concentric circles, circles, bars, dots and wavy lines. The meaning of the symbols varies in every painting, depending on the site shown, the religious inferences, the degree of information the authors have been allowed to convey (their ritual status) and the status of the intended audience.

In a sense, some of the symbols can be used like an alphabet but when put together they create a meaning that is totally accessible only to the creators and their immediate group.

When symbols are used together to form the ground plan of a design, they map the landscape, showing special features with important mythological relevance to the subject matter depicted. They also tell stories about events in the Dreaming. Thus, reproducing the designs becomes a religious act, a reaffirmation of belief in the creation ancestors and the absorption of their essential power.

Arnhem Land painting has a symbolic visual language distinctly different from that of other areas. In eastern Arnhem Land, each clan owns a wide range of patterns and designs that signify areas of land, natural features or specific objects. Representational figures of men, animals, fish and plants are incorporated into the art, but a full interpretation depends on the patterns and designs used in relation to the figurative element.

The giant carved trees, or dendroglyphs, of the southeast were made to mark initiation grounds and burial sites. The patterns of spirals, lozenges and zigzags denote territorial ownership. Ceremonies and trading visits between Aboriginal tribes were announced by messengers sent from one to the other. So that the messages would be received at their destination, messengers were given message sticks – incised with symbols and patterns – which would allow them to pass unmolested through strange country. The patterns not only identified the carrier by symbolising his territory, but, in some instances, they conveyed the message itself.

Symbols and signs continue to be part of traditional Aboriginal communication. Stones are left in patterns of tracks, and circles and lines are drawn in the sand as an aid to conversation and storytelling.

ROCK ART

Painting or engraving on rock is the oldest form of Aboriginal creative expression (see also pp. 79).For example, the finger-markings in the soft limestone walls of Koonalda cave, beneath the Nullarbor Plain in South Australia, were made around 20,000 years ago.

Rock art is predominantly magico-religious. Legends and songs tell of places where the ancestors 'put themselves on rock' and where their painted images are their very spirits.

Many engraving techniques have been used; lines are scratched through the surface of the rock, others are pecked, rubbed or abraded. Techniques for rock paintings include drawing with dry pebbles, rubbing large areas of ochre over the rock surface by hand, splattering paint on to the wall, stencilling a design on to the surface by blowing the paint around an object (such as a weapon or a human hand) pressed against the rock surface, finger painting and the most common technique, brush painting.

Aboriginal artists invariably had some intention in mind when they engraved thousands of patterns, animals' tracks and figures on rock surfaces. We can only guess at the purpose of many rock engravings, inferring their meaning and function through their association with contemporary cultural practice and symbolic art as well as through similarity of subject matter when compared to more recent paintings, interpreted by contemporary Aborigines.

On the other hand, some Aboriginal observers take into account not only the designs but their whole physical presence – the way in which they are grouped, and, most importantly, the natural features nearby. Because the engravings concerned hunting, magic or an ancestor spirit and because all these aspects of life throughout Australia directly related to geological formations, the living embodiments of Ancestral Beings, all engravings must be seen in relation to their environment and religious significance.

Many rock paintings are part of the living culture of Aboriginal people at these sites. It was the duty of certain people to refurbish the sacred paintings and to make the spirits 'fresh'. In so doing the artists restored the powerful presence of the ancestor at the site, they pleased him or her and thereby encouraged a plentiful supply of food and animals or the advent of rain. Many other paintings have involved aspects of magic or sorcery practices.

BODY ART

Body art is central to Aboriginal visual arts. In the desert the torso and face is covered with patterns of red and white plant down stuck to the body with blood. The northern people of Arnhem Land and off-shore islands paint the chests of young initiates and dancers with detailed clan patterns.

Funeral ceremonies are the focus of much body art. The body of the deceased is carefully painted with the ancestral designs of his or her clan; if a coffin is used, its lid may be painted instead, often on the inside. The designs guide the spirit to its resting place by representing the country where the spirit must go. Dancers coat their bodies with white clay to prevent pollution from the dead, which in turn could cause their own sickness and death.

Fine clay designs may be painted on a man's chest on several occasions in his life: at his initiation as a young man, at a major ceremony during his life, and at his death. At other times, elements of them, or sometimes the whole design, may appear in bark paintings. Women's body paintings are less complex.

Aboriginal dancer depicted c. 1910. Body painting is carried out for a wide variety of rituals.

BARK PAINTINGS

The art of bark painting has flourished over recent decades and has become the most widespread form of Aboriginal artistic expression throughout north Australia.

The bark used is taken from Eucalyptus tetradonta, 'stringy bark'. The materials used for painting on bark are red, brown, rust, yellow, black and white earth pigments, fixatives as well as a range of brushes and applicators. Throughout Arnhem Land, the pigments are ground with water on rough, flat stones and a fixative is added. The artists use a variety of simple brushes: a narrow strip of bark chewed at one end and held in the hand is used for the broader lines, and a thin stick about 7 cm long and softened at one end is used for the dots. The fine lines are drawn with a brush made from a few straight human hairs 7 – 10

Aboriginal stencilled painting in Carnarvon Gorge, Queensland. The purpose and meanings of such paintings are not clear, but they can be seen to symbolise the Aborigines' relationship with the land.

cm long, bound on to a thin twig. Up until the last few years, older, more skilled painters preferred to use the traditional fixatives from plant sources, notably the wild orchid. Modern fixatives have now usurped these natural binders. When used sparingly, chemical fixatives have ensured a longer life for the paintings by lessening the degree of flaking.

WOMEN'S WEAVING

Many women of traditional communities in the north have retained most of their ancient fibre craft skills. Bags and containers are made from hand-spun bark twine or woven fibre from the distinctive broad leaves of the coastal *Pandanus spiralis* tree. Some incorporate dyed materials and are decorated with feathers and ochre. Fibre and net bags are made for everyday use, although their origins lie in the teachings of the ancestors.

One of the most important ritual items is the feathered dillybag, a round-bottomed, conical shaped basket. Made of tightly twined pandanus interwoven with white and orange feathers, and having long strings of feathers hanging from the rim, dillybags are held or worn by initiates and hung in trees during ceremonial preparation.

MARKETING OF ABORIGINAL ART

Within the last decade Aboriginal art has become an important aspect of the economy of remote communities. Women produce bark paintings or carvings as well as a range of woven baskets, string bags and conical dillybags. The surfaces of women's softwood carvings at Yirrkala are finely gouged in the manner of wood blocks, then painted in natural ochres. Men,

in keeping with the traditional division of the sexes, concentrate on men's weapons and bark paintings.

There is considerable demand for Aboriginal traditional art within Australia and an increasing number of international exhibitions. The artworks are purchased by community-based art advisers. They are then transported to community centres of which there are now over 100.

Each centre follows the locally based policy of directly exhibiting the work in southern states in private galleries or selling paintings on a wholesale basis. Aboriginal art has attracted the interest of major art collectors and is now represented in all Australian galleries and an increasing number of important international contemporary art collections.

In the desert areas the interest in modern acrylic paintings has produced an explosion of talent. Many artists also work independently in towns of the outback particularly Alice Springs, in the Northern Territory, where tourism is an important component of the local economy.

Modern Aboriginal art includes painting, printmaking, contemporary crafts, ceramics and fabric printing. Urban artists have formed art cooperatives. Many of these artists have received formal art school education and their works, although diverse in style, reflect the urgent social and political considerations of Aborigines today.

Boomalli Aboriginal Artists' Co-operative in Sydney is one such focus for urban artists. An important issue facing all traditional artists is copyright of their designs and their use in Australia and elsewhere. Although the art is made for sale, traditional art is religious and is considered the exclusive copyright not only of the individual but of the clan or group as well.

There is, in a sense, an unspoken understanding on the part of the artists that the buyers will act as responsible custodians of the paintings. JI

Ceremonial ground designs from central Australia, photographed c. 1900.

Art of desert communities

The art of the desert is rarely representational; it is generally symbolic. The symbols used include single and concentric circles, straight lines, animal tracks and curving lines. These occur in all forms: as engravings, rock paintings, body patterns and ground designs, as well as decorations on weapons and utensils

The art of the desert reaches its fullest expression in the elaborate ceremonial ground designs made from plant down, earth ochres and feathers. These are found only in the central, northern and western areas of Central Australia.

Since 1971 desert artists have adapted their art to produce acrylic paintings on canvas, which have created a strong impact on the art community. Sales

of desert acrylic paintings from Papunya-Tula Aboriginal Art Cooperative, the founding group, are now a significant percentage of the local economy.

In many desert areas women paint with acrylics on canvas or make utensils. Three types of curved wooden carrying dish are made, each shaped to accommodate different functions: for winnowing seeds, carrying water and possessions and for digging. These *coolamons*, as they are known, are either painted or decorated on the convex surface with blackened designs burned into the wood with heated wire. This poker-work technique is a relatively recent development. Such designs originate in their own Dreaming stories about creation times. JI

Crafts

The history of the development of the decorative arts in Australia reflects changing cultural attitudes towards the UK, Europe, the USA and Asia. It also reflects changing relationships with art, design and industry, and social history. Institutions such as technical colleges, art schools, galleries and museums as well as a organisations and funding bodies have been influential in establishing and altering perceptions and values of taste, style, cultural meaning, technology and materials.

For most of the first century of European settlement in Australia, ideals were quite firmly fixed on the style and taste of 'home' countries. At first, however, cost and distance meant that few objects and artefacts were able to be brought to Australia, and early settlers and tradespeople were forced to be resourceful in developing new skills, and using the materials at hand in making furniture, utensils, tools and clothing. A furniture industry that used Australian timbers developed early, based on traditional forms. Ceramic and glass industries were also established to supply domestic needs, and a number of these, particularly potteries, survived well into the late twentieth century. Gold discoveries in the mid-nineteenth century encouraged the elaborate and highly skilled production, by such as J. M. Wendt (1830–1917) and Henry Steiner (1835–1914), of trophies, table-pieces and ornaments with Australian motifs and often using local curiosities such as emu eggs. Such new wealth in some states further encouraged imports, as well as local production of other decorative and useful wares.

THE ARTS AND CRAFTS MOVEMENT

Celebration of 100 years of European settlement in 1888 focused attention on expression of national identity through a range of products including the decorative arts. This coincided approximately with the development of art schools in technical colleges, and the establishment of art galleries and museums. The founding of Arts and Crafts Societies in most states in the early 1900s provided a focus for sharing information and marketing the work of many amateur and professional makers working individually in a range of activities from china-painting and embroidery, to leatherwork, metalwork, jewellery an woodcarving.

Practitioners ranged from architects (such as Alexander North (1858–1945) in Tasmania and Rodney H. Alsop (1881–1932) in Victoria) and teachers (such as Lucien Dechaineux (1869–1957) in Tasmania, H. P. Gill (1855–1917) in South Australia, J. W. R. Linton

Right *Silver trophy made by William Kerr, c. 1877, height 44 cm, Collection Powerhouse Museum, Sydney. Increased wealth as a result of the gold discoveries in the mid-nineteenth century led to the production of elaborate artefacts celebrating Australian subjects. This trophy, which won an award in the Sydney International Exhibition in 1879 for 'tasteful design', celebrates the first white Australian cricket team to tour England and depicts a match in progress underneath the mounted emu eggs.*

(1869–1947) in Western Australia, L. J. Harvey (1871–1949) in Queensland, and Lucien Henry (1850–96) earlier in New South Wales) committed to the ideals of the Arts and Crafts Movement. The Movement included hundreds of women similarly committed (such as designer Eirene Mort (1879–1977) in New South Wales, woodcarver Ellen Nora Payne (1865–1962) in Tasmania and potter Gladys Good (1890–1979) in South Australia) for whom these activities provided a creative yet practical and often professional activity. The Exhibition of Women's Work in 1907 in Melbourne displayed the extraordinary range of ability and production at the time.

The influences of the Arts and Crafts Movement and Art Nouveau lingered in the years between the two world wars with the use of Australian flora and fauna motifs, whereas Art Deco was seen in the design and fittings of buildings in the 1930s, and the products of some of the pottery and glass industries. From the late 1930s textile printing businesses (such as Frances Burke Fabrics (est. 1939), Annan Fabrics (est. 1941) and also Silk & Textile Printers Pty Ltd (est. 1939) provided fabrics for Modernist architects. Similarly, furniture using non-traditional materials and techniques (designed by, for example, Grant Featherston (1922–), Clement Meadmore (1929–) and Douglas Snelling (1916–85)) provided a contemporary alternative to not only the more common reproduction styles, but also to the innovative designs of, for example, Walter Burley Griffin (1876–1937) and Robert Prenzel (1866–1941) in the 1920s.

STUDIO CRAFTS

Studio crafts had been developed during the 1920s and 1930s by potters such as Gladys Reynell (1881–1956) and Merric Boyd (1888–1959), and jewellers such as Rhoda Wager (1875–1953) (and in the 1940s, Matcham Skipper (1921–)). This practice was encouraged by the example of British potter Bernard Leach from about 1940, and by the development of courses in technical colleges after World War II.

In ceramics, both the increasing interest in Oriental stoneware and a developing Modernist taste in the 1950s helped to displace the earlier decorative earthenware, and the use of Australian imagery. However, contemporary decorative design, which included Aboriginal as well as natural motifs, prevailed in the textile design of the 1950s as well as on a great deal of commercial pottery.

By the mid-1950s the Handweavers and Spinners Guild of New South Wales and the Potters Society of Australia, as well as state embroiderers' guilds, were providing information networks. The Sturt craft workshops (established in 1941) in New South Wales and the ceramics courses at East Sydney Technical College and the Royal Melbourne Institute of Technology were a few which provided training and a professional studio-crafts model from the early 1950s. Allan Lowe (1907–), Klytie Pate (1912–), Arthur Boyd (1920–) and John Perceval (1923–) were some working in decorative earthenware. Stoneware was largely initiated by Harold Hughan (1893–1987) from the 1940s, and by Ivan McMeekin (1919–93), Peter Rushforth(1920–), Les Blakebrough (1930–) and Col Levy (1933–) among many others in the 1950s.

INTERNATIONAL INFLUENCE

The 1960s brought a new expressionist emphasis from the USA, an element of irreverence initiated by British Pop art, and art-marketing through dealer galleries. Australians once more began to travel, while post-war migrants from Britain and Europe brought different traditions, attitudes and experiences, and were to provide new models.

As in other countries in the Western world, Australian craftspeople started to form a national organisational network from 1964, as part of an international network. By 1971, with the formation of the Crafts Council of Australia, there were Craft Associations (later Councils) in each state. These organisations provided information, training through workshops, exhibition opportunities, publications and, later, more complex entrepreneurial and lobbying activities.

In ceramics in the 1960s Marea Gazzard (1928–) and Peter Travis (1929–) used handbuilding techniques drawing on different cultural sources, Milton

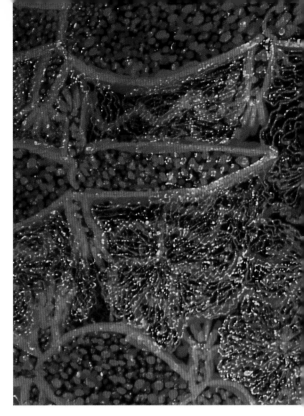

Right *Silk batik length made by Lena Pwerle at Utopia in Central Australia in 1985, height 270 x 90 cm, Collection Powerhouse Museum, Sydney. Some Aboriginal groups became well known in the 1970s and 1980s for their adaptations of traditional ground and body paintings to paint on canvas and printed and dyed textiles.*

Moon (1926–) and Eileen Keys (1903–92) worked in expressionist ways, while in South Australia Alex Leckie (1932–) and Bill Gregory(1942–) provided the early background for Australian funk and pop ceramics of the late 1960s and 1970s. Jewellers and silversmiths Helge Larsen (1929–) and Australian-born Darani Lewers (1936–) worked in the Scandinavian tradition in Sydney from 1961, while Wolf Wennrich (1922–91) had established a German influence in Melbourne by the early 1970s. A number of highly trained European women traditional weavers came from the 1950s, and by the late 1960s Jutta Feddersen(1931–), Australian Mona Hessing (1933–) and in 1971 Polish artist Ewa Pachucka (1936–), were making large sculptural fibre works. Schulim Krimper (1893–1971) made fine furniture in local timbers for over 30 years from the late 1930s, William Gleeson (1927–) was one of the earliest to develop modern designs in stained glass from the 1940s and Douglas Annand (1903–76) worked experimentally to make sculptural glass forms from the 1950s.

CRAFTS IN THE 1970s AND 1980s

Unprecedented funding for the arts, education and other social and cultural activities in the early 1970s included the establishment of a Crafts Board in the reconstituted Australian Council for the Arts in 1973 (established in 1969; from 1975 the Australia Council). This body provided the first real public funding for the contemporary crafts movement, and was soon supplemented by state government bodies. With these and the Crafts Council network, as well as the developing courses in art schools, programmes of

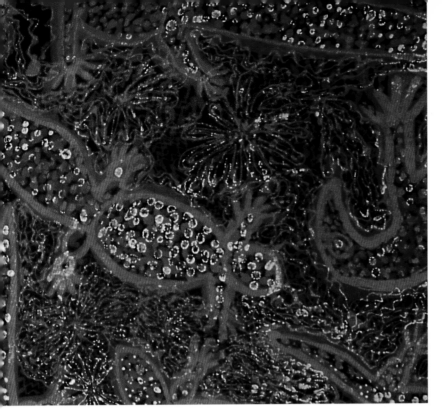

1970s. From the late 1970s and into the 1980s new national specialist groups formed or held biennial conferences for jewellery and metalwork, glass, leather, wood, fibre (wool, quilts, lace, tapestry and fibre) and paper. Regional galleries started to develop specialist media collections, such as ceramics at Shepparton and Newcastle, fibre at Ararat and Tamworth and glass at Wagga Wagga, and state and national art museums started to stengthen their contemporary crafts and design collections.

During the 1970s and 1980s several crafts workshops were established or developed in Aboriginal communities. Traditional motifs and forms were adapted, often onto non-traditional materials, for an external market. Amongst the items produced were screen-printed textiles from the Tiwi people on Bathurst and Melville Islands off Darwin, and batik from Ernabella and Utopia in Central Australia.

With a change in the economic climate in the 1980s, there was evidence that the idealism of the 1970s was shifting to a professional pragmatism. Highly qualified graduates emerged in all media with different perceived needs, and largely different attitudes to art, design, industry and society. The term craftsman had been replaced in the late 1970s by craftsperson or, increasingly, by the term designer-maker.

The aesthetic emphasis of the 1970s had been on natural materials and skilled, hand-made qualities. Practice shifted in the 1980s to include industrial and computer processes, commercial, found or alternative materials, and an eclectic post-modern style which was often characterised by bright colours, decoration, narrative, figurative and symbolic imagery.

Below *Klaus Moje (1936–) came to Australia from Germany in 1982 and was influential as a leading exponent of kiln-formed glass. This bowl form, made in Canberra in 1990, is in kiln-formed mosaic glass, fused, slumped into a plaster silica mould, ground and polished on both surfaces, 44.5 x 44 x 5 cm, Collection Powerhouse Museum, Sydney.*

residencies, visitors, travel, exhibitions, workshop and professional development and publishing were initiated. Exhibition, travel and study links became more established with other countries. Associated with these changes, there was a perceptible shift away from making functional forms towards making 'art-craft' objects for exhibition.

Areas such as woodwork, leatherwork and particularly glass production were revived and developed. With the decline of industrial glass-blowing, the ideals of the American studio glass movement, based on individual practice, found favour from the early

INTO THE 1990S

By the 1990s crafts practice had diversified to include professional followings in various areas. Traditional forms were produced for practical and decorative use, and sculptural and painterly works were produced for exhibition in an art context. Increasingly, craftspeople work to commission for a range of innovative design projects.

Largely because of a comparatively limited affluent collectors' market for 'art-craft' products, more practitioners sought new markets through commissions for corporate bodies and institutions, designing for customised industrial production, and designing and making large works for public spaces and furniture and fittings for the home and office. For the same reason, practitioners and their supporting agencies strengthened their involvement overseas through events such as trade fairs, expositions, cultural promotion activities and prestigious exhibitions.

GC

Architecture

Right *Rouse Hill House, in Rouse Hill, a suburb of Sydney, built 1813-18. Early town houses are Georgian in character.*

The development of Australian architecture can be understood in terms of three phases. From the first settlement until about 1890 it was overwhelmingly derived from Britain, and is best seen in relation to the architecture of other British colonies. From about 1890 until World War II American influence was increasingly important, as also were internal nationalistic tendencies. After World War II the influence of Europe was added to those of Britain and America, and most architects sought an international rather than a national character in their work. However, there was a strong minority national school centred on Sydney, and in more recent years a number of architects have again been concerned to emphasise national and regional characteristics.

The Australian colonies of the nineteenth century were not architecturally unified. Their climates and their circumstances differed markedly, and Perth is as far from Sydney as Aleppo from London. Therefore, architects in private practice were generally confined to a single colony. While Tasmania was under the administration of New South Wales its public buildings were to a greater or lesser extent controlled from Sydney, and this was also to be true of the Port Phillip District prior to its separation (as Victoria) in 1851. In the case of South Australia and Western Australia, even public buildings were designed autonomously. There is, therefore, no distinctively Australian character apparent before the middle of the last century.

SOURCES OF DESIGN

Single-storey houses were more common in the Australian colonies than in Britain. Some of the earlier house-plan forms in New South Wales were rows of rooms opening into each other or directly

from the exterior to permit the maximum of cross-ventilation, a simple equivalent of the H-plans which achieved the same effect in the Cape Colony (South Africa). The need for external access as well as for sunshading encouraged the adoption of the veranda, though to what extent it can be seen as an importation from India remains a moot point.

The early houses of New South Wales were generally symmetrical and are best described as Georgian. The leading architect was Francis Greenway (1777–1837) and his local Georgian work is regressive in relation to the Regency style of his and other buildings in Bristol prior to his transportation, though somewhat comparable with the work of John Soane. John Verge (1782–1861) was soon to practise in a more explicitly Regency manner, but this is the exception in New South Wales.

In Tasmania, a cooler climate and a slightly later date of settlement, especially in the north, encouraged a more urbane architecture, often Regency in style and sometimes with small verandas. Two-storeyed buildings were common, stucco surfaces were normal in the north, and walls were often pilaster. The first significant architect was John Lee Archer (1791–1852), who advanced the Neoclassical and the Greek Revival. It was James Blackburn (1803–54) who really developed the Greek, as well as the Norman, for churches and, for the first time in Australia, the picturesque Italianate for houses.

The contribution of non-British migrants was small in volume, but quite distinctive. The dissident Lutherans who reached South Australia in 1838 were the first of the Germans to re-establish their vernacular traditions in that colony, as did others, and subsequently in western Victoria and Queensland. These included *hufendorf* village planning (a medieval village plan with long strip allotments on either side of the main road), various traditional building forms, and *fachwerk* construction (the German form of half-timbering). Elsewhere smaller groups of Ticinesi (from the valley of the Ticino in Italian-speaking

Elizabeth Farm, Parramatta, New South Wales. Construction of this house started in 1793, making it one of the oldest European buildings in Australia. In its single-storey style it shows the transition from English-style cottage to Australian homestead.

The Hermannsburg Mission Church, a Lutheran church built by the Finke River in central Australia in 1877. German Lutherans added their own vernacular style to Australian architecture.

Switzerland), Swiss and French produced distinctive works, whereas the considerable number of Chinese arrivals, mainly after the gold rushes, built little and late. Their presence is attested mainly by joss houses, and even these were often designed by an English-born architect, as at South Melbourne, or built of non-traditional materials, such as corrugated iron at Atherton, in Queensland.

HIGH VICTORIAN

Between the discovery of payable gold in 1851 and the collapse of the local financial boom in the early 1890s, Victoria was the most architecturally active colony. The first years of the gold rushes saw the importation of many buildings, iron ones mainly from England and Scotland, but timber ones from America, India, Singapore and elsewhere as well. From the later 1850s Victoria saw the most extensive development of terrace housing, a form derived from Britain, but

soon characteristically ornamented with elaborate cast-iron decoration of a lacelike character, comparable, if only in broad terms, with that of New Orleans.

The ecclesiological Gothic Revival reached the Australian colonies from Britain almost undiluted. Designs for colonial churches were sent out by A. W. N. Pugin and by Joseph and Charles Hansom.

Some very gifted architects emigrated in person, notably William Wardell (1823–99), who had achieved a substantial reputation as a Gothicist before departing England. Wardell designed six Roman Catholic cathedrals in the various colonies, not all of which were built, and a number of austere but correct Roman Catholic churches in Victoria.

Local architects such as Edmund Blacket (1817–83) in Sydney and Leonard Terry (1825–84) in Melbourne designed conventional Gothic churches of some distinction. The American John Horbury Hunt (1838–1904), who at first worked for Blacket, developed a more innovative style, resembling that of the Gothic Revivalist William Butterfield, using bold masses of brickwork.

William Wardell was also the government's chief architect in Victoria, where his department produced classical work of some distinction, including a Government House which seriously rivalled Osborne House, Isle of Wight. These buildings are attributable not only to Wardell but to his very gifted assistants Peter Kerr (1820–1912) and J. J. Clark (1838–1913), of whom the latter was to become Colonial Architect for Queensland and to practise at other times in Sydney and Perth.

James Barnet (1827–1905), the Government Architect in New South Wales, had begun his career as a stonemason, but achieved in his post office buildings a distinctive version of the Italianate which seems to have overtones of European Neoclassicism.

Aerial view of Government House, Melbourne, designed by William Wardell in grand Victorian classical style.

THE SECOND EMPIRE STYLE

The Second Empire style made its first tentative appearance in Victoria in 1857, and Charles Tiffin (1833–?), Queensland Government Architect, constructed a crude version of Pierre Lescot's work at the Louvre in his Parliament House, Brisbane, of 1865–67. Characteristics of the Second Empire style included mansard roofs, pavilion planning and Irish ornament.

The government architecture of South Australia and Tasmania was not remarkable in the latter part of the century. The leading private practitioners, respectively, Edmund Wright (1824–88) and Henry Hunter (1832–92), were competent designers of no more than local standing.

AMERICAN INFLUENCE

The English Queen Anne Revival had an impact in Australia from the early 1880s, mainly in the form of a fashion for face red brick work, but later in the decade the American Romanesque style was introduced in the same material. This style was not seen as simply another decorative import, but as a valid basis for the development of a distinctive national architecture.

Towards 1890 there were technical developments, many of them also from the USA, which tended to transform local architecture even further – electric lighting, hydraulic lifts, telephones, prismatic pavement lights and steel framing. The first skyscraper had begun to be built in Melbourne in 1889, before the financial crisis and subsequent depression intervened.

THE NEW CENTURY

The red brick and some of the medievalising details of the Queen Anne style persist in the federation style. The roof is a deliberately complicated assemblage of hips and gables and covered typically in Marseilles tiles. These tiles, which are now so characteristic of Australia, are used little in France and hardly known at all in England. They were nearly all imported from Marseilles until World War I, but were subsequently made locally.

The impact of the Art Nouveau in Australia was generally limited to decorative elements such as wallpapers and ceramic tiles, but it was more pervasive in the buildings of the Victorian architect Robert Haddon (1866–1929), and his own decorative designs are themselves distinctive. Haddon's book, *Australian Architecture*, of 1908, and his other writings, comprise the first literary influence on a national scale.

From before the turn of the century Robin Dods

Right Page from Robert Haddon's influential book Australian Architecture (1908) *showing design in terracotta. Subtitled 'A technical manual for all those engaged in architectural and building work' the book was highly practical.*

(1868–1920), of Brisbane and later Sydney, began to make some experiments in abstract forms, especially as they could be rationalised in terms of climate control.

G. S. Jones (1865–1927) of Sydney experimented with blocklike shapes and intersecting planes in a modernistic cubist fashion best explained in relation to the American work of Irving Gill.

H. D. Annear (1865–1933) in Melbourne made selective use of Medieval, Georgian and Baroque sources, but is best known for the more austere vernacularising style which he evolved from the Arts and Crafts tradition. Annear's work was distinctive also for technical gadgetry such as sashes which slid up into the wall thickness, his own 'Australian fireplace' design, and a patent form of flush-panel timber door.

BETWEEN THE WARS

Although the federation style had often been associated with the deliberate introduction of Australian flora and fauna motifs, a different sort of nationalism was expressed by a revival of colonial Georgian forms early in the century, pioneered by W. Hardy Wilson (1881–1955). The style was characterised by symmetry, Georgian-inspired joinery and moulding.

The single most stimulating impact upon Australian architecture in the twentieth century was that

Right *House at Kew, Melbourne, c. 1910, with a roof made of Marseilles tiles in typical federation style.*

Below *Walter Burley Griffin's geometric design for Canberra, 1912.*

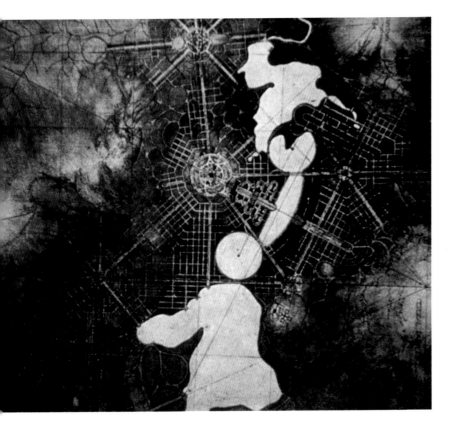

of the American Walter Burley Griffin (1876–1937), who in 1912 won the international competition for the design of the federal capital of Canberra, and subsequently settled in Australia and designed many extraordinary buildings in a highly personal and complex geometric style. However, his demonstrable influence upon local practitioners is remarkably slight in proportion to his fame and undoubted originality.

POST-WAR MODERNISM

The influence of international modernism made itself felt before World War II, but it was the war itself and the subsequent period of building restriction, amounting to more than a decade, which provided for the gestation of a local school of modern architecture.

One of the Melbourne pioneers, the geometrically inclined Roy Grounds (1905–81) had already made a substantial impact in the early 1930s. He was joined in 1953 by the writer and populist Robin Boyd (1919–71), whose buildings tend to be more brittle and insubstantial, and by a genuine member of the European Movement – the German refugee Frederick Romberg (1913–). In Sydney a post-war immigrant, the Austrian Harry Seidler (1923–) brought an even more authentic infusion of German Bauhaus design, and he reinforced its impact by a campaign of aggressive self-promotion.

The Nuts and Berries School

Nationalism was not forgotten. In Sydney, the architect Sydney Ancher (1904–79) attempted an unequivocally modern but distinctively Australian style. His later partner Ken Woolley (1933–) became the central figure of the Sydney School which tended to use tiles, rough-textured clinker bricks and stained timber (described by Robin Boyd as 'a tamed romantic kind of Brutalism').

The Nuts and Bolts School

In Melbourne, the architecture of the immediate post-war period was structuralistic and geometric – aptly described as the Nuts and Bolts school, as contrasted with the romantic Nuts and Berries school of Sydney.

The geometric tradition was initiated by Roy Grounds, beginning with an unbuilt project of 1948 for a house in the form of a three-pointed star. This was followed by round and triangular houses in and near Melbourne, and subsequently the inverted saucer of the Academy of Science in Canberra (1957–59), and the extraordinary, and not wholly felicitous, combination of rectangle, triangle and circle in the plan of the Melbourne Arts Centre, begun in 1959. Grounds' friend and later partner, Robin Boyd, experimented with structural shapes such as parabolic vaults in sprayed concrete (1952), and his Richardson House (1954–55), a wedge-shaped plan which bridged a creek bed by hanging from segmental arches on either side.

The Academy of Science, Canberra, designed in a continuation of the geometric tradition by Roy Grounds and built in 1957-59.

Below Tent-like structures designed by Daryl Jackson for the Bicentennial Exhibition. The Exhibition had to be constructed in such a way that it could be erected and dismantled at 34 different sites.

STRUCTURAL EXPRESSIONISM

The winning entry, in a competition to construct the swimming pool for the Melbourne Olympic Games of 1956, was submitted by a group of young designers, of whom Peter McIntyre (1927–) and Kevin Borland (1926–) were to remain prominent.

The form of the building was determined by a structure in which the roof trusses provided a horizontal tie between raking tiers of seating on either side, and the junctions at the top corners were tied back to the ground with cables. This was probably the first Australian building to be imitated overseas.

Other works in the Nuts and Bolts tradition included Peter McIntyre's own house, a triangle in section, carried on a stem to raise it above the flood level of the Yarra River.

Almost as striking as the Olympic Pool was the Myer Music Bowl of 1958, by Barry Patten (1927–) of Yuncken Freeman Brothers Griffiths and Simpson. This was arguably the world's first significant membrane structure, in which two vertical stanchions supported a skin of aluminium-clad marine plywood, tied back to ground level by cables. ML

COX, JACKSON AND SEIDLER

By the 1980s national architecture was dominated by three architects. Philip Cox (1939–) has written a number of works on Australian architectural history, and his early practice had a considerable component of conservation and restoration. His major buildings of more recent years have been increasingly structural expressionist. Cox's Yulara tourist resort at Uluru (Ayers Rock), Central Australia (1982), uses an elegant sail-like canopy for the roof. His Exhibition Halls at Darling Harbour (1986) are tied down at the corners in a highly contrived way which is almost reminiscent of Melbourne's Olympic Pool, but the

building is more directly related to British works such as the INMOS Factory in Wales, by Richard Rogers and Partners (1982), and the Renault Centre, Swindon, by Foster Associates (1983).

Another dominant architect is Daryl Jackson (1937–) of Melbourne, whose work cannot be so easily categorised. It tends to be arbitrary, informal and dextrous, but deftly steers clear of the extremes of structural expression, historical allusion and contextualism. His Great Southern stand for the Melbourne Cricket Ground (in association with Tompkins, Shaw and Evans, completed in 1992), exemplifies these qualities. One of Jackson's most distinctive works, the Australian Bicentennial Exhibition, which toured the country during 1988. This was a portable complex of fabric structures which travelled on a fleet of 70 vehicles, and was successively mounted at 34 different locations. The combination of masts, tensile fabric and guys gave the design a fortuitous resemblance to Cox's Yulara.

The third dominant practitioner, totally different in character, is Harry Seidler. Seidler is an unregenerate modernist whose principles have remained unchanged over four decades, though his work now tends towards more luxurious and refined finishes, such as glazed tiles or polished granite in place of exposed concrete. Seidler still commands a significant segment of the prestige commercial market (in the 1990s diminished because of economic recession), and the unmistakably classic quality of his buildings presents an anachronistic and embarrassing challenge to the more ephemeral fads of younger designers.

PARLIAMENT HOUSE

The international competition for Canberra's permanent Parliament House was won by the American firm of Mitchell/Giurgola in 1980. For the execution of the project their Australian-born employee Richard Thorp (1944–) was made a partner and Romaldo Giurgola (1920–) himself settled permanently in the country. The building was completed in 1988.

Parliament House is effectively buried in the crown of a prominent hill, but not that intended for the purpose in the original plan of Canberra executed by W. B. Griffin. The hill is cut into from two sides to expose the sweeping concave facades, but the location is marked unequivocally by a giant flagpole on four angled legs. The exposed portions are otherwise bland enough, and the overwhelmingly negative conception has undoubtedly spared Griffin's Canberra from undue violence.

LANDMARKS OF THE 1980S

A group of young designers practising under the name Biltmoderne have produced elegantly contrived and arbitrarily geometric designs, most characterised by their deliberate alienation from their environment, especially the natural environment. The approach is in fact more akin to furniture design, in which Biltmoderne also engage. More recently, the Melbourne architect Nonda Katsalidis (1951–)

The Sydney Opera House

The impact of the Danish architect, Joern Utzon, was almost as traumatic as that of W. B. Griffin some decades earlier, and likewise resulted from an international competition. The competition for the opera house was held in 1955–1956, and in January 1957 Utzon was announced the winner. Utzon did not last out even the completion of the Sydney opera house, much less develop any more extensive local projects or establish any local school.

Work began on the opera house site in 1959 and Utzon himself moved to Sydney in 1961. The cost began to escalate enormously, largely because it proved impossible to build the shells in anything like the intended form, and controversy built up until Utzon abandoned the project early in 1966.

The opera house was continued by other architects, and completed in 1973 in a form which superficially resembled the original but was much modified in plan and structure, and far more costly than had been estimated.

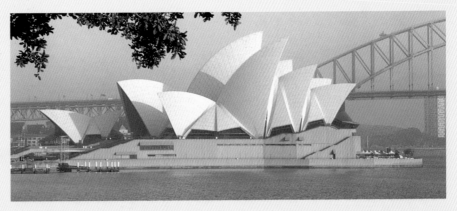

'The great merit of this building', according to the original assessors, had been 'the unity of its structural expression', a characteristic which had until now been more typical of Melbourne architecture, and one that had proved to be spurious in this first manifestation in Sydney.

Today the Sydney–Melbourne distinctions have been partially obscured,

or in some respects reversed. Glenn Murcutt (1936–), in New South Wales, developed a distinctive domestic style in corrugated iron. This was at first vernacular in character, but as larger and more urban commissions have come to dominate his work, it has evolved into an elegant structuralism with a more explicit expression of steel framing members.

ML

301

has worked in a less self-conscious yet even more exquisitely detailed manner, using lavish materials in a more urbane Europeanising tradition, as at the Deutscher House and Art Gallery (1987).

In Sydney, Alex Tzannes has produced more boldly classicising designs than any other Australian practitioner. Some of the better work in Brisbane by John Dalton (1927–) and Robin Gibson (1930–) is less sophisticated, but maintains a spirit of the Australian vernacular. The Queensland theme of the exposed timber frame has been resuscitated by designers such as Russell Hall in his house at Wilston (1986). In Darwin, Troppo Architects make a determined attempt to maintain a local tradition which has been more rigorously moulded by the tropical climate, houses raised on stilts, cross-ventilated, and roofed with corrugated iron.

CONSERVATION AND RESTORATION

It is because of this interest in the vernacular that conservation and restoration have come to play a formative role in the local architectural scene. An historical architecture which is largely of post-industrial date, geared to the local climate, and developed largely through the detached house, has retained a greater contemporary relevance than the more venerable traditions of older countries. Some of the leading historians, such as Robin Boyd and Philip Cox, have been leading practitioners as well. Clive Lucas of Sydney is the doyen of restorationists, known principally for his work on colonial Georgian buildings, but there are other figures as much involved in contemporary design as in restoration. Robert Riddel of Brisbane, for example, is an authority on the work of Robin Dods, and has partly restored and partly adapted Dods' Cunningham House, Brisbane (1987).

Recycling, as distinct from restoration, has boomed especially in Sydney with projects like the Powerhouse Museum (1984–88) and the Overseas Passenger Terminal (completed in 1987). The museum is, as the name implies, a converted and extended powerhouse which generated electricity for the tramways system. The old buildings remain externally intact, but have been revamped rather than restored, and have been joined by a glass-walled and barrel-vaulted building designed to evoke Joseph Paxton's Crystal Palace in London. The old Overseas Passenger Terminal has been trimmed down to a size compatible with the reduced volume and sporadic occurrence of passenger shipping, and imaginatively redesigned for what is now essentially a tourist use.

Domestic architecture has remained the medium for the most characteristic Australian expression. The veranda and its derivatives are almost as prominent today as they were in the second quarter of the nineteenth century in New South Wales. Equally alive in these days of post-post-modernism are the principles of picturesque design first expounded in Tasmania by James Blackburn and most characteristically expressed in the federation style of the early twentieth century.

THE 1990S

The new decade saw the culmination of a trend which had seemed initially to be the eccentric gimmick of one small practitioner. Glenn Murcutt (1936–) was employed soon after graduation by Ancher Mortlock Murray and Woolley, and exposed to the later phases of the Nuts and Berries School, but after beginning private practice in 1969 he pursued a different aspect of the vernacular, and soon became noted for his use of corrugated iron.

Murcutt was not the only or the first Australian designer to recognise that this material, though of industrial origin, was an authentic part of the Australian tradition and one with considerable aesthetic potential. He was, however, its most single-minded exponent. From 1975 onwards he won at least one, and usually more awards each year, and all were for small buildings, mainly houses. Murcutt has never been tempted either to expand his one-man practice or to accept larger commissions, and those buildings which have been slightly larger than the norm have been his least felicitous.

By the mid-1980s Murcutt was a national figure – the architect whose houses were of the greatest interest to readers of the glossies. His work was becoming increasingly refined, less and less like an architect-designed shed, and more and more approaching aerodynamic forms and using attenuated steel structural components. It began to converge with the structural expressionsim of Philip Cox and even John Andrews, less because he approached them than because they approached him.

In the 1990s, when postmodernism had filtered down to the meanest practices and decayed into facile gimmickry, and when the Euro-elegance of the genre promoted by Nonda Katsalidis had been strangled by the recession, the Murcutt school was left as an enduring focus for domestic design, and one with a meaningful connection to the larger works of other practitioners. In 1993 Murcutt was internationally recognised by the Alvar Aalto award. Murcutt reconciles the demands of popularism and connoisseurship, just as he also reconciles what previously had been quite disparate stylistic tendencies in contemporary Australian architecture.   ML

Fine art

In Australian art, there is a constant tension between the desire to represent uniquely local experience and the recognition that artistic tendencies in dominant cultures elsewhere – particularly the UK, Europe and the USA – are also replete with significant, and relevant, achievements. These contrary demands can be debilitating, driving artists into exile, or they can stimulate quite distinctive approaches: many seem content with highly conventional renderings of pleasing landscapes or famous figures, others question orthodoxy and create new ways of seeing both places and people. It is this play of forces which has been the major factor in conditioning artistic practice.

The institutions of Australian art have developed from the first major schools and galleries established in the 1860s and 1870s into the complex structure of private, corporate and government patronage that exists today. The art industry benefits from a large educational input, creating ever-increasing, more-informed audiences. The broader public has responded warmly to art that pictures everyday life by treasuring such images, particularly in reproduction, and by celebrating as cultural heroes – almost equivalent to sporting deities or entertainment stars – those few artists capable of creating icons of Australianness.

In contrast, there is often manifest a widespread aversion to art, particularly that cast in unfamiliar terms or in modes imported from elsewhere. There is, too, deep resentment of the association of art and privilege, of the superficial socialising of the art scene. And there is suspicion of the activities of the art market, especially of the spectacularly high prices paid for certain works of art – including the rare Australian works attracting a million dollars or more. But responses to art vary greatly throughout Australian society: a variety of audiences has evolved, ranging from small artists' cooperatives to a gallery-going public which regularly outnumbers those attending sporting events.

Painting and sculpture in Australia are best understood when seen as part of a wider range of visual arts practices, both professional and commercial, privileged and popular. This is so not only because the same artists have commonly worked in a variety of media, but because their subject matter constantly crosses social and economic boundaries. It will, however, be convenient to treat the public and the private faces of Australian art in turn, while recognising all the while their constant interplay.

This section concentrates on art by European Australians, and those recently immigrant, as another chapter deals with the much older and more diverse artistic traditions of Aboriginal Australians (p. 79 and pp. 290–2). These traditions, however, have often inspired white Australian artists, and in recent years their extraordinary renewal has had a profound impact on public consciousness of Australian art in general.

PUBLIC FACES

Measured by frequency of reproduction and by the attentions of gallery goers during the last two decades at least, the most popular visual images in Australia are certain paintings which depict, in heightened form, past moments of everyday experience.

A Break Away! by Tom Roberts (1856–1931) shows a mob of thirst-crazed sheep bursting from the bush, rushing a waterhole where many will drink themselves to death. The drover's desperate efforts to stop them are as evidently futile as those of his bowled-over dog. The frantic speed of men and animals contrasts to the still calm of the cause of all this drama: the drought-stricken countryside sparingly suggested in the upper right quadrant of the painting.

A Break Away! is typical of a group of paintings by Roberts which includes *Shearing the Rams*, *The Golden fleece* and *Bailed Up*. Each deals with an activity acknowledged during that centenary period as distinctively Australian, and does so in a relatively understated way.

This approach has invited some observers to recognise a celebration of the pastoral industry, vital to the economic health of the nation, while others have identified with the respect accorded the workers, from shearers to bushrangers. Nearly all iconic images are of aspects of country life and work; the city has been often painted but rarely celebrated. Love of the bush as an abstract ideal is scarcely surprising in a highly urbanised population, but it means that one of Aus-

Gallery viewers at an exhibition of Australian works at the National Gallery of Australia, Canberra. Numbers of attenders suggest that art rivals sporting events in popularity.

*Fred Williams (1927–82),
Oval Landscape (1965–66),
oil on canvas, 173.2 x 109.2
cm. Williams devised a new
way of painting Australia's
much-depicted landscapes
that drew upon the principles
of abstraction.*

The rapturous enjoyment of natural beauty that evidently inspired the artist to treat this subject as a pastoral lyric is matched by a recognition of the power and importance of the pastoral industry. Created during the 1888 centenary celebrations, and as part of the movement towards federation, it is scarcely surprising that paintings such as these joined the more overtly narrative treatments of bush life to become identified, then and since, with Australia's sense of national identity.

During World War I this kind of landscape became the most striking symbol of the values worth fighting for. Despite harsh treatment because of his ancestry, Hans Heysen painted gumtrees as heroic survivors. Streeton, Elioth Gruner and many others painted the slopes of the Great Dividing Range so often and so well that an Australian School of Landscape Painting formed, dominating the practice of art and all its institutions for two decades.

The School still provides the basis for much popular and amateur art. It was challenged, however, during and after World War II by artists for whom the landscape had become a place of estrangement, the arena of lost legends. Thus Sidney Nolan's *Ned Kelly* series of 1945–65 shows the insurrectionary bushranger as a creation of the cleared landscape, knowledgeable of its secret hiding places yet alienated within it. Ultimately, Kelly becomes a victim of the forces of law, yet is reborn as a myth: *Burning at Glenrowan/Siege at Glenrowan* (1946).

In the post-war years Nolan, and Russell Drysdale, saw in the drought-stricken areas of Central Australia an even less positive aspect of natural forces and social organisation: their nearly-empty deserts and deserted country towns are landscapes of despair.

Fred Williams (1927–82) and John Olsen (1928–) were the outstanding landscapists of the 1960s.

*Russell Drysdale (1912–81),
Walls of China (Gol Gol),
(1945), oil on hardboard,
76.2 x 101.6 cm, Art Gallery
of New South Wales, pur-
chased 1945. Drysdale
explored images of death and
despair in the parched landscapes of Central Australia.*

Reacting against advice that previous artists had exhausted the subject, and his sense that Australian vistas were monotonous and featureless, Williams set out to invent a distinctive landscape imagery based on the formal tenets of international abstraction, specifically those to do with flat, even space and gestural, impasto surfaces, as in *Oval Landscape* (1965–66). Olsen followed a similar path, as did many others influenced by expressionist approaches.

Landscape, however, was of little interest to the rising generation of non-figurative painters, conceptual and performance artists during the 1970s, and occurred only as a matter of ironic quotation or deliberate omission in the post-modernist art of the 1980s. It was, however, taken up very strongly by the revived film industry, which drew heavily on the broad popularity of both the Heidelberg School and desert imagery.

The imagery of the interior became an ideological, economic and social battleground during the 1970s as Aboriginal land rights and anti-uranium mining lobbies fought mining companies for symbolic ownership. So, too, the imagery of wilderness became a matter of extraordinary public consciousness, especially during the 1983 federal election. This occurred mostly in advertisements, posters and in media events, especially on television. The proliferation of ecological themes in art in recent years also reflects this increasing awareness of the fragility of the natural environment.

Sir Sidney Nolan

Sidney Nolan (1919–92) was born in Melbourne, the son of a tram driver. He took to painting in the 1930s, and attended a part-time course at technical school. In 1938 he became a foundation member of the Contemporary Art Society, thereby associating himself with radical art.

During his service in World War II, while based in Wimmera, northern Victoria, Nolan developed his interest in figurative and landscape painting. His landscapes painted during this time are now widely regarded as a crucial step in the modernisation of Australian landscape painting.

It was after the war, however, that he was to produce the paintings for which he is probably best known – the Ned Kelly series (1945–65). In these portrayals of the notorious bushranger, Nolan combined powerful images of Australian history and landscape which were to become thematic features of future work as, for example, in his paintings of explorers of Australia.

In the 1950s Nolan travelled in Europe, Africa, China and the Antarctic, and in 1954 he based himself in London. Here he produced paintings reflecting his travels as well as continuing to paint Australian themes.

Nolan explored many other artistic media including set design. Examples of his set designs include Covent Garden's *The Rite of Spring* (1962), *Samson and Delilah* (1981) and the Australian Opera's Il *Travatore* (1983).

The best known Australian artist of his generation, Nolan's works are exhibited in the world's leading galleries. He was knighted in 1981 and awarded the Order of Merit in 1985.

PRIVATE LIVES

Alongside the public face of landscape, portraiture and scenes from contemporary history, a more private theme has shaped Australian art. Whereas most early pictures of the colony served practical or official purposes, the sketch books of the wives of officers or businessmen, such as Sophia Campbell, and of itinerant artists, such as Augustus Earle, tend to observe everyday life from a more intimate perspective.

Grace Cossington Smith (1892–1984), The Lacquer Room (c. 1935), oil on paperboard on plywood, 74×90.8 cm, Art Gallery of New South Wales, purchased 1967. The painting is a study of both light and of middle-class mores.

Women artists have consistently found artistic interest in domestic scenes, and in those public places where social and gender difference is signalled quietly. Thus Grace Cossington Smith's (1892–1984) *The Lacquer Room* (c. 1935), set in the modernistic tea room of the major Sydney department store Farmer & Co., can be interpreted in several ways. It is, at once, a study of intense sunlight hitting equally strong artificial decor, of the manners of middle-class morning tea rituals and of the irruption of both at the intersection of many faces staring, as if into a flashing camera-eye.

With the exception of a brief period in the 1920s, when they were involved in the introduction of modern design, women artists played subsidiary roles in Australian art until the 1970s. The feminist movement has secured greater opportunities for women artists, as well as increased access to the full range of subjects and approaches enjoyed by their male colleagues.

Interest in the nature of sexuality is not confined to women artists: masculinity, its powers and its discontents, is a persistent concern of many male artists. Norman Lindsay (1879–1969), for example, created an impact with his highly literary presentations of erotic scenes in watercolour and oil.

The impact of deadly war machines on young male bodies struck many artists as part of the tragedy of the 1914–18 conflict: the bronze sculpture *Sacrifice* (1932), by Rayner Hoff (1894–1937), at the heart of the Anzac Memorial, Sydney, shows the spent youth laid across a shield held aloft by three women, themselves carved from a cannon shell.

Homoerotic imagery had a fugitive presence in Australian art until Donald Friend's celebrations of soldiers during the 1939–45 war, and Gareth Sansom and Juan Davila's transvestite figures during the 1970s and 1980s. The unimaginable shapes of repressed desires form the subject of much recent art, notably the many installations of sequenced photographs created by Bill Henson since 1981.

For some artists, women's bodies were the sites of a magical seduction: thus Bertram Mackennal's beguilingly lifesize bronze sculptures. For others, women were the bearers of evil, provokers of uncontrollable passions, and were thus ripe for distortion, even decimation. Albert Tucker saw the 'Victory Girls' of World War II as symptomatic of social decay, John Molvig was fascinated by the otherness of female sexuality during the 1950s, and Brett Whiteley traced the depredations of the English serial murderer Christie in the mid-1960s. Few male artists attempted to see the world from female perspectives, with the outstanding exception of Charles Blackman, who has done so consistently since the 1950s.

Certain themes common in other, comparable cultures are rare in Australian art. Unlike the

German Expressionists, for example, few artists have explored the excesses, transgressions and frightening scenarios of madness. Exceptions include the Angry Penguins mentioned above and Ken Unsworth's installation, *A Different Drummer* (1976), which figures the unbearable impact on the survivors of the death of a child through a lifelike toy drummer boy wired up so that he will continually march along the monkeybar structure and fall off. Unsworth does, however, share with other sculptors of his generation a willingness to work in a variety of media, from performance to painting.

URBAN LIVES

The city as the primary site of modernisation has had much less of a role in Australian art than that of Europe or the USA, for example. The same general shift – from treating the city as a public domain of progress in the nineteenth century to it becoming a stage for the enactment of individual alienation – has, however, been followed in Australian art.

Charles Kerry's successful publishing company issued many thousands of postcards of everyday life in the major cities, as well as developing a large repertoire of bush scenes and types..

In Melbourne during World War II the city did become home to the lost, the homeless, the damned and the demented in the art of the Angry Penguins (Sidney Nolan, Arthur Boyd, Albert Tucker and Joy Hester) and the Social Realists such as Noel Counihan.

After the war, the suburban sprawl of the major cities created new environments which artists such as John Brack (b. 1920) found chillingly empty manufactories of conformity. Children were seen as the major victim of this change. His *The Car* (1955) depicts the ideal nuclear family on show, oblivious to the landscape, framed by its dream of consumption.

Antipathy to suburbia also inspired the junk assemblages of the Annandale Imitation Realists in the early 1960s, but a gradual acceptance of the aesthetics of everyday popular culture subsequently emerged: in late 1960s hard-edge abstraction in Melbourne (Robert Rooney), and in its nostalgic presence in New Wave or Popism painting in the early 1980s.

The other great theme in the imagery of modernisation – the machine – does appear in Australian art, but less frequently than elsewhere. In 1935 photographer Harold Cazneaux was commissioned to illustrate the annual report of industrial giant Broken Hill Proprietary Ltd, aestheticising its Iron and Steel works in Newcastle in the internationally approved manner.

Machine imagery also inspired certain sculptors, especially Robert Klippel. *Opus 247 Metal Construction* (1965–68) is a welded construction of found objects such as discarded typewriters, machine parts and wooden tool moulds.

ABORIGINAL AND EUROPEAN ARTISTS

The Aboriginal peoples of Australia were the object of European artists' curiosity even before they were actually sighted. Cartographers invented mixtures of the exotic races known to them – from Asia and the Pacific Islands – and peopled the imaginary antipodes. The explorers' artists recorded the Aborigines as they did the flora and fauna, inaugurating a view of them as ethnographic specimens which persisted for many decades. Some explorers and early settlers found them 'noble savages', and noted their passing with evident regret. Benjamin Law made busts of the last two full-blood Tasmanians, Woureddy and Trucaninny in *c.* 1836 and subsequently Tom Roberts, Arthur Murch, Russell Drysdale and photographer Axel Poignant rendered them sympathetically. Jewish refugee artist Josl Bergner saw parallels between the sufferings of his people under the Nazis, and Arthur Boyd, David Boyd and Noel Counihan protested against the degradation of Aborigines in series painted around 1960, particularly Arthur Boyd's *Love, Marriage and Death of a Half-Caste*.

Others saw them as uncivilised and hostile natives, using caricature as a form of visual ridicule. Harsh treatment was rarely recorded, except where it was normal, as in many photographs of Aborigines in chains.

Racism was widespread in such popular imagery as cartoons. Since the gold rushes of the 1850s Asian peoples were regarded with deep suspicion. The *Bulletin* artists showed great skill in dramatically reducing complex ideas to a strikingly simple image, often grossly exaggerated racial stereotypes. Racist attitudes in art have been rare, but they persist in the popular media, especially at times of racial tension. An important counter to these attitudes has been the evident achievement of Aboriginal artists and, in recent years, of artists of immigrant background.

The 40,000-year-old traditions of Aboriginal art began to interest European anthropologists in the 1870s and began to be collected from around 1900. They held little appeal for European artists until the

John Brack (1920–), The Car (1955), oil on canvas, 41.0 x 101.8 cm, National Gallery of Victoria, purchased 1956. The painting shows a bleak view of flat and featureless suburban consumerism.

late 1920s when Margaret Preston (1875–1963), mindful of the impact of African and Pacific art on Picasso and the Cubists, perceived the usefulness of the abstract patterning in Aboriginal shield and body painting for her work and for Art Deco interior decoration. After some years she came to recognise the spiritual significance and the independent aesthetic power of this art, allowing it to shape her work more profoundly.

The best-known Aboriginal artist of the period, Albert Namatjira (1902–59), was celebrated for painting his region in the most popular Western manner, denigrated by the 1950s as the Gumtree School. Yet he, and his family and associates around Hermannsburg in the Northern Territory, were developing a unique version of the hybrid meeting of styles quite typical of modernism itself, evident in the work of Otto Pareroultja.

This ability to paint between Aboriginal and European culture has reached extraordinary heights in recent decades, in both Arnhem Land barks and western and central desert paintings using acrylic on canvas (pp. 291–2). It has also challenged the most inventive post-modernist artists, such as Imants Tillers whose *The Nine Shots* (1985) appropriates equally images from German Neo-expressionist George Baselitz and Papunya artist Michael Nelson Tjakamarra.

The current situation is marked by a diversification of conceptual concerns among avant-garde artists, a profound questioning of national and personal identity by immigrant artists, and the enormous impact of the painting on canvas, bark and other objects by Aboriginal artists. The energy, and the uniqueness, of Australian art at present derives from the sometimes converging, often conflicting but always stimulating interaction between these tendencies.   TS

Arthur Boyd (1920–), Persecuted Lovers (1964), oil, synthetic polymer paint and gouache on composition board, 137.2 x 182.9 cm, Art Gallery of South Australia, A R Ragless Bequest Fund 1964. Boyd protested against the inhumane treatment of Aborigines in paintings in the early 1960s.

Literature

The literature of Australia is essentially the written account of the European experience of Australia: only in recent years have Aboriginal people, or people from an Asian background, begun to contribute to it directly.

EARLY LITERATURE

Australian literature includes non-fictional prose as well as poetry and fiction, for non-fictional prose also represents an imaginative ordering of and a creative response to the experience of Australia. Early journals provide examples of this imaginative ordering. Some such journals, for example, comment that Australian forests are remarkable because the trunks of the trees are white, not brown. Such observations were striking because they represented something different and new to Europe. The notion of the bizarre otherside of the world, of the paradoxical antipodes, 'down under', where the patently impossible such as black swans would be discovered, was being confirmed as observable reality. There were few neutral facts about Australia.

An idea of Australia (*Terra Australis*) already existed before it was discovered. So, too, Australia was written about before Europeans settled on it. Some scholars maintain that the Yahoos of Swift's *Gulliver's Travels* (1726) derive in part from William Dampier's unflattering remarks on the Aborigines in 1688: 'The Hodmadods of Monanmatapa, tho' a nasty people, yet are gentlemen to these . . . who, setting aside their human shape, differ but little from brutes.' Throughout Europe, the journal of Captain Cook's voyages excited interest in the vast bowl of the Pacific, and Samuel Taylor Coleridge incorporated details from them into his *Rime of the Ancient Mariner*. The Great South Land was entering into the world of the European imagination.

With the awakening interest, several of the officers of the first fleet evidently arranged to have their account of the settlement at Botany Bay published as soon as they could get copy back to England. These individual responses rather than the more discreetly expressed official reports sought to convey something of the strange new world opened up by Cook: yet the anticipation of novelty and the bizarre was quickly countered by boredom and monotony. The size and distance of Australia, and the privations and hardship of settlement overwhelmed any response to the beauty of the wildflowers or to the spectacular colour of the birds. 'In Port Jackson all is quiet and stupid as could be wished', wrote Watkin Tench, the most accomplished of the early journal writers (1789).

The more prevalent commentary on the early Australian experience was statistical: that is, a summary and analytic account of what so far was known about the colony, rather than a personal response or personal commitment to it. By a quirk of fate, just as the sciences had developed more precise systems by which to order their material, Australia became available for scientific inquiry. Not only had the geography to be discovered, but all the exotic plant and animal life was there to be identified and catalogued. With the world of nature so extraordinary, it is not surprising that this preoccupied the minds of men and women. For it is remarkable how little vision, how little sense of destiny, there is in this early writing (the conventional heroics of, say, William Wentworth in 'Australasia: an Ode', 1823, are well-meant but not persuasive). Without that, and with no perceived dimension in history, the colonial imaginative orientation was all to the immediate perspective: 'where's no past tense; the ign'rant present's all', complained Barron Field, the unfortunately named author of the first volume of poetry in Australia, *First Fruits of Australian Poetry* (1819). One senses that this indifference is consistent with the notion of colonial luck, of fortunes made and lost, that subsequently was to be described as the fatalism inherent in the emerging Australian character.

In poetry and prose, the early writers tried to account for the unaccountable, to reconcile fact and fantasy, dream and reality. This was not wholly a misguided aspiration: the mirage persists in the landscape of the Australian mind; and the most telling Australian writing emerges from the fusion of fact and fiction. One fine early example is Alexander Harris' *Settlers and Convicts, by an Emigrant Mechanic* (1847). It has all the authenticity and conviction of a personal history and, Defoe-like, incorporates factual material (for example, accounts of the trial regarding the massacre of Aborigines at Myall Creek). Yet the narrator's history is not the author's. Like much colonial writing this book endorses a pattern of events that was to become archetypal: the cooperative relationship between two men working for themselves (mateship) and the eventual material success of the common man.

Very little of the early literature is concerned with the lives of the convicts, those social outcasts. Cultural embarrassment about them was a later indulgence; rather, the view was that they were brutes, and therefore unenlightening. Besides, the intention of the system was to negate any sense of individuality. From the ironic evidence of those convict ballads and songs which survived, the brutality seems to have been just as embedded in respectable society.

There was, however, considerable early interest in the ways of the Aborigines, but not in the Aborigines themselves. This was consistent with the developing European taste in travel literature, in which indigenous peoples were generalised figures, local, colourful and uncivilised. Books about the experience of migration on the whole concentrated on physical circumstances, on the new location as picturesque or formidable; they were narratives of events rather than representations of the immigrants' personal responses. One particular exception to this is the fear which accompanies the experience of being lost in the bush – a recurrent theme, treated with great seriousness in fiction and non-fiction alike. To be forced to admit the insufficiency of the self in face of the vast indifference of the land is the one great existential confrontation the Australian experience offers, from Alexander Harris to Patrick White's *Voss*, from the journals of the explorers to Douglas Stewart's suite of poems, 'The Birdsville Track', a century later.

The Australian experience contradicted any residual eighteenth-century notions of decorum, of balance between the nature of experience and the expression of it. Australia is simply too big, too far, too other. Early odes and poems express a want of achievable elegance in both the poet and the subject matter; satirical 'pipes' and ironic ballads seemed to get closer to the actual circumstances of early colonial life. Genteel or heroic verse and belle-lettristic prose all too readily became vapid, because more attentive to formal conventions than to finding the best means of articulating an identified or felt experience. Besides, much of this early writing is by those who only incidentally put pen to paper, or only for a brief season.

Few of the early figures were committed writers – but those who were, were impressive: Charles Harpur, Catherine Helen Spence, Henry Kendall and Marcus Clarke. Nineteenth-century writing in Australia was more commonly by amateurs than by men or women of letters, and so was directed quite consciously to a more general audience. This has continued to be a dominant characteristic of Australian literature: it tends to be generalist (even populist) as well as individually demanding. The two classic novels of the nineteenth century, Marcus Clarke's *His Natural Life* (1874) and Rolf Boldrewood's *Robbery Under Arms* (1888), both first appeared as serials in magazines, with all the suspense and heightened appeal of the episodic form; they are nonetheless serious for being popular fiction.

Adam Lindsay Gordon (1833–70), writing in the 1860s, the most acclaimed (and declaimed) of the colonial poets, wrote ballad poems but these are meant to be in the literary vein. Gordon was not a learned man. His reading of classical Greek verse resulted in insights no deeper than that 'Life is mostly froth and bubble', yet his melancholy, his sentimentalism, his nostalgia and his celebration of escape from stoic reflectiveness into the world of

Adam Lindsay Gordon (1833–70), author of ballads that captured the mood and pioneering spirit of the mid-nineteenth century.

manly action combined aspects of the bush ballad and the lyrical ballad and exactly caught the values and the attitudes of the mid-colonial temperament.

Henry Kendall (1839–82), the one Australian poet critically noticed by Oscar Wilde, was a more lyrical poet, a poet of the 'sweetest singer' type. Like Gordon, Kendall also attempted to write ballad verse and lines on various bush types. They were both conscious of the need to represent the common colonial experience in their poetry.

So, too, was the most ambitious of all of them, Charles Harpur (1813–68), a poet surprising in the range of his reading and knowledge, rugged and Wordsworthian, and intent on being the bard of his nation. Harpur, proudly a native-born Australian, was defeated by circumstance, but his poetry and his prose have extraordinary sturdiness, and he supplies the want of vision so lacking in those who first surveyed the colonies. More important, he is accurate if ponderous as he traces the pattern of light through the canopies of trees, or contemplates the intensity of a storm against the sphere of its impact, or measures the foreground against the background in a set description of the mountain ranges. He was prepared to review experience against a larger scheme of things, and to remark on the littleness of those who would be leaders in the new colony. Neither of these traits endeared him to his contemporaries, yet Kendall, for one, held him in very high regard. It has taken a hundred years to reach a proper estimation of his achievement.

LITERARY MELBOURNE

By the 1860s and 1870s there was a wealth of colonial experience to draw upon. Books of reminiscences appeared alongside explorers' journals. Old hands wrote of letting foolhardy 'new chums' (new arrivals) learn by their own mistakes, while explorers pushed their men, and their luck, in terribly new, terribly old terrain. Their efforts were heroic, but their fate was often ironic, if not tragic. This literature is almost classical in its manifest cautions against hubris.

There was also the wealth that had come from the gold rushes, and the social transformations that came with it. Old customs jostled alongside the new. Melbourne had become a substantial mid-Victorian city, with among other advantages a large public library, an active literary life and plenty of opportunity to publish. Writers gravitated to 'marvellous Melbourne'. Henry Kingsley, younger brother of Charles, had spent several years acquiring colonial experience and the material for the first widely accepted novel about Australia, *The Recollections of Geoffry Hamlyn* (1859), a pastoral romance of bold heroic actions and exaggerated fortune.

The *Bulletin*

As Australia approached the centenary of European settlement it began to take stock of itself. On the one hand, it claimed a dimension of history; on the other, it began a debate about its future which was to lead to federation.

Australian writing was becoming self-conscious and self-assertive – a tendency strongly encouraged by the Sydney *Bulletin* (commenced 1880) which urged its contributors to 'write Australian'. Joseph Furphy, one of the outstanding writers of the *Bulletin* school, supplied as an epigraph to his carefully sprawling novel of the Riverina, *Such is Life* (1903), the motto, 'Temper democratic; bias offensively Australian'. That sums up much of the *Bulletin* attitude, not least in its cheerful and ironic brashness. The *Bulletin* was a forum for nationalist sentiment and advocated federalism and republicanism in the debate with those who defended state rights or the imperial connection.

The major writers of the end of the century all published in the *Bulletin*,

Henry Lawson (1867–1922), poet and writer, often known as 'the people's poet'.

and a particular style is associated with it – laconic, humorous, realistic, and sympathetic to the bush worker or small selector (from 1860, farmers who took up small blocks of crown land). Its hallmark was the narrative ballad and the short prose sketch, or yarn; and the dominant figures were 'Banjo' Paterson (1864–1941), acknowledged as the author of Australia's alternative anthem, *Waltzing Matilda*, and Henry Lawson (1867–1922), whose short stories include some that are outstanding by any standard. Curiously, although federation with all its dawn imagery was to occur on the first day of the new century, Paterson and Lawson and their contemporaries show a pronounced yearning towards the past.

The *Bulletin* may have been characterised as the Bushman's Bible, but it also gave space to much more complex and advanced writers, such as the academic poet Christopher Brennan. It also gave room to one of the powerful stories of Barbara Baynton, whose chilling versions of bush experience challenge the comfortable masculine bush ethic of the *Bulletin* school.

AM

Andrew Barton ('Banjo') Paterson (1864-1941). Journalist, broadcaster, poet, short-story writer and novelist. His pseudonym, 'the Banjo', was taken from a racehorse owned by his family.

Marcus Clarke (1846–81) arrived in Melbourne in 1863, endured the misadventures of the new chum and then became the leading literary figure in the colony. His major work, *His Natural Life*, is the first Australian classic. It is a novel about the convict system in Van Diemen's Land, a story largely constructed from historical sources, but so shaped (especially in its revised version) as to forge some semblance of moral design in a world both pitiless and relentless.

Clarke addressed his novel to the world at large, though in his essays and short stories he wrote for a local audience. Rolf Boldrewood (1826–1915) had no such uncertainty of aim. His bushranging novel, *Robbery Under Arms*, first appeared just after the execution of the notorious Ned Kelly, and expresses in the colonial vernacular the point of view of a currency lad, the young Australian narrator.

WOMEN WRITERS

Although much has been made of 'the legend of the nineties' housed in the *Bulletin*'s Red Pages (its literary section), and the definition of the national character that took place there, its influence in determining the course of Australian literature is often over-estimated. A number of women writers, virtually excluded from literary history by the disproportionate attention given to the mainly masculine bush realists, had produced an extraordinary number of publications.

Ada Cambridge, Jessie Couvreur ('Tasma') and Rosa Praed all wrote of a more genteel Australia, but they were also all alert to the dreadful conditions of station life. Each of them maintained a more comfortable connection with England than suited nationalist sentiment and they have profited from recent feminist revisions of literary history.

Other areas of writing appeared at the end of the century. The work of anthropologists Baldwin Spencer and Francis Gillen among the Arunta people provided a systematic anthropological basis against which the value of such amateur compilations as Catherine Langloh Parker's collections of Aboriginal stories, beginning with *Australian Legendary Tales* (1896), could be acknowledged.

The common belief was that the Aborigines would inevitably disappear as a people. Daisy Bates, who spent a large part of her life among Aborigines on the Nullarbor, finally published an account of her experiences with the revealing title *The Passing of the Aborigines* (1938).

Mrs Aeneas Gunn wrote for young readers *The Little Black Princess* (1905) and also included Aboriginal material in her local classic autobiography, *We of the Never Never* (1908), about life on a property in the Northern Territory.

CHILDREN'S BOOKS

The rich vein of children's literature can be associated with this period, though there had been many works, mostly of an improving kind, throughout the preceding 50 years. Again, women writers are dominant. Ethel Turner's best-known novel *Seven Little Aus-*tralians (1894) and Ethel Pedley's *Dot and the Kangaroo* (1899) were very popular. So, too, were the many Billabong novels of Mary Grant Bruce, while May Gibbs' illustrated stories of Snugglepot and Cuddlepie, beginning with *Gumnut Babies* (1916), continue their appeal and invite comparison with the work of Beatrix Potter. Most popular of all is Norman Lindsay's *The Magic Pudding* (1918).

All this accomplished activity in writing for children suggests a more stable community than that reflected in the *Bulletin* stories. The prosperous years of the high Victorian age, and the big Edwardian houses and gardens which are a common point of departure in these books, provide the occasion for children with their natural curiosity to find their own way into the bush. In their writing, modern writers who grew up in those days, such as Patrick White (see p. 314) and Christina Stead, have fixed the source of their own troubled spirit in those apparently comfortable times and circumstances.

TOWN AND COUNTRY

The sense of a golden past is reinforced by the long literary lives of such figures as Mary Gilmore, Walter Murdoch and Miles Franklin. Mary Gilmore (1865–1962) became a legend in her own lifetime. In her poems and prose recollections she drew on her own memory, longer and more romantic than anyone else's, to tell of old ways and old days in Australia.

Walter Murdoch (1874–1970) was the most prolific essayist of the times – whimsical, genial, chatty, using the most inconsequential events as a basis for canny insights into deeper issues.

Miles Franklin (1879–1954), who had won early notice with her youthful *My Brilliant Career* (1901), went on to write a series of romantic pastoral novels, and to endow the annual Miles Franklin Award for the best Australian novel (the first award was to Patrick White for *Voss* in 1957). Others whose literary lives stretched over the best part of 50 years include Vance (1885–1959) and Nettie Palmer (1865–1964), leading figures in the cause for a national literature, and Katharine Susannah Prichard (1883–1969), a romantic realist novelist.

Although Australia is imagined as the wide brown land, the empty continent, it has always had mainly an urban population. That imbalance between imagination and experience has been persistent; at the beginning of the twentieth century there began to appear poems and novels both protesting against yet celebrating the crowding life of cities and Australia's incipient sprawl – against the city life of Louis Stone's *Jonah* (1911) and C.J. Dennis' *Songs of a Sentimental Bloke* (1915).

E. J. Banfield settled on Dunk Island in the Barrier Reef, and with his *Confessions of a Beachcomber* (1908) commenced a series of books celebrating natural history and commonsense philosophy as much as the exoticism of his tropic isle. Jack McLaren's *My Crowded Solitude* (1926) is more adventurous than reflective, but a comparable impulse to confront by oneself the otherness of the natural order can be seen here too. These books pass for fact; they read with as much interest as anything proposed in fiction. On the other side of Australia the young Bert Facey was proving himself through various rural experiences and, counter to the mateship myth, finding that he preferred his own company; but A. B. Facey's *A Fortunate Life* was not written down until much later in his life, nor published until 1981.

THE 1920S AND THE 1930S

World War I was to introduce change to Australia. Relatively little writing came out of the war directly – one fine exception is Frederic Manning's *The Middle Parts of Fortune* (1929; an expurgated edition, *Her Privates We*, appeared a year later).

But out of that war came C. E. W. Bean's massive official war history, in which he celebrates the image of the common soldier, the digger, seeing him as inheriting and encapsulating all the qualities of the bushman. In the first two volumes, *The Story of Anzac* (1921 and 1924), Bean endorsed the tradition of identifying a mythic dimension in Australian history. (This tradition would be reaffirmed in *Australia* (1930), Keith Hancock's reading of Australian history in terms of the national character.)

Change came in various forms. Much of the literature of the 1920s feels post-Edwardian rather than Jazz Age; Australia was on the whole resistant to modernism. D. H. Lawrence's brief visit in 1922 resulted in *Kangaroo* (1923), which with its moving sensitive descriptions of the bush encouraged more lyrical responses in place of harsh realism.

The decorativeness of Art Nouveau found expression in Australian poetry as well as painting, and *Vision*, a Sydney periodical articulating the enthusiasms of Norman Lindsay, flourished briefly (1923–24) but spectacularly as the focus for a particular creative energy, challenging small-minded middle-class proprieties ('wowserism' – a slogan supposedly invented by newspaperman John Norton (1850–1916), proprietor of the *Truth*, and anti-puritan), and launching the first two modern poets, Kenneth Slessor (1901–71) and Robert FitzGerald (1902–87).

In Slessor's carefully considered poems, the colourfulness of the images and an often somewhat theatrical figure as narrator or subject (a ghost at a window, a drowned man) tend to conceal a deep

Miles Franklin (1879–1954), author of several novels, of which the best-known is the first, My Brilliant Career *(1901), later made into a much-acclaimed film directed by Gillian Armstrong (1979).*

despair akin to that of existentialism. Slessor was no philosopher, but he was sensitive to the emotional and intellectual climate of his time.

FitzGerald wrote verse of a philosophically inquiring kind; he is remembered for his poems on time, memory and the relation between past and present. Between them, these two signalled the change in Australian poetry from colonial and Georgian romanticism to a more critically aware, ironic and personally expressive mode of writing.

Another poet, writing quite independently of all this activity in Sydney (which had overtaken Melbourne as the centre of literary activity, though most of the major publishing firms were still located in Melbourne), was John Shaw Neilson (1872–1942), a writer of extraordinarily delicate lyrical poetry. Arguably, modern Australian poets are best at the meditative lyric, a reflective poetic response to an actual or exactly remembered landscape, and Neilson can be placed at the head of this stream.

The most substantial novelist of the period was Henry Handel Richardson (1870–1946), and the change she introduces is in range and complexity. She was an expatriate writer, yet in spite of her distance from Australia she was concerned with local themes. *The Getting of Wisdom* (1910) is an unsentimental education, a portrait of the artist as a young girl at boarding-school. *Maurice Guest* (1908), set in Leipzig, shows the young provincial coming into contact with the avant-garde; a novel about an insufficiently grand passion, it maps out an ironic view of destiny. Her major work is the trilogy *The Fortunes of Richard Mahony* (1930), in which she had written of her father's generation, and of the nature of fortune and the individual's responsibility for it, in the manner of the great naturalist writers. The richly ambiguous closing paragraphs with their sense of the disappointment of life and the vast indifference of the landscape, convey a poignant image of the way destiny is felt to work in Australia.

Through the 1930s many who had begun to publish in the previous decade consolidated their careers as writers. As in other parts of the world, Australian writers were concerned with international political and social movements as well as with the immediate effects of the depression. They formed groups and societies and fellowships (though the Australian Literature Society had been formed as early as 1899), and debated social issues alongside points of ideology; they were essentially active.

In many respects this decade seemed a re-play of the legendary 1890s and the popular works of that period underwent a revival. A concern to identify the working-class origins of Australia led to excursions into the past in novels, poems and short stories – the leading historical novelists were Eleanor Dark and M. Barnard Eldershaw (Marjorie Barnard and Flora

Eldershaw). A comparable impulse, though looking for roots in another direction, was in the extensive popular literature of discovery. With the widespread advent of the car, both time and means were now available for independent exploration of the highways and by-ways of Australia. Being 'on the track' took on a new vigour, and there are numerous accounts of such journeys – William Hatfield's *Australia through the Windscreen* (1936), Thomas Wood's *Cobbers* (1934) and, in another mode, Ion Idriess' *Lasseter's Last Ride* (1931). With the instant success of that book, Idriess went on to publish numerous books about the outback and the remote coast, and established a market for popular travelogue and history that Frank Clune and others were quick to seize upon. That kind of writing is still probably the dominant mode of Australian writing.

Yet another place to look for roots was in Aboriginal culture, and late in the 1930s Rex Ingamells launched the Jindyworobak movement with his manifesto *Conditional Culture* (1938). Its extreme nationalism is matched by P. R. Stephensen's call for Australian culture to be based on the spirit of place, in his *The Foundations of Culture in Australia* (1936). Quite independently of these, Xavier Herbert's *Capricornia* (1938), a turbulent novel of racial prejudice and the Northern Territory happened to incorporate all these tendencies – social protest, the concern with origins, the outback, the Aborigines, and the spirit of Australia.

WORLD WAR II AND AFTER

The next and most considerable generation of Australian writers and artists began to emerge at the outset of World War II. For both groups the search was for an adequate symbolism. The famous 'Ern Malley' hoax, in which James McAuley and Harold Stewart constructed a set of meaningless but modernist poems, was part of it.

Christina Stead, who had long since moved overseas, was writing some of her greatest novels (*The Man who Loved Children*, 1940) but she would not be discovered until the 1960s.

McAuley, and other poets such as A. D. Hope, Douglas Stewart, Judith Wright, and just a little later David Campbell, would eventually set new standards for poetry in Australia. And like their contemporaries in painting, or Patrick White in fiction, they established Australia's presence before an international audience.

Patrick White's career, culminating in his Nobel Prize, belongs mainly to the post-war period; so, too, does that of Martin Boyd (1893–1972), even though he had won the first Gold Medal from the Australian Literature Society as early as 1928. White's novels, enormously ambitious in their vision and their symbolism, explore the spiritual possibilities of Australian experience. Boyd's novels are at once more personal and more universal. His interest is in the values of civilisation, and the destruction of these by

Patrick White

Patrick White (1912–90), the most famous of Australian writers and among the world's greatest novelists of the second half of this century, won the Nobel Prize for Literature in 1973. For 20 years before that his was a dominant influence on Australian writing. With him, Australian fiction ceased to be provincial in its themes and orientation; after White, Australian writing became more confident and more ambitious. Yet White's characteristically elaborate and highly charged style and his reliance on colourful symbolism sometimes became a stumbling block, for readers as well as writers.

He was born into a wealthy pastoral family, which, in the manner of the Edwardian era, still held strong attachments to England. His parents were determined that he should have a 'good' education; he was sent, at the age of 13, to Cheltenham College, England, and he never forgave his parents for what he regarded as a betrayal. He returned to Australia and worked as a jackeroo on a

sheep station for two years, and began writing at this time; then he returned to the UK, to study modern languages at King's College, Cambridge. After graduating in 1935 he moved to London and became a 'stage door johnny', a freqenter of theatre, and developed his passion for drama, which he maintained through his long career.

The affected world of the London intellectual struck him as increasingly parasitic and pointless. He served as an intelligence officer in the Middle East and there he met a Greek officer, Manoly Lascaris, who became his life-long partner. After the war they moved to Australia and White began his serious work, a range of remarkable novels in which he probed and tested the buried resources of the human condition, the complexity latent within simplicity, the extraordinary behind the ordinary, the poetry that redeems the mediocrity of modern life. He believed in 'a splendour, a transcendence above human realities', but equally was

disgusted by, and wittily satirical of, the suburban horrors of modern materialist society. At times his moral revulsion seems indistinguishable from aesthetic distaste; but always his writing is informed by a passion to probe, to discover new forms of meaning and knowledge, to enquire into the endless mystery of life.

White's novels include *The Aunt's Story* (1948), *The Tree of Man* (1955), *Voss* (1957), *Riders in the Chariot* (1961), *The Solid Mandala* (1966), *The Vivisector* (1970), *The Eye of the Storm* (1973), *A Fringe of Leaves* (1976) and *The Twyborn Affair* (1979). *Flaws in the Glass* (1981) he subtitled a self-portrait, a memoir rather than an autobiography. His plays, such as *The Season at Sarsaparilla* (1961), *Night on Bald Mountain* (1962) and *Signal Driver* (1983) established him as one of Australia's finest non-naturalist playwrights. Just before his death he read, and approved, David Marr's magnificent biography, *Patrick White: A Life* (1991).

AM

events such as the great wars; likewise, he is interested in the operation of the past within us (the proposed collective title of his 'Langton' novels) and the beauty and sorrows of humanity. Another considerable writer to emerge at this time was Hal Porter (1911–84), initially with his short stories and later with his autobiographical works, especially *The Watcher on the Cast-iron Balcony* (1963).

The founding of literary magazines such as *Southerly* (1939) and *Meanjin* (1940), the increased involvement of the Commonwealth Literary Fund in publishing and, after the war, in promoting Australian literature through a series of lectures, and the commencement of the study of Australian literature at universities, all supported the activities of this remarkable generation. By the 1950s, they had the confidence to present universal perceptions through the use of local material, to reveal the extraordinary behind the ordinary. Cultural myth was fascinating to them, but they had escaped the preoccupation with the merely local; and a second wave of gifted writers – Randolph Stow, Christopher Koch, Thomas Keneally – carried on the momentum of their achievement.

Writers of all kinds were inspecting the past to disentangle cultural myth from historical reality, sometimes in order to assert the myth. This was true of poetry and drama as well as prose. The first volume of Manning Clark's *History of Australia* was published in 1962; Donald Horne's *The Lucky Country* (1964) remained an often-revised success; George Johnston analysed the legendary and the likely Australian in a partly autobiographical novel, *My Brother Jack* (1964); writers as various as Hal Porter, Donald Horne and Graham McInnes wrote autobiographies which concentrated on adolescence and confirmed that as the definitive age for the shaping of the Australian character; while other acclaim was being won by biographers such as John Hetherington and social historians such as Alan Moorhead.

Patrick White (1912-90), novelist, short-story writer and playwright. In 1973 he became the first Australian to win the Nobel Prize for Literature.

TRADITIONAL AND MODERN

The late 1960s and early 1970s provided the opportunity for even wider activity – street theatre, underground poetry, happenings – as a young generation asserted its voice, whether in response to the counter-culture or in reaction to Vietnam. In the age of Aquarius, California was the promised land, and younger writers modelled themselves on what came from the West Coast (USA). In part, this was a reaction against a different conscription, a desire to be seen as liberated and international rather than confined and Australian.

There need be no such antagonism of course, and the best stories of Frank Moorhouse, Michael Wilding and Peter Carey, prominent writers of short stories at this time, move comfortably between the two poles – they take their subject matter from whatever happens to interest them.

One of the poets to emerge in the 1970s as a major figure, Les Murray, has reassessed cultural and social myth in Australia; he identifies spiritual values in the secular world, and combines the vernacular with the traditional.

Peter Porter has combined traditional and modern in verse of classical elegance; and that formulation is reflected also in the novels, stories, poems and essays of David Malouf, and the poems of Gwen Harwood. Bruce Dawe, like Murray, prefers to write in the plain language of the common man, and his satires make use of the speech rhythms and intonations of the vernacular.

THE 1980s

Thomas Keneally is a prolific novelist with a recurrent motif: an individual of no particular importance thrust into a moment of historical significance or public notice. In that motif he represents the recurrent intersection in Australian fiction between the ordinary and the elevated, a literature at once popular and serious. Another prolific and well-regarded novelist of this period is Thea Astley. All of these writers are prize-winners, and most have an international reputation. Keneally was several times short-listed for the Booker Prize in England, before winning it in 1982 with *Schindler's Ark*, a novel as much factual as fictive. Peter Carey, who has escalated his fragmentary short stories into the novel, also won the Booker Prize in 1988 with *Oscar and Lucinda*.

After the feminist movement of the 1970s, women writers have featured prominently. Not all of them are committed to that cause in their writing: Shirley Hazzard is an elegant and morally powerful novelist, and *The Transit of Venus* (1980) consciously draws on literary tradition as it explores the relation between character and destiny. Feminist sympathies are more visible in the novels and stories of Barbara Hanrahan, Helen Garner, Kate Grenville and Elizabeth Jolley. In non-fictional prose Robyn Davidson's *Tracks* (1982) works through those ideas to come to a less insistent, perhaps more Aboriginal view of the relation between place and identity – an issue of increasing interest in contemporary writing.

New writers continued to appear throughout the 1980s – Tim Winton, Brian Castro, Janette Turner Hospital and Glenda Adams in fiction, and in poetry Robert Adamson, John Tranter, Robert Gray and Kevin Hart. Dimitris Tsaloumas and Antigone Kefala are examples of writers coming from a non-English background, and signal the increasingly multicultural dimension in Australian writing.

Four late-nineteenth-century actors and actor-managers: (from left to right) George Rignold, J. C. Williamson, Harry Rickards and Bland Holt.

writer; and discouraged recognition of the indigenous star. Two notable exceptions were the brilliant Nellie Stewart (1858–1931), star of pantomime, Gilbert and Sullivan, opera and comedy, and Gladys Moncrieff (1892–1976), the musical comedy star 'Our Glad', to whom the mantle fell in the 1920s. They were two of the greatest 'people's' stars Australia has seen.

The 1870s and 1880s saw the rise of other successful actor-managers such as George Darrell, Alfred Dampier and Bland Holt, who felt more positively about the local writing talent. With his manager, J. H. Wrangham, Dampier (?1848–1908) wrote the classic *Marvellous Melbourne* (1886) and in 1894 took his adaptation of Rolf Boldrewood's *Robbery Under Arms* (1888) to London. Darrell (1841–1921), a debonair and fashionable actor, wrote 55 plays and starred in most of them. But the most extravagant actor-manager was Bland Holt (1853–1942), who produced sensation dramas and adaptations of imported plays. His The *Breaking of the Drought* (1902), an adaptation from the English playwright Arthur Shirley, was one of the first plays with a contemporary setting and the cause of political protest over its realistic representation of drought devastation. Holt also presented many Marcus Clarke and Garnet Walch pantomimes.

The gradual gentrification of the theatre from the 1870s on led to further censorship particularly of bushranging plays and this extended to the silent movies about the Kelly Gang at large at the time which captured the popular imagination. Edward I. Cole's itinerant Bohemian Dramatic Company were the chief exponents with plays such as *Captain Moonlight* and *Thunderbolt*.

J. C. Williamson's chief rival on the national scene was the William Anderson Dramatic Company, which began producing first-class melodrama in the 1890s. Anderson built a vast entertainment empire, including touring companies, Wonderland City, at Tamarama, Sydney, and his own King's Theatre in Melbourne. He showed his enterprise by mounting the popular plays of the actors Bert Bailey and Edmund Duggan, the first of a new style of indigenous bush comedy-drama, which, though based on the skills of vaudeville and melodrama, pointed forward to a recognition of Australian realism. For wealth and variety the theatre was at its height and the success continued until the outbreak of World War I.

South Australia had early become part of this touring circuit but Western Australia had been behind the rest in the development of professional theatre. The discovery of gold in Kalgoorlie in 1893 changed that. Perth became a boom town and the Theatre Royal was built in 1897 and His Majesty's Theatre in 1904. Theatres were also built in the goldfields and touring managements who travelled by train, ship and buggy around the continent began to venture more frequently across the Nullarbor Plain. Some followed the agricultural shows around from state to state, carrying their own improvised theatres with them. One such was Kate Howarde, a tent-show manager for 30 years who wrote her own bush comedies.

But tastes were changing. The new literary theatre movement in London led by Harley Granville Barker was about to find its champion: the popular character actor Gregan McMahon (1874–1941), probably Australia's first theatre director in the modern sense.

In 1911 McMahon founded the Melbourne Repertory Society, an amateur organisation devoted to quality theatre. His professional work for the concert producers J. and N. Tait led to a lifetime patronage of his productions of modern realist writers such as Ibsen and Galsworthy; and his association with Bernard Shaw led to him presenting the world premiere in 1936 of *The Millionairess*. In his obituary in 1941 the *Age* newspaper called him 'the Granville Barker of Australia'. The title was apt but it failed to take account of the profound differences between the British repertory movement, which was professional, and the Australian, which was amateur.

In 1908 the Adelaide Repertory Society was founded and was followed in due course by similar groups in every state, mixing serious intention with social cachet. Nevertheless, until the 1960s it was through the amateur movement that progressive thought came to the Australian theatre.

THREATS TO THE THEATRE

By 1910 the arrival of cinema had begun to divert many major figures in the theatre to film. Theatre partnerships were broken up and a new hierarchy

Stiffy (Nat Phillips; left) and Mo (Roy Rene). Stiffy and Mo's sometimes risqué vaudeville routines made them Australia's most famous double act during and after World War I.

was established. With cinema draining away the working-class audiences, theatre became even more apparently middle class. Nellie Melba returned in 1911 to head the J. C. Williamson Opera Company, and the Firm began to align themselves with more elegant theatre forms. In competition were Harry Rickards' Tivoli circuit of vaudeville and its rival, the variety circuit run by Benjamin and John Fuller. While the cockney Rickards' stars were largely imported the Fullers' style was Australian and created many stars, among them the comedians Jim Gerald, Maud Fanning, Queenie Paul, Roy Rene and Nat Phillips.

The outbreak of World War I completed the transformation which the coming of film had begun. Phillips and Rene became Australia's most famous double act as Stiffy and Mo. One of the great wartime successes was the Fullers' Christmas pantomime *The Bunyip* in 1916, written and composed by Phillips, Ella Airlie and Herbert de Pinna.

An influenza pandemic in Australia in 1918, which took many lives, had a devastating effect upon the entertainment industry. In 1920 J. C. Williamson merged with J. and N. Tait, concert producers. The five Tait brothers dominated the commercial theatre in Australia until the death of Sir Frank Tait in 1965.

The year 1920 also saw the formation of the Allan Wilkie Shakespeare Company. Wilkie was a Scotsman and he and his wife, Frediswyde Hunter-Watts, were Shakespearians of the old school. They toured Australia and New Zealand, India and South Africa until 1930, when they moved to Canada.

This period was a high point in the new middle-class theatre. Dion Boucicault jun. and his wife Irene Vanbrugh toured to Australia three times in the 1920s, Oscar Asche twice, Anna Pavlova twice and Melba twice. In 1932 J. C. Williamson brought out the Casson Thorndike Company with Sybil Thorndike's memorable Saint Joan. Operetta was also at its height and in 1921 Gladys Moncrieff gave her first performance of the role with which she remained identified, the *Maid of the Mountains*.

The literary theatre, meanwhile, was making its protest against this lavish escapism. Louis Esson (1879–1943), journalist and playwright, was one of a group of Melbourne writers, artists and socialists who were the first to develop a dialectic about an Australian dramatic literature and the first to determine that its source lay in a working-class culture. Esson's style owed much to such theorists as Shaw and Wilde, and later Yeats, Synge and O'Neill.

Such literary movements were only one symptom of the division that had grown by this time between popular entertainment and middle-class culture. The day of the actor-manager had passed and the entrepreneur had arrived.

In 1929 the depression was on its way. The theatre now had a double battle for survival, against the cinema and the economy. By 1930 all but two theatres in Sydney had closed or been converted into cinemas for Hollywood movies. The infant film industry had died. The only new avenue for employment was radio, which had come to Australia in 1923. By the 1940s the radio actors were Australia's stars.

In the middle-class theatre the style was changing too. Behind the change was a concern for cultural advancement and the persistent thought that Australia should possess its own indigenous theatre – an idea disseminated by the amateurs. The 1930s and 1940s were particularly rich in innovative amateur theatres. Some were socialist, some were social, some were devoted to Australian writing, some were a mixture of professional and amateur management. The quality of performance was often high and the relationship to the profession close. For the performer the training stage was the amateur theatre; but for the playwright the way into the profession was still closed. Those who wanted more from their theatre had to find it abroad. And many, such as Sumner Locke Elliott, Leo McKern, Peter Finch, Coral Browne, Keith Michell, Ron Randell and later Zoe Caldwell, were lost to Australia.

THE TRUST

For the writer the first breakthrough into the commercial theatre came in 1948 with Sumner Locke Elliott's wartime comedy *Rusty Bugles*. It was first

The Ham Funeral in a production by the Sydney Theatre Company in 1989. Patrick White's surrealist first play, it was written in 1947, but did not receive its first performance until 1961.

Events, however, contrived against progress in this direction. A play competition turned up as co-winner Ray Lawler's *Summer of the Seventeenth Doll* (first produced, 1955) and before he knew it Hunt found himself the producer of a world-wide success. It raised the hopes of writers and actors alike and there followed a series of original works, the most lasting of which were Richard Beynon's *The Shifting Heart* (1956), Alan Seymour's *The One Day of the Year* (1959) and Patrick White's *The Ham Funeral* (1961).

At this point the rift between the popular and middle-class taste became apparent. At the outset, the Trust had set up national ballet, opera and theatre companies. The first two, offering traditional fare, in due course became the Australian Ballet and the Australian Opera. But the Trust was not prepared for a generation of playwrights determined to expose the more disreputable aspects of Australian life. The Trust Players were abandoned after three years.

FESTIVALS

Further controversy came in with the establishment of the Adelaide Festival of Arts in 1960 as a biennial March event, aimed at rivalling the Edinburgh Festival. Australia already had one festival of the kind in the Festival of Perth, held annually since 1954 in the grounds of the University of Western Australia; but Adelaide quickly outflanked it as an international event and remains the major Australian festival.

Though they featured stars of some import, the early festivals are chiefly remembered for the Board of Governors' banning of Alan Seymour's *The One Day of the Year* and Patrick White's *The Ham Funeral*. The plays were refused performance, the first because it was seen as an attack on the Returned Services' League, a powerful conservative lobby; and the second because of certain unpleasant images in the text. Both plays were promptly performed elsewhere and have since earned the status of classics. The founder of the Festival, Professor John Bishop, died in 1964 and the directorship became a rotating appointment. Among the luminaries have been Sir Robert Helpmann, Jim Sharman and the Edinburgh Festival founder, Lord Harewood.

performed by the amateur Independent Theatre in Sydney, where the army slang earned it a ban by the New South Wales chief secretary; but it went on to a national tour. The play remained an isolated Australian hit until the establishment of the first government patron of the performing arts, the Australian Elizabethan Theatre Trust, in 1954. It began, albeit hesitantly, a new deal for the Australian theatre which over the next two decades transformed the whole structure of the industry.

J.C. Williamson had responded vigorously to the end of World War II with *Oklahoma!* (1947) and a wealth of other popular musicals, culminating in *My Fair Lady* (1959). But to Australia the ultimate civilising event was the British Council's gift to Australia in 1948 – Laurence Olivier and Vivien Leigh in a trio of plays sumptuously designed by Cecil Beaton; and in its wake Prime Minister Chifley invited the British director Tyrone Guthrie to advise on a proposal for a National Theatre. Guthrie's advice, however, was that the government should spend its money sending promising artists overseas to train and work. The proposal was not well received. Impatient for action, a group of businessmen led by H.C. Coombs, governor of the Reserve Bank, launched a campaign to establish, in 1954, commemorating the young queen's visit to Australia, an Australian Elizabethan Theatre Trust.

The Trust, as it came to be known, was funded partly by the federal government and partly by private donation; and its aim was to improve the standards of classic and original work by providing subsidy and expertise. It soon found, however, that it must itself become an entrepreneur. It brought Hugh Hunt from Britain as its first director and purchased an old theatre in Newtown, Sydney, which it renamed the Elizabethan. Hunt's first season confirmed that he was one in spirit with Tyrone Guthrie. It was a company led by Ralph Richardson and Sybil Thorndike, with a season of Terence Rattigan plays.

CLIMATE OF CONFLICT

Other incidents in the 1950s demonstrated the growing cultural ambitions of an affluent society. One was the Sydney Opera House design competition held in 1955–1956, won by the Danish architect Joern Utzon. The building, with its vast white sails set against the blue of Sydney Harbour, is today one of the architectural wonders of the twentieth century. Its construc-

The Adelaide Festival Theatre. Established in 1960, the Adelaide Festival soon became established as the country's major arts festival.

The 1960s proved a turning point for the theatre. The bright new generation of playwrights such as Ray Lawler, Alan Seymour, Ray Mathew, Richard Beynon and Anthony Coburn, who had been encouraged by the Trust, set off to seek their fortunes abroad. The flag was held by the returned expatriate Patrick White (p. 314), whose work for the theatre made a sharp move away from realism towards a medley of poetry, symbol and vaudeville. It was a first step towards the discovery of an indigenous style of theatre which accommodated the rhythms and language of Australian life more fittingly than the European forms which had dominated the writing of the 1950s. The movement would begin in earnest in 1967.

Several other elements combined to make the late 1960s the most innovative period this century. The theatre management of J. C. Williamson was failing and new entrepreneurs were springing up to challenge it. Music-hall theatre restaurants were attracting a new carriage-trade audience that had long ceased to go to the legitimate theatre. The dashing impresario Harry M. Miller confronted the censors with the American gay comedy *The Boys in the Band* (1969), followed by *Hair* the same year and *Jesus Christ Superstar* (1972). The Vietnam war was at its height; a growing ambition for cultural independence swept the country.

tion, however, was plagued by the same conflicts. They led to the resignation of the architect in 1966 and the building was completed in 1973 by a panel of architects assembled by the state government (see also p. 301).

It was, of course, this climate of conflict which produced Australia's comic phenomenon, Barry Humphries, whose monstrous suburban housewife Edna Everage first appeared in revue in 1958. Though he is now an international star, Humphries' style of comedy is grounded in this period of cultural awakening which lashed out at the suburban dream.

Another event marking the close of the 1950s was the establishment in 1959 of the National Institute of Dramatic Art (NIDA) in Sydney. This was the first government-funded drama school and its graduates number most of the major stage and screen actors today. Schools in other states followed in the 1970s.

Harry Miller's major contribution – and the innovation which accounted for his remarkable, too brief success – was the promotion of new talent and original work. In particular, he gave opportunity to the director Jim Sharman, then only 22. His productions of *Hair* and *Jesus Christ Superstar* took him to an international career and opened the way for others to divide their work between Australia and the world. Another of Miller's protégés was the playwright David Williamson, whose first success, *The Removalists* (1971), was taken into the commercial theatre by Miller and to London. It was the first of the contemporary plays to make the leap from the back streets. Williamson followed it with hits such as *Don's Party* (1973), *The Club* (1978), *Travelling North* (1980) and *Emerald City* (1987). Today the most popular playwright in Australia's recent history, he is equally successful as a filmwriter in Sydney and Los Angeles.

This time the foreign influences in the theatre were not middle class or classical but the theatre of protest. In 1968 a performance at Sydney's tiny socialist New Theatre of the American protest play *America Hurrah!* was banned by the New South Wales chief secretary, bringing about unprecedented public defence. The banning of other plays and films followed, particularly in Victoria and Queensland. The outcry led first to a ridiculing of existing laws, and subsequently to their reassessment.

This climate of protest gave opportunity to new writing. Backstreet nurseries for the new theatre

Barry Humphries as the Australian housewife Edna Everage, before she became a 'Superstar'. Later a somewhat ambiguous parody of show-business types, Edna Everage was conceived as a satire on late-1950s consumerist suburban society.

sprang up. The early plays from La Mama and the Pram Factory (two converted factories in Carlton, Melbourne) were comic assaults on convention and fresh, free-wheeling expressions of the Australian language. In Sydney, a parallel theatre movement was less political and more celebratory; and its centre was the little Nimrod Street Theatre, a former stable. It was in these theatres that the working-class theatre tradition began to reassert itself, breaking down the old realist conventions in favour of the vaudeville routine.

History has assigned these Sydney and Melbourne groups the most lasting significance; but elsewhere experiment was equally prolific. There were travelling players, happenings, love-ins and reinterpretations of the classics. Universities were a vital centre of experiment, spawning political and avant-garde theatre, open-air and open-space theatre and theatre-in-the-round. Most of today's innovative directors, designers and actors had their origins in such groups.

THE AUSTRALIA COUNCIL

The ferment of new writing and performance was only a small part of the dramatic changes taking place in the Australian theatre. The most important – the one which indeed generated much of this ferment – occurred in 1968 when Prime Minister Gorton announced the establishment of the Australian Council for the Arts, Australia's government patronage of the performing arts, today known as the Australia Council.

The principal lobbyist for such a Council had been H. C. Coombs, founder of the Australian Elizabethan Theatre Trust. The Trust had begun to fill the yawning gaps that existed in the performing arts; but a grander and more even-handed structure was now needed. The first executive director was Jean Battersby, a modern languages academic who held the post until 1976. The first budget was $1.5 million; today, it is $50 million.

The Council was structured to comprise a governing council of policy-makers, an executive officer and staff and panels of peer advisers; and the same structure obtains today. The existence of the Council soon forced the state governments to rethink their responsibilities and within five years each of the states had set up their own arts advisory and ministerial funding systems.

A monument to this new thinking was the cultural centre. While the old commercial theatres were being torn down and replaced by office blocks, local government began constructing new performing arts centres. The Sydney Opera House opened in 1973, Perth's Concert Hall in 1973, Adelaide's Festival Centre in 1974, Alice Springs' Araluen Centre in 1984, the Victorian Arts Centre concert hall and theatre in Melbourne in 1982 and 1985, respectively, Brisbane's Cultural Centre in 1985 and Darwin's Performing Arts Centre in 1986. (The cities of Perth and Hobart had the vision to restore the two finest baroque theatres left in Australia, His Majesty's in Perth, and the Theatre Royal in Hobart.)

Whatever the passions and divisions engendered by the arrival of the Australia Council, the result was a burgeoning of activity such as the arts had hardly seen before. The first action of the Theatre Board, as it came to be known, was to nominate a theatre company in each state to become the recipient of a major grant, thus creating a series of regional organisations.

REGIONAL THEATRES

In Adelaide, the South Australian Theatre Company already existed, established by John Tasker under the umbrella of the Trust.

The National Theatre at the Playhouse, in Perth, metamorphosed from the amateur Perth Repertory Club, was then the major house. In 1986 it became the Western Australian Theatre Company.

In Melbourne, the Union Theatre Repertory Company, started in 1947 as a semi-professional company on the University of Melbourne campus by John Sumner, had risen to become Melbourne's major regional theatre. It is now the Melbourne Theatre Company. Sumner, who came to national attention in 1955 as the director of *Summer of the Seventeenth Doll*, dominated Melbourne legitimate theatre for 30 years. He retired in 1987.

The choice of company in Sydney, in 1968, was not so clear. There were four competing companies: the Independent Theatre, with a policy of 'world standard' theatre; the Ensemble Theatre-in-the-round with a strong American-style vitality; the Community Theatre, which provided theatre for Sydney's North Shore; and the Old Tote Theatre Company, an offshoot of NIDA. Though its history was brief and fragile, its politics were sound and the Old Tote was selected. In 1973 it expanded into the Opera House Drama Theatre but its reign was short-lived; it went into liquidation in 1978. The state government replaced it with the Sydney Theatre Company in 1979.

Brisbane in 1968 boasted no major professional theatre but it had a number of small semi-professional groups, notably the Brisbane Repertory Company, known as La Boite (from their theatre-in-the-round) and the Twelfth Night Theatre. In the event the state government chose to create by statute in 1969 the Queensland Theatre Company (now granted the Royal prefix) and appointed Alan Edwards as founding director, a position he held until 1987.

Doris Fitton (1897–1985), actress, co-founder in 1935 and controlling force of the Independent Theatre in North Sydney. Actors who worked with the company, which closed in 1977, include Peter Finch, Keith Michell and Barry Humphries.

Timothy Schwerdt (left) and John Blair (right) as Moorli and the Leprechaun in the play of the same name by Aboriginal writer Jack Davis. This production was staged in 1994 by the Riverina Theatre Company, based in regional New South Wales.

The history of the Tasmanian Theatre Company (1972–84) housed at the Theatre Royal, Hobart, was not so successful. With a large theatre and a small population, repeated attempts to retain a theatre company in Hobart failed. Its single success has been the long-running children's theatre, the Salamanca Theatre Company.

COMPANIES

The years 1969–70 saw a whole stream of vintage productions and new experiment by artists hitherto starved of resources. They also saw the rise of new companies and the death of others.

In Sydney, the Independent Theatre did not long survive. The Ensemble lost its vitality. The Community Theatre went into decline. The Nimrod Street Theatre with its new, vulgarian Aussie style, flourished and in 1973 moved to larger premises in Surry Hills (now known as the Belvoir Street Theatre). The old theatre became the home of a new group dedicated to all-Australian theatre, the Griffin Theatre Company. The Q Theatre, which for some years had been providing lunch-hour theatre at Circular Quay, sought a new home at Penrith, at the foot of the Blue Mountains, to create theatre for the working and unemployed community. In the 1980s theatres changed hands again. It was the Nimrod's turn to fail. It moved from Belvoir Street, and the building was bought by a syndicate of the theatre profession. The old Community Theatre, now the Northside Theatre Company, was for a period the most prosperous small theatre in Australia.

In Melbourne, the Pram Factory opened in 1970 as a home for the Australian Performing Group. Their experiments in athletic performance bred a circus troupe which in due course became Circus Oz, which tours internationally. The group's comedy style also influenced the comedy cabaret for which Melbourne became known in the 1970s. The Australian Performing Group died in 1981. A further breakaway group, led by the actor/director Graeme Blundell, formed Hoopla, later the Playbox Theatre Company, which took over the lease of Harry M. Miller's little Playbox Theatre in Elizabeth Street in 1977. It now has its own two-theatre home, the CUB Malthouse, a converted brewery in South Melbourne.

In Adelaide and Brisbane, the gap between the state theatre company and the other theatres proved unbridgeable and has remained so. The lively Theatre 62 in Adelaide in the 1960s struggled for a decade and died. The avant-garde groups, the Sheridan Theatre and Troupe have passed on. By the late 1980s the Stage Company (for a while the serious opposition to the South Australian Theatre Company) had closed their doors. In Brisbane, the pattern is the same. La Boite, the most advanced of the groups, remains semi-professional. Twelfth Night is gone. Several attempts have been made to provide theatre to the vast stretches of northern Queensland. The most substantial has been the touring New Moon Theatre Company, based in Townsville.

The Playhouse history in Perth has not been an even one and in the 1980s the company was twice bankrupted and several times dark. It had to fight for audiences and subsidy with the Hole in the Wall Theatre, housed first in a small theatre-in-the-round in Leederville and since 1984 in the converted Subiaco Town Hall. Both companies produced popular and classical plays and largely shared their audience.

The two companies amalgamated in 1991 to form the State Theatre Company of Western Australia, but the political and financial problems remained unresolved and in 1993 it went into liquidation. The most significant aspect of the Playhouse's work was the introduction of the black playwright Jack Davis to the theatre in 1979. Davis is now in the forefront of Australian writing and began his own theatre company, Marli Byoli, under the umbrella of the Western Australia Theatre Company. The development of his work, with his director, Andrew Ross, has created a place for Aboriginal actors which has now extended to all parts of the theatre industry and bred the first generation of black playwrights. (Ross founded his own company, the Black Swan Theatre Company, with a policy of employing multiracial actors.) The development of these artists and their perspective is the greatest advance the Australian theatre has made in the 1980s and made possible the spontaneous success of the Aboriginal musical *Bran Nue Dae* (1990) by Jimmy Chi, the most significant dramatic evidence that Australia is a multicultural society.

KB

Playwriting

The theatre began to develop in Australia, in the nineteenth century, at a time when theatre throughout the European and colonial worlds was primarily an actor's medium. The effect of this, together with the influence of commercial entrepreneurs whose repertoire consisted almost entirely of English and, later, American successes, has meant that local playwriting has not until recently had a central place in the Australian theatre. The alienation of playwrights from the professional stage is the most important factor in the faltering development of Australian drama. Apart from a brief period in the late nineteenth century it was not until the late 1960s that Australian playwriting began to assume a central place in the professional repertoire.

The earliest dramatists produced a number of plays which used parent styles, from the English tradition, to explore local themes. Charles Harpur (1813–68) wrote an eccentric but still interesting Shakespearian drama in verse, *The Bushrangers* (1853) (see also p. 311). Before him David Burn (?1799–1875) had also written a romantic drama called *The Bushrangers* (1829), as well as a number of literary-historical dramas. Edward Geoghegan (?1813–?) wrote a lively musical comedy, *The Currency Lass* (1844), which is still in the repertoire. As a convict Geoghegan was unable to admit authorship but during the 1840s he produced, anonymously, a series of workable genre plays for the professional theatre.

In the second half of the nineteenth century, there was a great increase in local writing. The 1870s and 1880s, particularly, remain the only period in Australian playwriting, until recently, when Australian authors had access to the major commercial stages of the country and could command a popular audience. Garnet Walch (1843–1913) was a prolific adapter of overseas scripts, but also injected a distinctively larrikin brand of Australian folk humour into his pantomimes and farces. One of his most successful pantomimes, *Australia Felix* (1873), was republished in 1988. Alfred Dampier (?1848–1908) acted, produced and also wrote nationalistic bush melodramas of a kind which became increasingly popular towards the end of the century, and which continued to be an important part of the repertoire of the early Australian film industry (see also p. 309). George Darrell (1841–1921) wrote, with one eye on the 'home' market, a large number of relaxed melodramas which exploited in a good-humoured colonial style the colourful bush legend which was being created in the 1890s. His only surviving play, *The Sunny South* (1883), is still occasionally revived.

The last triumph of this golden age of Australian commercial playwriting was Bert Bailey and Edmund Duggan's melodramatic stage version of the stories of 'Steele Rudd', *On Our Selection* (1912). The play was enormously successful and spawned a series of 'Dad and Dave' plays, movies, radio serials and finally a television series, which have given Australia its own particular 'hayseed' tradition.

Also in 1912 the playwright who often now is called 'Australia's pioneer dramatist', Louis Esson (1879–1943), produced his first successful play, a Shavian political comedy entitled *The Time is Not Yet Ripe*. Esson represents the beginnings of modernity in Australian playwriting – a modernity which, in spite of some anti-realistic experimentation, found its fullest expression, as in other post-colonial cultures, in the realism of 'local colour'. The short, grim bush plays which are Esson's best, such as *Dead Timber* (1911) and *The Drovers* (1920), were the first in a long line of stark tragedies of the harshness of outback life which continued well into the 1950s.

REALISTIC AND NON-REALISTIC TRADITIONS

Many of the most interesting dramatists of the 1930s and 1940s were women. Katharine Susannah Prichard (1883–1969), Henrietta Drake-Brockmann (1901–68), Dymphna Cusack (1902–81) and 'Betty Roland' (1903–) are among the most important. Between them they produced an important group of plays, in a style consistent enough to be called a school – that of bush realism. These plays explored the effect which outback life had on individual human souls, showing the harshness of the environment reflected in a hardening of character and, often, an embitterment of the individual spirit.

Two of the most successful plays of the school were Prichard's *Brumby Innes* (1927) and Roland's *The Touch of Silk* (1942). In contrast to the well-made, sometimes melodramatic realism of the bush plays was the looser naturalism of Sumner Locke Elliott's (b. 1917) downbeat war play, *Rusty Bugles* (1948), and, more influentially, the verse dramas of Douglas Stewart (1913–85), whose plays *The Fire on the Snow* (1941) and *Ned Kelly* (1942) have been studied by generations of Australian schoolchildren.

In 1955 Ray Lawler (1921–) produced what is still Australia's best-known and most-loved play, *Summer of the Seventeenth Doll*, in which the bush tradition is finally brought into the city and laid to rest. 'The Doll' sparked a brief resurgence of well-made realistic playwriting, now set in the growing working-class suburbs of the cities.

The appearance after 'The Doll' of Richard Beynon's *The Shifting Heart* (1960) and Alan Seymour's *The One Day of the Year* (1960) and other slum dramas, created for a brief time the impression that a new

also on traditions of the popular theatre such as vaudeville. White returned, in the late 1970s and the 1980s, to produce several plays which explored styles, such as surrealism and symbolism, and themes, such as individual spiritual alienation in materialist society, which have been largely neglected in the mainstream of Australian drama.

THE NEW WAVE

In the late 1960s there began a sudden and extraordinarily energetic resurgence of Australian theatre which was to a large extent fuelled by new playwriting. The young, mostly male, writers of this movement began to create a new mythology of Australianness, as part of the upsurge of cultural nationalism which characterised the late 1960s and early to mid-1970s. At the time John Romeril (1945–), Jack Hibberd (1940–), Alexander Buzo (1944–) and David Williamson (1942–) were seen as another new school of writers, creating a comic, affectionately satirical image of Australian society based to a large extent on a young, awkward, male character stereotype which came to be known as the 'son of ocker'. The later development of these writers reveals them to be very different from each other, in form and subject, but they became the core group in what has come to be called the New Wave of Australian playwriting.

The New Wave was characterised by an enthusiastic eclecticism, as writers, as well as directors, looked back through the entire modern theatre and pillaged its styles to serve their often nationalistic but sometimes highly individualistic goals.

The two main writers' theatres were the Australian Performing Group (APG), in Melbourne, and the Nimrod Theatre, in Sydney. Apart from the work of Romeril, Hibberd, Buzo and Williamson, they brought to prominence Barry Oakley (1931–), Bob Ellis (1942–), Ron Blair (1942–), Alma de Groen (1941–) and Jim McNeil (1935–82). Two writers who had had their first plays produced well before the New Wave but who produced their best work in the revitalised, some said liberated, theatrical climate of the early 1970s were Dorothy Hewett (1923–) and Peter Kenna (1930–87). Hewett, in particular, has continued into the 1980s to produce a series of adventurous plays in which she explores in a wide variety of different styles and, from a woman's perspective, the theme of the romantic quest for the self.

By the end of the 1970s the initial apparent coherence of the New Wave had broken up. The only playwright of the original group who continued to produce radical work was Romeril, who after the demise of the APG turned his energies to the new community and educational theatres. He remains to this day one of Australia's most prolific, hard-work-

school of urban realism was developing, but by 1960 the movement was already losing momentum and it became clear that the new plays were in fact a culmination of the realistic tradition begun by Louis Esson.

In 1961 the novelist Patrick White (1912–90) launched the first of a series of controversial forays into the theatre which continue to this day. There had been a hidden tradition of non-realistic modernist drama, dating back to the 1910s, but White was the first to achieve success, and notoriety, in the professional theatre, with *The Ham Funeral, The Season at Sarsaparilla, A Cheery Soul* and *Night on Bald Mountain* all appearing between 1961 and 1963 (see also p. 320).

The plays were experimental, by Australian standards, employing an expressionist style but drawing

ing, but critically neglected playwrights. Hibberd drifted away from the self-consciously populist style with which he identified himself in the early to mid-1970s, and began to work in a more exotic, deliberately 'advanced' style. Buzo began to pursue with increasing subtlety themes of personal and interpersonal morality, which came to be seen as unfashionable in the materialist society of the late 1970s. Only Williamson continued, partly through his highly successful move into the film industry, to hold a wide popular audience.

New writers

By the late 1970s a new batch of young writers was emerging, so that for the first time there were two generations of Australian playwrights working together. The most important of the young writers were Louis Nowra (1950–) and Stephen Sewell (1953–), who brought a new political seriousness to the theatre and were the first major playwrights to break completely free from the nationalist concern with 'Australianness' which had hitherto dominated much Australian playwriting. Both writers explore the interrelations between individual characters and the social, political and economic world which is the context of their actions, and which their actions help to make.

Some of the most important new writing of the 1980s was by a new group of urban black playwrights, especially Robert Merritt (1945–) and Jack Davis (1918–) (see also p. 323). Davis, already a distinguished poet and public figure when he turned to playwriting in the early 1980s, writes about the lives of black people after colonisation and the difficulties which urbanised Aboriginal communities face, within themselves and in relation to the dominant white society, as they struggle towards a post-colonial conception of Aboriginality. It is a sign of the comparative richness of modern Australian theatre that this black struggle emerged on white stages only a few years after the white writers themselves began to explore their own post-colonial conception of white 'Australianness'. It was the challenge of the late 1980s that white Australians themselves should begin to see themselves as a colonising, rather than a colonised, people.   JMcC

Dance

Dance has an interesting history in Australia, a dynamic present and the potential for an even more diverse and creative future. Although the stylistic sources for most Australian theatre dance can be traced back to Europe or the USA, there is a firmly established individual approach and a generosity of movement which is considered characteristically Australian. There is also a growing interest in Aboriginal dance, and a new spirit amongst Aborigines and Torres Strait Islanders of sharing those aspects of their dances which do not remain in the private domain of their cultures.

Australia's increasing cultural, business and tourism contacts with the Asian nations to its north – particularly Indonesia and Japan – are bringing fresh influences to dance and theatre generally. Isolation from the world's great dance centres – even the distances between its own cities – has in the long run encouraged Australians to go their own way creatively. But the debilitating effects of the 'cultural cringe', which made so many Australians cling to their colonial ties with Britain, took many decades to shake off.

Curiously, for such a distant continent in times of slow sea travel, nineteenth-century Australians had a remarkable influx of visiting dancers to augment the efforts of their resident performers. *Giselle* was performed in Australia less than 15 years after its Paris première in 1841. That same year, 1855, Aurelia Dimier from the Paris Opera, danced Lise in her production of *La Fille Mal Gardée*, and Lola Montes was shocking audiences with her celebrated *Spider Dance*. In 1893, the resident entrepreneur J. C. Williamson (see pp. 317–18) set up a classical company of 100 dancers – 90 of them local performers. But the first international ballet star to visit Australia was Adeline Genée, whose arrival in 1913 with members of the Imperial Russian Ballet and a repertoire which included *Coppélia*, *Le Cygne* and *Les Sylphides*, was a revelation to the enthusiastic audiences.

Anna Pavlova's Australian tours in 1926 and 1929 sparked an even greater response from a cross-section of the community, establishing a devoted following for classical ballet and inspiring a new generation of performers which included the young Robert Helpmann. Nothing, however, had prepared Australian audiences for the exhilarating impact of Colonel de Basil's touring companies in the 1930s. They not only spiced the appetite for dance, but they made a more lasting contribution than their predecessors through the people who stayed behind as World War II broke out in Europe while they were on tour in Australia. Most important of these was Edouard Borovansky, who, with his wife Xenia,

Miranda Coney of the Australian Ballet dancing in Of Blessed Memory. *Choreographed by Stanton Welch, it had its world premiere in Melbourne in 1991 and was performed in London in 1992. Design by Kristian Fredrikson, music by Joseph Canteloube.*

founded the company and the school which bore his name. The Borovansky Ballet, with its direct line to the theatrical innovations of Diaghilev's Ballets Russes in the early part of the century, shaped the taste of Australian dancegoers for theatricality with their classicism.

From the mid-1940s to his death in 1959, Borovansky managed to keep sufficent continuity in his company to develop Australian classical dancers, the most celebrated of them being Kathleen Gorham and Peggy Sager. Amongst his company's repertoire of vivid short works from the Diaghilev repertoire, and a slow build-up to the full-length classics, Borovansky choreographed his own ballets. These included some of the first on Australian themes – *Terra Australis*, *The Black Swan*, *The Outlaw* – to be offered to a mainstream dance audience. Another de Basil dancer, Helene Kirsova, had founded a company in 1941, but it crumbled under competition from Borovansky. Companies were also founded in Adelaide by Joanne Priest and in Melbourne by Laurel Martyn, whose Victorian Ballet Guild became Ballet Victoria and built up a diverse repertoire over 30 years. In a different area of dance, another European artist who had settled in Australia at the outbreak of war, Gertrud Bodenwieser, was imparting the essence of her expressive dance to students in Sydney. She, too, localised her creative works in a way that many Australian-born choreographers seemed reticent to do at that time, and her influence is still to be found in some of the most creative branches of the artform.

Classical ballet is, however, the pivotal style in Australia. After the death of Borovansky, the Australian Ballet was formed in 1962 with substantial government assistance. Peggy van Praagh was its founding artistic director, bringing her considerable production skills from Sadler's Wells Theatre Ballet. She was succeeded in 1975 by Robert Helpmann, who

had been her co-artistic director since 1965, although she returned in 1978 after the departure of Anne Woolliams (1976–77) and ahead of Marilyn Jones (1979–82). Maina Gielgud took over as artistic director in 1983.

The Australian Ballet is well regarded internationally for the technical finesse of the dancers in a repertoire built on the classics, and more recent works by choreographers ranging from Balanchine to Bejart, Cranko to Kylian. There is also some original Australian content such as Graeme Murphy's version of *Nutcracker*, and short works by company members such as Stephen Baynes' *Catalyst* and Stanton Welch's *Of Blessed Memory*. Over 30 years, the Australian Ballet has had many outstanding dancers, including Lucette Aldous, Marilyn Jones, Marilyn Rowe, Ulrike Lytton, Kelvin Coe, John Meehan, Danilo Radojevic, Garth Welch, David Burch and Gary Norman. In the 1990s, its principals included Miranda Coney, Lisa Pavane, Steven Heathcote, David McAllister and Greg Horsman.

The enormous size of the continent – Sydney to Perth is like London to Moscow – and its political division into States, has led to the growth of regional companies based in the capital cities.

The West Australian Ballet, established in 1953 by another former de Basil dancer, Kira Bousloff, is the oldest continuing company. Since 1983 Barry Moreland has directed and choreographed the major contributions to its wide-ranging repertoire, mingling great works from the past such as *Giselle* with balletic versions of *Romeo and Juliet*, and *Hamlet*, punctuated with more abstract contemporary pieces.

The Queensland Ballet, founded by Charles Lisner in 1960, has a similar approach to communicating through well-known narratives brought to the stage. Under the direction of Harold Collins since 1979, this company has nurtured performers and choreographers through its particular versions of *Salome*, *The Tempest* and *Carmen*, amongst others.

The Sydney Dance Company, founded by Suzanne Mustiz in 1965, has been directed since 1977 by

The Sydney Dance Company in Poppy. *Choreographed by Graeme Murphy,* Poppy *is based on the life of Jean Cocteau. Design by Kristian Fredrikson, George Gittoes and Gabrielle Dalton, music by Carl Vine.*

The Bangarra Dance Theatre Australia in Praying Mantis Dreaming, *choreographed by Stephen Page, music by David Page. The work is inspired by the Yirrkala people of North East Arnhem Land in the Northern Territory. The first full-length production was in 1992, and it merges three distinct styles of dance – traditional Aboriginal, Torres Strait Island and contemporary dance.*

Graeme Murphy, who is also its chief choreographer. The company has toured its largely original repertoire extensively in Australia and overseas. Working with a core group of individual artistic talents, headed by dancer Janet Vernon, Murphy has developed a body of memorable works ranging from *Poppy*, his tribute to Jean Cocteau, through a variety of Australian themes to a dance version of Karol Szymanowski's opera, *King Roger*.

The Australian Dance Theatre, also established in 1965, was the only State company to have a modern dance base. Elizabeth Dalman's foundation principles have changed with succeeding artistic directors, but the company remains one of the country's most eclectic under its latest director, Meryl Tankard. An Australian whose performing career flourished as a member of Pina Bausch's company, her name was added to its title on her appointment in 1993 to make it the Meryl Tankard Australian Dance Theatre.

Perhaps the most exciting, and often the most original dance comes from the smaller groups. Some of these, such as Dance North in Townsville, currently under the artistic direction of Cheryl Stock, have survived for decades and grown with the community around them. Others have made their mark and gone. Great diversity is to be found between the post-modern rigour of Russell Dumas' Dance Exchange and the social relevance of One Extra Company, first under its founding director Kai Tai Chan and then his successor, Graeme Watson. Paul Mercurio, star of the film *Strictly Ballroom* (see p. 336), emerged from the Sydney Dance Company to start his own company, the Australian Choreographic Ensemble (ACE), in 1992. In Perth, another outstanding choreographer of a new generation, Chrissie Parrott has launched a company under her own name with great success. Danceworks in Melbourne works from a strongly individual creative base, as does Expressions in Brisbane, Tasdance in Hobart, Leigh

Warren and Dancers and Outlet Dance in Adelaide, 2 Dance Plus in Perth, Darc Swan in Sydney and vis-à-vis Dance Canberra, launched with Sue Healey as artistic director in 1993.

Amongst the many contrasting groups, one of the most interesting developments has been the growth of Aboriginal and Torres Strait Island dance contributions, nurtured by the Aboriginal and Islander Dance Theatre school which has spawned its own professional group under the direction of Raymond Blanco. In addition, one of its former students, Stephen Page, is artistic director of Bangarra Dance Theatre and choreographing works which blend the concerns of traditional and urban Aboriginal people. Both have toured overseas, and each offers one of the strongest challenges of stylistic fusion versus separate identity to be found in Australian dance.

JS

Music

The first European music documented in Australia was military, and the social gulf between free settlers and convicts was such as to ensure that there would be 'high' and 'low' cultures from the beginning, though it should be remembered that the soldiery shared more with the convicts than with their officers or the gentry. Music was further impoverished by the assault on the Aborigines and their culture, of which music was a rich and complex part.

From the beginning, therefore, there were strong social polarisations whose effects have endured: Australia has musically (and in other ways) adhered to British and, later, American models and influences, and its own art music has, until recently, resisted the influences of Aboriginal and traditional (or folk) music.

FOLK

The serious collection and study of both Aboriginal and folk music began late. The doctor and botanist, John Lhotsky, the composer Isaac Nathan (a forebear of Sir Charles Mackerras) and Dom Rosendo Salvado (prior of the Benedictine Abbey, New Norcia, Western Australia) were among the very few in the nineteenth century to pay attention to Aboriginal music and to try to use it creatively. Thorough modern study of this music began only with the work of Alice Moyle, her student Catherine Ellis and their school.

Herbert Henry ('Smoky') Dawson (1913–), a country singer and rodeo showman. In the 1920s he wrote a song about bushranger Ned Kelly's younger brother, whom he had met on a farm. Later he went on to tour his own show regularly around Australia and to front his own radio programme.

Creative use of the idiom this century has been sparse and controversial with some seeing it as cultural pillage and others as tokenism. It influenced John Antill's large-scale ballet *Corroboree* (1946) and it has been a continuing inspiration to Peter Sculthorpe and Moya Henderson.

One of the earliest of the twentieth-century collectors of folksongs was the poet and musician John Manifold; others have built upon his work. Naturally, these songs have mostly been adapted tunes of the British Isles with words pertaining to the local situation, especially the plight of convicts, the endurance of the squatters, stockmen and shearers, as well as the gold rushes. They were, as the poet Judith Wright observed, 'often hard and crude, almost always womanless'. There is an irony in this dominance of the concerns of pastoral Australia (which persists in Australia's modern mythology) because, even in the nineteenth century, Australia was one of the most urbanised countries in the world.

The best known of these traditional songs is *Waltz-*

Some like it hot. Lynette and Her Redheads, jazz band, late 1920s. A large number of jazz bands of the period either featured female performers or were exclusively female.

ing Matilda (words by A. B. ['Banjo'] Paterson), others being *Botany Bay, Bound for South Australia* and *The Old Bark Hut*. This folk tradition has diverged in the later twentieth century; alongside the scholarly collection and publication of authentic folksong has been the powerful influence of the American folk revival in its Australian Country and Western manner. This latter has involved such performers as Tex Morton, Slim Dusty, Reg Lindsay and Eric Bogle as well as groups like 'Redgum' and 'The Bushwackers'. Since 1973 an annual National Country Music Festival has been held in early January in Tamworth, the 'hillbilly heaven' in northern New South Wales.

JAZZ

Except for the persistently domesticated nature of the work of such people as the prolific lyricist and composer Jack O'Hagan, who produced such successful songs as *Our Don Bradman*, and *Along the Road to Gundagai*, popular music in Australia has largely been (for commercial no less than political reasons) subordinate first to British then to American influences. One of the few examples of a reversal of this trend was the phenomenal success of the songs of May Brahe whose *Bless this House* sold 90,000 copies internationally in 1943 and significantly underwrote the publishing activities of Boosey & Hawkes (supporting works of Stravinsky, Bartok and Britten).

Mass culture was, in the nineteenth century, associated with music hall, melodrama and family piano evenings – all of it decidedly English Victoriana. More cosmopolitan influences came with the gold rushes; then after World War I the American domination began in jazz and dance music as well as popular songs (assisted by the developments in radio and recording).

Large numbers of jazz and dance bands operated in this period as 'jazz became the anthem of youthful energy and liberation'. A striking number of women were involved with these bands. The depression slowed the progress of jazz but it accelerated with the influx of USA servicemen into Australia during World War II. Graeme Bell in Melbourne (the 'All Stars' was his best-known band) and Ray Price in Sydney (the 'Port Jackson Jazz Band') were prominent exponents of Dixieland whereas Don Banks (later an eminent classical composer) was involved with the Modern Jazz movement in Melbourne. The popularity of the 'Varsity Five' in Brisbane during the late 1950s–early 1960s points to the greater attraction of jazz among the middle class and undergraduates in Australia at that time; a surprising number of famous jazz musicians have had a tertiary education (for example, Ade Monsbourgh, 'the father of Australian jazz', who formed the Melbourne University Rhythm Club in 1937). This observation is especially interesting in view of the origins of the music; however, various forms of rock 'n roll (or simply rock) – earlier considered a rather working-class and teenage style – have more recently been in the ascendancy, especially among students.

ROCK

Johnny O'Keefe ('The Wild One') was an early star of Australian rock, helped by the popular ABC–TV programme 'Six O'Clock Rock' (begun in 1959), and from 1974 'Countdown' was of comparable popularity. Despite a reputation for conservatism, the ABC has been a trend-setter in this as in other areas (for example, with its rock/youth radio station, 2JJ/JJJFM). The American-born entrepreneur Lee Gordon was the midwife to Australian rock; this fact, plus the strong English influences (especially 'The Beatles') meant, according to the experts, that in the 1960s Australian rock was essentially imitative. Subsequently, as Aboriginal and bush-ballad influences began to be absorbed, Australian musicians produced a 'stream of gruff, tough, snarling rock music that is now recognised internationally as among the most durable and impressive ever recorded'. Such bands as 'AC/DC', 'Little River Band', 'INXS' and 'Men at Work' became extremely widely known and supported.

The success of the band 'Midnight Oil' points to a noteworthy fact: there is a far greater concern with political and environmental issues in Australian than in American or British rock music. Such bands as 'Cold Chisel' have sung about steel workers and the working class generally, but the huge support for Peter Garrett (the singer in 'Midnight Oil') as a Nuclear Disarmament candidate in the 1984 federal election attests to the wider social appeal of the music. The phenomenon may be associated with the fact that pubs, with their necessarily mixed audiences, have been where most Australian bands have practised and developed their styles and skills.

Apart from such rare boundary crossing as that by Don Banks (who not only operated in both the jazz and classical worlds, but wrote for both together, for example, 'Nexus') and the appearance of the rock group 'Tully' with the Sydney Symphony Orchestra and conductor John Hopkins at the rumbustious final night of the 1970 Prom Concerts, popular and 'serious' musical worlds have had little interaction in Australia, though the New South Wales Conservatorium of Music established a jazz department in 1973.

EARLY MUSIC MAKING

Public music-making of a serious kind began at the establishment of the colony when *God Save the King* was the first work ever performed (though it is interesting that Surgeon George Worgan of the London musical family, had a piano among his goods on the first fleet). Service bands were integral to musical life for more than half a century, augmenting theatrical and concert orchestras as public concerts began to flourish. The first recorded concerts were held in Sydney and Hobart in 1826 and Philharmonic Societies were formed in 1833.

The year 1836 is significant: W. Vincent Wallace ('the Australian Paganini') arrived in Sydney and John Deane also moved there with his family after 14 years' contribution to the secular and religious musical life of Hobart (then a centre of some importance). Sydney thereafter became the musical capital of the colony but within a generation had ceded this title to the more prosperous Melbourne (regaining it only after World War II). Wallace and Deane's arrival in Sydney not only boosted concert life but also revivified musical teaching. Stephen H. Marsh brought the latest English methods of sight-singing when he arrived in 1842; this was important because choral music was a staple of the musical life of the colony and these new methods allowed untrained people – especially workmen – to participate in ensemble singing.

The first music festival was held in St Mary's (Catholic) Cathedral, Sydney, in January 1838. Another grander one ran over four days to commemorate the opening of Edmund Blacket's Great Hall at the University of Sydney in 1859; the programme included Handel's *Messiah* and Haydn's *Creation*, done with a chorus of 250 and an orchestra of 50.

AC/DC in 1992, Australia's most internationally successful rock band.

OPERA

In the meantime, the first real composer, Isaac Nathan, had arrived in the colony in 1841: he threw himself vigorously into Sydney's musical life and in 1847 presented the first opera written in Australia, his *Don John of Austria*. Opera had, in fact, been presented fairly regularly, beginning with Shield's ballad-opera, *The Poor Soldier* (Sydney, 1796); Barnett Levey's Theatre Royal, which was built in 1833 as an adjunct to his Royal Hotel, was a venue for regular seasons of ballad-opera. Genuine Italian opera first appeared in Sydney in 1843 with Rossini's *The Barber of Seville*; others rapidly followed and these seasons, together with the expansion of musical skill beyond the upper classes (which Marsh's sight-singing methods had facilitated), led to complaints of degradation of public taste.

An enormous enhancement of operatic life occurred in 1861 with the arrival in Melbourne of the Irish-American impresario, W. S. Lyster. From then until his death in 1880 he provided that city and numerous other centres with an amazingly varied and successful repertoire. His family and company influence could be said to have continued through the consortium which his accountant George Hudson formed with J. C. Williamson (see pp. 317-18) in 1882 (though 'the Firm', as it came to be called while it virtually dominated Australian theatre until the 1970s, concentrated almost exclusively on overseas-proven musical comedy, with imported stars).

The repertoire of Lyster's company – which ranged from *The Bohemian Girl* to *Lohengrin*, taking in *Oberon*, *Les Huguenots* ('produced in lavish splendour') and *William Tell* on the way – was well in excess of 50. An indication of the scale of its activities is the fact that in the seven years after 1861 the company gave 1,459 performances.

ORCHESTRAS

The next significant developments were in the 1880s. One was the appointment of Joshua Ives to the first chair of music in Australia (at the University of Adelaide) and another was the spate of musical activity associated with the 1888 centennial celebrations and the Melbourne International Exhibition of that year, in particular the formation of a 68-strong orchestra specifically for the occasion. This was directed by Frederic Cowen who brought the key players with him from England, several of whom remained in Australia. The appointment of the flamboyant and bohemian G. W. L. Marshall-Hall as Professor of Music at the University of Melbourne (1891) further stimulated orchestral music there. One of his professorial successors, Bernard Heinze, was also a dynamic and innovative conductor.

An orchestra had been established in Sydney in 1889; it was called the Sydney Symphony Orchestra after 1908 when its principal conductors were the Englishmen Joseph Bradley and Arundel Orchard (later the second director of the Conservatorium there). After the opening of the New South Wales State Conservatorium in 1916, the orchestra, which the foundation director, Henri Verbrugghen, conducted, became the major source of orchestral music in Sydney until, with the formation in 1932 of the Australian Broadcasting Commission (the ABC, now the Australian Broadcasting Corporation), the present Sydney Symphony Orchestra was born (initially as a permanent ensemble of 25).

After World War II, orchestras developed greatly especially following the appointment of Eugene Goossens as conductor of the Sydney Symphony Orchestra and director of the Conservatorium in 1947. Charles Mackerras was the first Australian-born Chief Conductor (1982–85) and this precedent was followed up with Stuart Challender's appointment in 1987 (d. 1991).

By 1993, the ABC was maintaining orchestras in Brisbane (71 permanent players), Sydney (96), Melbourne (92), Hobart (46), Adelaide (66) and Perth (86). Other significant orchestras include the Queensland Philharmonic Orchestra in Brisbane (31), the Australian Chamber Orchestra (20) and the Australian Opera and Ballet Orchestra (69) in Sydney, the State Orchestra of Victoria (69) in Melbourne. Innumerable professional/amateur orchestras flourish across the country, most with regular concert schedules.

BANDS AND CHOIRS

For many years the ABC also supported dance bands, the most famous being the Sydney Band (disbanded 1976) directed successively by Jim Davidson, Jim Gussey and Eric Jupp. The Commission also supported vocal ensembles, the best known being the Adelaide Singers (abolished 1976). The existence of such choruses is a reminder of the strong choral tradition inherited from Britain. Other traditions were important, too: under the influence of the German settlers (in South Australia and Queensland, but later elsewhere) the *Liedertafel*, or concert-giving gentlemen's song club, was an important social and political as well as musical institution.

Carl Linger (composer of *Song of Australia*) in Adelaide and R. T. Jeffries in Brisbane, as well as the Cowen concerts of 1888, were among the important influences in sustaining the choral movement. In more recent years every state capital has supported a large major choir, the most active and accomplished being the Sydney Philharmonia Society and the Melbourne Chorale while the University Musical

National opera

In both opera and ballet Australia has followed a modified British model and established strong national, touring companies. The Australian Opera was essentially begun in 1956 by the Elizabethan Theatre Trust with its Mozart bicentennial season. Between W. S. Lyster's death (1880) and that time numerous seasons had been provided by visiting companies but also by two 'National Operas'.

Various Italian companies had visited Australia in these years (the last of them in 1949) but the biggest seasons were those of Thomas Quinlan (1912 and 1913) – with an amazing repertoire including Wagner's *The Mastersingers, Tristan and Isolde* and *The Ring* – and Benjamin and John Fuller (1934–35) with the repertoire of 14 operas sung in English.

Eugene Goossens presented several notable productions at the Sydney Conservatorium in the 1950s while the rival 'National' organisations were established by two formidable women, Gertrude Johnson in Melbourne and Clarice Lorenz in Sydney; some of the singers whom they nurtured before

their demise in the mid-1950s remain among today's great names. They ended bankrupt so the action by the Elizabethan Trust was timely.

In 1970 the Australian Opera was formally constituted; this company has, despite numerous managerial vicissitudes, reached a size and standard where, in a typical year, it gives 230 performances in three or more cities in a repertoire of about 16 operas performed at high international levels of quality. It maintains a full-time chorus of 50, a children's chorus of about 40 and regularly engages comparable numbers of soloists.

Increasingly the Australian opera cooperates with the four State Opera Companies (in Perth, Adelaide, Melbourne and Brisbane). All of them have conservative repertoires although in recent years, especially with Richard Meale's *Voss* (1986), Larry Sitsky's *The Golem* (1993) and an annual Opera Workshop, the AO has begun to recognise its obligations (as a substantially subsidised company) to Australian composers.

JC

Huge crowds at the annual Opera in the Park, given by the Australian Opera as part of the Sydney Festival.

Societies, which have held a national Inter-Varsity Choral Festival annually since 1950, have been notable institutions.

Major churches, especially those in the capital cities, have also supported choral music, mostly in the British tradition, with a decline into pseudo-folk in Catholic churches following the Second Vatican Council. Richard Connolly opposed this unfortunate trend and, in collaboration with the eminent poet James McAuley, produced some fine music for congregational use while Nigel Butterley's *Hail True Victim* is one of the great hymns of the twentieth century.

CHAMBER ENSEMBLES

Chamber music flourished after World War II, beginning with Richard Goldner's formation of Musica Viva late in 1945. He paid for this society's full-time string quartet (led by Robert Pikler) until 1951; during its life it travelled widely to give 200 concerts each year. After 1955 Musica Viva began to import overseas groups and has grown to be the biggest entrepreneurial organisation of its type in the world. Several of the tertiary institutions (and in the later 1940s, the Queensland government) have maintained full-time string quartets and, to a lesser extent, other ensembles.

MUSIC TEACHING

Many of these ventures, and numerous others, have been supported by the Music Board of the Australia Council which (since its own beginnings in 1968) has also encouraged the commissioning of Australian music; another of its projects has been substantial funding of the Australian Music Centre in Sydney which produces and distributes scores and recordings of Australian music. This Centre has a battle against the conservatism of music education in Australia.

Teaching of music is sporadic in primary and secondary schools while there are tertiary institutions which cover academic and practical aspects of music in all the capitals (several, in most of them) and in a number of major country centres (for example, Bathurst and Lismore in New South Wales). Private teachers, however, constitute the majority of those teaching music and exceed by more than fourfold the total numbers employed in primary, secondary and tertiary education.

The domination of recording and publishing by overseas interests makes the task of the few imaginative teachers extremely difficult and very little Australian music finds its way on to syllabuses (a situation that is in clear contrast to what now pertains in the teaching of literature).

COMPOSERS

Prior to World War II there was very little knowledge by any musicians – composers, performers or critics – of European or North American trends and Asia was a closed book. The German-educated Alfred Hill, for instance, clung tenaciously to the Mendelssohnian inheritance; Septimus Kelly (English and German-educated) wrote in a conservative idiom but his early death in World War I ended an extremely promising career.

Only Percy Grainger and Henry Tate thought seriously about the nature of an authentic Australian music. Grainger had the technical skill to match his ideas; he wanted his counterpoint to have a pungent 'democraticness' that matched the Australian character and wanted a wide sweep in his melodies to match the breadth of the landscape. Tate was a distinctly lesser creative figure though his ideas were stimulating: notably in his book, *Australian Musical Possibilities* (1924), he encouraged composers to listen to and learn from the sound of wind in the trees and, well in advance of the French composer Olivier Messiaen, advocated bird song as a rich source of melodic material.

After World War II, Keith Humble studied in the exhilarating environment of Paris; Richard Meale and Peter Sculthorpe worked in the USA, and Nigel Butterley studied with Priaulx Rainier in London. These last three became the Australian avant-garde in the 1960s with Meale and Butterley having an additional influence as concert and radio programmers with the ABC. Meale's *Las Alboradas*, Butterley's *Laudes* and Sculthorpe's Sixth String Quartet were the outstanding works of the period – all of them chamber music. Each has gone on to bigger things: Meale is now best known for his opera *Voss*, with David Malouf's libretto from Patrick White's great novel, Sculthorpe with a long list of quartets and the *Sun Music* series, and Butterley with his fine opera *Lawrence Hargrave Flying Alone* and *In the Head, the Fire* (a work for voices and instruments) which won the Italia Prize in 1966.

Other composers of their generation who have consistently produced music of quality include Larry Sitsky (in Canberra) – who has also edited critical editions of Busoni's music – and Colin Brumby in Brisbane, who has several operas and choral works in his output. In Melbourne, George Dreyfus has used folksongs extensively and achieved amazing popularity with his score for the television series 'Rush'.

Sculthorpe has also had a powerful influence as a member of the Department of Music at the University of Sydney. His students have included Alison Bauld (now in London), Anne Boyd (who in 1990 was appointed Professor of Music at the University of Sydney), Barry Conyngham (Melbourne and the Dean at Wollongong), Brian Howard (Perth) and Ross Edwards (Sydney). They have imbibed Sculthorpe's concern with colour and a certain static and reflective approach to rhythm and harmony and, like him, show clear influences of Asia amongst which the gamelan orchestra and the music of Toru Takemitsu are noteworthy.

Vincent Plush has, instead, looked eastwards across the Pacific to both North and South America, while Graham Hair (currently Professor of Music in Edinburgh) has a strong affinity with composers from New York and the northeastern intellectual tradition. Gerard Brophy and Riccardo Formosa have been especially influenced by such Italian composers as Franco Donatoni.

Richard Mills (Brisbane), who is also a percussionist and conductor, is perhaps the most technically accomplished of Australia's younger composers. Carl Vine, another performer who is a prolific and fluent composer, has written several ballet scores amongst many other works.

WOMEN IN MUSIC

In music, no less than in Australia's literature and painting, women have made striking contributions to Australian life. Apart from such singers as Nellie Melba, Ada Crossley, Marjorie Lawrence, Marie Collier, Joan Hammond and Joan Sutherland, and such instrumentalists as Eileen Joyce, Daisy Kennedy and

Percy Grainger (1882-1961). From an early age Grainger lived in Europe and the United States, but always considered himself an Australian composer.

Below Dame Nellie Melba (1861–1931). Australia has produced several opera singers who have gained international reputations. Melba, who was born Mitchell and took the name Melba in honour of the city where she was brought up, enjoyed an almost legendary status, especially in London, where she sang regularly at Covent Garden from 1889 to 1909.

Right Dame Joan Sutherland, in her farewell performance with the Australian Opera in 1990, in Meyerbeer's Les Huguenots. Sutherland's reputation has become as big in its own way as Melba's was, and has been gained on a more international stage. She was nicknamed 'La Stupenda' on account of her vocal technique.

Bertha Jorgensen (in 1948, as leader of the Melbourne Symphony, she was the first woman to lead an Australian orchestra and one of the first anywhere) there has been a striking number of Australian women composers.

Margaret Sutherland was a distinguished pianist as well as composer, the first of Australia's modern composers, in fact. The opera *The Young Kabbarli* (1965) is one of her most important works.

Peggy Glanville-Hicks spent most of her life away from Australia; like Margaret Sutherland she studied composition with Fritz Hart in Melbourne and was later a student of Vaughan Williams, Egon Wellesz and Nadia Boulanger. She wrote four operas, four ballets, several film scores and numerous orchestral and vocal pieces, many with oriental influences.

Among the middle generation are Gillian Whitehead (composer of several dramatically introspective operas) and Moya Henderson who has written theatre pieces (including the comic short opera *Stubble*), cabaret songs (*Conversations With My Dogs*) and

The Dreaming, a lyrical, elegiac piece for string orchestra, with an Aboriginal dedication.

Ros Bandt, who is a fine recorder player with the renaissance quartet 'La Romanesca', produces impressive sound sculptures by making recordings in such spaces as large water tanks and pipes while Elena Kats-Chernin and Lisa Lim are interesting and promising younger writers of more orthodox concert music. The publisher Louise Dyer (founder of *L'Oiseau-Lyre Edition*) was another Australian woman with a considerable musical significance, particularly on the international scene.

INSTRUMENT-MAKING

Instrument-making is a frequently overlooked aspect of this diverse musical life. Aboriginal bands have naturally employed their traditional instruments but George Dreyfus and Colin Bright are virtually the only 'serious' composers to use the didgeridoo in concert music. The metal frame and tuning system which Octavius Beale devised for his Sydney-built pianos (patented in 1902) were extremely important for the remarkable dispersal of this instrument into the otherwise impossibly hot country districts.

Australia has several important organ builders: Ronald Sharp of Sydney has been part of the return to traditional 'tracker action' organs but he has also employed new technology – for example, to facilitate choice of registration in his larger instruments, such as the splendid one in the Concert Hall of the Sydney Opera House.

Performers from around the world seek out the recorders of Fred Morgan (Daylesford, Victoria) and the harpsichords of Bill Bright (of Barraba, New South Wales). The Fairlight computer-synthesiser was developed in Sydney from 1975–78 and has been widely accepted by performing groups and a variety of composers, including Bruce Smeaton the successful film composer and Martin Wesley-Smith of the Sydney Conservatorium.

The composer Moya Henderson has developed the Alemba, a fascinating percussion instrument which is a set of tuned pentangles (over a wide compass) with resonating chambers: it is capable of sounds ranging from the deepest bell-like throb to a glacial brilliance.

Two hundred years after the transplantation of European culture, Australia has a rich musical life of high standard and considerable diversity. Its essential problems remain those of colonial and subservient economies and societies – the fight to resist domination while being alert to the best that the rest of the world can offer, and the struggle to keep its best musicians working 'at home with the tribe' rather than succumbing to the allure of overseas. JC

Aborigine playing a didgeridoo. Although commonly considered as the typical Aboriginal musical instrument, didgeridoos were only used by Aborigines native to the northern third of the continent. The instrument provides rhythm and a drone rather than melody.

Film

The first actuality films were made in Sydney and Melbourne in 1896 by Marius Sestier, on an imported Lumière Cinematographe: they included a record of that year's great horse-racing event, the Melbourne Cup. As the novelty spread, similar pictures were presented with imported material as 'acts' in variety theatres, soon followed by picture shows in vast tents, open-air cinemas and purpose-built 'hard-tops' by 1910. The travelling rural 'picture show man' took films to isolated communities, setting up in local halls. Demand was insatiable: American, British and European productions dominated the programmes.

On 13 September 1900 the Salvation Army's Limelight Department premiered its production *Soldiers of the Cross* in the Melbourne Town Hall. Devised by Army Commandant Herbert Booth and Major Joseph Perry, it was described as an 'illustrated lecture': the two-hour presentation employed film, lantern slides and music and was the first important use of film for drama and propaganda.

With *The Story of the Kelly Gang* in 1906 and other long dramas, Australia arguably pioneered the modern feature film, bypassing the one- or two-reel dramas that were standard overseas. This pre-war period established recurrent motifs – such as city versus bush, sport, life in the outback, the convict, gold rush and bushranging eras – and character types, such as the resourceful bush heroine and city slicker villain.

More than 250 silent feature films were made (to 1930). Though most of their work is now lost, the reputations of directors Franklyn Barrett and Ray-

mond Longford have endured, and Longford's *The Sentimental Bloke* (1919) is the acknowledged classic of the era. Just prior to the coming of sound, Norman Dawn's costly epic *For the Term of His Natural Life* (1927) and the films of the three McDonagh sisters brought a new Hollywood-style sophistication.

Actuality films, documentaries and newsreels were mainstays and thousands were produced: the weekly *Australasian Gazette* newsreel, travelogues, industrials (industrial documentaries to promote products and their producers) and the like were perennials. In 1911 cinematographer Frank Hurley accompanied the Mawson Antarctic expedition (see p. 286), beginning a lifetime career of documenting the remote and exotic. His contemporary Francis Birtles traversed the inland, filming a still unknown continent and the life of its Aboriginal inhabitants.

The protracted conversion to talkies around 1930 restructured production. Two studios – Cinesound (Sydney) and Efftee (Melbourne) – became the most prolific producers of features and documentaries. Ken G. Hall's feature dramas and comedies (including the *Dad and Dave* series) set new production standards and enjoyed considerable success. Independent producer Charles Chauvel closed the decade with *Forty Thousand Horsemen* (1940), revealing, as in his subsequent films, his epic vision of Australia. Their alumni included Peter Finch, Chips Rafferty, Cecil Kellaway, Errol Flynn and Ann Richards.

From 1939 to 1945 the industry geared to the war effort. The enormous influence of the *Cinesound Review* and *Australian Movietone* newsreels was supported by outstanding front-line cameramen, such as Damien Parer.

After the war, a new government film studio (today known as Film Australia) encouraged documentaries, as did a national system of free 16-mm-film lending libraries, which distributed these and other films for education and community use, in accordance

The Sentimental Bloke (1919) a classic silent feature film, made by Raymond Longford starring Lottie Lyell (right). The film was based on the successful poem, The Songs of a Sentimental Bloke, by C. J. Dennis (1915) – a humorous love story told in dialect verse.

Frame blow-up from a film of the 1896 Melbourne Cup, one of the earliest pieces of Australian film footage.

Film still from My Brilliant Career, *directed by Gillian Armstrong in 1979, based on Miles Franklin's autobiographical novel of 1901. Judy Davis (1955–), who played Sybylla Melvyn (seated on right), went on to star in international films.*

with the precepts of British documentarist John Grierson. Commercial organisations, such as Shell Oil Company, also supported documentaries: John Heyer's *The Back of Beyond* (1954) was a major international success. The film society movement and film festivals emerged. Despite significant work by Hall, Chauvel and others, however, feature production faltered and became reliant on financial and artistic control from overseas.

In 1969–70, the Gorton government established mechanisms for assisting the industry, including an investment corporation, a national film and television school, and an experimental film fund. Feature production revived; the renaissance has been sustained and has won unprecedented international success with such films as Peter Weir's *Picnic at Hanging Rock* (1975), Phil Noyce's *Newsfront* (1978), George Miller's *Mad Max* (1979), Gillian Armstrong's *My Brilliant Career* (1979), Bruce Beresford's *Breaker Morant* (1980), Nadia Tass' *Malcolm* (1986), the Paul Hogan vehicle *Crocodile Dundee* (1986), Jocelyn Moorhouse's *Proof* (1991) and Baz Luhrmann's *Strictly Ballroom* (1992). The success of these films culminated in the Oscar awards won by Jane Campion's *The Piano* (1993). In 1988 the government established a Film Finance Corporation to stabilise the industry's financial base.

RE

Broadcasting

SOUND RECORDING

The first Australian recordings were probably made on the tinfoil cylinder phonograph: an apparatus built by Victorian scientist Alexander Sutherland was in use by 1878. The Edison phonograph arrived in 1890; Douglas Archibald and A. C. Haddon made recordings of eminent Australians, Aboriginal music and prominent singers (though few now survive).

Popularisation was rapid. Overseas companies such as Edison and Columbia dominated the market for machines and recordings: by 1907, annual imports passed one million records. In 1898, Allan and Co. of Melbourne made the earliest known Australian commercial recordings, including recitations by the poet 'Banjo' Paterson. They were followed in 1903 by Edwin Henderson in Sydney, releasing vaudeville performers and brass band music on his 'Federal' and 'Australia' labels. Against overseas competition such ventures proved short-lived. Apart from piano rolls, whose manufacture began in 1919 and still continues, Australian-based recording and manufacture was not solidly established until the mid-1920s, when the disc had supplanted the cylinder.

Over this period Australian singers such as Nellie Melba, Peter Dawson, Florrie Forde and Billy Williams built international careers by recording in England. But by 1930 the local studios of Vocalian, Parlophone, World and Columbia offered an outlet for Australian performers whose work now effectively supplemented imports and could gain radio airtime. Dance bands and songs from musical comedies and films were staples: topical songs like *Our Don Bradman* and *Kingsford Smith*, *Aussie is Proud of You* celebrated local heroes. *Along the Road to Gundagai* defined the cherished myths of the Australian bush. Such overt Australiana remain characteristic today.

The Great Depression forced closures and mergers resulting in a single overseas-owned producer/manufacturer: EMI. In turn, World War II stimulated the industry. Post-war, distinctive styles of country music and jazz expanded the repertoire. EMI's dominance was challenged by new Australian companies releasing cover versions of American hits before the originals went on sale, just as the introduction of the microgroove LP and EP eclipsed the standard 78 rpm disc.

The arrival of rock and roll in the mid-1950s heralded an era of widening opportunities for Australian performers and composers. Television joined radio as a promotional outlet. The industry continued to diversify, as further independent companies emerged. International recording organisations attracted Australian artists from the mid-1960s: Dame Joan Sutherland, the Seekers, the Easybeats, Olivia Newton-John, Helen Reddy and Peter Allen among them. Some became expatriates. More recently, Australian-produced recordings by such groups as 'INXS', 'Midnight Oil', 'Men at Work' enjoyed significant international as well as local success.

CD, record and cassette sales in the early 1990s were about 42 million units annually, the great majority manufactured in Australia.

RADIO

Regular broadcasting began in November 1923 by 2SB (later 2BL) Sydney, closely followed by stations in Melbourne and Perth. Initial programmes included live recitals or concerts using makeshift studios. By 1929 there were five radio sets for every 100 Australians, the proportion doubling every seven years thereafter. In a sparsely populated country radio provided instant communication – for individuals and for the masses. The growth of broadcast services was paralleled by development of the two-way 'pedal wireless' in the outback, allowing communication between remote homesteads and with such services as the Flying Doctor (see p. 239) and the School of the Air (see p. 245).

The division between commercial and government broadcasting dates from 1932, with the establishment of the Australian Broadcasting Commission (ABC). Modelled on the British Broadcasting Corporation, it rapidly became a national network, developing distinctive programming for children (*The Argonauts Club*), for rural listeners (*The Country Hour*) and an authoritative news service. Later, it developed the international service of Radio Australia and, in 1993, International Television Australia (ITVA).

Early radio broadcasters: Reginald Sharland and Annie Croft, in the 1920s.

EGINALD SHARLAND
and

Before television, radio structured the day: there were breakfast programmes, mid-morning 'sweep while you weep' serials for the housewife, and afternoon children's serials; in the evening, the family gathered to enjoy variety shows, quiz programmes and plays. Saturday brought sporting events, especially horse racing: race callers developed a distinctive, graphic style. Before short-wave broadcasts became practical, live Test cricket matches were re-created synthetically in the studio, complete with sound effects (from information cabled from London as it happened).

As the commercial networks developed in the late 1930s and 1940s, stars such as Jack Davey, Bob Dyer and Roy Rene 'Mo' became celebrities commanding huge audiences and big sponsors. Production and syndication of pre-recorded programmes was a major part of the radio industry, and enjoyed a sizeable export market. Significantly, characteristically Australian programmes such as *Dad and Dave* and the rural saga *Blue Hills* were never exported.

The advent of television (from 1956) coincided with development of the transistor radio: the former took the sponsor base and the latter made complete reorientation of programming possible. Radios became portable: programmes more localised and specialised. News, music, chat shows and talkback became staples: morning 'drive time' replaced evening as the prime slot.

From the 1970s on, there has been considerable growth in the number and diversity of stations. In 1993, the ABC had three main domestic networks and operates over 100 AM and 400 FM stations/transmitters. There are 163 commercial stations (AM plus FM) and over 200 community or public stations.

TELEVISION

In 1885 Henry Sutton, a Ballarat inventor, designed – but could not build – a theoretically feasible television system which he named the 'Telephane'. Others resumed practical experiments in the 1920s: Tom Elliott and Val McDowell made test transmissions in Brisbane from 1934 to 1939. Regular telecasting did not begin until 16 September 1956 on TCN9, Sydney. (Colour was added in 1975.) The arrival of television coincided with the staging of the Melbourne Olympic Games.

As for radio, there were commercial stations (initially two in most capital cities), supported entirely by advertising revenue, and the ABC network which carried no advertising. Despite recent changes to the ABC, and addition of a second government network (SBS) for specialist and foreign-language programmes, this rationale is unchanged.

Within a decade, 90 per cent of homes had sets:

Bob Dyer goads a contestant in his popular 1960s TV quiz show, Pick-a-Box. *His most famous catchphrase was 'The money or the box?' The contestant had to pick between the two, without knowing the contents of the box. A contestant who refused the money sometimes ended up with a booby prize.*

At first, American programmes dominated: by 1958, Australian content – including news, sport and variety – amounted to less than 45 per cent of airtime. The 1960s brought regulations setting minimum quotas of Australian programming, and stimulated production by independent houses and the networks themselves.

Early variety programmes were localised, with some radio personalities – and formats – successfully transferring. Networking brought national programmes such as Bob Dyer's *Pick-a-Box*, Bobby Limb's *Sound of Music* and *The Graham Kennedy Show* (a weekly compilation of the long-running *In Melbourne Tonight*). In 1965 the landmark *Mavis Bramston Show* revealed the satirical potential of television and, like the *Norman Gunston Show* a decade later, the most distinctive and unexportable aspects of the Australian sense of humour. Drama began tentatively, with studio-bound chapter plays and one-shots, and later regular series. Former radio producer Hector Crawford's *Homicide*, launched in 1961, and a succession of other long-running police shows, successfully competed for audience share with imported products. In turn, series as diverse as *Skippy*, *Number 96* and more recently, *Neighbours*, *A Country Practice* and *Home and Away* have dominated national ratings and been widely exported. Beginning with *Against the Wind* in 1978, quality mini-series with historical Australian themes – such as *A Town Like Alice* and *Bodyline* – have added a further dimension.

even though, in the beginning, a set could cost three months' wages. The weekly family visit to the movies, like the evening around the radio, were things of the past. Glued to the small screen in the darkened living room, family togetherness took on a new meaning. People rearranged their social calendars to suit programming schedules.

Anne Haddy (left) as Helen Daniels in Neighbours, *a television soap opera successfully marketed in Europe. One of the original cast members, Anne received a Penguin award in 1987.*

Characteristics of programmes

Australia's remoteness and distinctive history have produced vigorous media industries in which innovation and nationalistic self-expression have coexisted with the desire to imitate. Australia's small population and production base could never match, quantitatively, the flood of English-speaking films, records and programmes from overseas for which it was an eager market: nor did it always finance and control its own means of production and dissemination.

Yet the Australian Commonwealth and the technology of film and sound recording came into being at about the same time and indeed recorded the formal foundation of the nation. Through choice and necessity Australians have always been among the most intense *per capita* producers and consumers. They have contributed significantly to the world's screen and sound heritage, both artistically and technically.

Pre-television radio illustrates the ambivalence. Foreign programmes were rarely heard, yet neither was the Australian accent: cultivated BBC diction was standard. Pre-recorded series, made with Australian performers, were often derived from overseas scripts or characters – children's serials *Superman* and *The Air Adventures of Biggles* for instance – and later exported. Even so, the most popular (and today the best remembered) programmes were often those with strongly nationalistic content, broad humour and little exportability.

Desite the growing confidence, increased cultural recognition and official support of recent times, in world terms the industry remains small and its best performers, directors and camera operators continue to be enticed to greener pastures overseas.

RE

VIDEO

The home video-cassette player/recorder (VCR) has rapidly become as ubiquitous as the television set. Principal use is for off-air recording and selective viewing, but the rental and sale of pre-recorded videos for home use has rapidly become a major retail industry. The accessibility of 'X' rated material which cannot be televised or shown in cinemas is an important component of this market.

As elsewhere, video competes with broadcast television for the viewer's attention, has affected cinema attendances and has largely supplanted the use of film for non-theatrical purposes, including home movies.

CURRENT STRUCTURE

The ABC operates national radio and TV networks throughout city and rural areas, and SBS a TV and radio service in major cities (see pp. 249–51). Commercial radio comprises AM and FM stations in networks and independent groupings: non-commercial community stations also operate on both AM and FM. Some networks and stations have extensive production facilities and produce, purchase and market programmes.

In the film world, independent production companies initiate most projects. Most state governments maintain film offices or corporations which act as producers, investors or advisers, and in some cases provide production facilities. At the national level, the Australian Film Commission provides marketing and overseas representation services, and funds cultural activities and developmental projects; the Australian Film Finance Corporation provides investment; Film Australia is the government production house. Three cinema chains (Greater Union, Hoyts and Village) dominate exhibition and a handful of American and Australian companies dominate distribution. Production, distribution and marketing for both film and television are increasingly intertwined.

As for records and videos a small number of Australian and overseas companies dominate production, manufacturing and marketing, with many independent companies also active. Retail mechanisms for sound recordings and video are converging, and some companies are increasingly active in both fields. The Australian Record Industry Association (ARIA) and the Video Industry Distributors' Association (VIDA) represent the major companies.

The Sydney-based Australian Film, Television and Radio School is a national government body offering training in media skills. The Canberra-based National Film and Sound Archive (NFSA) preserves and provides access to Australian recordings, films, TV and radio productions and related materials. RE

Serious current affairs, such as the long-running *Four Corners*, was dominated by the ABC until commercial networks moved strongly into the field in the 1970s, the most notable being the Nine Network's *60 Minutes*. With rare exceptions, such as Peter Luck's compilation series *This Fabulous Century* in 1976, documentaries have not been a major ingredient of commercial programming.

Sport – especially football and cricket – has always figured largely in weekend and late-night schedules and, for major events, dominates prime time. Australian technical innovations, such as 'Racecam', have made coverage more dramatic; the medium itself has brought about sporting innovations such as the controversial *One Day Cricket*.

The ABC network effectively covers the country while SBS reaches the major population centres. There are 41 commercial TV stations arranged in three networks (Seven, Nine and Ten) covering major cities and allied, in various configurations, to regional stations. *Per capita* viewing hours (average 19 hours 20 minutes per week) are declining: video and satellite services are widening viewer choice (97 per cent of Australia's 5.85 million household have television).

Popular entertainment

Circus

The origins of the Australian circus may be traced to England where a renaissance of this form of entertainment began to take place in the late eighteenth century. Entertainments by rope dancers were given in New South Wales as early as 1833. The first circus exhibitions in the colonies were given in timber and corrugated iron amphitheatres in the colonial capitals in the years leading up to the first gold rushes. These were modelled upon English counterparts. The establishment of inland communities and trade routes in the wake of the gold rush era encouraged the development of the travelling circus and, with it, the adoption of the tenting system. From these early itinerant troupes flowered the travelling circus companies that travelled the colonies. Until well into the present century, the circus was one of the most popular forms of entertainment in Australia. At the peak of their popularity, the colonial circuses of Ashton, Burton, St Leon and others were well-organised combinations of men, women, horses, wagons, brass bands and paraphernalia.

A family of German musicians, the brothers Wirth, who provided the music for Ashton's Circus in 1881–82, later established their own circus. In the present century Wirth Bros Circus was the largest and most famous circus in Australia. Other popular Australian circuses were those of the Perry family, who began their travels in central Queensland in the 1880s but whose links with Australian show business are traced as far back as the 1840s; FitzGerald Bros Circus, which was the largest circus in Australia in the period 1892–1906 and the first to be organised along lines characteristic of the great American circus companies; and Bullen Bros Circus, which, although organised as early as 1924, won its widest acclaim in the post-war era.

At least 10 circus companies of American origin visited the Australian colonies. Among these circuses were America's largest – those of Cooper & Bailey (1876–77), W. W. Cole (1880–81) and the Sells Brothers (1892). In contrast, there was a paucity of visiting British circuses due to the more difficult and expensive proposition of transporting a circus company by a longer and less-placid sea route.

In the face of the rising cost of star acts, increasingly militant musicians and the proliferation of the cinema throughout the country districts, the transition by the Australian circus companies from horse-drawn to motorised transport during the 1920s was timely. A motorised circus could cover more territory quicker than was previously possible, thus generating greater revenues to cover their increasing overheads. The largest circuses, particularly Wirth's, had relied heavily on rail transport since 1888.

By the 1920s acts regularly alternated between circus and vaudeville, thus affording artists greater continuity of employment and maximisation of financial reward. The circus remained a popular form of entertainment in both city and country in the inter-war period: there were more than 30 circuses on the road in the 1920s and 1930s. During World War II, the activities of all circuses were curtailed. Most closed up while the daily movement and activities of the largest circus, Wirth's, were severely limited by strict petrol rationing. The post-war period saw a flowering of the circus in Australia once more and by the mid-1950s there were 17 circuses travelling Australia.

The introduction of television in 1956 may be cited as the largest single factor that has brought about the decline of the Australian circus in recent decades, although a gradual qualitative decline appears to have been apparent since the 1920s. That a sizeable portion of the Australian public still appreciates circus entertainments of a high quality is attested by the visits in recent years of the Moscow State Circus and by the televised spectacles of major American and European circuses. In the 1990s, the outlook for a renaissance of the Australian circus and, with it, the

Right Performance by the Flying Fruit Fly Circus. Starting as a project for schoolchildren in New South Wales in 1979, the circus has gone on to tour Australia and establish a wide reputation, still using young performers.

re-creation of a tradition of performing skills, is positive. There are alternative circus groups scattered throughout all states and territories of Australia, many of which owe their initial inspiration to groups such as Circus Oz and the Flying Fruit Fly Circus.

The Australian circus may be credited with producing two of the greatest 'stars' of the international circus. These were the acrobatic equestrienne, May Wirth (1894–1978), an adopted daughter of the Wirth family; and the part-Aboriginal tightwire artist, Con Colleano (1899–1973), whose family started out with its own circus from Lightning Ridge (northern New South Wales) in 1910.

MUSIC HALLS

The English music hall tradition was created when light entertainment was combined with another English institution – the tavern. In Australia, 'musical nights' were first held in Sydney drinking houses in the late 1830s. A music hall movement began in Melbourne during the gold rushes and, by the mid-1860s, gained a foothold in Sydney with the opening of the Royal Alhambra in King Street.

The early Australian music hall was an inferior establishment to its English counterpart. 'More often than not [the Australian music hall] was housed in a plain, spartan building, and provided entertainment for audiences that wanted light music, gaiety, ribald and sentimental songs, recitations, comedy and animal turns, and a chorus of girls.' Although some music halls along the English model were opened in the latter quarter of the nineteenth century they supplied neither food nor drink as was the English custom. The music hall generally never enjoyed the same degree of popularity in Australia as it did in England, although various music halls-cum-restaurants have done a flourishing trade in Sydney and Melbourne since the 1960s. Of a more certain history was the development of a rich Australian variety and vaudeville tradition.

CLUBS

The post-war era saw the establishment of Returned Servicemen's League, Football and Workers' clubs. These have been financed virtually by the profits from poker machines, the more opulent clubs boasting dance floors, billiard rooms, swimming pools, restaurants, cocktail lounges and card-rooms. A club circuit began to burgeon in the 1960s and became the employer of hundreds of entertainers as the dance hall and vaudeville circuit suffered a demise following the introduction of television.   MStL

Sport

ABORIGINAL SPORT

Aboriginal sport was closely linked to economic and cultural needs. For example, tree-climbing competitions among children were in part a training for food-gathering, and the Queensland game of *Murri Murri*, involving throwing toy spears at a rolling wooden disc, developed a hunting skill. Games involving boomerang-throwing had clear economic relevance. Children's play involving food preparation, tracking, and animal and bird imitation was also largely preparation for life; and physical activity such as running, swimming and jumping developed strength and stamina. Other pastimes, such as dancing, had cultural implications; but there were activities such as ball-spinning and string-figure making that were predominantly for amusement.

There is some evidence of competition between individuals and tribes, and the physical prowess demonstrated by the 1868 Aboriginal touring cricket side to England indicates that athletic ability was cultivated for much the same reasons – a preparation for war and employment – as influenced their European conquerors.

ORIGINS OF AUSTRALIAN SPORT

Australian sport derived from its British and Irish origins. Both had long and extensive sporting traditions, and both developed and codified new sports during the century that Australia was initially being colonised. Australians took up these sports, both old and new, often giving them an Australian emphasis, and they invented some of their own. The major developments were in cricket, horse racing, boxing, and, later, football.

Cricket was recorded as early as 1803, and there were cricket clubs in New South Wales and Tasmania by the 1830s. Soldiers and civilians played against each other and among themselves in primitive conditions using rudimentary equipment. Crowds of up to 2,000 attended, and wagers in both money and kind were heavily laid. Cherrywood bats, ti-tree stumps and bails, joint use of rough paddocks with sheep or horses, bare feet and rustic technique did not deter the enthusiasm or the ambition of Australia's cricketers.

As both new colonies and new settlements were formed the cricket club and the cricket ground joined the church, the pub and the racecourse as essential adjuncts, the Melbourne Cricket Club, for example, being formed within three years of the foundation of

CRICKET IN AUSTRALIA

Colony/State	First record of game	First recorded club	First inter-colonial/ interstate game	Entry into Sheffield Shield
NSW	1803	Military CC 1826 Australia CC	v Victoria 1856	1892
Tasmania	1826	Hobart CC 1832	v Victoria 1851	1977
Western Australia	1835	Perth CC 1835	v Victoria 1893	1947
Victoria	1838	Melbourne CC 1838	v Tasmania 1851	1892
South Australia	1846	Adelaide CC 1846	v Victoria 1875	1892
Queensland	1844	Albion CC 1844	v NSW 1864	1926

the town in 1835. Teams representing separate colonies (Port Phillip versus Launceston) first met in Tasmania in 1851, and New South Wales met Victoria in March 1856 initiating a contest that has lasted, with one gap in 1865, ever since.

In 1861–62 a touring English side was brought out, largely to teach the colonials how to play cricket. The tourists lost only two matches, each to teams of 22. In 1867 the gap narrowed, in 1874 Victoria and New South Wales beat the tourists and in 1877 an Australian eleven (significantly named) won the first 'Test' match against England by 45 runs.

A white touring side of 11 Australians, all but three native-born, went to England in 1878, winning 10 and losing 4 of 19 eleven-a-side games, including an astonishing nine-wicket victory over an England-strength Marylebone Cricket Club side at Lord's in May. A win over England at the Oval in August 1882 led to a mock obituary in the *Sporting Times* in affectionate remembrance of the death of English cricket whose 'body will be cremated and the ashes taken to Australia'.

By the 1890s Australian cricket was at least equal to England's. Its large, hard grounds, its warm climate, its budding egalitarianism and its growing confidence had fashioned a distinctive cricketing style of fast, high over-arm bowling (Spofforth, Turner), forceful

Steeplechase from the early nineteenth century. The growth of horse racing led to the foundation in 1861 of the Melbourne Cup, now one of the premier handicap races in the world.

batting (Bonnor, Murdoch, Hill), sharp fielding (Blackham) and fierce competitiveness (Giffen). By 1902 21 series had been played, 10 of them in the 1880s. At the end of the 1888 series the score stood at England 16, Australia 10; by the end of 1902 it was England 28, Australia 26.

In horse racing it was more difficult to match Australian with British, but by the end of the century visitors such as Nat Gould, journalist and author, had no doubt that 'they knew how to race in Australia'. Racing began officially in 1810 in traditional mode: weight-for-age, or age-grouped fields, often with two horses running best-of-three heats. Intercolonial rivalry led, as in cricket, to match races, between New South Wales and Victorian champions in 1857, to a Champions Cup in Melbourne in 1859, and, eventually, to the first Melbourne Cup in 1861.

The Melbourne Cup has become central to the tradition of Australian horse racing. It broke with British practice in that it was a handicap, hence more of a lottery. It was linked with Australia's fastest-growing city whose expansion was based upon the discovery of gold, a city that became in the 1870s 'Marvellous Melbourne' and by the 1880s provided crowds of up to 100,000 for the Cup. Each year there seemed to be a different drama – of outsiders victorious, of the result foretold in dreams, of favourites losing. The development of its mystique reflected, like cricket, the Australian attitude to life.

Horse-racing personalities included bookmakers such as Joe Thompson 'The Leviathan', E. N. Abrahams 'The Count' and Sol Green; jockeys such as Tom Hales (Melbourne Cup with Flaneur in 1880 and 500 winners from 1,700 mounts) and Tom Corrigan, who died tragically from a race-fall in 1894; and trainers such as Etienne de Maistre (Archer) and Walter Hickenbotham, who trained Carbine. Carbine rivals Phar Lap as Australia's greatest hero of the turf, winning the 1890 Melbourne Cup with 10 st 5 lb (66 kg), although another great horse of the time, Flaneur, retired as a three-year-old undefeated to stud after 15 wins, including the 1880 Melbourne Cup.

Betting made fortunes for bookmakers and for two others, George Adams with his Tattersall's lottery and John Wren with his totalisator betting where the payout was not determined by a price (for example, 5–1) but on the stake money held at the start, divided by the number of successful selectors.

Boxing was a direct, early input from Britain. The first recorded bare-knuckled fist fight took place in April 1803 at Sydney, and a visiting English champion, Sam Clark, was knocked out by Young Kable of Windsor in 1824. Australia continued to produce fighters who took on visiting champions. Larry Foley, native-born son of a schoolmaster, became a labourer, a street-fighter and a Catholic larrikin gang-leader who won a 71-round bout with the Protestant Sandy

Imperial pride

The emulative strain that led colonial Australians to match themselves particularly against Englishmen but also against Americans was a pronounced feature of the formative years of Australian sport, and it is a characteristic that has not diminished.

There was a clear-headed recognition and acknowledgement among Australian journalists and public figures of the reasons for this –

a combination of a wish to prove that 'Jack was as good as his master', and that Australians, by demonstrating prowess in sport, proved that they were of good imperial stock.

The triumphs at Lord's (and at the Oval on the 1882 tour), on the Thames, at the American 1876 centennial and in the boxing ring were hailed as exemplars of both independent nationhood and of imperial ties.

BM

Ross in 1871. He was unbeaten in bare-knuckled contests, outmatching even the legendary Englishman Jem Mace. Not a big man (5 ft 9 in, 10 st 4 lb; 175 cm; 65 kg) he relied on agility and punching power.

Albert Griffiths, 'Young Griffo', an undisciplined genius who was once called 'the fastest thinking brainless boxer in history', began a line of Australian boxers denied their rightful world titles by their isolation in Australia and the chicanery of promoters overseas – or so the story goes. Moving from bare-knuckle to gloved fights (the former were made illegal in 1884) he won a world featherweight title against the American Torpedo Billy Murphy in Sydney in 1890 – but the Americans refused him recognition. He died, an alcoholic, in New York in 1927. Foley fathered the line of skilful Australian boxers, Griffiths that of unlucky, hard-done-by geniuses.

Boxing was a sport for heroes, crooks and gamblers. So, too, were professional athletics ('an honest pedestrian [foot-runner] is so rare as to be a human phenomenon'), sculling and rowing.

In rowing, Australia could claim its first world champion, Edward Trickett of New South Wales, who

was backed by his supporters in 1876 to go to England to defeat Englishman Joseph Sadler on the Thames almost a year before Australia won the first cricket Test. Other champions followed: Bill Beach and Henry Searle, the latter, the 'Clarence Comet', dying on a return voyage from England in 1889.

Searle was not above fixing the result of a heat to get the price right in a final, but sculling, corrupt as it was, was as nothing to foot-running and, later, to cycling which fell from popularity largely because the results seemed often to come as less of a surprise to the competitors than to the betting spectators.

Professional foot-running, cleaned up, persisted into the present century. The Stawell Gift, the oldest continuing foot-race in the world, having been first held in 1878, providing an annual Easter carnival. But the professionals, as in rowing, where schools and university boat clubs began to monopolise the sport after 1890, gave way to the growth of amateur athletics, given a boost by the revival of the Olympic Games at Athens in 1896 where Edward Flack, an Australian accountant holidaying in England, went to win both the inaugural 800 m and 1,500 m races and compete in the marathon and the lawn tennis.

In football, the Australians chose to go it alone. The dominant code in the majority of states and with a substantial presence in the rest is Australian Rules football, a game invented, codified and refined initially in Melbourne, at about the same time as the Melbourne Cup was breaking with British practice (see also p. 100).

Most English, Scottish and Irish migrants to the goldfields would have known of, or played, versions of folk or school football that proliferated back home. Attempts to standardise and regulate the rough and ready games were about to take place in England; in Victoria the lead was taken by a squatter's son recently returned from Rugby School, Thomas Wentworth Wills, who was also a cricketer of note (the

Australian Rules football match in 1879, one of the first sporting events to be played under electric light.

343

colonial W. G. Grace). He, together with his cousin Henry Harrison and other respectable middle-class young men, got together to form clubs to play a game that would fill in the gap between cricket seasons.

Its essence has not changed greatly from its first codification in 1858. It was to be manly but not dirty, it was to avoid the hacking and scrumming that in other codes looked like brawling, and a premium was placed on open play in a setting in which space was no problem. Since then, modifications and developments of the rules and tactics of the code have maintained those early precepts. As a consequence the game has enlisted fervent and widespread support; but only in Australia.

For the first 20 years of its existence the game in Melbourne was largely the preserve of the respectable, but its attractions soon enlisted the support of the growing working class in suburbs such as Essendon, Fitzroy and, most famously, Collingwood.

A league competition, the Victorian Football Association formed in 1874, predated the English Football League by 14 years. It became the Victorian Football League in 1896, formed by eight breakaway clubs who wished to maximise the profits from crowds which were, *per capita* of population, the largest to watch any sport in the world at that time (with the exception of the Melbourne Cup).

Soccer football, one of the two divergent paths taken by the game in England in the 1870s (Ireland had to wait until 1884 to have a codified game that, intriguingly, much resembled Australian Rules), did not properly strike root in Australia until after World War II, although there were expatriate clubs in Melbourne in the 1880s.

Rugby football, the other strain, was played in the University of Sydney in the 1860s, the first meeting of the club being recorded in June 1865. Games were between clubs or against visiting British ships' crews; but in the 1870s other clubs were founded, sufficient for the Southern Rugby Union to be formed in 1874. In 1876 the game started in Queensland, and the Queensland Rugby Union was formed in 1882, the same year in which a New South Wales representative team went to New Zealand, a return visit occurring two years later. By the turn of the century two more sides from New Zealand and two from Britain had visited Australia. An Australian side first went to Britain in 1908.

By the end of the century every game and sport that had been played or was being played in the British Isles had been played or was being played in the Australian colonies. North American sports, too, were in vogue, notably lacrosse and baseball.

The widening of Australia's competitive sporting horizon was already under way by the turn of the century. Rugby footballers had played against New Zealanders; boxers, wrestlers, rifle-shooters, rowers against Americans; an athlete and a tennis player (Edward Flack) against representatives of 10 other nations present at the Athens Olympics. The major sports established in the nineteenth century – cricket, football and horse racing – continued to flourish in the twentieth. Against the traditional foe, England, Australia established an ascendancy that was threatened only rarely and for very short periods.

CRICKET

In the years immediately following World War I, Australia overtook England in Tests won, winning 12 out of 15 played in the first three series. Warwick Armstrong, captain for the first two of these, brought an abrasive arrogance into the rivalry that ensured the primacy of the Ashes as a barometer of Anglo-Australian sporting rivalry. After World War II, dourness (from both sides), confrontation and controversy gave cricket what was to many an unpleasant aspect.

Domestic and international cricket in Australia was transformed in 1977 by the creation of a highly professionalised group of international cricketers – Australian, West Indian, English, South African, Pakistani and (one) New Zealander – who developed, mainly for television presentation through Kerry Packer's Channel 9 network, a colourful extension of traditional Test match cricket and, more intensively and more popularly, of one-day, limited-over matches.

Floodlighting, distinctive coloured uniforms, white balls and black sight screens, fielding circles, use of multiple cameras and on-field microphones made the game a bane to traditionalists, and a joy to the populace. The breakaway itself ended by 1979, but the one-day games have remained a distinctive and most popular feature of Australian cricket.

The Sheffield Shield first-class domestic cricket competition (instituted in 1892–93) became notable, particularly between the wars, for high scoring. New South Wales dominated the competition until the mid-1960s, since when Western Australia has been the premier cricketing state. To 1993, New South Wales won the Shield 41 times (all but 5 of those by 1965–66), Victoria 26 times, South Australia 13, and Western Australia 13. Queensland and Tasmania had still to win the Shield.

International one-day cricket match between Australia and New Zealand in 1982-83. In the late 1970s and early 1980s Australian cricket broke some of the hallowed traditions of the game, introducing, among other innovations, night-time floodlit matches, coloured clothing in place of all-white outfits, and on-field television microphones.

AUSTRALIA V. ENGLAND CRICKET TESTS			
	A won	E won	Drawn
1901-12	15	14	9
1920-38	22	15	12
1946-93	50	33	54

HORSE RACING

Australian horse racing, as parochial in its way as Australian Rules football, continued to be a major sporting interest. Equine heroes, heroines and geldings, among them Phar Lap, winner of the 1930 Melbourne Cup and accounted by many to have been Australia's greatest racehorse although foaled in New Zealand, engaged great public devotion.

Scandals of various sorts – the doping of the second favourite Big Philou hours before the 1969 Melbourne Cup, the pulling of another jockey's leg by Schumacher in the 1961 AJC Derby, the use of remote-controlled batteries in saddles at Rosehill (Sydney) in 1969, the 'ringing-in' of better horses for inferior ones at Flemington in 1931, Murray Bridge (SA) in 1934, Casterton (Victoria) in 1972, and at Eagle Farm (Brisbane) in 1984 – all continued to add characteristic flavour to the sport.

Successful jockeys and trainers also continued to become notable public figures. Among the former were Jim Pike (Phar Lap's jockey), Scobie Breasley (who also enjoyed great success in England), George Moore (who rode over 1,000 winners but failed to win a Melbourne Cup), Roy Higgins and Malcolm Johnstone (whose mounts in 1979–80 won over $1 million in stake money). Trainers such as James Scobie (Melbourne Cups in 1900, 1922, 1923 and 1927), Jack Holt 'The Wizard of Mordialloc' (1933) and Jack Telford (Phar Lap's trainer) have been out-matched in recent times, in terms of stake money won, by Tommy Smith ($1 million in 1973–74, $2 million in 1979–80 and $3 million in 1984–85) and Bart Cummings (who was the first to win $1 million in a season), and trained Melbourne Cup winners.

RUGBY UNION

Like cricket, Australian Rugby Union extended its range of opponents in the twentieth century, but its major contests were against New Zealand (which has heavily outplayed it since internationals began in 1903), South Africa, which showed equal superiority in the 29 matches played between 1933 and 1971, and teams from the Home Countries, either united as the British Lions, or separately as England, Scotland, Wales and Ireland.

Since World War II France (1948), Fiji (1952), Tonga (1973), Japan (1975), USA (1976 – although one game was played in California in 1912), Argentina (1979), Italy (1983), Canada (1985) and Western Samoa (1993) have been added to Australia's list of opponents.

For a brief period in the mid-1980s Australia was arguably Rugby Union world champion, winning all four internationals on a British Isles tour in 1984, and

Other Cricket Tests

Australia met South Africa in Tests for the first time in 1902 in South Africa, and played 53 Tests in 10 series until 1970. Dominant early, Australia won only two Tests and lost eight (including the last five played) in the final decade of the rivalry.

West Indies became Test opponents from 1930–1931; by 1993, 77 matches had been played, Australia winning 30, West Indies 26 (16 of them since 1980), 20 being drawn and 1 being memorably tied in Brisbane in 1960.

Australia first met India in a Test series in 1947–48; by 1993, 47

matches had been played, Australia winning 24, India 9 and 14 being drawn including a tied Test at Madras in 1986. Pakistan has been met 37 times since 1956, Australia winning 12, Pakistan 10 (including a victory in the first match) and 15 being drawn.

New Zealand played only once, in 1946, before 1973 but by 1993 had met Australia 25 times, with Australia winning 10, New Zealand 6 and 9 games being drawn. Seven official Tests have now been played against Sri Lanka, with Australia winning four, the rest being drawn.

BM/WV

AUSTRALIA IN FIRST-CLASS INTERNATIONAL CRICKET (to 1993)

Opponent	First tour of Australia (First Test)	First tour by Australia (First Test)	No. of Test tours to Australia	No. of Test tours by Australia
England	1861–62 (1877)	1878* (1880)	33	32
South Africa	1910–11 (1910)	1902–03 (1902)	3	7**
West Indies	1930–31 (1930)	1955 (1955)	10	6
New Zealand	1898–99 (1973)	1877–78 (1946)	4	7
India	1947–48 (1947)	1955–56 (1956)	6	6
Pakistan	1964–65 (1964)	1956 (1956)	7	7
Sri Lanka	1984 (1988)	1982 (1983)	2	2

*An Aboriginal side toured England in 1868.
**One Test series was played in England in the 1912 Triangular Tournament.

For many years in the shadow of its neighbour, New Zealand, Australian Rugby Union rose to pre-eminence by winning the World Cup in 1991, beating England (the players in the white jerseys) in the final.

beating New Zealand in New Zealand in 1986, but since then New Zealand has resumed its customary dominance. Nevertheless in 1991 Australia won the inaugural World Cup.

The game in Australia is largely confined to New South Wales and Queensland, having only a vestigial following in the southern states and the west. It retains, somewhat unjustly, an image of private school, university and middle-class support, caricatured by cartoon association with tweed coats and the phrase 'The Rah-Rahs' supposedly characteristic of the cries of the supporters.

RUGBY LEAGUE

Rugby League on the other hand, although like Union, confined almost wholly to New South Wales and Queensland, is seen as a working-class game. Founded in 1907 as a breakaway from Union which refused to countenance payment of players, it was played first at international level against a team of New Zealand professionals (the 'All Golds'). A domestic competition involving six clubs began in 1908, and a touring side went to Great Britain in 1908–09. Since that time over 200 tests have been played, mainly against Britain, New Zealand and France but also against Papua New Guinea and South Africa with Australia ahead in victories against all opponents.

Australian Rugby League developed in the 1980s a

world dominance marred only by occasional surprise defeats by New Zealand and, for the first time in 10 years, by Great Britain in 1988. Based on the strength of the New South Wales clubs competition (which comprises clubs from Brisbane, the Gold Coast, Canberra, Newcastle and Wollongong as well as from Sydney) the sport is now arguably Australia's strongest in international terms.

FOOTBALL

The strongest domestic football code, Australian Rules football has, apart from only partially successful efforts to meet Irish Gaelic footballers at a game with compromise rules, been entirely confined to Australia. The Victorian Football League has become the Australian Football League and now involves teams from Sydney, Brisbane, Perth and Adelaide. It remains the premier competition, although of recent years state sides from Western Australia and South Australia, largely comprising players born in those states but playing in the VFL and AFL, have been able regularly to defeat Victoria itself and in 1992 the AFL premiership itself went to Perth, courtesy of the West Coast Eagles.

Club loyalty, particularly to such teams as Collingwood, Carlton and Essendon – although it is characteristic of supporters of all clubs – manifested in large attendances, giant banners, cheer squads and the wearing of club colours in scarves, hats, general attire

AFL (VFL) PREMIERSHIPS 1897–1993		
1897-28	1929–59	1960–93
Collingwood 7	Melbourne 8	Hawthorn 9
Fitzroy 7	Collingwood 6	Carlton 8
Essendon 6	Essendon 4	Essendon 5
Carlton 5	Geelong 4	Richmond 5
Melbourne 2	Carlton 3	Melbourne 2
Richmond 2	Richmond 3	North Melb 2
South Melb 2	Fitzroy 1	Geelong 1
Geelong 1	Footscray 1	St Kilda 1
	South Melb 1	West Coast 1
		Collingwood 1

Australian Rules Football match between Hawthorn and North Melbourne, 1992. Although not played anywhere else in the world and with its own distinctive set of rules, the fast-moving and open Australian Rules football has continued to outpace other codes in popularity.

and even hair keeps the code popular if parochial. Sponsorship has not been difficult to enlist, and the game has become both more colourful and more commercialised. A number of players, distinguished by their skill, physique and ferocity, or all three, have attained heroic status, at least in Melbourne.

Club primacy has varied over the 95 years of the VFL's and AFL's existence, as the Premiership table of roughly 30-year periods shows. The decline of Collingwood and Fitzroy is particularly noticeable, also the rise of Hawthorn and the relative consistency of Carlton and Essendon.

SOCCER

Soccer, the world's most popular football code, is the weakest of the four played widely in Australia (there is, in addition, some expatriate and romantic dabbling in American gridiron and Irish Gaelic football).

English and Scottish middle-class immigrants formed soccer clubs in Sydney and Melbourne in the 1880s, and areas such as Newcastle and Wollongong also supported the game. It did not prosper, although a number of international games were played against Canada, Czechoslovakia, England, India, New Caledonia, New Zealand and Palestine between the wars.

Post-war southern European immigration enlarged support for the code, which became organised principally on ethnically based clubs (for example, South Melbourne Hellas and Sydney Croatia). Tours by leading European clubs became a regular feature of the season, and Australia entered the World Cup qualifying rounds in 1965, abruptly leaving after two defeats by North Korea. After again failing to qualify in 1969, Australia won an Asian zone tournament to go to West Germany in 1974 where it lost two and drew one of its games. It has failed to qualify for the finals of the four Cups held since.

In 1977 a National Soccer League was formed with clubs from Sydney, Melbourne, Adelaide, Brisbane and Canberra. It has undergone a number of organisational changes and apart from occasional successes by Adelaide City and West Adelaide has, in its various forms, been dominated by Sydney and Melbourne clubs, which retain pronounced European nationalist affiliations.

At the international level there is evidence of improving standards, Australia progressing to the final of the Special Bicentenary Gold Cup by defeating Argentina, the then world champions, 4–1 only to lose 0–2 to Brazil. In the 1988 Olympic Games Australia advanced to the quarter-final stage, losing 0–3 to the Soviet Union. At Barcelona in 1992 the 'Olyroos' were placed fourth, the best performance ever by a national adult side.

GOLF

Golf is reported to have been played in Tasmania in the 1820s, but not until the 1880s did the sport begin in earnest in Australia. A game for respectable society, it held its first national championships for women in August 1894, and for men in November 1894. Professionals were employed by clubs from their earliest days (Melbourne GC 1891, Sydney 1896) and a Professional Golfers' Association was formed in 1911, seven years after the first Open Championship held at Botany, Sydney and won by the Hon. Michael Scott of Melbourne.

Not until after World War II did an Australian win a major overseas tournament, Jim Ferrier winning the US Professional Golfer's Association tournament in 1947. Peter Thomson was the first to win a British Open, in 1954, winning it on four further occasions. David Graham won the US Open in 1981 (having won the USPGA in 1979). Other Australian winners of major tournaments include Norman von Vida (British Open 1960) and Greg Norman, also the British Open in 1987 and again in 1993.

GOLF IN AUSTRALIA

Colony	First Reports	First Clubs	
New South Wales	1840s	Australia	1882
Victoria	1847	Flagstaff Gardens	1850
South Australia	1870s	Adelaide	1892
Queensland	1880	Brisbane	1890
Western Australia	1895	Perth	1895
Tasmania	1820s	Newlands	1896

LAWN TENNIS

Lawn tennis, invented by an Englishman in the 1870s, was established in Australia by 1878, clubs being formed in both Sydney and Melbourne in that year. In 1896 Flack, the runner, also played lawn tennis for Australia in the inaugural Olympics. Australia and New Zealand, playing as 'Australasia', entered the Davis Cup competition in 1905, winning it for the first of six times in 1908. In 1924 Australia competed separately for the first time, losing to the USA in the Challenge Round. In 1939 this result was reversed.

In 1946 there began one of the most extraordinary sequences in sporting history. Every year between then and 1968 Australia appeared in the Challenge Round, 23 times in all, being victorious on 15 occasions – all between 1950 and 1967. Since then Australia has won the Cup on four further occasions, the most recent in 1986.

The glory days of Davis Cup triumphs, usually over the USA, were matched by successes at Wimbledon. Norman Brookes of Melbourne was the first Australian to win the men's singles, in 1907. Between 1952 and 1971 Australians won the title 14 times (Rod Laver 4, John Newcombe 3, Lewis Hoad 2, Roy Emerson 2, Francis Sedgman, Ashley Cooper and Neale Fraser once each). Margaret Smith (Court) won three Ladies' titles between 1963 and 1970.

In the US Open, Australian men took the title 15 times in the 23 years 1951–73, including seven in succession 1956–62. Francis Sedgman, Ken Rosewall, Neale Fraser, Roy Emerson, Rod Laver and John Newcombe all won twice, Mal Anderson, Ashley Cooper and Fred Stolle once each. Also, between 1962 and 1973 Margaret Smith (Court) won five women's titles.

This golden age of Australian tennis was achieved against representatives of the world's richest and most powerful nation, and while it lasted to a great extent replaced the traditional cricketing rivalry with Britain as a yardstick of national pride.

Regarded by many informed commentators as the greatest male tennis player of them all, Rod Laver swept all before him for years. He was the last man to win the Grand Slam of Wimbledon and the US, French and Australian Opens in the same year, which he did in 1969, and is the only player ever to have performed the feat twice, having previously achieved it as an amateur in 1962.

SWIMMING AND ATHLETICS

In athletics and swimming, too, the 1950s and 1960s saw Australia victorious especially at Olympic level and particularly so at the 1956 Games held in Melbourne which produced double-gold medallists in sprinting (Betty Cuthbert) and in swimming (Murray Rose). Dawn Fraser, who was to go on to win three more gold medals in successive Olympics to 1964, won her first at Melbourne.

On the running track, Herb Elliott, unbeaten as an adult in any mile or 1,500 m race, won an Olympic 1,500 m title at Rome in 1960, and held the world mile record, at 3 min, 54.5 s for four years, from 1958 to 1962. John Landy, another Australian, had held it (at 3 min, 57.9 s) from 1954 to 1957.

SAILING

Australian sailing began in the 1820s on Sydney Harbour and on the Derwent River in Hobart. Yacht clubs were formed in Victoria (1856), Sydney (1862), Tasmania (1874), Brisbane (1866), Perth (1865). Ocean yacht racing began in the 1860s, and Australia won its first world championship in 1958 and its first Olympic gold medal in 1964, having first competed in yachting at Helsinki in 1952.

Victories in the 1980s

In tennis, Pat Cash won the men's singles at Wimbledon in 1987, the same year the Australian cricket team won the one-day World Cup held in India and Pakistan. The Rugby Union Wallabies won all four internationals on a tour of Great Britain and Ireland in 1984 (and beat the All Blacks in New Zealand in 1985), and the Rugby League tourists went on two undefeated tours of Great Britain in 1982 and 1986.

Even in athletics and swimming, where Australia had to compete not only against Americans but against heavily state-funded Soviet and East German teams, some triumphs were recorded. At the Los Angeles Olympics (boycotted by the communist world) four gold medals were won, one each in athletics and swimming, one in weightlifting and one in cycling. At the Seoul games in 1988, with no major boycott in operation, Australia won three gold medals – Debbie Flintoff-King in the women's 400 m hurdles, Duncan Armstrong in the 200 m freestyle swimming, and the women's hockey.

The most notable triumph of all in the 1980s was the winning of the America's Cup in September 1983 at Newport, Rhode Island. BM

Two years previously *Gretel* lost Australia's first challenge for the America's Cup by four races to one. In 1967 *Dame Pattie* lost 0–4 to *Intrepid*. In 1971, amid Australian criticism of American sportsmanship, *Gretel II* lost 1–4 again to *Intrepid*. In 1974 *Southern Cross* lost 0–4 to *Courageous*. In 1977 *Australia* lost 0–4 again to *Courageous*, and in 1980 *Australia* lost to *Freedom* 1–4.

The Alan Bond syndicate-owned, Ben Lexcen-designed *Australia II* won an elimination series for the right to challenge *Liberty* in September 1983. Three–one down after four races of the best of seven Australia's seventh challenge looked to be as hopeless as the rest; but a remarkable revival, culminating in a victory in the seventh race, witnessed widely throughout Australia in the early hours of the morning on television, gave *Australia II* the Cup, though it was lost to America again off Perth in 1987. Since then, Australian entries have failed to reach the final series of races.

Left *Evonne Goolagong, later Evonne Cawley, playing in the Australian Open in 1972. The first top-rank Aboriginal tennis player, for a decade she was amongst the top five women players of the world.*

Ben Lexcen (designer) and John Bertrand (helmsman) at the victory parade in Perth for the America's Cup, won by Australia II *in 1983.*

OLYMPIC AND COMMONWEALTH GAMES

Australians have participated in every summer Olympic Games – one of only three nations to do so – since the establishment of the modern Games in Athens in 1896. Success on this particular world stage has been limited with the significant exception of the 1956 gathering in Melbourne at which 35 medals were won, 13 of them gold. As might be anticipated greater success has been obtained at the Empire (now Commonwealth) Games where the competition is less fierce.

SPORTING ORGANISATIONS

Having originally developed at the club, local and colonial level the organisation of Australian sport began to operate at a national level with the prospect and reality of federation.

By the end of the first decade of federation Australia's major sports, other than horse racing, had formed Australia-wide sporting bodies. Cricket, which had provided national teams since 1877, came under an official national Board of Control in 1905.

In football the National Football League, supposedly to control Australian Rules football, was founded in 1906, but real control has remained vested in the various state Football League bodies – for example, the Victorian Football League founded in 1896 as a breakaway from the Victorian Football Association (1877). Another breakaway, the Australian Rugby Football League, was founded in 1907 to coordinate the development of the professional defection from the New South Wales Rugby Union. A soccer federation of sorts had existed since 1880, but not until 1923 was the Football Association of Australia founded. It became the Australian Soccer Federation in 1957.

The exception was Rugby Union football which continued under state control, principally that of the New South Wales Rugby Union (Southern Union, 1874: renamed in 1892), until the creation of the Australian Rugby Union in 1949.

Lawn tennis came under a national Association in 1904, and the Amateur Athletics Association, founded in 1897, was in existence when federation came. The Australian AAA became the Amateur Athletics Union in 1927.

There is a number of coordinating sports organisations whose operations cover a spectrum of sports. These include the Australian Olympic Federation and the Australian Commonwealth Games Association which are responsible for all activities relating to the sending of teams to those events. The Australian Institute of Sport was founded in 1981, partly as a response to the poor Australian performance at the

Other twentieth-century champions

Mention must be made of a number of other notable twentieth-century champions in a variety of sports in order to indicate the continuing range of Australian sporting activity.

In boxing, Jimmy Carruthers (world bantamweight champion 1952–54), Johnny Famechon (world featherweight champion 1969–70), Lionel Rose (world bantamweight champion 1968–69) and, latterly, Jeff Fenech, another bantamweight, Geoff Harding, Lester Ellis and Barry Michaels have maintained what is to some an inglorious tradition of excellence.

Stuart McKenzie, winner of the Diamond Sculls of Henley Royal Regatta, England, for five successive years 1957–61, was in the mould of Trickett and Searle.

Walter Lindrum's phenomenal success on the billiard table (a world-record break of 4,137 in 1931) caused the rules to be changed.

Jack Brabham won the motor car racing World Drivers' Championship three times (1959, 1960 and 1966), and Alan Jones did so in 1980.

In cycling, Hubert Opperman between the wars, Russell Mockridge and Syd Patterson afterwards ranked among the world's best.

Heather McKay was undefeated in women's squash for 18 years, and lost only two matches in her entire career (1960–1979), a feat unmatched in any sport anywhere in the world.

A country of bush and beaches has also necessarily provided sportsmen and women associated with those features. Woodchopping and shearing champions such as the Heckenbergs, Charlie Winkel and Jack O'Toole (axemen) and Jack Howe in the 1890s and Kevin Sarre in the 1950s and 1960s (shearing) have become local legend, as has, more recently, David Foster, winner of over 100 woodchopping championships.

The surfing and particularly the surf life-saving movement is a notable symbol of Australia. It has produced world champions such as 'Midge' Farrelly (1963), Wayne Bartholomew (1978) Mark Richards (1979–83), Tom Carroll (1983–85), Damien Hardman (1987) and Barton Lynch (1988) and a number of national characters in the ironman, surf life-saving's glamour event involving surf-skiing, board paddling, swimming and beach running.

BM

1976 Olympics, as a central institute where the best athletes in the country could be trained using modern sports science and experienced coaches. Originally located solely in Canberra it has now decentralised many of its activities, simultaneously widening the range of sports covered. The Australian Sports Commission followed three years later with a brief to provide a more coordinated approach to sports development in Australia. Its primary objectives are to maximise funding for sport from the private sector, to provide leadership in improving Australia's international performance, and to increase the general level of participation in sport by Australians.

Standing somewhat apart is the Confederation of Australian Sport, founded in 1976 at a time of despair following the poor performance at the Montreal Olympics and a general decline in Australian tennis, swimming and running. Representative of over 120 affiliated national sporting organisations it acts as a lobby group and, through a number of committees,

involves itself in such matters as sports coaching, development, sports research and the annual Sport Australia awards.

Sports in universities, colleges of advanced education and schools have separate organisations, as do, since 1983, sports administrators. Each state and territory has a department or a division of a department concerned with sport and recreation (under a variety of titles), and local authorities throughout Australia provide, as they think appropriate, support for club and community sporting and recreation facilities.

BM/WV

Australian sporting bodies

The following (not exhaustive) list shows the development of national sporting bodies. It indicates the range of Australian sports activity, and, more recently, the involvement in sport of the handicapped and the disadvantaged.

1897 Amateur Athletics Association
    (Australian Amateur Athletics Union 1927)
1904 Lawn Tennis Association
1905 (Cricket) Board of Control
1906 National Football League (Australian Rules)
    National Ice Skating Association
1907 Australian Rugby Football League
1909 Amateur Swimming Union
1910 Women's Hockey Association
1911 Australian Bowling Council
    Professional Golfers' Association
1914 Australian Olympic Council (became
    Australian Aero Club (re-established 1926))
1921 Ladies' Golf Union
    Universities Sports Association
    Amateur Weightlifting Federation
1923 Football Association of Australia (became
    Australian Soccer Federation 1961)
1924 Amateur Boxing Union
1925 Hockey Association
    Rowing Council
1926 Women's Basketball Association (Netball
    Association 1970)
1927 Power Boat Association (reorganised 1933)
1928 Auto Cycle Council
    British Empire Games Association
1930 Schools Sports Council
1931 Women's Cricket Council
    Lacrosse Council
1932 Ski Federation
    Women's Amateur Athletic Union
    Vigoro Association
1933 Table Tennis Board of Control (reorganised as
    Table Tennis Association 1937)
1934 Squash Rackets Association
1935 Badminton Association
1936 Clay Target Association
1939 Basketball Federation

1945 Rough Riders' Association
1946 Gymnastic Federation
1948 Polocrosse Association
    Amateur Fencing Association
1949 Canoeing Federation
    Australian Rugby Union
    Softball Association
    Croquet Association
    Equestrian Federation
1950 Gliding Association
1951 Ice Skating Council
    Water Ski Association
1953 Confederation of Australian Motor Sport
1954 Deaf Sports Federation
    Modern Pentathlon Association
1956 Australian Council for Health, Physical
    Education and Recreation
    Amateur Pistol Shooting Association
1963 Kart Association
    Volleyball Association
1964 Little Athletics Union
1969 Amateur Soccer Association
1971 Orienteering Federation
1974 Ski Patrol Association
    Association of Veterans' Athletic Clubs
1975 Ballooning Federation
1976 Confederation of Australian Sport
1977 Paraplegic and Quadriplegic Sports
    Federation
    National Soccer League
    Blind Sports Federation
1978 Korfball Association
    Indoor Soccer Federation
    Touch Association
1979 Bowhunters' Association
    National Basketball League
1981 Australian Institute of Sport
    Amputee Sporting Association
1984 Australian Sports Commission
    Transplant Olympic Association
1986 Sport and Recreation Association for Persons
    with an Intellectual Disability
1988 Mountain Bike Association

The physical continent

TOPOGRAPHY

Adams, P., *Place and Space in Australia* (Melbourne, 1988).
Cameron, E. E. and Cogger, H. G. (eds.), *Arid Australia* (Sydney, 1978).
Davies, J. L. and Williams, M. A. J. (eds.), *Landform Evolution in Australasia* (Canberra, 1978).
Jeans, D. N. (ed.), *Australia: A Geography*, Vol. 1 (Sydney, 1986).
Jennings, J. N. and Mabbutt, J. A. (eds.), *Landform Studies from Australia and New Guinea* (Canberra, 1967).
Johnson, K., *The AUSMAP Atlas of Australia* (Cambridge 1992).

Video recording
Australia: The First Four Billion Years (Gamma Films, Leichhardt NSW, 1986).

GEOLOGICAL STRUCTURE

BMR Palaeogeographic Group, *Australia – Evolution of a Continent* (Canberra, 1990).
Brown, D. A., Campbell K. S. W. and Crook, K. A. W., *The Geological Evolution of Australia and New Zealand* (Oxford, 1967).
Veevers, J. J. (ed.), *Phanerozoic Earth History of Australia* (Oxford, 1984).

CLIMATE

Australian Bureau of Meteorology, *Climatic Atlas of Australia* (Canberra, 1988).
Australian Bureau of Meteorology, *Climate of Australia* (Canberra, 1989).
Australian Bureau of Meteorology, *Climatic Averages* (Canberra, 1989).
Crowder, R. B., *The Wonders of the Weather* (Melbourne, 1994).
Linacre, E. and Hobbs, J., *The Australian Climatic Environment* (Brisbane, 1977).
Pittock, A. B. et al., *Climatic Change and Variability: A Southern Perspective* (Cambridge, 1978).
Tapper, N. and Hurry, L., *Australia's Weather Patterns: An Introductory Guide* (1993).

Video recording
Drought (Golden Dophin Productions, Newport NSW, c. 1983).

SOILS

CSIRO Division of Soils, *Soils: An Australian Viewpoint* (London/Melbourne, 1983).
Christie, E. K., *Pastoralism and Ecology in Arid Australia* (Melbourne, 1986).
Evans, G., *Acid Soils in Australia: The Issues for Government* (Parkes ACT, c. 1991).
McDonald, R. C., *Australian Soil and Land Survey Field Handbook* (2nd edn, Melbourne, 1990).
Russell, J. S. and Isbell, R. F. (eds.), *Australian Soils: The Human Impact* (St Lucia QLD, 1986).

Video recordings
Assault on the Land (Box Hill College of TAFE, Melbourne, c. 1989).
Dirty Problems (Video Education Australasia, Bendigo VIC, c. 1991)
Dreamtime to Dust: Australia's Fragile Environment (Australian Museum, Sydney, 1991).

Audiocassettes
The Vanishing Continent: Australia's Degraded Environment (6 cassettes, Hear a Book, North Hobart TAS, 1991).

WATER RESOURCES

Surface water
Crabb, P., *Australia's Water Resources: Their Use and Management* (Melbourne, 1986).
Department of Primary Industries and Energy and Australian Water Resources Council, *Review of Australia's Water Resources and Water Use* (2 vols, Canberra, 1985).
Department of Resources and Energy, *Water 2000: A Perspective on Australia's Water Resources to the Year 2000* (Canberra, 1983).
Industry Commission, *Water Resources and Waste Water Disposal* (Canberra, c. 1992).
Pigram, J. J. J., *Issues in the Management of Australia's Water Resources* (Melbourne, 1986).
Warner, R. F. (ed.), *Fluvial Geomorphology of Australia* (Sydney, 1988).

Groundwater
Australian Water Resources Council, *1985 Review of Australia's Water Resources and Water Use* (2 vols, Canberra, 1988).
Brown, M. and Lubczenko, V., *Groundwater and Salinity in the Murray Basin* (Murray Darling Basin Commission, VIC, 1991).
Crabb, P., *The Murray Darling Basin: A Resource at Risk* (Melbourne, 1993).
Habermehl, M. A. 'Groundwater in Australia', *Memoirs of the 18th Congress of the International Association of Hydrogeologists*, Vol. 1 (Cambridge, 1985).
Habermehl, M. A., 'The Great Artesian Basin, Australia', *BMR Journal of Australian Geology and Geophysics*, 5: 9–38 (1980).
Jacobson, G., Habermehl M. A. and Lau, J. E., *Australia's Groundwater Resources* (Canberra, 1983).
Lau, J. E., Commander, D. P. and Jacobson, G. 'Hydrogeology of Australia', *Bulletin of the Bureau of Mineral Resources, Geology and Geophysics*, 227 (1987).
Quiggin, J., *Salinity in the Murray River System: An Illustrative Model* (Canberra, 1985).

VEGETATION

Australian Surveying and Land Information Group, *Atlas of Australian Resources*, 3rd series, Vol. 6 (Canberra, 1990).
Beadle, N. C. W., *The Vegetation of Australia* (Cambridge, 1981).
Dyne, G. R. (ed.), *Flora of Australia*, Vol. 1, Introduction (Canberra, 1981).
Groves, R. H. (ed.), *Australian Vegetation* (Cambridge, 1981).
Higgins, G. and Hermes, N., *Australia, the Land Time Forgot: The Origins of our Land, Plants and Animals* (Frenchs Forest NSW, 1988).
Hill, R. S. (ed.), *History of the Australian Vegetation: Cretaceous to Recent* (Cambridge, 1994).
Huntley, B. and Webb, T. III (eds.), *Vegetation History* (Dordrecht, 1988), pp. 237–306.
Low, T., *Wild Food Plants of Australia* (North Ryde NSW, 1991).
Pyne, S., *Burning Bush: A Fire History of Australia* (New York, 1991).
Zola, N., *Koorie Plants, Koorie People: Traditional Aboriginal Food, Fibre and Healing Plants of Victoria* (Melbourne, c. 1992).

Video recordings
A Curious and Diverse Flora (CSIRO/Australia Academy of Science, Melbourne, c. 1981).
Like Nowhere Else: Australia's Unique Environment (Film Australia, Lindfield NSW, 1991).
Nature of Australia: A Portrait of the Island Continent (Australian Broadcasting Corporation, Sydney, 1988).

FAUNA

Archer, M. and Clayton, G. (eds.), *Vertebrate Zoogeography and Evolution in Australasia: Animals in Space and Time* (Carlisle WA, 1984).
Cogger, H. G., *Reptiles and Amphibians of Australia* (Sydney, 1992).
Schodde, R. and Tidemann, S. C. (eds.), *The Complete Book of Australian Birds* (Sydney, 1986).
Strahan, R. C. (ed.), *The Australian Museum Complete Book of Australian Mammals* (London, 1988).

THE RAINFORESTS AND REEFS

Figgis, P. and Mosley, G., *Australia's Wilderness Heritage*, Vol. 1 (Sydney, 1988).
Ritchie, R., *Seeing the Rainforests in Nineteenth Century Australia* (Sydney, 1989).
Webb, L.J. and Kikkawa, J. (eds.), *Australian Tropical Rainforests* (Melbourne, 1990).

THE GREAT BARRIER REEF

Bennett, I., *The Great Barrier Reef* (Sydney, 1992).
Cannon, L. R. G., *Exploring Australia's Great Barrier Reef: A World Heritage Site* (North Ryde NSW, 1989).
Hopley, D., *The Great Barrier Reef: Ecology and Management* (Melbourne, 1989).
Mather, P. and Bennett, I., *A Coral Reef Handbook: A Guide to the Geology, Flora and Fauna of the Great Barrier Reef* (Chipping Norton NSW, 3rd edn, 1993).
Murdoch, L., *Discover the Great Barrier Reef Marine Park* (Townsville, n.d.).
Steene, R. C., *The Reader's Digest Book of the Great Barrier Reef* (Sydney 1990).

Video recordings
The Great Barrier Reef (Aussie Holiday Videos, Kingsgrove NSW, c. 1987).
The Reef (Australia Heritage Series, Melbourne, 1987).

THE NORTH

Young, E. A., 'Aborigines and Land in Northern Australian Development', *Australian Geographer*, 19 (1): 105–16 (1988).

Video recordings
Arafura to Alice (Film Australia, Lindfield NSW, 1980).
Kakadu: Land of the Crocodile (Kestrel Films, Melbourne, 1986).
Kamira: Pina yanirlipa ngurrurakurra [Kamira: We're Going Back to our Country] (Ngurrangka Video NT, 1986).
Land of Nature's Dreaming: The Northern Territory's Top End (Panorama Australia, Adelaide, n.d.).
Return to the Dreaming (Opus Films, Castlemaine VIC, 1988).
Shake'im this Country (Northern Territory Aboriginal Sacred Sites Protection Authority, Hawthorn Audio Visual, Carlton VIC, 1986).
The Last Great Cattle Drive (Film Australia, Lindfield NSW, 1988).
The Rise of the Crocodile (Sorena Pty Ltd, Sydney, 1988).

ENVIRONMENTAL ISSUES

Australian Council of National Trusts, *Save the Bush* (Canberra, 1990).
Australian Heritage Commission, *Australia's National Estate* (Canberra, 1985).
Australian Heritage Commission, *The Heritage of Australia: The Illustrated Register of the National Estate* (Melbourne, 1981).
Bates, G. M., *Environmental Law in Australia* (Sydney, 1983).
Bolton, G., *Spoils and Spoilers* (2nd edn, Sydney, 1993).
Castles, I., *Australia's Environment: Issues and Facts* (Canberra, 1992).
Mather, G. and Laurence, C., *Managing Your Urban Bushland: A Guide for Urban Councils* (Sydney, 1993).
Mulvaney, D.J. (ed.), *The Humanities and the Australian Environment* (Canberra, 1981).
Sagazio, C. (ed.), *The National Trust Research Manual* (Sydney, 1992).

Smith, B., *Documents on Art and Taste in Australia: The Colonial Period 1770–1914* (Melbourne, 1975).

Video recording
The Charge of the Greens: Green Thinking, Green Politics and Green Issues (Video Education Australasia, Bendigo VIC, c. 1991).

WORLD HERITAGE

Masterworks of Man and Nature: Preserving our World Heritage (Sydney/London 1992).

Information kit
World Heritage (Department of the Environment, Sport and Territories, G.P.O. Box 787, Canberra ACT 2601).

The Aboriginal heritage

PREHISTORY TO 1788

Flood, J., *Archaeology of the Dreamtime* (Sydney, 1982).
Godden, E. and Malnic, J., *Rock Paintings of Aboriginal Australia* (Sydney, 1982; rev. edn, New Haven, Conn., 1990).
Layton, R., *Australian Rock Art: A New Synthesis* (Sydney 1992).
Mulvaney, D. J., *The Prehistory of Australia* (London, 1975).
Mulvaney, D. J. and White, J. P. (eds.), *Australians to 1788* (Sydney, 1987).
White, J. P. and O'Connell, J. F., *A Prehistory of Australia, New Guinea and Sahul* (Sydney, 1982).

Video recording
Dreamings: The Art of Aboriginal Australia (Film Australia, Sydney 1988).

SOCIAL ORGANISATION

Bell, D., *Daughters of the Dreaming* (Melbourne, 1983).
Berndt, R. M. and Tonkinson, R. (eds.), *Social Anthropology and Australian Aboriginal Studies* (Canberra 1988).
Hiatt, L., *Kinship and Conflict* (Canberra, 1965).
Keast A. (ed.), *Ecological Biogeography of Australia* (The Hague, W. Junk, 1817–52 (1983)).
Maddock, K., *The Australian Aborigines: A Portrait of their Society* (London, 1972).
Myers, F. R., *Pintupi Country, Pintupi Self* (Washington DC, 1986).
Pring, A. (ed.), *Women of the Centre* (Apollo Bay VIC, 1990).
Spencer, B. and Gillen, F. J., *The Native Tribes of Central Australia* (London 1899).
Stanner, W. E. H., 'Aboriginal Territorial Organisation: Estate, Range, Domain and Regime', *Oceania* 36:1–25 (1965).
Tonkinson, R., *Living the Dream in Australia's Western Desert* (New York, 1978).

Video recordings
Sing Loud, Play Strong (video recording of festival of Aboriginal rock music, Central Australian Aboriginal Media Association, Alice Springs NT, 1988).
Ways of Thinking (video recording of the Walpiri community of Central Australia, Ronin Films, Sydney, c. 1990).

RELIGION

Berndt, R. M., *Australian Aboriginal Religion* (Leiden, 1974).
Harris, J., *One Blood: Two Hundred Years of Aboriginal Encounter with Christianity* (Sutherland NSW, 1990).
Kolig, E., *The Silent Revolution: The Effect of Modernization on Australian Aboriginal Religion* (Philadelphia, 1981).
Morphy, H., *Journey to the Crocodile's Nest* (Canberra, 1984).
Morphy, H., *Ancestral Connections* (Chicago, 1991).
Moyle, R., *Songs of the Pintubi* (Canberra, 1979).
Stanner, W. E. H., *On Aboriginal Religion*, (Sydney, 1963).

History since European contact

1770–1850

Blainey, G. *Our Side of the Country. The Story of Victoria* (Hawthorn VIC, 1984).

Burroughs, P., *Britain and Australia 1831–1855* (Oxford, 1967).

Cameron, J. M. R., *Ambition's Fire. The Agricultural Colonisation of Pre-Convict Western Australia* (Nedlands WA, 1981).

Connell, R. W. and Irving, T. H., *Class Structure in Australian History* (Melbourne, 1980).

Crowley, F. (ed.), *A New History of Australia* (Melbourne, 1974).

Fletcher, B., *Colonial Australia before 1850* (Melbourne, 1976).

Kociumbas, J. *Oxford History of Australia*, Vol. 2 (South Melbourne, 1992)

Martin, G. (ed.), *The Founding of Australia* (Sydney, 1978).

Nicholas, S. (ed.), *Convict Workers: Reinterpreting Australia's Past* (Cambridge, 1988).

Pike, D., *Paradise of Assent, South Australia 1829–1857* (Melbourne, 1967).

Reynolds, H., *The Other Side of the Frontier* (North Queensland, 1981).

Robinson, P., *The Women of Botany Bay* (Sydney, 1993).

Robson, L., *A History of Tasmania*, Vol. 1 (Melbourne, 1983).

Shaw, A. G. L., *Convicts and the Colonies* (London, 1966).

Sturma, M., *Vice in a Vicious Society* (St Lucia QLD, 1983).

Video recording
Elizabeth Macarthur: A Great Pioneer (Equality Videos, Prahran VIC, 1992).

Audiocassettes
Bound for Botany Bay: A Journal of the First Fleet (2 cassettes, Australian Broadcasting Corportation, Sydney, c. 1987–88).

1850–1900

Clark, M., *A Short History of Australia* (2nd edn, South Melbourne, 1981).

Clark, M., *The Ashton Scholastic History of Australia* (Sydney, 1988).

Clarke, F. G., *Australia: A Concise Political and Social History* (Sydney, 1992).

Foss, P. (ed.), *Island in the Stream: Myths of Place in Australian Culture* (Sydney, 1988).

Hughes, R., *The Fatal Shore: A History of the Transportation of Convicts to Australia 1787–1868* (London, 1987).

Molony, J., *The Penguin Bicentennial History of Australia* (Ringwood VIC, 1987).

Video recording
Beginnings with Thomas Keneally (British Broadcasting Corporation London, 1987).

AUSTRALIA IN THE WORLD WARS

Alcorta, Frank X., *Australia's Frontline: The Northern Territory's War* (North Sydney, 1991).

Alford, R. N., *Darwin's Air War: 1942–45, an Illustrated History* (Darwin, 1991).

Bean, C. E. W. (ed.), *Official History of Australia in the War of 1914–18* (12 vols, Sydney, 1921–42).

Bean, C. E. W., *Anzac to Amiens* (Canberra, 1961).

Butler, A. G. (ed.), *Official History of the Australian Medical Services, 1914–18* (3 vols, Canberra, 1937–43).

Connell, D., *The War at Home* (Sydney, 1988).

Hall, R. A., *The Black Diggers: Aborigines and Torres Strait Islanders in the Second World War* (Sydney, 1989).

Hardisty, S. (ed.), *Thanks Girls and Goodbye! The Story of the Australian Women's Land Army 1942–45* (Ringwood VIC, 1990).

Long, G., *The Six Years War* (Canberra, 1973).

Long, G. (ed.), *Official History of Australia in the War of 1939–45* (22 vols, Canberra, 1952–77).

McKernan, M., *The Australian People and the Great War* (Sydney, 1980).

McKernan, M., *All In! Australia During the Second World War* (Melbourne, 1983).

McKernan, M. and Browne, M. (eds.), *Australia: Two Centuries of War and Peace* (Canberra, 1988).

Robertson, John, *Australia Goes to War* (Sydney, 1984).

Smith, H. and Moss, S. (eds.), *A Bibliography of Armed Forces and Society in Australia* (Canberra, 1987).

Video recordings
Gallipoli, the Fatal Shore (Australian Broadcasting Corporation, Sydney, 1990).
Thanks Girls and Goodbye! (Newground Productions/Film, Victoria 1988).

AUSTRALIA SINCE 1945

Bolton, G., *The Oxford History of Australia*, Vol. 5 (Melbourne, 1990).

Crowley, F., *Modern Australia 1939–70. A Documentary History of Australia*, Vol. 5 (Melbourne, 1973).

Jupp, J. (ed.), *The Australian People* (North Ryde NSW, 1988).

McQueen, H., *Social Sketches of Australia* (Harmondsworth, 1978).

The Chifley Government
Crisp, L. F., *Ben Chifley: A Biography* (London, 1960).

May, A. L., *The Battle for the Banks* (Sydney, 1968).

Millar, T. B., *Australia in Peace and War* (Canberra, 1978).

The Menzies Years
Menzies, R. G., *Afternoon Light* (Melbourne, 1967).

Menzies, R. G., *The Measure of the Years* (Melbourne, 1970).

Murray, R., *The Split. Australian Labor in the Fifties* (Melbourne, 1970).

Simms, M., *A Liberal Nation. The Liberal Party and Australian Politics* (Sydney, 1982).

The Liberals in decline
Colman, P., *Obscenity, Blasphemy and Sedition* (Sydney, 1974).

Frost, F., *Australia's War in Vietnam* (Sydney, 1987).

Pemberton, G. (ed.), *Vietnam Remembered* (Sydney, 1990).

Whitlam and Fraser
Horne, D., *A Time of Hope* (Sydney, 1980).

Oakes, L. and Solomon, D., *The Making of an Australian Prime Minister* (Melbourne, 1984).

Whitlam, E. G., *The Whitlam Government, 1972–75* (Ringwood VIC, 1985)

Labor's return
d'Alpuget, B., *Robert J. Hawke* (Ringwood VIC, 1984).

Arnold, J., Spearritt P. and Walker, D. (eds.), *Out of Empire* (Melbourne, 1993).

Brennan, F., *Sharing the Country* (Ringwood VIC, 1991).

Carew, E., *Paul Keating, Prime Minister* (North Sydney, 1992).

Kelly, P., *The Hawke Ascendancy* (London, 1984).

Kelly, P., *The End of Certainty. The Story of the 1980s* (St Leonards VIC, 1992).

Maddox, G., *The Hawke Government and Labor Tradition* (Ringwood VIC, 1989).

ABORIGINAL–EUROPEAN RELATIONS

Gilbert, K. (ed.), *Living Black* (Ringwood VIC, 1978).

Mattingley, C. and Hampton, K. (eds.), *Survival in Our Own Land* (Adelaide, 1988).

Read, P., *Charles Perkins: A Biography* (Ringwood VIC, 1990).

Reynolds, H., *The Law of the Land* (Ringwood VIC, 1987).

Rose, D., *Hidden Histories* (Canberra, 1991).

Government

FINANCING FEDERALISM

Brennan, G. et al., *Taxation and Fiscal Federalism* (Canberra, 1988).

Commonwealth of Australia, *Commonwealth Financial Relations with Other Levels of Government* (annual series, Canberra).

Drysdale, P. and Shibata, H. (eds.), *Federalism and Resource Development: The Australian Case* (Sydney, 1985).

Mathews, R. L. and Jay, W. R. C., *Federal Finance* (Melbourne, 1972).

THE LEGAL SYSTEM

Allars, M., *Introduction to Australian Administrative Law* (Sydney, 1990).
Castles, A. C., *An Australian Legal History* (Sydney, 1982).
Crawford, J., *Australian Courts of Law* (2nd edn, Melbourne 1988).
Lane, P. H., *An Introduction to the Australian Constitution* (5th edn, Sydney, 1990).
Reynolds, H., *The Law of the Land* (Ringwood VIC, 1987).

Video recording
Warriors and Lawmen (examines Aboriginal/European law, Focal Video, Sydney, 1985).

The Economy

1890–1945

Boehm, E. A., *Twentieth Century Economic Development in Australia* (Melbourne, 1979).
Lowenstein, W., *Weevils in the Flow: An Oral Record of the 1930s Depression in Australia* (South Yarra VIC, 1978).
Maddock, R. and McLean, I., *The Australian Economy in the Long Run* (New York, 1987).
Schedvin, C. B., *Australia and the Great Depression* (Sydney, 1970).

Video recording
Bread and Dripping (Wimins Films/Australian Film Commission, 1981).

Audiocassette
Stony Broke and Walking: They Said You'd Own Your Own Farm (1 cassette, Australian Broadcasting Corporation, Sydney,1991).

MANUFACTURING INDUSTRY

Forsyth, P. (ed.), *Microeconomic Reform in Australia* (Sydney, 1992).
Industry Commission, *Annual Report 1991–92* (Canberra,1992).
Terry, C., Jones R. and Braddock, R., *Australian Microeconomic Policies* (3rd edn, Sydney, 1988).

AGRICULTURE

Australian Bureau of Agricultural and Resource Economics, *National Agricultural Outlook Conference* (Canberra, 1993); *Quarterly Review of the Rural Economy* (various issues, 1990–93); *Rural Industry in Australia* (Canberra, 1983).
Campbell, K. O. and Fisher, B. S., *Agricultural Marketing and Prices* (3rd edn, Melbourne, 1991).
Chisholm, A. H. and Dumsday, R. G., *Land Degradation: Problems and Policies* (Cambridge, 1987).
National Farmers Federation, *Australian Agriculture – the Complete Reference on Rural Industry* (3rd edn, VIC,1991/92).
Williams, D. B. (ed.), *Agriculture in the Australian Economy* (Sydney, 1990).

Video recording
Wheat Today, What Tomorrow? (Environment Audio Visuals, Castlemaine VIC, c. 1987).

THE MINERALS AND ENERGY SECTOR

Collis, B., *Snowy: The Making of Modern Australia* (Sydney, 1990).
Unger, M., *Voices from the Snowy* (Kensington NSW, 1989).

Video recordings
The Snowy: A Dream of Growing Up (Film Australia, Lindfield NSW, c. 1989).
The Power of Water: Building the Snowy Scheme (Film Australia, Lindfield NSW, c. 1991).

TRANSPORT

AR Publishing, *Aviation Report: Weekly News and Analysis of Aviation Business, Policy and Technology in the Australian Region* (Sydney, 1990–).

Audiocassettes
Apple Computer Australia, *The Opinion-makers Forum, March 1992* (1 cassette, Frenchs Forest NSW, 1992).
Rag, Sticks and Wire: A Social History of Australian Aviation (4 cassettes, Australian Broadcasting Corporation, Sydney, c. 1990).

BANKING AND FINANCE

Australian Financial System Inquiry, *Final Report* (Canberra, 1981).
Carew, E., *Fast Money 3: The Financial Markets in Australia* (Sydney, 1991).
House of Representatives Standing Committee on Finance and Public Administration, *A Pocket Full of Change* (Canberra, 1991).
Kennedy, B. and Kennedy, B., *Australian Money* (Sydney, 1987).
Lewis, M. K. and Wallace, R. H. (eds.), *The Australian Financial System* (Melbourne, 1993).
Valentine, T. J. *Interest Rates and Money Markets in Australia* (Sydney, 1991).

TRADE RELATIONS

Video recording
Australian Trade Commission, *Overseas and Undersold: Developing Australia's Export Culture: China* (Film Australia, Lindfield NSW, 1988).

Society

POPULATION

Castles, I., *Year Book Australia*, No. 71, Chapter 6, pp. 253–91 (Canberra, 1988).
Day, L. H. and Rowland, D. T. (eds.), *How Many More Australians? The Resource and Environmental Conflicts* (Melbourne, 1988).
Gray, A., 'Some Myths in the Demography of Aboriginal Australians', *Journal of the Australian Population Association*, (1985) 136–49.
Hugo, G., *Australia's Changing Population* (Melbourne, 1986).
National Population Inquiry, *Population and Australia: A Demographic Analysis and Projection* (first main report of the National Population Inquiry, Canberra, 1975).
Rowland, D. T., *Ageing in Australia: Population Trends and Social Issues* (Melbourne, 1992).
Ruzicka, L. and Caldwell, J., *The End of Demographic Transition in Australia* (Canberra, 1977).
Jing Shu and Siew Ean Khoo, *Australia's Population Trends and Prospects 1992* (Canberra, 1993).

LANGUAGE

Collins, P. and Blair, D. (eds.), *Australian English. The Language of a New Society* (Brisbane, 1989).
Blake, B. J., *Australian Aboriginal Languages* (Sydney, 1981).
Bradley, D. and Bradley, M., *English in Australia* (Melbourne, 1984).
Clyne, M. G., *Community Languages*. The Australian Experience (Cambridge, 1991).
Delbridge, A. *et al.* (eds.), *The Macquarie Dictionary* (2nd edn, Sydney 1991).
Dixon, R. M. W., *The Languages of Australia* (Cambridge,1980).
Dixon, R. M. W., *Australian Aboriginal Words in English: Their Origin and Meaning* (Melbourne, 1990).
Horvath, B. M., *Variation in Australian English* (Cambridge, 1985).
Lo Bianco, J., *National Policy on Languages* (Canberra, 1987).
Mitchell, A. G. and Delbridge, A., *The Pronunciation of English in Australia* (Sydney, 1965).
Torre, S., *The Macquarie Dictionary of Australian Quotations* (Sydney, 1990).

VALUES

Clark, M., *A Short History of Australia* (London, 1987).

Connell, R. W. and Irving, T. H., *Class Structure in Australian History* (2nd edn, Melbourne, 1992).

Encel, S., *Equality and Authority: A Study of Class, Status and Power in Australia* (Melbourne, 1970).

Encel, S., *Out of the Doll's House: Women in the Public Sphere* (Melbourne, 1991).

Horne, D., *Money Made Us* (Ringwood VIC, 1976).

Hughes, R., *The Fatal Shore* (London, 1987).

Mackay, H., *Being Australian* (Chatswood NSW, 1988).

Mackay, H., *The Australian Dream* (Lindfield NSW, 1990).

Mackay, H., *Reinventing Australia: The Mind and Mood of Australia in the Nineties* (Sydney, 1993).

Video recording
Beliefs, Values and Customs (for secondary school students, Film Australia, Sydney, c. 1987).

RURAL–URBAN DIFFERENCES

Costar, B. and Woodward, D., *Country to National: Australian Rural Politics and Beyond* (Sydney, 1985).

Craig, R. A., 'Maintaining the Peripheral Workforce – the Role of Ideology in Family Farming in Australia' (Annual Conference of the British Sociological Association, Cardiff, Wales, 1983).

Encel, S. and Berry, M. (eds.), *Selected Readings in Australian Society* (Melbourne, 1987).

Kelly, S., 'City Folk, Country Folk: Demographic and Attitudinal Urban–Rural Differences', *Family Matters*, 24 (1987), 43–5.

Lawrence, G., *Capitalism and the Countryside: The Rural Crisis in Australia* (Sydney, 1987).

New South Wales Women's Advisory Council, *Women on the Land* (Sydney, 1985).

Van Dugteren, T. (ed.), *Rural Australia: The Other Nation* (Sydney, 1978).

MULTICULTURALISM

Australian Council on Population and Ethnic Affairs, *Multiculturalism for all Australians* (Canberra, 1982).

Australian Ethnic Affairs Council, *Australia as a Multicultural Society* (Canberra, 1977).

Dare, T., *Australia: A Nation of Immigrants* (rev. edn, Frenchs Forest NSW, 1988).

Dugan, M. and Szwarc, J., *'There Goes the Neighbourhood!' Australia's Migrant Experience* (Melbourne, 1984).

Foster, L. and Stockley, D., *Multiculturalism: The Changing Australian Paradigm* (Melbourne, 1984).

Foster, L. and Stockley, D., *Australian Multiculturalism: A Documentary History and Critique* (Melbourne, 1988).

Jupp, J. (ed.), *Ethnic Politics in Australia* (Sydney, 1984).

Martin, J. I., *The Migrant Presence: Australian Responses 1947–1977* (Sydney, 1978).

Wilton, J. and Bosworth, R., *Old Worlds and New Australia* (Ringwood VIC, 1984).

Video recordings
Immigration: The Waves that Shaped Australia (Film Australia, Lindfield NSW).

The Last Dream: A Special Report by John Pilger (3 video recordings, Central Independent Television (UK)/Australian Broadcasting Corporation, 1988).

HEALTH

Australian Institute of Health and Welfare, *Australia's Health* (Canberra, 1992).

Bates, F. and Linder-Pelz, S., *Health Care Issues* (Sydney, 1987).

Better Health Commission, *Looking Forward to Better Health* (3 vols, Canberra, 1986).

Broadhead, P., 'Social Status and Morbidity in Australia', *Community Health Studies* 9 (2): 87–98 (1985).

Broom, D., *Damned If We Do: Contradictions in Women's Health Care* (North Sydney, 1991).

Crichton, A., *Slowly Taking Control? Australian Governments and Health Care Provision 1788–1988* (Sydney, 1990).

Davis, A. and George, J., *States of Health: Health and Illness in Australia* (2nd edn, Sydney, 1993)

Hill, S. *et al.*, *Where the Health Dollar Goes* (Melbourne, 1988).

Lee, S. H. *et al.*, *Health Differentials for Working Age Australians* (Canberra, 1987).

McMichael, A. J., 'Social Class and Mortality in Australian Males', *Community Health Studies* 9 (3): 220–30 (1985).

O'Leary, T., *North and Aloft: A Personal Memoir of Service and Adventure with the Flying Doctor Service in Far Northern Australia* (Brisbane, 1988).

Pearn, J. (ed.), *Pioneer Medicine in Australia* (Brisbane, 1988).

Tatchell, M. (ed.), *Perspectives on Health Policy* (Canberra, 1984).

Thomson, N. J., 'Assessment of Aboriginal Health Status' (National Medical Research Council/Menzies Foundation Workshop: Research Priorities to Improve Aboriginal Health, Alice Springs, 1986).

Video recording
Getting Better (Corroboree Films, Randwick NSW, c. 1987).

Audiocassettes
Your Health Rights (6 cassettes, Australian Consumers' Association, South Yarra VIC, 1991).

EDUCATION

Alice Springs School of the Air, *Welcome to the Alice Springs School of the Air* (Alice Springs NT).

Department of Employment, Education and Training (DEET), *Education at a Glance* (Canberra, 1988).

Department of Employment, Education and Training (DEET), *Higher Education in Australia* (Canberra, 1993).

Karmel, P. H., 'Trends in Australian Education 1970–1985', *International Journal of Educational Research*, 2: 127–36 (1988).

Saha, L. J. and Keeves, J. P. (eds.), *Schooling and Society in Australia: Sociological Perspectives* (Canberra, 1990).

Tardif, R. (ed.), *The Penguin Dictionary of Australian Education* (Sydney, 1989).

Yates, L., *The Education of Girls: Policy Research and the Question of Gender* (Melbourne, 1993).

THE MEDIA

Chadwick, P., *Media Mates: Carving up Australia's Media* (Melbourne, 1989).

Communications Update (Communications Law Centre, P.O. Box 1, Kensington NSW 2033).

Cunningham, S. and Turner, G. (eds.), *The Media in Australia: Industries, Texts, Audiences* (Sydney, 1993).

Gee, M., *Media Guide*, annual (45 Flinders Lane, Melbourne).

Media Information Australia, quarterly (Australian Film and Television School, 13–15 Lyon Park Road, North Ryde NSW 2113).

Media Watch (Journal of the Institute of Public affairs (NSW), 56 Young Street, Sydney NSW 2000).

Shawcross, W., *Rupert Murdoch: Ringmaster of the Information Circus* (London, 1992, rev. edn. 1993).

CHILD CARE

Bessant, B. (ed.), *Mother State and Her Little Ones: Children and Youth in Australia 1860s–1930s* (Melbourne, 1987).

Brennan, D., *Towards a National Child Care Policy* (Melbourne, 1982).

Brennan, D., *The Politics of Australian Child Care: From Philanthropy to Feminism* (Cambridge/Melbourne, forthcoming).

Brennan, D. and O'Donnell, C., *Caring for Australia's Children: Political and Industrial Issues in Child Care* (Sydney, 1986).

Langford, P. and Sebastian, P. (eds.), *Early Childhood Education and Care in Australia* (Kew VIC, 1979).

Wearing, B., *The Ideology of Motherhood* (Sydney, 1984).

Video recording
Quality Affordable Child Care Australia-wide (Interim National Child Care Accreditation Council, Sydney, 1992).

UNEMPLOYMENT

Cass, B., 'Income Support for the Unemployed in Australia:

Towards a More Active System', Issues Paper No. 4 of the Social Security Review (Canberra, 1988).

Corden, W. M., *The Wages Push and Macroeconomic policy: The Dilemmas Ahead* (Canberra, 1982).

Jones, B., *Sleepers, Wake! Technology and the Future of Work* (Melbourne, 1982).

Senate Standing Committee on Employment, Education and Training, *Wanted: Our Future. Report into the Implications of Sustained High Levels of Unemployment Among Young People* (Canberra, 1992).

Wheelwright, E. L. and Buckley, K. (eds.), *Essays in the Political Economy of Australian Capitalism*, Vol. 4 (Sydney, 1980).

Video recording
Work (for secondary school students, Film Australia, Lindfield NSW, c. 1986).

THE TRADE UNIONS

Creighton, W. B. *et al.*, *Labour Law* (Sydney, 1983).

Kitay, G. B. and Powe, P., 'Exploitation at $1,000 per Week? The Mudginberri Dispute', *The Journal of Industrial Relations* (1987).

Martin, R. M., *Trade Unions in Australia* (Ringwood VIC, 1980).

Plowman, D. *et al.*, *Australian Industrial Relations* (rev. edn, Sydney, 1981).

Rawson, D. W., *Unions and Unionists in Australia* (Sydney, 1978).

Rawson, D. W. and Wrightson, S., *Australian Unions 1984* (Sydney, 1985).

Simms, M., *Militant Public Servants* (Sydney, 1987).

Smith, R., *Politics in Australia* (Sydney, 1993).

Stilwell, F., *The Accord and Beyond* (London, 1986).

EQUAL OPPORTUNITY LEGISLATION

Affirmative Action Agency, *Annual Reports* (Canberra, 1989–).

House of Representatives Standing Committee on Legal and Constitutional Affairs, *Half Way to Equal: Report of Inquiry into Equal Opportunity and Equal Status for Australian Women* (Canberra, 1992).

Video recordings
A Fair Go For All (Television Makers, Sydney, 1989).

Getting it Right: Good Human Resource Management (FM–TV Australia for Equal Employment Opportunity Trust, 1988).

Hats in the Ring (Municipal Association of Victoria, c. 1988).

Implementing EEO in Local Government (Department of Local Government, NSW, 1988).

The Sikh Hat Trick: For General Staff (University of Melbourne Equal Opportunity Unit, Parkville VIC, c. 1987).

SOCIO-ECONOMIC INEQUALITY

Broom, D. H., *Unfinished Business: Social Justice for Women in Australia* (Sydney, 1984).

Collins, J., *Migrants in a Distant Land: Australian Post-war Immigration* (Sydney, 1988).

Connell, R. W. and Irving, T. H., *Class Structure in Australian History* (Melbourne, 1980).

Jamrozik, A., *Class, Inequality and the State: Social Change, Social Policy and the New Middle Class* (South Melbourne, 1991).

Jennett, C. and Stewart, R. G., *Three Worlds of Inequality: Race, Class and Gender* (South Melbourne, 1987).

Miller, J., *Koori: A Will to Win* (London, 1985).

O'Leary, J. and Sharp, R. (eds.), *Inequality in Australia: Slicing the Cake, the Social Justice Collective* (Port Melbourne, 1991).

Pettman, J., *Living in the Margins: Racism, Sexism and Feminism in Australia* (North Sydney, 1992).

Sawer, M. and Simms, M., *A Woman's Place* (2nd edn, North Sydney, 1992).

Video recording
Women 88 (Overview of women's achievements in various fields, Film Australia, Lindfield NSW, 1987).

Science and technology

THE ORIGIN AND DEVELOPMENT OF SCIENCE

Moyal, A., *A Bright and Savage Land: Science in Colonial Australia* (Sydney, 1986).

Todd, J., 'Science at the Periphery: An Interpretation of Australian Scientific and Technological Dependency and Development Prior to 1914', *Annals of Science*, 50: 33–58 (1993).

GEOLOGY AND BIOLOGY

Branagan, D. F. and Townley, K. A., 'The Geological Sciences in Australia – a Brief Historical Review', *Earth Science Reviews*, 12: 323–46 (1976).

Carr, D. J. and Carr, S. G. M. (eds.), *Plants and Man in Australia* (Sydney, 1981).

Grenfell Price, A., *Island Continent* (Sydney, 1972).

Stanbury, P. and Phipps, G., *Australia's Animals Discovered* (Sydney, 1980).

MacLeod, R. (ed.), *The Commonwealth of Science* (Melbourne, 1988).

Vallance, T. G., 'Origins of Australian Geology', *Proc. Linn. Soc. NSW*, 100: 13–43 (1975).

ANTARCTICA

Fifield, R., *International Research in the Antarctic* (Oxford, 1987).

Lovering, J. F. and Prescott, J. R. V., *Last of Lands – Antarctica* (Melbourne, 1979).

Parsons, A., *Antarctica: The Next Decade* (Cambridge, 1987).

Reader's Digest, *Antarctica: Great Stories from the Frozen Continent* (2nd edn, Sydney, 1990).

Swan, R. A., *Australia in the Antarctic* (Melbourne, 1961).

Triggs, G. (ed.), *The Antarctic Treaty Regime* (Cambridge, 1987).

Walton, D. W. H. (ed.), *Antarctic Science* (Cambridge, 1987).

GENERAL

Encel, V., *Australian Genius: Fifty Great Ideas* (Sydney, 1988).

Video recording
Desperately Seeking Solutions (Film Australia, Lindfield NSW, 1987).

Culture and the arts

CRAFTS

Cochrane, G., *The Crafts Movement in Australia: A History* (Sydney, 1992).

Ioannou, N. (ed.), *Craft in Society: An Anthology of Perspectives* (Fremantle WA, 1992).

Isaacs, J., *The Gentle Arts: Two Hundred Years of Women's Domestic and Decorative Arts* (Sydney, 1987).

Timms, P., *Australian Studio Pottery and China Painting* (Melbourne, 1986).

Zimmer, J., *Stained Glass in Australia* (Melbourne, 1984).

ARCHITECTURE

Boyd, R., *Australia's Home* (Melbourne, 1962).

Fraser, M. *et al.*, *The Heritage of Australia* (South Melbourne, 1981).

Freeland, J. M., *Architecture in Australia* (Melbourne, 1967).

Haddon, R., *Australian Architecture* (Melbourne, 1908).

Herman, M., *The Early Australian Architects and their Work* (Sydney, 1954).

Irving, R. (ed.), *The History and Design of the Australian House* (Melbourne, 1985).

Johnson, D. L., *Australian Architecture 1901–1951* (Sydney, 1980).

Lewis, M., *Victorian Primitive* (Melbourne, 1977).

Video recording
Mind Made (Pepper Audiovisual/South Australian Film Corporation, 1978).

FINE ART

Burn, I. *et al.*, *The Necessity of Australian Art* (Sydney, 1988).

Chanin, E. (ed.), *Contemporary Australian Painting* (Sydney, 1990).

Eisler, W. and Smith, B., *Terra Australis, the Furthest Shore* (Sydney, 1988).

Kerr, J. (ed.), *The Dictionary of Australian Artists: Painters, Sketchers, Photographers and Engravers to 1870* (Melbourne, 1992).

McCormick, T., *First Views of Australia 1788–1825* (Sydney, 1987).

Newton, G. F., *Shades of Light: Photography and Australia 1839–1988* (Canberra, 1987).

Pike, A. and Cooper, R., *Australian Film 1900–1977* (Melbourne, 1980).

Scarlett, K., *Australian Sculptors* (Melbourne, 1980).

Smith, B., *European Vision and the South Pacific* (Melbourne, 1959, 2nd edn Sydney, 1984).

Smith, B., *Australian Painting 1788–1970* (Melbourne, 1962, 2nd edn, 1971, additional chapters on painting 1970 to 1990 by T. Smith, Melbourne 1991).

Sturgeon, G., *The Development of Australian Sculpture 1788–1975* (London, 1978).

Sturgeon, G., *Contemporary Australian Sculpture* (Sydney, 1991).

Sutton, P. (ed.), *Dreamings: The Art of Aboriginal Australia* (New York, 1988).

Thomas, D. (ed.), *Creating Australia: Two Hundred Years of Art 1788–1988* (Sydney, 1988).

White, R., *Inventing Australia. Images and Identity 1688–1980* (Sydney, 1981).

Willis, A. M., *Picturing Australia: A History of Photography* (Sydney, 1988).

Video recording
Contemporary Painting 1950–1979 (Film Australia, Lindfield NSW, 1989).

LITERATURE

Critical studies

Berndt, R. M. and Berndt, C. H., *The Speaking Land: Myth and Story in Aboriginal Australia* (Ringwood VIC, 1989).

Dutton, G. (ed.), *The Literature of Australia* (rev. edn, 1976).

Fitzpatrick, P., *After 'The Doll': Australian Drama Since 1955* (London, 1979).

Green, H. M., *A History of Australian Literature* (rev. by D. Green, 2 vols, London, 1984).

Healy, J. J., *Literature and the Aborigine in Australia* (2nd edn, St Lucia QLD, 1989).

Hergenhan, L. (ed.), *The Penguin New Literary History of Australia* (Ringwood, VIC, 1988).

Kramer, L. (ed.), *The Oxford History of Australian Literature* (Melbourne/Oxford, 1981).

Wilde, W. H., Hooton J. and Andrews, B., *The Oxford Companion to Australian Literature* (Melbourne/Oxford, 1985).

Anthologies

Davis, J. *et al.*, *Paperbark: A Collection of Black Australian Writings* (1990).

Heseltine, H. (ed.), *The Penguin Book of Australian Verse* (Harmondsworth/Ringwood VIC, 1972).

Heseltine, H. (ed.), *The Penguin Book of Modern Australian Verse* (Ringwood VIC, 1981).

Kramer, L. and Mitchell, A. (eds.), *The Oxford Anthology of Australian Literature* (Melbourne/Oxford, 1985).

Murray, L. A. (ed.), *The New Oxford Book of Australian Verse* (Oxford, 1986).

Wallace-Crabbe, C. (ed.), *The Golden Apples of the Sun: Twentieth-Century Australian Poetry* (Melbourne, 1980).

Video recording
Australian Literature: A Discussion with Dame Leonie Kramer and Tang Zhengqiu (University of Sydney, Department of English, 1987).

THEATRE

Brisbane, K. (ed.), *Entertaining Australia* (Sydney, 1991).

Carroll, D., *Australian Contemporary Drama 1909–1982* (Berne, 1985).

Holloway, P. (ed.), *Contemporary Australian Drama* (rev. edn, Sydney, 1987).

Irvin, E., *Australian Melodrama, Eighty Years of Popular Theatre* (Sydney, 1981).

Irvin, E., *Dictionary of Australian Theatre 1788–1914* (Sydney, 1985).

Love , H. (ed.), *The Australian Stage, a Documentary History* (Sydney, 1984).

Parsons, P. and Chance, V., *A Companion to Theatre in Australia* (Sydney, 1993).

Radic, L., *The State of the Play* (Ringwood VIC, 1991).

Rees, L., *A History of Australian Drama* (2 vols, Sydney, 1978).

Tait, V., *A Family of Brothers* (Melbourne, 1971).

Thorne, R., *Theatre Buildings in Australia to 1905* (2 vols, Sydney, 1971).

West, J., *Theatre in Australia* (Sydney, 1978).

Williams, M., *Australia on the Popular Stage 1829–1929* (Melbourne, 1983).

MUSIC

Atherton, M., *Australian Made; Australian Played* (Sydney, 1990).

Covell, R., *Australia's Music: Themes for a New Society* (Melbourne, 1967).

Johnson, B., *The Oxford Companion to Australian Jazz* (Melbourne, 1987).

Love, H., *The Golden Age of Australian Opera* (Sydney, 1981).

BROADCASTING

Bertrand, I. (ed.), *Cinema in Australia: A Documentary History* (Sydney, 1989).

Bridges, N., *Wonderful Wireless* (Sydney, 1983).

Hall, K. G., *Australian Film: The Inside Story* (Sydney, 1980)

Kent, I., *Out of the Bakelite Box* (Sydney, 1983).

Long, J. and Long, M., *The Pictures that Moved – a Picture History of the Australian Cinema 1896–1929* (Melbourne, 1982).

Moran, A. and O'Regan T. (eds.), *The Australian Screen* (Ringwood VIC, 1989).

Pike, A. and Cooper, R., *Australian Film 1900–1977* (Melbourne, 1980).

Shirley, G. and Adams, B., *Australian Cinema: The First Eight Years* (Sydney, 1983).

Stratton, D., *The Avocado Plantation* (Sydney, 1991).

Video recordings
The Cinema of Charles Chauvel (Australian Film and Television School, Sydney, 1982).

Tony Buckley (interview with film producer, Australian Film and Television School, Sydney, 1986).

Television series
The Australian Image (produced by N. Hildyard and R. Edmondson, Australian Capital Television, 1988).

POPULAR ENTERTAINMENT

Fotheringham, R. (ed.), *Community Theatre in Australia* (Sydney, 1992).

McGregor, C., *The Australian People* (Sydney, 1980).

St Leon, M., *Spangles and Sawdust – the Circus in Australia* (Melbourne, 1983).

Video recording
Amazing Scenes: A Look at Some Australian Fringe Theatre (Film Australia, Lindfield NSW, *c.* 1980).

SPORT

Pollard, J., *Australian Cricket* (Sydney, 1982).

Pollard, J., *Australian Rugby Union* (Sydney, 1984).

Vamplew, W. *et al.*, *The Oxford Companion to Australian Sport* (Melbourne, 1992).

Vamplew, W. and Stoddart, B., *Sport in Australia: A Social History* (Cambridge, forthcoming).

Index

Every effort has been made to obtain permission for use of the photographic material listed below; if any errors or omissions have occurred the publishers would welcome these being brought to their attention.

PHOTOGRAPHS. x, M. K. Guy/V. K. Guy Ltd; 2bl, Cliff. D. Ollier; 2br, John Mason; 3bl, Cliff D. Ollier; 3br, R. F. Isbell; 5b, CRAE Remote Sensing and Image Processing Group, Canberra; 7t, John Mason; 8–9, Ron Ryan/Coo-ee Picture Library; 9b, Ron Ryan/Coo-ee Picture Library; 13t, R. F. Isbell; 15, Ron Ryan/Coo-ee Picture Library; 17b, Snowy Mountains Authority; 18b, R. F. Isbell; 21, main picture, Peter Valentine; inset (tl), Snowy Mountains Authority; inset (bl), Snowy Mountains Authority; inset (tr), Coo-ee Picture Library; inset (br), John Mason; 22, Kathie Atkinson; 23, main picture, Coo-ee Picture Library; 24, CSIRO Division of Wildlife and Ecology; 25t, John Mason; 25b, main picture, Graeme Chapman; inset, John Mason; 26bl, CSIRO Division of Wildlife and Ecology; 26br, 27tl, Coo-ee Picture Library; 27tr, ANT/Natural History Photographic Agency; 27b, Coo-ee Picture Library; 28t, Ron Ryan/Coo-ee Picture Library; 28b, 29, CSIRO Division of Wildlife and Ecology; 31, Coo-ee Picture Library; 33tl, Peter Valentine; 33tr, Michael Trenerry, photographer; 33, main picture and inset, 34, Peter Valentine; 35t, Kathie Atkinson; 35b, Fred Bavendam/Oxford Scientific Films; 38–9, 38t, Kathie Atkinson; 38b, Coo-ee Picture Library; 39t, Kathie Atkinson; 39b, Bill Wood/Bruce Coleman Ltd; 40, 41, Peter Valentine; 42, Elspeth A.Young; 43, Coo-ee Picture Library; 44, main picture and inset, Prof. David Harris, University College London; 45, Ron Ryan/Coo-ee Picture Library; 46, Ron Ryan/Coo-ee Picture Library; 48, Coo-ee Picture Library; 49, Australian Heritage Commission; 50, Ron Ryan/Coo-ee Picture Library; 51, Australian Heritage Commission; 52, Barry Skipsey/Northern Territory Tourist Commission; 53, Cliff D.Ollier; 56, Coo-ee Picture Library; 57, John Mason; 58–9, 60, Kathie Atkinson; 62, 65, 66–7, 67, 68, Coo-ee Historical Picture Library; 72, Kathie Atkinson; 75, Coo-ee Picture Library; 77, 78, Coo-ee Historical Picture Library; 79l, Coo-ee Picture Library; 79r, Kathie Atkinson; 80–1, Mitchell Library/State Library of New South Wales; 82, Rex Nan Kivell Collection/National Library of Australia; 86t, courtesy of the National Portrait Gallery, London; 86b, National Maritime Museum, Greenwich; 87, Coo-ee Historical Picture Library; 88, Historic Houses Trust of New South Wales; 89, Coo-ee Historical Picture Library; 90, National Library of Australia; 91, Tourism Tasmania; 93, Coo-ee Historical Picture Library; 95, Mitchell Library/State Library of New South Wales; 97, Coo-ee Historical Picture Library; 99t, 101, National Library of Australia; 103, Coo-ee Historical Picture Library; 104, Historic Memorials Committee, Parliament House, Canberra; 107, National Capital Planning Authority; 109, National Library of Australia; 110, 111t, Coo-ee Historical Picture Library; 111b, Australian War Memorial; 112, National Capital Planning Authority; 114, National Library of Australia; 115, The Snowy Mountains Hydro-Electric Authority; 117t, Mirror Australian Telegraph Publications; 117b, National Library of Australia; 118, Mirror Australian Telegraph Publications; 120t, The Board of Works, Melbourne, State Government of Victoria; 120b, Coo-ee Historical Picture Library, with the authority and knowledge of Email Ltd; 121, ACP Publishing Pty Ltd; 123t, 123b, National Library of Australia; 124, Ron Ryan/Coo-ee Picture Library; 127, 130, 131, Coo-ee Picture Library; 132, Hon. R. J. Hawke AC; 135, Office of the Prime Minister; 136, Rex Nan Kivell Collection/National Library of Australia; 138, Coo-ee Historical Picture Library;

139, Mitchell Library/State Library of New South Wales; 141, Coo-ee Historical Picture Library; 143, National Library of Australia; 144, Coo-ee Picture Library; 145, Collection, Art Gallery of Western Australia; 146, Peter West/AUSPIC; 149, Hon. Simon Crean; 151, Hon. Andrew Peacock; 152, Senator Bjelke-Petersen; 153, Janine Haines; 154–5, National Capital Planning Authority; 156, Tourism Tasmania; 157 Peter West/AUSPIC; 159t, Reserve Bank of Australia; 159b, National Capital Planning Authority; 161, Peter West/AUSPIC; 162, Coo-ee Historical Picture Library; 164t, Mirror Australian Telegraph Publications; 164b, Elaine Pelot Kitchener; 164-5, Ron Ryan/Coo-ee Picture Library; 166, Coo-ee Picture Library; 168-9, National Library of Australia; 170, Railways of Australia; 171, 172, 174, 175br, Coo-ee Historical Picture Library; 177t, National Library of Australia/Lindsay Estate; 178, David Jones Ltd; 182–3, Coo-ee Picture Library; 184, Qantas; 186, Coo-ee Picture Library; 187, Ron Ryan/Coo-ee Picture Library; 188, Snowy Mountains Authority; 189, Australian Wool Corporation; 192, Kathie Atkinson; 193, 195, The BHP Company Ltd; 196, Snowy Mountains Authority; 197, 198, 200, Coo-ee Picture Library; 202r, State Rail Authority; 207t, Coo-ee Picture Library; 207b, Qantas; 209b, Snowy Mountains Authority; 210, Australia Post; 212, reproduced by courtesy of Telecom Australia; 213, Reserve Bank of Australia; 214, National Australia Bank; 215, National Library of Australia; 218, Andrew Campbell/*Canberra Times*, 18 August 1988; 220, Ron Ryan/Coo-ee Picture Library; 222l, 222r, Coo-ee Picture Library; 223l, 223r, Ron Ryan/Coo-ee Picture Library; 224, New South Wales Government: Department of Planning; 225, Collection: John Oxley Library, Brisbane; 226, National Library of Australia; 228, Ron Ryan/Coo-ee Picture Library; 229, Coo-ee Historical Picture Library; 230, Ron Ryan/Coo-ee Picture Library; 232, New South Wales Government: Department of Planning; 233, M. K. Guy/V. K. Guy Ltd; 235, Hulton Deutsch/Reuters; 236, 237, Ron Ryan/Coo-ee Picture Library; 239, Royal Flying Doctor Service of Australia; 241, Ron Ryan/Coo-ee Picture Library; 242, Kathie Atkinson; 243, Streetwize Comics; 244, Julian C. Liberto, photographer; 245, Royal Flying Doctor Service of Australia; 246, 249, Ron Ryan/Coo-ee Picture Library; 252l, Kathie Atkinson; 252r, Coo-ee Picture Library; 253, 254, 256, Ron Ryan/Coo-ee Picture Library; 257, Coo-ee Historical Picture Library; 259, Mitchell Library/State Library of New South Wales; 260, Ron Ryan/Coo-ee Picture Library; 262, Coo-ee Picture Library; 264, Kathie Atkinson; 265, Peter West/AUSPIC; 267, Ron Ryan/Coo-ee Picture Library; 268, P. Masterson/CSIRO Division of Radiophysics; 270, Tourism Commission of New South Wales; 273, Coo-ee Historical Picture Library; 274, Kathie Atkinson; 275, 276, CSIRO Division of Radiophysics; 279, Kathie Atkinson; 281, National Library of Australia; 282t, 282b, courtesy of CSIRO Division of Entomology; 283, Coo-ee Picture Library; 284, Ron Ryan/Coo-ee Picture Library; 285, National Library of Australia; 286t, OTC Public Affairs; 286b, Patrick G.Quilty; 288, Art Gallery of New South Wales; 290l, Coo-ee Historical Picture Library; 290r, Ron Ryan/Coo-ee Picture Library; 291t, 292, Coo-ee Historical Picture Library; 293, 294–5, 295, photographs courtesy Powerhouse Museum, Sydney; 296t, 296b, Historic Houses Trust of New South Wales; 297b, Ron Ryan/Coo-ee Picture Library; 299t, Coo-ee Historical Picture Library; 299b, 300t, National Capital Planning Authority; 300b, Daryl Jackson; 301, Sydney Opera House/Peter Garrett; 303, National Capital Planning Authority; 304, Art Gallery of South Australia; 305t, Collection, Art Gallery of Western Australia; 305b, reproduced by permission of the Australian National Gallery, Canberra; 306t, reproduced with permission of Lyn Williams; 306b, 307, Art Gallery of New South Wales; 308, National Gallery of Victoria, Melbourne; 309, Art Gallery of South Australia; 310,311b, 313, Mitchell Library/State Library of New South Wales; 315, National Library of Australia; 316, Jerry Bauer/Hodder & Stoughton; 318, Mitchell Library/State Library of New South Wales; 319, Performing Arts Museum, Victorian Arts Centre; 320, Sydney Theatre Company/Stuart Campbell; 321t, Tourism South Australia; 321b, Performing Arts Museum, Victorian Arts Centre; 323t, Elizabethan Theatre Trust; 323b, Riverina Theatre Company/Lee Verral; 325t, Nick Tate; 325b, Sydney Theatre Company/Sesh Roman; 327t, The Australian Ballet; 327b, Sydney Dance Company/Branco Gaica; 328, Bangarra Dance Theatre Australia Ltd/Paul Sweeney; 329t, Smoky Dawson; 330, Albert Productions, Sydney, Australia; 332, Sydney Festival and Carnivalé; 333br, The Australian Opera; 334, Ron Ryan/Coo-ee Picture Library; 335b, 335t, National Film and Sound Archive; 336, National Film and Sound Archive/New South Wales Film and Television Office/Margaret Fink; 337, Coo-ee Historical Picture Library; 338t, National Library of Australia; 338b, Grundy Television; 340, Sydney Festival and Carnivalé; 343, Coo-ee Historical Picture Library; 344–5, Ron Ryan/Coo-ee Picture Library; 346, Allsport; 347, Ron Ryan/Coo-ee Picture Library; 348, Allsport; 349t, Coo-ee Picture Library; 349b, Mirror Australian Telegraph Pictures.

MAPS AND DIAGRAMS. 6b, reproduced with the permission of the Australian Geological Survey Organisation; 17, based on information from Snowy Mountains Engineering Corporation Ltd, *Australia, Surface Water Quantity and Quality* (Canberra 1983); 21, after Carnahan, J. A., 'Vegetation', in Jeans, D. N. (ed.), *Australia: A Geography* (Sydney 1977, pp. 175–95); 203, 204, derived from material which is © Commonwealth Copyright, AUSLIG, Australia's national mapping agency. The material has been reproduced with the permission of the General Manager, Australian Surveying and Land Information Group, Department of Administrative Services, Canberra, ACT, Australia; 208, source: Department of Transport and Communications; International Civil Aviation Organisation; 209, source: Department of Transport and Communications; 224, based on information from Rowland, D.T., 'Population Growth and Distribution', in United Nations, *Population of Australia*, ESCAP, (Bangkok 1982, p.16); Australian Bureau of Statistics, *Australian Demographic Statistics*, March Quarter 1988, Australian Bureau of Statistics Catalogue No. 3101 (Canberra 1988); Jing Shu and Siew Ean Khoo, *Australia's Population Trends and Prospects* 1992, Bureau of Immigration Research, Australian Government Publishing Service (Canberra 1993); 227, based on information from *Year Book Australia*, No. 71, Bureau of Statistics (Canberra 1988, p.263); *Expanded Community Profile, Australia 1991*.

The Editor

Susan Bambrick is Pro Vice-Chancellor, La Trobe University and Head of its Albury-Wodonga Campus. Prior to this appointment she held posts at the University of New England, Coffs Harbour Centre (Director 1991–93) and the Australian National University (Master of University House 1986–91 and Dean of Students 1984–86). Susan Bambrick is a Fellow of the Australian Institute of Energy and a member of the executive of the Science and Industry Forum at the Australian Academy of Sciences. She has travelled extensively in the United States, Canada and New Zealand and has published widely on the economics of the minerals and energy industries. She was awarded the OBE in 1983 for service to education.

Contributors: Christopher Anderson; Susan Bambrick; John Barrett; Arthur J Birch; R V Blanden; H M Boot; David F Branagan; Deborah Brennan; Katharine Brisbane; Dorothy H Broom; Sarah Bunney; Alan Burnett; Robin Burnett; R N Byron; K S W Campbell; John Carmody; John A Carnahan; Barbara Chambers; Athol Chase; Anthony H Chisholm; Michael Clyne; Grace Cochrane; Clive Coogan; Catriona Cook; Ann Daniel; Peter J Davies; M F Day; Ray Edmondson; Frank Fenner; Christopher Findlay; P M Fleming; Brian H Fletcher; J-P L Fonteyne; Bill Gammage; S C B Gascoigne; Alan Gibson; Ian Gray; M A Habermehl; Barbara Hilliard; Andrew Hopkins; Ian Inkster; Jennifer Isaacs; R F Isbell; R V Jackson; Stan Jarzynski; Christine Jennett; Ian Keen; Peter Kershaw; J W Knott; Frank Lewins; Miles Lewis; Stuart Macintyre; Campbell Macknight; Bill Mandle; Robin Marks; Russell L Mathews; John McCallum; John Merritt; Helen Mills; Adrian Mitchell; John Mulvaney; Cliff D Ollier; Max Pettini; John D Pitchford; David Pope; Keith Powell; Patrick G Quilty; W J Rankin; Don Rawson; Peter Read; Andrée Rosenfeld; David K Round; Donald T Rowland; Claire Runciman; Lawrence J Saha; Marian Sawer; Richard Schodde; Helen Sim; Marian J Simms; Terry Smith; Mark St Leon; Peter Sutton; Jill Sykes; Peter Valentine; T J Valentine; Wray Vamplew; Alan Walsh; Paul Wild; Elspeth A Young; J W Zillman; Leslie Zines.

metres
2000+
1000-2000
200-1000
0-200

0   250   500   750   1000 km
0   100   200   300   400   500 miles